Written under the auspices of the Center for International Affairs, Harvard University

Transnational Relations and World Politics

Transnational Relations and World Politics

Edited by Robert O. Keohane and Joseph S. Nye, Jr.

Harvard University Press, Cambridge, Massachusetts 1972

Library of Congress Catalog Number 76–178076

The essays in this volume originally appeared in a special issue of *International Organization* entitled "Transnational Relations and World Politics," Vol. XXV, No. 3 (Summer 1971)

Printed in the United States of America

CONTENTS

Preface vii

Transnational Relations and World Politics: An Introduction.
Joseph S. Nye, Jr., and Robert O. Keohane ix

Part I. Transnational Relations: The Nature of the Beast 1

Transnationalism and the New Tribe.
James A. Field, Jr. 3

Transnational Economic Processes.
Edward L. Morse 23

The Politics of Transnational Economic Relations.
Robert Gilpin 48

The Growth of International Nongovernmental Organization in the Twentieth Century.
Kjell Skjelsbaek 70

Part II. Transnational Organizations 93

The Multinational Business Enterprise: What Kind of International Organization?
Louis T. Wells, Jr. 97

The Ford Foundation as a Transnational Actor.
Peter D. Bell 115

The Roman Catholic Church: A Transnational Actor.
Ivan Vallier 129

Contemporary Revolutionary Organizations.
J. Bowyer Bell 153

Part III. Issue Areas 169

Private International Finance.
Lawrence Krause 173

Governments and Airlines.
Robert L. Thornton 191

Labor and Transnational Relations.
Robert W. Cox 204

Transnational Networks in Basic Science.
Diana Crane 235

Transnationalism in Space: Inner and Outer.
Edward Miles 252

Security and a Transnational System: The Case of Nuclear Energy.
Lawrence Scheinman 276

PART IV. TOWARD PEACE AND JUSTICE? 301

Transnational Participation and International Peace.
Donald P. Warwick 305

National Autonomy and Economic Development: Critical Perspectives on Multinational Corporations in Poor Countries.
Peter B. Evans 325

Multinational Business and National Economic Goals.
Raymond Vernon 343

Transnational Relations as a Threat to the Democratic Process.
Karl Kaiser 356

Transnational Relations and World Politics: A Conclusion.
Joseph S. Nye, Jr., and Robert O. Keohane 371

SELECTED BIBLIOGRAPHY 399

PREFACE

The idea for this volume began over dinner in Boston in June 1968. With several other new members of the Board of Editors of *International Organization* we were trying to articulate our sense of dissatisfaction with the study of international organization. We felt that an "Everest syndrome" prevailed. Scholars studied organizations simply because "they are there." We agreed that new approaches were needed. But we also agreed that calls for "new approaches" had often been interpreted as calls for ever more esoteric methodology that contributed to an overemphasis on easy to study yet frequently trivial aspects of international organization like roll-call voting in public international assemblies. We decided to edit a special volume that would, in our view, put the horse back in front of the wagon by first describing patterns of interaction in world politics and then asking what role international institutions do or should play.

Our reaction against the overemphasis on intergovernmental organization and our desire to start from the patterns of interaction in the world led us to theorize in terms of transnational relations. We make no claim to having "discovered" transnational relations. Others, like Raymond Aron, Philip Jessup, Karl Kaiser, Horst Menderhausen, and James Rosenau, used the concept long before we did. As students of Stanley Hoffmann (and thus of Aron) we started our theorizing in terms of Aron's conception of "transnational society." We found this unsatisfactory, however, because it did not direct attention to governmental manipulation of transnational relations. During our work on this volume we have grown progressively more interested in the interaction between governments and transnational society and in transnational coalitions among subunits of governments. Thus, this volume gradually shifted its emphasis from different international organizations to a broader paradigm for approaching world politics.

Many people have helped us with this volume. We were four at the start of the venture. Harold K. Jacobson and Oran Young, who wisely chose transnational sabbaticals abroad rather than writing about transnational relations at home, helped us both to formulate our ideas and to find suitable authors. During 1969 we exchanged outlines and ideas with them and with others in such diverse settings as New York, Washington, Cambridge, Geneva, and Bellagio. Our focus of transnational relations owes a great deal to our previous work in integration theory and the behavior of small states, as well as to the stimulus of friends and critics like Hayward Alker, Stanley Hoffmann, Raymond Hopkins, Samuel Huntington, Karl Kaiser, Nan Keohane, Van D. Ooms, Donald J. Puchala, and Philippe Schmitter.

A crucial element in the production of this volume was the opportunity to bring together authors already expert on various subjects to confront our theoretical speculations. We are indebted to Robert Bowie, also a tireless critic, and the Center for International Affairs of Harvard University for supporting and hosting the Center for International Affairs Conference on Transnational Relations, June 4–5, 1970. We are equally indebted to the authors who attended, both for the provocativeness of their ideas and their willingness to react to our often unclear conceptions, and to the contributions of other participants. The result was a conference at which scholars from four different disciplines actually talked to, rather than past, each other.

We found the technique of asking for short memos rather than polished papers a very useful way of organizing the conference. Before the conference we prepared a memo describing our approach and a list of specific points for each author to address in a memo of his own. After the conference we sent a letter to each author detailing the comments made during the conference which we felt he should take into account in writing his essay. Subsequently, we read, commented on, and reread the essays that finally appear here. The result, we hope, is a volume that is more than merely a collection of essays.

We were helped by Jorge Domínguez and David Leyton-Brown who acted as rapporteurs at the conference and as subsequent critics of our work. Marina Finkelstein, Anita Yurchyshyn, and Carolyn Leigh have given us many pages of useful editorial suggestions. Karen Trimmer has suffered through more drafts of the introduction and conclusion—but always with good humor—than we had right to expect. Many colleagues on the Board of Editors of *International Organization* and at Harvard University, Swarthmore College, and elsewhere have offered useful criticisms. Several of our students at Harvard, Swarthmore, and Columbia University, captive audiences for drafts of work that appear here, also made helpful suggestions. Finally, we wish to note that we have enjoyed working together. Our ideas are thoroughly intermixed. The order of our names was determined by a flip of a coin during a long distance telephone call, and the labor in this volume has been equally shared. Criticism will be equally shared as well!

ROBERT O. KEOHANE
JOSEPH S. NYE, JR.

Transnational Relations and World Politics:

An Introduction

JOSEPH S. NYE, JR., AND ROBERT O. KEOHANE

STUDENTS and practitioners of international politics have traditionally concentrated their attention on relationships between states. The state, regarded as an actor with purposes and power, is the basic unit of action; its main agents are the diplomat and soldier. The interplay of governmental policies yields the pattern of behavior that students of international politics attempt to understand and that practitioners attempt to adjust to or control. Since force, violence, and threats thereof are at the core of this interplay, the struggle for power, whether as end or necessary means, is the distinguishing mark of politics among nations.[1] Most political scientists and many diplomats seem to accept this view of reality, and a state-centric view of world affairs prevails.[2]

It is obvious, however, that the interactions of diplomats and soldiers do not take place in a vacuum. They are strongly affected by geography, the

JOSEPH S. NYE, JR., a member of the Board of Editors of *International Organization,* is professor of political science in the Government Department of Harvard University and program director of the Center for International Affairs, Harvard University, Cambridge, Massachusetts. ROBERT O. KEOHANE, also a member of the Board of Editors, is associate professor of political science at Swarthmore College, Swarthmore, Pennsylvania.

[1] This is, of course, the orientation of Hans J. Morgenthau, but it also reflects the general point of view of eminent scholars like Raymond Aron and Kenneth N. Waltz. See Morgenthau, *Politics among Nations: The Struggle for Peace and Power* (4th rev. ed.; New York: Alfred A. Knopf, 1967); Aron, *Peace and War: A Theory of International Relations,* trans. Richard Howard and Annette Baker Fox (New York: Frederick A. Praeger, 1967); and Waltz, *Man, the State and War: A Theoretical Analysis* (Topical Studies in International Relations No. 2) (New York: Columbia University Press, 1959).

[2] International lawyers and economists seem less prone to accept the state-centric paradigm as much of the literature in international economics and international law indicates. See, particularly, the works of Richard Cooper, Raymond Vernon, and Philip Jessup.

nature of domestic politics in the various states, and advances in science and technology. Few would question that the development of nuclear weapons has dramatically altered the nature of twentieth-century international politics or deny the importance of internal political structure for relations between states. From the state-centric perspective geography, technology, and domestic politics comprise aspects of the "environment" within which states interact. They provide inputs into the interstate system but for considerations of analytic convenience are considered to be outside the system.

The environment of interstate politics, however, does not include only these powerful and well-known forces. A good deal of intersocietal intercourse, with significant political importance, takes place without governmental control. For example, among the major Western countries this includes most trade, personal contact, and communication. Furthermore, states are by no means the only actors in world politics. Arnold Wolfers noted more than a decade ago that "the Vatican, the Arabian-American Oil Company, and a host of other nonstate entities are able on occasion to affect the course of international events. When this happens, these entities become actors in the international arena and competitors of the nation-state. Their ability to operate as international or transnational actors may be traced to the fact that men identify themselves and their interests with corporate bodies other than the nation-state."[3]

Although Wolfers and others have pointed out the importance of intersocietal interactions and "transnational actors" in international affairs, the impact of these phenomena on world politics has often been ignored both in policy-oriented writings and more theoretical works.[4] When they have been recognized, they have often been consigned with the factors mentioned above to the environment of interstate politics, and relatively little attention has been paid to them or to their connections with the interstate system. This

[3] Arnold Wolfers, "The Actors in World Politics," in *Discord and Collaboration: Essays on International Politics,* ed. Arnold Wolfers (Baltimore, Md: Johns Hopkins Press, 1962), p. 23. This essay was first published in 1959 in William T. R. Fox, ed., *Theoretical Aspects of International Relations* (Notre Dame, Ind: University of Notre Dame Press, 1959). Other political scientists who have departed from the state-centric paradigm are John W. Burton, *Systems, States, Diplomacy and Rules* (Cambridge: Cambridge University Press, 1968); James N. Rosenau, ed., *Linkage Politics: Essays on the Convergence of National and International Systems* (New York: Free Press, 1969); Karl Kaiser, "Transnationale Politik: Zu einer Theorie der multinationalen Politik," *Politische Vierteljahresschrift,* 1969 (Special Issue, No. 1), pp. 80–109; and Horst Menderhausen, "Transnational Society vs. State Sovereignty," *Kyklos,* 1969 (Vol. 22, No. 2), pp. 251–275.

[4] The most striking examples of neglect of transnational relations and complete concentration on state policies appear in the literature on the North Atlantic Treaty Organization (NATO). See, for example, Henry A. Kissinger, *The Troubled Partnership: A Re-Appraisal of the Atlantic Alliance* (New York: McGraw Hill Book Co. [for the Council on Foreign Relations], 1965). On the more theoretical side the editors of a recent volume of essays on international relations note that, despite ardent disagreement over methods, "each author clearly conceives the subject to consist of the individuals and groups who initiate and sustain the actions and interactions of nation-states." Klaus Knorr and James N. Rosenau, eds., *Contending Approaches to International Politics* (Princeton, N.J: Princeton University Press, 1969), p. 4.

volume, by contrast, focuses on these "transnational relations"—contacts, coalitions, and interactions across state boundaries that are not controlled by the central foreign policy organs of governments. It treats the reciprocal effects between transnational relations and the interstate system as centrally important to the understanding of contemporary world politics.

A glance at the table of contents will reveal that we are interested in a wide variety of transnational phenomena: multinational business enterprises and revolutionary movements; trade unions and scientific networks; international air transport cartels and communications activities in outer space. Yet, we do not explore transnational relations simply "because they are there"; on the contrary, we hope to use our analysis to cast light on a number of empirical and normative questions that are directly related to the contemporary concerns of statesmen and students of international affairs.

These questions can be grouped into five broad areas of inquiry: 1) What seems to be the net effect of transnational relations on the abilities of governments to deal with their environments? To what extent and how have governments suffered from a "loss of control" as a result of transnational relations? 2) What are the implications of transnational relations for the study of world politics? Is the state-centric view, which focuses on the interstate system, an adequate analytic framework for the investigation of contemporary reality? 3) What are the effects of transnational relations on the allocation of value and specifically on asymmetries or inequalities between states? Who benefits from transnational relations, who loses, who controls transnational networks, and how is this accomplished? 4) What are the implications of transnational relations for United States foreign policy? Insofar as the United States is indeed preponderant in transnational activity, what dangers as well as opportunities does this present to American policymakers? 5) What challenges do transnational relations raise for international organizations as conventionally defined? To what extent may new international organizations be needed, and to what extent may older organizations have to change in order to adapt creatively to transnational phenomena?

We elaborate these questions later in this introduction and return to them in the conclusion, drawing on evidence presented in the various essays to document our assertions, reinforce our speculations, and propose hypotheses for further research. We do not pretend to be definitive; we realize that we are just beginning to explore this field and that even our best-documented beliefs are only provisional. We hope to stimulate inquiry, not to codify knowledge.

Before considering these five broad questions in detail, however, it is necessary to define the two aspects of transnational relations on which we concentrate in this introduction—transnational interactions and organizations—and to analyze some of their effects on interstate politics. Definition and description therefore take priority at this point, although our broader and more speculative inquiries should not be forgotten. We return to them beginning with section III of this introduction.

I. Transnational Interactions and Organizations

In the most general sense one can speak of "global interactions" as movements of information, money, physical objects, people, or other tangible or intangible items across state boundaries. We can distinguish four major types of global interaction: 1) communication, the movement of information, including the transmission of beliefs, ideas, and doctrines; 2) transportation, the movement of physical objects, including war matériel and personal property as well as merchandise; 3) finance, the movement of money and instruments of credit; 4) travel, the movement of persons. Many international activities involve all four types of interaction simultaneously. Trade and warfare, for example, both require coordinated movements of information, physical objects, money, and persons; so does most personal participation by individuals in foreign societies—"transnational participation"—as discussed in Donald P. Warwick's essay.

Some global interactions are initiated and sustained entirely, or almost entirely, by governments of nation-states. This is true of most wars, a large amount of international communication, considerable trade, and some finance. These we consider "interstate" interactions along with conventional diplomatic activity. Other interactions, however, involve nongovernmental actors—individuals or organizations—and we consider these interactions "transnational." Thus, a transnational interaction may involve governments, but it may not involve only governments: Nongovernmental actors must also play a significant role. We speak of transnational communication, transportation, finance, and travel when we refer to nongovernmental or only partially governmental interactions across state boundaries. Thus, "transnational interactions" is our term to describe the movement of tangible or intangible items across state boundaries when at least one actor is not an agent of a government or an intergovernmental organization.[5]

Another way of looking at transnational interactions, and of distinguishing them from interstate interactions, is to refer to a diagram that we found useful in thinking about the subject. The classic paradigm of interstate politics, depicted in figure 1, focuses on governments as the agencies through which societies deal politically with each other. Interstate politics is conceptually distinguished from, although linked indirectly to, domestic politics; transna-

[5] As our conclusion explains at greater length, "transnational interactions" constitute only one aspect of "transnational relations" by our definition. Yet, most of the essays that follow focus on transnational interactions and transnational organizations. Thus, in order to understand the essays, our definition of transnational interactions is crucial.

tional interactions are ignored or discounted. Governments may, however, interact through intergovernmental organizations; thus, this is included in the classic paradigm.

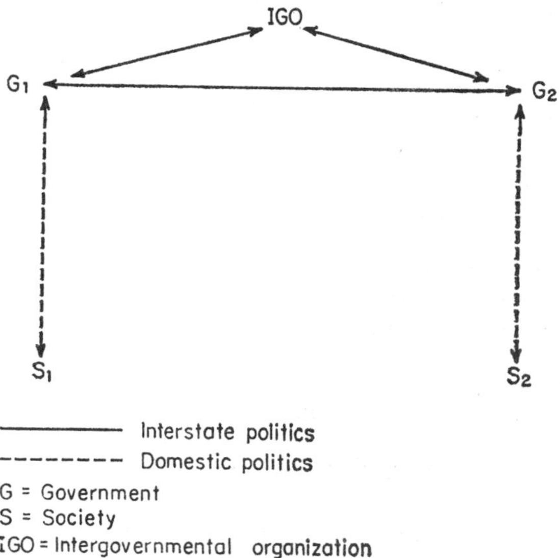

Figure 1. A state-centric interaction pattern

The additional lines drawn in figure 2 indicate what we mean by transnational interactions. For each of the interactions represented by these lines at least one of the actors is neither a government nor an intergovernmental organization. The point can be made somewhat differently by referring to J. David Singer's distinction between two ways in which individuals and organizations in a given society can play roles in world politics: 1) They may participate as members of coalitions that control or affect their governments or 2) they may play direct roles vis-à-vis foreign governments or foreign societies and thus bypass their own governments.[6] Only the second type of behavior is transnational by our definition.

At the Center for International Affairs Conference on Transnational Relations the objection was raised that a definition such as ours concentrates exclusively on the position of an actor—whether within a government or outside it—and does not raise the question of whether governmental actors necessarily play governmentally defined roles. It was pointed out that even high officials may take actions that cannot be ascribed to their status as governmental actors. Military officers in the United States, for example, frequently share common interests with military men in allied countries and may sometimes act in con-

[6] J. David Singer, "The Global System and Its Subsystems: A Developmental View," in Rosenau, p. 24.

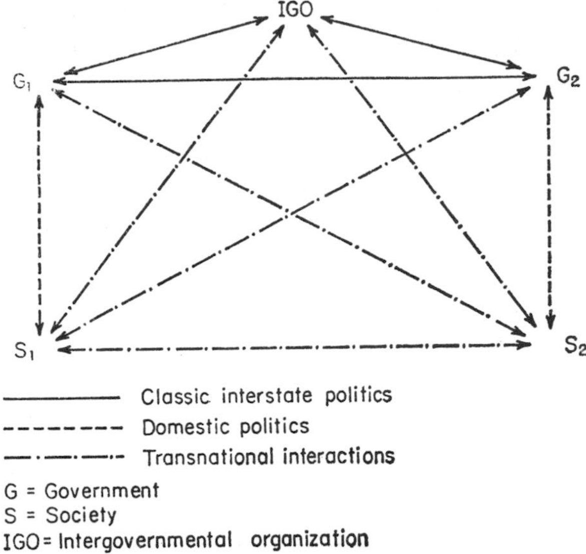

Figure 2. Transnational interactions and interstate politics

cert with these foreign military officers against other elements of the American government to achieve common political goals.[7] Leon N. Lindberg and Stuart A. Scheingold have noted the development of coalitions among agricultural officials from various countries of the European Economic Community (EEC): "The Ministers of Agriculture of the six and their aides and advisors, charged with primary negotiating responsibility along with the Commission, have come to share preoccupations and expertise. They are subject to similar constituency demands, engaged in annual budget battles against their respective Ministers of Finance, and they seek the same general goals of improving the conditions of farmers and of modernizing agriculture. Indeed, in the eyes of many of their colleagues in other governmental ministries, they have come to form 'an exclusive club, thoroughly defended by impenetrable technical complexities.'"[8]

The position of a governmental actor, however, is more visible and thus more easily known than his behavioral role. Furthermore, an actor's position is classifiable in one of three categories—governmental, intergovernmental, or nongovernmental—whereas his role may slide back and forth between the three. Even with perfect knowledge it would become extremely difficult and ultimately arbitrary to say exactly where a governmental agent stops playing

[7] Robert O. Keohane, "The Big Influence of Small Allies," *Foreign Policy*, Spring 1971 (Vol. 1, No. 2), pp. 161–182.

[8] Leon N. Lindberg and Stuart A. Scheingold, *Europe's Would-Be Polity: Patterns of Change in the European Community* (Englewood Cliffs, N.J: Prentice-Hall, 1970), p. 160. Their quotation is from "How Not to Rule the Roost: More Trouble in the Poultry Market," *Common Market*, July 1963 (Vol. 3, No. 7), p. 131.

a governmentally defined role and begins to act "on his own." Furthermore, since the essays in this volume focus primarily on nongovernmental activities and organizations, a definition that stresses the governmental/nongovernmental/intergovernmental distinction focuses attention on the relationships with which we are most concerned here. For a first approximation that can be easily applied in widely varying essays, therefore, we use the narrower and more precise definition, centering on the position of an actor, rather than a broader and vaguer definition in terms of role. In the conclusion, in which we contrast a world politics paradigm with the state-centric paradigm, we reintroduce the dimension of role and discuss the problems and prospects that it raises. The reader should be aware, therefore, that in this introduction we use the phrase "transnational relations" as shorthand for "transnational interactions and organizations," whereas in the conclusion we also consider relations between governmental actors that are not controlled by the central foreign policy organs of their governments.

Many transnational interactions take place without the individuals involved leaving their localities or the organizations maintaining any branches outside their countries of origin. Domestic industries, trade unions, and farmers engage in international trade without necessarily changing their loci of activity; bankers can move vast sums of money without leaving their offices; student groups may broadcast their views via world television while remaining in Paris, Cambridge, or Tokyo; the *New York Times* would somehow be obtained in other world capitals even if it did not maintain sales offices abroad. Thus, purely domestic organizations, such as national trade unions, can participate in transnational interactions.

Yet, we are also concerned with the activities of nongovernmental organizations that do operate regularly in several states. Transnational relations by our definition therefore include the activities of transnational organizations, except within their home states, even when some of their activities may not directly involve movements across state boundaries and may not, therefore, be transnational interactions as defined above. Thus, the activities of IBM in Brazil or Unilever in the United States are within the context of transnational relations even though some of these activities may take place entirely within Brazil, on the one hand, or the United States on the other. It would seem extremely artificial, for example, to exclude an arrangement made between Standard Oil Company of New Jersey and the French government from the arena of transnational relations merely because all negotiations for the agreement may have taken place in Paris.[9]

Multinational business enterprises, international trade union secretariats,

[9] It would seem equally absurd, on the other hand, to consider a grant by the Ford Foundation to Newark, New Jersey, or the sale of computers by IBM in Des Moines, Iowa, to be transnational activities. Thus, we exclude from transnational relations the activities of transnational organizations within their home states if the organizations retain such national identification.

global religious organizations, and far-flung foundations are all transnational by our definition. This does not imply, however, that they are staffed by "citizens of the world" or that they are necessarily controlled by individuals from several states. In fact, most transnational organizations remain linked primarily to one particular national society. Multinational enterprises tend to be managed by citizens from the home state; thus, according to Sidney Rolfe, 21 percent of the employees, but only 1.5 percent of the managers, of 150 United States–based multinational enterprises in the 1960s were non-American.[10] In this volume J. Bowyer Bell points out that transnational revolutionary movements often aspire to become nationalist regimes, and Peter D. Bell shows that the Ford Foundation's international staff remains predominantly American. These organizations are transnational by our definition, but they are not "geocentric."[11] An organization becomes geocentric only when the composition of its leadership and its pattern of behavior indicate that it has lost all special ties to one or two particular states.

Intergovernmental organizations often devote considerable effort to assuring that they will be geocentric in fact as well as in name: One need only note the continuing attempts by less developed states in the United Nations to assure "equitable geographical distribution" of positions in the secretariat. Transnational organizations, by contrast, are rarely established as such but usually evolve gradually from national organizations. Furthermore, they frequently do not have autonomous constituent units—such as the states in intergovernmental organizations—to insist on geocentricity. Thus, transnational organizations tend to become geocentric gradually and quite frequently move in that direction only after pressure has been brought from outside, particularly by host governments.[12]

II. Some Effects of Transnational Relations on Interstate Politics

How do transnational interactions or organizations affect interstate politics? At the most general level our contention is that these transnational relations increase the sensitivity of societies to one another and thereby alter relationships between governments. This point is illustrated by two examples, one from the area of international trade and finance, the other from global mass communications.

[10] Sidney Rolfe, *The International Corporation* (Paris: International Chamber of Commerce, 1969), p. 76.

[11] For these terms see Howard V. Perlmutter, "The Tortuous Evolution of the Multinational Corporation," *Columbia Journal of World Business*, January–February 1969 (Vol. 4, No. 1), pp. 9–18.

[12] To encompass transnational organizations as well as interactions figure 2 would have to be three-dimensional. Transnational organizations would appear on the third dimension, linked to governments, national societies, and intergovernmental organizations by a variety of interactions. Since such a representation is beyond our artistic powers, the reader will have to be content with the reminder that transnational relations under our definition include these organizational activities as well as the interactions that figure 2 depicts.

Richard N. Cooper has convincingly argued the case for the economic arena: As the decision domains of business and banking transcend national jurisdictions, small changes in one state's policies may have large effects on the system.[13] The essay by Lawrence Krause in this volume makes a similar point. States may be able to reduce their sensitivity to outside influence but only at the high price of reducing the concomitant benefits which result from their intercourse.

As a result of global mass communications various groups in different societies, such as radical students, military officers, or racial minorities, can observe each other's behavior and copy it when it seems appropriate. Thus, student radicals may suddenly develop similar political demands and tactics without direct contact with one another. Their international "conspiracies" are carried on in public and transmitted with the assistance of attentive media. Precursors of this phenomenon can be found, but its scale, scope, and speed are largely products of global television. Although its immediate effects are on the sensitivity of one state's domestic politics to that of another, its secondary effects—or the effects of efforts to halt unwanted communication—may well have consequences for interstate politics.

We can become more specific by suggesting five major effects of transnational interactions and organizations, all with direct or indirect consequences for mutual sensitivity and thereby for interstate politics. Four of these may result from transnational interactions even without the presence of transnational organizations, although transnational organizations may produce them as well; the fifth effect necessarily depends on the presence of transnational organizations as autonomous or quasi-autonomous actors. We summarize these effects under the following headings: 1) attitude changes, 2) international pluralism, 3) increases in constraints on states through dependence and interdependence, 4) increases in the ability of certain governments to influence others, and 5) the emergence of autonomous actors with private foreign policies that may deliberately oppose or impinge on state policies. Our categorization does not pretend to be exhaustive or definitive but is rather designed systematically to suggest some effects of transnational relations on interstate politics.

Transnational interactions of all types may promote *attitude changes* which may have possible consequences for state policies. As Warwick's essay suggests, face-to-face interactions between citizens of different states may alter the opinions and perceptions of reality of elites and nonelites within national societies. Transnational communication at a distance, transmitted either electronically or through the printed word, may also promote attitude changes.

[13] Richard N. Cooper, *The Economics of Interdependence: Economic Policy in the Atlantic Community* (Atlantic Policy Studies) (New York: McGraw-Hill Book Co. [for the Council on Foreign Relations], 1968), especially chapters 3, 4, and 6.

Similar results may follow, although probably less directly, from transnational transportation, travel, and finance. World peace may not, as the IBM slogan has it, come through world trade, but buying a Toyota or a Fiat may very well influence one's attitudes toward Japanese or Italians.

New attitudes can also be fostered by transnational organizations as they create new myths, symbols, and norms to provide legitimacy for their activities or as they attempt to replicate Western beliefs, life-styles, or social practices elsewhere in the world. Thus, James A. Field, Jr., traces the activity of missionaries and the "cultural package that accompanied the Protestant gospel" in the nineteenth century as well as the economic and evangelical activities of multinational business enterprises in the twentieth century. Peter B. Evans argues that advertising by these multinational enterprises affects popular attitudes in less developed societies to the detriment of their autonomy and economic development; Robert W. Cox refers to the multinational enterprise as the new hero of functionalist theory. Cox also gives examples of the justifications for transnational economic activity developed not only by corporations but also by certain union leaders. Examining the ideas of some trade unionists, Cox perceives an emerging "policy of symbiosis" between the trade union and the corporation in which both share power and through which unions would replace nation-states as the chief countervailing force to corporate dominance of the world economy.

It is clear to Cox and to other authors in this volume that the nation-state will not be as easily replaced as such visions might imply. Indeed, many of the essays in this volume focus on the role of the state in transnational networks. Bowyer Bell observes that even transnational revolutionaries usually seek power within a state, although they may draw support from outside; Peter Bell and Ivan Vallier focus a good deal of their attention on relations between the Ford Foundation and the Roman Catholic church, on the one hand, and the nation-states within which they operate on the other. Whereas Krause and Raymond Vernon argue for new international agreements to accommodate increases in transnational exchanges, Robert Gilpin speculates that governments will be led to support regional intergovernmental organizations as defenses against global transnationalism. A welter of divergent trends, predictions, and proposals emerges from these essays. What is clear to anyone, however, is that the attitudes produced by transnational relations will not necessarily lead to either universal concord or to the continued growth of transnational relations themselves.

A second effect of transnational relations is the promotion of *international pluralism*, by which we mean the linking of national interest groups in transnational structures, usually involving transnational organizations for purposes of coordination. The essay by Kjell Skjelsbaek documents the rapid growth of international nongovernmental organizations which link national organizations having common interests. After their creation these transnational organizations may stimulate the creation of new national affiliates and thus contribute to the internationalization of domestic politics. But transnational organizations themselves are apparently the product of increasing specialization of societies combined with the phenomena of transnational communication, travel, and transportation which allow people to perceive the possibilities for transnational organizations and to implement their visions. The creation of organizational linkages, as the essay by Edward Miles indicates, may in turn affect attempts by national groups to influence governmental policy.

It is interesting to note that the first two suggested effects of transnational relations are similar to those that have been most frequently observed by students of European integration. The "cybernetic" school of theorists has stressed the effect of transactions on mass attitude changes, whereas the "neo-functionalist" approach emphasizes the roles of interest groups and elites, or international pluralism.[14] Theorists of both varieties attempt to specify certain effects of transnational relations that are likely to constrain governments and make their policies more cooperative.

A third effect of transnational relations, the creation of *dependence and interdependence,* is often associated with international transportation and finance. The essays by Krause and Edward L. Morse focus on this relationship, and the essays by Field, Gilpin, Robert L. Thornton, and Vernon also give it a good deal of attention. Yet, as we have suggested above, one may also become dependent on a transnational communication network or on transnational travel. Even totalitarian states, if their governments want to keep pace scientifically, may have to allow their scientists to read foreign journals and to participate in international conferences. States may also become dependent on transnational organizations, particularly if those organizations provide something—goods, services, information, managerial skills, religious legitimacy—that they need.

Dependence is translated into policy most directly when certain policies which a government might otherwise follow become prohibitively costly. Integration into a world monetary system may make it impossible for a state to follow an autonomous monetary policy without drastic changes in its economy; dependence on foreign companies for technology, capital, and managerial skill may deter less developed countries from following highly nationalistic and socialistic economic policies. Where transnational organizations become important within a host society, they may alter the patterns of domestic interests so that certain governmental policies become prohibitively costly politically even if they might be feasible economically. Furthermore, new actors, such as multinational enterprises, with new patterns of behavior may raise

[14] See Peter J. Katzenstein, "Hare and Tortoise: The Race toward Integration," *International Organization,* Spring 1971 (Vol. 25, No. 2), pp. 290–295.

difficulties for bureaucratized governments that tend to follow standard operating procedures when reacting to change. Following an effective policy toward a new transnational actor may therefore be too costly on bureaucratic grounds.

Coping with dependence and interdependence raises special problems for large states. Small or weak states may well be able to make their decisions solely by considering the costs and benefits of various alternative policies to themselves, taking into account, of course, the probable reactions of other states. More powerful states, however, must also consider the effects of their own policies on the system of transnational relations. Insofar as the state benefits from a particular set of linked transnational arrangements, it will need to exercise care lest a reversion to autonomy in one area sets off retaliatory measures by other large states that could—quite apart from their direct effects on the first state—destroy the entire system. Yet, only if statesmen perceive both interdependence and system-fragility will they allow considerations such as these to constrain their actions. Perceptions of transnational relations by governmental elites are therefore a crucial link between dependence or interdependence, on the one hand, and state policies on the other.

We have just noted that transnational relations may make all states dependent on forces that none of them controls. But they may have a less evenhanded result as well by creating *new instruments for influence* for use by some governments over others. Among powers of roughly equal weight both sides may be able to take advantage of these instruments, as in the use of the Pugwash Conferences on Science and World Affairs by the United States and the Union of Soviet Socialist Republics to explore questions of arms control. But among unequal states transnational relations may merely put additional means of leverage into the hands of the more powerful states, located at the center of the transnational networks, to the disadvantage of those which are already weak.

Governments have often attempted to manipulate transnational interactions to achieve results that are explicitly political: The use of tourists as spies or the cultivation of sympathetic ethnic or religious groups in other states are examples of such "informal penetration."[15] Governments may also seek, however, to direct the flow of economic transactions to their own politico-economic ends. Through the use of tariff and quota policies powerful governments may attempt to affect the flow of international trade—for example, they can discourage manufacturing in less developed countries by levying higher tariffs on imports of processed and semiprocessed goods than on raw materials. Or, as the essay by Krause indicates, governments may try to

[15] See Andrew M. Scott, *The Revolution in Statecraft: Informal Penetration* (Random House Studies in Political Science, 551) (New York: Random House, 1965); and Richard W. Cottam, *Competitive Interference and Twentieth Century Diplomacy* (Pittsburgh, Pa: Pittsburgh University Press, 1967).

produce changes in international monetary arrangements by unilateral or multilateral action. Insofar as states become dependent on one another, some states may acquire new means by which to influence others.

Transnational organizations are particularly serviceable as instruments of governmental foreign policy whether through control or willing alliance. This has been evident in the use of United States–based multinational business enterprises by the American government. Thus, in the mid-1960s the United States sought to retard the development of France's nuclear capability not by sending an ultimatum or launching a war but by forbidding IBM-France to sell certain types of computers to the French government. The United States has also used its influence over United States–based multinational enterprises as a means of internationalizing its embargoes against the People's Republic of China (Communist China) and Cuba.[16] Cox gives examples of British and American trade unions which, following private foreign policies similar to the public foreign policies of their governments, interfere in the domestic politics of other countries to combat real or imagined communism. Even when there is no explicit coordination, transnational organizations can be useful to states. The Ford Foundation has been one of few American links to many Arab states since 1967. Vallier argues that states which hold key positions in transnational resource systems are able, often with decisive advantage, to draw on, and to some degree mobilize, all the "funds" that the system encompasses.

The fifth effect of transnational relations on interstate politics depends on the presence of transnational organizations as *autonomous* or quasi-autonomous *actors* in world politics. Several essays in this volume discuss such organizations—revolutionary movements, trade unions, multinational business enterprises, and the Roman Catholic church among others—that maintain private foreign policies. In some cases these organizations possess enormous resources: In 1965 some 85 business enterprises each had annual sales larger than the gross national products of some 57 voting members of the United Nations.[17] As Krause points out, in the monetary field the resources in the hands of some twenty banks can, at least in the short run, render nugatory the efforts of national monetary authorities even in very powerful countries. Thus, autonomous transnational organizations are potential and sometimes actual opponents of governmental policy in a wide variety of areas—whether the policy is liberalizing divorce in Italy, living at peace with Israel in the Middle East, enforcing economic plans in France, or maintaining a strong balance-of-payments position in the United Kingdom. The conflict between govern-

[16] For a discussion of some of the controls used by the United States for these purposes see Jack N. Behrman, *National Interests and the Multinational Enterprise: Tensions among the North Atlantic Countries* (Englewood Cliffs, N.J: Prentice-Hall, 1970), chapter 7, pp. 101–113.

[17] G. Modelski, "The Corporation in World Society," *The Year Book of World Affairs, 1968* (London: Stevens & Sons [under the auspices of the London Institute of World Affairs], 1968), pp. 64–79.

ment and transnational organizations may reflect the policies of a home government standing behind the transnational organization, but it may also result from differences between the policies of a host government and those of a transnational organization, without the home government, if any, becoming involved in the dispute.

Where home governments are involved, the presence of transnational organizations may exert a distinctive effect on the interstate relations that develop. Thus, it would be difficult to understand British-Iranian relations during 1951–1953 or American-Cuban relations between 1959 and 1961 without appreciating the role of certain international oil companies in both situations.[18] In these cases actions by the oil companies almost certainly aggravated existing interstate conflicts. It is possible, however, for a transnational organization also to facilitate good relations between states; certainly, these same oil companies have tried to foster cooperation between the United States and the Arab world. Their efforts have, in turn, been partially foiled by a very powerful transnational force—namely, Zionism—which has worked effectively for good American relations with Israel even at the expense of United States relations with Israel's adversaries. Not only may a struggle between transnational organizations, or between transnational organizations and states, lead to interstate conflict; interstate conflict, such as the Arab-Israeli conflict, may lead to struggles for influence among transnational organizations or movements. The interrelationships are complex and often reciprocal, but they can hardly be ignored.

III. Transnational Relations and "Loss of Control" by Governments

Our observations about changes in world politics do not deny that governments remain the most important players in the game. Although transnational organizations are immensely more plentiful and significant now than before 1914 or 1945, governments have attempted since World War I not only to maintain but also to extend their control over outside forces and events. Previously ignored areas of activity have been brought within the regulation and concern of governments. International monetary flows, for example, were of much less importance to governments before 1914 than they are now. In those years few governments consciously attempted to plan economic growth or to promote full employment at home. As Cooper has stressed, new tasks for governments "place greater burdens on the available instruments of policy" and make it more difficult to accept "the intrusions of international economic integration on national economic policy."[19] Thus, the sensitivity of govern-

[18] For a discussion of these cases see Michael Tanzer, *The Political Economy of International Oil and the Underdeveloped Countries* (Boston: Beacon Press, 1969), chapter 24, pp. 319–348.
[19] Cooper, p. 151.

ments to changes elsewhere increases as governments become more ambitious. Increased aspirations for control and increased interdependence go hand in hand.

It therefore becomes clear that to pose questions such as we did at the outset in terms of an alleged "loss of control" is to put the issue in a misleading way. Governments have generally not been able to control their environments successfully for long periods of time whenever those environments have changed rapidly as a result of large-scale social forces or advancing technology. Small and middle powers, and even great powers within a balance-of-power system, have had to accustom themselves to a very small degree of environmental control; they have had to adjust to changes rather than to shape the forces of history. It may be that United States policymakers have less control now than in the 1950s, but it was the 1950s that were exceptional, not the present.

As governments become more ambitious, however, the impact of transnational relations does create a "control gap" between the aspiration for control and the capability to achieve it. The essays by Morse, Krause, and Vernon discuss various facets of this problem. At the same time, as Vallier and Evans argue, transnational relations may redistribute control from one state to another and benefit those governments at the center of transnational networks to the disadvantage of those in the periphery.

It seems better, therefore, to raise the issue of governmental control as a question for investigation rather than to prejudge the issue at this point in terms of "loss of control." It is clear that governments are becoming more ambitious and that this forces them to react to, and often to adapt to, transnational interactions and organizations. The further governments seek to extend their reach, the more they involve themselves with the environment of interstate politics and particularly with transnational relations. Insofar as they are unwilling to pay the price for complete control, they must contend with relatively autonomous transnational forces. From the analyst's perspective, therefore, their behavior becomes more and more difficult to predict without a rather detailed knowledge of transnational relations. Our next question is therefore posed: Does the phenomenon of transnational relations make the state-centric paradigm inadequate for understanding contemporary world politics?

IV. Transnational Relations and the State-Centric Paradigm

Sophisticated proponents of the state-centric view have observed transnational interactions, and they have certainly not been blind to the fact that actors other than states exist. Yet, they have deliberately excluded transnational relations from the interstate system on the grounds that their direct political importance is small and that their indirect effects enter, along with domestic factors, into the formation of national foreign policies. Although this conclusion has partially relied on a definition of politics merely in terms of state behavior, it does contain a solid core of insight. States have been and remain the most important actors in world affairs, acting both directly and through intergovernmental organizations to which states, and only states, belong. States virtually monopolize large-scale, organized force which remains the ultimate weapon and a potent bargaining resource. Thus, there would be no point in ignoring the nation-state. Instead, one might ask the following questions: Should more attention be paid to the effects of transnational relations on interstate relations, and is the state-centric paradigm adequate if we wish to explore these effects? Evans has expressed this feeling pungently although in a somewhat "loaded" way: "It is not interesting to exclude traditional state behavior and then study the residual only. What is interesting is the contamination of interstate relations by transnational relations."[20]

If we depart from a state-centric, institutional definition of politics, the need for a broader focus becomes evident immediately. The classic model as depicted in figure 1 normally assumed as a definition of world politics the actions and interactions of states. Students of domestic politics, however, have moved away from such exclusive reliance on the state and have focused more broadly on the process by which societies make binding decisions.[21] The problems with definitions such as David Easton's are well known: Departing from a traditional, narrow view of politics seems to lead one to a definition without clear limits. Until we adopt a broader definition, however, we continue to view governments as more clearly unique than they are, and we are foreclosed from examining the politics of trade unions, industrial corporations, or schools. Likewise, with international politics, a definition of politics in terms of state behavior alone may lead us to ignore important nongovernmental actors that allocate value and that use means similar to those used by governments to achieve their ends.

We therefore prefer a definition of politics that refers to relationships in which at least one actor consciously employs resources, both material and symbolic, including the threat or exercise of punishment, to induce other actors to behave differently than they would otherwise behave. Using this definition of politics, we define world politics as all political interactions between significant actors in a world system in which a significant actor is any somewhat autonomous individual or organization that controls substantial resources and participates in political relationships with other actors across state

[20] This is a close paraphrase of a remark made by Evans at the Center for International Affairs Conference on Transnational Relations, Harvard University, June 4–5, 1970.

[21] For a discussion of this trend see David Easton, "Political Science," *International Encyclopedia of the Social Sciences,* ed. David L. Sills (17 vols.; n.p: Macmillan Co. and Free Press, 1968), Vol. 12, pp. 282–298.

lines.[22] Such an actor need not be a state: At any point where a transnational organization employs techniques such as economic boycotts, airline hijackings, or religious excommunication to achieve the modification of other actors' behavior, it is behaving politically. International oil companies, for example, insofar as they act to maintain political stability in producing countries, are transnational political actors by this definition.[23]

If the effects of transnational relations were slight, variable, and perhaps transitory, consigning them to a vaguely specified and generally ignored environment would be acceptable as a parsimonious simplifying device. Yet, this entire volume testifies to the fact that the effects of transnational relations are much more important and pervasive than that. Knowing the policies and capabilities of a set of governments may not allow us accurately to predict outcomes or future characteristics of the system if significant transnational interactions or powerful transnational organizations are involved. Even if states in some sense "win" confrontations with transnational forces, their anticipation of these forces, and of the actions of transnational organizations, may lead states to alter their policies in advance to avoid costly confrontations.

Transnational relations are not "new," although, as Skjelsbaek's essay indicates, the growth of transnational organization in the twentieth century has been spectacular. Yet, our contention is not only that the state-centric paradigm is inadequate for reasons indicated above but also that it is becoming progressively more inadequate as changes in transnational relations take place. As a partial view of international politics it was more useful in the past than in the present, and it is still more useful now than it is likely to be in the future. The essays shed some light on changes in transnational relations; the conclusion to this volume attempts to draw the evidence together in order to buttress the case that has been sketched above and to introduce our alternative "world politics paradigm" as a substitute for the state-centric analytic framework.

V. Transnational Relations and Values

Thus far in this essay we have been viewing transnational relations largely from an empirical perspective, but they can also be evaluated normatively. This immediately raises the question of who benefits from transnational relations. It could be argued that transnational relations enrich and strengthen the strong and the rich—in short, the most modernized, technologically adept segments of the world—because only these elements are able to take full advantage of its network of intersocietal linkages. The continuing debate on the effects of multinational business enterprises on welfare, for example, has

[22] These definitions borrow heavily and consciously, although with substantial modification, from an essay by Oran R. Young, "The Actors in World Politics," in *The Analysis of International Politics,* ed. James N. Rosenau, B. Vincent Davis and Maurice A. East (Glencoe, Ill: Free Press, forthcoming).

[23] For an analysis of the activities of these corporations see Tanzer.

raised numerous questions about the value of transnational relations for less developed countries in particular.[24] Many of the essays in this volume, particularly those in parts III and IV, raise questions of this kind. In producing a volume that emphasizes transnational interactions and organizations we mean to point out their importance, not necessarily to celebrate their effects.

Some would regard transnational relations as a new name for the old phenomenon of imperialism. As one scholar has noted, however, the word "imperialism" is "entirely at the mercy of its user."[25] It is sometimes used to describe virtually any relationship across state boundaries between unequals that involves the exercise of influence. If this definition is used, "imperialism" includes most of world politics and thereby becomes virtually devoid of analytic value.

Imperialism may be used, however, in a more restricted although not very precise way to refer to cross-national relationships in which unequal power is used to achieve "unfair" allocations of value. Some actors, whether states or not, exploit others. Given an agreed concept of "fairness" (which is, of course, the chief difficulty) some transnational relations would presumably be "imperialistic" and others would not. Yet, the ambiguities present even in this use of "imperialism" are so great that we would rather ask directly about the effects of transnational relations than inquire whether a given set of transnational relations is "imperialistic" or not. Focusing on "asymmetries" or "inequalities" seems more useful to us than trying to employ older terms encrusted with many layers of ambiguous or contradictory meaning.

The reader should therefore bear in mind while reading these essays Harold Lasswell's definition of politics in terms of "who gets what." Do the activities of multinational business enterprises, trade unions, or the Ford Foundation redistribute economic resources? If so, in what direction does the flow go? Do these transnational organizations, or transnational interactions generally, differentially affect the welfare, security, or autonomy of various states or regions? To what extent are the effects unidirectional and to what extent are cross-currents more typical, with some benefits and some costs for each state or region? Once again, the conclusion attempts to draw together evidence from the essays in order to give at least a tentative answer to these questions.

24 For some recent works on the subject see Charles P. Kindleberger, *American Business Abroad: Six Lectures on Direct Investment* (New Haven, Conn: Yale University Press, 1969); Harry Magdoff, *The Age of Imperialism: The Economics of U.S. Foreign Policy* (New York: Monthly Review Press, 1969); and Harry Johnson, "The Efficiency and Welfare Implications of the International Corporation," in *The International Corporation: A Symposium,* ed. Charles P. Kindleberger (Cambridge, Mass: M.I.T. Press, 1970), pp. 35–56.

25 Hans Daalder, "Imperialism," in the *International Encyclopedia of the Social Sciences,* Vol. 7, p. 108.

VI. Transnational Relations and United States Foreign Policy

As Field points out in his essay, Americans have always had a propensity for transnational activity. The United States has the world's most highly modernized, as well as its largest, economy. American social units such as corporations, foundations, labor organizations, and universities involved in transnational activities often have annual budgets greater than those of the governments in whose territories they operate. Vernon and Peter Bell indicate in their essays that perhaps three-fourths of the world's multinational enterprises and 29 of 32 foundations with assets over $100 million have their origins in the United States. In ironic counterpoint hostility toward the American colossus is one of the few ties uniting the revolutionary movements described by Bowyer Bell.

At the same time it would be a mistake to view transnational activities as a purely American game, let alone a United States government game, particularly if one looks at recent trends. Stephen Hymer and Robert Rowthorn have concluded from an analysis of comparative growth of European and American firms that the future will see increasing European direct investment in the United States as multinational firms from the Old World vie with those from the New World to "establish world-wide market positions and protect themselves from the challenges of each other."[26] Rainer Hellmann has pointed out that although American direct investment in Europe is more than double European direct investment in the United States, if one includes portfolio investments the totals are almost exactly equal. Furthermore, "since 1967 European companies have for the first time increased their direct investments in America more rapidly than American firms increased theirs in Europe."[27] Apart from the economic realm America is by no means dominant even now: The United States is not the center of transnational political parties, revolutionary movements, or the Roman Catholic church. It is, however, the most important focus of transnational activity in basic science and one of the major centers of transnational trade unionism. Not all roads lead to New York; some still lead to Rome, Peking, Geneva, or even Damascus.

We can therefore see an emerging dialectic between American predominance, at least in the economic area, and European or Japanese challenges, with less developed states as bystanders, victims, or junior partners as the case may be. Such a dialectic raises the question of whether United States foreign policy should seek to defend, ignore, or countervail the transnational effects of American society. Is the United States like an elephant in a hen-

[26] Stephen Hymer and Robert Rowthorn, "Multinational Corporations and International Oligopoly: The Non-American Challenge," in Kindleberger, *The International Corporation,* p. 81.

[27] Rainer Hellmann, *The Challenge to U.S. Dominance of the International Corporation,* trans. Peter Ruof (Cambridge, Mass. Dunellen, University Press of Cambridge, Mass., 1970), p. 306. Hellmann estimates that 60 percent of worldwide direct investment originates in the United States while 30 percent originates in Europe (p. 305).

house—so powerful that it causes problems regardless of its intentions—or is the United States more like Great Britain in the late nineteenth century—still dominant, but imperceptibly losing the advantages on which its dominance is based? Although few authors in this volume confront these questions directly, most of the essays are highly relevant to such problems of foreign policy. The reader should be aware of these policy issues as he reads this volume; we return to them in the conclusion.

VII. Transnational Relations and International Organization

A discussion of the effects of transnational relations on values and of America's role in transnational networks raises the inevitable further question of intergovernmental cooperation to control these effects and to limit or legitimate American dominance. It is clear that most if not all governments will find it very difficult to cope alone with many aspects of transnational relations in the decade of the 1970s and thereafter. In reading this volume students of international organizations, international politics, and international law will surely ask themselves what tasks intergovernmental institutions can be expected to assume in their attempts to influence and control transnational trends. Outer space, the oceans, and the internationalization of production are only three of the most obvious areas in which intergovernmental control may be demanded in the form of new international laws or new international organizations or both. The new laws and organizations will have to take into account important nongovernmental actors, perhaps including them in the organizations as well as acknowledging them in the laws. Whether governments will cooperate more successfully in regulating transnational relations than in controlling each other's conflict behavior remains to be seen.

Yet, a few tentative steps in this direction can be discerned. The European Economic Community aspires to convert its trade bloc into a single currency area during the 1970s.[28] Less sweeping alterations have been made in Atlantic and global intergovernmental arrangements in the area of monetary policy to cope with disruptions caused by transnational financial activity. There has been considerable discussion in Europe of developing an EEC-wide incorporation law to assist the growth of European multinational corporations to combat the "American challenge."[29] By declaring the sea to be "the common heritage of mankind" the United Nations General Assembly has taken a symbolic step toward controlling the activities of transnational organizations, such as multinational business enterprises, as well as the activities of states in their exploitation of the sea and seabed for commercial and military purposes. The recent Treaty Prohibiting the Emplacement of Nuclear Weapons on the Sea-

[28] *New York Times*, February 10, 1971, p. 1.

[29] Hellmann, p. 301. See also J.-J. Servan-Schreiber, *The American Challenge*, trans. Ronald Steel (New York: Avon Books, 1969).

bed and Ocean Floor has limited states' rights to use the seabed by banning atomic arms, and limits on the encroachments of transnational organizations are likely to follow.[30] The United Nations Conference on the Human Environment, to be held in 1972, will certainly have to come to grips with the transnational, as well as governmental, actors that help determine environmental improvement or decay.

Most of these are small steps, significant only if they represent the opening edge of a wedge. Whatever their impact, it is clear that none of them was taken automatically; individuals had to perceive present and future problems and act on them before governments could be expected to cooperate. Basic research, directed at describing and explaining important phenomena, is a necessary prerequisite to such anticipation of future difficulties as well as to intelligent policy analysis and recommendations after problems have been identified. Students of international law and organization should therefore become involved in the study of transnational relations not merely for the sake of understanding reality but also in order to help change reality. The essays that follow are intended not only to improve our understanding but also to improve the ways in which we can increase the general welfare by controlling the forces that shape our lives.

Transnational Relations and World Politics

PART I

TRANSNATIONAL RELATIONS: THE NATURE OF THE BEAST

Our introduction has indicated why we are interested in transnational relations and has suggested what some of their effects on world politics may be. But it is surely difficult to evaluate our claims about transnational phenomena until one has some information about their history, scope, and significance. The essays in part I are designed to provide such information as well as to forward a variety of arguments about the causes and future of transnational relations.

In the first essay James A. Field, Jr., examines the broad sweep of transnationalism in the nineteenth and twentieth centuries, arguing that "the nationalist pail was always seen as half-full or better when in fact it was half-empty and leaking." After surveying the transnational activities of individuals in the nineteenth century and the "organizational revolution" that began about 1870, Field contends that the years since World War II have seen the development of transnational groups linked not by common nationality but by functional ties—intellectual, professional, and familial. Supported by a rapidly advancing communications and transportation technology, these groups, according to Field, are creating a new world culture and contributing to the decline, or at least the alteration, of the national state.

Edward L. Morse extends this line of thought to the economic present, contending that "the politicization of economics and the creation of economic value for political goods are what transnational processes are all about." Morse argues that the major industrialized, non-Communist states are indeed becoming more interdependent, particularly as a result of economic processes, and that the sensitivity of national economies to one another is increasing—with significant consequences for policy as well as for theory.

Although Robert Gilpin accepts the proposition that economics and politics are intertwined, he introduces a skeptical note with his argument for the primacy of politics. He regards the rise of transnational relations as dependent, in the mid-twentieth century, on a Pax Americana that has provided "the security and political framework for the expansion of transnational economic activity." Yet, he sees this political framework as resting on a precarious set of politico-economic bargains—particularly between the United States and West Germany and the United States and Japan. Far from accepting the "erosion of the nation-state" thesis, Gilpin concludes that "the role of the nation-state in economic as well as in political life is increasing."

In the final essay of part I Kjell Skjelsbaek assembles substantial amounts of data, much of it new, to indicate the rapid growth of international nongovernmental organizations since about 1900 and particularly since 1940. He then proceeds to formulate some hypotheses about the reasons for this growth and for its concentration among developed Western states. It appears that domestic pluralism and high levels of economic development are associated with international pluralism and, in particular, that specialization within advanced societies creates the need for transnational linkages between functionally defined groups—Field's "New Tribe," or perhaps new tribes.

These essays hardly present a unified or definitive portrait of our subject. The strokes are painted with broad brushes, often in bold colors, and the various artists, working on the same canvas, cannot always agree on the features that should be highlighted. Indeed, Gilpin suggests more shadows. Yet, since we desire neither to promulgate a doctrine nor to found a school, this intellectual disorder dismays us no more than "a sweet disorder in the dress" disturbed the poet, Robert Herrick, when he wrote that its manifestations "Do more bewitch me, than when art / Is too precise in every part." Like the ladies Herrick admired we seek to arouse interest and encourage further inquiry rather than to achieve an ordered consistency at the price of dullness.

Transnationalism and the New Tribe

James A. Field, Jr.

I. The National Image

Among the striking developments of modern history the growth of nationalism and the proliferation of nation-states must surely take high place. To numerous peoples in the post-Napoleonic era the possibility of modeling themselves on England and France seemed both desirable and feasible in a time when language groupings, the reach of political and economic control systems, and the capabilities of armaments appeared roughly to coincide. Together with patriotisms reinforced by popular education and increasing literacy these phenomena emphasized the defensibility of both the spiritual and the military frontiers. The result, in the latter half of the nineteenth century, was a series of wars of national unification which were followed in the twentieth century by great efforts to defend the nationality thus gained, socially, through such devices as immigration restriction, economically, by tariffs and various autarchic experiments, and militarily, in two great wars.

For Europe and North America this period of the flowering national state was also a time of notable economic advance. One result of this prosperity was a great expansion of scholarship and education, and while forms and techniques often proved transferable from country to country, much of the content did not. In colleges and universities the developing history curriculum froze in the nationalist pattern as the French endlessly refought their revolution, the British wrote the history of their liberties and the Germans that of their geist, and the Americans celebrated their freedoms and their frontier. Of such later specialities as diplomatic history and international relations, products in large degree of the early twentieth-century peace movement and of the telegrams of 1914, much the same can be said. The nation appeared to be the crucial actor, and in the interplay of these juridically equal sovereign units the diplomats and soldiers held the high ground.

No doubt, it could hardly have been otherwise. The visible trappings of na-

James A. Field, Jr., is Isaac H. Clothier Professor of History, Swarthmore College, Swarthmore, Pennsylvania.

tionalism—triumphal arches, military display, royal funerals—were unquestionably impressive. The age sat so well for its portrait that few concerned themselves with what lay under the skin or questioned whether the political map, so good for empires, wars, and treaties, did not conceal as much as it revealed or whether other kinds of maps—soil type and rainfall, religion and educational level, railroad mileage and coal production—might not yield information of more enduring significance.

The concentration on politics tended to mask the problem of what was necessary to the successful national state. Did it require a sovereign, linguistic and religious unity, and a traditional enemy? Were agricultural self-sufficiency and juxtaposed iron and coal essential? How important was it to have a national hero, a national history, and a national literature? Whatever the chosen criteria few states could ever meet them all. While almost anyone could muster up a Scanderbeg, there was still only one Shakespeare, and throughout the period the contrast of maxi-, mini-, and non-nation remained. Some parts of the nineteenth-century world lacked the first requisites of the national state. Some states were minuscule and unimportant. The Habsburg and Romanov empires, like those of the Ottomans and Manchus, had very different histories, structures, and possibilities than the West European national states.

Even in Europe, where it all began, some states were much more successfully "sovereign" or "national" than others, and the futures of even the most successful were soon at hazard. France, the ideal eighteenth-century nation and long the terror of Europe, entered a nineteenth-century decline with a stable population and poorly located resources. Almost from the start the security of the newly united German Empire was affected by its dependence on imported food and petroleum. At their moment of greatest triumph the British found themselves vulnerable as their growing population came to depend on overseas food and their navy, which had to ensure the food supply, on overseas oil. In the intellectual realm as well problems developed as new formulations—Pan-Slavism and Pan-Germanism, the Western Hemisphere Idea, international socialism—either emphasized the lack of fit between state and nation or questioned the ideal itself.

None of this, of course, was ever really a secret. At the time of Alexis de Tocqueville and again at the turn of the century there came reiterated predictions of the emergence of the United States and Russia as the two superpowers. From at least the 1870s a nervous recognition of national vulnerability could be detected in continental preoccupation with conscription schemes, British invasion scares and debates on naval policy, the phenomenon of imperialism, and the development of alliance systems. Yet, this very recognition, stressing as it did the roles of soldiers and diplomats, tended to obscure the underlying trends. The actions and attitudes of governments, like those of scholars, music hall entertainers, and ordinary citizens, emphasized the national state. But much of the picture, it may be argued, lay in the eye of the beholder. The nationalist pail was always seen as half-full or better when in fact it was half-empty and leaking.

II. The Invisible Hand

Looking for a moment beyond international rivalry and conflict, it is perhaps possible to describe the main business of the world since 1800 as the product of three great interrelated processes. The first of these, originating in the countries bordering the North Atlantic, was the development of an ever-changing modernity compounded of the thrust toward freedom, self-determination, liberalism, and nationalism, the rapid advance of science and technology, and the rush toward industrialization and urbanization. Paralleling, and in large measure the consequence of this modernization, was the completion by Europeans and Americans of the process of discovery and exploration; the settlement of useful distant empty areas and the establishment of patterns of world trade; and then the shrinking and linking of the world through improved communications, expanded commerce, the export of Western techniques and attitudes, and the imposition in some cases of Western political control.[1] The third main trend, flowing from what preceded, involved a large variety of efforts, both at home and abroad, to eliminate or mitigate the perceived resulting evils.[2]

In all three of these categories much—perhaps most—of the work was "transnational" in nature, reaching across state boundaries and initiated by or acting upon private individuals and groups. In the struggles for freedom, self-determination, and national identity one may instance such paradoxically transnational individuals as the Marquis de Lafayette, Tadeusz Kosciuszko, Tom Paine, and the "titled freebooter" Lord Cochrane and such groups as the Philhellenes, Garibaldians, Fenians, and Zionists. From the beginning the scientists were citizens of the world; the secrets of the new technology proved impossible to contain; entrepreneurs could and did migrate. If a few governments were active in exploration, they by no means monopolized the field, while colonization, the development of world trade, and the export of Western techniques were predominantly nongovernmental affairs. The efforts to cushion the impact of the new developments gave rise both to transnational action groups and to exportable reforms. Among the humanitarians there developed an international peace movement and international campaigns for

[1] European aspects of these developments are dealt with in David S. Landes, *The Unbound Prometheus: Technological Change and Industrial Development in Western Europe from 1750 to the Present* (Cambridge: Cambridge University Press, 1969); their export to the wider world is the subject of William Woodruff, *Impact of Western Man* (New York: St. Martin's Press, 1967).

[2] One should perhaps add, as an important background factor, the extraordinary continuing growth of world population.

the abolition of the slave trade and of slavery, for women's rights, and for temperance. Working class groups supported the international labor movement, international socialism, and anarchism. From the managers there came a network of private treaties—trusts, cartels, and the like—designed to regulate competition abroad as well as at home.

In much of this activity, of course, private and public sectors found themselves intertwined; governments would intermeddle, and private groups would seek governmental aid. Equally, among the actors, governments were the most unitary, the most visible, and the easiest to watch and describe. But while the apparatus of the state continued to grow throughout the period, and particularly from the latter part of the nineteenth century, its role (at least until the perfection of control systems that came with the First World War) was less one of initiating policy than of responding to conditions produced by nongovernmental factors whose influence increasingly transcended national boundaries.

These factors, in the first instance, seem largely economic. As well as for immense material development, the nineteenth and twentieth centuries were notable for great fluidity as capital, labor, and entrepreneurial and technological skills acquired a mobility never before approached. Much the same, indeed, could be said of land and its associated natural resources; for while these, in the first instance, were where one found them, they too became "movable" through improved transportation, new discoveries, obsolescence, or substitution. How this fluidity, primarily the work of private individuals and groups, greatly influenced their own and other societies and governments can be seen in the developments in transportation, in population movement, and in agriculture and industry that turned a fragmented localized world into a unified market economy.

The steady improvement in modes of transportation and the concomitant reduction in costs profoundly affected national interests. In the first half of the nineteenth century the skills of American shipwrights and navigators threatened the maritime position of Great Britain; in the second half the coming of steam and of the iron ship helped kill off the American merchant marine. The Suez Canal, the work of a private French company, emptied the South Atlantic, hastened the shift from sail to steam, brought increased European pressure upon the Far East, and led through the British occupation of Egypt to the partition of Africa. The railway, a British invention, revolutionized the economies of northern Europe, the United States, and certain British overseas possessions and interest areas; and while railroad construction, in various instances, was subsidized by the state for strategic or economic reasons, the end result was the creation of regional rather than discrete national networks. By the 1880s the world that mattered could be pretty well defined in terms of railroad track. Where railroads had been built, and only there, the maritime trade routes had been extended inland to exploit, on a wholly unprecedented scale, the noncoastal, nonriverine world.

The increased mobility which resulted from improved transportation brought great changes in the distribution of population groups and in the political map. To the revolution already wrought by the introduction of Europeans and Africans into the New World, the nineteenth century added its own transnational embellishments. The advance of individual Americans into "foreign" territory—Oregon, Hawaii, Texas, California—made the role of the federal government in expansion less that of initiator than of registrar of deeds. Emerging from their ghettos, escaping their disabilities, and engaging in such cosmopolitan activities as finance, the arts, and socialist agitation, the Jews so distinguished themselves as transnational actors as to become the objects of a virulent transnational anti-Semitism. As the century wore on, an increasing outflow of European emigrants peopled the Americas, South Africa, and the Antipodes, while the Japanese began to spread eastward across the Pacific. On the far side of the world Indians moved into Burma and the overseas Chinese settlements grew.

If much was individual, much of the movement of population groups was also the result of organized nongovernmental effort. In the presumed interest of the groups themselves the American Colonization Society exported free Negroes and founded Liberia; starving Irishmen were shipped to America to build railroads and improve Tammany Hall; the Mormons trekked to Utah to set up their own theocracy. In the interest of both parties to the transaction American railroads organized a massive recruitment and transportation of Europeans to colonize the Plains states. Primarily in the interest of others, the slave trade being dead but hard jobs remaining, Chinese coolies were exported to the Western Hemisphere to bring about, among other things, the first United States immigration restrictions, while a similar transport of Indians to Pacific and Indian Ocean islands, to East and South Africa, and to the Caribbean, stored up problems for the future.

These transfers of people and of skills had powerful consequences for world agriculture and industry. With the opening of new areas and the introduction of new crops once-local agricultural products—maize, tobacco, sugar, the potato—gained worldwide distribution, creating new commercial links, modifying age-old patterns of life, and alleviating, for the moment, the Malthusian checks. Two such products, one a fiber and one a foodstuff, had widest transnational impact, influencing societies throughout the world in ways no government could hope to control.

The labors of planters, slaves, and Eli Whitney, together with the skills of British textile engineers, made cotton the most important commodity in nineteenth-century commerce. Spun and woven by steam, it rapidly became the basis of a spreading Industrial Revolution—the cloth that clothed the world, the destroyer of indigenous textile industries, the spearhead of Western penetration of Asia and Africa. With the help of Cyrus McCormick, the railroad builders, and new handling and marketing techniques, the wheat farmers of the Americas, the Antipodes, and the Ukraine fed the growing industrial populations of the North Atlantic world while at the same time undermining that world's traditional agriculture.

So population movement and improved transportation led increasingly to regional specialization. The world began to separate into areas of primary production and areas of industrial processing. That the power of the developed North Atlantic area was greater than that of the outer feeder regions early became apparent, as in the curious history of guano, a commodity briefly in vogue as a fertilizer. For a couple of decades at midcentury the demands of British, American, and German farmers made this product the primary basis of Peruvian prosperity. In response to these demands the Chincha Islands, products of centuries of avian effort, were loaded aboard ship by a labor force especially imported from China. So impressive a new El Dorado brought out the old conquistadors. Briefly, in 1864–1866, the islands were seized by Spain. But soon the deposits were exhausted, substitute manures were developed, the Peruvian economy collapsed, the Spanish went home, and the Chinese remained.[3]

Examples of this kind of transnational development could be multiplied. A harder problem is how to categorize them. The controlling decisions were made at the "center" with ramifications extending from Spain to China. But the "center" itself stretched from the United States to Germany, and the decisionmakers were nongovernmental and dispersed. To some, doubtless, the process appears to have been a type of imperialism. But the only identifiable imperialist would seem to be the invisible hand, and in any case the center, while acting upon the outer areas, also acted upon itself.[4]

If the coming of the world market economy and the triumph of industrialization placed the outer areas at the mercy of the developed regions, the developed regions themselves faced similar problems at home. As cotton was joined by other imported raw materials, their industries became increasingly dependent upon supplies from outside; external supplies in the form of cheaper foodstuffs, however necessary to the growing urban population, threatened the livelihood of the farmers; the changes in energy sources that came with the shift from wood to coal (as later to falling water, oil, and uranium) profoundly affected the relative status of the industrializing areas. As the century drew to a close, Europe still appeared to be the center

[3] A. H. Church, "Guano," *Encyclopædia Britannica: A Dictionary of Arts, Sciences, and General Literature* (9th ed.; 24 vols.; Boston: Little, Brown, & Co., 1875–1888), Vol. 9, pp. 233–235.

[4] Jonathan V. Levin, *The Export Economies: Their Pattern of Development in Historical Perspective* (Cambridge, Mass: Harvard University Press, 1960); W. M. Mathew, "The Imperialism of Free Trade: Peru, 1820–70," *Economic History Review,* December 1968 (Vol. 21, No. 3), pp. 562–579.

of the world. But the network of interdependence worked both ways, and questions could be asked about the sovereignty of a continent, let alone of its constituent states, that could not feed or clothe itself.

In coping with this continuous reshaping of the world by the growing transnational economy little leverage was available to even the greatest of national states. That leverage was desired was evidenced at the end of the century by the resurgent popularity of tariffs and subsidies. These, on occasion, proved helpful to developing enterprise; they also proved capable of dealing localized lethal blows, for example, to West Indian and Hawaiian sugar planters. But when faced with the full force of transnational technological innovation, most notably in diminished transportation costs, their long-run defensive value was small.

III. The Propagation of Useful Knowledge

The interaction between center and periphery was not, needless to say, limited to the exchange of goods. Inevitably, the merchants and shipmasters, the emigrants and entrepreneurs, carried their intellectual baggage with them, and the years of developing economic interdependence also saw a growing transfer of knowledge, skills, and attitudes. Predominantly, although not wholly, an extension of the North Atlantic culture and predominantly the work of private individuals and groups, the process in time attained a strength that conservative dynasties and nationalist groups would struggle against in vain. While it has been to some extent overshadowed by concentration on political history, imperialism, and decolonization, the transfer began long before the imperialists got going and would continue at an accelerated pace after the flags were hauled down.

In the promotion of cultural interchange the resident stranger—merchant, diplomat, or refugee—has had a long history, and as the world shrank, his number rapidly increased. Carrying the skills of the Industrial Revolution, British artisans and entrepreneurs crossed the English Channel and the Atlantic Ocean. To the old windows on the West at St. Petersburg, Smyrna, and Nagasaki the nineteenth-century traders added Canton, Shanghai, and a host of other establishments. New countries were brought into diplomatic relations with the "civilized world"; alien rulers established themselves in Asia, Africa, and the islands of the Pacific; a burgeoning foreign missionary movement deployed its workers around the globe. If the influence of these alien enclaves was by no means always one-way and if diplomats and missionaries at times reversed their roles, they nevertheless served importantly in the transmission of culture from the center.

From such contacts, and from their demonstration of the values of modernity, came the growth of transnational "synarchy," the joint or cooperative rule of insiders and outsiders. For while the term has principally been used to describe the Chinese custom of co-opting qualified barbarians—Mongols, Manchus, and ultimately Europeans and Americans—to assist in governing the empire,[5] it in fact describes a fairly general response of coherent traditional societies seeking to cope with externally induced change. In the relations of the West with the traditional civilizations the history of synarchy goes back to the Age of Discovery. But its great period came in the nineteenth and twentieth centuries with the explosive growth of European power and with the appearance on the world scene of those ecumenical busybodies, the Americans.

Already in the late eighteenth century Samuel Grieg and some other Scottish officers had modernized the Russian navy. In the nineteenth century French officers staffed the army of Mehemet Ali in Egypt, the elder Moltke served in the army of the sultan of Turkey, and Colonel Charles Gordon in China and Egypt. As the century moved on, increasing numbers of European technicians and advisers were recruited for the service of Japan, of the modernizing kings of Siam, and of the Chinese Empire. Most notable, perhaps, of all nineteenth-century synarchists was Sir Robert Hart, for more than forty years director of the Chinese Maritime Customs Service. But his preeminence, and the numerical predominance of Europeans in far places, should not obscure the special situation and role of the Americans.

From the first years of its independence the United States was a notably transnationalist society, a country in which the nationalist pail was always half-empty. The universal nature of the American ideology, compounded of Enlightenment thought and evangelical religion, gave to the citizens of the new republic a feeling of identity with humanity at large and a sense of responsibility for its future. To European revolutionaries, as to those desirous of resisting European pressures, the American emphasis on self-determination and progress made the new society a model. To modernizers on whatever continent their faith in the virtues of education and applied science, as well as their practical skills, had similar appeal, while their remote location and their commercial rather than political bias made their help acceptable.

All this encouraged the role of missionary and of mediator between Europe and the outer world, and the American tendency toward synarchy, in contrast to the European great-power emphasis on power and coercion, can be illustrated by a sufficiency of examples. As a sampling of the positions held by these New World transnationalists in the century or so following independence one may list: a head of the Bavarian Council of Regency and a commander of the Russian Black Sea fleet; a commodore of the Argentine, an admiral of the Chilean, and the commander in chief of the Mexican navies; two Ottoman chief naval constructors and the builder of the Moscow–St.

[5] John K. Fairbank, "Synarchy under the Treaties," in *Chinese Thought and Institutions*, ed. John K. Fairbank (Chicago: University of Chicago Press, 1957), pp. 204–231.

Petersburg railway; a president of Nicaragua, a prime minister of Samoa, and a nativist prime minister of the Hawaiian Kingdom; two Chinese generals fighting the Taiping Rebellion and the Taiping "foreign secretary"; an inspector general of the Japanese navy and a chief of staff of the Egyptian army; the organizers of the Imperial University at Tokyo, the first dean of the Chinese Imperial University, and a series of foreign policy advisers in Japan and Korea.[6]

The concentration of the invited synarchists on educational, administrative, and military matters reflected the interests of their hosts. The assumptions of the sending societies of the West as to what was needed in the periphery were equally reflected in a variety of purposeful transnational philanthropic activities intended to assist victims of war or disaster and to uplift those presumed to be dwelling in darkness. Nineteenth-century contributions for relief of the Cape Verde Islands, Greece, Syria, Ireland, and Armenia not only benefited the recipients in greater or lesser degree but had, at times, unanticipated effects, for example, on the pattern of American immigration. From the Greek episode, additionally, came an important precedent: In the future the giver and not the receiver would administer the relief, and transnational aid would bring transnational interference. Nongovernmental though it was, this kind of helpfulness had, on occasion, clear political motivation, as in private American effort during the Civil War to reduce tension with England by assisting the unemployed Lancashire textile operatives. Toward the end of the century much of this work became internationalized in organizations like the Red Cross and Red Crescent, but predominant control remained in the North Atlantic centers of funds and administrative expertise.[7]

More widespread, more persistent, and more important than the relief of intermittent disaster was the philanthropy that expressed itself in the rapid growth of the Protestant (and predominantly Anglo-American) foreign missions movement. For although success in conversion was only moderate and the hope that the world might be evangelized in one or two generations proved illusory, the missionary stations served importantly as show windows for the West, and the cultural package that accompanied the Protestant gospel proved profoundly effective as a social solvent. Most significant, perhaps, of all the missionary contributions was the introduction into the traditional so-

[6] American synarchists can be discovered in quantity in Merle Curti and Kendall Birr, *Prelude to Point Four: American Technical Missions Overseas, 1838–1938* (Madison: University of Wisconsin Press, 1954), and in such regional works as Tyler Dennett, *Americans in Eastern Asia: A Critical Study of the Policy of the United States with Reference to China, Japan, and Korea in the 19th Century* (New York: Macmillan Co., 1922); James A. Field, Jr., *America and the Mediterranean World, 1776–1882* (Princeton, N.J: Princeton University Press, 1969); Fred H. Harrington, *God, Mammon, and the Japanese: Dr. Horace N. Allen and Korean-American Relations, 1884–1905* (Madison: University of Wisconsin Press, 1961); and Robert S. Schwantes, *Japanese and Americans: A Century of Cultural Relations* (New York: Harper & Brothers [for the Council on Foreign Relations], 1955).

[7] Merle Curti, *American Philanthropy Abroad: A History* (New Brunswick, N.J: Rutgers University Press, 1963).

cieties of the idea that change—of the individual by conversion or education, of the environment by the use of Western techniques—was possible.

Here the missionary emphasis on education was of crucial importance. In Asia, Africa, and elsewhere the evangelical emphasis on the Word of God and on a Bible-reading Christianity placed a high premium on literacy and gave rise to remarkable developments in vernacular elementary education. The results were measurable not only in increased literacy but also in an impetus (as in the Ottoman Empire) to linguistic nationalism and in the inculcation throughout Asia (as notably in China with the arrival of the Young Men's Christian Association movement) of novel ideas of female and vocational education and of social concern. Success in primary education was followed by demands for more advanced schools, and, as the philanthropy of the many which had supported the first missionary efforts came to be joined by the philanthropy of the prosperous few, there came the foundation of Robert College at Constantinople, of the Syrian Protestant College at Beirut, and of Christian colleges in India, China, and Japan.

The expansion of the curriculum beyond the elementary level had important cultural consequences. Like the orientalists of the East India Company in the years before T. B. Macaulay's famous minute the missionaries had generally worked to preserve their clients' cultures, to avoid deracination, and to emphasize the vernacular as the language that could reach the heart. Like the orientalists the missionaries lost out to the twin pressures of an expanding curriculum, with its enlarged requirements for texts and teachers, and of the desires of their ambitious clients. In both cases the westernizers defeated the Westerners, and in both cases the consequences were profound. In India the spread of English proved of critical importance to the unification of the subcontinent; both there and elsewhere the proliferation of missionary institutions of higher learning gave further and important impetus to the extension of English as a world language.[8]

The growth of the missionary educational establishment was paralleled by other developments in the transnational propagation of useful knowledge. In the early nineteenth century both Turkey and Egypt had sent students to Europe, and American missionaries had educated some Greeks and South Sea islanders in the United States. The education of the Chinese Yung Wing at Yale in the fifties and of the Japanese Niishima Jo at Amherst in the next decade was followed in the seventies by the Chinese Educational Mission and the Japanese Iwakura Mission. From this time the stream grew steadily with training of Chinese and Japanese in America, Indians and Africans at Ox-

[8] Kenneth S. Latourette, *A History of the Expansion of Christianity* (7 vols.; New York: Harper & Brothers, 1937–1945); Clifton Jackson Phillips, *Protestant America and the Pagan World: The First Half Century of the American Board of Commissioners for Foreign Missions, 1810–1860* (Harvard East Asian Monographs, 32) (Cambridge, Mass: East Asian Research Center, Harvard University, 1969); Field, pp. 350–359.

bridge, London, and Sandhurst, Africans and Indochinese in Paris, and (following the Russo-Japanese War) Indians and Chinese in Japan. At the same time a transfer of institutional forms was taking place, with the extension of extramural accreditation to institutions throughout the British Empire, and with the foundation, by the Japanese and others, of universities on the Western model. By the end of the century there had developed a worldwide educational structure, loose and uncoordinated it is true, but one which opened wide the doors to Western knowledge and whose products would play increasingly important roles in national, transnational, and international affairs.[9]

IV. The Organizational Revolution

The latter part of the nineteenth century saw the commencement of what would later come to be known as the organizational revolution.[10] The increasing importance of organized collectivities, especially in the economic realm, introduced new forces into the transnational picture. Like the work of conversion and education, and like the work of the early synarchists, the bartering and chaffering of shipmaster and supercargo had been largely an affair of individuals. But as the economic business of the world advanced from trading to development—to harbor improvement, the construction of railways, tramlines, and telegraph systems, and the operation of large-scale mines and plantations—it became company business with implications for government at both ends of the transaction. Formerly, in regions of doubtful security, extraterritoriality and consular protection had generally met the needs of the individual; but the new scale of transnational operations brought forth novel problems in diplomacy and in the extension of commercial and international law.

The new scale first became visible, as the Industrial Revolution moved on, in the increasing availability of European capital for export. Gathered by private groups such as the Barings and the Rothschilds, it followed the emigrating Europeans to the United States to finance a greater industrial revolution which by the century's end would be challenging Europe. As the French and Germans joined the capital accumulators, Europeans became the world's bankers with mortgages on Latin America, Turkey and Egypt, the Chinese Empire, and Russia and the Balkans.[11] Such large investments raised serious

[9] The concern for the useful aspects of the Western stock of knowledge showed itself in the concentration on such fields as engineering, business and economics, and education. See, e.g., the list of studies elected by Chinese students in American universities in Kwang-ching Liu, *Americans and Chinese: A Historical Essay and a Bibliography* (Cambridge, Mass: Harvard University Press, 1963), pp. 31–32.

[10] Kenneth E. Boulding, *The Organizational Revolution: A Study in the Ethics of Economic Organization* (New York: Harper & Brothers, 1953).

[11] Ralph W. Hidy, *The House of Baring in American Trade and Finance: English Merchant Bankers at Work, 1763–1861* (Harvard Studies in Business History, 14) (Cambridge, Mass: Harvard University Press, 1949); Herbert Feis, *Europe, the World's Banker, 1870–1914* (New York: W. W. Norton & Co., 1965).

problems of protection. In predictable circumstances, as in the Anglo-American connection, normal legal remedies and the recruitment of American partners proved generally sufficient; elsewhere the bankers, like farmers, manufacturers, and workers faced by other transnational problems, called on government for assistance. Again, as with their tariffs and labor legislation, the governments responded. Questions of equal opportunity drew them into rivalry, problems of default brought out the gunboats, and there followed the seizure of Latin American customs houses, the foreclosure of the Egyptian mortgage, and the exaction of additional security from China.

With the money went the promoters seeking to extend the range and increase the productivity of the world economy and to turn a profit in the process. By the first decade of the twentieth century projects for Turkish, African, and Chinese railways and for Chinese flood control had reached such dimensions as to involve entrepreneurs, governments, and in some cases the eleemosynary sectors. As with the bankers a generation before and the frontiersmen a generation before that, the activities of the promoters now made diplomatic problems for their governments. That the magnitude of their activities had also given them some of the attributes of government was early recognized. In assembling his 1904 collection of Chinese and Korean treaties and conventions the American diplomat W. W. Rockhill proceeded on the assumption that the private agreements regarding railroad concessions and mining rights were as important for Chinese relations with the outer world as were the more formal treaties.[12]

The development in Europe and America of the large manufacturing corporation introduced a new transnational actor. The product, above all, of the new communications technology—railroad and telegraph, typewriter and telephone—these corporations were impressive enough at home. Even before the merger with United States Steel Corporation Andrew Carnegie was producing more steel than all England. Increase in size was followed by increase in range as the visible hand of the managers came to replace the invisible hand of the market. The same urge for rationalization and stability that led at home to vertical integration and to trusts, pools, and cartels also led outward to sources of raw materials and to important marketing areas.[13] This outward thrust was made possible by a series of advances in international

[12] John A. DeNovo, "A Railroad for Turkey: The Chester Project of 1908–1913," *Business History Review*, Autumn 1959 (Vol. 33, No. 3), pp. 300–329; Jerry Israel, "For God, For China and for Yale," *American Historical Review*, February 1970 (Vol. 75, No. 3), pp. 796–807; Paul Varg, *Open Door Diplomat: The Life of W. W. Rockhill* (Urbana: University of Illinois Press, 1952), p. 128.

[13] John Kenneth Galbraith, *The New Industrial State* (Boston: Houghton Mifflin Co., 1967), considers this rationalization in purely domestic terms; Harry Magdoff, *The Age of Imperialism: The Economics of United States Foreign Policy* (New York: Monthly Review Press, 1969), provides a Marxist description of the American outward reach. Some idea of the limits of administrative possibility prior to the development of the new tools can be gained from Leonard D. White, *The Federalists: A Study in Administrative History* (New York: Macmillan Co., 1959), pp. 466–506, and *The Jacksonians: A Study in Administrative History, 1829–1861* (New York: Macmillan Co., 1954), pp. 530–551.

communications which complemented the completion of the railroad networks and the triumph of steam upon the oceans. In 1866 the Atlantic cable linked the telegraph networks of Europe and North America; in the 1870s India, the Far East, and South America were tied in; and the same decade brought the establishment of the General Postal Union and the International Bureau of Weights and Measures. By the turn of the century the transnational corporation had become clearly visible—soap manufacturers had developed plantations in Africa and the Pacific, oil refiners had established their marketing organizations in Africa and Asia, fruit companies served their Caribbean plantations with their own shipping lines, and copper companies had bought up Latin American mineral deposits. Most significant, perhaps, for the future were the 28 American-owned plants that had been established in Europe to engage in such up-to-date activities as meat packing and the manufacture of electrical machinery, cash registers, and sewing machines.[14]

The exportation in the latter part of the nineteenth century of such complicated systems as railroads and large-scale mining operations and the appearance of the multinational corporation emphasized the increasing and unanticipated differences between the industrialized areas of the world and the outer feeder regions. Just as the growing urban complexes of Europe and North America were coming more and more to dominate their hinterlands, so these same complexes, and with them the North Atlantic region as a whole, were gaining on the outer world. This differential was vastly greater than it had been at the start of the century when trade between the center and the periphery (as between city and farm) had involved an exchange of goods on roughly the same level of sophistication and when, except in the crucial areas of navigation and entrepreneurship, geographical differences had been more important than different levels of skills. By 1900 the productive centers of the North Atlantic rimlands had gained a near monopoly of modern industry, organizing skills, and capital. Between these regions moved the greater part of the world's trade, and the workings of so powerful a system were visible everywhere, not least, perhaps, in the rhetoric and behavior of the imperialists.[15]

The conclusions of the imperialists covered only part of the picture, for the growing split between "world city" and "world farm" brought with it an ever-closer interdependence. Much of the early trade between the North Atlantic and the outer regions had been in luxuries which could, if necessary, be dispensed with; but by the twentieth century the luxuries of the few had

[14] Frank A. Southard, Jr., *American Industry in Europe* (Boston: Houghton Mifflin Co., 1931), p. xiii. Mira Wilkins, *The Emergence of Multinational Enterprise: American Business Abroad from the Colonial Era to 1914* (Cambridge, Mass: Harvard University Press, 1970), sheds much new light on this subject.

[15] Since all sizable states had their own domestic underdeveloped areas—Scotland, Prussia, Sicily, the American South and West—these workings were also visible at home in urbanization, the depopulation of the hill country, and agrarian protest.

given way to the necessities of the increasingly influential many as the center's need for raw materials was balanced by the periphery's need for fabricated products. This situation raised questions about the ability of national states—and ultimately even of the strongest of these—to fulfill their classic responsibilities of ensuring the prosperity and security of their citizens. Increasingly, indeed, these functions came to seem incompatible. As dependence on transnational economic developments and the rising expectations of the home population emphasized the welfare function, national security planning was complicated by problems of strategic materials, technological complexity, and rising costs. More and more, as time passed and technology advanced, defense became the prerogative of the very rich. As early as the 1880s some had predicted that American economic competition would force the powers of Europe to forswear their costly armaments. In the years after World War II these predictions appeared to have been fulfilled.

Despite its excessive nationalisms, its autarchic experiments, and its destructive wars the twentieth century witnessed a continuing spread of transnational systems and a remarkable growth of international nongovernmental organizations. In this process, as earlier, advances in the technology of transportation and communication played a crucial role. Pipelines and powerlines extended the economic network; road nets and the trucking industry gave land transport a flexibility approximating that in a fluid medium; increasingly, for both people and commodities, the airplane (and particularly the long-range jet) reduced all geography to a series of great circles.

Profiting from these developments and from great advances in telecommunications, the bankers and managers (like the scholars and philanthropists) pressed on with their work of functional transnational integration. By the end of the 1920s American corporations were reported to control more than 1,000 European subsidiaries together with sizable, if smaller, numbers in Canada and Latin America. In the Union of Soviet Socialist Republics there developed a notable example of corporate synarchy as American engineering firms were brought in to assist in the industrialization of the country.[16] The increasing importance of petroleum brought windfall wealth to distant deserts, led Western capital and Western technicians into new areas, and created a new diplomacy of corporation executives, sheiks, and colonels. In the quarter century after World War II there came an extraordinary expansion of transnational direct investment by the major American corporations (as by Swiss drug manufacturers, German automobile makers, and by British, Italian, and Japanese concerns). Not least remarkable of transnational developments was the astonishing growth of airborne tourism which provided, for

[16] Southard, pp. xiv, xv, 11–14, and 203–206. For statistics on the development of 187 selected corporations see James W. Vaupel and Joan P. Curhan, *The Making of Multinational Enterprise: A Sourcebook of Tables Based on a Study of 187 Major U.S. Manufacturing Corporations* (Boston: Division of Research, Graduate School of Business Administration, Harvard University, 1969).

countries endowed with scenery, antiquities, or big game, a startlingly large share of the national product and which linked, in symbiotic community of interest, beachboys and barmen on tropic isles with the designers and manufacturers of some of the most sophisticated equipment known to man.

V. New Culture and New Tribe

The consequences of the shrinking and linking of the world, of increased wealth and increased mobility, of the spread of Western knowledge and the growth of transnational organization extended far beyond the political issues of security and welfare. At the same time that these were being called into question, the cultural foundations of the traditional societies and the presumed cultural uniqueness so central to so many nationalisms were being undermined. This process involved the development of two cultures—better, perhaps, two levels of culture—one global and the other local, national, or provincial. Some rough earlier analogues could be seen in the extension of Roman and Moslem rule, in the imposition of Spanish control systems on the indigenous population of the Americas, and in the British domination of India. But the latter-day phenomenon was notably less political and depended more on contagion than on conquest.

That the old bottles were inadequate to the new vintages was early visible in the area of language where the replacement of religion by commerce as the prime transnational activity brought with it the need for a new Latin. The first answers appeared in the spread of regional lingua francas—Pidgin, Swahili, bazaar Malay—to which could perhaps be added as specialized technologically determined examples, Morse Code and the International Code of Signals. Analogous responses to the new needs developed even in the major cultures in the shift from classical to vernacular Chinese, in the extensive absorption (as in Japanese and "Franglais") of foreign locutions, and in the adulteration, so frequently deplored in letters to *The Times,* of English by American. As early as the 1880s conscious recognition of the problem had led to purposeful attempts at a solution with the invention in that single decade of four "universal languages" of which one, Esperanto, survived to enjoy a considerable boom between the wars.

Yet, whatever the merits of Esperanto, it turned out in the end that the universal language had been around all the time. The mid-twentieth century brought the triumph of English which the missionary educator Cyrus Hamlin had long before seen as "destined to form a bond of sympathy between the nations, beyond any other language."[17] To the demands of wartime interallied

[17] Cyrus Hamlin, *Among the Turks* (New York: R. Carter & Brothers, 1878), p. 282. That this was not a purely Anglo-Saxon conceit may be seen in a still earlier description of English by Pierre Aronnax: "Cette langue . . . est à peu près universelle." Jules Verne, *Vingt mille lieues sous les mers* (Paris: J. Hetzel et Cie., 1869), chapter 8.

cooperation, the needs of transnational corporations and of advanced scientific instruction, and the requirements of expanding tourism the language of the Bible and Shakespeare provided the answer. The triumph on such an extensive scale of the language of commerce over the language of diplomacy suggests both the power and the nature of the transnational phenomenon.

The nineteenth-century spread of lingua francas was paralleled by the appearance of a new transnational culture. Not since the Renaissance had the West experienced such important literary and cultural mergings. Together with the influence of English writers in America, the translation of Russian authors into English, and the Germanization of Shakespeare came the dominance of German and Italian composers and of French painters and the vogue for Indian and Far Eastern literature, philosophy, and art. The emergence of this new nineteenth-century cosmopolitan high culture was followed in the twentieth century by that of a new low one. Over the course of the years there had emanated from Great Britain a whole series of games played with balls of which one, soccer, ultimately attained the dignity of casus belli; the subtitled or dubbed motion picture commenced that homogenization of teen-ager and stenographer that television pushes on apace; the movement of Western military forces added the educational impact of the post exchange to the revolution of rising expectations.

The energy, the curiosity, and the prosperity of the creators of the new culture raised a new problem. To the question of who owned the rubber of Liberia or the copper of Chile was added another: Who owned the national treasures of Greece or Italy or France or England? Since Napoleon I, and increasingly with the growth of industrial wealth, archeological artifacts and works of art had gravitated to where the money was. The Elgin marbles adorned the British Museum; Cleopatra's needles stood in Paris, London, and New York; Renaissance paintings decorated the Louvre and the Metropolitan. To the nationalists, who had long ignored these matters, the process came in time to seem a predatory cultural imperialism to be cured by laws forbidding export; to the transnationalist, who had seen the objects first, it was a process of discovery, preservation, and integration into the larger culture. It was, after all, a Frenchman who deciphered the Rosetta stone; a German had dug up a Mycenae ignored by the Greeks; Englishmen and Americans excavated ancient Crete and Egypt; an American from Hawaii introduced the world to Italian primitive painting and one from Massachusetts made the Japanese aware of their artistic past.

So while transnational pressures were eroding local cultures and traditional ways, the representatives of the new trends were working to preserve. As the conflict of interest between cargo cultist and academic anthropologist would show in high relief, the westernizers tended to be much more thoroughgoing than the Westerners. Nevertheless, the development of the new transnational and cosmopolitan culture raised hard problems. Given the importance of narcissistic history to nineteenth- and twentieth-century nationalism, as perhaps to all feelings of group identity, it was galling to find one's past preserved, one's history written, and one's literature interpreted by outsiders. While primitive societies had long been subjected to this treatment, the disproportionately large resources available to Western scholars, and above all to the Americans, had by mid-twentieth century made the problem one of world-wide dimensions.

Not unnaturally, the creation of a transnational economy and the formation of a transnational cultural superstructure led to new social groupings. The new dispensation, in due course, came to be visible in terms of people. The demands of the Industrial Revolution and the opening of new areas had encouraged the expatriation of the strong-backed and the technically and entrepreneurially skilled; their fruits permitted the expatriation of the prosperous. By 1900, whether for business or for pleasure, some 15,000 Americans were reported resident in London; by 1910 some 55,000 were living abroad. To the growth of such foreign enclaves, by no means limited to Americans, the twentieth century would contribute notably through the diaspora of the central European intellectuals, the movements of the armies, the expansion of the international civil service, and the growth of the transnational corporation.[18]

The consequences of increased mobility and improved communication went well beyond matters of residence or occupation. By the end of the nineteenth century international marriage, long-known among the European aristocracy, had extended to intercontinental marriage as members of the British and other European upper classes, drawn by their admiration of American wealth, embarked upon this sex-linked form of synarchy.[19] Nor was this development a purely North Atlantic one; on the other side of the globe the development of opportunity and shared interest brought marriages of American teachers and diplomats to Japanese girls and of Chinese, Japanese, and Koreans to Americans. In mid-twentieth century student and GI brides greatly expanded the phenomenon which, while geographically exogamous, was in terms of role endogamous. As with the intellectuals and managers, so with the family: The developments of transnationalism had led to the appearance of a new and growing tribe, functionally rather than geographically or ethnically defined.

[18] By 1965 the American population abroad was estimated at 1.4 million. In 1970 the United Nations and consular colony in New York totaled some 27,000. On the migration of European intellectuals see Laura Fermi, *Illustrious Immigrants: The Intellectual Migration from Europe, 1930–41* (Chicago: University of Chicago Press, 1968); on the migration of talent generally see Walter Adams, ed., *The Brain Drain* (New York: Macmillan Co., 1968).

[19] Transatlantic marriage is discussed in Dixon Wecter, *The Saga of American Society: A Record of Social Aspiration, 1607–1937* (New York: Charles Scribner's Sons, 1937), pp. 405–416.

VI. Whose Challenge?

In the years following the Second World War the growing range and expanding activity of the high-technology–high-production world opened increasing opportunity for assimilation to the New Tribe. Throughout the world the educated, the energetic, and the unscrupulous left the country for the metropolis. Much of this movement had important transnational implications. On the one hand, the demands of the industrialized areas, crossing cultural and political boundaries, drew Puerto Ricans to New York, Pakistanis to London, and southern Europeans northward to the new bidonvilles. On the other hand, the establishment of branch plants and subsidiaries by transnational corporations tended to attach segments of local populations to the interests of nonnational enterprise and in other ways to limit the economic sovereignty of the state. In such a context the managerial choice between moving the plant and moving the labor came to have large social and political implications. But whether within or across national boundaries the osmotic aspects of brain drain and brain gain and the expanded activity of the knowledge industry worked for further definition of the two levels of culture, of world city versus world farm, and of New Tribe versus old tribes.

Hardly surprisingly, the existence of all these pressures—economic, cultural, social—elicited some lively political responses both from the governments of the national states and from revolutionary groups aspiring to replace them. The omnipresence of the New Tribe brought quarrels reminiscent of those between national monarchs and universal church. But resistance, whether expressed economically in tariff and subsidy, politically in expropriation or revolution, or culturally in Aryan art and socialist realism, proved generally palliative at best. If the New Tribe, like the Old Church, depended for its effective functioning on the sufferance of local political authorities, the latter still had to tread carefully when trifling with salvation.

The multiplication of new sovereignties which followed both world wars only emphasized the limitations of the state.[20] For the newer, less developed, and less solidly established of these, whose gross national product was in many cases inferior to the output of major North Atlantic corporations, transnational pressures were almost irresistible. Seen in nationalist terms the answer to their problems was to hold fast to tradition while catching up with the advanced areas of the world. But this answer, in most cases, proved to be no answer at all. The choice between sovereignty, autonomy, and no foreign in-

[20] The number of independent sovereignties, something under 50 in 1900, has subsequently more than tripled. This passion for independence has produced its share of curiosities: Nauru, a phosphate island in the Pacific Ocean (area eight square miles, population c. 6,000) which maintains a high standard of living by exporting itself; Anguilla, a would-be independent island in the Caribbean, the majority of whose "nationals" live in the greater New York area; Israel, a state located in one continent, administered by an elite from another, and with much of its tax base located in a third. The list could of course be extended.

vestment and a development program which involved acceptance of the new synarchy of the transnational corporation was seldom a very real one. Furthermore, as the brain drain clearly showed, it was much easier to join up than to catch up.

More generally, in spite of incidents of violent resistance, the response of states both great and small involved a shift of function. Where corporations had assumed some of the attributes of sovereignty, now governments involved themselves in the productive process. At home questions of welfare came to predominate, industries were nationalized, and ministries of agriculture, transport, communications, and tourism were added to the government. Abroad, with war priced out of the market for all but the very rich (or in some cases the very poor), the new role involved a considerable divestiture of sovereignty. Together with unprecedented international cooperation in economic planning, administration, and enterprise there developed a complex mix of stabilizing, developing, and uplifting efforts. In some of these areas, where the new requirements proved too large for the traditionally responsible bankers, philanthropists, or corporations, governments themselves became transnational actors as public moneys supplemented private postwar relief, as transnational education was expanded, and as the Peace Corps and various technical missions took up the roles of the missionaries and synarchists.

So the erosion, or at least the transformation, of the national state continued. With the diminution of cold-war tensions and the resultant low-profile leadership throughout the great-power world the emperor's clothes became less and less visible. At the same time that many states appeared too small to wield the traditional prerogatives of sovereignty, they also seemed too big (or too obviously linked with the transnational world and the New Tribe) to hold the loyalty of all their citizens. With the disappearance of the enemy over the border came the search for new enemies, the exacerbation of internal nationalisms—Welsh, Scotch, Breton, black, and that of the Woodstock Nation—and the phenomenon of transnational student revolt. The decline of international tension and the efficiency of global communications had opened the way to threats of ethnic or generational conflict.

Such startling developments could hardly have been anticipated by earlier generations, although eighteenth-century thought and nineteenth-century optimism had looked forward to a coming world culture. Enlightenment thinkers had foreseen the unification of mankind through expanded commerce, the application of science to transportation, and the extension of the federal principle. The Victorians had anticipated the parliament of man. So attractive a vision gained devotees outside the North Atlantic area and, as the nineteenth century wore on, individual Latin Americans and Chinese saw in railroad and steamship, in steam and electricity, the means for the unification of all nations.[21] But with time the picture changed as concentration on the social question at home, the partition of Africa and the pressure on China, and the excitement of turn-of-the-century wars gave rise to J. A. Hobson's *Imperialism* (1902) and to Lenin's 1916 sequel on the same subject.[22]

Although the views of Hobson and Lenin are still persuasive to undergraduates and other reactionaries, the clearer vision appeared in the contemporary description by the English journalist and reformer W. T. Stead of the "Americanization" of the world. Since events had already outpaced language, Stead had problems with terminology. There was much truth in the idea of "Americanization" as indicative of the branch of Western society most active in the transnationalizing process, and similar thoughts had been expressed by Richard Cobden some 60 years before as well as by American patriots of the revolutionary generation.[23] But the label, of course, was also a paradoxically national one. These same terminological problems remain: How "American" is the "American challenge"? Has the world been—is it being—Anglo-Saxonized or Americanized or Westernized? If only because of the present role of Japan, none of these terms fits well, nor are they welcomed by those who, however appreciative of the spread of Greek culture, Roman law, and Arabic numbers, look askance at similar contemporary developments. For the moment, and until we get a good name for the New Tribe, the student is forced back upon "non-" and "trans-" compounds, Mumfordian adjectives, and similar barbarisms.

Despite these difficulties—better, perhaps, precisely because they exist—the transnational phenomenon deserves attention. For many years the process was best understood, in whatever country, in terms of the colors on the map, the civilizing mission of the nation-state, and "The March of the Flag." More recently it has been fashionable to disparage the whole business as cultural or economic "imperialism." Should we now look at the process in early nineteenth-century terms as evidencing the march of progress, or of liberty, or of steam? Or should we consider it under more modern rubrics as reflecting the spread of software or of the gestalt? Granting that nationalism has been, and in some cases perhaps can still be, an extraordinarily energizing force, it should prove useful to look beyond the flags, the traditional curricular formulations, and the political map.

[21] In 1870 the Argentine Juan Bautista Alberdi foresaw the coming of the "global village" ("pueblo-mundo"): Arthur P. Whitaker, *The Western Hemisphere Idea: Its Rise and Decline* (Ithaca, N.Y: Cornell University Press, 1965), p. 65. For a similar Chinese vision see Ssu-yü Teng and John K. Fairbank, *China's Response to the West: A Documentary Survey, 1839–1923* (New York: Atheneum Publishers, 1963), p. 136.

[22] J. A. Hobson, *Imperialism: A Study* (London: James Nisbet & Co., 1902); V. I. Lenin, *Imperialism: The Highest Stage of Capitalism—A Popular Outline* (Little Lenin Library, Vol. 15) (rev. trans.; New York: International Publishers, 1939).

[23] W. T. Stead, *The Americanization of the World; Or, the Trend of the Twentieth Century* (New York: H. Markley, 1902); Richard Cobden, "England, Ireland, and America," in *The Political Writings of Richard Cobden* (2 vols.; London: T. Fisher Unwin, 1903), Vol. I, pp. 5–119; Field, pp. 2–24. Although Stead (like Cobden) thought well of the process, some had reservations: See, e.g., John McFarland Kennedy, *Imperial America* (London: Stanley Paul & Co., 1914).

Transnational Economic Processes

Edward L. Morse

Changes in the structure of the global economy have resulted in a withering of governmental control of certain activities presumed to be de jure within the domain of governments. The international monetary crises of the 1960s have demonstrated the emergence of financial markets that seem to operate beyond the jurisdiction of even the most advanced industrialized states of the West and outside their individual or collective control. The flourishing of multinational corporations has affected the national science and economic growth policies of highly developed and less developed states alike by restricting the freedom of those governments to establish social priorities. Tariff reductions carefully and arduously negotiated on a multilateral basis through the General Agreement on Tariffs and Trade (GATT), through bilateral arrangements, or through emergent regional economic organizations have similarly increased the number of relatively nonmanipulable and unknown factors which must be accounted for in planning a wide spectrum of domestic and foreign economic policies—from regional development policy or anti-inflationary efforts on the domestic side to the international exchange rate of a state's currency.

Whether these factors have become so significant as to render obsolete the state-centric view of international political and economic relations is a question which can be answered only when the limits upon restrictions on governmental operations become more clearly defined. It is, however, now obvious that the state-centric view must at least be modified and supplemented by additional frames of reference so that the factors which have impaired the efficacy of state-level decisionmaking processes can be more coherently analyzed.

This essay is concerned with one set of factors salient in twentieth-century international relations which cannot satisfactorily be dealt with through traditional references to autonomous national states. These factors are predomi-

Edward L. Morse is assistant professor of politics and international affairs at the Woodrow Wilson School of Public and International Affairs and a faculty associate of the Center of International Studies, Princeton University, Princeton, New Jersey.

nantly economic and are associated with changes in the global economy over the course of the past 100 years. In particular, this essay is concerned with describing those economic trends which have served to undermine the traditional state-centric view. In addition to this descriptive task, this essay is also concerned with explanations of the growth of transnational economic activities. In both instances the present endeavor inevitably covers issues of great controversy. On the one hand, proponents of the state-centric view have offered cogent reasons for maintaining, if modifying, the traditional perspective by treating phenomena such as multinational corporations, international economic organizations, and multinational economic treaty commitments as "environing conditions" which have restricted but not invalidated the state-centric view. On the other hand, even among those who accept the evidence that these external factors ought to be isolated and analyzed apart from national governments, there is no consensus on a theory which would explain the development of these factors or indicate their relevance.

I have chosen to focus my attention on an empirical rather than a theoretical issue—namely, whether there exists in contemporary international economic relations an isolable set of factors which can be fruitfully thought of as transnational and, if so, what the significance of those factors is for the foreign and domestic policies of various states. In so doing I have evaded the task of formulating a theoretical explanation of the growth of transnational economic activities. Neither I nor others have yet been able to develop or test a theory which would be adequate to that task. When such a theory is developed, however, it will clarify what are currently the most arguable questions concerning international economic relations. Among these are the following questions: Is the level of international economic interdependence increasing or decreasing? Is such a change in economic interdependence universal or regional? Is the growth in transnational activities the consequence of permanent changes in international affairs in general or of the particular and transitory political configuration of forces which developed after World War II? Do transnational economic activities raise fundamental political questions about the ability of the modern nation-state to control them? Do the dynamics of transnational processes suggest a prognosis of stability or of instability in international affairs? Finally, what are the consequences of this prognosis for international peace?

I. Economic Activities as Transnational Processes

If transnational interactions are understood as "the movement of tangible or intangible items across state boundaries when at least one actor is not an agent of a government or an intergovernmental organization,"[1] it immediately becomes obvious why a transnational perspective on international affairs should

[1] Joseph S. Nye, Jr., and Robert O. Keohane, introductory essay to this volume, p. xii.

focus on economic activities. Virtually any "tangible" item involved in such processes is likely to have a significant economic dimension in that it can be treated as a commodity or service to which monetary value can be attached. Whether it is a question of goods, information, or money itself, its presence is likely also to entail certain costs for the governments or societies involved. This economic aspect of transnational activities is central for several additional reasons.

First, transnational processes seem to have arisen in the contemporary international system after the technological revolution induced persistent economic growth in the highly developed or modernized societies of Western Europe. The remarkable development of first the British and later other Western economies in the nineteenth century through the "extended application of science to problems of economic production" enabled these societies to mobilize resources on an unprecedented scale.[2] This mobilization of economic resources coupled with revolutionary innovations in the fields of transportation and communication enabled Western states to expand their power and influence, if not their rule, over the rest of the planet. The linking up of the various states of the world through this process of growth in transnational economic phenomena was accompanied by an unprecedented mobility of certain factors of production (population, capital) as well as of output.[3]

Second, these economic activities were transnational, as defined above, as a result of the kind of political regimes in which the industrialization process first occurred. These states were, by and large, liberal democracies. Very little of the initial growth in trade was a result of planned governmental activities. Rather, the responsibility for taking advantage of the economic potential of new technological innovations was usually in the hands of private industrialists and bankers whose main incentive was the profit motive. Given the nature of the regimes involved international economic activities were bound to have some transnational element, and these were generally private business enterprises.

Third, with the onset of sustained economic growth in what are now the most highly modernized societies economic values became a central substantive focus of political and other social activities. This was the case for several

[2] Simon Kuznets, *Modern Economic Growth: Rate, Structure, and Spread* (Studies in Comparative Economics, No. 7) (New Haven, Conn: Yale University Press, 1966), p. 9. A similar definition has been used to describe the revolution of modernization in human affairs; see C. E. Black, *The Dynamics of Modernization: A Study in Comparative History* (New York: Harper & Row, 1966), pp. 1–9.

[3] For example, overseas emigration from Europe was at a level of some 257,000 per year in 1846 and increased to a rate of 1.4 million per year at the outbreak of World War I. Thereafter the rate precipitously declined. Similarly, world trade increased at an accelerating rate through the first half of the nineteenth century, reaching a per decade rate of growth of 61.5 percent in the 1840s and declining to about 47 percent at the outbreak of the First World War. It, too, later declined drastically. With the rapid growth of world trade in the century before World War I the share of the foreign trade sector in the national product also generally increased in the industrializing societies. More complete data on the period between the 1830s and 1960 can be found in Kuznets, pp. 285–358.

reasons. First, economic values were central to the new secularism which accompanied the breakdown of the feudal system and which is one of the distinguishing characteristics of modern life. Second, with the growth of their domestic economies expectations of affluence became generalized in all societies. Through this "revolution of rising expectations" political goods grew to assume more and more the substantive characteristic of economic goods. Thus, the growth of the "welfare state" and of governmental policies for health care, minimum wages, and the like reinforced the secular evaluation of public policy.[4] Third, those transnational ideologies which developed as explanations of a world characterized by sustained economic growth focused on economic activities. For liberalism this focus appeared in a dichotomy of economic and political activities. The modern state was thought to be the upshot of a historical development which permitted economic activities to flourish internationally as political controls over the activities of individual citizens were dismantled. For Marxism-Leninism the withering of the state would result from economically determined processes which would enable "man" to overcome his alienation so as to develop freely his own individual capacities. In both cases the ideal was a transnational and universal humanitarianism based on the transcendence of the nation-state and the development of the potential of high levels of industrialization.

The central position of economic activities in transnational processes has been reinforced by the more recent revolution in nuclear technology and its impact on international affairs. As a result of the development of nuclear technology traditional foreign policy goals involving territorial accretion have become so politically and economically costly as to be virtually prohibitive. The well-known paradox of the inutility of force in the relations of those states which have been stalemated by the "balance of terror" has made it possible for international economic activities to increase tremendously in political significance.[5] As the use of traditional instruments of force has receded in importance, plays for power and position subsequently have appeared in the international monetary and commercial systems.[6]

[4] For an important and stimulating discussion of the relationship between political and economic aspects of modernization in terms of the growth of public as opposed to private goods see Karl de Schweinitz, Jr., "Growth, Development, and Political Modernization," *World Politics,* July 1970 (Vol. 22, No. 4), pp. 518–540. De Schweinitz views political growth as the process by which the output of public goods is increased. This political output is jointly consumed by all members of the polity—whether or not they wish to consume them: "Everyone must consume political goods. Although I can choose to consume cigarettes, automobiles, or transistor radios, I have no choice but to consume the armed forces of the United States, the space program of NASA, the judicial system, the FBI, the Federal Reserve Authority, or the National Labor Relations Board." (P. 525.)

[5] For an elaboration of this paradox see Pierre Hassner, "The Nation-State in the Nuclear Age," *Survey,* April 1968 (No. 67), pp. 3–27; and Hans J. Morgenthau, "The Four Paradoxes of Nuclear Strategy," *American Political Science Review,* March 1964 (Vol. 58, No. 1), pp. 23–35.

[6] For an elaboration of this argument see my article, "The Transformation of Foreign Policies: Modernization, Interdependence, and Externalization," *World Politics,* April 1970 (Vol. 22, No. 3), pp. 379–383; and Klaus Knorr, *On the Uses of Military Power in the Nuclear Age* (Princeton, N.J: Princeton University Press, 1966), pp. 21–34.

International economic policies have increased in political importance for three different kinds of states for three different sets of reasons. First, in the case of the industrialized societies of the West the post–World War II attempt to create an "Atlantic Community," first through the Marshall Plan and later through the negotiation of tariff dismantling through GATT, involved an amalgamation of security and welfare objectives. On the one hand, the community was seen as an attempt to foster higher levels of interdependence among Western industrialized states so as to reinforce, through economic recovery and economic growth, their collective defense against Communist expansion. On the other hand, the accrual of the welfare benefits of higher levels of trade was also viewed as an end in itself.[7] Second, in East-West relations trade policies formulated in virtually all Western states during the 1960s were based on the notion that foreign economic policy could foster political liberalization in Eastern Europe.[8] Third, in the case of relatively nonmodernized societies economic policies have grown in importance as a result of the relative impotence of these societies when compared to relatively industrialized states. Without the capacity to sustain traditional foreign policies based on the use of force the leaders of these states have collectivized their demands for a greater share of the world's wealth by supporting efforts to redistribute that wealth through trade and aid agreements with the wealthier societies of both East and West.

As a result of these three reasons the same general conclusions can be reached: Economic change and economic policy have become central foci of international politics in the twentieth century. Any general theory which is to succeed in explaining the reasons why this focus has grown in importance must take into account the shift in the substance of international politics from a concentration on instruments of force to an emphasis on economic statecraft.[9]

II. The "Myth of National Interdependence" Reexamined

If the politicization of economic activities accounts for their place in a discussion of transnationalism, it does not provide an explanation of the emer-

[7] The same combination of "security" and "welfare" goals could be found among the various incentives for European integration. On the one hand, European unification was viewed as a means of putting an end to the divisive nationalisms which had been seen as a root of warfare and upheaval in Europe in the century preceding World War II. On the other hand, it was seen as the means of creating a market sufficiently large to support modern industrial growth. For a discussion of these motives in terms of functional, federal, and confederal approaches to European unity see Altiero Spinelli, *The Eurocrats: Conflict and Crisis in the European Community*, trans. C. Grove Haines (Baltimore, Md: Johns Hopkins Press, 1966), pp. 3–25.

[8] For the most comprehensive review of political aspects of East-West trade see Samuel Pisar, *Coexistence and Commerce: Guidelines for Transactions between East and West* (New York: McGraw-Hill Book Co., 1970).

[9] The increased importance of economic relationships as a major concern of international politics is further explained by Susan Strange in "International Economics and International Relations: A Case of

gence and growth of what may be called transnational economic activities. As I suggested above, a discussion of transnational economic activities ought to be concerned with two issues: 1) the empirical question of whether transnational activities exist and 2) the theoretical question of what sort of theory is necessary to explain the emergence of transnational activities and the dynamics of their growth. It is the former issue to which the following discussion is largely directed. Problems arising from the theoretical issue are discussed in section IV.

Any discussion of the nature of transnational economic processes must relate the emergence of transnational economic relations to relatively recent changes in international relations and include the magnitude of the growth of international economic activities. Because a theory to explain this growth is lacking, even the empirical concern of describing trends is confronted with frequently contradictory evidence.[10] Some writers see these trends as supportive of the thesis that transnational economic activities have grown in volume as well as significance during the past century.[11] Others see the trends as reflective of a substantially decreased significance in the external sector for virtually all societies which followed the growth in this sector before World War I.[12] These contradictions apparently reflect our inability to perceive clearly the dynamics of change since we are in the midst of a process which is as yet incomplete. As a result trends have become clearly discernible, but, as one student of modern economic growth has argued, "the final shapes of these characteristics are presently hidden from us. This limitation, however, should affect primarily questions of degree rather than kind, of intensity rather than being. It will be most important to bear this limitation in mind in evaluating the specific empirical coefficients—their stability and variability over time and space."[13]

There are several possible ways to organize a discussion of transnational economic trends. One would involve the specification of the nongovernmental participants including corporations, financial organizations, and other group-

Mutual Neglect," *International Affairs* (London), April 1970 (Vol. 46, No. 2), pp. 304–315; and my article, "The Politics of Interdependence," *International Organization*, Spring 1969 (Vol. 23, No. 2), pp. 311–326.

[10] Several of these contradictory interpretations are reviewed in my article in *International Organization*, Vol. 23, No. 2; and in Oran R. Young, "Interdependencies in World Politics," *International Journal*, Autumn 1969 (Vol. 24, No. 4), pp. 726–750.

[11] See Kuznets; and Richard N. Cooper, *The Economics of Interdependence: Economic Policy in the Atlantic Community* (Atlantic Policy Series) (New York: McGraw-Hill Book Co. [for the Council on Foreign Relations], 1968).

[12] The most extreme statement of this viewpoint is found in Kenneth N. Waltz, "The Myth of National Interdependence," in *The International Corporation: A Symposium*, ed. Charles P. Kindleberger (Cambridge, Mass: M.I.T. Press, 1970), pp. 205–223. See also Karl W. Deutsch and Alexander Eckstein, "National Industrialization and the Declining Share of the International Economic Sector, 1890–1959," *World Politics*, January 1961 (Vol. 13, No. 2), pp. 267–299; and Karl W. Deutsch, Chester I. Bliss, and Alexander Eckstein, "Population, Sovereignty, and the Share of Foreign Trade," *Economic Development and Cultural Change*, July 1962 (Vol. 10, No. 4), pp. 353–366.

[13] Kuznets, pp. 15–16.

ings which are highlighted in this volume. Alternatively, the pattern of interactions can be specified at a systemic level which would isolate a set of activities analytically separable from the nation-state focus. Although an ideal long-run goal, this would require the definition of a theoretical framework which is beyond the scope of this essay, and it would carry the discussion far from its focus of transnational economic activities. Instead, I have chosen to treat both the general trends in economic activities and the controversial debate over them through a discussion of developments in international economic interdependence.

Although it can lead such a discussion astray, a focus on international economic interdependence is central to a discussion of transnational economic processes. Transnational processes and international interdependence refer, in effect, to overlapping sets of phenomena. Interdependent behavior may be understood in terms of the outcome of specified actions of two or more parties (individuals, governments, corporations, etc.) when such actions are mutually contingent.[14] These parties, then, are interdependent with respect to specific issue areas and not to the whole spectrum of their activities. None of the actions involved is understood to be fixed. Nor need they be consciously perceived as mutually contingent or dependent, although such perception would be necessary if interdependence was to be manipulated by one or more of the parties involved. In this sense strategic interaction would be a subset of interdependence and would involve specified goal-oriented behavior on the part of at least two parties.

Interdependence as defined above need not involve transnational processes. For example, the security of two states may involve a set of interdependent relationships but also involve no nongovernmental actors and therefore not necessarily be transnational. Similarly, transnational activities could exist without affecting the level of interdependence among certain groups. I presume this to be frequently the case with such less-tangible phenomena as ideolo-

[14] There are other definitions which have been offered for "interdependence." Each has a different focus and therefore gives rise to different sets of questions. This one focuses on state actions and consequently lends itself to questions regarding the ability of a state's leadership to attain its objectives and its level of control over activities both within and beyond its borders. Interdependence has also been defined in systemic terms and in terms of the growth of political output or political goods.

In systemic terms, for example, interdependence has been defined "in terms of the extent to which events occurring in any given part or within any given component unit of a world system affect (either physically or perceptually) events taking place in each of the other parts or component units of the system." Young, *International Journal,* Vol. 24, No. 4, p. 726. This definition lends itself to the formulation of hypotheses about the systemic effects of increases (or decreases) in the levels of interdependence: "The higher the ratio of interdependencies among the component units of a world system to interdependencies within the component units, the greater the proportion of any given unit's resources that will be devoted to external affairs." Ibid., p. 741.

In terms of political goods or "public goods" (those goods which, if consumed by any single member of a group, cannot feasibly be withheld from other members of the group) interdependence would be defined as a function of the scope and number of political goods produced in a group. See, for example, Norman Frohlich and Joe Oppenheimer, "Entrepreneurial Politics and Foreign Policy," *World Politics,* forthcoming.

gies. By and large, however, I would hypothesize that *as transnational processes increase in number and in scope for a specified set of states, the level of interdependence among them similarly increases.* Although subject to empirical verification this would seemingly be the case because state objectives would become increasingly a function of intersocietal interdependence.

I treat this hypothesis as an assumption in the discussion below. Even though the focus on international economic interdependence raises operational difficulties which are as intractable as those of transnational economic relations, the concept is useful for two reasons. First, much of the debate over changes in international economic relations has revolved around the question of whether there has been a secular increase in the level of international economic interdependence over the past century. Second, given the hypothesis stated above a number of questions about transnational economic processes are covered in a discussion of international interdependence.

The discussion of international interdependence is controversial even before an attempt is made to measure the phenomenon or to trace longitudinal trends in its growth. Arguments against the usefulness of conceptualizing international politics in terms of notions of interdependence have recently been brought together in an essay by Kenneth Waltz, "The Myth of National Interdependence." An analysis of Waltz's argument, therefore, serves as a useful foil for the present discussion. Waltz argues that "a comparison of the conditions of internal and external interdependence will make it clear that in international relations interdependence is always a marginal affair."[15] While Waltz's analogy may be an apt one, his conclusion does not follow from his assumption. This is apparently a result of Waltz's bias against "the mistaken conclusion . . . that a growing closeness of interdependence would improve the chances of peace."[16] Waltz's view that an increase in international interdependence would be destabilizing for international society as a whole is probably correct. Yet, his bias against the concept results in a failure to define it explicitly and also in the complacent belief that international affairs are more "stable" than other views might imply.

The concept of interdependence ought to be viewed in neutral terms without the value judgments of optimists who invoke a harmony of interest theory or of pessimistic prophets of doom. Even here the analogy between international and domestic society remains appropriate. This distinction, however, need not imply that in international society interdependence is always marginal. What it does imply is that the level of political integration outside the state is, by definition, lower than that within it. Interdependence, as defined above, has to do with the ability of statesmen to achieve those goals which have been set for them when goal attainment is contingent upon activities

[15] Waltz, in Kindleberger, p. 206.

[16] Ibid., p. 205.

pursued elsewhere. For example, the margin within which any Western industrialized state can establish the rate of exchange for its currency is a function of market mechanisms in the international monetary system and the tolerance of other governments. If a government devalues its currency beyond this margin in order to enjoy the trade benefits which accrue to an undervalued currency, it can be certain that foreign governments will retaliate—for example, by devaluing their currencies proportionately or by refusing trade credits—in order to nullify unfair advantage. The margin of autonomy and the limitations put on it are indices of monetary interdependence. By postulating that interdependence is always a marginal affair internationally Waltz's analysis avoids the most interesting set of questions. This has to do with the political effects of interdependence on both patterns of international behavior (the functioning of the international monetary system in the example cited) and on domestic politics (the mix of anti-inflationary and growth policies implied by the example).

Waltz continues his argument against the utility of the concept of interdependence through an elaboration of the classic dichotomy between the state and international society. His argument on interstate interdependence is based on the traditional dictum of statecraft which says that all states are alike in that their leaders must maximize state security. Within the domestic order, however, there is a functional division of labor: "The domestic order is composed of heterogeneous elements; the international order is composed of homogeneous units. . . . The international order is characterized by the coaction of like units. . . . Because the units that populate the international arena are the same in type, interdependence among them is low even if those units are of approximately equal size. . . . This last point can be stated as an iron law; high inequality among like units *is* low interdependence."[17]

Classical trade theory would tell us that the logic of Waltz's argument is quite correct. Homogeneous units would find little need for trade-offs based on comparative advantage, and the level of interdependence among them would thus be low. His argument at this point therefore depends on the empirical generalization that international society is composed of like units. But is it? The Rankean assumption that states are alike in that their leaders maximize security seems terribly antiquated to a contemporary observer. Waltz's generalization may, in fact, have held for the powers of classic diplomacy. These powers were all European, their leaders were educated in similar types of schools, they spoke the same language of diplomacy and understood the same signals, and their expectations for change were relatively low. Today the number and type of international actors appear to be historically unparalleled.[18] The international system is composed of some 120 states that

[17] Ibid., p. 207.

[18] For a stimulating discussion of changes in the types of international actors and their current diversity see Oran R. Young, "The Actors in World Politics," in *The Analysis of International Politics,* ed. James N. Rosenau, B. Vincent Davis, and Maurice A. East (Glencoe, Ill: Free Press, forthcoming).

vary tremendously in size, level of economic development, cultural heritage, type of political system, language, style, and expectations. In addition, the diversity of governmental and nongovernmental organizations, corporations, and other types of actors which form the linkages of transnational society present a world foreign to Waltz's system of like units.

The capstone of Waltz's argument is that the international system since 1945 has been based on two superstates, highly unequal to all the others, from which follows, given his "iron law" of inequalities, that interdependence today is at such low levels as to be specious. Waltz then turns to evidence from trade and investment transactions to bolster his argument. This thesis can be challenged on four counts. One is theoretical; a second involves distortions which result from a security-focused view of international politics; a third comes from a logical fallacy; and a fourth from further omissions in longitudinal economic analysis of trends.

On the theoretical level the problem encountered in the writings of Waltz flows from the nature of his implicit definition of interdependence. This definition skirts the major issues involved in the study of international interdependence or of transnational society. We want to know what units are interdependent in terms of specified sets of activities (e.g., technology or transportation), geographical or functional areas (e.g., the North Atlantic region or international trade), and in terms of specified state objectives (e.g., security, peace, wealth). To speak of interdependence on a general level of abstraction without specifying these matters can result only in fruitless disputation over its empirical existence or its usefulness as a concept.

The second problem found in Waltz's analysis involves distortions which stem from his security focus of international politics. The traditional objective of the units of international society has been termed security maximization. It is that set of security objectives which comes immediately to mind when Waltz speaks of a bipolar world in which two states share the "pinnacle of power."[19] But is this world one of low interdependence? We can clarify this point by looking at the converse of interdependence, namely, autonomy. In the bipolar system does the security of any state—even of the two at the "pinnacle of power"—involve autonomous actions only? Or does the security of the whole system depend upon contingent actions taken (or not taken) by the major states? An affirmative answer to the latter question flies directly in the face of Waltz's argument. Here evidence is far more substantial than conventional wisdom. This evidence has been described elsewhere as "the most outstanding example of menacing cultural lag in our world today."[20] It has to do with the accelerating pace of technological change and the conse-

[19] Waltz, in Kindleberger, p. 207.

[20] Hornell Hart, "The Hypothesis of Cultural Lag: A Present-Day View," in *Technology and Social Change*, by Francis R. Allen et al. (New York: Appleton-Century-Crofts, 1957), p. 428.

quent exponential growth of destructive capacity rather than 1) growth in areas governed by single political systems and 2) growth in the "area in which human beings can kill each other from a given base."[21] The effects of these changes in technology, power to govern, and power to destroy taken together have been described as follows:

> In atomic cultural lag, the leading variable is the maximum area within which, at any given date, people could be killed from a given base. The lagging variable is the ability to prevent this accelerating power from damaging or destroying the kind of civilization which is valued within the accepted frame of values. . . .
>
> Although the killing area had been growing with acceleration since before the dawn of history . . . in 1900 it was still almost negligible compared with the governing area. . . . From that date [1912] onward, however, the killing area increased precipitately. In 1944 it surpassed the size of the largest governing area ever attained. . . . The development of refueling in the air, and the development of bombers of still greater range, have extended the potential killing radius to globe-encircling dimensions.[22]

Developments in both destructive power and delivery power since these lines were written mean that with respect to "survival" the world has never before been as interdependent as it is today—size of states notwithstanding. Nor have the transnational aspects of defense and security ever been so striking.

The third problem stems from Waltz's logical fallacy of first asserting that the world is less interdependent given its present "two pinnacles of power" and then supporting this assertion with evidence drawn from trade and investment flows. The fallacy once again results from the failure to conceptualize interdependence in terms of specific state objectives, activities, and parameters of action. On the one hand, the "iron law" is one which is drawn from "high politics"—from actions concerned with maximizing security and prestige. The evidence, on the other hand, is drawn from areas of "low politics"—activities whose objective concerns the maximization of wealth and welfare.[23] The connection between the two spheres is one which is not specified in any way. In addition, there is another logical gap in this argument. Waltz has generalized from interactions between the United States and the Union of Soviet Socialist Republics to the structure of global society. At best, his generalization ought to be restricted to Soviet-American interactions. Even if levels of interdependence between the two societies could be shown to have been reduced during this century, this does not permit one to leap to conclusions about relations between member states of the European Economic Community (EEC), of the Council for Mutual Economic Assistance (CMEA), or of any other region however defined.

[21] Ibid.

[22] Ibid., p. 432.

[23] For an elaboration of this argument see my article in *World Politics,* Vol. 22, No. 3, pp. 377–383.

The fourth set of problems encountered by Waltz and others who argue that there has been a decrease in the level of economic interdependence in international society during the course of the last 50 years is, perhaps, the most intriguing for our purposes. It also raises exceedingly complex questions of analysis. Since it involves changes in the levels of various types of economic interactions as well as transformations in the global economy, it is worth dwelling on at some length.

III. Trends in Transnational Economic Activities

Evidence of changes in the nature of international economic interdependence and the consequent growth of transnational economic society can be found in transaction data and in the expected consequences of an increased sensitivity of domestic economic activities to external stimuli. Most analysis has focused on the former, while the latter has recently also been submitted to rigorous examination.[24]

Transaction analysis can focus on trade and investment figures as well as on evidence drawn from the mobility of persons. The findings of these analyses are well known, but it is useful to review some of them briefly. In most cases a similar set of trends obtains. There are two general characteristics of these trends in transnational economic activities during this century which ought to be singled out in any discussion of transnational processes. The first trend is the almost continuous process of change and transformation which these activities have been undergoing. The second is the appearance of 1914 as a watershed year regardless of what set of activities is considered.

The accelerated increase in the mobility of persons, for example, was one of the first consequences of the application of technology to modes of transportation. Innovations in shipping, in railroad construction, and, later, in the automotive and aviation industries had several effects: Speeds of transportation increased at an exponential rate of growth after 1820,[25] capacity similarly increased, and costs of transportation declined precipitously.[26] The relative openness of borders to immigration in the nineteenth century, the desire to leave one's homeland because of famine, repression, or revolution, and the attraction of material betterment in North America, northern Europe, or Australia resulted in an unprecedented movement of persons across borders, espe-

[24] For examples of the former see Waltz, in Kindleberger; Deutsch and Eckstein, *World Politics,* Vol. 13, No. 2; and Deutsch, Bliss, and Eckstein, *Economic Development and Cultural Change,* Vol. 10, No. 4. For examples of the latter see Cooper; and Ingvar Svennilson, *Growth and Stagnation in the European Economy* (Geneva: United Nations Economic Commission for Europe, 1954).

[25] See Bruce M. Russett, *Trends in World Politics* (Government in the Modern World) (New York: Macmillan Co., 1965), pp. 7–10. J. Edwin Holmstrom has pushed the exponential growth curve back several millennia to the use of wagons and the consequent increase of capacity over "man-transport" and pack animals. See his book, *Railroads and Roads in Pioneer Development Overseas: A Study of Their Comparative Economies* (London: P. S. King & Son, 1934), p. 56.

[26] This decrease in transportation costs also, of course, affects global trade. See Cooper, pp. 65–66.

cially away from Europe. The era of most rapid rate of growth was the 30-year period preceding World War I after which there was a precipitous decline in international migration.[27] By the outbreak of World War II there was a virtual halt in both absolute terms and as a percentage of total world population in the international flow of persons. In order to determine the effects of these changes on international interdependence (and vice versa) we must ask why the decline occurred.

The lowering of barriers to migration represented an obvious growth in transnational society however defined. This growth was primarily the result of technological change. Its coming to a halt after World War I was not, on the other hand, attributable to technological change. Rather, it was the result of conscious governmental policy designed for social and political reasons to restrict mass movements of population. Does this mean that as a result of a decline in population movements across territorial boundaries the world has become less interdependent? The contrary would seem to be the case. Governmental intervention occurred as a means of controlling and stabilizing this form of interdependence. As Gunnar Myrdal has described it, "the doors are closed at the very time when cheaper travel makes movement easier and the spread of knowledge opens up new vistas and horizons. The closing of the boundaries is also one of the many factors leading to an absurd intensification of national allegiances which is continuously weakening that basis of international solidarity upon which international policy has to be built."[28]

At the same time that shifts in population declined in intensity the means of supporting such shifts increased through further reductions in transportation costs. What has occurred, then, is an even further increase in personal mobility which is obscured by national actors. Some idea of the phenomenal increase in personal mobility can be gained if we focus for a moment on the post-World War II growth in international travel. The number of persons arriving from abroad in the various states of the world has doubled every decade since World War II. Figures for three representative years are: *1948,* 40,601,200; *1958,* 81,487,900; *1968,* 168,752,300.[29]

While the decrease in migration levels seems to indicate a lower level of international interdependence, the effects of this enormous growth in personal mobility on interdependence cannot be underestimated. A large and increasing number of travelers go abroad for business purposes, and this itself

[27] For details on the volume of international migration in aggregated as well as disaggregated form (by country of origin and country of entrance) see Svennilson, pp. 65–68; Kuznets, pp. 51–56; and Gunnar Myrdal, *An International Economy: Problems and Prospects* (New York: Harper & Brothers, Publishers, 1956), chapter 7.

[28] Myrdal, p. 95.

[29] Figures are drawn from the United Nations *Statistical Yearbook* (12th and 21st eds.; New York: Statistical Office of the United Nations, 1961, 1969). The number of international travelers during 1970 has been estimated at over 200 million. The largest part of this travel, some 50 percent, represented exchanges among persons residing in the industrialized societies of Western Europe and North America.

helps partially to explain the growth in postwar trade. In addition, international travel has the important, if diffuse, effect of "broadening the horizons" of citizens of all countries to varying degrees. This also is an important, if incommensurable, aspect of transnational society (increases in domestic travel notwithstanding).

In addition, a large number of persons travel abroad to seek employment. When, as in the EEC, this mobility of labor is a result of consciously and jointly executed policy on the part of a group of states, "transnational problems" are inevitably generated. Free movement of labor leads to a "transnationalization" of problems of labor relations—social security, health benefits, health insurance, and family remissions. Some of these affect the balance of payments of individual countries and governmental intervention in foreign as well as domestic sectors.

Capital mobility has exhibited a pattern of growth not unlike that of the mobility of persons. There was a remarkable increase in the flow of investment in the century preceding the First World War (a rate of increase of 64 percent per decade before 1914), a retardation during the Great Depression, and another vast increase in flow after 1950. Generalizations are far more tenuous with regard to capital flows, and a complete account of capital movements to support such generalizations is outside the scope of this essay.[30] Nonetheless, certain general features of this pattern can be summarized.

First, in spite of the parallel between the phenomenal growth of capital flows during the nineteenth century and the emergence of European empires, "a substantial proportion of these capital flows [at least half] went to developed countries."[31] Although the shares of portfolio capital versus credit and of private versus public sector contributions shifted (in each case toward the latter) after 1950, the share invested in developed countries remained high. In both periods the findings indicate substantial asymmetry in the structure of the global economy with centralization of control institutionalized in the highly industrialized states. At the same time two-way capital flows between advanced countries developed after 1950, although American businessmen have been much less reluctant to take advantage of international investment opportunities than have their European counterparts. In any case, it remains true that, even with the increase in capital mobility since 1950, investment abroad represents a smaller share of domestic savings in lending countries than it did a century ago.

What accounts for the increased mobility of capital since 1950? Why should such an increase result in a higher level of interdependence, at least among

[30] For a more complete discussion based on a disaggregation of capital flows see Kuznets, pp. 321–334, for the period between 1820 and 1960; Cooper, pp. 82–91, carries the discussion through the middle of the 1960s. A discussion of some of the political effects of these flows in the postwar period is found in the essay by Lawrence Krause in this volume.

[31] Kuznets, p. 327.

advanced industrialized societies? Richard N. Cooper has outlined several factors which have fostered capital mobility. Among those he lists are "the desire by an investing firm to exploit some quasi-monopoly it holds, whether special skills, patent rights, or 'good will' "; the recovery of Europe and the return to currency convertibility by the end of 1958; the consequences of the implementation of the Treaty Establishing the European Economic Community (Rome Treaty); the general improvement in the European political position; and the sense of security which followed the dampening of the cold war.[32] These factors, in short, were mainly political, but they were aided by improvements in the structure of capital markets and a general "widening of business horizons."

This does not refute Waltz's claim that a situation different from the pre-1914 conjecture obtains in a world in which two powers appear to be little dependent on the rest of the world. It does, however, severely restrict his position when we ask to what set of factors this dependence pertains. Waltz himself notes that "the higher the costs of disentanglement, the higher the degree of dependence," but he argues that even for the United States it would be a "hard blow" to absorb a sudden and general loss of trade outlets or of investments.[33] It is difficult, then, to understand why he concludes that the United States, like the Soviet Union, is "little dependent on the rest of the world."[34] Waltz's argument is based on the improbability that recipient countries would be willing to accept a future loss which would arise from their nationalization of American-owned capital. Such a situation would imply a high level of interdependence.

Additional evidence of increased interdependence arising from capital mobility accrues from another source, namely, the tendency of the structure of the international monetary system to breed crises. This system can be described as one in which a great deal of interdependence has developed but centralized authority capable of formulating policy has not. The consequence is that governments are forced to coordinate their decisionmaking processes with regard to monetary matters—a process which is not easy given the number of countries involved but which is facilitated by the unacceptability for all governments concerned of the costs of either retrenching to a position of relative autonomy or of fostering a unification of their currencies.

There is an important reason why it can be expected that international crises, such as the ones characteristic of the international monetary system in the late 1960s, will appear in a system in which there exist high levels of interdependence but weak structures for international policy coordination. This is because transnational interactions result in losses of governmental control over the foreign activities of citizens. This has been the case especially with short-

[32] Cooper, pp. 88–90.

[33] Waltz, in Kindleberger, p. 216.

[34] Ibid., p. 214.

term capital flows associated with the multibillion dollar Eurodollar market. Private transactions may bring about situations in which governments are forced to take action but often with their freedom of action restricted. As transnational interactions of this sort increase, the possibilities of effective decisionmaking in a purely national setting, of isolation or of national encapsulation, become less likely. Therefore, control becomes a more difficult problem, especially insofar as knowledge of the effects of interdependence is still limited.

The third kind of economic transaction which enters the argument about transnational society has to do with foreign trade and the importance of the international sector as a component of gross national product (GNP) in an economy. Here, again, we find the familiar trend, and the controversy is over its interpretations. The transactions involve both commodities and services.

In historical terms this pattern has been described as follows:

> The time pattern of the international flows of resources and goods contrasts sharply with this movement [of technological knowledge]: the rapid acceleration in the rate of increase of these flows that began in the 1820s was followed by the markedly disrupting effects of the two world wars of this century and of the political institutional changes that were the consequences partly of these wars, partly of the spread of modern economic growth under auspices that militated against the widening of peaceful international economic flows. The decline in the rate of increase of such flows that began with World War I, extended to the end of World War II, and only currently is being compensated for by the high rate of some of these flows since the early 1950s, is in contrast with the apparently continuous and perhaps accelerated rise in the transnational stock of useful knowledge. . . . [35]
>
> This high rate of growth of foreign trade between the 1820s and 1913 was in sharp contrast to the much lower rate of slightly over 10 per cent shown for the period back to the mid-eighteenth century; and it dropped sharply over the five decades that followed 1913, to about 21 per cent per decade—despite the remarkably high rate for the 1950s. . . . [36]

There is a series of questions which must be asked with regard to these trends in determining the political importance of these transnational activities. The first has to do with the share of the international sector in the domestic economy in terms of GNP: Does a decreased share imply as an automatic consequence a lower level of international interdependence and, consequently, a decrease in the importance of transnational society? A second question has to do with structural change in the countries involved and asymmetric patterns of interactions: Does a reduction in the number of great-power interactions imply a lower level of interdependence for the system as

[35] Kuznets, pp. 294–295.

[36] Ibid., p. 305.

a whole? A third question most appropriately raised at this juncture has to do with the limitations of transaction analysis in measuring the scope of transnational society: Are transactions in themselves appropriate indicators of interdependence?

The first question is crucial to the argument that interdependence has been decreasing. It is here that the work of Karl Deutsch has played a central role.[37] Deutsch has used a series of indicators to argue the case that as societies become more industrialized, at least after a certain threshold, national introversion increases. Evidence is drawn not only from the foreign trade sector but also from international migration data, letters sent abroad, and elite interviews. The evidence drawn from foreign trade is crucial to his argument. The data Deutsch used is widely accepted as valid, and his conclusions are widely agreed upon.[38] For the older industrialized states of the West the share of the foreign trade sector in GNP was much greater before World War I than it is today. Even though this share rose in the 1950s above its depression levels, it has still not reattained the earlier levels. In addition, the share of the foreign trade sector has not risen for the more recently developed countries, including those of the Soviet bloc. The major questions to be asked, then, are why this is so, and what are the implications of this for trends in international interdependence.

The first question is somewhat easier to deal with than is the second. In the first place, the initial growth of the foreign trade sector was somewhat extraordinary. It reflected the suddenness with which businessmen and other groups were able to take advantage of the revolution in transportation discussed above. As domestic economies continued to grow, it was natural for the relative proportion of the foreign trade sector to decline. Second, the period was one of trade liberalism, reflecting "a policy decision by the United Kingdom, the economic leader of the time, to foster international division of labor and freer trade. . . . "[39] In the later period there was a series of political decisions designed to foster policies of autarky rather than of trade liberalism for two sets of reasons which, in a sense, grew out of the experiences of World War I.[40] These resulted in a decline after World War I both in intra-European

[37] See Deutsch and Eckstein, *World Politics*, Vol. 13, No. 2; and Deutsch, Bliss, and Eckstein, *Economic Development and Cultural Change*, Vol. 10, No. 4. In addition, the following works should be consulted: Karl Deutsch et al., *France, Germany and the Western Alliance: A Study of Elite Attitudes on European Integration and World Politics* (New York: Charles Scribner's Sons, 1967); and Karl Deutsch, "Transaction Flows as Indicators of Political Cohesion," in *The Integration of Political Communities*, ed. Philip E. Jacob and James V. Toscano (Philadelphia: J. B. Lippincott Co., 1964), pp. 75–97.

[38] Kuznets, however, disagrees with Deutsch's findings for the pre-1914 period. He finds "that the trends in the trade proportions of the older developed countries in the period before World War I were generally and significantly upward, not downward." Kuznets, p. 316.

[39] Ibid., p. 319.

[40] There were other effects of the war which fostered stagnation in economic growth. Among these were financial losses, losses of manpower, of overseas markets, and a withering of the psychology of free trade; see Svennilson, pp. 18–20 and 41–61.

trade and in Europe's share of world trade. On the one hand, governmental controls introduced during the war were maintained as part of preparation for future wars. On the other hand, the aftermath of the Bolshevik Revolution coupled with the controls instituted during the war years and the depression in the non-Communist states demonstrated that national economic policies, which required relative isolation from the world economy, could be used to control domestic economic growth. In short, as Kuznets has remarked, "It is hardly a surprise that the *international* dislocations that marked the post-1913 period depressed the *international* flows to a much greater extent than the *national* economic activity of the developed nations. . . ."[41]

What, then, was the relationship between a lower share of the foreign sector and international interdependence? In one sense the data itself cannot tell us. For, if interdependence is understood as a function of state objectives, then the declining share of the foreign trade sector after World War I and the stagnation of world trade in the interwar period were partly reflected in the costs governments were willing to accept in order to enhance the autonomy of their economies. Thus, the stagnation in economic growth reflected, in part, the enormous cost of national autonomy once high levels of international interdependence obtain. As national economies grow and become more potentially specialized, the potential welfare effects of trade liberalization may increase interdependence even in the absence of higher absolute or relative levels of trade.

In addition, the structure of trade has changed considerably since the pre-1914 period. Today the greatest powers do not trade substantially with each other as they did in the earlier period.[42] At the same time the terms of trade for primary products, the principal exports of less developed countries, has appreciably worsened while trade in manufactures for manufactures between industrialized non-Communist states has increased substantially. What this means is that the structure, not necessarily the level, of interdependence has shifted in terms of the international economy. The upshot is a complex structure of relationships; some of these relationships represent a thickening web of interdependence and others do not. Evidence drawn from the share of the international sector is, in short, inconclusive. Indeed, it raises as many questions as it answers. It means that a mapping of interdependencies is not as simple as would be implied from this sort of transaction analysis. It also implies that interdependence is a rather important affair laden with significant political effects that are obscured when its importance is minimized.

The second major question posed above pertains to structural changes in the countries involved in this web of interdependence and to asymmetric

[41] Kuznets, p. 321. The reasons, of course, are far more complicated than the highlights outlined above. Fuller treatment is found in Kuznets and in Svennilson.

[42] Yet, there is some importance in the fact that these do not represent the same specific states.

patterns of interaction. This, too, is a controversial issue and far too complex to be treated completely in this essay. It is relatively misleading to generalize about patterns of interdependence without reviewing asymmetries within them. The units of international society themselves vary tremendously and this variety is further reflected in relations between them. Moreover, just as there have been changes in the structure of individual political systems, there have also been complex changes in their relationships. Some of these changes have been more rapid than others and have resulted from political considerations such as the growth of the Communist system and its relative isolation from the global economy. Others have been more evolutionary and have reflected the processes of economic growth. As new relationships have developed, others have withered. Thus, simultaneous trends such as the growing closeness of the industrialized states of the West, the isolation of the Communist bloc, and the disintegration of the European-centered empires give the appearance of both disintegration and the creation of new forms of international institutions.

One of the forms of social disintegration most commented upon in economic and political literature is the increased gap between relatively modernized societies and latecomers to the modernization process. This gap is indicative of one of the most disintegrative aspects of social change in general and economic change in particular in the twentieth century.[43] Paradoxically, the poorer societies have benefited from some of the concomitants of the modernization process but have also suffered because of their inability to handle the wide spectrum of problems which accompany this process. They have, for example, been able to reduce mortality rates through the application of advanced medical techniques but have not been successful in reducing fertility rates. They have developed pockets of modernity in their major cities but only at the cost of bifurcating their own social structures between traditional and modern sectors. But most of all, in terms of the global economy, they have relied primarily on export sectors based on specialization in primary products for which the terms of trade have continuously deteriorated for over one-third of a century. At the same time these less developed societies have failed to significantly increase trade between themselves. The divisions in the international economy which this implies, i.e., the apparently increased dependence of less developed societies upon the more modernized world and their sustained isolation from one another, seem to make arguments about increased levels of international interdependence difficult to accept. However, if we accept for the moment the hypothesis that the process of change in international society involves the appearance of newly integrated structures of rela-

[43] It is this disintegrative quality of modernization which Marion Levy has in mind when he argues that "the structures of modernization, once they have reached certain levels of development, constitute a sort of universal social solvent." Marion J. Levy, Jr., *Modernization and the Structure of Societies: A Setting for International Affairs* (Princeton, N.J: Princeton University Press, 1966), p. 14.

tionships and the disintegration of others, the argument is incomplete until an attempt is made to identify these new structures.

Economic historians have pointed out that one of the most marked features of international trade in the mid-twentieth century has been the phenomenal growth of trade in such commodities as machinery and transportation equipment between relatively advanced societies and a contraction in trade between them in textiles, primary products, and other miscellaneous processed materials which were products of the first wave of industrialization.[44] Traditional trade relationships involving an exchange of "land-using," or primary, products for "labor-using" manufactures has, in short, shifted toward trade in manufactures for manufactures. As Cooper has pointed out, "exports of manufactures have grown from less than 40 per cent of world trade in 1928 to nearly 60 per cent in 1966. During the period 1953–64, world exports of manufactures rose 228 per cent, compared with a growth of 84 per cent in other products."[45] Most of this increase in trade, then, represents an increased share of trade for industrialized countries.

In short, along with a perceivable "disintegration" in the global economy reinforced by the isolation of Communist-bloc countries from the growth in trade there has been a growing interdependence among industrialized societies with respect to the benefits they mutually derive from trade with one another. This growth in interdependence has been reinforced by changes in forms of decisionmaking for the "global economy." These decisionmaking structures are of two types, although sometimes, as in the case of the International Monetary Fund (IMF), the same organization deals with both sets of problems. Some relate to the way non-Communist industrialized societies regulate and adjust the political problems which stem from their growing interdependence. Thus, a set of trade, mutual problem-solving, and monetary arrangements has arisen to foster the coordination of decisionmaking. These arrangements include the IMF, the Organisation for Economic Co-operation and Development (OECD), the Group of Ten, the EEC, etc., and all have become centers of important political action as economic activities have grown to reflect the changing power relationships between industrialized states. Other arrangements relate to decisionmaking for rich and poor societies alike. General problems of global liquidity to finance trade, of market arrangements, and of loans and aid for development also have been centered more and more in international organizations. The upshot has been a centralization of decisionmaking for international economic affairs, itself, perhaps, the most important indirect index of international interdependence.

It might be objected that this increased centralization of economic decisionmaking only reflects the greater dependence of less developed societies on

[44] See Svennilson, pp. 175–180.

[45] Cooper, pp. 60–61.

wealthier ones. This, indeed, is the case because it is virtually impossible for any less developed society to achieve goals associated with increased levels of modernity in isolation from global activities. But the same generalization obtains for more advanced societies in other policy areas. The result is that no society, however economically advanced, can achieve the entire spectrum of its goals in isolation. Thus, the degree of interdependence with regard to such goal achievement remains significantly asymmetric because of the split between advanced and less developed societies and the centralization of decisionmaking primarily in the hands of the former.

There is an additional asymmetry in these interdependent relationships. It has to do with the relative size of societies measured in terms of GNP. It is this asymmetry which has, in part, led Deutsch and others to conclude that as societies become more industrialized, at least up to a point, the share of their external sectors declines. But one still finds, as Kuznets has pointed out, "that foreign trade proportions are positively correlated with the level of economic development as measured by per capita income, once the size factor is taken into account, [and this] lends further support to the inference that small countries can attain economic growth *only* through heavy reliance on foreign trade. . . ."[46]

These asymmetric relationships give rise to several qualifications to some of the generalizations made above concerning the political implications of interdependent relations. First, there is a divergence among societies in terms of their willingness to grant decisionmaking power over economic activities to supranational groupings. Since a large, highly developed society such as the United States is relatively more capable of insulating itself from effects of interdependence, its leadership is less willing to give up decisional power and will opt for coordination of economic policies when such coordination is necessary. Second, these asymmetries are reflected in the relative negotiating strength of the various states when decisions with respect to the transnational effects of interdependence are imposed upon them. It is this kind of asymmetry in power which has been apparent in the decade-long process of negotiating new credit facilities within the IMF and the Group of Ten in which the American position on special drawing rights (SDRs) eventually won out. Moreover, these asymmetries notwithstanding, there is a great deal of evidence that interdependence, at least among more industrialized states, has increased with respect to international economic activities of all sorts in recent years. While the situation is relatively complex, the general trends which created it remain clear.

A third question which must be dealt with in determining the political implications of transnational phenomena concerns the nature of the evidence available for measuring changes in international interdependence and, spe-

[46] Kuznets, p. 302.

cifically, the adequacy of transaction data to provide sufficient information about the scope and growth of transnational society. This sort of evidence is utilized by Deutsch when, for example, he argues that "European integration has slowed since the mid-1950's, and it has stopped or reached a plateau since 1957-58."[47] Deutsch's data is based on flows of international trade, mail, travel, and the exchange of students. In particular, Deutsch bases his statistical computations on the "Index of Relative Acceptance—the RA index—which measures the percentage by which the volume of actual transactions (such as, for instance, trade) between two countries exceeds or falls short of the hypothetical amount that would be proportional to the overall share of each of these two countries in the total flow of transactions among all countries of the world."[48] Analyzing structural integration among the six, Deutsch has found that "if the RA index of structural integration . . . had continued to grow in the 25 years after 1938 at the same rate as it did from the eve of World War I to the eve of World War II, the index in 1963 would have reached 94 per cent, far above the 77 per cent it actually did."[49]

Are we to conclude, however, that the movement toward European integration stopped before the Rome Treaty was implemented? How could one then explain the need to coordinate anti-inflationary policies in 1963 or the effects of the French devaluation and German revaluation of 1969 on the EEC common agricultural policy? Two sets of problems seem to lead one to question Deutsch's conclusions. One has to do with transaction analysis itself, and the other has to do with what Deutsch omitted from his analysis.

The reliability of transaction data in providing evidence for growth or decline in interdependent relationships has recently been questioned. Oran Young, for example, has argued that some of the most significant aspects of the growth of transnational interdependence "do not manifest themselves in iterative transactions."[50] For example, the empirical reference to volatile factors such as trade and mail flows "make dubious indicators of long-term secular trends at best."[51] Equally important, perhaps, is the failure of Deutsch to take into account such indirect and relatively intangible measures of interdependence as the fragility of the international monetary system in which interdependence gives rise to predictable crises, the increased sensitivity of domestic economic activities to external phenomena, the growth of capital mobility, and the increased expectations of gain by business in an increasingly interdependent international system.

The second problem with transaction analysis has to do with what it omits. Cooper has leveled a succinct attack on the thesis that the international eco-

[47] Deutsch et al., p. 218.

[48] Ibid., p. 220.

[49] Ibid., p. 221.

[50] Young, *International Journal*, Vol. 24, No. 4, p. 733.

[51] Ibid., p. 734.

nomic system was more interdependent or more highly integrated before 1914 than it is today. Cooper has argued that there are several important reasons why a comparison of the contemporary international economy with that of the pre-1914 period is not appropriate. First of all, governments everywhere have assumed far more extensive responsibilities for assuring the achievement of minimum standards of welfare including employment and salary levels. "These new tasks," Cooper argues, "place greater burdens on the available instruments of policy" and result in the increased sensitivity of the domestic economy to international activities.[52] Second, the perfection of communication links between all advanced industrialized societies increases the knowledge of investors of opportunities to achieve higher interest rates on short-term capital than ever before. Finally, even though tariff barriers were relatively low before 1914, there were other barriers to trade including, especially, shipping costs that have since been significantly overcome: "Thus, the integration of the pre-1914 world economy was something of an illusion. While the pre-1914 world was integrated in the sense that government-imposed barriers to the movement of goods, capital and people were minimal, those imposed by nature were much greater and economic integration was not high in the sense used here: quick responsiveness to differential earning opportunities resulting in a sharp reduction in differences in factor rewards."[53]

IV. Explaining Transformations in International Society

These recent trends in international economic relationships have been the subject of much debate and controversy. These debates pertain to fundamental questions about international politics. Is there a permanent nation-state focus of international society which stems from the fragmentation of the state system into relatively autonomous political systems, or has the emergence of transnational phenomena substantially altered that fragmented universe? Is transnationalism something new, or has it been even more marked in other epochs such as the sixteenth and seventeenth centuries when the state system coexisted with "transnational remnants" of medieval Christendom? Has the system been disintegrating from its relatively more homogeneous status of a century ago, or has the web of interdependence grown tighter?

The divergent interpretations implied by these questions probably result from the variety of biases and analytic foci in current writings. For some the focus of analysis is ideological, and the explanation offered has something to do with the rise of the "new diplomacy" associated with the apotheosis of liberalism under Woodrow Wilson or of Marxism under Lenin.[54] A second

52 Cooper, p. 151.

53 Ibid., p. 152.

54 See, for example, Arno J. Mayer, *Political Origins of the New Diplomacy, 1917–1918* (Yale Historical Publications, Study No. 10) (New Haven, Conn: Yale University Press, 1959).

framework focuses on the instruments of force, and the explanation pertains to the revolution in weaponry which occurred simultaneously with the collapse of the Euro-centered international political system and the emergence of Soviet-American relations as the central ordering axis of the international system.[55] A third focus is a more general one and pertains to the revolution of modernization and its concomitant, continuous, and enormous (probably exponential) growth of knowledge.[56]

The controversies which emerge from contrasting these different frameworks are not likely to be decidedly resolved in the near future. Clarifications and refutations may readily be made, but the underlying controversies will remain as long as no theoretical breakthroughs develop which can settle the matter by explaining the interrelationships between trends such as those discussed in this essay. My own bias in this analysis would lead me to argue that changes in international economic and political relations over the past century have been dramatic and transformational. The growth of transnationalism, it seems to me, is a direct offshoot of the phenomenal growth in knowledge, knowledge which cannot be monopolized by any one society but which is inherently transnational. Indeed, the foundation of transnational society can be viewed, to borrow Kuznets's phrase, as the increasing "transnational stock of knowledge." As he has argued, the basis of modern economic growth and therefore the basis of transnational phenomena is "the increase in the stock of useful knowledge and the extension of its application. . . . " He has further asserted that "no matter where these technological innovations emerge . . . the economic growth of any given nation depends upon their adoption. In that sense, whatever the national affiliation of resources used, any single nation's economic growth has its base somewhere outside its boundaries—with the single exception of the pioneering nation, and no nation remains the pioneer for long. Indeed, this dependence of a single nation's growth on the transnational stock of useful knowledge is implicit in the concept of an economic epoch. . . . "[57]

The relationship between the processes of modernization which Kuznets and others have described and the growth of transnational society is little more than a hunch. Although no one has been able to make a theoretical linkage between the two, it is likely that efforts will be made in this direction in research during the next decade. Evidence for this linkage which presently exists is little more than indirect. It has to do with such phenomena as the monetary crises outlined above, with perceived "technology gaps" and political

[55] Something of this is found in Kenneth E. Boulding, *Conflict and Defense: A General Theory* (Center for Research in Conflict Resolution Publication) (New York: Harper & Brothers, Publishers, 1962), but the notion is widespread.

[56] Kuznets, p. 286.

[57] Ibid., pp. 286–287. For a more general view of the phenomenon of modernization defined in terms of cumulative growth of knowledge see Black, pp. 7ff.

responses to them in Europe and elsewhere, and with international efforts to coordinate national policies so that transnational phenomena can be brought under control. Above all, it seems to me, it has to do with the politicization of economically derived values which has had as a concomitant the increased sensitivity of national economic policies to external activities.

The increased scope of governmental activities in all states, but especially in the most advanced industrialized states, is the major link between the general processes of modernization and transnational phenomena. This increased scope is everywhere associated with the emergence of the "good life" as a major political goal. For governments to provide the general welfare they must get involved in the provision of social services, guarantees of minimal levels of individual consumption, and the like. At the same time specialization of national production increases with modernization just as the possibility of autarky diminishes. From the latter develops the major incentive to international economic cooperation—fear that the inability to pursue an autarkic policy will lead to the cutoff of foreign markets and sources of supply without which the good life could not be attained.

Both the increased scope of governmental attitudes and the increasing incentives for internationally coordinated policies, coupled with such transnational activities as those associated with capital mobility, bring me to the point with which this essay began, namely, the merging of economic and political phenomena which is a characteristic of contemporary domestic and international life. The mark of our current dilemmas and the failure of our major ideologies result significantly from our predisposition to think of political and economic activities in separate terms. If modern society bears any resemblance to primitive societies it is precisely in this realm. The age of transnational society is one in which only holistic accounts will suffice. The politicization of economics and the creation of economic value for political goods are what transnational processes are all about. One can no longer be conceptualized independently of the other.

This mark of contemporary international affairs is one of the substantive bases for claiming that things simply are not the same as they were during the period of classic diplomacy. International relations today correspond neither to the theories of power politics characterizing an "anarchic international system" nor to the utopias of world government depicting a single international society, although aspects of both are found everywhere. Foreign policy and international relations are, rather, in an intermediate and transitional position and assume mixed and diverse forms. Whichever direction they move in during the coming decades, toward increased autonomy or toward the creation of new institutions to control transnational processes, no development will arise without having momentous significance for the whole set of international relationships.

The international corporations have evidently declared ideological war on the "antiquated" nation state. . . . The charge that materialism, modernization and internationalism is the new liberal creed of corporate capitalism is a valid one. The implication is clear: the nation state as a political unit of democratic decision-making must, in the interest of "progress," yield control to the new mercantile mini-powers.
—Kari Levitt, "The Hinterland Economy,"
Canadian Forum, July–August 1970 (Vol. 50, Nos. 594–595), p. 163.

While the structure of the multinational corporation is a modern concept, designed to meet the requirements of a modern age, the nation state is a very old-fashioned idea and badly adapted to serve the needs of our present complex world.
—George W. Ball, "The Promise of the Multinational Corporation," *Fortune,* June 1, 1967 (Vol. 75, No. 6), p. 80.

The Politics of Transnational Economic Relations

ROBERT GILPIN

I

THESE two statements—the first by a Canadian nationalist, the second by a former United States undersecretary of state—express a dominant theme of contemporary writings on international relations. International society, we are told, is increasingly rent between its economic and its political organization. On the one hand, powerful economic and technical forces are creating a highly integrated transnational economy, blurring the traditional significance of national boundaries. On the other hand, the nation-state continues to command men's loyalties and to be the basic unit of political decision. As one writer has put the issue, "The conflict of our era is between ethnocentric nationalism and geocentric technology."[1]

George W. Ball and Kari Levitt represent two contending positions with

ROBERT GILPIN is professor of politics and international affairs and faculty associate, Center of International Studies, Princeton University, Princeton, New Jersey.

[1] Sidney Rolfe, "Updating Adam Smith," *Interplay,* November 1968 (Vol. 2, No. 4), p. 15.

respect to the political implications of contemporary economic and technical forces and especially of their primary agent, the multinational corporation. Whereas Ball advocates the diminution of the powers of the nation-state in order to give full rein to the productive potentialities of the multinational corporation, Levitt argues for a powerful Canadian nationalism which could counterbalance American economic domination. What appears to one as the logical and desirable consequence of economic rationality seems to the other to be an effort on the part of American imperialism to eliminate all contending centers of power.

The issues raised by these contrasting positions are central to any evaluation of the impressive growth of transnational economic relations since the end of the Second World War. In specific terms the issue is whether the multinational corporation has become or will become an important actor in international affairs, supplanting, at least in part, the nation-state. If the multinational corporation is indeed an increasingly important and independent international actor, what are the factors that have enabled it to break the political monopoly of the nation-state? What is the relationship of these two sets of political actors, and what are the implications of the multinational corporation for international relations? Finally, what about the future? If the contemporary role of the multinational corporation is the result of a peculiar configuration of political and economic factors, can one foresee the continuation of its important role into the future?

Fundamental to these rather specific issues is a more general one raised by the growing contradiction between the economic and political organization of contemporary international society. This is the relationship between economic and political activities. While the advent of the multinational corporation puts it in a new guise, the issue is an old one. It was, for example, the issue which in the nineteenth century divided classical liberals like John Stuart Mill and the German Historical School represented by Georg Friedrich List. Whereas the former gave primacy to economics and the production of wealth, the latter emphasized the political determination of economic relations.[2] As this issue is central to the contemporary debate on the implications of the multinational corporation for international relations, I would like to discuss it in brief outline.

The classical position was, of course, first set forth by Adam Smith in *The Wealth of Nations*.[3] While Smith appreciated the importance of power, his purpose was to inquire into the nature and causes of wealth. Economic growth, Smith argued, is primarily a function of the extent of the division of

2 An analysis of the argument is provided by Edmund Silberner, *The Problem of War in Nineteenth Century Economic Thought*, trans. Alexander H. Krappe (Princeton, N.J: Princeton University Press, 1946).

3 Adam Smith, *An Inquiry into the Nature and Causes of the Wealth of Nations*, ed. Edwin Cannan (New York: Modern Library, 1937).

labor which in turn is dependent upon the scale of the market. Much of his attack, therefore, was directed at the barriers erected by feudal principalities and mercantilist states against the free exchange of goods and the enlargement of markets. If men are to multiply their wealth, Smith argued, the contradiction between political organization and economic rationality had to be resolved in favor of the latter.

Marxism, the rebellious ideological child of classical liberalism, erected the concept of the contradiction between economic and political relations into a historical law. Whereas classical liberalism held that the requirements of economic rationality *ought* to determine political relations, the Marxist position was that the mode of production *does* determine the superstructure of political relations. History can be understood as the product of the dialectical process—the contradiction between evolving economic forces and the sociopolitical system.

Although Karl Marx and Friedrich Engels wrote amazingly little on the subject of international economics, Engels in his famous polemic, *Anti-Dühring,* dealt explicitly with the question of whether economics or politics was primary in determining the structure of international relations.[4] Karl Dühring's anti-Marxist theory maintained that property relations resulted less from the economic logic of capitalism than from extraeconomic political factors. Engels, on the other hand, using the example of the unification of Germany in his attack on Dühring, argued that economic factors were primary.

Engels argued that when contradictions arise between economic and political structures, political power adapts itself to changes in the balance of economic forces and yields to the dictates of economic development. Thus, in the case of nineteenth-century Germany, the requirements of industrial production had become incompatible with feudal, politically fragmented Germany. Though political reaction was victorious in 1815 and again in 1848, it was unable to prevent the growth of large-scale industry in Germany and the growing participation of German commerce in the world market.[5] In summary, Engels argued that "German unity had become an economic necessity."[6]

In the view of both Smith and Engels the nation-state represented a progressive stage in human development because it enlarged the political realm of economic activity. In each successive economic epoch the advancing technology and scale of production necessitates an enlargement of political organization. Because the city-state and feudalism were below the optimum for the scale of production and the division of labor required by the Industrial Revo-

[4] The relevant sections appear in Ernst Wangermann, ed., *The Role of Force in History: A Study of Bismarck's Policy of Blood and Iron,* trans. Jack Cohen (New York: International Publishers, 1968). The best exposition of Marxist theories of economic relations is P. J. D. Wiles, *Communist International Economics* (New York: Frederick A. Praeger, 1969).

[5] Wangermann, p. 13.

[6] Ibid., p. 14.

lution, they prevented the efficient utilization of resources and were superseded by larger political units. Smith considered this to be a desirable objective; for Engels it was a historical necessity.

In our era this Marxist emphasis on the historical law of development has been made by many writers—Marxists and non-Marxists—in discussing the contemporary contradiction between the nation-state and the multinational corporation. This position that economic forces are determining the structure of international relations has been put most forcibly by the economist, Stephen Hymer. In an intriguing article entitled "The Multinational Corporation and the Law of Uneven Development" Hymer has argued that contemporary international relations are rapidly being reshaped by "two laws of economic development: the Law of Increasing Firm Size and the Law of Uneven Development."[7]

The law of increasing firm size, Hymer argues, is the tendency since the Industrial Revolution for firms to increase in size "from the *workshop* to the *factory* to the *national corporation* to the *multi-divisional corporation* and now to the *multinational corporation*."[8] The law of uneven development, he continues, is the tendency of the international economy to produce poverty as well as wealth, underdevelopment as well as development. Together these two economic laws will produce the following consequence:

> A regime of North Atlantic Multinational Corporations would tend to produce a hierarchical division of labor between geographical regions corresponding to the vertical division of labor within the firm. It would tend to centralize high-level decision-making occupations in a few key cities in the advanced countries, surrounded by a number of regional sub-capitals, and confine the rest of the world to lower levels of activity and income, i.e., to the status of towns and villages in a new Imperial system. Income, status, authority, and consumption patterns would radiate out from these centers along a declining curve, and the existing pattern of inequality and dependency would be perpetuated. The pattern would be complex, just as the structure of the corporation is complex, but the basic relationship between different countries would be one of superior and subordinate, head office and branch office.[9]

In contrast to the position of liberals and Marxists alike who stress the primacy of economic relations nationalists and the so-called realist school of political science have emphasized the primacy of politics. Whereas the liberal or Marxist emphasizes the production of wealth as the basic determinant of social and political organization, the realist stresses power, security, and national sentiment. Thus, whereas Ball predicted to a session of the Canadian House of Commons that economic logic would lead to the eventual total inte-

[7] The article appears in J. N. Bhagwati, ed., *Economics and World Order* (New York: World Law Fund, 1970).

[8] Ibid., p. 1.

[9] Ibid., pp. 2–3.

gration of Canada and the United States, Levitt and other Canadian nationalists prefer national independence to a higher standard of living.

Although himself a proponent of economic liberalism, the late Jacob Viner made one of the best analyses of the relationship of economic and political factors in determining the structure of international relations and concluded that political and security considerations are primary. In his classic study, *The Customs Union Issue,* Viner analyzed all known cases of economic and political unification from the perspective of whether the basic motivation was political or economic.[10] Thus, whereas Engels interpreted the formation of the Zollverein as a response to the industrialization of Germany and the economic necessity of larger markets, Viner argued "that Prussia engineered the customs union primarily for political reasons, in order to gain hegemony or at least influence over the lesser German states. It was largely in order to make certain that the hegemony should be Prussian and not Austrian that Prussia continually opposed Austrian entry into the Union, either openly or by pressing for a customs union tariff lower than highly protectionist Austria could stomach."[11] In pursuit of this strategic interest it was "Prussian might, rather than a common zeal for political unification arising out of economic partnership, [that] had played the major role."[12]

Whereas liberalism and Marxism foresee economic factors leading to the decline of political boundaries and eventually to political unification, Viner argued that economic and political boundaries need not coincide and may actually be incompatible with one another. The tendency today, he pointed out, to take the identity of political and economic frontiers for granted is in fact a quite modern phenomenon and is even now not universal. With respect to tariffs, the concern of his study, the general rule until recently was that political unification was greater than the area of economic unification. Furthermore, any attempt to further economic unification might undermine political unification; this was the case with respect to the American Civil War and is the case today in Canada.[13]

Viner concluded his argument that economic factors are of secondary importance to political unification with the following observation which is highly relevant for the concerns of this essay:

> The power of nationalist sentiment can override all other considerations; it can dominate the minds of a people, and dictate the policies of government, even when in every possible way and to every conceivable degree it is in sharp conflict with what seem to be and are in fact the basic economic interests of the people in question. To accept as obviously true the notion that the bonds of

[10] Jacob Viner, *The Customs Union Issue* (Studies in the Administration of International Law and Organization, No. 10) (New York: Carnegie Endowment for International Peace, 1950).

[11] Ibid., pp. 98–99.

[12] Ibid., p. 101.

[13] Ibid., pp. 95–101.

> allegiance must necessarily be largely economic in character to be strong, or to accept unhesitatingly the notion that where economic entanglements are artificially or naturally strong the political affections will also necessarily become strong, is to reject whatever lessons past experience has for us in this field.[14]

The contemporary argument that interstate relations will recede in face of contemporary technological developments and will be replaced by transnational relations between large multinational corporations was anticipated in the 1930s by Eugene Staley. In a fascinating book, *World Economy in Transition,* Staley posed the issue which is our main concern: "A conflict rages between technology and politics. Economics, so closely linked to both, has become the major battlefield. Stability and peace will reign in the world economy only when, somehow, the forces on the side of technology and the forces on the side of politics have once more been accommodated to each other."[15]

While Staley believed, along with many present-day writers, that politics and technology must ultimately adjust to one another, he emphasized, in contrast to contemporary writers, that it was not inevitable that politics adjust to technology. Reflecting the intense economic nationalism of the 1930s, Staley pointed out that the adjustment may very well be the other way around. As he reminds us, in his own time and in early periods economics has had to adjust to political realities: "In the 'Dark Ages' following the collapse of the Roman Empire, technology adjusted itself to politics. The magnificent Roman roads fell into disrepair, the baths and aqueducts and amphitheatres and villas into ruins. Society lapsed back to localism in production and distribution, forgot much of the learning and the technology and the governmental systems of earlier days."[16]

II

This rather lengthy discussion of the relationship between economics and politics argues the point that, although the economic and technical substructure partially determines and interacts with the political superstructure, political values and security interests are crucial determinants of international economic relations. Politics determines the framework of economic activity and channels it in directions which tend to serve the political objectives of dominant political groups and organizations. Throughout history each successive hegemonic power has organized economic space in terms of its own interests and purposes.

Following in this vein, the thesis of this essay is that transnational actors

[14] Ibid., p. 105.

[15] Eugene Staley, *World Economy in Transition: Technology vs. Politics, Laissez Faire vs. Planning, Power vs. Welfare* (Publications of the Council on Foreign Relations) (New York: Council on Foreign Relations [under the auspices of the American Coördinating Committee for International Studies], 1939), pp. 51–52.

[16] Ibid., p. 52.

and processes are dependent upon peculiar patterns of interstate relations. Whether one is talking about the merchant adventurers of the sixteenth century, nineteenth-century finance capitalists, or twentieth-century multinational corporations, transnational actors have been able to play an important role in world affairs because it has been in the interest of the predominant power(s) for them to do so. As political circumstances have changed due to the rise and decline of nation-states, transnational processes have also been altered or ceased altogether. Thus, as the French economist François Perroux has observed, the world economy did not develop as a result of competition between equal partners but through the emergence and influence of great national economies that successively became dominant.[17]

From this perspective the multinational corporation exists as a transnational actor today because it is consistent with the political interest of the world's dominant power, the United States. This argument does not deny the analyses of economists who argue that the multinational corporation is a response to contemporary technological and economic developments. The argument is rather that these economic and technological factors have been able to exercise their profound effects because the United States—sometimes with the cooperation of other states and sometimes over their opposition—has created the necessary political framework. By implication, a diminution of the Pax Americana and the rise of powers hostile to the global activities of multinational corporations would bring their reign over international economic relations to an end.

The basic point was made some years ago by E. H. Carr when he wrote that "the science of economics presupposes a given political order, and cannot be profitably studied in isolation from politics."[18] An international economy based on free trade, Carr sought to convince his fellow Englishmen, was not a natural and inevitable state of affairs but reflected the economic and political interests of Great Britain. The regime of free trade had come into existence and was maintained by the exercise of British economic and military power. With the rise after 1880 of new industrial and military powers with contrasting economic interests, namely, Germany, Japan, and the United States, an international economy based on free trade and British power became less and less viable. A proponent of appeasement, Carr advocated in defense of the Munich Pact that England work with these challenging powers, particularly Germany, to create a new international system which reflected the changed balance of economic and military power and interests in the world.

Perhaps the most effective way to defend the thesis that the pattern of international economic relations is dependent upon the structure of the interna-

[17] Perroux's theory of the dominant economy is set forth in his "Esquisse d'une théorie de l'économie dominante," *Economie appliquée,* April–September 1948 (Vol. 1, Nos. 2–3), pp. 243–300.

[18] Edward Hallett Carr, *The Twenty Years' Crisis, 1919–1939: An Introduction to the Study of International Politics* (2nd ed.; New York: St. Martin's Press, 1954), p. 117.

tional political system is to review the origins of the Pax Britannica, its demise with the First World War, and the eventual rise of a Pax Americana after the Second World War. What this history clearly reveals is that transnational economic processes are not unique to our own age and that the pattern of international economic activity reflects the global balance of economic and military power.

Each successive international system that the world has known is the consequence of the territorial, diplomatic, and military realignments that have followed history's great wars. The origins of the Pax Britannica lie in the complicated series of negotiations that followed the great upheavals of the Napoleonic wars. The essential features of the system which were put into place at that time provided the general framework of international economic relations until the collapse of the system under the impact of the First World War.

The first essential feature of the Pax Britannica was the territorial settlement and the achievement of a balance of power among the five Great Powers.[19] This territorial realignment can be divided into two parts. In the first place, on the continent of Europe the territorial realignments checked the ambitions of Russia in the east and France in the west. Second, the overseas conquests of the continental powers were reduced at the same time that Great Britain acquired a number of important strategic overseas bases. As a result the four major powers on the Continent were kept in check by their own rivalries and by offshore Britain which played a balancing and mediating role.

British naval power, the second essential feature of the Pax Britannica, was able to exercise a powerful and pervasive influence over global politics due to a fortunate juncture of circumstances. Great Britain's geographical position directly off the coast of continental Europe and its possession of several strategic naval bases enabled it to control Europe's access to the outside world and to deny overseas colonies to continental governments. As a consequence, from 1825 when Great Britain warned France not to take advantage of the revolt of the Spanish colonies in America to the latter part of the century, the greater part of the non-European world was either independent or under British rule. Moreover, the maintenance of this global military hegemony was remarkably inexpensive; it thus permitted Great Britain to utilize its wealth and energies in the task of economic development.

Third, using primarily the instruments of free trade and foreign investment in this political-strategic framework, Great Britain was able, in effect, to restructure the international economy and to exercise great influence over the course of international affairs. As the world's first industrial nation, Great

[19] Albert H. Imlah, *Economic Elements in the Pax Britannica: Studies in British Foreign Trade in the Nineteenth Century* (Cambridge, Mass: Harvard University Press, 1958), chapter 1.

Britain fashioned an international division of labor which favored its own industrial strengths at the same time that it brought great benefits to the world at large. Exchanging manufactured goods for the food and raw materials of other nations, Great Britain was the industrial and financial center of a highly interdependent international economy.

One may reasonably argue, I believe, that in certain respects the regime of the Pax Britannica was the Golden Age of transnationalism. The activities of private financiers and capitalists enmeshed the nations in a web of interdependencies which certainly influenced the course of international relations. In contrast to our own era, in which the role of the multinational corporation in international economic relations is unprecedented, the private institutions of the City of London under the gold standard and the regime of free trade had a strategic and central place in world affairs unmatched by any transnational organization today. Prior to 1914 the focus of much of international relations was the City of London and the private individuals who managed the world's gold, traded in commodities, and floated foreign loans. Though this interdependence differs radically in kind from the internationalization of production and the immense trade in manufactured goods which characterize our own more industrialized world economy, this earlier great age of transnationalism should not be overlooked. In exaggerated acknowledgment of the political importance of the transnational actors which dominated this age J. A. Hobson in his book on imperialism asked rhetorically whether "a great war could be undertaken by any European State, or a great State loan subscribed, if the house of Rothschild and its connexions set their face against it."[20]

The foundations underlying the Pax Britannica and the transnational processes it fostered began to erode in the latter part of the nineteenth century. On the Continent the industrialization and unification of Germany profoundly altered the European balance of power. France, too, industrialized and began to challenge Great Britain's global supremacy. Overseas developments of equal or potentially greater magnitude were taking place. The rapid industrialization of Japan and the United States and their subsequent creation of powerful navies ended British control of the seas. No longer could Great Britain use its naval power to deny rivals access to the globe. With the decline of British supremacy the imperial struggle for the division of Africa and Asia began, leading eventually to the outbreak of the First World War.

The war completed the destruction of the pre-1914 system. As a consequence of the duration and intensity of the conflict one sector after another of economic life was nationalized and brought into the service of the state. The role of the state in economic affairs became pervasive, and economic nationalism largely replaced the laissez faire traditions upon which so much of pre-

[20] J. A. Hobson, *Imperialism: A Study* (3rd rev. ed.; London: G. Allen & Unwin, 1938), p. 57.

war transnationalism had rested. Not until the Second World War would political relations favor the reemergence of extensive transnational activity.

The failure to revive the international economy after the First World War was due to many causes: the policies of economic revenge against Germany; the ill-conceived attempt to reestablish the gold standard; the nationalistic "beggar-my-neighbor" policies pursued by most states, etc. In terms of our primary concern in this essay one factor in particular needs to be stressed, namely, the failure of the United States to assume leadership of the world economy, a role Great Britain could no longer perform. Whereas before the war the City of London provided order and coordinated international economic activities, now London was unable and New York was unwilling to restructure the international economy disrupted by the First World War. The result was a leadership vacuum which contributed in part to the onset of the Great Depression and eventually the Second World War.

For our purposes two developments during this interwar period hold significance. The first was the Ottawa Agreement of 1932 which created the sterling area of imperial preference and reversed Great Britain's traditional commitment to multilateral free trade. The purpose of the agreement between Great Britain and the Commonwealth, an action whose intellectual roots went back to the nineteenth century, was to establish a regional trading bloc effectively isolated from the rest of the world economy. Germany in central Europe and Japan in Asia followed suit, organizing under their hegemonies the neighboring areas of strategic and economic importance. "This development of trading blocs led by great powers," one authority writes, "was the most significant economic development of the years immediately preceding the second World War. As always the breakdown of international law and economic order gave opportunity to the ruthless rather than to the strong."[21] Such a system of law and order the international gold standard had provided. Under this system transnational actors could operate with little state interference. With its collapse nation-states struggled to create exclusive spheres of influence, and trade relations became instruments of economic warfare.

The second important development from the perspective of this essay was the passage of the Reciprocal Trade Agreements Act in June 1934. The purpose of this act was to enable the United States government to negotiate reductions in tariff barriers. Followed in 1936 by the Tripartite Monetary Agreement, the act not only reflected the transformation of the United States into a major industrial power but also represented the first step by the United States to assert its leadership of the world economy. Furthermore, it demonstrated the potential of bilateral negotiation as a method to achieve the expansion of multinational trade even though the immediate impact of the act was relatively minor. World trade continued to be dominated by preference sys-

[21] J. B. Condliffe, *The Commerce of Nations* (New York: W. W. Norton & Co., 1950), p. 502.

tems, especially the sterling area, from which the United States was excluded. The importance of this prewar situation and the determination of the United States to overcome this discrimination cannot be too greatly emphasized. The reorganization of the world economy was to be the keynote of American postwar planning.

III

American plans for the postwar world were based on several important assumptions. In the first place, American leadership tended to see the origins of the Second World War as largely economic.[22] The failure to revive the international economy after the First World War and the subsequent rise of rival trading blocs were regarded as the underlying causes of the conflict. Second, it was assumed that peace would be best promoted by the establishment of a system of multinational trade relations which guaranteed to all states equal access to the world's resources and markets. Third, the main obstacles to the achievement of such a universal system, Americans believed, were the nationalistic and discriminatory measures adopted in the 1930s by various European countries—trade preferences, exchange controls, quantitative restrictions, competitive currency depreciations, etc.

The importance of economic considerations in American postwar planning has led in recent years to a spate of writings by revisionist historians who interpret these efforts as part of a large imperial design.[23] While this literature does serve to correct the simple-minded orthodox position that the cold war originated as a Communist plot to achieve world domination, it goes much too far and distorts the picture in another direction.

There is no question that the creation of a system of multilateral trade relations was in the interests of the United States. Preference systems ran directly counter to American basic interests as the world's dominant economic power and a major trading nation. It does not follow from this fact, however, that American efforts to achieve such a system were solely self-serving and unmotivated by the sincere belief that economic nationalism and competition were at the root of the Second World War. Nor does it follow that what is good for the United States is contrary to the general welfare of other nations.

The American emphasis on postwar economic relations represented a long tradition in American thought on international relations. The American liberal ideal since the founding of the Republic has been the substitution of commercial for political relations between states.[24] In the best free trade tradition

[22] The basic source for this period is Richard N. Gardner, *Sterling-Dollar Diplomacy: The Origins and Prospects of Our International Economic Order* (expd. ed.; New York: McGraw-Hill Book Co., 1969).

[23] The most ambitious statement of this thesis is Gabriel Kolko, *The Politics of War: The World and the United States Foreign Policy, 1943–1945* (New York: Random House, 1968).

[24] See the study by Felix Gilbert, *To the Farewell Address: Ideas of Early American Foreign Policy* (Princeton, N.J: Princeton University Press, 1961).

trade relations between nations are considered to be a force for peace. Furthermore, as a nation which felt it had been discriminated against by the more powerful European states, the United States wanted a world in which it would have equal access to markets. Universal equality of opportunity, not imperial domination, was the motif of American postwar foreign economic planning.

This naive American faith in the beneficial effects of economic intercourse was reflected in the almost complete absence of attention to strategic matters in American postwar plans. In contrast to the prodigious energies devoted to the restructuring of the international economy little effort was given to the strategic and territorial balance of the postwar world. This neglect is explicable in large part, however, by the prevailing American assumption that a universal system based on an integrated world economy and on the United Nations would replace the traditional emphasis on spheres of influence and the balance of power.

If one accepts the revisionist argument that imperial ambition underlay American postwar plans, then the cold war should have been between the United States and Western Europe, particularly the United Kingdom, rather than between the Union of Soviet Socialist Republics and the United States. The bête noir of American planners was European discrimination and especially the imperial preference which encompassed a high percentage of world trade and exercised considerable discrimination against American goods. American plans for the postwar era were directed against the British in particular. Beginning with the framing of the Atlantic Charter in 1941 and continuing through the negotiation of the Lend-Lease Act (1941), the Bretton Woods Agreement (1944), and the British loan (1945), the thrust of American policy was directed against Commonwealth discrimination.

In light of the intensity of these American efforts to force the United Kingdom and other European countries to accept a multilateral system it is important to appreciate that they were abandoned in response to growth of Soviet-American hostility. As American leadership came to accept the Soviet diplomatic-military challenge as the major postwar problem, the United States attitude toward international economic relations underwent a drastic reversal. In contrast to earlier emphases on multilateralism and nondiscrimination the United States accepted discrimination in the interest of rebuilding the shattered West European economy.

The retort of revisionists to this argument is that the American-Soviet struggle originated in the American desire to incorporate Eastern Europe, particularly Poland, into the American scheme for a global empire. This effort, it is claimed, clashed with the legitimate security concerns of the Soviet Union, and the cold war evolved as the Soviet defensive response to the American effort to expand economically into the Soviet sphere of influence. If the United

States had not been driven by the greed of its corporations, American and Soviet interests could easily have been accommodated.

There are sufficient grounds for this interpretation to give it some plausibility. Certainly, American efforts to incorporate Eastern Europe and even the Soviet Union into the world capitalistic economy raised Soviet suspicions. Although the American view was that the withdrawal of the Soviet Union from the world economy following the Bolshevik Revolution had been a contributing factor to the outbreak of the Second World War and that a peaceful world required Soviet reintegration, the Russians could easily interpret these efforts as an attempt to undermine communism. No doubt in part they were. But it is a long jump from these American efforts to trade in an area of little historical interest to the United States to a conflict so intense and durable that it has on several occasions taken the world to the brink of thermonuclear holocaust.

A more realistic interpretation, I believe, is that the origins of the cold war lie in the unanticipated consequences of the Second World War. The collapse of German power in Europe and of Japanese power in Asia created a power vacuum which both the United States and the Soviet Union sought to fill to their own advantage. One need not even posit aggressive designs on either side to defend this interpretation, although my own position is that the Soviet Union desired (and still desires) to extend its sphere of influence far beyond the glacis of Eastern Europe. To support this political interpretation of the cold war it is sufficient to argue that the power vacuums in Central Europe and the northwestern Pacific created a security dilemma for both powers. In terms of its own security neither power could afford to permit the other to fill this vacuum, and the efforts of each to prevent this only increased the insecurity of the other, causing it to redouble its own efforts. Each in response to the other organized its own bloc, freezing the lines of division established by the victorious armies and wartime conferences.

One cannot understand, however, the pattern of the cold war and its significance for international economic relations unless one appreciates the asymmetric situations of the United States and the Soviet Union. Whereas the Soviet Union is a massive land power directly abutting Western Europe and the northwestern Pacific (primarily Korea and Japan), the United States is principally a naval and air power separated from the zones of contention by two vast oceans. As a consequence, while the Soviet Union has been able with relative ease to bring its influence to bear on its periphery at relatively much less cost in terms of its balance of payments, the United States has had to organize a global system of bases and alliances involving an immense drain on its balance of payments. Moreover, while the Soviet system has been held together largely through the exercise of Soviet military power, economic relations have been an important cement holding the American bloc together.

These economic and strategic differences between the two blocs have been crucial determinants of the postwar international economy and the patterns of transnational relations which have emerged. For this reason some attention must be given to the interplay of economic and political factors in the evolution of relations between the three major components of the contemporary international economy: the United States, Western Europe, and Japan.

Contrary to the hopes of the postwar economic planners who met at Bretton Woods in 1944, the achievement of a system of multilateral trade was soon realized to be an impossibility. The United Kingdom's experience with currency convertibility, which had been forced upon it by the United States, had proven to be a disaster. The United Kingdom and the rest of Europe were simply too weak and short of dollars to engage in a free market. A further weakening of their economies threatened to drive them into the arms of the Soviet Union. In the interest of preventing this the United States in cooperation with Western Europe had to rebuild the world economy in a way not envisaged by the postwar planners.

The reconstruction of the West European economy involved the solution of three problems. In the first place, Europe was desperately short of the dollars required to meet immediate needs and to replenish its capital stock. Second, the prewar European economies had been oriented toward colonial markets. Now the colonies were in revolt, and the United States strongly opposed the revival of a world economy based on a colonial preference system. Third, the practices of economic nationalism and closed preference systems between European states and their overseas colonies had completely fragmented the European economy.

The problem of rehabilitating the economy of the Federal Republic of Germany (West Germany) was particularly difficult. The major trading nation on the Continent, its division into Soviet and Western zones and the Soviet occupation of Eastern Europe had cut industrial West Germany off from its natural trading partners in the agricultural German Democratic Republic (East Germany) and the East. The task therefore was to integrate the industrial Western zones into a larger West European economy comprising agricultural France and Italy. The failure to reintegrate industrial Germany into the larger world economy was regarded to have been one of the tragic errors after World War I. A repetition of this error would force West Germany into the Soviet camp.

The American response to this challenge is well known. Through the Marshall Plan, the Organization for European Economic Cooperation (OEEC), and the European Coal and Steel Community (ECSC) the European economy was revived and radically transformed. For our purposes one point is significant. In the interest of security the United States tolerated, and in fact promoted, the creation of a preference area in Western Europe which discriminated against American goods. At first the mechanism of discrimination was the nonconvertibility of European currencies; then, after the establishment of the European Economic Community (EEC) in 1958, discrimination took the form of one common external tariff.

The economic impact of economic regionalism in Western Europe was not, however, completely detrimental to United States–European trade. One can in fact argue that regionalism gave Europe the courage and security to depart from traditions of economic nationalism and colonialism. The establishment of a large trading area in Europe turned out to be more trade-creating than trade-diverting. As a consequence American and European economic ties increased and the United States continued to enjoy a favorable balance of trade with its European partners.

With respect to Japan the United States faced a situation similar to that presented by West Germany. Although Japan was not severely damaged by the war, it was a densely populated major trading nation exceptionally dependent upon foreign sources of raw materials, technology, and agricultural products. With the victory of the communists on the Chinese mainland Japan's major prewar trading partner came under the control of the Soviet bloc. Furthermore, Japan suffered from discrimination by other industrialized states both in their home markets and in their overseas colonial empires. The exclusion of the Japanese from South and Southeast Asia practiced by the Dutch, French, and British had been a major cause of Japan's military aggression, and the continued existence of these preference systems threatened its economic well-being. Separated from the Soviet Union by a small body of water and economically isolated, Japan's situation was a highly precarious one.

As in the case of West Germany the task of American foreign policy was to integrate Japan into the larger world economy and lessen the attraction of markets controlled by the Communist bloc. While this history of American efforts to restructure Japan's role in the world economy is less well known than is the history of its European counterpart, the basic aspects deserve to be emphasized. In the first place, the United States brought pressures to bear against Dutch, French, and British colonialism in South and Southeast Asia and encouraged the integration of these areas into a larger framework of multilateral trade. Second, over the strong opposition of Western Europe the United States sponsored Japanese membership in the International Monetary Fund (IMF), the General Agreement on Tariffs and Trade (GATT), and other international organizations.[25] Third, and most significant, the United States in the negotiations leading to the Treaty of Peace with Japan granted Japan privileged access to the American home market.[26]

[25] For the history of these efforts see Gardner Patterson, *Discrimination in International Trade: The Policy Issues, 1945–1965* (Princeton, N.J: Princeton University Press, 1966), chapter 6.

[26] Frederick S. Dunn, in collaboration with Annemarie Shimoney, Percy E. Corbett, and Bernard C. Cohen, *Peace-Making and the Settlement with Japan* (Princeton, N.J: Princeton University Press, 1963), chapter 7.

At the same time that these developments in the economic realm were taking place, through the instrumentalities of the North Atlantic Treaty Organization (NATO) and the Treaty of Peace with Japan, Western Europe and Japan were brought under the protection of the American nuclear umbrella. In Europe, Japan, and around the periphery of the Soviet Union and the People's Republic of China (Communist China) the United States erected a base system by which to counter the Soviet advantage of geographical proximity. Thus, with their security guaranteed by this Pax Americana, Japan, Western Europe, and, to a lesser extent, the United States have been able to devote the better part of their energies to the achievement of high rates of economic growth within the framework of a highly interdependent transnational economy.

Just as the Pax Britannica provided the security and political framework for the expansion of transnational economic activity in the nineteenth century, so this Pax Americana has fulfilled a similar function in the mid-twentieth century. Under American leadership the various rounds of GATT negotiations have enabled trade to expand at an unprecedented rate, far faster than the growth of gross national product in the United States and Western Europe. The United States dollar has become the basis of the international monetary system, and, with the rise of the Eurodollar market, governments have lost almost all control over a large segment of the transnational economy. Finally, the multinational corporation has found the global political environment a highly congenial one and has been able to integrate production across national boundaries.

The corollary of this argument is, of course, that just as a particular array of political interests and relations permitted this system of transnational economic relations to come into being, so changes in these political factors can profoundly alter the system and even bring it to an end. If, as numerous writers argue, there is a growing contradiction between the nation-state and transnational activities, the resolution may very well be in favor of the nation-state or, more likely, of regional arrangements centered on the dominant industrial powers: Japan, the United States, and Western Europe.

IV

This argument that contemporary transnational processes rest on a peculiar set of political relationships can be substantiated, I believe, if one analyzes the two most crucial relationships which underlie the contemporary international economy. The first is the relationship between the United States and West Germany, the second is that between the United States and Japan.

While the American–West German special relationship is based on a number of factors including that of mutual economic advantage, from the perspective of transnational activities one factor is of crucial importance. In simplest terms this is the exchange of American protection of West Germany against the Soviet Union for guaranteed access to EEC markets for American products and direct investment. In both agricultural commodities and manufactured goods the United States continues to enjoy a very favorable trade balance with Western Europe. With respect to direct investment the subsidiaries of American corporations have been able to establish a very powerful position in Western Europe since the beginning of the EEC in 1958.

Without this overall favorable trade balance with Western Europe and West German willingness to hold dollars, the American balance-of-payments situation might, the West Germans fear, force the United States to reduce its troop strength in West Germany. As such a move could lessen the credibility of the American nuclear deterrent, the West Germans are very reluctant to make any moves which would weaken the American presence in Western Europe. Consequently, while the significance of American direct investment in Europe for the American balance of payments is unclear, the West Germans are unwilling to take any action regarding this investment which might alienate American opinion and lessen the American commitment to Western Europe.

The importance of the military dependence of West Germany on the United States for continued access to EEC markets for subsidiaries of American corporations was revealed several years ago. In the early 1960s President Charles de Gaulle of France launched an offensive against increasing American economic penetration of Western Europe. While the major part of this effort was directed against "the hegemony of the dollar," a parallel attempt was made to arrest and possibly reverse the flow of American direct investment in Western Europe.[27]

The initial move of the French government was to prevent further American direct investment in France. This effort, however, soon proved to be self-defeating. Denied permission to establish or purchase subsidiaries in France, American corporations were welcomed into one of France's partners in the EEC and thus still had access to the French market. That France acting alone could not solve the problem was driven home to the French when General Motors Corporation, denied permission to locate in France, established one of the largest automobile assembly plants in Western Europe across the border in Belgium.

In response to this situation de Gaulle sought to obtain West German cooperation against American investment in EEC countries. Together these two most powerful of the six could dictate a policy which the others would be forced to accept. Through the instrumentality of the Franco-German Friendship Treaty of 1963, therefore, de Gaulle sought to form a Bonn-Paris axis

[27] For this history see Robert Gilpin, *France in the Age of the Scientific State* (Princeton, N.J: Princeton University Press [for the Center of International Studies, Princeton University], 1968), chapter 3.

directed against American hegemony in Western Europe. While the terms of this treaty go beyond our immediate concerns, two aspects are important. In the first place, de Gaulle wanted West Germany to join France in taking a stand against American investment. Second, he wanted to see joint West German–French cooperative efforts in science, technology, and industry in order to lessen European dependence upon the United States in these areas.

Although there was sentiment in West Germany favorable to taking measures to limit the rapidly growing role of American subsidiaries in EEC countries, the West German government refused to take any action which might weaken the American commitment to defend Western Europe. The United States government not only reminded the West Germans that a continued American military presence was dependent upon West German support of measures to lessen the American balance-of-payments deficit, West Germany was also pressured to increase its military purchases from the United States and to avoid competitive arrangements with France. Largely as a result of these American pressures the Friendship Treaty was in effect aborted and the first serious counteroffensive of the nation-state against the multinational corporation collapsed. It is clear, however, that the outcome of this tale would have been altogether different if West Germany had desired greater military and economic independence from the United States.

Turning to the other pillar of the contemporary transnational economy, the American-Japanese special relationship, mutual economic interest is an important bond, but the primary factor in this relationship has been the security issue. In contrast to the American–West German situation, however, this relationship involves American protection and a special position for the Japanese in the American market in exchange for United States bases in Japan and Okinawa. The asymmetry of this relationship compared with that between the United States and West Germany reflects the differences in the economic and military situations.

As mentioned earlier the basic problem for American foreign policy with respect to Japan was how to reintegrate this highly industrialized and heavily populated country into the world economy. Given communist control of mainland Asia and the opposition of European countries to opening their markets to the Japanese this meant throwing open the American economy to Japanese exports. As a consequence of this favored treatment the Japanese have enjoyed an exceptionally favorable balance of trade with the United States. For security reasons the United States has not only tolerated this situation but, with a few exceptions, has not restricted Japanese imports or forced the Japanese to open their economy to American direct investment.

In contrast to the situation prevailing in Europe the purpose of American military base structure in Japan is not merely to deter local aggression against the Japanese; rather, it is essential for the maintenance of American power and influence throughout the western Pacific and Southeast Asia. Without access to Japanese bases the United States could not have fought two wars in Asia over the past two decades and could not continue its present role in the area. Largely because of this dependence upon Japanese bases for its strategic position around the periphery of Communist China, the United States has been willing to tolerate in a period of balance-of-payments deficit the $1.5 billion annual trade surplus Japan enjoys vis-à-vis the United States.

In the case of both the American-European and the American-Japanese relationships new forces are now at work which threaten to undermine the foundations of contemporary transnational relations. In the case of United States–European relations the most dramatic change is the decreased fear of the Soviet Union by both partners. As a consequence both Americans and Europeans are less tolerant of the price they have to pay for their special relationship. The Europeans feel less dependent upon the United States for their security and are more concerned with the detrimental aspects of close economic, military, and diplomatic ties with the United States. The United States, for its part, is increasingly sensitive to European discrimination against American exports and feels threatened by EEC moves toward the creation of a preference system encompassing much of Western Europe, the Middle East, and Africa. As the Mansfield amendment to reduce United States military forces in Europe reveals, Americans, too, are less willing to pay the cost of maintaining a large military force abroad.[28]

With respect to the relationship of Japan to the United States, strategic and economic changes are undermining the foundations of transnationalism. At the same time that Communist China is receding as a security threat to the United States and Japan, economic strains are beginning to aggravate relations between the two countries. In the eyes of the United States Japan's economy is no longer weak and vulnerable, necessitating special consideration by the United States. As a consequence the demands of American interests for import curbs against Japanese goods and for the liberalization of Japanese policies on foreign direct investment are beginning to take precedence over foreign policy and strategic considerations. Nor does the United States continue to accept the fact that the defense burden should rest so heavily on it alone. Underlying the Nixon Doctrine of American retrenchment in Asia is the appreciation that a greater Japanese military effort would not only reduce American defense costs but would also cause the Japanese to divert resources from their export economy and relieve Japanese pressures in the American market.

The Japanese for their part resent the fact that they are almost totally dependent upon the United States for their security and economic well-being.

[28] United States, Congress, House, *Amending the Military Selective Service Act of 1967 to Increase Military Pay; To Authorize Military Active Duty Strengths for Fiscal Year 1972; And for Other Purposes,* H.R. 6531, 92nd Cong., 1st sess., 1971, Amendment No. 86.

While they of course want to maintain a strong position in the American market and feel particularly threatened by protectionist sentiment in the United States, they are growing increasingly concerned about the price they must pay for their close association with the United States. Moreover, they feel especially vulnerable to American economic pressures such as those that have been exerted to induce Japan to permit direct investment by American corporations. But the dominant new factor is the Japanese desire to play a more independent role in the world and to enjoy the prestige that is commensurate with their powerful and expanding economy.

In the cases of both American-European and American-Japanese relations new strains have appeared which threaten to undermine the political framework of transnational economic activity. Diplomatic and military bonds tying Europe and Japan to the United States have weakened at the same time that economic conflicts have intensified and have become less tolerable to all three major parties. As a result the favorable political factors that have facilitated the rapid expansion of transnational processes over the past several decades are receding. In their stead new political forces have come into play that are tending to isolate the United States and to favor a more regional organization of the international economy.

On the other hand, one must readily acknowledge that the multinational corporation and transnational processes have achieved tremendous momentum. It is not without good reason that numerous authorities have predicted the demise of the nation-state and the complete reordering of international life by 200 or 300 "megafirms."[29] Perhaps, as these authorities argue, the multinational corporation as an institution has sufficiently taken root in the vested interests of all major parties that it can survive the vicissitudes of political change. History, however, does not provide much comfort for this train of thought. As Staley and Viner have suggested, the contradiction between the economic and political organization of society is not always resolved in favor of economic rationality. Moreover, whatever the outcome—the preservation of multilateral transnational processes, a reversion to economic nationalism, or the division of the globe by economic regionalism—the determining consideration will be the diplomatic and strategic interests of the dominant powers.

V

Prior to concluding this essay one crucial question remains to be treated: What, after all, has been the impact of transnational economic activities, especially the multinational corporation, on international politics? In answer to this question both Marxists and what one might call the transnational ideol-

[29] Howard V. Perlmutter, "Some Management Problems in Spaceship Earth: The Megafirm and the Global Industrial Estate," *Academy of Management Proceedings, 29th Annual Meeting, Chicago, August 24–27, 1969*, pp. 59–93.

ogists see these transnational processes and actors as having had a profound impact on international relations. Some go much further. By breaking the monopoly of the nation-state over international economic relations the multinational corporation is claimed to have altered the very nature of international relations.

Under certain circumstances and in relation to particular states there can be little doubt that the multinational corporation has, and can exercise, considerable influence over domestic and international relations. One could mention in this connection the international petroleum companies, for example. But in general there is little evidence to substantiate the argument that the multinational corporation as an independent actor has had a significant impact on international politics. As Staley has convincingly shown in his study of foreign investment prior to World War II, where business corporations have exercised an influence over political developments they have tended to do so as instruments of their home governments rather than as independent actors.[30]

Contemporary studies on the multinational corporation indicate that Staley's conclusion continues to hold true. While the evidence is indisputable that the multinational corporation is profoundly important in the realm of international economic relations, its political significance is largely confined to its impact on domestic politics where it is an irritant to nationalistic sentiments. In part the resentment has been due to the unwarranted interference by foreign-owned corporations in domestic affairs; this has especially been the case in less developed countries. More frequently, nationalistic feelings have been aroused by the predominant positions multinational corporations may hold in the overall economy or in particularly sensitive sectors.

Despite all the polemics against multinational corporations there is little evidence to support the view that they have been very successful in replacing the nation-state as the primary actor in international politics. Where these business enterprises have influenced international political relations, they have done so, like any other interest group, by influencing the policies of their home governments. Where they have tried to influence the foreign and economic policies of host governments, they have most frequently been acting in response to the laws of their home countries and as agents of their home governments. In defense of this argument it should be noted that a Canadian study of American direct investment in Canada focused its concern almost exclusively on the extraterritorial application of American law (antitrust laws, the Trading with the Enemy Act, and balance-of-payments regulations).[31] As Canada has a higher percentage of foreign ownership than any

[30] Eugene Staley, *War and the Private Investor: A Study in the Relations of International Politics and International Private Investment* (Garden City, N.Y: Doubleday, Doran & Co., 1935).

[31] *Foreign Ownership and the Structure of Canadian Industry,* Report of the Task Force on the Structure of Canadian Industry (Ottawa: Queen's Printer, January 1968).

other industrialized country and as this study was one of the most thorough which any government has conducted on foreign direct investment, its conclusions are especially significant.

Contrary to the argument that the multinational corporation will somehow supplant the nation-state, I think it is closer to the truth to argue that the role of the nation-state in economic as well as in political life is increasing and that the multinational corporation is actually a stimulant to the further extension of state power in the economic realm. One should not forget that the multinational corporation is largely an American phenomenon and that in response to this American challenge other governments are increasingly intervening in their domestic economies in order to counterbalance the power of American corporations and to create domestic rivals of equal size and competence.

The paradox of the contemporary situation is that the increasing interdependence among national economies, for which the multinational corporation is partially responsible, is accompanied by increased governmental interference in economic affairs. What this neo-mercantilism constitutes, of course, is one response to the basic contradiction between the economic and political organization of contemporary international society. But in contrast to the opinion of a George Ball who sees this conflict resolved in favor of transnational processes, the internationalization of production, and actors like the multinational corporation, nationalists in Canada, Western Europe, and the less developed world favor upholding more powerful states to counterbalance large multinational corporations.

Similarly, the impetus today behind the EEC, Japan's effort to build an economic base less dependent on the United States, and other moves toward regionalism reflect in part a desire to lessen the weight of American economic power; in effect, these regional undertakings are essentially economic alliances between sovereign governments. Although they are altering the political framework within which economic forces will increasingly have to operate, the basic unit is and will remain the nation-state. For better or for worse it continues to be the most powerful object of man's loyalty and affection.

The Growth of International Nongovernmental Organization in the Twentieth Century

KJELL SKJELSBAEK

I. INTRODUCTION

TRANSNATIONAL interactions have been defined as "the movement of tangible or intangible items across state boundaries when at least one actor is not an agent of a government or an intergovernmental organization."[1] Correspondingly, transnational organizations can be defined as transnational interactions institutionalized. There may be several reasons why participants in transnational interactions may find it convenient to found a permanent organization and to endow it with a certain amount of authority to coordinate their interaction. First of all, the intensity of a particular kind of interaction may rise to such a level that more personnel and other resources are needed to regulate and facilitate the process. The most economical way of responding to this need may be to establish a joint secretariat. Second, although the intensity of exchanges between each pair of interacting entities may be constant, the number of participants may increase. This process results in a problem of coordination and the need for a coordinating agent in the form of, for example, an international body. To put it slightly differently,

KJELL SKJELSBAEK, a staff member of the International Peace Research Institute in Oslo, is presently a visiting scholar at the Mental Health Research Institute at the University of Michigan, Ann Arbor, Michigan. The author would like to express his gratitude to the International Peace Research Institute, the Fund for Peace in New York, the Norwegian Advisory Council on Arms Control and Disarmament, the Norwegian Research Council for Science and the Humanities, the United States Educational Foundation in Norway, and the Center for International Affairs, Harvard University, Cambridge, Massachusetts, for financial support, practical assistance, and scholarly guidance. This article is identifiable as PRIO publication 22–14.

[1] Joseph S. Nye, Jr., and Robert O. Keohane, introductory essay to this volume, p. xii. Cf., Adrea Rosenberg, "International Interaction and the Taxonomy of International Organizations," *International Associations*, November 1967 (19th Year, No. 11), pp. 721–729.

institutionalization tends to follow multilateralization. Third, although neither of the above conditions may obtain, an organization may be founded to achieve fast action in emergencies requiring joint operation. Finally, an organization, and in particular its officers, may serve as mediator and arbitrator in situations of conflict and competition between interacting members. Such activities are, for example, promoted by the Inter-American Commercial Arbitration Commission.

The relative importance of these and other possible causes of the institutionalization of transnational interactions is hard to assess, but the impressive increase in many kinds of transnational interactions since World War II has in fact been paralleled by a considerable increase in the number of transnational organizations.[2] Today there are probably somewhere between 2,500 and 3,000 transnational, nonprofit organizations in the world; the exact number depends on which definition of transnational organization one prefers. If profitmaking organizations, that is, multinational business enterprises, are included, the figures will be much higher, but I have left them out since they are discussed elsewhere in this volume.[3] Some of the nonprofit organizations with which I am concerned, for example, the International Red Cross, are well known to the public and to students of international relations. Others are seldom mentioned in mass media but have a recognized standing in the world of international organizations and have occasionally caught the attention of scholars. Most of the organizations are, however, rather inconspicuous; some of them perform important functions for their members and the societies they represent, while others are of moderate significance even to them.

Transnational organizations operate in a variety of fields. Organizations concerned with commerce, industry, health, medicine, and natural science are particularly numerous. But there are also organizations in the areas of sports, religion, international relations, art, economics and finance, agriculture, education and technology among others.[4] Some examples of transnational organizations will indicate the range of their activities: Among the more important organizations are the International Air Transport Association (IATA), the International Olympic Committee (IOC), the World Council of Churches (WCC), the International Commission of Jurists (ICJ), and the World Federation of Trade Unions (WFTU).[5]

[2] Much statistical information on transnational interaction has been collected and utilized by Robert Cooley Angell in his *Peace on the March: Transnational Participation* (New Perspectives in Political Science, No. 19) (New York: Van Nostrand Reinhold Co., 1969).

[3] See the essays by Louis T. Wells, Jr., and Raymond Vernon in this volume. For an effort to list and classify multinational business enterprises see A. J. N. Judge, "Multinational Business Enterprises," in *Yearbook of International Organizations*, ed. Eyvind S. Tew (12th ed.; Brussels: Union of International Associations, 1968–1969), pp. 1189–1214.

[4] See the *Yearbook of International Organizations*, p. 13. Characteristics of organizations and processes in some of the particular fields are discussed by the authors in parts II and III of this volume.

[5] The functions of the IATA are interestingly described by Robert L. Thornton in this volume; the essay by Robert W. Cox in this volume deals with problems of international trade unions.

For an organization to be "transnational" two minimal requirements must be met: At least two different countries must be represented in the organization and one of the representatives must not be an agent of a government. In practice it would probably be wise to specify that at least one-half of the members of the multilateral organization should not act in a governmental capacity. In either case, however, the criteria for a transnational organization should emphasize membership composition.

The empirical part of this essay is based on data collected by the Union of International Associations (UIA) and by myself on the basis of UIA definitions of various kinds of organizations.[6] Unfortunately, the UIA uses a legalistic criterion to distinguish between intergovernmental organizations (IGOs) and international nongovernmental organizations (NGOs). This criterion defines IGOs as organizations established by intergovernmental treaty, as specified in a United Nations Economic and Social Council (ECOSOC) resolution of 1950, regardless of the character of their membership.[7] Most but not all IGOs include only governmental members, and in practice many NGOs have both governmental and nongovernmental members. Thus, the UIA's list of NGOs is somewhat different from and generally more restrictive than a list of transnational organizations compiled according to the membership criteria suggested earlier.[8] I have altered the UIA definition in one way by excluding approximately 250 business and professional groups within the European Economic Community (EEC) and the European Free Trade Association (EFTA). These organizations are officially recognized as international interest groups by either the EEC or EFTA and cooperate with these IGOs but are still often merely subcommittees of larger European NGOs and should therefore not be counted twice.[9]

Most of my aggregate data has been drawn from UIA publications, particu-

[6] The Union of International Associations in Brussels is itself an interesting transnational actor. It was founded in 1907 to serve as a documentation center on international governmental and nongovernmental organizations, their activities and meetings. The UIA also works to promote research in the same field and to publicize studies. I have found its publications very useful and appreciate the time spent by its staff in consultation with me.

[7] "Any international organization which is not established by inter-governmental agreement shall be considered as a non-governmental organization. . . . " ECOSOC Resolution 288 (X), February 27, 1950.

[8] There are several additional differences between the lists that can be briefly mentioned. The UIA excludes bilateral organizations, of which there appear to be few, organizations in which one national delegation is completely dominant through the budget or by means of the voting arrangements, and ephemeral organizations established to organize a single international meeting. It also excludes organizations without a formal structure. Moreover, universities, colleges, churches, and religious missions fall outside the scope of the UIA. On the other hand, the UIA definition includes some organizations that are formally subunits of others if they act relatively independently and elect their own officers. Thus, eleven international trade union secretariats of the WFTU as well as the WFTU itself are included. Profit-making organizations are, of course, excluded.

[9] EEC business and professional groups have been studied by Jean Meynaud and Dusan Sidjanski; see *Groupes de pression et coopération européenne* (Paris: Centre d'études des relations internationales, 1967); and *Les Groupes de pression dans la Communauté européenne* (2 vols.; Montreal: Université de Montreal, 1969).

larly from the tenth (1964–1965) edition of the *Yearbook of International Organizations,* and has been coded and put on punch cards.[10] I have also collected my own data on the basis of a questionnaire which was mailed to the secretaries-general of all IGOs and NGOs in 1967.[11]

II. The Development of the NGO World

The NGO world is growing and changing in many ways. New organizations are added and old ones disappear. New countries become represented and others see their relative share of influence reduced. New functions are performed, new procedures adopted, and more channels of information established. Internal structures of organizations are reformed. These changes affect the importance of NGOs in the world. It is hard to form a conclusive opinion about the role they are playing today and harder still to predict their future significance. For both purposes, however, knowledge of the past development of the NGO world puts us in a better position for analysis and evaluation.

Development means changes in certain dimensions. Particularly important for the assessment of the strength and size of the NGO world are the following dimensions:

1) *Domain* of the NGO world—the number of units or NGOs in the global system.
2) *Number of national representations*—the number of countries that have individual citizens, national organizations, and/or governmental agencies affiliated with an NGO.
3) *Scope* and *intensity* of NGO activity—the number of functions which an NGO performs (scope) at certain rates (intensity).
4) *Interconnection* of the NGO world—the degree of cooperation between NGOs. The more NGOs cooperate with each other instead of fighting or remaining isolated, the more effective they presumably are in performing their functions and upholding their independence vis-à-vis IGOs and nation-states.

Increases in one or more of these dimensions are defined as growth. Two more dimensions are included, however, because they seem to be politically significant:

5) *Distribution of NGOs by field of activity*—the distinction between those

[10] None of the tables from UIA publications appears in its original form since I have split and regrouped the data.

[11] The representative quality of the returned questionnaires turned out to be very high; see Kjell Skjelsbaek, "Peace and the Systems of International Organizations" (Magister's thesis, University of Oslo, 1970), chapter 3.

6 #6.

organizations concerned with, for example, sports and those mainly concerned with influencing the international political situation.

6) *Distribution of NGOs across countries*—the variation in peacemaking potential between NGOs limited in their membership and activities to one region of the world and those NGOs whose membership and activities are evenly distributed.

The theoretical justification for these two dimensions is elaborated in subsequent parts of this essay.

These six dimensions are treated individually. The validity of their empirical indicators often leaves much to be desired because data on more satisfactory variables simply does not exist.

The first dimension, the *domain* of the NGO world, is by far the easiest to operationalize. The variable used is the number of independent organizations. The first NGO—the Rosicrucian Order—is said to fit the UIA definition since 1694 which makes it a unique phenomenon for nearly one and one-half centuries.[12] Figure 1 shows the number of NGOs founded during

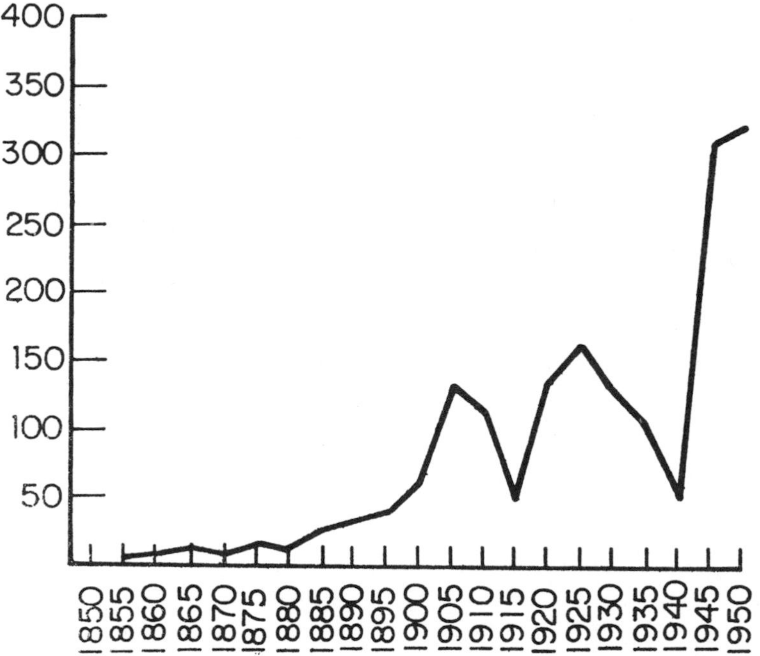

Figure 1. Number of NGOs founded per five-year period, 1850–1954

[12] The traditional history of the Rosicrucian Order began in Egypt about 1500 B.C. It is an educational and fraternal order whose teachings present a system of metaphysical and physical philosophy to help the individual utilize his natural talents to better advantage. There are about 100,000 members in 53 countries. Cf., the *Yearbook of International Organizations,* pp. 976–977; and G. P. Speeckaert, *The*

each five-year period since 1850.[13] The most striking characteristic of the trajectory is the general upward trend interrupted by two very marked dips at the time of the world wars. Unfortunately, it has not been possible to calculate the net increases for the periods before 1950, but in all probability they were negative immediately before and during the wars as in the case of IGOs.[14] Grave international conflicts apparently curtail the formation of NGOs.[15]

Reliable biennial data for the years 1954–1968 makes it possible to calculate mean percentage increases in different periods (see table 1). Although mergers and splits do take place in the NGO world, there are more of the former than of the latter. The high growth rates in table 1 can therefore not be attributed to a relatively high number of splinter groups.

Table 1. Active NGOs, 1954–1968

Year	Number of NGOs	Percentage increase
1954	1,012	—
1956	975	−3.7
1958	1,060	8.8
1960	1,255	18.4
1962	1,324	5.5
1964	1,470	11.0
1966	1,685	14.6
1968	1,899	12.7
Mean increase per annum, 1954–1968		4.7
Mean increase per annum, 1962–1968		6.2

SOURCE: *Yearbook of International Organizations* (5th–12th eds.; Brussels: Union of International Associations, 1955–1969).

The second dimension of the NGO world is the *number of national representations.* The figures for this variable, presented in table 2, indicate a steady increase in the number of national representations which means that NGOs on the average now involve more countries than in previous years. This is par-

1,978 International Organizations Founded since the Congress of Vienna: A Chronological List (Documents for the Study of International Nongovernmental Relations, No. 7) (Brussels: Union of International Associations, 1957), p. 1.

13 Data for figure 1 is derived from Speeckaert, p. 1.

14 Skjelsbaek, "Peace and the Systems of International Organizations," chapter 4, p. 7.

15 It could be argued that the causal relationship operates in reverse, i.e., that NGOs make up an integrative subsystem of world society and that, if the integrative subsystem weakens, conflicts will erupt. In my mind there is an interplay beween the two factors, but interstate conflicts still have more effect on NGOs than the other way around. However, this may well be changed in the future as the NGO world expands. For an interesting theoretical justification of this kind of thinking see Paul Smoker, "Nation State Escalation and International Integration," *Journal of Peace Research,* 1967 (Vol. 4, No. 1), pp. 61–75.

tially due to the increasing number of states in the world, but this is probably not the entire explanation.[16] The increase is not due, however, to any increased percentage of universal organizations. In fact, the proportion of regional organizations increased until at least 1962. This is shown in table 3.[17]

Table 2. National representations in NGOs, 1951–1966

Year	Mean	Standard deviation	N	No information
1951	21.0	—	583	240
1956	22.3	—	897	76
1964	23.7	19.9	1,458	12
1966	25.7	—	1,416	269

SOURCES: "La Participation des états aux organisations internationales," *International Associations,* October 1957 (9th Year, No. 10), tables 2 and 3, pp. 708–709; *Yearbook of International Organizations* (10th ed.; Brussels: Union of International Associations, 1965).

Table 3. Distribution of regional NGOs, 1954–1962

	Percentage by year			
Continent	1954	1956	1960	1962
Europe	55.1	60.7	65.0	61.1
Americas	33.5	28.0	24.6	25.5
Africa	6.3	4.8	4.6	7.0
Asia	5.1	6.5	5.7	6.4
Sum	100.0	100.0	99.9	100.0
N	158	186	280	298
Percentage of all NGOs	13.9	18.2	24.2	25.0

SOURCE: E. S. Tew, "Représentations nationales dans les organisations internationales," *International Associations,* November 1963 (15th Year, No. 11), tables K and L, pp. 694–695.

The *scope* of an NGO is defined as the number of functions an NGO per-

16 Sixty-one percent of the organizations surveyed expected to gain new national branches in the future in spite of the small likelihood of a corresponding increase in the number of nation-states and territories.

17 The organizations were classified as regional on the basis of their names. I have tried this procedure myself and found it very difficult. There is a basic confusion about the term region. The UIA does not distinguish between region and continent which makes it hard to place Arab organizations or NGOs with members from Western Europe and North America only. Moreover, the name of an organization may be misleading, and it may have one or two members from other regions. Israel, for example, is represented in some European organizations. The blurred lines between regions may be annoying to the researcher, but they may be functional for other purposes. Cf., the discussion about the peace relevance of NGOs, section V of this essay.

forms. Since it is unclear how a "function" should be defined, it is impossible to operationalize this concept. NGO programs now appear to be more encompassing and diversified than before. Probably more important is the fact that new organizations formed every year engage in new activities hitherto not taken up at the international level. In spite of the importance of this dimension, however, an attempt at empirical verification of the hypothesized expansion of scope must be temporarily postponed.

Intensity of activity can be measured by numbers of paid staff members and budgets. About one-third of all NGOs in 1964 had no paid staffs; they were administered by elected secretaries on a voluntary basis. Another one-third of the NGOs had staffs of one to three persons. The average for all organizations, however, was nine which indicates that a few large NGOs have more staff personnel than all the others together. Unfortunately, dispersion measures cannot be computed for other years, but the means are given in table 4 together with the corresponding mean size of budgets. It is clear that no trend toward larger mean size of staff or budget is evident for NGOs.[18]

Table 4. Budget and paid staff of NGOs, 1954–1964

	Budget			Paid staff		
Year	Mean[a]	N	Percentage response	Mean[a]	N	Percentage response
1954	710	327	32	—	—	—
1958	610	477	45	12.5	478	45
1960	587	521	42	8.3	491	39
1964	629	417	28	9.0	615	42

SOURCES: "Un Réseau inextricable?" *International Associations,* October 1958 (10th Year, No. 10), tabulation and table 3, pp. 682–683; E. S. Tew, "The Organizational World," *International Associations,* December 1960 (12th Year, No. 12), tables 3 and 4, pp. 734–735; *Yearbook of International Organizations* (10th ed., 1965).

[a] In thousands of US $.

There is no comparative data over time on relationships between NGOs or the degree of *interconnection* between them, but this dimension of growth is nevertheless so important that it deserves brief discussion. The increasing number of organizations in various fields of activity probably leads to a need for coordination which in turn may beget new "super-NGOs" as coordinating

[18] Staff and budget indicators are, of course, closely related—the gamma correlation equals .88. Missing data represents a difficult problem since many organizations, particularly the smaller ones, are loath to report the size of their staffs and budgets. But since these are probably the same organizations every year, the general trends shown may be reliable even though the particular means may be incorrect.

mechanisms.[19] My hypothesis, therefore, is that interaction between NGOs and between NGOs and other actors is increasing. The base from which this increase would take place is fairly substantial: In 1964 about one-third of all NGOs reported some kind of formal relationship with two or more other NGOs, and a slightly smaller fraction had formal relationships with IGOs in the form, for example, of consultative status.[20]

The fifth dimension, the *distribution of NGOs by field of activity,* is roughly measured by the data presented in table 5. IGOs are also included in these figures, but, since they comprise only about 10 percent of the total, they constitute only a minor problem. Many of the organizations founded in these three time periods no longer exist, but the death rate is claimed to be approximately equal in the largest categories.[21] A more important problem is the difficulty of defining and classifying the various fields of activity. Because one man, G. P. Speeckaert, has done the classification, the consistency is relatively high, although he has not entirely escaped the problems posed by organizations working in several fields.

Despite all of these reservations some of the changes indicated in table 5 are large enough to be considered significant. Most notable is the category of economic and financial organizations. They constituted 12.5 percent of the number of organizations founded in the period after World War II compared with only 3.3 percent before 1914. Commercial and industrial organizations show a similar, although less marked, pattern. It is remarkable, however, that the relative number of pure science organizations is diminishing. Scientists seem to have organized internationally at an early period, and much of the expansion and diversification in the postwar period must have taken place within the existing organizations. Applied science, however, is an area with an increasing number of international organizations.[22]

A more valid indicator than the number of organizations founded is the total number of organizations active at various points in time. Very reliable data is now available for NGOs alone for the period 1964–1968. Relative dis-

[19] Descriptions of several "super-NGOs" are found in J. J. Lador-Lederer, *International Non-Governmental Organizations and Economic Entities: A Study in Autonomous Organization and* Ius Gentium (Leiden: A. W. Sijthoff, 1962), p. 66. According to a recent count there are almost 100 superorganizations consisting partly or exclusively of other NGOs; cf., A. J. N. Judge, "International NGO Groupings," *International Associations,* February 1969 (21st Year, No. 2), pp. 89–92.

[20] For details see Skjelsbaek, "Peace and the Systems of International Organizations," chapter 3, p. 13. Negative relationships are formalized neither in the NGO world nor in the nation-state world; see ibid., appendix B, p. 1, for a discussion of negative alliances. Negative, or at least competitive, relationships may exist between NGOs of different ideological color. The most clear-cut ideological divisions are probably found between trade unions; cf., Cox, in this volume.

[21] Speeckaert, p. xiv.

[22] The mean number of national representations is different for the different categories of organizations. In general the means are lowest in those areas that are most relevant for politics. Commercial NGOs have, for example, about fifteen representations on an average which is half the mean number of countries represented in sports organizations.

Table 5. International organizations founded, 1693–1954

Field of activity	Percentage by year		
	1693–1914	1915–1944	1945–1954
General, press, documentation	6.3	3.5	5.6
Philosophy, ethics, peace	7.1	5.0	4.0
Religion	5.3	3.8	2.9
Social science	1.8	1.2	2.1
Economics, political economy, finance	3.3	9.5	12.5
Labor	8.6	3.0	5.2
Law, administration	10.0	9.2	8.6
Relief, education, youth and women's movements	8.6	11.6	12.1
Commerce, industry	5.7	8.3	9.2
Philology, languages	5.5	2.0	.9
Pure science	10.6	6.5	4.9
Medicine, health	9.4	10.5	9.6
Engineering, technology	2.9	4.1	4.6
Agriculture, domestic science	4.9	5.1	6.0
Transport	2.0	4.5	4.5
Art	2.0	5.6	4.7
Sports	5.1	5.0	1.7
Literature	0	1.2	.2
Geography, history	.8	.9	.7
Sum	99.9	100.5	100.0
N	509	666	803

SOURCE: Speeckaert, p. xiii.

NOTE: About 400 organizations, for which the foundation date is missing, are not included in the table. Most of them are not in existence today. Cf., "The Development of the International Structure," *NGO Bulletin,* July 1952 (4th Year, Nos. 6–7), p. 247.

tribution by field of activity appears to be quite stable, but the long-run trends mentioned earlier are clearly discernible.[23]

I hypothesize that the relative number of NGOs has been growing precisely in those areas that are most politically relevant and in which national governments are likely to be most active. If this is so, the consequences may be far-reaching. Governments may respond to NGO expansion in several ways: by curbing NGO activities by establishing an IGO; by trying to influence their respective states in the relevant NGOs; or by trying to nationalize the particular types of activity. Conversely, the composition of the membership of NGOs may be such that it not only brings different national nongovernmental groups together but also facilitates contacts between governmental and nongovern-

[23] For details see Kjell Skjelsbaek, "Development of the Systems of International Organisations: A Diachronic Study," *Proceedings of the International Peace Research Association Third General Conference* (IPRA Studies in Peace Research) (3 vols.; Assen, the Netherlands: Royal Van Gorcum, 1970), Vol. 2, pp. 90–136; and "Peace and the Systems of International Organizations," chapter 4, p. 25.

mental sectors. At least some of the European agricultural organizations seem to have this potential. In short, all kinds of bargains can be struck.

The final dimension to be discussed is the *distribution of NGOs across countries.*[24] It goes almost without saying that the particular configuration of organizations across countries to a large extent determines the culture of the NGO world and its acceptance in various national societies. To simplify this analysis I divided the 219 countries in the world in 1969 into eight categories or regions on the basis of economic and political similarity rather than territorial contiguity or geographical proximity.[25] The eight regions are:

Northwest—North America and Western Europe plus Australia, Cyprus, Israel, Japan, New Zealand, and the Republic of South Africa. This label obviously refers to political, not geographical, position.

Latin America—all countries in the Western Hemisphere except the United States and Canada.

Arab World—all members of the League of Arab States plus Iran and the Arab ministates.

Western Asia—all other Asian states not ruled by communist parties.

Communist Asia—the Democratic People's Republic of Korea (North Korea), the Democratic Republic of Vietnam (North Vietnam), the Mongolian People's Republic, and the People's Republic of China (Communist China).

Eastern Europe—the communist-ruled states in Europe.

Black Africa—all non-Arab countries in Africa not under colonial rule or ruled by white elites in 1969.

Other—all other nation-states and territories.

Two of these regions, the Northwest and Eastern Europe, are "developed," and two regions, Eastern Europe and Communist Asia, consist exclusively of Communist countries.

Since the Northwest has a disproportionate share of involvement in international organizations in general and in NGOs in particular, three subregions will be looked at separately: North America, Canada and the United States; northern Europe, the members of the Nordic Council; the EEC group, the six members of the European Economic Community. This classification is not very different from others derived by empirical methods.[26]

24 The term "country" is used here instead of state because many units that ordinarily do not classify as independent states may have representatives in NGOs, e.g., Hong Kong.

25 The classification was based on the PRIO list of countries and territories obtainable from the International Peace Research Institute. See also Nils Petter Gleditsch, "The Structure of the International Airline Network" (Magister's thesis, University of Oslo, 1968); and Skjelsbaek, "Peace and the Systems of International Organizations," appendix L, pp. 1–3. The complete distribution of countries in regions is found in ibid., appendix A, pp. 1–2.

26 To my knowledge the most thorough effort to define regions empirically has been done by Bruce M. Russett in *International Regions and the International System: A Study in Political Ecology* (Chicago:

Table 6 shows the distribution of national representations in NGOs, regional and universal, across the various regions. I have not corrected for the different number of countries or for population size in each region, but it is still quite clear that the Northwest is much overrepresented. At the opposite ex-

Table 6. National representations in NGOs, 1951–1966

Region	Percentage by year					
	1951	1956	1960	1962	1964	1966
Northwest	66.2	63.5	58.3	57.8	54.5	53.5
Latin America	15.5	17.2	16.4	15.9	16.5	16.6
Arab world	3.5	5.4	4.8	5.2	5.2	5.3
Western Asia	6.6	6.7	8.5	7.4	7.7	8.3
Communist Asia	.1	.4	.3	.3	.5	.5
Eastern Europe	7.9	6.6	7.5	7.7	8.0	7.9
Black Africa	.2	.3	3.5	4.8	6.7	6.8
Other	0	0	.9	1.0	.9	1.1
Sum	100.0	100.1	100.2	100.1	100.0	100.1
N	12,249	20,027	24,144	28,827	34,486	36,341
Number of NGOs	583	897	—	—	1,458	1,416
Missing data	240	76	—	—	12	269
North America	6.0	5.2	4.6	4.6	4.5	4.3
Northern Europe	12.2	11.3	10.2	10.0	9.3	9.4
EEC group	20.9	20.0	18.9	18.4	17.0	16.4

SOURCE: As for table 2 plus "Ninety-Seven Sovereign States and the International Non-Governmental Organizations," *NGO Bulletin*, May 1952 (4th Year, No. 5), table 1, p. 215.

treme is Communist Asia. This region is virtually excluded from the NGO world.[27] The Latin American share of the total is probably closest to what may be considered "just," taking into account the number of countries and the size of the population in this region. All the other regions are more or less underrepresented, especially Western Asia. There has been an important decrease in the percentage of representations of the Northwest during the past fifteen years, however, and the shares of the subregions have been re-

Rand McNally & Co., 1967). One of Russett's variables is comemberships in IGOs. I have done a similar factor analysis with NGO comemberships, and the differences from Russett's findings were small indeed.

27 Cluster and factor analysis bring out the four countries as a very distinct and isolated group. It is interesting to note that the National Liberation Front (NLF) of the Republic of Vietnam (South Vietnam), which probably would have clustered with the same countries had the organization been considered a separate political entity by the UIA, was represented in eleven NGOs in 1966. Some of these belonged to the international "establishment" and had consultative relations with the UN specialized agencies. A general evaluation of revolutionary organizations as transnational actors is found in J. Bowyer Bell's essay in this volume. The number of NGOs with world revolution as their primary concern seems to be very low.

duced in roughly the same proportion. The other regions are, by and large, stable. Black Africa is the significant exception. The remarkable influx of African representatives into NGOs is of course partly due to the liberation of former colonies.[28] There are far more ties between African countries and the NGO world now than in the beginning of the 1950s.

The number of national representations is only one indicator of a country's involvement in international organizations. Other indicators are the number of officers of the particular nationality, headquarters and secondary offices located on its territory, the number of international meetings held there, presumably administered by the local NGO branch, and financial contributions. Data exists for several of these variables at different points in time. In all cases the trend is roughly similar to that of the number of national representations. The percentage of the Northwest has diminished and the share of Black Africa has increased. But the differences between the variables are more interesting than the similarities. For this comparison it is sufficient to look only at the Northwest (table 7). Two conclusions can be drawn from the data.

Table 7. Role of the Northwest in international organizations, 1951–1968

	Percentage by year								
Indicator	1951	1954	1956	1958	1960	1962	1964	1966	1968
Site of publication	—	93.3	—	—	91.3	—	—	—	—
Site of headquarters[a]	93.2	93.2	—	92.0	—	90.8	89.4	88.7	87.1
Officers	—	—	—	—	88.4	—	—	—	—
International meetings[a]	87.0	83.3	83.3	84.3	77.5	76.8	78.6	75.5	—
Site of secondary offices[a]	—	—	—	76.6	—	68.9	64.4	58.9	57.5
Representations	66.2	—	63.5	—	58.3	57.8	54.5	53.5	—

SOURCES: As for table 6 plus "Répartition par matières et par pays des publications périodiques des ONG internationales," *NGO Bulletin,* December 1953 (5th Year, No. 12), pp. 505–507; and the following articles in *International Associations:* Geneviève Devillé, "Les Réunions internationales en 1958," June 1959 (11th Year, No. 6), table 4, pp. 444–445; Eliane Dolo-André, "International Periodicals," October 1959 (11th Year, No. 10), pp. 704–710; Geneviève Devillé, "Le Développement géographique de la coopération internationale," December 1962 (12th Year, No. 12), pp. 799–803; "The Leaders of International Organisations and Their Nationality," May 1967 (19th Year, No. 5), pp. 354–355; "Geographical Distribution of International Meetings 1956–1966," February 1968 (20th Year, No. 2), pp. 92–93; and Kjell Skjelsbaek, "Location of Headquarters of International Organizations (1960–1968)," January 1970 (22nd Year, No. 1), pp. 36–37.

[a] Figures for IGOs and NGOs combined.

First, the higher the level in the organizational structure at which involvement takes place, the larger is the percentage of Northwest representation. Second, the higher the organizational level, the more slowly the percentage

[28] Corresponding IGO figures show an increase from 1.5 percent in 1956 to 18.0 percent in 1966 for Black Africa; see Skjelsbaek, "Peace and the Systems of International Organizations," chapter 4, p. 3.

of Northwest representation diminishes. Although there is a visible development in the direction of a more egalitarian distribution of involvements in NGOs, there are still gross biases particularly with respect to the decision-making nuclei of the organizations. The NGO world will experience strains when less developed countries become more conscious of this and when and if Communist countries want to become more active participants.[29]

To summarize, although the available data is not as complete and valid as one might wish, a reasonably clear picture of different trends of development has emerged. The number of NGOs has annually grown at a rate of about 6 percent. Most NGOs have small secretariats and, if the pattern of the past can be extended into the future, little prospect of enlarging them. On the other hand, a majority of NGOs has added new national branches and is likely to continue to do so. Over the past 100 years relatively more NGOs have tended to operate in fields that are also of great concern to national governments, for example, economics, finance, commerce, industry, and technology. There is a clearly diminishing concentration of NGO involvement in capitalist, developed countries and a rising number of NGO involvements in African countries. Because this is partly explained in terms of decolonization, changes in this dimension will be relatively smaller in the immediate future.

III. Some Causes of the Development of NGOs

The causes of these trends are complex, and the following discussion does not pretend to provide definitive answers to the questions that inevitably arise. It is rather an attempt to formulate some relevant hypotheses.

A glance at table 6 immediately suggests that two characteristics of national societies are particularly conducive to participation in NGOs: 1) a high degree of technological and economic development and 2) a pluralistic ideology. In general it appears that the more economically developed a country is, the more involved it will be in NGOs.[30] Whether the average degree of pluralistic ideology has increased over time is harder to assess although suggestive evidence is available to confirm a relationship between this variable and NGO membership also.[31]

29 There are already signs of skepticism expressed by delegates from less developed countries within ECOSOC. The Soviet delegation, too, has several times criticized "infringement of national sovereignty" by, for example, Western-dominated civil rights NGOs. See Persia Campbell, "United Nations Report: Do NGO's Have a Role?" *International Development Review*, September 1969 (Vol. 11, No. 3), p. 37.

30 Pearson's correlation between an index of economic development and the number of representations in NGOs was .64 in 1964; cf., Skjelsbaek, "Peace and the Systems of International Organizations," chapter 5, p. 26.

31 The hypothesis can be tested by comparing countries equally developed economically but with different degrees of pluralism. An approximate method may serve as an illustration. Suppose that the countries of the Northwest are generally more pluralistic than the countries of Eastern Europe but about

Economically developed, pluralistic societies are clearly more likely to have a multitude of national interest groups than are less developed, less pluralistic societies. In addition, these societies are also more likely to have interest groups that will expand transnationally. As economic and technological development proceeds, specialization ensues with the result that some categories of persons, groups, or industries are no longer large enough to constitute functional communities that can satisfy their members' needs. Functional communities are hardly less important to people now than earlier, and, if they cannot be organized satisfactorily on the national level, the logical procedure, particularly with relatively decreasing communication and transportation costs, is to make them transnational. The shortage of personnel is naturally first experienced in small and medium-size countries which, other things being equal, should be more involved in transnational organizations.[32]

If the development of the NGO world is to a large extent the result of economic and technological development, there is good reason to believe that the number of NGOs will increase in the years ahead—assuming that the international system is not marked by increased tension or revived nationalism. With a modest growth rate of 5 percent per year from 1968, there will be 9,049 NGOs in the world in the year 2000. The correlation with economic and technological development also makes it likely that more countries will participate actively in such organizations as they reach a higher stage of development. Japan's participation in NGOs, for example, has increased despite the obstacles of language and distance: In 1964 it ranked sixteenth with representation in 611 NGOs. Thus, the mean number of national representations will increase in the future as it has done in the past, although not as fast as in the past because the artificial effect of decolonization will be absent. After some years there will be a ceiling effect because many NGOs need not, and

equally developed economically. Then the mean number of national representations in NGOs should be higher in the former region, which indeed it is:

Region	Mean number of NGO representations	Mean degree of economic development	Mean size of population
Eastern Europe (7 countries)	322	.758	42.7
Northwest (21 countries)	763	1.096	22.7

In calculating the mean degree of economic development the mean for all countries in the world weighted by their population is zero. The average deviation is one. This tabulation also suggests that the size of population (presented in millions) may be a factor of importance, and it probably is in an intricate way.

[32] A list of countries ranked according to the number of NGOs in which they are represented gives a good indication of this, but, after dividing by the size of their population, the tendency stands out much more clearly. The six countries that have most NGO representations per million inhabitants are: 1) Israel, 2) Norway, 3) Switzerland, 4) Denmark, 5) Finland, and 6) New Zealand. Countries with less than one million people have been excluded.

should not, be universal. Many problems are local and can be dealt with effectively by limited-membership organizations.[33]

If my hypothesis about the transnational consequences of specialization is correct, it partly explains why many NGOs are so small. Although most leaders of organizations wish to increase their domains, many organizations will expand only within certain limits determined by the number of persons having the same special interests. However, a large number of organizations, such as political parties, trade unions, and religious organizations, are based on widespread interests. Their potential domain is large indeed, and these mass-support organizations will generally continue to grow in proportion to the improvement of communications and economic conditions. The two types of NGOs have different capabilities: The first kind is based on expertise; the second kind has influence by leading and representing large segments of the public in various societies.

Different levels of economic and technological development may also explain different distributions of involvement across various fields of activity. The impression derived from table 5 is that relatively more NGOs have recently been established in fields closely connected with politics—finance, industry, and technological development—than in less political areas. It is in exactly these fields that the most developed states were most active.[34]

IV. NGO Increase and the Analysis of International Relations

The state-centered view of world affairs, the interstate model which still enjoys so much popularity in the study of international relations, has now become too simplistic as a result of new developments in the global system, particularly since World War II. The interstate model is especially unfit for projections and predictions about the future. Another model is proposed that I regard as more realistic but also far more complex.

There are two reasons why the interstate model is inadequate. First, the above analysis, as well as much of the other material in this volume, shows that nation-states are not the only actors on the world scene. Some NGOs probably have more power and influence in their respective fields than some of the smaller nation-states. The same applies to several IGOs and undoubt-

[33] In addition, there may be many regional NGOs with members exclusively from nation-states that are in the process of forming a political union. The best example is the high number of business and professional groups within the EEC. I have reserved the term "local international organization" for bodies that intentionally limit their domain geographically but not in accordance with the borders of a prospective political union. The Mediterranean Social Sciences Research Council (MSSRC), for example, is a local NGO.

[34] Most organizations in these fields were not only more "developed" in their membership composition but also more Western on the East-West political dimension; see Skjelsbaek, "Peace and the Systems of International Organizations," chapter 5, p. 20.

edly to many multinational business enterprises which have more employees and a larger production output than most countries.[35]

The crucial question for our analysis, however, is whether these organizations are so dependent on the consensus of governments for their operation that they merely carry out common governmental policies or whether they formulate and pursue policies of their own, sometimes even in opposition to governments. Only to the extent that they formulate and pursue independent policies are they independent actors in world affairs.[36]

Independence from governmental control may be denoted as "extranationalism." Extranationalism differs from transnationalism, which is defined in terms of activities across state borders by nongovernmental actors, and supranationalism, which implies that organizations have some formal authority over governments as in the case of the Commission of the European Communities. Extranational actors may have de facto authority in fields governments seldom regulate themselves, for example, the execution of research programs. They may also have a say in matters in which governments are involved but that are to a certain extent beyond governmental competence and control. IATA actions against certain governments in connection with airplane hijacking are a case in point. The IATA has sometimes effectively put pressure on governments for release of a plane, but it has been less successful with the semigovernmental, semi-international Arab guerrilla organizations.

The second reason for the inadequacy of the interstate model of world affairs is connected with the first. States are not like ships that have unified structures of command and can pursue only one course of action at a time. States are not necessarily unified: One group may engage in transnational processes and organizations to thwart actions of other groups, for example, the government. Thus, political parties with similar views frequently discuss common policies and problems in their respective NGOs; multinational business enterprises may have interests that run counter to the wishes of governments and other groups in the countries in which they operate. Functionally similar groups in different societies may therefore organize themselves to change the policies of governments; conversely, governments may ally to change the actions of transnational organizations. This can be done directly by issuing orders to the secretariats in the case of IGOs and indirectly by gaining control over the national branches of NGOs. Transnational organizations are not just another category of social actors on the world scene: They permeate the old ones, nation-states, and vice versa.

An alternative model of the global system should therefore include IGOs,

[35] Only seventeen countries have gross national products greater than the annual output of General Motors Corporation; see Jonathan F. Galloway, "Worldwide Corporations and International Integration: The Case of INTELSAT," *International Organization*, Summer 1970 (Vol. 24, No. 3), table 2, p. 511.

[36] I do not mean primarily "high politics." Most of these organizations operate in other fields and their possible influence on "high politics" is mainly indirect but not, a priori, negligible.

	Nation-state	IGO	NGO	Multinational business enterprise	
Nation-state	1	5	9	13	150
IGO	2	6	10	14	250
NGO	3	7	11	15	2500
Multinational business enterprise	4	8	12	16	1000

Figure 2. Proposed model of the global system. The figures outside the matrix have been approximated.

NGOs, and multinational business enterprises as well as nation-states.[37] Figure 2 directs our attention toward relations between various types of actors, as well as between states, IGOs, NGOs, and multinational enterprises. Cell 3, for example, represents policies of states toward NGOs; cell 9 indicates the converse relationship. This is not the place to discuss all the cells in the matrix, but each one of them may be the point of departure for research projects and policy recommendations. In the case of IGO-NGO relationships, for example, there is a notable asymmetry on both a quantitative and qualitative level. Quantitatively, the relationship is asymmetric because a limited number of IGOs have connections with a very large number of NGOs, while each of these NGOs only has official connections with from one to six or seven IGOs. Qualitatively, some NGOs feel that they trade information and expertise for the dubious prestige of being on a list of selected consultants.[38] Focusing on another set of relationships—that between IGOs and multinational business enterprises—it has been suggested that one way to finance IGOs would be to permit them to tax such enterprises on the ground that these organizations benefit from the general peace and prosperity of the international level at which they operate.[39]

[37] Many of the ideas in this section are the result of several seminar discussions directed by Johan Galtung at the International Peace Research Institute.

[38] Conversely, some IGOs may feel that NGOs are too afraid of losing their independence to be willing to participate in joint programs.

[39] Johan Galtung, "Non-Territorial Actors and the Problem of Peace" (Revision of a paper delivered at the World Order Models Conference, Northfield, Massachusetts, June 18–24, 1969), pp. 23–24. See also G. Modelski, "The Corporation in World Society," *The Year Book of World Affairs, 1968* (London: Stevens & Sons [under the auspices of the London Institute of World Affairs], 1968), pp. 64–79.

Two factors make the model more complex than the relatively simple matrix in figure 2 may indicate. In the first place, there are numerous overlapping memberships in the system. A given individual is the citizen of a state which is member of several IGOs. He may simultaneously, however, be a member of a trade union that belongs to one or more NGOs, and he may work in a plant that is part of a multinational business enterprise. Second, NGOs themselves are often linked in superorganizations as discussed earlier. Thus, the predominantly horizontal perspective presented should be supplemented by a vertical perspective encompassing the connections between individuals at the bottom and super-NGOs at the top. This also cannot be illustrated in a two-dimensional presentation.

The suggested model is now very complex and comprises an almost infinite number of relationships. No researcher can possibly study all of them simultaneously, but, by using the total model as his point of departure, he will be more aware of the aspects he excludes from consideration when he singles out certain categories of relationships for closer scrutiny. Moreover, he may find that the same general theories are applicable in the most different parts of the model. Finally, he will be more conscious of the many possible future paths of development of the global social structure. The proposed model seems to be more useful than the old interstate model for people interested in "social engineering" at the world level.

V. Consequences of NGO Development for Peace

The possible consequences of the development of the NGO world for peace cannot be analyzed unless some criteria of "a peaceful world" have been laid down. They can hardly be specified without running into an ideological discussion. I consider two conditions essential to a state of peace: 1) the substitution of positive relationships and interactions for violence or potential violence and 2) the absence of exploitation so that interacting parties benefit about equally from their relationship.[40]

A variety of arguments has been offered over the past few decades to show

[40] The second dimension may also be denoted as social justice or equality. It is included in the definition of peace because the lack of such qualities in the international system frequently has the same consequences as do wars—spiritual and physical destruction of human beings. Since 1945 more people have probably died from malnutrition and lack of medical care than in military battles. Since exploitation typically takes place in an egalitarian social structure, the net result is often referred to as structural violence. Revolutionaries are often willing to use personal or direct violence to end structural violence, while people that profit from such a structure may claim that they can prevent violence in the traditional sense of that term through their control of the system. The Pax Romana is the classic example of this kind of a situation. In my opinion nothing is gained by trading one kind of violence for another if the change does not result in fewer degraded and lost human lives. For a discussion of these problems see Herman Schmid, "Peace Research and Politics," *Journal of Peace Research,* 1968 (Vol. 5, No. 3), pp. 217–232; Johan Galtung, "Violence, Peace, and Peace Research," *Journal of Peace Research,* 1969 (Vol. 6, No. 3), pp. 167–192; and Johan Galtung and Tord Høivik, "Structural and Direct Violence: A Note on Operationalization" (Oslo: International Peace Research Institute, 1970). (Mimeographed.)

that international organizations, including NGOs, contribute to the prevention of war or the threat of war. For example, it is argued that positive interactions may take place within the organizations; that functional organizations may perform such useful functions that governments are reluctant to launch conflicts for fear of disrupting them; and that functional cooperation may "spill over" into other areas where force is more likely to be used, that is, into areas of "high politics."[41] This study provides no data that bears directly on these arguments.

Another argument in favor of NGOs is that they contribute to the blurring of regional as well as national boundaries. In my opinion, however, exclusive regional integration and the substitution of interregional conflict for international conflict is no improvement at all since larger units can engage in larger wars. Numerous NGOs and several functional IGOs recruit members and operate according to functional needs, disregarding ideological and political barriers.[42] If all international organizations did that and there were many of them, the world would be an intricate web of overlapping memberships and affiliations. Japanese, for example, would sit together with Chinese for regulation of fisheries, with Americans to organize radio satellite systems, and with Indians for the advancement of Buddhism. Adversaries and competitors in one connection would be allies and collaborators in another. If the argument holds for IGOs, it should be truer still for NGOs since most governments permit their citizens to have contacts that they do not for political reasons maintain themselves.[43]

The data indicates, however, that about one-fourth of all NGOs do not fit the ideal description but declare themselves as regional organizations. On the other hand, many of them do not take their self-imposed limitations very seriously, and cluster and factor analysis of NGO comemberships in regional, local, and universal organizations reveal regional tendencies but no sharp borders.

41 The "spillover" hypothesis has been seriously contested lately in a number of articles in the *Journal of Common Market Studies*. See, for example: Stanley Hoffmann, "European Process at Atlantic Cross-purposes," February 1965 (Vol. 3, No. 2), pp. 85–101; Karl Kaiser, "The U.S. and the EEC in the Atlantic System: The Problem of Theory," June 1967 (Vol. 5, No. 4), pp. 388–425; Ernst B. Haas, "*The Uniting of Europe* and the Uniting of Latin America," ibid., pp. 315–343; Paul Taylor, "The Concept of Community and the European Integration Process," December 1968 (Vol. 7, No. 2), pp. 83–101; and Andrew Wilson Green, "Review Article: Mitrany Reread with the Help of Haas and Sewell," September 1969 (Vol. 8, No. 1), pp. 50–69.

42 Cf., David Mitrany, *A Working Peace System: An Argument for the Functional Development of International Organization* (Chicago: Quadrangle Books, 1966). When Mitrany introduced this kind of argument, he was thinking of functional IGOs. A counterargument is that such a world structure for many purposes will be ineffective and give rise to serious problems of coordination. Some states will be involved in some functional agencies while others will not and may even be supporting competing ones. Agencies in related functional fields may quarrel over the lines between their respective areas of responsibility.

43 The multilateral setting of international organizations forces national delegations to have direct and indirect contacts with representatives from countries they ordinarily avoid interaction with, but sometimes exclusions and withdrawals take place. Several attempts to exclude countries from IGOs are well known. My own data gives reason to believe that such cases are very rare in NGOs.

It is particularly interesting that a systematic, pairwise analysis of NGO representations of the divided countries of the world—the Germanies, Chinas, Koreas, and Vietnams—showed that in each case there were *more* comemberships between them than expected on the basis of each country's total number of comemberships. IGO comemberships, however, were almost nonexistent. Most extreme was the relationship between the two Germanies: In 1964 the Federal Republic of Germany (West Germany) was represented in 93 percent of the NGOs in which the German Democratic Republic (East Germany) was represented. It is not known to what extent these channels are used for positive interaction between national delegations, but they are at least potentially important.

Although it is difficult to construct a simple measure of the degree to which NGO relations are affected by regional and/or political borders, some figures on NGO comemberships in Europe will at least shed some more light on this.[44] The following tabulation presents the normed mean number of NGO comemberships between and within political blocs in Europe in 1964. The figures in parentheses are the number of pairs.

	West	Neutral	East
West	161 (156)	(104)	(91)
Neutral	116	74 (56)	(56)
East	71	55	65 (42)

The countries were classified according to their military alliances with the United States and the Union of Soviet Socialist Republics. The figures are normed so that the mean number of memberships over all pairs equals 100; thus, scores over 100 indicate more comemberships than the average, and scores under 100 indicate fewer comemberships. It is remarkable that the score is lower for intra-East pairs (65) than for East-West pairs (71). This means that East European countries generally have more NGO contacts with Western states than with each other.

This data is only suggestive; for further confirmation one must look at the kinds of organizations in which interbloc contacts take place. One study of

[44] Europe was chosen because the continent is relatively homogeneous in terms of economic and technological development, the distances are short, and the East-West conflict is the only overriding, political conflict dimension. An extended discussion is found in Skjelsbaek, "Peace and the Systems of International Organizations," chapter 5, pp. 31–34.

the NGOs in which both the Soviet Union and the United States are represented reports that these organizations are mainly concerned with high-consensus issues. In addition, they have a lower level of activity and a less centralized decisionmaking structure than other NGOs.[45] If this holds generally for interbloc organizations, the score of 71 for the East-West relationships may be misleadingly high. Nevertheless, NGOs are less affected by the alliance structure than are interactions like international trade, airline connections, and diplomatic exchanges.[46]

The second criterion for peace is that all interacting parties should benefit about equally from their relationship. One actor should not be able to exploit another. At first sight participation in NGOs has little to do with exploitation. However, if one looks at all NGOs—what I loosely have called the NGO world—instead of each separate organization, the picture is quite different. As shown above less developed countries partake much less in NGOs than do developed countries, and they are especially poorly represented in the central organs of these organizations. Thus, the distribution of NGOs does not contribute much to the reduction of unequal opportunities in the global system. Furthermore, if a high density of NGO comemberships with a group of national societies results in a higher degree of integration between them which, in turn, leads to more power for that group, then NGOs at present contribute to the consolidation and improvement of the already dominant group of countries in the world, the Northwest. However, within that region they probably favor small and medium-size countries most. As a consequence the evaluation of NGOs as a peace- and justice-producing factor depends very much on whether one has a global or more limited perspective.[47] It also depends on whether one takes into consideration the activities of NGOs and not only their distribution. Some of them undoubtedly do a good job of improving conditions in less developed countries regardless of the Northwest bias of their membership composition. But these organizations are nevertheless open to the suspicion of neo-colonialism.

The only real solution to this problem lies in the establishment by less developed countries of their own organizations whenever possible and their collaboration with the rest of the NGO world through these organizations.

45 Louis Kriesberg, "U.S. and U.S.S.R. Participation in International Non-Governmental Organizations," in *Social Processes in International Relations: A Reader,* ed. Louis Kriesberg (New York: John Wiley & Sons, 1968), p. 479.

46 The comparisons were made by means of chi-squares calculated on the basis of matrices corresponding to the tabulation on p. 440. The difference between NGOs and IGOs in this respect is negligible. A very interesting general study of NGOs as a means of East-West interaction has been done by Paul Smoker, "A Preliminary Empirical Study of an International Integrative Subsystem," *International Associations,* November 1965 (17th Year, No. 11), pp. 638–646.

47 On the other hand, in less developed regions there seems to be a closer coupling between general rank and amount of involvement in NGOs. The single best indicator of general rank, in my mind, is gross national product. However, the hypothesis about regional differences with regard to this relationship has not been carefully tested.

This will admittedly be a difficult task considering the relative absence of the two factors which have been so conducive to the formation of NGOs in other parts of the world—a highly developed technology and economy and some kind of pluralistic ideology. Although I would hope not, such organizations may be met by skepticism and resentment from people with vested interests in existing organizations. On the contrary, I hope that the proposed arrangement will serve two purposes: 1) to give less developed countries an opportunity to establish and run NGOs according to their own ideologies and needs and 2) to link developed and less developed countries to each other in a more symmetric way than is the case now, particularly in order to solve problems common to both groups.

Whether or not this happens, it is clear that the institutionalization of transnational interactions in nongovernmental organizations is continuing apace and that in a variety of ways it may be an important factor in future patterns of world politics. Students of international relations as well as policymakers must come to understand this new phenomenon clearly to ensure that it promotes peace to the greatest possible extent.

PART II

TRANSNATIONAL ORGANIZATIONS

Part II focuses on transnational organizations, but the essays themselves are quite diverse. Louis T. Wells, Jr., considers the best known set of transnational organizations, multinational business enterprises, and Peter D. Bell discusses the offspring of one of these enterprises, the Ford Foundation. On the less economic side of transnational relations Ivan Vallier analyzes the Roman Catholic church as a transnational actor, and J. Bowyer Bell explores transnational revolutionary movements. Since these organizations are quite dissimilar, the authors' conclusions cannot be neatly summarized. Many points made in part II refer only to one organization or set of organizations.

All four authors attempt to respond to three questions that we asked. The first question referred to internal control within each organization: How internationalized is decisionmaking? The answer to this question must be that none of these organizations is "geocentric" as defined in the introduction, although movements in that direction can be discerned. Vallier indicates that while Italians have been predominant within the official personnel of the

Holy See, a new trend toward "internationalization" seems to be emerging. Peter Bell notes that 87 percent of the staff involved in the international activities of the Ford Foundation at the end of 1969 were Americans, and Wells observes that an even higher proportion of top managers in American-owned multinational business enterprises are United States nationals. Finally, Bowyer Bell suggests that transnational revolutionary movements remain overwhelmingly national in membership as well as in organization: "The revolutionary operates almost entirely as an actor within his national framework or as an exile from national power."

In the second question we asked about the relationships between transnational organizations and governments. Vallier, Peter Bell, and Bowyer Bell devote extensive attention to this aspect and indicate the general nature of these relationships, while Vallier specifies quite exactly how the church's relationships with states vary from state to state and how they have changed over time. To function effectively all transnational organizations have to strike bargains with states. The relationships can vary from mutually friendly alliances to wary and uneasy absence of overt hostility. One can therefore analyze "amity and enmity" between transnational organizations and nation-states as well as between states.[1]

The essay by Wells approaches the relationship between transnational organizations and states from a somewhat different perspective. He argues that centralized multinational business enterprises, which can transfer resources readily across national jurisdictions, constitute a more serious threat to national sovereignty than firms that grant more autonomy to their subsidiaries. He therefore considers explicitly a problem that the other authors treat implicitly—the relationships between the decisionmaking structure of a transnational organization and its external behavior. Wells contends that decisionmaking structures of business enterprises are largely determined by the types of activities in which the firms engage. Firms marketing small numbers of relatively standardized products tend to organize on a geographical basis and to centralize decisionmaking, whereas firms that sell many products, with considerable product innovation, tend to organize on a product basis and to grant considerably more autonomy to their subsidiaries. According to Wells firms in the latter category are less threatening to host-country autonomy than are centralized enterprises.

In their treatments of the relationship between internal structure and the environment Vallier and Bowyer Bell, in partial contrast to the focus of Wells, emphasize the influence of environment on structure. Vallier sees the "notions of office, status, and authority" altered as a result of changes in the environment within which the Roman Catholic church operates and, in particular,

[1] See the essay by Arnold Wolfers, "Amity and Enmity among Nations," in his book, *Discord and Collaboration: Essays on International Politics* (Baltimore, Md: Johns Hopkins Press, 1962), pp. 25–35.

the normative context of its action. Bowyer Bell argues that success for revolutionary movements, given the nature of the external situation, requires organization on a national basis: "To broaden the struggle is to risk dilution; to narrow the scope offers the hope of success."

In the third question we asked about the relationships between the particular transnational organization and other transnational actors. Here it is Vallier and Bowyer Bell who provide the most extensive treatments, although Peter Bell describes the relations of the Ford Foundation with other aid donors—of which some are transnational organizations—and with Ford Motor Company. Vallier carefully details patterns of the church's interaction with other Christian transnational organizations and communism and indicates how these competitive struggles have affected the evolution of the Roman Catholic church as an organization. Bowyer Bell outlines some of the many attempts to create unity in the revolutionary Left and argues that these attempts have been largely unsuccessful. Even among ideological allies one sees a pattern of competition and dispute along with some cooperative activity. Wells does not explore the relationships between multinational business enterprises, but from other work in the field it seems clear that these are generally characterized by a mixture of conflict and cooperation that can be summarized as "monopolistic competition."[2]

Although the answers to our three questions do not constitute a unity, they suggest interesting comparisons. In general the transnational organizations discussed in these essays tend to be dominated by persons of one nationality, at least in leadership positions; they compete with other transnational actors operating in the same fields of activity; and they stand in a variety of more or less uneasy relationships with states. Their actions toward their environments are strongly affected by their international organizational structures and vice versa. These generalizations, however, are only a beginning. Our basic concern is to stimulate students of world politics to answer questions such as those we have asked and to do so more thoroughly and systematically than we have done in this volume.

[2] See Charles P. Kindleberger, *American Business Abroad: Six Lectures on Direct Investment* (New Haven, Conn: Yale University Press, 1969), chapter 1, especially p. 11. See also Stephen Hymer and Robert L. Rowthorn, "Multinational Corporations and International Oligopoly: The Non-American Challenge," in *The International Corporation: A Symposium,* ed. Charles P. Kindleberger (Cambridge, Mass: M.I.T. Press, 1970), pp. 57–91.

The Multinational Business Enterprise:

What Kind of International Organization?

Louis T. Wells, Jr.

I. Introduction

The recent growth in the size and number of private business enterprises that operate in many countries has generated a great deal of speculation as to whether a form of international organization has been created which is able to frustrate the policies of the traditional nation-state. The enterprise with subsidiaries scattered around the globe clearly has the potential to evade the influence of many governmental policies. The firm can circumvent a tight monetary policy in one country by having an affiliate borrow in another country and transfer the funds across national borders. If direct transfers of capital from abroad are restricted, transfer prices, royalty payments, or open accounts between affiliates can be adjusted to bring in the needed financial resources. If taxes are high in one jurisdiction, profits that would be subject to tax can be shifted to another tax jurisdiction through manipulation of affiliate transactions. National labor unions and comparatively harsh labor legislation can be frustrated by moving production to facilities in another country when strikes or higher costs threaten a particular market. A governmental program aimed at increasing technical and managerial training to provide a larger domestic supply of skilled personnel may only generate technicians or managers for the multinational enterprise to shift out of the country, back to its head office or to other countries. Technology developed in one country—often through governmental support and often related to defense needs of governments—can be leaked quickly to other countries through the communication network of the multinational enterprise. If the multinational enterprise exercises many of these options, it is an entity that must be understood in any analysis of international relations.

Louis T. Wells, Jr., is assistant professor at the Graduate School of Business Administration, Harvard University, Boston, Massachusetts. This essay is part of a larger study of the multinational enterprise and the nation-state financed by the Ford Foundation and by the Division of Research of the business school.

There has also been speculation that multinational enterprise based in the United States is simply an extension of American culture and political interests abroad. The proponents of this view blame the multinational enterprise for carrying American products to countries where they are not in the best interests of the nationals. They note that almost all the top corporate executives of the enterprises are American.[1] The United States government is thought by some critics to use foreign subsidiaries of American companies to carry out its policy aims—whether those aims are to discourage trade with Communist countries, to provide cheap sources of raw materials, or, according to some, to increase the dependence of less developed countries on the United States.

Whether the multinational enterprise actually uses this potential to frustrate the policies of various governments depends a great deal on how the enterprise is organized. One could picture an enterprise with a head office that manipulates subsidiaries in dozens of countries to fulfill objectives that transcend the objectives of any single part of the enterprise located in any one state, or one could envisage the existence of a loosely knit group of companies in different countries, all having a financial relationship and drawing to a certain extent on a common technology and trade name but for the majority of decisions acting like national companies of the host countries. The implications for international relationships are very different for the two models. If decisionmaking is highly centralized, governments are likely to feel increasingly threatened; they might respond by lashing out at the multinational enterprise, or they might try to reach agreements with other governments in order to control the new entity that is escaping the jurisdiction of individual governments. On the other hand, the loosely knit system may pose much less of a threat to the existing order. Each subsidiary unit is likely to respond to the incentives and threats of the country in which it is located in order to maximize its life and profits. Initial feelings of frustration on the part of the government may be tempered as it discovers that it can exercise control over the local subsidiary. But the implicit assumption of most governmental officials is that the multinational enterprise is best described by the model of centralized decisionmaking. The analyst would feel somewhat secure if he could classify the multinational enterprise at one end or the other of such a scale. But as so often is the case, the real world is complex.

Most complicated organizations have elements of centralization and decentralization mixed together. The multinational business enterprise is no exception. What makes a brief description of the multinational enterprise difficult in a short essay is not the complexity of a single firm—the organiza-

[1] Kenneth Simmonds, "Multinational? Well, Not Quite," *Columbia Journal of World Business*, Fall 1966 (Vol. 1, No. 4), p. 118. Simmonds concluded that one-fifth of the total employment of the fifteen largest United States industrial corporations was foreign, but only 1.6 percent of their top corporate managers entered the United States after age 25 or remained outside the United States.

tion of the Roman Catholic church is perhaps more complex—but the wide range of forms in which the multinational enterprise appears. In addition, the organization of most multinational enterprises goes through a series of changes as the firm develops. Although the term "multinational enterprise" is not well defined, there are at least 200 or 300 firms whose operations are sufficiently global that most observers would call them multinational. Even though the variety of organizational forms within these 200 or 300 firms is great, there is sufficient pattern in the development of the enterprises that useful analytic frameworks are appearing. Some parts of one of these frameworks are presented in this essay.[2]

II. Growth of Multinational Enterprises

The rapid growth of firms that could be called multinational is generally recognized. The existence of important firms operating in many countries has been with us for quite a while. By 1900 a number of American companies had major investments abroad (Otis Elevator Company and Singer Company, for example). By the first decade of this century books that dealt with American investment began to appear in Europe. Titles from this period, such as *The American Invaders,* have a familiar ring today.[3]

The growth of United States foreign investment accelerated dramatically during the 1950s, as illustrated in the first tabulation. By 1966 there were 187 firms that qualified as "multinational," using as the definition of a multinational enterprise an American firm that was large enough to be included in *Fortune's* 1966 list of the 500 largest corporations and that had manufacturing activities in six or more foreign countries. It is this list of firms that provided the basis for the study of the multinational enterprise from which many of the findings in this essay are drawn.[4]

Year	1929	1946	1950	1957	1960	1964	1966
Amount (in billions of US $)	7.5	7.2	11.8	25.2	32.8	44.4	54.6

[2] The material in this essay draws heavily on work done by John Stopford, Lawrence Fouraker, and Lawrence Franko. The results of a study of the organization of the multinational enterprise, authored by John Stopford and Louis T. Wells, Jr., will soon be published by Basic Books, Publishers. See also Lawrence E. Fouraker and J. M. Stopford, "Organizational Structure and Multinational Strategy," *Administrative Science Quarterly,* June 1968 (Vol. 13, No. 1), pp. 47–64; Stopford, "Growth and Organizational Change in the Multinational Firm" (D.B.A. diss., Graduate School of Business Administration, Harvard University, 1968); and Lawrence G. Franko, "Strategy Choice and Multinational Corporate Tolerance for Joint Ventures with Foreign Partners" (D.B.A. diss., Graduate School of Business Administration, Harvard University, 1969).

[3] F. A. MacKenzie, *The American Invaders* (London: Grant Richards, 1902).

[4] This sample was common to several studies conducted under the general direction of Raymond Vernon in connection with the project, "The Multinational Enterprise and the Nation-State," financed by the Ford Foundation. Data for the first tabulation is drawn from the United States Department of Commerce *Survey of Current Business.*

The second tabulation, showing the growth of manufacturing subsidiaries of 187 multinational enterprises outside the United States and Canada, indicates the spread of the subsidiaries of these firms. Since Canadian subsidiaries have generally been handled as domestic operations by the managers of these firms, they have been excluded in this tabulation.

Year	1901	1913	1919	1924	1929	1939	1945	1955	1960	1967
Number of subsidiaries	41	86	119	187	330	546	615	1,003	1,789	3,203

These 187 enterprises probably accounted for more than 80 percent of United States foreign investment. The average reported worldwide sales of these enterprises was $927 million in 1964; the typical firm had 22 percent of its sales outside the United States. It is clear that the potential for these enterprises to transfer resources across national boundaries is very large.

Of course, not all multinational enterprises have their origins in the United States. Well known are such European firms as the Royal Dutch Shell group and Unilever. There are at least 49 large European firms for which foreign assets, earnings, employees, or sales account for 25 percent of the total for the firm.[5] But the United States represents the largest single home base of such enterprises and the source of the largest multinational firms.

III. Spread of Manufacturing Enterprises

The corporate policies that led to the spread of American investment in manufacturing abroad have been far from the planned exploitation of foreign markets that has been described by some authors. The early investments of most firms in manufacturing abroad were defensive actions to keep the enterprises from losing markets that they had gained almost by accident. Only later did global strategies and centralization of policymaking occur. The amount of this centralization has differed dramatically from firm to firm.

The innovation of new products that has occurred in response to high income and high labor costs in the United States provides a natural base for exports.[6] As the demand for these new products increases abroad, orders often simply appear on the doorstep of American firms. The export business grows. But as enterprises in other countries learn how to make the products and as their markets become large enough to support a plant, this export market is

[5] Sidney E. Rolfe, *The International Corporation* (Paris: International Chamber of Commerce, 1969).

[6] See Louis T. Wells, Jr., "Test of a Product Cycle Model of International Trade: U.S. Exports of Consumer Durables," *Quarterly Journal of Economics,* February 1969 (Vol. 83, No. 1), pp. 152–162; and Robert B. Stobaugh, Jr., "Where in the World Should We Put That Plant?" *Harvard Business Review,* January–February 1969 (Vol. 47, No. 1), pp. 129–136.

threatened. Even though the export business has grown in a rather unplanned way, it has become important to some individuals within the firm. A number of managers whose main responsibility is providing foreign markets are eager to defend the importance of retaining these sales. The phenomenon will be familiar to students of other kinds of bureaucracies in which vested interests are important determinants of policy. The threat of losing exports to a foreign manufacturer often leads managers to decide that the American enterprise should build its own plant abroad to maintain its market. The enterprise slowly becomes multinational without having a conscious plan for doing so.

Autonomous Subsidiaries

These early subsidiaries that are set up abroad to manufacture locally what was previously exported are typically rather autonomous entities. They are often managed by fairly loyal company men who are sent out in much the same spirit that Roman governors were sent out to the colonies.[7] Little direct control is exercised by the parent company over its subsidiaries. Since the operations are not critical to the strategy of the enterprise, the enterprise can tolerate a wide range of behavior in the periphery. The parent can have some confidence that major policy decisions will be made by managers of the subsidiaries in ways that would be consistent with the company policies with which they have been indoctrinated. For detailed decisions the local manager is essentially a free man.

One of the most important influences on the decisions of the local manager is his desire to retain autonomy.[8] As long as he maintains profitable operations and can avoid turning to the rest of the system for funds, he can at least delay the exercise of control from above. If he needs cash, he is likely to borrow locally rather than turn to the parent company. If the government is restricting credit, he is likely to behave as a local firm does and wait until he can borrow locally instead of using the ability of the enterprise to borrow elsewhere. Since a record of profits is important in retaining autonomy, the manager is likely to fight for transfer prices that show profits in the subsidiary even though they might not minimize the total taxes of the whole multinational enterprise. Similarly, he is likely to be aggressive in trying to supply export markets; he will try to utilize his excess capacity even though long-run costs may be lower elsewhere in the enterprise.

The enterprise can live for a while with a structure that requires subsidiaries to report only to the president of the system. However, as the importance of

[7] See Antony Jay, *Management and Machiavelli: An Inquiry into the Politics of Corporate Life* (New York: Holt, Rinehart & Winston, 1967), for a fascinating and instructive attempt to apply some of the concepts of political analysis to the management of a large business enterprise. This particular analogy is drawn from Jay.

[8] See Robert B. Stobaugh, Jr., "Financing Foreign Subsidiaries of U.S. Multinational Enterprises," *Journal of International Business Studies*, Spring 1970 (Vol. 1), pp. 43–64.

overseas manufacturing increases, an international division is usually established to which the subsidiary managers report. The international division serves both to concentrate the abilities of the few international managers on the most important problems and to provide a training ground to develop more general managers with international experience. Initially, the international division does not interfere greatly with the autonomy of successful subsidiaries.

Some evidence of the independence of subsidiaries when the country manager reports only to a remote vice-president of the international division is provided by data on the use of joint ventures by multinational enterprises. Local partners can be tolerated only when the subsidiary has a great deal of freedom to maximize its own interests. Since a partner shares only in local profits, policies dictated from above that could shift profits elsewhere in the system for the good of the multinational enterprise lead to such conflicts that local partners can no longer be tolerated. Of the 187 multinational enterprises examined those that had a structure which required the local manager to report only to a remote vice-president with no intervening structure had local partners in 43 percent of their manufacturing operations in countries in which joint ventures were not required by the government. For the other firms the number was only 21 percent.

This is hardly the exploitative kind of enterprise pictured in some of the attacks on multinational business. Consistent system objectives generally reach far-flung subsidiaries only indirectly and in a modified form. Subsidiaries behave much like local firms with a few annoying exceptions, for example, the tendency of new managers to ignore local customs until the penalties of behaving as if they were at home are made painfully clear.

However, when the international division is established, a process is begun that *can* lead to a great deal of control over the local subsidiary. But not every firm moves toward centralization. The most certain result is an almost irreversible commitment on the part of the enterprise to international business. The careers of several highly placed managers in the firm are based on the success of overseas operations. They are likely to deal with weak performance in a subsidiary even if a little more control is exercised over the successful units in the periphery.

The continued growth of foreign business appears to lead almost inevitably to the end of the international division.[9] The division was established originally to maximize the use of a scarce resource in the firm, management with international know-how, and to provide a training opportunity to increase the quantity of this resource. As the international division succeeds, it provides its own destruction. As it becomes large, other parts of the organization fear its power and want its profits included in their operations. Sufficient inter-

[9] See Fouraker and Stopford, *Administrative Science Quarterly*, Vol. 13, No. 1.

national skills have been developed so that the division's activities can be split and assigned, with international personnel, to other parts of the organization.

Area versus Product Commitment

The choice of organizational structure is one of the most frustrating issues for the manager of a large enterprise. The selection that is made is critical in determining the response of the local subsidiary to local governmental policies. Typically, the businessman is committed to some very basic concepts of organizational structure. These include the principles that there should be an unambiguous chain of command, with each man having one clear boss, and that responsibility for the performance of subordinate units should be assigned to an individual. If the nature of decisions is complex, an ideal organization based on these principles is simply very difficult to develop. The manager who must decide what way to divide the assignments of the international division when it is disbanded is faced with difficult trade-offs. He must decide questions such as whether his West German appliance plant manager should report to a European headquarters that covers a number of product lines in the area or to an appliance division in the United States that is responsible for appliance manufacture all over the world. If the manager assigns responsibility on the basis of geographical area, he may ease coordination within Europe for a number of product lines. Marketing policies most appropriate for the region and rationalization of production facilities can best be entrusted to an area manager. But there is a cost entailed in this route. The most advanced know-how for the product line is likely to be in the product division in the United States. If the product-division manager sees no profits allocated to his unit for using scarce knowledgeable men to transfer know-how to the West German subsidiary, he is likely to be stingy with assistance. On the other hand, if the responsibility is vested in the product division, geographical area coordination is likely to be minimized. It will be difficult to establish common marketing policies in Europe for the appliance and other lines of the enterprise. Duplicate distribution channels are likely to be built, and advertising programs are likely to overlap and conflict. The number of plants may proliferate beyond what "rational" planning would dictate.

The manager faces a dilemma. He hesitates to give up his principles of unity of command and clear responsibility which would be sacrificed if he were to try to live with both forms of organization. The subsidiary manager would have to report to two kinds of bosses, and each would have only very limited responsibility assigned to him.

The choice, as one might guess, is far from random. Firms that have few products usually go the area route. Such firms most commonly sacrifice little on the technological transfer side because they tend to be firms that do little new product development. Area coordination becomes the critical element of strategy. Marketing and production techniques can become relatively standardized. Area-wide planning to transfer successful marketing strategies, to coordinate marketing programs, and to lower costs through production rationalization are critical parts of the international strategy of those firms. On the other hand, firms with many products usually assign responsibility for overseas operations to product divisions. New product developments are transferred more easily, but area coordination is difficult.

The choice is one that has important implications for the behavior of local subsidiaries of a multinational enterprise. Transnational actors that emerge under the area choice are very different from those that develop from the product route.

The Area Organization

The choice of an area organization is the most interesting to those who are looking for transnational actors that exercise many of the options that are open to multinational enterprises. The decision to organize subsidiaries on a geographical basis leads to the removal of a great deal of autonomy from the individual subsidiary to a higher level in the firm. The multinational enterprise that is organized on an area basis is the firm that is most likely to shift funds from subsidiary to subsidiary to avoid controls that an individual government tries to impose. Its production rationalization generates large amounts of trade between subsidiaries and allows it to manipulate transfer prices to shift significant amounts of profits from one jurisdiction to another. If there is a bête noire of the host government's desire for control, it is the area-organized multinational enterprise. It is probably also more independent of the home government's incentives or controls over capital exports than are other multinational enterprises. Although it is an organization that is most difficult for a host government to control, this kind of firm can also bring advantages that other multinational enterprises cannot. It is likely to locate its production facilities in patterns much more like those that the theory of comparative advantage would suggest. Longer runs of different parts might be made in two countries with trade of parts for local assembly. The result will probably be more efficient use of resources in both countries. But increased international efficiency comes at a cost of sovereignty to the nation-state.

The removal of decisionmaking power from the local subsidiary is easily traced. It begins when area structures appear within the international division. The next step is a reorganization of the enterprise into divisions with geographical responsibilities. There may be, for example, a division responsible for the Western Hemisphere, one for Europe, one for the Middle and Far East, and one for the rest of the world. Answers to questionnaires which I distributed to managers of multinational enterprises indicate that area-organized firms are the ones that are standardizing marketing and production policies for large geographical areas. Not surprisingly, joint ventures begin to disappear and few more are entered when the enterprise starts to organize along area lines. A recent study of joint ventures has indicated that the change to an area organization is typically accompanied by a "peaking" of instability of joint-venture arrangements, through buying out the local partner's interests or selling off the parent's equity within three years of the change of organization structure.[10] The change to an area organization is also accompanied by a reduction in the number of entries into new joint ventures. Firms that had an area organization within the international division or which were organized at the division level by geographical areas in 1966 had joint ventures in only 16 percent of their manufacturing operations in countries in which they had relative freedom to choose their ownership structure. The equivalent figure for other firms was a significantly different 36 percent.

The area-organized multinational enterprise is the one most likely to have subsidiaries that do not respond like local firms to governmental incentives. The enterprise has the ability to see the advantages of and to implement policies that maximize the interests of the system, even if they come at a cost of profits to an individual subsidiary. These firms may bring advantages to the host country, but they are frustratingly difficult to control. Their ability to ignore the interest of a single subsidiary often extends to policies that do not maximize the interest of an operation in the country in which they originated. When cheaper sources are found abroad for a product, the system is likely to transfer production to the cheaper country and to import the product back into the United States. Transfer pricing for foreign assembly might well be set up to reduce United States taxes and duties. These firms are truly transnational actors.

The Product Organization

Much less centralized in its structure is the multinational enterprise that chooses the product form of organization. An enterprise that decides to partition its organization by product line rather than by geographical area seems to be unable and unwilling to remove a great deal of autonomy from the individual subsidiary. Evidence of this autonomy is provided by the retention of joint ventures and the continued entry into new ones by this form of organization. The study of joint-venture instability referred to earlier found that changes to worldwide product divisions were not accompanied by significant purchases of the interests of local partners or sales of the parent company's equity in joint ventures.[11] The firms that were organized by product division in 1966 had local partners in 30 percent of their foreign manufacturing operations in that year.

[10] Franko, "Strategy Choice and Multinational Corporate Tolerance for Joint Ventures with Foreign Partners."

[11] Ibid.

The decision to assign responsibilities by product line is typically taken by enterprises that have a wide range of products. The firm finds more need for close coordination within product groups than it does by geographical area.

Product diversity is strongly associated with a policy of developing new products. The local subsidiary is much more likely to move on to new models of a product than it is to fight a war of cost reduction by production rationalization and maximum use of area-wide marketing policies. Area standardization is not critical to the enterprise's strategy. Many more decisions are likely to be left to the local manager who will try to maximize the interests of the subsidiary. This subsidiary will behave much more like a local firm in responding to governmental policies than will the subsidiary of an area system. The product division enterprise is a transnational actor but perhaps a much less frustrating one for the host government than is the area-structured firm.

Other Organizations

Obviously, this brief presentation has oversimplified the types of multinational enterprises that manufacture abroad. Some firms choose organizations that are mixtures of these forms. In these enterprises some of the products may be handled on an area basis, others by worldwide product divisions. But the analytic framework applies equally well to these enterprises.

More important to those interested in understanding decisionmaking processes in the multinational enterprise is the emergence of a new form of organization in recent years—the grid structure. A few managers have been willing to drop the heretofore sacred principles of unity of command and clear assignment of responsibility. These managers have not been willing to choose between area and product divisions but have the subsidiary report to both kinds of bosses. The frustrations of those working in such an organization will be familiar to academic readers who have been lost in the maze of a university organization in which responsibilities for disciplines (economics, political science, etc.) cross with responsibilities for programs (undergraduate, graduate, professional schools). Not surprisingly, the grid form is being tried in enterprises that have a great deal of product and area diversity.

The grid form of business organization has not existed long enough to provide a very clear indication of the degree of autonomy it grants the local subsidiary. The enterprising subsidiary manager, like the enterprising professor, can perhaps survive with a great deal of autonomy. Very limited data (on three firms) indicates that grid enterprises stay away from local partners in overseas manufacturing operations. This may be a clue to a tendency to remove autonomy from the local subsidiary in the grid structure. In fact, this may be the case par excellence of the need to rely on indoctrination of subsidiary managers into the company philosophy for management control. However, local partners are hard to indoctrinate with corporate myths.

If the grid form of organization is successful in avoiding the dilemma faced in product versus area choice, it will, no doubt, grow in importance. We will have to await new data in order to form a firm basis for deciding the nature of this transnational actor.

IV. The Extractive Enterprise

The history of foreign investment by American enterprise for raw material extraction is rather different from the story of the manufacturing enterprise.[12] While the history of the manufacturing enterprise is one of continued centralization for some firms and only partial centralization for others, the history of the extractive enterprise in international business typically begins with centralization and currently includes some efforts at decentralizing the structures in certain parts of the organization.

Involvement by American firms with overseas sources of raw materials has been planned by the headquarters management from the earliest years much more carefully than were the initial investments in manufacturing abroad. Cheap sources of raw materials from other countries for American manufacturing and marketing operations could not be left to a partially loyal, rather autonomous manager who was far from the central office. Shipments had to occur on schedule to meet the needs of the United States plants; quality had to be right. With the need to control schedules and quality closely came a communication network that enabled most important decisions that affected the foreign operations to be made in the United States headquarters. Rubber plantations maintained by Firestone Tire and Rubber Company in Liberia, for example, had direct radio connection to Akron which enabled quick control of these important operations long before rapid airplane connections were available. If the extractive operations of multinational enterprises behaved as a local firm did, it was only a coincidence. The host government quickly felt the frustration of trying to induce the local manager to respond to its wishes; the local manager, however, typically did not have the authority to do so. Transfer prices, volume of shipments, choice of carriers, etc., were almost always decided in the United States. As the local tax authorities soon discovered, the important financial records were also kept in head offices. Here was a transnational actor that fit many of the characterizations of the centralized decisionmaker. Management of extractive operations has changed only little to this day except in the very important cases in which direct local governmental participation in management, through holdings of equity or rights acquired in the concession agreement, has driven a wedge into the absolute power of the headquarters.

12 See Raymond Vernon, "Foreign Enterprise and Developing Nations in the Raw Material Industries," *American Economic Review*, May 1970 (Vol. 60, No. 2), pp. 122–126.

Joint ventures with local partners for extractive operations have come only through insistence by the host government and only when its bargaining power was great.[13] The partner has usually been a state agency. The resistance of the enterprise to any threat to its centralized control has been broken only when technology or marketing control has slipped out of the hands of the oligopolists.

In activities other than their purely extractive operations, extractive-oriented firms have developed looser organizations. As the enterprises discover the potential of foreign markets for their raw materials, they set up manufacturing and distribution operations in other countries to provide outlets for the output of mines, wells, and plantations. Most of these facilities were initially in advanced countries, but markets in less developed countries are increasing in importance. Many extractive firms have been able to take a large portion of their profits through oligopolistic pricing of the raw material (copper, for example) or of processed intermediates (aluminum, for example). The point at which profits can be taken depends on the location of the oligopolistic control. In the downstream stage when oligopolistic control is not possible, a great deal of autonomy can be given to anyone who can dispose of the output of the controlled states. The incremental costs of additional output from the upstream stages are usually low; what the multinational enterprise needs are users that are tied to it as a unique or major source of supplies. Joint ventures have been frequent at the downstream stages. Between 1960 and 1967 petroleum firms that were examined entered joint ventures with local partners in 53 percent of their manufacturing operations. Mining firms included local partners in 71 percent of their manufacturing activities. These facilities often reported through a completely different part of the organization from that which controlled the extractive operations.

Only when different activities of the extractive multinational enterprises are segregated can one understand their role as transnational actors. Extractive operations have remained tightly controlled from the center; the overseas manufacturing and distribution operations of the same firms have typically been given much more autonomy.

V. Centralization by Function

Centralization and decentralization are terribly crude concepts. Rarely are decisions in different functional areas of business uniformly centralized or decentralized in a particular organization. The evidence is clear, however,

[13] See Louis T. Wells, Jr., *The Evolution of Concession Agreements* (Economic Development Reports, No. 117) (Cambridge, Mass: Harvard Development Advisory Service, 1969). Joint ventures with other multinational firms have, of course, been common. There was little chance for conflicts of interest; both parties were interested in quality and regularity of supply. There was no chance that the partner would sell to the firms that were outside the oligopoly.

that certain decisions are more likely to be centralized than others in a multinational enterprise. Unfortunately, too little is known about decisionmaking processes in the various functional areas of the enterprise. A study currently in progress promises to shed some light on how financial decisions are made.[14] Tentative results seem to indicate a complex pattern with firms moving from considerable autonomy in the subsidiary, through a great deal of centralization with attempts to maximize profits from financial transactions, to a system based on rules of thumb as the enterprise matures and as foreign operations account for a larger portion of earnings.[15] When foreign operations are small, the gains from having a specialized staff to solve complicated financial problems appear to be outweighed by the costs of the staff. As the problems become more important, the staff begins to pay for itself. However, when the problems reach a certain complexity, optimization becomes too difficult, and rules of thumb are substituted for ad hoc analysis. A study of consumer durables has shed some light on decisions in the marketing area.[16] The study indicates that marketing decisions for one industry are more likely to be centralized when foreign operations as a whole account for a large part of a firm's business and when an individual subsidiary is itself relatively large. This study also found a great deal of variation in the degree of centralization by the type of marketing decision that was examined. For example, product design decisions were much more centralized than decisions on prices and advertising. Standardization of decisions on price was found for products that were easily transported from one market to another. Transportability presumably increased the possibility that outsiders would perform arbitrage in response to price differences. Advertising tended to be more standardized when the media flowed across boundaries.

Studies of financial and marketing decisions indicate that in order to identify the locus of decisionmaking in a multinational enterprise the kind of decision in question must be specified. The crude concept of centralization versus decentralization does, however, provide some help in predicting the amenability of a given multinational enterprise to its use as a tool of governmental policy or the response of the enterprise to governmental incentives and penalties. Some broad generalizations can be made on the basis of the organizational structures described thus far.

14 Sidney M. Robbins and Robert B. Stobaugh, Jr., under the auspices of the study, "The Multinational Enterprise and the Nation-State," directed by Raymond Vernon.

15 See Stobaugh, *Journal of International Business Studies,* Vol. 1.

16 Richard Aylmer, "Marketing Decisions in the Multinational Firm" (D.B.A. diss., Graduate School of Business Administration, Harvard University, 1968); and Robert Buzzell, "Can You Standardize Multinational Marketing?" *Harvard Business Review,* November–December 1968 (Vol. 46, No. 6), pp. 102–113.

VI. Influence of Governments

Host Government

The official in the host government that faces a multinational enterprise which grants a great deal of autonomy to its subsidiary can feel somewhat confident that many policies which affect local companies will elicit somewhat similar responses out of the local subsidiary of the foreign firm. Incentives for exports are likely to induce the local manager to consider export markets. Credit restrictions are likely to pinch the foreign subsidiary. New taxes are less likely to generate shifts in transfer prices that negate the effects of higher tax rates. Within limits the host government can control the subsidiary. These limits are approached only when the subsidiary's actions are sufficiently injurious to the multinational enterprise that the parent company responds by restricting the freedom of a local manager. If the enterprise is not organized to do this easily, the host government may be able to exercise a great deal of control over the subsidiary.

However, the centralized organization presents a different picture for the host government. The subsidiary manager is not very responsive to local incentives and penalties. Decisions such as who supplies what market are made at a higher level. The higher level will not ignore local governmental policies, but the outcome of the calculations that result from a governmental policy change may be different from what it would be if the subsidiary were free to maximize its own interest. Export market allocation might, for example, be based on long-run average cost curves when the subsidiary would be responsive to profits on incremental costs. In addition, means are readily at hand to evade direct governmental controls. Accounts payable to other affiliates might be allowed to lag, for example, to accumulate funds when credit is tightened.

The host government does not, of course, bargain with an enterprise; it negotiates with an individual who has personal goals that may be different from the goals of the enterprise. The negotiator who is sent from the headquarters to arrange an agreement with the host government may be motivated by a desire to return with as many concessions as other firms have received. In his eagerness to show his bargaining skills to his supervisors, the negotiator may obtain concessions that have little value to the enterprise.[17] Many cases could be described in which the company representative bargained determinedly for relief from local taxes even though the savings would be almost exactly offset by the higher United States taxes that result from the loss of foreign tax credits.

On the other hand, the multinational enterprise also does not bargain with

[17] See Raymond Vernon, "Indonesia's Policies toward Foreign Direct Investment," Djakarta, September 15, 1969. (Mimeographed.)

a monolithic structure. The various agencies of the host government may have different interests. Not unusual is the case of a United States subsidiary of a foreign enterprise that was under pressure from United States customs officials to increase the transfer price of goods imported from foreign affiliates to raise the duty and, at the same time, under pressure from the Internal Revenue Service to lower the transfer price so that the resulting higher reported profits would mean more United States income taxes.[18]

The interests of pressure groups in the host country are likely also to be varied. Businessmen who supply a foreign investor with inputs are likely to align themselves with the multinational enterprise; those that view him as a competitor are likely to seek other allies against the foreigner.

Home Government

Little hard evidence is available to estimate the ability of the home government to influence its firms when they operate in foreign countries. One or two policies of the United States government are frequently cited as examples of the use of the multinational enterprise to extend national power. Yet, the fact that so few examples are presented as illustrations of attempts at control by home governments suggests that their role may have been very limited.

The extraterritorial application of the United States Trading with the Enemy Act is the most commonly cited example. Rarely mentioned is the recent attempt of the American government to limit United States investment in Namibia as long as the Republic of South Africa refuses to honor United Nations directives. In addition, there are a few defensive threats posed in support of American investment abroad such as those contained in the Hickenlooper amendment.[19] But these are hardly in the nature of aggressive use of multinational enterprises for the ends of the home country's government.

The argument is often presented that aid flows are conditioned on open reception of American foreign investment. However, the fact that large amounts of aid have continued to move to countries that are tough on American investors (for example, India, Pakistan, and Peru) indicates that this is at most a minor factor in determining the recipients of American assistance. This is not to deny that a local Agency for International Development (AID) (or United States embassy) official sometimes gets carried away by the arguments of potential American investors or by an ideological commitment to free enterprise. Nonetheless, his support of the multinational firm can be

[18] United States Congress, Joint Economic Committee, *A Foreign Economic Policy for the 1970's, Hearings,* statement by Robert B. Stobaugh, Jr., before the Subcommittee on Foreign Economic Policy, 91st Cong., 2nd sess., July 29, 1970, pp. 874–887.

[19] First Hickenlooper amendment to the *Foreign Assistance Act of 1961, United States Code,* Vol. 22, section 2370(e).

quickly eroded when word reaches Washington that he is upsetting the local government.[20]

It is too simple to say that the home government never attempts to use the multinational enterprise to further its policies, but it is probably fair to say that the historical use of this vehicle for foreign policy by the United States government has been very limited.

Too little empirical work has been done on the ways in which the policies of the United States government and multinational business influence each other; even less is known about the relationship between multinational enterprises that originate in other countries and their relationships to their home governments. One can only guess that these relationships will vary considerably and in systematic ways. In countries where communication, trust, and coordination between government and business have historically been close, one would expect the cooperation to continue for some time when its business firms go abroad. It is not surprising to find occasional confusion on the part of host-government officials in less developed countries when they are negotiating terms of entry for Japanese business, for example. Some say that they are not always sure when they are talking to a businessman or when the businessman is an official of the Japanese government. One might expect similar coordination between French firms and the French government where historically the relationship has been close. But the separation and mistrust that have characterized business-government relations in Anglo-Saxon countries will probably continue for some time to characterize their relationship when the firms go abroad.

An alliance of a multinational enterprise with the government of the country in which it originated can be short-lived. As foreign business begins to supply a large portion of its income, it may become less and less eager to follow policies that coincide with the desires of the home government. Tightened credit in the home country may send the multinational enterprise to the Eurocurrency markets. Balance-of-payments problems at home may lead the multinational enterprise that fears devaluation or controls on capital exports to aggravate the problems by withholding remissions of profits from overseas. Increasing costs of local labor may be countered by moving production overseas more rapidly than would have taken place in the absence of a multinational firm with the ability to transfer technological and marketing know-how across international boundaries.

Especially for non-American enterprises threats by the home government may become less frightening. As foreign business grows, the portion subject

[20] This is consistent with my experience of having a United States ambassador instruct United States government employees not to cooperate with me when I was advising an African government in negotiations with a United States investor. The instructions of the local ambassador were quickly reversed when complaints reached Washington.

to pressure by the country of origin may come to represent only a relatively insignificant source of profits to the firm.

VII. Conclusion

Multinational business enterprises are clearly important transnational actors. They move large amounts of resources across international boundaries. Some of them have organizations that centralize decisionmaking processes so that these resources can be used to fulfill objectives that may be at variance with those of a particular country in which a subsidiary is located. These firms have at their disposal many tools for frustrating governmental policies, but the policies that they frustrate may be those of the host government or those of the home government.

Some multinational enterprises may seem to form alliances with governments. Yet, as they grow and begin to take a more global view, these alliances may prove to be no more lasting than those of nation-states. Common interests may dominate the alliances initially, but the interests may diverge as the home market becomes just one more piece in the multinational system. Threats of the home government may be taken less seriously as the threatened part of the business becomes relatively small.

The organizational structures of multinational enterprises are not very different from those that characterize other international organizations. Their ability to coordinate policies of units in the periphery can be analyzed in ways that are similar to the analysis of other organizations. The kinds of management problems faced by the multinational enterprise are similar to those of governments. A highly centralized system is limited in its ability to span diversity. If it expands too much, it has tendencies to grow baronies in the periphery that begin to maximize local interests rather than those of the center. Elements within the organization build alliances which keep the enterprise from behaving according to some centralized set of goals.

The fact that some of these organizations are operating in a coordinated fashion or that they even seem to have the potential for doing so makes them appear to governments as a challenge to their control. The result is a feeling of frustration on the part of governmental officials that results in occasional lashing out at foreign investment. In many cases these attacks may appear to an economist to hurt the national interest. However, the set of objectives that determines governmental actions is no less complex than that of the multinational enterprise. The desire of the government to retain control leads to attacks on enterprises that appear to challenge its sovereignty.

The multinational enterprise is important because of its ability to move resources across international boundaries. It is also important, in some instances, as a transnational actor that makes decisions without regard to the direct interests of its operations in any single country. It is equally important because of the responses that it engenders from governments of nation-states that react to its potential for weakening their control. There is, however, a great deal of danger in treating multinational enterprises as homogeneous entities. Enterprises differ greatly in their organizational structures, and these structures, moreover, change over time. For many purposes a better understanding of the role of the multinational business enterprise in international affairs can be obtained by turning to the concepts of the organization specialist and the frameworks of political analysis than by relying solely on the models of the economist.

The Ford Foundation as a Transnational Actor

PETER D. BELL

"FOUNDATIONS," private, nonprofit institutions that make grants for public purposes, depend for their existence on the private accumulation of great wealth and on fiscal and moral incentives for its philanthropic use. Several European foundations, including the Calouste Gulbenkian Foundation, the Volkswagen Foundation, the Krupp Foundation, and the Nuffield Foundation, are now comparable in organization and size to the American leaders. But modern foundations, independently directed and professionally staffed, are principally an invention of twentieth-century industrial society in the United States.[1] Of 32 foundations with assets exceeding $100 million, 29 are American.

Those American foundations with international activities tend to be the larger ones. *The Foundation Directory* of 1967 reports that some 21 percent (or $160 million) of the grants from the 237 largest foundations were for international activities, compared to 2 percent (or $9 million) of the grants from 6,566 intermediate and small foundations. The number of foundations which made international grants increased from 33 in 1963 to 152 in 1966. Grants for international activities were allocated among the following purposes: 1) international studies, mainly in the United States (36 percent); 2)

PETER D. BELL, currently the representative of the Ford Foundation in Chile, wrote this essay while a research associate on leave from the foundation in 1969–1970 at the Center for International Affairs, Harvard University, Cambridge, Massachusetts. The views which he expresses are his own and not necessarily those of the Ford Foundation.

[1] According to the 1969 *Directory of European Foundations* (Turin: Agnelli Foundation) only three European foundations have assets which exceed $100 million, whereas *Philanthropic Foundations in the United States: A Brief Description* (New York: Foundation Center, 1969), p. 15, reports that there are 29 such American foundations. This booklet states that there are about 22,000 foundations in the United States with estimated total assets of $20.5 billion, at market value, and annual expenditures of some $1.5 billion. About 250 have resources of over $10 million and are termed "large foundations" by the Foundation Center.

education (29 percent); 3) technical assistance (19 percent); 4) health and medicine (8 percent); and 5) all other activities (8 percent).[2]

It is clear from these figures that in terms of international expenditures foundations do not approach states or even the United States Department of State in importance. Nonetheless, the resources and attention of the larger foundations, especially the Ford Foundation and the Rockefeller Foundation, can be critically important in specific sectors of other societies. Earlier in this century, for example, the Rockefeller Foundation led worldwide campaigns for the eradication of hookworm, malaria, and yellow fever without regard to "nationalisms, geographical frontiers, and political differences and difficulties."[3] The Green Revolution that has captured much recent attention is based on strains of rice and wheat developed by international research institutes sponsored by the Ford and Rockefeller foundations. The two foundations have supported population activities internationally, and the Ford Foundation has promoted economic planning in much of the less developed world. The Ford Foundation is the largest financial supporter of social science research in Latin America, and it has been a major force in the development of Latin American studies in the United States.

The political significance of these activities depends, of course, on the context. In Brazil, for example, Ford Foundation support enabled social scientists fired from the University of São Paulo for their political views to remain at work in São Paulo rather than joining the brain drain to developed countries. Another illustration of the contextual importance of foundation roles is Ford Foundation support of family planning, for example, through grants to the Colombian Association of Medical Faculties. Such grants may be viewed variously as a pilot project by the Ministry of Health, an opening wedge for the United States Agency for International Development (AID), an affront to the moral superiority of the Roman Catholic church, and a counterrevolutionary move against "third-world" Marxists. More specifically, grants may affect competing organizations in family planning and the distribution of power within the grantee association. These factors interlace with the interests cited earlier. The playing out of these competing and complementary interests might conceivably affect relations within families, between political parties, between church and state, and between the recipient country's government and the United States.

Foundations are significant transnational actors not only because of the direct outcome of their grants but also because of their direct and indirect influence on other actors in world politics. Yet, we know very little about

[2] Data from Marianna O. Lewis, ed., *The Foundation Directory* (3rd ed.; New York: Russell Sage Foundation [for the Foundation Library Center], 1967), tables 11, 16, and 23 on pp. 27, 39, and 46, respectively.

[3] Raymond B. Fosdick, *A Philosophy for a Foundation* (New York: Rockefeller Foundation, 1963), p. 1.

foundations in comparison with and in relation to those actors. Congressional hearings, journalistic articles, and several scholarly studies have recently added to our knowledge, but understanding of foundations, especially as they operate transnationally, is still inadequate.[4] The mythology of foundations holds that their motives should not be impugned nor their operations questioned. One Ford Foundation trustee describes foundations as encompassed by "such an aura of respectable honor that the layman does not know what goes on within the arcanum."[5] Credit (and blame) is held to rest with grantees rather than grantors. Foundations are viewed as nonpolitical, professional, and bland.

This account of the Ford Foundation as a transnational actor is based on personal observation rather than on scientific study. I have chosen the Ford Foundation both because of its size and importance and because of my experience on the staff of the foundation since 1964, largely in Brazil but also more widely in Latin America. Although the Ford Foundation occupies a special place among foundations, it does illustrate a number of general points about foundations as transnational actors.

I. Programs and Purposes

After acquiring the estates of Henry Ford and Edsel Ford in 1950 the Ford Foundation enlarged its interests from charities and schools in the state of Michigan to a program of national and international scope. Its overarching purpose was "to advance human welfare." Its assets in 1968 totaled approximately $3.6 billion, four times those of the Rockefeller Foundation, the second largest foundation in the United States. In recent years its annual budget, mainly for institutional grants, has averaged about $250 million. One-fifth to one-quarter of the Ford Foundation budget has been spent on international activities. This sum is nearly one-half of that contributed by all other foundations combined but only a miniscule portion of governmental resources for such purposes as foreign aid and cultural exchange. The Ford Foundation, like other large foundations, justifies its role less by the size of its resources than by the institutional qualities which give it special opportunities for independence, flexibility, persistence, professionalism, speed of action, and the capacity for innovation, experimentation, and demonstration.

The Board of Trustees of the Ford Foundation confers quarterly on broad policy direction, approves major budget allocations, and chooses the foundation president and its own members. The president, who is also a trustee, oversees the management of the foundation. He is assisted by six vice-presi-

[4] A rare and evocative attempt to examine the attitudinal proclivities and political effects of foundations is made by Irving Louis Horowitz and Ruth Leonora Horowitz, "Tax-Exempt Foundations: Their Effects on National Policy," in *Science*, April 10, 1970 (Vol. 168, No. 3928), pp. 220–228.

[5] Charles E. Wyzanski, Jr., remarks before the Examiner Club, Cambridge, Massachusetts, May 7, 1956.

dents; two vice-presidents head the administrative and financial divisions, and four direct the International Division, and the divisions of National Affairs, Education and Research, and Humanities and the Arts. Each of the divisions is in turn subdivided into more specialized efforts.

The International Division is today made up of 1) an Office for European International Affairs; 2) an Office for Population; and 3) offices for the three major less developed regions of the world, Asia and the Pacific, the Middle East and Africa, and Latin America and the Caribbean. The first two offices, plus the divisional office of the vice-president which is responsible for activities of a supraregional nature, are located in the foundation's New York headquarters and serve constituents in the United States and abroad. The three regional heads also reside in New York, but most of the work of their offices is carried out by sixteen field representatives and staffs located overseas. Most foundations which make grants abroad operate from their home bases, sending out short-term study missions and concentrating in specialized fields of activity. In contrast, the Ford and Rockefeller foundations have posted resident staffs abroad and charged them to develop relatively broad-gauge programs.

The broad purposes of the Ford Foundation program were shaped by an outside committee in anticipation of the large gifts of 1950. In November 1948 the Board of Trustees charged H. Rowan Gaither, chairman of the RAND Corporation, to gather together "the best thought available in the United States as to how this Foundation can most effectively and intelligently put its resources to work for human welfare."[6] A year later, in the aftermath of World War II and at the onset of the cold war, the Gaither report postulated "the establishment of peace" as the priority area of Ford Foundation activity.

The report suggested four subareas of activity: 1) the mitigation of tensions which threaten world peace; 2) the development among peoples of the world of the understanding and conditions essential to permanent peace; 3) the improvement and strengthening of the United Nations and its associated international agencies; and 4) the improvement of the structure and procedures by which the United States government and private American groups participate in world affairs. The report also noted the inappropriateness of the Ford Foundation taking "an official part" in diplomacy or international affairs.

Operationally, the international purposes of the Ford Foundation were initially pursued through three distinct programs: International Training and Research (ITR), International Affairs, and Overseas Development. Between 1952 and 1966 ITR awarded some $240 million in grants, primarily to American universities for graduate training and research in "non-Western studies."

[6] Henry Ford II to H. Rowan Gaither, Jr., November 22, 1948, *Report of the Study for the Ford Foundation on Policy and Program,* H. Rowan Gaither, Jr., chairman (Detroit, Mich: Ford Foundation, November 1949), p. 10.

In 1966 ITR was reduced and folded into the three regional development offices of a new International Division. Passage of the International Education Act of 1966 had heralded governmental acceptance of the responsibility for supporting international studies, but, to the disappointment of the universities and the foundation, the act has never been funded by Congress.

The International Affairs Program, operating like ITR from the foundation's New York headquarters, supported conferences, exchanges, efforts to improve international organizations, and studies of international problems. Among the objectives which the program pursued were development of an Atlantic partnership, cooperation with Pacific "neighbors," and increased understanding with the Union of Soviet Socialist Republics and Eastern Europe. Relatively small compared to either the old ITR or Overseas Development Program, the program continues as the Office of European and International Affairs.

The Gaither report's view that poverty, hunger, and disease "produce unrest and social instability, and these, when aggravated by ignorance and misinformation, produce a climate conducive to conflict,"[7] provided the rationale for initiating the foundation's development program. The Ford Foundation devoted some $500 million to development assistance between 1951 and 1959. Just as the Rockefeller Foundation after World War I had posited "an interrelated world in which disease stopped at no boundaries and respected no flags —a world in which political differences were irrelevant in the face of human suffering,"[8] now the Ford Foundation announced that it "must be concerned with society as a whole, and, in an era when both problems and solutions disdain national boundaries, it must be prepared to act globally."[9]

If the impulses which led the Ford Foundation beyond the United States were largely ethical and nonpolitical, the criteria which guided its allocation of staff time and grant resources to different areas of the world were in large measure geopolitical; issues of peace and war were questions not only of poverty and suffering but also of politics and power. Describing the foundation's decision in the early 1950s to concentrate on Asia and the Near East, Merle Curti has said: "These areas seemed particularly important in view of major tensions that threatened world peace, in view also of proximity to the Soviet Union and Communist China and the opportunity for channeling rising nationalism into constructive human purposes within a democratic framework."[10] The establishment of Ford Foundation activities in Africa in 1958 followed the achievement of Ghanaian independence; the initiation of the

[7] *Report of the Study for the Ford Foundation on Policy and Program,* p. 26.

[8] Fosdick, p. 15.

[9] *The Ford Foundation in the 1960s,* Statement of the Board of Trustees on Policies, Programs, and Operations (New York: Ford Foundation, July 1962), p. 3.

[10] Merle Curti, *American Philanthropy Abroad: A History* (New Brunswick, N.J: Rutgers University Press, 1963), p. 581.

Latin American program in 1959 swiftly followed Fidel Castro's victory in Cuba.

II. Participation and Politics in Decisionmaking

The Ford Foundation is predominately an American organization in the location of its home office, the origin and allocation of its resources, and the composition of its Board of Trustees and staff. Although most of the sixteen trustees also head organizations with international outreach, only John H. Loudon, chairman of the Board of Directors of Royal Dutch Petroleum Company, is not an American. At the end of 1969, 61 members (13 percent) of the 463-member professional staff of the International Division were not Americans, and only thirteen of the non-Americans were involved in the development of foundation program areas as opposed to the implementation of grant projects.

Responsibility for the day-to-day decisionmaking and management of the development assistance program is decentralized. The heads of the regional offices in New York coordinate the country programs under their aegises, but within the Ford Foundation it is the field representatives who initiate the requests for grants. Such requests are approved in turn by the relevant head, vice-president, and president. These initiatives are rarely denied or importantly amended partly because of prior communication between the field and New York headquarters and partly because New York recognizes that the critical expertise exists in the field. The representatives are empowered to approve smaller awards by themselves—for example, grants for travel and study and graduate fellowships. In a 1966 self-study twelve of the sixteen representatives seemed satisfied with the level of their delegated authority.

Although Ford Foundation trustees and staff generally agree that the decentralized pattern of decisionmaking increases the effectiveness of the development program, their opinions vary about how decisions should be made within the field offices and the extent to which greater local participation and accountability should be structured into the decisionmaking process. In no field office are members of the representative staff nationals of the host country, and only a small (if increasing) number of locally appointed consultants are nationals. Most consultation with local opinion remains ad hoc. Nevertheless, the three regional and sixteen country programs vary in accordance with the local culture, conditions, and the personalities and proclivities of staff. Field representatives of the foundation tend to become representatives for the countries in which they are located.

The frequent assertion by the Ford Foundation that it is "nonpolitical" needs to be qualified. First, as suggested above, the priority given to the mitigation of tensions rather than to activities like the prevention of disease, typified by early Rockefeller Foundation activities abroad, assumes the need for explicitly political considerations. But even the Rockefeller Foundation's "disregard for nationalisms" had political connotations in a period when the League of Nations was under debate. The conscious selection of one country above others for assistance is necessarily political; so is positing a world in which assistance should be aimed at problems regardless of national boundaries. Second, granting funds affects the distribution of resources, including power, within (often critically important) institutions. The criteria for selection may be scientific or professional, but the meaning of who gets what is manifestly political.

Foundations, as private American philanthropies, nurture a set of values which are often left implicit. Irving Horowitz and Ruth Horowitz explain the liberalism of foundations as a "function of their precarious social and political location between government and business"—a way of steering a difficult course toward public acceptance.[11] The liberalism of the Ford Foundation enables it to look upon its third-sector status as a contribution to pluralism, and the foundation's advocacy of pluralism becomes a part of the foundation's ideology and a necessity for its survival. The foundation, then, favors liberalism, pluralism, gradualism, and rational, scientific, and technocratic reform. It has been especially sympathetic and generous toward governing parties like the Congress party in India and the Christian Democratic party in Chile and toward such areas as economic planning and agricultural policy even in countries with military governments like Pakistan and Brazil.

The Ford Foundation is sometimes viewed by foreigners as essentially American in attitude and values and therefore as alien and threatening (or comforting, as the case may be). For example, Joseph C. Kiger has noted that the emphasis of foundations on education itself reflects an implicit American faith that "by study and learning the world will become a better and better place in which to live."[12] The harmony-of-interests assumption underlying the belief that more knowledge promotes peace may be ingenuous; it almost certainly coincides with the interests of an industrial power in relation to less developed countries. Even when the Ford Foundation is viewed as an instrument genuinely advancing human welfare, its officers tend cautiously to hope that kindlier views of America result. Francis X. Sutton, deputy vice-president of the International Division, for example, "retains confidence that successful and competent people will have a trusting view of this country and be understanding and forthcoming partners in new ventures."[13]

Finally, vocal elements of opinion in the United States and abroad perceive

[11] Horowitz and Horowitz, *Science,* Vol. 168, No. 3928, p. 224.

[12] Joseph C. Kiger, *Operating Principles of the Larger Foundations* (New York: Russell Sage Foundation, 1954), p. 62.

[13] Francis X. Sutton, *American Foundations and US Public Diplomacy* (New York: Ford Foundation, 1968), p. 10. This pamphlet has been reprinted from United States, Congress, House, Committee on Foreign Affairs, *The Future of United States Public Diplomacy, Symposium,* before the Subcommittee on International Organizations and Movements, 90th Cong., 2nd sess., 1968.

the Ford Foundation to be both ideological and political. In the United States Congress southern conservatives attack the liberalism and internationalism of the foundation; populists criticize its unchecked concentration of power. In 1916 the Industrial Relations Commission accused foundations like the Rockefeller Foundation and the Carnegie Endowment for International Peace of being instruments for extending capitalist control over education and welfare. In 1952 the Cox committee in Congress investigated foundations for "un-American or subversive activities" which tend "to weaken or discredit the capitalistic system as it exists in the United States and to favor Marxist socialism."[14] Abroad, anti-imperialists of the Left and ultranationalists of the Right see the Ford Foundation as a threat to vital values. The reformist bent of the foundation satisfies neither the revolutionaries nor the defenders of the status quo.

III. Ford Foundation Relations with Other Actors

The Ford Foundation claims its "independence" as its major asset and distinguishing characteristic. The foundation's appropriations are not subject to any body beyond the Board of Trustees. Its trustees are self-perpetuating; its income is generated from its own endowment, and its budget is not overburdened with fixed commitments. Foundations are not only free to take risks and to fail at times, they are expected to do so. In the real world, however, independence is a relative concept. This section examines Ford Foundation relations with several other classes of actors.

Grantees

Theoretically, prospective grantees have no influence on a foundation. Practice, of course, wanders from theory. The Ford Foundation's "leverage" for exacting changes from the grantee is greatest during the pregnant negotiations. But insofar as the foundation acts not as a judge of proposals but as an entrepreneur of ideas, it has to bargain even at this stage. Moreover, disapproval of a proposal may be interpreted as "disapproval" of an institution more widely and thereby takes on importance beyond the funds involved. Conversely, approval of a proposal, especially one from a less developed country, may signify international "approval." The most effective way for an institution to counter Ford Foundation "arrogance" is not to need its money or blessing.

Once a grant is made, the Ford Foundation's principal sanctions are threats of not supplementing an initial grant with a second one and, in cases in which the original terms may have been violated, of suspending or terminating payments on a grant in progress. Moreover, because of the experience, vantage

[14] E. E. Cox, representative from Georgia, chaired the Select Committee to Investigate and Study Educational and Philanthropic Foundations and Other Comparable Organizations which Are Exempt Federal Income Taxation until his death in December 1952. Quotations are from Kiger, p. 92.

point, and professionalism of its staff the Ford Foundation enjoys varying degrees of influence as an informal institutional and policy advisor, a clearinghouse of information, a coordinator of disparate professional and intellectual "communities," and a pacesetter among development assistance agencies. Sutton has described the ideal foundation-grantee relationship as "that of a partner with resources and competence, but one who also makes exactions and is attentive to the performance of others."[15]

Grants are the Ford Foundation's principal instruments of policy; yet, they are imperfect instruments for fulfilling the foundation's goals. It is the recipient who must fulfill the objectives of the grant, and often the objectives are in terms of more freedom and autonomy (even from the foundation). Moreover, straight-line solutions to the foundation's lofty goals are impossible. Foundation officers are usually compelled either to take some leaps of faith in justifying grants or to settle for more modest and immediate justifications on the terms of the grantee institution.

Other aid donors

The Ford Foundation maintains a variety of relations with other aid donors in foreign countries ranging from multilateral, bilateral, and international agencies to other private foundations and national organizations. Especially relevant for the foundation in defining such relations are its own budget size, focus of effort, quality of staff, speed of action, flexibility, residence in country, and nongovernmental status.

Relations with other donors are generally cooperative. The Ford Foundation sometimes exchanges information about programs and plans, and it sometimes uses its good offices to present prospective clients. The foundation may collaborate intimately with the Rockefeller Foundation, for example, in sponsoring international research centers in agriculture. In Brazil the Ford Foundation and AID cooperated in economics and law, areas in which the respective staffs felt a professional and policy congeniality, but the foundation was wary of AID in some other areas both because of AID's emphasis on short-term political objectives and the inadequacy of its professional resources.

A division of labor with other assistance agencies influences the role of the foundation. For example, the Ford Foundation purposely withholds assistance from fields already relatively well covered, such as public health and medicine, in favor of areas as yet uncovered. Moreover, the foundation tends to concentrate its resources directly in human resource development, whereas intergovernmental organizations, for example, will pay for infrastructure and construction costs. The foundation itself never accepts funds from other agencies.

The Ford Foundation sees itself as a leader and pacesetter among other

[15] Sutton, p. 7.

donors. It has opened the way in sensitive and untried fields, for example, in population activities throughout the world and in Latin America in the social sciences. The Ford Foundation has encouraged with advice and money the growth of development institutions, including planning ministries, science councils, development banks, and foundations in foreign countries. Moreover, the foundation's organization and practices have influenced the mode of foreign assistance: A bill has been passed by the United States Congress, for example, to establish a government-funded but publicly directed Inter-American Social Development Institute in Latin America along foundation lines.[16]

Ford Motor Company

When Henry Ford and his lawyers established the Ford Foundation in 1936, their principal objectives were probably the maintenance of family control over Ford Motor Company, the avoidance in large measure of the inheritance tax, and the fashioning of a largely family instrument for philanthropy. Until the 1950s the assets of the foundation were entirely Ford Motor Company shares. Now, however, the foundation and Ford Motor Company are quite separate organizations, and independence in policy and operations is generally observed between them. Over the years the foundation has divested itself of approximately 70 percent of its Ford Motor Company shares and reinvested in over 100 different holdings.

Two members of the Ford family currently sit on the Ford Foundation's board, but the board long ago ceased to be the preserve of the family and its confidants. Benson Ford shows relatively little interest. Henry Ford II is an active member but tries to assume the role of a citizen at large rather than of a representative of his family or company.

Perhaps out of deference to Ford Motor Company unwritten foundation policy once prescribed Ford cars for the field offices around the world. That policy, which was, ironically, sometimes violated by field staff as a matter of principle, no longer exists. In conformance with recent tax legislation the foundation now buys its cars strictly on the basis of comparative shopping. The foundation will probably continue to divest itself of Ford Motor Company stock partly to signify its disassociation from the company and partly to seek higher yield investments.

The public sometimes links the Ford Foundation and Ford Motor Company because of the similarity of names. Members of the Left link them ideologically. At best, they see the foundation as an instrument of the company's public relations, at worse, as a more or less sophisticated attempt to maintain the status quo, including the capitalist system. In Brazil the name "Ford" has

[16] United States, Congress, *Foreign Assistance Act of 1969,* part IV: "Inter-American Social Development Institute," P.L. 91–175, 91st Cong., 1st sess., *United States Statutes at Large,* Vol. 83, pp. 821–824.

not prejudiced the foundation. Nationalists are generally proud of the surging automobile industry which signifies growth and new prestige. The spectacular failure of Fordlandia, the company's speculative venture in Brazilian rubber in the 1930s, gives "Ford" an endearing quality to some Brazilians.

Because of the confusion of names and consequent association the Ford Foundation and Ford Motor Company sometimes exchange information in countries in which they both maintain operations. Occasionally, controversial grants may adversely (or favorably) affect the sale of automobiles. Confusion between the foundation and company persists even in the United States. For example, farm-owners' organizations in California protested a foundation grant to the Center for Community Change, which they identified with Cesar Chavez, by threatening to boycott Ford trucks. A grant in the early 1960s to the Mozambique Institute in Tanzania, the educational wing of the Mozambique Liberation Front (FRELIMO), produced a Portuguese boycott of Ford cars and an additional item of friction in negotiations over United States bases in the Azores. The initial grant was not supplemented by another one—a more probable result of the concern of the Department of State than of Ford Motor Company.

United States Government

The Ford Foundation regards itself as a vital element in the American pluralistic system and as sacrosanct from United States government intervention. However, the foundation has recently been reminded by congressional hearings, new tax legislation, and treasury searches of its files that the scope of its freedom is circumscribed by the government.

Although the Ford Foundation is enjoined from "lobbying" (except in behalf of its self-preservation), it does attempt to inform the debate of public issues and the discussion of governmental policies and actions. Foundation officers and staff testify upon invitation before congressional hearings on subjects ranging from educational television and international education to world hunger and federal aid to the arts. Moreover, foundation-supported institutions like the Brookings Institution and Resources for the Future provide the government and public with independent studies on policy issues.

Abroad, the Ford Foundation does not regard itself as an instrument of United States government policy, but it does feel constrained not to contradict United States policy blatantly or to embarrass the government. Staff may disagree with United States policy and try to influence it as individual citizens but not as Ford Foundation representatives. The foundation sometimes has acknowledged its national origins by assisting American schools abroad or by endorsing travel on United States flagships for balance-of-payments purposes.

United States embassies are sometimes unhappy about Ford Foundation assistance to "anti-American" or "subversive" groups, and on occasion embassies have tried "unofficially" to warn against it. Usually, however, embassies welcome the foundation's presence as part of the American presence.

Under certain circumstances, when United States–host-government relations are jeopardized, the Ford Foundation's good offices have facilitated communications and eased tensions. The head of the Middle Eastern program, for example, believes that in his region "the Foundation has value first as a window to the west. . . . As one link after another with the Arab world is broken, the importance of the foundation grows."[17] The foundation has also fostered better communications with East European countries by funding exchanges and meetings like the Pugwash Conferences on Science and World Affairs.

AID is the main United States government agency abroad with which the Ford Foundation has most frequent contact. David E. Bell, vice-president of the foundation's International Division, was formerly administrator of AID in Washington and McGeorge Bundy, president of the foundation, has pleaded for greater public commitment to and governmental effort in the foreign assistance area: "We believe in foreign aid on every ground—of humanity, of peace, and of our own American interest."[18] AID often seeks the expertise of Ford Foundation staff in fields like education and population. Foundation collaboration may also be sought, however, because it legitimates AID's support for the program. Foundation staff in the field are somewhat wary of AID because of its frequent organizational reforms, staff discontinuities, and use of aid for political purposes.

Host governments

The conditions for and promise of foundation work are importantly dependent on host governments. At a minimum Ford Foundation presence in a foreign country depends on host-government consent. Although the Ford Foundation has never been expelled from a country, it has left several times because conditions for program continuation were considered absent. As is the case for all other corporations the juridical personality of the foundation and its special dispensations from taxes and duties as a philanthropy are defined by host governments. Moreover, in many instances the continuation of foundation projects depends on eventual host-government financing and support.

The ways in which governments view the Ford Foundation depend on local circumstances. Governments first see the foundation as an outside source of funds and expertise. By mutual understanding in Pakistan, for example, all grants, even to private institutions, must be formally requested by the presi-

[17] J. Donald Kingsley, "Notes on Program Puzzles in the Middle East" (Paper prepared for the Meeting of the International Division, Ford Foundation, Mexico City, December 4, 1969), pp. 6–7.

[18] "The President's Review," *The Ford Foundation Annual Report: October 1, 1967–September 30, 1968* (New York: Ford Foundation, 1968), p. xvi.

dent's secretariat and made part of the government's development program. A similar situation pertains to Ghana. In Kenya a Ford Foundation advisor was the principal draftsman of Sessional Paper Number 10 of 1965, a major ideological statement of the government. Especially in Asia and Africa foundation advisors have helped shape governmental policies in population, agriculture, and education, and the foundation tends to be viewed by governments as generally supportive, albeit discriminatingly so. In other areas, particularly in Latin America, the Ford Foundation is more distant from government. There, too, the foundation selectively assists governmental programs and agencies, but it is viewed and views itself as a pluralistic influence in those societies.

Even in cases in which the foundation resists identification with the host government, it also avoids unnecessary provocation of the government. An attempt is made to maintain criteria which are professional, scientific, and nonpolitical. Academic freedom and other civil liberties are supported not so much as abstract principles but as essential conditions of work. In Brazil, for example, during the wave of governmental repression of intellectuals in 1969 the foundation decided to adhere to its existing projects as long as grantees had minimal conditions for continuation, and it showed unusual administrative and financial flexibility in facilitating such conditions. In São Paulo, where several distinguished social scientists were forcibly retired, the foundation helped to establish an independent center for continuing their research. Two other "retirees" were made consultants to the foundation. In 1966, when the military regime in Argentina violently intervened at the University of Buenos Aires, physically assaulting professors and students, the Ford Foundation helped scores of Argentine scientists to resettle in other Latin American countries more respectful of academic freedom.

The Ford Foundation is well aware that if it tried to challenge governments in the political arena it would sacrifice its own legitimacy and effectiveness. When governments intervene in scientific inquiry and the practice of the professions, then the foundation is on firmer ground. In such circumstances governments themselves are likely to be divided and international scientific and professional communities supportive of their beleaguered colleagues.

IV. Conclusion

Moral and developmental goals, technocratic and professional standards, and relative institutional independence endow large foundations with a degree of legitimacy and political aloofness. But the ideological biases (and blinders) and the distributive powers of foundations give them political coloring within controversial and sensitive areas of American society. When basically American foundations like the Ford and Rockefeller foundations venture beyond the United States, they are apt to become even more manifestly political not only as they are perceived by but also as they interact with other organizations. Foundations are part of the total configuration of world politics, varying in significance according to the institutions, problems, and geopolitical areas at issue.

The importance of foundations as transnational actors does not result from their dominance in policy areas deemed important by governments. The relationship between foundations and governments is more subtle. Under varying circumstances foundations support activities which might have been financed by governments and thus themselves bear the risk of failure or reaction. Foundations inform and evaluate governmental policies, serve as resource bases for ideas and talent, and even legitimate or undermine governmental programs and actions by supporting them or failing to do so. Foundations also influence, if only by assisting, other transnational and national actors which, in turn, affect domestic and world politics. In short, consideration of foundations as transnational actors does not impair our view of the importance of governments. Instead, it gives us a richer picture of the complexity of world politics.

The Roman Catholic Church:

A Transnational Actor

Ivan Vallier

The notion of the Roman Catholic church as a transnational actor is both intriguing and elusive. Its global empire, and thus its transnationality, ties it to many situations, no two of which are exactly alike. Its center in Rome coordinates and shapes the actions of the subsidiary field units by supplying them with general norms, symbolic leadership, and authoritative decisions. Each of the field units possesses, in turn, a certain autonomy vis-à-vis the center; the field units make demands on the center, may provide it with new ideas, and often generate key resources for the center, for example, loyalties, money, and skills.

Yet, these complex, internal features are not the whole story. The Roman Catholic church as a system competes with other actors that are also agencies of religious values or autonomous centers of power. In this essay I discuss the church's struggles in relation to three of these competitors: nation-states, transnational political movements (communism), and other Christian religions. In each instance I identify some patterns of church action and suggest how they have affected its organizational features. The main analytic theme underlying these discussions is that changing forms of competition require new types of action and that, in the course of developing these capacities, various levels of the Catholic church system become prominent, with the role of the center changing accordingly.

The center-periphery patterns of the church system are not static through time nor uniform from one segment of the periphery to another at any given time. The historical pattern of center-periphery relations has been one of increasing operational autonomy for the peripheries, in the choice of means and the combination of resources, and a corresponding gain in the religiosymbolic

Ivan Vallier is professor of sociology at the University of California, Santa Cruz.

importance of the center. This broad trend is, however, held back by the persistence of more traditional sectors, for example, in which the nation-state stands between the Catholic center and its peripheries or situations in which the center feels the necessity to exert authoritative control over peripheral segments. Much of the increased autonomy of the peripheries has resulted from the changing bases of religious control in certain types of societies. As countries grow more secular and tolerant of religious differences, the Catholic church realizes that its policies and appeals need to be tied increasingly to "local" or contextual needs which means that elites in the peripheries must be given more freedom to maneuver.

I. The Catholic Church System

The formal organization of the contemporary Roman Catholic church has three central features: 1) The whole earth's surface is divided into territorial units—dioceses, abbacies, vicariates, prefectures apostolic—that are designated as noncollegiate moral persons by Canon Law. These territorial divisions are mutually exclusive, and the lines can be modified only by the pope. Each territorial division is governed or ruled, through papal authorization, by a residential bishop or a person of equivalent or near-equivalent rank. Territories that are "fully established," i.e., where the hierarchy has been erected in its completeness, fall under the Sacred Congregation of the Bishops; those that are still mission territories come under the Sacred Congregation for the Evangelization of Peoples.[1] In some instances a territory poses a special problem, for example, the Union of Soviet Socialist Republics, and is assigned to a pontifical commission. 2) Each territorial unit in the church is connected by a vertical system of authority and administration to the transnational center of the church, the Holy See. The bishop of the Holy See is the pope who is elected from among the members of the Sacred College of Cardinals. The cardinals, of course, are selected by preceding popes. The Holy See is the authoritative center of the world church as well as its sacramental, ceremonial, and bureaucratic center. As head of the Catholic church the pope is assisted by bodies of ecclesiastical advisors, specialized ministries, and juridical units (tribunals). Each of these auxiliary papal units is the apex of another subsidiary system. Thus, the Office of the Secretary of State has charge of transactions between the Holy See and civil powers and as such heads up the papal diplomatic corps. Technically, the Holy See is located in the Basilica of St. Peter; however, as an organization it is nearly coincident with the State of the Vatican City—a sovereign territory of approximately 108 acres guaranteed to the church by the Lateran Treaty of February 11, 1929. 3) The main trunk of the church's organized life extends vertically from the parish priest up

[1] Until 1967 its name was the Sacred Congregation for the Propagation of the Faith.

to the bishop and then to the papal apex and its immediate auxiliary units. This central line of vertical organization is, in turn, supplemented by a number of specialized "task forces" or transnational systems that have emerged at various points in history to carry on particular kinds of work or service for the church. Each of these religious orders, monastic families, secular institutes, missionary societies, or apostolic movements has its own "transnational" system that is formally linked to the pope, either through the Sacred Congregation of the Religious or some other curial unit.[2]

The pope is given formal control over a number of specialized structures and categories of actors which may be utilized to further the church's goals. The problem of establishing stable conditions (or sociopolitical parameters) for the work of the church in particular states is handed over principally to members of the Vatican's diplomatic corps, nuncios and internuncios. The tasks of supervising the extensive range of decisionmaking, management, and discipline within the church's formal structures throughout the world are given to the Roman Curia. The problem of advancing the spiritual frontiers of the church in new territories or in the "pagan world" is tendered, at the professional level, to the specialized missionary orders. These, in turn, attempt to form and mobilize nonprofessional or lay-based movements for evangelization (in coordination with local ordinaries, of course). For the cure of souls and the preservation of the faith—keeping the membership committed and involved—the pope appoints bishops who, in turn, organize pastoral, educational, and welfare programs.

There are four main areas of specialization within the international church: diplomacy, evangelism, administration, and "shepherding," or pastoral work. Each area of specialization is built around a relational system. Within this system nuncios are oriented to officials of sovereign states, curial officials, as the pope's executives, are linked with the subpapal decisionmakers in the entire church, missionary elites are focused on "non-Catholic" peoples, and the residential bishops are concerned with the priests and faithful within their dioceses. Generalized control at the center is a prerequisite for all other activities. In turn, relations between the Holy See and sovereign states are critical for regular religious work in the field. Without the proper "working conditions" at the national level the church cannot proselytize and cannot make

[2] For additional details on the formal features of the church and its governmental system consult one or more of the following works: T. Lincoln Bouscaren, Adam C. Ellis, and Francis N. Korth, *Canon Law: A Text and Commentary* (4th rev. ed.; Milwaukee, Wis: Bruce Publishing Co., 1966), pp. 155–175; Peter Canisius van Lierde, *The Holy See at Work: How the Catholic Church Is Governed,* trans. James Tucek (New York: Hawthorn Books, 1962); Robert A. Graham, *Vatican Diplomacy: A Study of Church and State on the International Plane* (Princeton, N.J: Princeton University Press, 1959), pp. 127–154; and Charles Pichon, *Le Vatican* (Les Grandes Etudes contemporaines) (Paris: Editions A. Fayard, 1960). See also *Annuario pontificio* (Vatican City: Tipografia Poliglotta Vaticana), the official, annual publication of the Holy See which details all major organizational units within the church, indicates their status, and includes the names of personnel.

contact with the residential bishops and, through them, with the faithful.

These four areas of specialization exhibit certain functional interrelationships. The "internal-political" area (curial structures) grows out of the problem of establishing the principles of power and authority throughout the whole church. It is the matrix of formal power and executive control. The "external-political" area (in which the nuncios work) handles the church's relationships with political sovereigns and secures the conditions of access to their territories. If satisfactory conditions are obtained, then the "external-religious" area (in which missionaries are active) emerges as a primary focus of activities. Successful missionary work eventuates in the need for developments in the "internal-religious" area, carried on by residential bishops or pastors. In other words, the central groundwork for all operations is the establishment of international authority and political control.[3] Without a clear basis of authoritative decisionmaking and the legitimacy of the papal center all action breaks down. If international control is established, then efforts can be directed to establish "working conditions" (or the political parameters) to carry on religious activities—the work of the papal diplomatic corps. If political access is provided, attention can be directed to the task of building a local church through missionary work and preparation for the establishment of dioceses. Concentrations of members, in turn, pose the central task, the work of bishops—the provision of sacramental services, the cure of souls, and the maintenance of the religious community. Figure 1 illustrates the areas of responsibility and activity of the various churchmen.

Contributions to religious system

Areas of Specialization	Establishment of internal authority and control	Securement of conditions for work in political systems	Capture of loyalties for the church	Protection and control of church members
Internal-political	Papal bureaucrats			
External-political		Papal nuncios		
External-religious			Missionaries	
Internal-religious				Residential bishops

Figure 1. Areas of specialization within the Roman Catholic church

The total membership of the Roman Catholic church is approximately 560 million persons distributed in major regions of the world in roughly these

[3] The balance of power among these categories, especially the relationship between the residential bishops and the Holy See, has become the focus of a general controversy within the church. Many bishops, led by Leon Joseph Cardinal Suenens of Belgium, want a more decentralized, collegial system with full participation in the center's decisions. Although their major focus is papal authority, especially since *Humanae Vitae* (1968), the Roman Curia is also implicated. For a report on an interview with Cardinal Suenens on these issues see José de Broucker, "L'Unité de l'eglise dans le logique de Vatican II," *Informations catholiques internationales,* May 15, 1969 (No. 336, Supplement), pp. I–XVI.

proportions: 250 million in Western, Central, and Eastern Europe; 200 million in the countries of Latin America; 50 million in North America; 25 million in Africa; 35 million in Asia; and 3 million in Oceania (including Australia and New Zealand).[4] The professional personnel of the church numbers about 1.6 million, including nearly 380,000 priests (diocesan and religious), 960,000 sisters, 150,000 brothers, and about 2,500 bishops (residential and titular). The main constituency of the church is in areas that are typically designated as the Western world even though sizable Catholic segments are dispersed throughout the populations of the South Pacific, in countries such as Vietnam and Ceylon, and, of course, in the Philippines, central Africa, and North Africa. There are an estimated 8 million Catholics in the Soviet Union and another 3 million in the People's Republic of China (Communist China). Despite long and concerted missionary efforts in places like India and Japan Catholics remain a miniscule fraction of their populations.

In its central goals and corporate tradition the Roman Catholic church is first, last, and perhaps always a religious organization. As such its main activities and programs are focused on propagating sacred truths, consolidating religious loyalties and commitments, and creating and renewing sacred structures. In pursuing these objectives and in claiming for itself the role of religious leadership the church automatically assigns itself a role as a "moral authority." The church authors statements and generates ideas that are intended to make up the moral foundations of social order.[5] "Right" relations between men, between classes and collectivities, and between states are as much its concern as the Catholic's "right" relations to the sacramental activities that channel and bestow grace. The church's conceptions of the good society are, of course, based on divine law and Christian teachings. Moreover, the church has fashioned a transnational organization that provides it with a visible center from which its moral principles can be communicated and through which it attempts to exercise influence and social control.

The Roman Catholic church, obviously, holds in its possession many of the crucial resources (organizational and cultural) that we would consider requisite to generate and sustain a position as moral leader. Yet, in carrying out its work as a transnational actor, the church has earned some special informal reputations. Most prominent is its reputation for rigidity which implies that the church will not compromise or meet others halfway. Instead of working as a member of a team, the church usually goes it alone. This rigidity is closely connected in observers' minds with another trait, dogmatism, a corporate

[4] For figures by country see *Bilan du monde: Encyclopédie catholique du monde chrétien*, Vol. 2 (Collection église vivante) (2 vols.; Paris: Casterman [for the Centre de recherches socio-religieuse, Brussels, and the Centre église vivante, Louvain], 1964).

[5] The "social encyclicals" of certain popes since the late nineteenth century concern basic moral and social positions: *Rerum Novarum* (1891), *Quadragesimo Anno* (1931), *Mater et Magistra* (1961), *Pacem in Terris* (1963), and *Populorum Progressio* (1967).

posture that bespeaks "having *the* truth." Its moral laws and central doctrines are held as eternal verities, not open to debate, modification, or change. The church is also reputed to be bureaucratic. Sustaining this reputation is the church's stress on formal rules, privilege of office, hierarchical structure, "official" behavior, and officiousness, symbolized by the bureaucratic complex, the Roman Curia. These global reputations tend to be combined into overarching phrases—the church is "a centralized authoritarian institution"; "a dogmatic, conservative religious bureaucracy"; and "a triumphalistic, aggressive church."

During the past ten years the church's leading progressives have been attempting to change the global reputation of Roman Catholicism. Stimulated and encouraged by the charismatic pastoral initiatives of Pope John XXIII and by their legislative victories during the sessions of Vatican II, these "new men" are promoting the church in both national and transnational spheres as a human servant, a community of people of God, a pilgrim searching its way through man's troubled history, a collegial body of leaders responsible to one another and for human betterment, and an open-ended enterprise which values historically conditioned truth along with its more absolute and eternal laws.[6] All of these new images and themes have helped to modify the general reputation of the church. It now appears more approachable, more human, and more like a *mater et magistra* than a severe, authoritarian father.

At the present time the church stands in one of its most important periods of change and transition. Its broad parameters have been appreciably modified, providing it with new normative referents and differing conceptions of task. Correspondingly, notions of office, status, and authority have undergone noticeable changes: Where formal status earlier legitimated the exercise of authority, authority now depends increasingly on the qualities of the person who occupies the office as well as on the style with which his admonitions and directives are tendered. One-way vertical communication—from top to bottom—is rapidly being eclipsed by both reverse and lateral patterns. Italian priests and cardinals have been predominant within the official personnel of the Holy See, but now a new pattern of "internationalization" is emerging, with French, German, and American clergy occupying strategic positions. In regard to structural additions the church has established new secretariats for ecumenism, justice and peace, and nonbelievers. It has also created the Synod of Bishops whereby representatives of the world episcopate periodically convene in Rome to assist the pope.[7] The new Theological Com-

[6] The significance of these changes in theological, sociological, and historical terms is examined in depth by Thomas F. O'Dea, *The Catholic Crisis* (Boston: Beacon Press, 1968).

[7] On the nature of recent, official changes in the relations between bishops and the Holy See, as well as in the organization of the Roman Curia, see Pope Paul VI's "motu proprio," *Pro Comperto Sane* (August 6, 1967) and his apostolic constitution, *Regimini Ecclesiae Universae* (August 15, 1967). These actions preceded the first meeting of the Synod of Bishops, September–October 1967. See "L'Esprit du concile l'emporte," *Informations catholiques internationales,* November 1, 1967 (No. 299), pp. 13–17; and Giancarlo Zizola, "Le Nouveau Visage de la Curie romaine," *Informations catholiques internationales,* July 15, 1968 (No. 316), pp. 27–32.

mission, which met for the first time in 1969, draws leading thinkers together as an advisory body.

II. The Catholic Church and Nation-States

The complex struggles that have taken place between the Holy See and temporal sovereigns during the past 500 years have brought the Holy See to a systemic position that has the following broad features: 1) The papacy stands, in all but a token way, differentiated from temporal or territorial bases of power. The appropriation of the Papal States by Victor Emmanuel II in 1870 marks the decisive event in this process. Between 1870 and the signing of the Lateran Treaty in 1929 the Holy See made its way in international affairs as a spiritual sovereign which meant, in customary international law, that it enjoyed full juridical status. With the Lateran Treaty the Holy See was provided with the small geographical territory in Rome that is called the State of the Vatican City. This temporal base guarantees the Holy See a token, but real, claim to political sovereignty, though in no way can the Vatican state be characterized as a nation-state.[8] 2) Although the papacy or Holy See possesses sovereign status in both spiritual and temporal realms, the crucial fact is that all but a few of the 560 million Catholics who make up the church's constituency live within the borders of other sovereign entities, or nation-states. To reach Catholics and to affect the course of *intra*national ecclesiastical developments the Holy See must initiate various kinds of transactions across the borders of nation-states. Whenever the Holy See takes up pastoral policies, educational activities, or missionary work, it is faced with the problems of legitimating itself to national governments, gaining access to politically sovereign territories, securing guarantees for pursuing its religious work, and preserving and strengthening relationships between local churches and the transnational center in Rome. In many ways a continuing validation of the Holy See's spiritual authority is highly dependent on its capacities as a political and diplomatic actor.

The problem that I have chosen to examine in this section, even though in a very preliminary way, concerns the conditions under which the actions of the church's transnational center can affect domestic situations. From the perspective of nation-states this problem has to do with the differing kinds of border rules that are defined for the Holy See and the degree to which one or another set of border rules impedes, neutralizes, or facilitates the actions of the Holy See. In its relationships with nation-states the Holy See undoubtedly holds as an ideal a situation in which it has free or untrammeled access to a country, in which the government guarantees to protect and support the Catholic faith, and in which the Holy See's controls over central ecclesias-

[8] The subtleties of papal sovereignty are ably described by Graham, especially pp. 157–302.

tical matters are fully specified and legalized in the form of an international agreement or concordat. This ideal is seldom achieved, although in the 1887 concordat negotiated between the government of Colombia and the Holy See something very near to the ideal was realized.[9] Among other things this concordat, which is still in effect today, defines Catholicism as the official religion of Colombia; binds the state to protect the church and to "enforce respect for it and its ministers"; provides the church with "complete liberty and independence of the civil power"; gives the church rights to acquire and administer property; allows for the unhindered establishment of religious orders and associations; tenders to the church a central role in all types of public education, including a provision that makes religious instruction obligatory in all schools; places the power of making episcopal appointments in the hands of the Holy See while recognizing, however, the role of the president of the republic in making recommendations. The Colombian situation not only presents the Holy See with an open boundary but also harnesses the political sovereign to the cause of the church.

The opposite situation is exemplified by nation-states that deny access to the Holy See. Many of the Communist-bloc countries have adopted this policy, legitimating it in terms of political realities. The Holy See is defined as either an agent of political ideologies that may subvert national goals or as an ally of states that are considered political enemies. Communist China denies access to the Holy See and prohibits Catholics from carrying on relationships with Rome. Catholics, like members of other religions, are grouped politically by the regime into "national associations." Individuals who refuse to enter these associations are considered enemies of the state and are punished accordingly. While Catholics are permitted to carry on regular sacramental activities, ecclesiastical appointments are controlled by the government. Bishops are named to vacant sees but remain unauthorized by the pope. According to a recent report more than 40 bishops have been seated on these terms during the past twenty years.[10] However, one must not generalize from this case to other "Communist" situations. Cuba, though lying within the circumference of Soviet power, not only hosts a papal nuncio but dispatches an ambassador to the Vatican. The Polish People's Republic is also an interesting case. It is a Communist-bloc country but also a major center of European Catholicism. In 1945 the Polish government unilaterally revoked the concordat of February 10, 1925, and set about to transform Catholicism into a national church. Cycles of conflict between the state and the hierarchy have occurred since then, and

[9] The full text of the Concordat between the Republic of Colombia and His Holiness the Supreme Pontiff Leo XIII is provided in J. Lloyd Mecham, *Church and State in Latin America: A History of Politico-Ecclesiastical Relations* (rev. ed.; Chapel Hill: University of North Carolina Press, 1966), pp. 126–131.

[10] See Léon Trivière, "1949–1969: Les Chrétiens devant le défi chinois," *Informations catholiques internationales*, February 1, 1969 (No. 329), pp. 26–32.

there is no diplomatic representative of the Vatican in Poland. Even so, the relationship between the Polish state and the Polish hierarchy is now regulated by a modus vivendi, and it is important to record that twenty Polish bishops traveled to Rome in 1962 for the opening session of Vatican II.

Between the two extremes of high, privileged access, on the one hand, and the denial of access on the other hand several additional types of situations confront the Holy See. One important group of nation-states, most of which are Catholic countries, limit the Holy See's influence over internal church affairs by holding tenaciously to patronage rights, those powers that were conceded historically by popes to temporal sovereigns who were deemed strategic for protecting the Catholic faith and for promoting its geographical expansion. Rights of patronage, such as those tendered to the Spanish sovereigns around the beginning of the sixteenth century—the *patronato real*—grant the temporal ruler control over episcopal appointments, the erection of dioceses, the privilege of the placet on all papal communications, and in many other ways subordinate the church to political authority.[11] The temporal sovereigns agree, in turn, to protect the church, to aid it financially, to extend its influence, and to provide the clergy with special privileges such as exemption from military status and provisions for special ecclesiastical courts. Many of the independent states that have developed out of these kingdoms maintain some or all of these patronage rights and, on those bases, effectively restrict the influence of the Holy See. Yet, these same states, including Argentina, Peru, Spain, and Venezuela, carry on full-fledged diplomatic relationships with the Vatican. There is, then, a combination of political openness to Rome and restricted ecclesiastical access. The trend, undoubtedly, is toward a relinquishment of patronage rights as evidenced in the recent agreements between the Holy See and the governments of Argentina and Venezuela.[12]

The other group of nation-states which deserve consideration consists of countries that have established and institutionalized the principle of separation of church and state, e.g., Brazil, Chile, France, Mexico, and Portugal, as well as the United States. Although particularities mark each case, the broad picture is freedom of religious activities for all groups in these states. Diplomatic ties with Rome vary considerably.[13] Brazil, Chile, and Portugal receive papal nuncios; France (according to the *Annuario pontificio per l'anno 1960*) receives a pronuncio; apostolic delegations reside in Canada, Mexico, the United

[11] For a detailed study of the history of the *patronato real,* its original provisions, and its subsequent implications for political and ecclesiastical developments in Latin America see Mecham.

[12] The features of these agreements are reported by John J. Kennedy, "The Legal Status of the Church in Latin America: Some Recent Developments," in *The Church and Social Change in Latin America,* ed. Henry A. Landsberger (International Studies of the Committee on International Relations, University of Notre Dame) (Notre Dame, Ind: University of Notre Dame Press, 1970), pp. 165–171.

[13] The information on diplomatic arrangements between the Holy See and particular countries is for 1960 and is drawn from the *Annuario pontificio per l'anno 1960* (Vatican City: Tipografia Poliglotta Vaticana, 1960), pp. 981–1001.

Kingdom, and the United States. States, in turn, may or may not dispatch representatives to the Vatican. Brazil, Chile, France, and Portugal are represented by ambassadors; Mexico and the United States are not represented diplomatically. Despite these differences in diplomatic arrangements and some of the special circumstances that, as in Mexico and Portugal, qualify the generalization that a separation of church and state automatically implies equal treatment of all religious groups by the government, the boundaries of these countries are relatively open to the initiatives of the Holy See, if not directly and diplomatically, then indirectly through its transnational auxiliaries. Chile, France, and the United States are among the countries that have gone furthest in institutionalizing church-state separation and in endorsing religious pluralism. These are also countries that permit the church unusually favorable opportunities for transacting business across their boundaries. Although the governments shoulder no responsibilities for protecting, preserving, or promoting the Catholic faith or any other religion, they have set a course whereby international religious relationships can be freely formed and developed. The Holy See appears to have assumed that these open, universalistic situations are less favorable to its interests than those, as in Colombia, where privileged access and political support are guaranteed. In my judgment this assumption is mistaken. While it may be true that the Holy See possesses certain particularistic advantages in situations like that in Colombia, its influence is largely limited to traditional expressions and, no less important, is based on anachronistic arrangements. On the other hand, in places like Chile, France, and the United States its influence has to be won in competition with other religions and political ideologies, and it has a potential for expressing this influence in other than traditional ways.

The broad distinctions I have made in the kinds of situations that nation-states present to the Holy See indicate, preliminarily, some of the conditions that bear on the Holy See's capacities to influence both political and ecclesiastical domestic situations. Where a nation-state shuts the Holy See and its transnational auxiliaries out of its territory, the transnational capacities of the church are obviously blocked. Though pastoral messages from Rome or news of the public activities of the pope may seep into the country, the Holy See's organized influence cannot penetrate its borders. Local church units in these states either adapt politically or disintegrate.

Where a nation-state retains remnants of patronage rights, the Holy See is relatively limited in its capacity to control and promote the church within the state's boundaries. The transnational influence of the church is more likely to be transmitted through diplomatic channels to the governing political groups which then may or may not modify the situation of the Catholic church. Most governments that hold to patronage arrangements are not basically worried about the vigor or quality of the Catholic faith but retain portions of ecclesiastical control in order to shape the church into a political ally.[14] It seems that wherever one finds a Catholic country in the West that is unsure of itself politically, it will attempt to maximize the scope of political control over ecclesiastical affairs. The greater these political controls, the greater is the likelihood that the church within its territory will be fashioned to serve political ends. The problem that these countries face is one of developing a secular theory of political legitimacy and applying it fully as a basis of civic order.

Nation-states that present open boundaries to Rome and that have separated church and state provide the Holy See and its transnational units the greatest possibilities for influence. Transactions and the development of effective relationships between the center and its peripheries can proceed as each situation requires. If these open nation-states happen to become a strategic focus of competition between Catholics and other religious or political groups, the Holy See and the Vatican may assume very important roles by mobilizing resources from other parts of the Catholic system and by deploying them (or at least offering them) to local hierarchies, by formulating transnational normative appeals, and by encouraging and rewarding innovative thrusts that emerge in local encounters.

These brief examples are perhaps sufficient to indicate that the church, as a transnational actor, confronts the nation-state under differing sets of conditions and that each set requires specialized problem-solving initiatives by the center.[15] Whereas the papal diplomatic corps plays a strategic role vis-à-vis nation-states that are bound up with the church legally and politically, the nuncios are not the key to problems of competition that arise between Catholic workers and communist workers in a Brussels factory. The type and extent of action by the transnational center of the church vary with the local situation and much depends on the kind of access the nation-state allows the Holy See.

It is also clear that the church's transnational actions have different consequences for national situations because the parameters that constrain problem-

[14] The transnational church has recently stated in clear terms that rights of patronage and decisions on all ecclesiastical matters belong only to the church. The text of *Christus Dominus,* the decree on the Bishops' Pastoral Office in the Church of October 28, 1965, promulgated during the fourth and final session of Vatican II, states "that in the future no rights or privileges of election, nomination, presentation, or designation for the office of bishop be any longer granted to civil authorities." See chapter 2, article 20.

[15] For those who wish to look into church–state–Holy See relations in particular countries see, as a beginning, A. C. Jemolo, *Church and State in Italy, 1850–1950,* trans. David Moore (Philadelphia: Dufour Editions, 1961); Victor D. Du Bois, "New States and an Old Church [Guinea, Congo (Brazzaville), and the Ivory Coast]," in *Churches and States: The Religious Institution and Modernization,* ed. Kalman H. Silvert (New York: American Universities Field Staff, 1967), pp. 51–79; Guenter Lewy, *The Catholic Church and Nazi Germany* (New York: McGraw-Hill Book Co., 1964); Joseph N. Moody, ed., in collaboration with E. Alexander et al., *Church and Society: Catholic Social and Political Thought and Movements 1789–1950* (New York: Arts, 1953), especially Moody's monographic contribution on France, pp. 93–186; and William Ebenstein, *Church and State in Franco's Spain* (Research Monograph 8) (Princeton, N.J: Center of International Studies, Woodrow Wilson School of Public and International Affairs, Princeton University, 1960).

solving efforts differ. If the Catholic church in a particular country encompasses a major part of the population in its membership and is under high threat, is low on crucial resources, and stands in a state that allows the transnational church full access across its borders, then it is likely that the transnational level of church control and its organizational capacities will be focused on that national situation. The Holy See may erect new dioceses (thus adding new types of episcopal leadership); it may formulate normative demands that will place Catholic churches in other states under responsibility to transfer resources to the beleaguered church; or it may draw on its own funds and elite groups to undertake special missions or engage in particular kinds of institution building.

All of these actions and inputs will help reshape the conditions of local competition. These shifts, in turn, will directly affect domestic political developments, intergroup conflict or alliance, and cultural and symbolic meanings. The transnational capacities of the church are mediated through different systems of religious control according to national context. If an extensive Catholic infrastructure exists throughout the occupational and political sectors of a national society, initiatives from the center may be rapidly amplified or interrupted depending on the national church's orientations to the Holy See and the type of directives that it sends.

The intervention of the Holy See against the French worker-priest movement in 1953 produced major splits within the Catholic church in France. These, in turn, aggravated an already tense political situation in that country. Catholics constitute a majority of the French population, and, since they are deeply divided politically, any authoritative action by the transnational center that involves a politically important issue (and the worker-priest movement was certainly such an issue) produces widespread consequences for French political life. On the other hand, the encyclical *Humanae Vitae* (1968) has not polarized French Catholics to any great extent for at least two reasons: Many French Catholics have already resolved the contraception problem in ad hoc ways, and the encyclical did not have direct political meaning. Action from the center has different consequences at the national level depending on the issue, the relationship to and importance of Catholics in the society, the history of the church's posture toward Rome, and the degree and basis of unity or division among Catholics. The Holy See can take initiatives vis-à-vis the church in the United States with fewer political consequences for the state because United States Catholics are not divided into deeply institutionalized factions that reflect national political cleavages. The effects of the center's actions on the American Catholic system are expected to be more indirect and "individually transmitted." From these perspectives the power of the Holy See vis-à-vis the nation-state can only be assessed by examining types of national situations and types of initiatives taken by Rome.

III. The Catholic Church and Communism

The most salient "other" in the environment of the Roman Catholic church during the past 50 years has been communism. Communism not only promotes an intriguing faith and aspires toward world domination but also shows a capacity for developing local "communities," regional centers, national parties, and international networks and structures. It also makes political control at the level of the nation-state one of its main procedural objectives. Thus, when it gains political control, it can translate many of its norms and behavioral models into national policies and back them up with ultimate force. On these and other merits the Communist system presents the church—equally committed to a body of religious truths and equally aspiring to transnational dominance—with a formidable situational problem.

Although the struggle has undergone several important evolutionary changes and a number of significant social, economic, and political consequences have been produced by these encounters, I am interested in identifying some of the ways in which this threat has affected the church as a problem-solving system: What lines of specialization has the church drawn on or created in these encounters? Has the threat of communism increased the transnational activities of the church? Has it stimulated innovation and internal change? Has it altered relations between the church and other organized centers of power? My answers are preliminary, not conclusive.

The Catholic church, as far back as the nineteenth century, tried to deal with the threat of "secular faiths" (including communism) through preaching, condemnations, or papal pronouncements. When the communists gained control of Russia, a major European state, the church shifted quickly to diplomacy. For more than ten years the Holy See tried, but failed, to induce Soviet leaders to enter into an agreement whereby the church could continue its regular work in that country.[16] As organized Communist influence moved west, into France, Germany, and Italy, the church began to supplement its diplomatic and normative strategies with new lines of associational activity in local settings. Through new concepts of action and specialized training methods laymen were mobilized as "religious agents" of the institutional church. A whole new fund of motivational resources was generated in the lay sector, and part of this was channeled into political movements that combined Catholic ideologies of modernization and national organizations into major Christian Democratic parties as, for example, in France, Germany, Italy, and later Chile and Venezuela. The organizational strategies of the competitor—the communists—in open-field situations (in which the church could not rely on political regimes to protect its interests) forced the church to develop new kinds of structural and motivational resources. But these developments were not the

[16] An extensive report on this phase is provided in Graham, chapter 13.

products of any single level of organization and action but grew out of the combined efforts of local, national, and transnational centers of church activity. Pope Pius XI called for a worldwide program of Catholic Action as early as 1922, but this normative initiative could not yet be coupled with concrete structural units.[17] Some models of field action were emerging in the peripheries (for example, the *Jeunesse ouvrière chrétienne* movement founded by Joseph Cardinal Cardjin in Belgium), and they were rapidly legimated by the center and more or less generalized as structural solutions.

The direction that Catholic Action took in Italy during the late 1920s and early 1930s was essentially parochial in its organizational principle and divided laymen into age-sex categories (adult male, adult female, male youth, female youth).[18] In many ways it was quite passive vis-à-vis the environment due to the political problems it raised for the Italian regime. Furthermore, the church had secured certain guarantees from the regime that would protect it from communism. In France, by contrast, a more open battlefield situation emerged; Catholic Action vigorously responded to its environment and focused on occupational, residential, and functional areas of French society.[19] These different patterns of structural development reflected the nature of the competition and the parameters within which it took place.

The next phase in this encounter, beginning in the 1950s, shifted the main battlefield from national settings in Europe to the low-income countries, or the third world. Latin America emerged as a crucial test site for the church because nearly two-fifths of its members live in those countries and the secular Left was already well organized in many regions. Moreover, the local hierarchies were short on personnel, funds, action models, and laymen who could be mobilized to extend the church's influence to new groups and marginal strata. Under these conditions—high threat, low resources in local units, and quite open national boundaries—the transnational church, in close cooperation with local hierarchies, swung into action. Problem-solving strategies were transferred from other sectors of the world church, funds poured in, new contingents of trained personnel were deployed, and a variety of new institution-building sequences were begun. Since the dominant ideological motif was "radical social change," many church leaders began to formulate

[17] *Ubi Arcano Dei* (1922).

[18] On the development of the Catholic Action movement in Italy, its internal problems, and its significance for political variables (including the Christian Democratic party) see Jemolo, chapters 6 and 7; Gianfranco Poggi, *Catholic Action in Italy: The Sociology of a Sponsored Organization* (Stanford, Calif: Stanford University Press, 1967); and Joseph LaPalombara, *Interest Groups in Italian Politics* (Princeton, N.J: Princeton University Press, 1964), pp. 57–59, 360–366, and 404–412.

[19] The development and influence of Catholic Action in France are examined at length by William Bosworth, *Catholicism and Crisis in Modern France: French Catholic Groups at the Threshold of the Fifth Republic* (Princeton, N.J: Princeton University Press, 1962). One of the most influential essays on the principles of Catholic Action in relation to civil and political life is "Catholic Action and Political Action" by Jacques Maritain in his book *Scholasticism and Politics*, trans. Mortimer J. Adler (Garden City, N.Y: Image Books, 1960), pp. 185–211.

new concepts and norms that could tie Catholic loyalties to the need for social change. To accomplish this the church needed new structures and additional resources. Innovation in the fields of social service, human community, and pastoral leadership, together with related efforts, was aimed toward capturing the loyalties of status groups that had become prime targets of the secular Left—peasants, urban poor, intellectuals, and students.[20] The contest was focused on the capacity of each side to mobilize these status groups which meant, on the practical level, that Catholics had to demonstrate that they could provide new economic, social, and political rewards. In Chile this competition stimulated a strategy of Catholic-based reform politics combined with a series of specialized programs aimed toward improving the living conditions of the minorities. In Brazil, under quite different national conditions, the innovative trend among Catholics took a more radical, political cast and made special attempts to develop a political consciousness among the masses.[21]

There have been three consequences of these recent struggles of the church with the secular Left in third-world situations: 1) The lateral ties between national episcopal systems have been upgraded and strengthened not only within the perimeters of Latin America but also between Latin American hierarchies and those of Belgium, Canada, the Federal Republic of Germany (West Germany), France, the United States, and other countries. In short, these struggles have created a new integrative basis among hierarchies that does not directly involve the Roman center and, simultaneously, have increased the operational power of the national hierarchies as systems vis-à-vis the center. The gathering in Rome of bishops from all over the world during the Second Vatican Council helped consolidate some of these new alliances and ties. 2) The range of organizational specialization in local church systems has expanded and thereby increased the dispersive or centrifugal forces at the boundaries between church and society. New flexibilities emerged and Catholics gained new freedoms. These changes helped, in part, to open the way for the growth of a Catholic Left which has now formed some collaborative ties with Marxists. Although the center helped generate these new developments, it has little control over them. The church now has an emerging basis on which it can compete with other revolutionary groups, but, in gaining this added capacity, it has also created a major integrative problem. 3) The center has had to expand its institutional culture in order to provide a norma-

[20] The evolutionary and cross-national configurations in the church's problem-solving efforts are examined in Ivan Vallier, *Catholicism, Social Control, and Modernization in Latin America* (Modernization of Traditional Societies Series) (Englewood Cliffs, N.J: Prentice-Hall, 1970); and Ivan Vallier, "Extraction, Insulation, and Re-Entry: Toward a Theory of Religious Change," in Landsberger, pp. 9–35.

[21] On developments between Catholic movements and politics in Brazil consult Thomas G. Sanders, "Catholicism and Development: The Catholic Left in Brazil," in Silvert, pp. 81–99; Emanuel de Kadt, *Catholic Radicals in Brazil* (London: Oxford University Press, 1970); and Thomas C. Bruneau, "Conflict and Change in the Brazilian Catholic Church" (Ph.D. diss., Department of Political Science, University of California, Berkeley, 1970).

tive and symbolic framework capable of accommodating Catholic values and the concept of radical social change. As recent encyclicals such as *Populorum Progressio* (1967) indicate, the center is attempting to broaden its predominately West European concerns. Although this newer phase of pastoral leadership at the global level was seriously damaged by Pope Paul VI's encyclical *Humanae Vitae,* which reiterated the church's teachings against artificial birth control methods, a break with the European–North American axis and a new focus on the third-world sector seems to have developed and is likely to be further developed in the near future.

The church's evolving encounter with communism has compelled it to restructure its organizational life along lines that could give it competitive power. I do not imply that it has succeeded in stopping its enemy; yet, some of the structural changes that have taken place in the Communist system, for example, the development of polycentrism, may have their roots in the competition that Catholic forces have presented in states like France, Italy, and West Germany.[22] Moreover, the communists have learned that the Catholic church does not disappear if it is cut off from the center as in the Czechoslovak Socialist Republic, Poland, and the Socialist Federal Republic of Yugoslavia. It is also worth mentioning that the church has, at least until now, retained its unitary, transnational features with its center intact, while the Communist center is in dispute. Finally, the Catholic church has been able to keep itself formally differentiated from important political centers; communism, on the other hand, fuses "church and state" at all levels.[23] This is undoubtedly a major source of its present evolutionary problem.[24]

[22] For a discussion of change in the Communist system see Zbigniew Brzezinski, "Threat and Opportunity in the Communist Schism," *Foreign Affairs,* April 1963 (Vol. 41, No. 3), pp. 513–525; Richard Lowenthal, *World Communism: The Disintegration of a Secular Faith* (New York: Oxford University Press, 1964); Vernon V. Aspaturian, *The Soviet Union in the World Communist System* (Integration and Community Building among the Fourteen Communist Party-States, Vol. 3) (Stanford, Calif: Hoover Institution on War, Revolution, and Peace, Stanford University, 1966); and Edward M. Bennett, ed., *Polycentrism: Growing Dissidence in the Communist Bloc?* ([Pullman]: Washington State University Press, 1967).

[23] Lowenthal attaches fundamental significance to this "Caesaro-papist" feature of modern totalitarianism:

> The ideological disintegration of world communism . . . raises the question of why it has proved impossible to maintain a single doctrinal authority for a movement ruling a plurality of independent states—why the unity of doctrine could not survive the diffusion of power. The answer must be sought in the "Caesero-papist" nature of modern totalitarianism, with its inseparable unity between ideology and state power: here lies the fundamental difference between the structure of international communism and that of the Catholic Church. A spiritual movement may preserve its world-wide doctrinaire unity so long as . . . it refrains from seeking to exert political power directly. But in a movement constructed on the Byzantine model, where loyalty to the faith and obedience to the state coincide, ideological fragmentation is bound to follow the growth of political pluralism. [Lowenthal, pp. 234–235.]

[24] In a more speculative vein the East-West contest can be viewed as taking place between two transnational systems, and within each system instrumental and expressive problems exist. Each system faces the imperatives of developing transnational areas of specialization with corresponding control centers that, on the one hand, carry forward instrumental activities—economic growth, educational development—and, on the other hand, handle expressive activities—the articulation of collective ideals, promotion

IV. The Catholic Church and Other Christians

The Roman Catholic church has always maintained that it is the exclusive and authoritative representation of Christ on earth, a position that automatically defines other Christian bodies as distortions, usurpers, and systems based on error. This confessional arrogance, reinforced by doctrinal absolutism and rigid field policies, has kept the boundaries between Catholicism and other Christian religions very distinct. Rules regarding mixed marriage, participation in other Christian rituals, and confessional burial grounds have helped maintain this fixed, separated posture.

The tense historical pattern that emerged between Roman Catholicism and the other Christian religions has begun to break down within the past 25 years.[25] Several developments have played a part: 1) There has been a rapid growth of the amalgamating tendencies among major Protestant bodies and

of integrative norms, and the symbolic representation of "religious" beliefs. In the Communist system both areas of specialization have been anchored in the same concrete structures up and down the vertical scale. By contrast, the West is much more internally differentiated, with the Judeo-Christian system and its representative bodies performing the expressive role and the major nation-states, such as the United States, performing the instrumental role. In this perspective the transnational features of the Roman Catholic church play a crucial role because its center is structurally differentiated from the main centers of the West's instrumental power.

This combination of the two areas of specialization within the Western system provides it with tremendous advantage vis-à-vis the Communist system mainly because the religious system can (but may not) function as an expanding base of integrative and legitimate action as changes occur in the instrumental sector. On the other hand, the Communist system—the fusion of "church" and "state" (the instrumental and expressive functions in concrete structures)—finds that its failures in the instrumental sector carry direct and thus negative implications for its "religious sector." Similarly, its "religious" norms are tendered as capable of being operationalized into concrete, instrumental structures. These norms lose their overarching autonomy and flexibility, becoming norms that have to demonstrate practical payoffs or lose their meaning.

On this basis I suggest that the primary matrix of transnational developments in the West is the changing relationship between the Roman Catholic church and the United States. Respectively, these two actors represent the main foci of expressive and instrumental leadership. Moreover, certain symbolic and organizational alliances have already been forged at the international level, for example, in Latin America and in Southeast Asia, notably in the Republic of Vietnam (South Vietnam). These two systems gained somewhat charismatic ascendancy between 1960 and 1963—the era of the "two Johns," Pope John XXIII and John F. Kennedy. Their interrelationships were not only symbolized by the fact that Kennedy was the first Catholic president of the United States but also on the basis of their shared interests in Latin America since the Cuban revolution. For a few years the Western system took on a new grace and grandeur.

Since 1963 the relationship between the two actors has become more complicated, perhaps even more structurally interconnected. The "field operations" of United States technical assistance programs and those of the church often overlap in interesting, if not productive, patterns. It is to be expected that Washington-Rome relations will undergo new and significant changes in the next two decades with the not unlikely possibility that these relations will raise many of the issues and tensions distinctive to the "church-state" problem, although this time at the transnational level rather than at the level of the nation-state as in the past.

25 In his encyclical *Mortalium Animos* (1928) Pope Pius XI condemned the ecumenical developments that were taking shape among Protestants. Twenty years later the Holy Office refused the invitation of ecumenical leaders to participate in the first assembly of the World Council of Churches. In 1964 *Unitatis Redintegratio*, the decree on ecumenism formulated by Vatican II, was promulgated. By 1967 the Holy See appointed fifteen official observers to the Fourth Assembly of the World Council of Churches (WCC) held in Uppsala. See P. Beaupère, "De la condamnation à la collaboration," *Informations catholiques internationales*, July 1, 1968 (No. 315), pp. 31–32.

an establishment of cooperative links between Protestant and Orthodox churches. These developments fall under the broad heading of the "ecumenical movement."[26] Preparatory stages and alliances in particular functional spheres gathered speed from the late nineteenth century through the 1920s. Interdenominational mergers began to occur in the 1930s, and plans were made by international Protestant leaders to establish a "world council of churches," but the interruptions of World War II postponed these activities until 1948. For the first time Protestant and Orthodox leaders were joined in common efforts within the circumference of a transnational structure. 2) The steady advances of secular values, religious indifference, and revolutionary politics throughout the Western world have appreciably eroded the institutional strengths of Christianity. In the course of a century or less the "Christian" system has become a peripheral rather than a dominant field of action, stimulating denominations and formerly confident bodies like the Roman Catholic church to open up possibilities for new alliances. As religious values and ecclesiastical influence have declined, interaction and cooperation among Christians have increased. 3) There has been a growing recognition by top Catholic strategists that the days of traditional political alliance are gone forever. This recognition, however ambiguous and preliminary, is perhaps the most important source of Catholic ecumenical posture. Throughout most of its history the Catholic church has been able to secure important guarantees of religious monopoly in major regions of the world through alliances with kings, princes, empire builders, and nation-states. But as the separation principle is more widely applied and as the high levels of unpredictability that democratic polities inject into constitutionally based Catholic guarantees are recognized, the church is forced to choose "another dancing partner." One possibility is a new emphasis on "religious coalitions and alliances" with "other Christians" rather than ties with nation-states. 4) Roman Catholic leaders have grown aware of the need for new institutional principles as the basis of local church life and personal participation. The structural features of urban, industrial, and pluralistic societies, as in the Netherlands, the United Kingdom, and the United States, suggest that the vitality of Catholic life depends in greater and greater degree on incorporating the norms of rank-and-file participation, congregational voluntarism, and subsidiarity into the routine operations of the church system. These features have been basic to many Protestant churches. As the Catholic church begins to value them, it moves structurally, and even theologically, closer to the Protestants. This is a subtle process of learning from the environment.[27]

26 Background materials are provided by Ruth Rouse and Stephen Charles Neill, eds., *A History of the Ecumenical Movement, 1517–1948* (2nd ed.; Philadelphia: Westminster Press, 1967).

27 An exchange process appears to be taking place: As Roman Catholics move toward certain "Protestant-type" structures and ideas, Protestants (via national and international organizations) are taking on some of the features of the Roman Catholic system.

The Holy See is working on several levels of ecumenical activity. The pope has engaged in symbolic meetings with, for example, the archbishop of Canterbury and, in Jerusalem, the patriarch of Constantinople. A Secretariat for Christian Unity was established in 1966 with Augustin Cardinal Bea, a German Jesuit, assuming its first phase of leadership. The growth of increasingly cordial relations with the World Council of Churches is suggested by several specific developments. First, the Holy See dispatched official observers to the Fourth Assembly of the World Council of Churches held at Uppsala in the summer of 1968; second, Pope Paul VI visited the headquarters of the WCC in Geneva in 1969; and third, a number of unofficial, but nonetheless important, interfaith projects have been developing.

It appears that the present phase, though partially overshadowed by Pope Paul VI's encyclical *Humanae Vitae,* is one of "jockeying for position" on the part of all the central Christian elites who are seriously interested in ecumenism. The Roman Catholic church has moved quickly to foster open lines of communication with other Christian bodies and to provide official structures for limited kinds of collaboration, but it has not yet shown how it intends to respond to major issues, such as authority, ministry, and the sacraments. Certainly, the papacy is a major issue and, in my judgment, is the center of the whole problem of ecumenical development. However much the papacy may be criticized by Catholics and non-Catholics, it is an especially significant bargaining point for the church. Though it may undergo modifications in both structural detail and functional scope, the principle of a global apex of sacred authority and religious symbolism will be enhanced, rather than eclipsed, by future changes.

V. Systemic Trends

Have the basic features and functional position of the Roman Catholic church changed over the past century? If so, how can the changes be explained? Is there any basis for attributing significance to the contemporary church vis-à-vis national powers, international developments, or supranational trends? There is no doubt that the church's position and importance in international life differ from their situation 100 years ago.

1) The church today is a much more integrated, international organization. I do not claim that it has less internal conflict or that there is more adherence to central doctrines by the members, but I do propose that the church in the 1970s shows more structural integration, indicated by a heightened increase of communication and contact between the center and the peripheries; a more integrated linkage between national hierarchies and the Holy See by virtue of the decrease in Gallicanist, Febronianist, and Josephite tendencies; and a higher rate of transactions between national church systems, indicated by

personnel transfers, material aid, and cooperative plans. The international church has gained structural strength because it has been able to move beyond an earlier, segmental pattern in which national governments played a key "intermediary" role.

2) The contemporary church, in contrast to its situation 100 years ago, is much more dependent for its prestige and influence on its spiritual and moral leadership because it has lost major forms of organized political support. The progressive differentiation of ecclesiastical elites and structures from political units came about voluntarily in some instances and by force in others. This differentiation has several sources: a) an abandonment of the traditional establishment principle by many governments, for example, by Brazil in 1890; France, 1905; Mexico, 1917; and Chile, 1925; b) the recognition by the papacy, first articulated by Pope Leo XIII in the late 1880s, of the legitimacy of all forms of government, including democracy, and, more importantly, the papal teaching that Catholic members are duty-bound to respect and obey their governments if broad moral laws are observed; c) the church's gradual recognition of the needs of all men and the need to promote the basis of a moral order that extends beyond that of the family, tribe, nation, or particular faith. These suggest that a whole new perspective has emerged regarding church relations with society and, as a corollary, a different conception of the basis of religious legitimacy and moral leadership.

3) The contemporary Catholic church is much less oriented toward "confessional expansion" reflected in the extensive missionary enterprises that were promoted during the late nineteenth century and until the end of World War II. The church is currently focusing on upgrading its confessional bases within "Catholic" countries and gaining access to behavioral spheres that are central to the urban-industrial sector of international life. Earlier marks of membership—knowledge of catechism, baptism, regular ritual participation, and priestly obedience—are being increasingly overshadowed by criteria of Christian influence: worldly actions that reflect Christian ethics; mature spiritual judgment in spheres of behavior and decisionmaking; professional, artistic, and intellectual contributions of a Christian-Catholic nature to the life of total societies; a closer congruence between stated beliefs and daily behavior. Several factors have helped reduce the militant, proselytizing posture of the church. With the breakup of the traditional colonial systems the church has had to revise its conceptions of missionary purpose and the relationship of direct proselytization to political development. Also, the growth of the ecumenical idea has helped reduce, though not erase, the church's aggressive confessional posture toward other Christians working in Catholic-linked territories or in field situations in which Catholics hold a major interest. Identities at the Christian level, and in some cases at the broader religiosocial level, are replacing Roman Catholic ones. Finally, the church's capacity to hold its

own and to make headway with new status groups (workers, campesinos, urban poor, and other minorities) is increasingly recognized as dependent on its willingness to provide concrete programs of help, to build new types of social services, and to foster the development of modern institutions.

4) There is a growing appreciation by the church hierarchy of the needs, aspirations, and opinions of the Catholic rank and file. The church's deliberate efforts to mobilize the laity into an apostolic labor force, illustrated in the mandated programs of Catholic Action since the 1920s, indicated to officials that a delegation of responsibility could not be very effective unless some provisions were made for the layman to be heard and, eventually, to share in the distribution of power. On one level, the Council of Laymen, established by Pope Paul VI in 1967, provides a formal basis for bringing the voice of laity into the Roman Curia. In many dioceses and parishes laymen have become members of pastoral councils, and there are indications that this type of arrangement will become a part of church activities at the national level. Pastoral councils at this level have been developed in the Netherlands and planned in the United States. Thus, for the first time in its long history the church is developing a grass-roots participative principle for the laity which promises to align its religious and ecclesiastical life more closely with the laity and its needs. In addition, it opens the possibility of strengthening the voluntary, associational pattern which is so crucial for organized religions in urban, industrial society. This trend is accompanied by, and even stimulated by, a growth in the concept of "functionality" in organizational arrangement. As a result the needs or felt needs of the church's membership take on first-order importance, and the structure of the church will change to allow both an expression of these needs and their further development. One hundred years ago it was simply assumed that the pope or a bishop, even the parish priest in many situations, could confidently give authoritative decisions and lay down rules without any protest from below. That day has largely passed.

In short, the church today, in contrast with the church 100 years ago, is more integrated as a single system, more dependent on spiritual and social capacities for influence, more concerned with consolidation and competence than with numerical and territorial expansion, and more vulnerable to demands and influence of the rank and file. Taken together, these changes do not sustain a conclusion that the church is more influential or important today than it was a century ago. No single generalization is possible. Instead, it is necessary to look at specific arenas of institutional activity that hold the manifest interests of the church and to examine in each its structural and cultural capacities.

The central, or transnational, structures of the Roman Catholic church have begun to play more specialized roles in aggregating demands and giving normative support for universal human values. Forced to give up temporal political responsibilities, the transnational center of the church has gained more freedom to assert general stands on controversial issues and ethical problems. Through these processes the church has moved up in the hierarchy of social control toward a systemic position as a global pastor. At the same time the center has had to yield more autonomy and flexibility to its major field units. These freedoms have tended, in turn, to help these units anchor themselves more firmly in their respective environments and to connect in more suitable ways the felt needs of the members with the formal features of the church. As rank-and-file Catholics gain more recognition and influence in the operational work of the local church, they are more inclined to relate to the church voluntarily. This voluntarism shifts the basis of commitment from fear of transgressing rules to an interest in making corporate contributions. When this takes place, the member is prepared to move out into the secular world as a loyal, but autonomous, Christian. In short, the upward extension of the center from a more political level of the international system to a global, pastoral position at the religious level is being accompanied at the lower end of the church system by a new type of integration between the Catholic layman and secular society.

VI. Observations on the Nation-State Model

The nation-state has lost much of its earlier capacity to control its environment and to that extent it has become a less important unit for explaining both *intra*national and *inter*national patterns. However, we cannot make generalizations applicable to all nation-states but must think of identifying types of nation-states with particular attention to 1) the degree to which they are bound up with higher levels of coordination and control (e.g., military alliances, scientific communities, economic systems) and 2) the position of power or leadership they hold in those higher level systems. A nation-state that is closely linked with extranational systems and that holds key positions of power and prestige in those international systems is, in fact, no longer a nation-state but a transnational actor. Its internal division of labor, for example, extends beyond the national arena into various transnational spheres, and its "actions" in critical encounters have the backing and benefits of many sectors of the transnational system that it leads. The contemporary United States cannot be fruitfully studied as a bounded nation-state; instead, it must be studied as a transnational system in which the territory of the United States constitutes its symbolic center and major (but not exclusive) resource base. In earlier periods the features of the United States as a bounded geographical territory and its features as a social system coincided; space and structure mirrored each other. This is no longer true. While physical territory has remained nearly constant, the structural system of the United States has become transnational or extranational in many of its most important role systems.

One indication of these developments is the widespread growth of roles that are differentiated to handle the problems of promoting and defending the "Western capitalistic system" against strictly national interests. I would suggest, however, that many of the specialists in "technical diplomacy," communications media, military affairs, scientific activities, and political life are oriented to the further development of the Western system rather than to the specific welfare of the United States. Moreover, the United States cannot be "saved" without saving the transnational system and its main institutional features. This overlap of the United States as a concrete entity with the Western system as a transnational actor is one of the reasons why Americans who work transnationally to prop up the wider system are often misunderstood. As United States citizens they are symbolically aligned with the "national" interests of their sovereign government, yet their roles have principal relevance to the functioning of a major transnational system. By the same token it is clear that by holding the "center" position in the Western system national interests and transnational interests are intimately fused.

The situation is quite different for a nation-state that is minimally bound up with wider systems of control and coordination and holds low prestige and power in the international arena, for example, Australia. Its actions as a nation-state are much more "national," and in its encounters with external actors its gains or losses are much more dependent on its capacities as a nation-state rather than as a transnational actor. Although many social scientists still insist on "comparing states" as if they were equivalent units, this is unfruitful.[28] Unless the notion of social structure is expanded to encompass the relational patterns that national societies display in the international and transnational arenas, we cannot expect very much by way of "empirical laws" or theoretical illumination.

These brief remarks are perhaps sufficient to cast doubt on any abstract assertion about the significance of either "the" nation-state or "the" international system. Instead, it seems necessary to work with types of relational systems—competitive, collaborative, integrative—and then, for any given level, to identify the main actors and their structural features. In some instances the structural features of the main actors will be equivalent to the nation-state and, by implication, the nation-state will become an important explanatory variable. In other relational systems the actors will be in control of transnational resources and possess transnational capacities. For these systems the relevant explanatory level is transnational, not national.

Now it may be that increased interaction between the S-S and the S-G points in figure 2 of the introduction do erode the power of the nation-state. Yet, this perspective does not take us very far, mainly because the relational

[28] On this problem and other basic problems in comparative research see Ivan Vallier, ed., *Comparative Methods in Sociology* (Berkeley: University of California Press, 1971).

contexts within which the state is positioned are not brought into the model. Furthermore, there seems to be an implicit assumption that the quantity of S-S and S-G interaction is a good indication of systemic power.

Some nation-states, as centers of power and action, are losing ground in the international arena; others are not. The difference, however, is not due to variations in interaction between points S-S and S-G but to variations in the positions that nation-states occupy in crucial resource systems (within which I include centers of coordination and control, symbolic centers, and material resources). Those states that hold key positions in transnational resource systems can draw on, and to some degree mobilize, all the "funds" that the system encompasses, often with decisive advantages. At the same time such a nation-state has the obligation to defend and maintain the transnational system that it leads.

From this perspective the notion of competition between transnational actors and nation-states is misleading. A better distinction is one between actors that can operate as transnational control centers (thus being capable of organizing and allocating resources from many types of lower-order units) and those that cannot. The units that fight for these crucial transnational positions may be nation-states, churches, professional societies, or political movements. Moreover, it is not fruitful to think that the only important kinds of transnational centers are political since political power is only one kind of control. The number of transnational positions that will be competed for at a given time varies according to the extent of structural specialization in the role systems of societies and according to the number of major theological camps that are competing within the boundaries of the global culture.

Contemporary Revolutionary Organizations

J. Bowyer Bell

During the past century revolutionary organizations have, in the name of mankind, sought the violent transformation of the existing international framework. Their aim has been the liberation of nations submerged by fate or repressed by coercion and the destruction of the entire nation-state system, considered a passing phase of history. Even those revolutionary organizations dedicated to a specific national struggle have tended to see the triumph of their cause as a step toward a conflict-free world society in which the basic aspirations of all will have been achieved.[1] In the heyday of anticolonial revolts nationalism per se tended to dominate the ideology of the various movements. In the last decade, with fewer countries to liberate from a foreign oppressor and more to be liberated from domestic regimes supported by worldwide imperialism, the universal ideological context of the revolutionary struggle has become more pronounced. Today most, but by no means all, revolutionary movements proclaim an allegiance to world revolution; nevertheless, as in the past, most continue to act as covert governments or illegal armies, underground or in exile, and to represent not the universal but the particular. Such organizations may have deep sympathies, even specific alliances, with fellow national revolutionary organizations or legitimate governments, but they are often comparable, if not parallel, to normal international arrangements. Even the most militant movements in the vanguard of world revolution, despite all their paraphernalia of antinational ideology, are

J. Bowyer Bell is a research associate at the Center for International Affairs, Harvard University, Cambridge, Massachusetts.

[1] The basis for this essay is a seemingly indeterminable number of interviews with retired and practicing revolutionaries in North America, Western Europe, the Middle East, and Africa carried out during the past five years. For the most part and for obvious reasons research concerning covert organizations is largely qualitative. For a more extensive analysis of contemporary revolutionary movements see my *The Myth of the Guerrilla, Revolutionary Theory and Malpractice* (New York: Alfred A. Knopf, forthcoming), which also contains a selected bibliography from existing academic and polemic literature of revolution.

nearly always established on a national basis and act as alternative national regimes. At best, revolution in one country may be actually allied with similar revolutions, but rarely is it submerged in a fully integrated, universal transnational movement.

The result is that the revolutionary operates almost entirely as an actor within his national framework or as an exile from national power. His organization, a counterstate, aspires to achieve de facto national control from a self-proclaimed de jure status. His loyalties, concerns, and organizational activities are directed toward acquiring power in a specific national arena. His movement may be illegal, but his role is essentially similar to that of any national actor that seeks to provide an alternative power structure or regime. Like the regime he may seek allies outside the nation-state but for national purposes. Even if his movement is dedicated to the elimination of "nationalism" as an obstacle to a greater world society, he does not necessarily see any immediate contradiction between his national and revolutionary roles any more than does the priest who answers the demands of both Caesar and the church. Thus, there is not really any conflict between the "national" aspirations that absorb nearly all his attention and his revolutionary goals since the latter will be achieved partly as a result of the former.

When the nation-state is liberated but world revolution not yet accomplished, the movement may face unforeseen "contradictions." Successful revolutions that produce ideologically similar states—battles won in a world struggle—unexpectedly place severe strains on the concept of fraternal solidarity. To the dismay of Arab revolutionaries the two Ba'ath states of Iraq and Syria have become bitter opponents as have the two Yemeni republics. Then, too, there have been disconcerting ideological divisions within revolutionary ranks: The "mother cells" in Peking or Moscow propound contradictory doctrine. Even within specific national liberation battles the revolutionary troops often turn on each other, whether in the jungles of Angola or the streets of Amman. Nevertheless, the need for *a* revolutionary movement remains very great and the existence of a universal dream apparently compelling. In a previous generation Menahem Begin and the *Irgun Zvai Leumi* were satisfied to seek Israel, not a better and transformed world society, and General George Grivas and the National Organization of Cypriot Fighters (EOKA) sought *enosis,* union with Greece, not a classless millennium.[2] Contemporary revolutionaries, however, insist that they fight under a supranational banner. In this they do not necessarily differ greatly from many of their revolutionary ancestors of the nineteenth century who fought for the future in the ranks of the world proletariat or, in turn, from their predecessors who, whatever their

[2] Grivas accepted the similarity in the aspirations of EOKA and those of the Algerians, but as a pure nationalist and a Christian he denied the legitimacy of communist "national liberation" struggles as formulated by Mao Tsetung.

nationality, fought under the universal banner of the rights of man. The newer generation, largely huddled on the "red" Left of the political spectrum, has adopted, if not digested, world ideologies, however irrelevant, and has thereby joined—in theory—the world movement.

I. Organizational Efforts

To provide definition and to give form to the amorphous world revolutionary movement or movements various organizational efforts have been proposed or undertaken and various universal strategies suggested or initiated. The three prime advocates of revolution, Cuba, the People's Republic of China (Communist China), and the Union of Soviet Socialist Republics, have from the first sought to create webs of revolution but usually from a national base. As a result in some unliberated nation-states (e.g., Bolivia, Guatemala, and Venezuela) three parallel but exclusive parties exist, each claiming priority and each owing ideological allegiance, if nothing more, to the admired center—Moscow, Peking, or Havana. These centralizing structures, with or without a formal secretariat, are transnational organizations of national parties that generally recognize Peking, Moscow, or Havana as the first among equals. Universal ideologies that have not secured a power-base, i.e., a liberated nation-state, like the Anarchists or the Fourth (Trotskyite) International, have escaped centralization but at the cost of coherence and the benefits of a secure sanctuary.

All of these ideologically pure world organizations are amenable to analysis as transnational parties. Their ancestors are the various internationals and their coevals are the Christian Democratic and Socialist parties. None, however, is as universal as the Zionist movement that demanded the loyalty of "citizens" of many states to establish, or reestablish, a nation-state in Palestine. None is as peculiar as the Irish Republican Brotherhood invading Canada in the name of the invisible Irish republic. The traditional national party structure of revolution has become standard, although contemporary revolutionaries have sought new forms to carry revolution on to a higher world plane.

In the years after Fidel Castro's victory in 1959 the three major states that advocated revolution, Communist China, Cuba, and the Soviet Union, failed to cooperate in the name of world revolution. The only lasting organization of note that evolved out of various efforts was the Organization of the Solidarity of the Peoples of Africa, Asia, and Latin America, or "Tricontinental," founded in Havana in January 1966. Open to most revolutionary parties (i.e., Marxists-Leninists) Tricontinental has had regular conferences;[3] it issues a

[3] A very substantial number of revolutionary organizations are proclaimed Marxists-Leninists—an umbrella word for "good, radical guys." Despite the plethora of ideological publications churned out by revolutionary societies (the mimeograph still seems to be mightier than the AK-47), many revolutionaries have too often read one book—and the wrong one at that: The Irish Republican Army (IRA) should have read Begin and not Tom Barry in 1956, and Ernesto "Ché" Guevara is hardly the ideal guide for the Palestinian fedayeen.

wealth of publications and maintains a secretariat and various offices abroad. Tricontinental, however, has not succeeded in uniting all revolutionary factions. The Sino-Soviet split devastated the possibilities of revolutionary solidarity. The differences in Soviet and Cuban aspirations in Latin America also dissipated considerable revolutionary ardor. As the foundation for a coherent and centralized world revolutionary struggle Tricontinental has proven to be more of a facade to maintain the ideal of solidarity than a viable structure. Tricontinental is little more than a central office, a clearinghouse for propaganda, and an outward symbol of revolutionary idealism.

Most important, however, has been the development of what might be called the Tricontinental revolutionary gospel for the present anti-imperialist struggle. Together with a considerable amount of apocalyptic rhetoric—"Victory or Death!"—it presents specific universal rules for revolution. Based not on the old gospel of Karl Marx and Lenin or the apostates Mikhail Bakunin or Trotsky but on the testament of Mao Tsetung, Ho Chi Minh, Vo Nguyen Giap, Fidel Castro, et al., the new gospel has been ideologically comforting and emotionally satisfying.

Linked with the Tricontinental new gospel is an emphasis on the strategy of Ché Guevara. Guevara viewed the world divided between the submerged masses and the powerful imperialists, led by the United States. The imperialists can be defeated by a simultaneous series of peoples' wars instigated without the necessity of long political preparation and fought largely by peasant guerrillas spreading out from *focos* of insurrection. Guevara's strategy of guerrilla revolution built on Asian communist theorists and the Cuban experience. It has thus far had extensive appeal but no notable success. Just as the new gospel on which it is based has been open to deviant interpretation, this new strategy has often proven faulty in the field. Repeated failures—Argentina, Guatemala, Peru, and Venezuela—have led revolutionaries to extensive modification of this strategy and consequently to alternative methods of action: urban terror (in Brazil) or novel tactics such as kidnapping (in Guatemala and Uruguay). Nevertheless, the basic theory of guerrilla revolution evolved by Mao, practiced by Giap, successful in Algeria and Cuba, and perhaps misused by Guevara remains basic to most revolutionary thinking. Divisions are deep and disputation endless, but the inspiration of the gospel is undeniable. The guerrilla revolution has become the strategy par excellence, replacing the political insurrectionist approaches of Lenin or those of the Anarchist terrorists. Thus, despite bitter ideological differences and overt conflicts between the great revolutionary powers, there appears to be a relatively coherent, contemporary revolutionary strategy, difficult to apply and open to interpretation but offering the possibility of success.

Even if there is not a specific organizational structure for world revolution, the conviction of the committed is that there *is* a world revolutionary society, perhaps organized by national parties, perhaps in ideological disarray, but nevertheless real. Revolutionaries in Mozambique feel a solidarity with those in Laos, the People's Democratic Republic of Yemen (Southern Yemen), or Peru as long as the common ideology is the new gospel. Each feels that he fights one tentacle of the imperialist octopus; each is encouraged by the war in Indochina; each admires the same heroes (Giap and Castro), reads the same authors (Mao and Guevara), and leads much the same life for much the same purposes. Whatever their ideological differences revolutionaries, as professionals, have much in common.

Africa

In Africa many revolutionary organizations that maintain an existence as counterstates claim de jure existence and negotiate agreements, pacts, and even, in some cases, alliances without any visible indigenous base of operations. Thus, six of the liberation movements operating against the Portuguese—as revolutionary organizations, not as governments-in-exile—signed an alliance creating the Conference of National Organizations in the Portuguese Colonies (CONCP) with a secretariat, publicity offices, and a program of meetings and conferences. The three major CONCP movements have also negotiated military cooperation pacts with the South African National Congress (ANC) and the Zimbabwe African People's Union (ZAPU) in Rhodesia. Rivals of one or all of the CONCP-ANC-ZAPU bloc, the Zimbabwe African National Union (ZANU), the Pan-African Congress (PAC), the *Comité Revolucionário de Moçambique* (Coremo), and *Govérno Revolucionário de Angola no Exilio* (GRAE), have in turn formed pacts and alliances (ZANU-PAC and Coremo-GRAE). From time to time African liberation movements with political or military affinity, similar sponsors, or similar rivals hold summit conferences. In January 1969, for example, the CONCP-ANC-ZAPU group plus the South West Africa Peoples Organization (SWAPO) held a guerrilla summit conference in Khartoum attended by friends, sympathizers, and substantial delegations of revolutionary groups aligned with Moscow in the existing ideological disputes of the Left.[4] The Khartoum summit was something between an international conference of political parties and an international meeting of states. None of the guerrilla movements at Khartoum had as yet declared a government-in-exile, but all had acted and continued to act as counterstates.[5] While in 1963 the Organization of African Unity (OAU) had established a more inclusive National Liberation Committee with

[4] See "A Report of the International Conference in Support of the Peoples of the Portuguese Colonics and Southern Africa: Khartoum, January 18–20, 1969," *African Communist*, Second Quarter 1969 (No. 37), pp. 13–24.

[5] Only one African liberation movement, GRAE, has declared a government-in-exile. Most African states that have relations with the liberation movements treat them as "movements," not as "governments."

headquarters in Dar es Salaam to aid the struggle against white-supremacist governments, the liberation movements found the committee had few funds and even less power; each organization continues to act independently of the liberation committee, dealing directly with friendly movements and governments as was the case at Khartoum.[6]

Attempts to manipulate foreign revolution for national purposes—Germany transporting Lenin to Russia in his sealed railway car or the French alliance with the American revolutionaries—have long been recognized. It simply constitutes one state rearranging another state's society so that the successor regime will be more amenable to reason, less capable of harm, or more ideologically orthodox. By and large, but by no means entirely, those "manipulated" perceive the "interference" as advantageous.[7] They anticipate replacing or seizing the existing state structure and perhaps continuing such de facto relations, i.e., manipulation, on a de jure basis. Thus, on the day of victory the revolutionary organization anticipates making formal agreements with past friends and thereby transforms "manipulation" into a conventional state-to-state relationship. With few exceptions all of the African liberation movements optimistically foresee victory as the establishment of an African state in their particular area, Mozambique or Zimbabwe (Rhodesia), not a single, revolutionary African entity, much less a world revolutionary society. In fact, their ideas tend to stress the importance of the armed struggle in creating national consciousness and racial pride.[8] Such a transformation—a humiliated "native" turning into a proud Zimbabwe by fighting the white Rhodesians—intends or foresees merely one more nationalism despite the formal bows to the "One-Africa" concept. Thus, in Africa the major form of transnational interaction is the rather conventional one between legal governments

[6] In Africa those regimes which host liberation headquarters play the dominant part in the movements' contacts. Tanzania insists on monitoring shipments of arms and has taken action, largely unsuccessfully, to prevent intramovement divisions or to end undesirable practices which may be criminal or viewed as politically counterproductive. Zambia formally prohibits armed entry and too visible training and has also threatened expulsion as a result of intramovement divisions or undesirable practices like torture. Both governments prefer effective liberation movements that do not greatly disturb domestic peace or, particularly in the case of Zambia, make retaliation probable.

[7] The Mozambique Liberation Front (FRELIMO) long recognized that the rivalries between the Soviet Union and Communist China to "sponsor" the organization had caused the most severe internal strains. FRELIMO's president, Eduardo Mondlane, who had managed to acquire Western support as well, barely managed to prevent a split. After his assassination in February 1969 FRELIMO managed to struggle through until autumn before a split occurred. On the other hand, the long-range purposes of the Soviet Union and Communist China to win friends and hurt the white bastion to the south are not seen as particularly "dangerous" nor the prospect of Russian or Communist Chinese domination particularly likely. The belief that self-proclaimed friends can be managed even when supping with a short spoon is universal. In the Middle East *Al Fatah* was quite aware that Syrian aid during 1965–1967 was not directed toward a Palestinian goal but to embarrassing Jordan and Egypt. *Al Fatah* leaders did not mind, in fact, they largely supported, Syrian policy as long as the aid continued. After 1967 Syria, suspicious of *Al Fatah*'s first loyalty to the Palestinian cause and the nonideological front policy, sponsored a Palestinian Ba'ath fedayeen movement, *Al Sa'iqa*.

[8] This is the Fanon thesis that to be free and proud a man must struggle for liberation, not be presented with "independence."

and "illegal" parties. Relations between illicit groups and the organizations founded by them are, in general, either those of shadow governments or of ideologically aligned parties. Very few foresee the transformation of the existing African state system by revolution and so most prime loyalties are to the national party or the inchoate nation-state, not to Africa or the world at large.[9]

Latin America

Both Africa and Latin America have the same multitude of parties dividing and reuniting, the same delight in ideological disputation, and the same quarrels of personality and prejudice—although Latin America is free from tribal clash. In Latin America there are several major revolutionary currents—Castroite, Trotskyite, Maoist, Guevarist—along with the orthodox communists and a wide variety of independents. Only the most primitive continental organizational structures exist outside the Moscow-oriented communists, who are largely but not entirely adverse to the armed struggle, and the Castroite network based in Havana. The Havana-based Latin American Solidarity Organization (OLAS) ties together the major groups of Castroites and is a more effective centralizing factor than those available to the Fourth International or to Maoist splinter groups. Finally, some coherence is supplied by a small number of sympathetic continental publications. In balance, however, Latin America is less coherently organized than Africa where the various revolutionary movements sign formal alliances and the special liberation committee of the OAU provides a revolutionary framework.

There is another notable difference between Latin American and African revolutionary movements. The concept of "One Latin America" is less alien to Latin Americans than the concept of "One Africa" is to Africans. Ché Guevara's final bungling Bolivian mission, for example, made a faltering attempt to establish several Andean *focos* which, when ignited, would create an Andean revolution, not simply a Bolivian or Peruvian insurrection, and lead to another Vietnam by tying down more American troops, bleeding the center of imperialism, and thus contributing a major victory to the ultimate triumph of world revolution. Just what Guevara foresaw as the structure of successful revolution is as vague as his "Two, Three Vietnams" strategy. Yet, in Latin America, more than in Africa, there is a feeling of unity among revolutionaries of various persuasions. Once the revolution triumphs, the Latin Americans may be somewhat less committed to micronationalism—e.g., a

[9] All the liberation movements in southern Africa recognize that they have a single opponent and that victory probably cannot be won in a single area—Angola or Mozambique. Rather than concentrate on one area, assuming that this was ideologically and militarily possible, most movements have accepted the strategy of many wounds—various guerrilla fronts producing greater attrition than a single blow. In practice, except for the ANC-ZAPU alliance and to a lesser degree the ZAPU-FRELIMO agreement, tactical cooperation has been nil; in some cases, particularly in Angola, the competing movements have fought each other.

liberated Bolivia—and somewhat more interested in continental liberation.[10] Latin American revolutionaries do not have to become as involved in nation building by means of the armed struggle as do African revolutionaries and can, therefore, have a broader vision of a continental future.

These revolutionary visions of the future have not, however, been closely defined or extensively articulated. The theory of national liberation in Latin America, under whatever guise, resembles that of nineteenth-century nationalism: Once the nation-state is "liberated" all problems will disappear in the new revolutionary society. In Latin America some may feel that, as the canon promises, the state may wither away; most others feel that after the revolution succeeds the problem of the nation-state will simply not be particularly relevant. In the meantime there exists an unarticulated, fraternal society of revolutionaries, bound as it has been for generations by similar aspirations, often joint exile, and a common heritage of political action. The loyalties of this society often transcend specific political differences and are probably more significant than the various continental structures like OLAS.

In Latin America, then, relations between revolutionaries are relations between members of similar parties conveniently labeled with national titles combating similar opponents conveniently labeled nation-states. One can find however, as in Africa, many Latin American revolutionaries who are devout nationalists and whose first loyalty usually will be to their own nation-state—depending on what question they are asked or what sacrifice they are required to make. Yet, unlike the African variety, Latin American revolutionary nationalism rests on a nationalist tradition as well as on a tradition that stresses Latin American unity and a rediscovered Indian heritage. This tradition of unity has, however, been limited to a Latin American context. While some lip service is given to the future revolutionary society beyond the bounds of Latin America, Ché Guevara's expedition to the Congo has been the only transcontinental action on a level beyond fraternal greeting.

That Guevara and a group of Cubans did, in fact, go to Africa to fight for the revolution indicates that the localism of Africa and Latin America, the national particularism of the latter and the continental isolation of the former, is not complete. The older and more conventional revolutionary parties, still organized around the national delegation and often at the call of the "mother" state's ambitions, had little relevance for a man like Guevara who was not only beyond parties but also beyond the lures of nationalism. Wherever injustice and oppression existed, as defined by Guevara, there all men should fight under whatever was the friendly, local flag. Since none could be free until the nexus of oppression, i.e., the United States, could be eliminated,

[10] This is largely an intuitive—certainly not a quantitative—judgment based on conversations with those involved. The Africans, never having had nation-states, stress nation building through the armed struggle far more than a distant, if desirable, "One Africa."

Guevara's strategy was to begin revolution everywhere and hope that it would ignite often enough to entangle the United States in "Two, Three Vietnams." Then, in the fullness of time, bearded and brave, the new generation would come down from its various Sierra Maestras and transform the world.

This doctrine had a certain charismatic, simplistic appeal as a strategy of goodwill and fraternal unity, but it led only to one tactical disaster after another. The revolution did not "catch" in the Congo, in the various *focos* in Latin America, or any place else. Yet Guevara, rather than the staid and comfortable bureaucracies of revolutionary-socialism, for the first time in 50 years introduced the practice of permanent revolution, long hallowed in word and ignored in deed even by purist Peking. By strength of will alone Guevara sought to drag revolution from the nationalist morass, great-power domination, and narrow regional interest to the high ground of brotherhood. There were many to applaud the effort to universalize the struggle but few in Latin America or elsewhere to follow his example.

During the past generation there have been few causes that have attracted international volunteers in the name of an ideological crusade. Despite Guevara there have not been international brigades such as those in Spain in the thirties. Individuals have been attracted to alien revolutionary causes and sympathetic, self-seeking governments have offered "volunteers"; but most revolutionary organizations fighting for national liberation have been exclusive, fearful of contaminating the purity of their cause by "internationalizing" their armed struggle. Efforts have been made, for example, in Latin America during the fifties, to form international brigades, but their overall impact has been minimal and the concept ill received. Since many revolutions are guerrilla based, the technical difficulties of absorbing many alien volunteers are great—international brigades are only useful in brigade-size wars. There has often been strategic or tactical cooperation between like-minded revolutionaries, for example, during the communist insurrections in Asia in 1948, but revolution by an organization without a national base, without aspirations as an alternative nation-state, has been rare indeed. Even Guevara's foray into the Congo was in the specific name of a specific national revolutionary movement. His Cubans were volunteers in another's cause even if they saw it as their own. Success would not have dissolved the Congo but only turned it into a mother cell for further struggles of national liberation. In one area of the world, however, revolutionary organizations are dedicated to the elimination of the existing nation-state structure, not simply to the substitution of allied, ideologically pure, and liberated states in the traditional framework.

The Arab World

The Arab world has for centuries harbored the dream of a pan-Arab nation stretching from the Indus River to the Atlantic Ocean. Such an Arab nation, though created by a variety of contradictory means, would override the various schismatic differences of religion, language, race, economics, and politics. It would have a universal character, incorporating in an as yet vague form true Arab unity. Definitions of the obstacles to unity have varied greatly as have the means used to achieve it, but existing local or parochial interests have been regarded as the prime obstacles, only occasionally superseded by the manipulation of distant powers. Essentially, Arab revolutionary organizations in the mid-twentieth century have attacked existing Arab political structures and regimes as obstacles to immediate unity. Once in power they then perpetuate their own existence as the basis for further unity. This strategy of unity is seen as a reverse, but creative, mitosis: Individual states swallow each other until a universal nation-state results. Thus, under whatever formula, the various Arab ministates will be ultimately combined. This probably was, for example, the strategy behind the creation of the United Arab Republic in 1958 and the Federation of Arab Republics in 1971.[11] The relentless failure of the antimitosis strategy has not persuaded existing powers that the road to unity lies elsewhere than in universal Arab conversion to specific existing organizations or ideologies. All roads in Arab politics—the way of the Ba'ath, Iraqi or Syrian, the true path of Islamic purity, the fashionable route of socialism as espoused by Gamal Abdel Nasser—will lead to unity even if the parallel ways often lead instead to open conflict. Thus, almost all Arab political figures act part of the time as Arab unifiers since the ultimate and ideal, if distant, goal is unity—a unity that will first deny, if not disguise, the particular and then merge all in one.

There have regularly been, however, ideologies that sought not to become the central cell of ultimate unity but to displace, hopefully simultaneously, all existing structures defined as obstacles to the Arab nation. The Ba'ath, for example, saw their ideals as universally applicable, although, given the opportunity, they were willing to seize power in one area under the assumption that localization and responsibility would not dilute their universal appeal. After a generation the ideals of the Ba'ath still have some general attraction, but the narrow and self-interested policies of the two wrangling Ba'ath governments in Iraq and Syria, the decline in the already vague intellectual content of the ideology, and the disappearance of the early charismatic leaders have reduced Ba'ath revolutionaries to apologists for or appointees of specific, and not particularly revolutionary, regimes. The far more militant Arab Na-

[11] There are two conservative strategies for unity as well. One of these, that of the Moslem Brotherhood, should probably be considered revolutionary since it seeks to overturn the existing "atheistic regimes" in the name of a universal Islamic state. The Moslem Brotherhood is banned in almost all Arab states and is viewed by Arab radicals as an anachronistic, reactionary movement. The traditional regimes have sought unity through the strategy of federation, either dynastic (as was the case with Iraq and Jordan) or institutional (as is the case with the League of Arab States or the Trucial states). Neither the Islamic nor the federal road has led any nearer to the goal than has the strategy proposed by the revolutionaries.

tional Movement of George Habash has tended to fill the extremist vacuum.

Urging freedom, unity, and socialism, the Arab National Movement, much like the Ba'ath, sought the elimination of all the existing structures, orthodox, revolutionary, or colonial. Successful only in Southern Yemen, the movement even there found that unity with the Yemen Arab Republic was prevented, among other reasons, by doctrinal differences. After the 1967 Arab-Israeli War, the Palestinian-dominated movement reconsidered and accepted a new strategy: The road to unity lay through the Palestine gates; the previous attacks on mininationalism and Palestinian parochialism were to a degree unwarranted; victory in Palestine would simultaneously transform the Arab world and create an Arab nation. The victory in Palestine could and would be secured not by the existing—and discredited—Arab regimes but through a general transformation of the Arab masses who would, in conjunction with the Palestinians, sweep out the Israelis and found not only a free Palestine but also the single Arab nation.[12] Habash and the members of the Arab National Movement perceive their "party" as a revolutionary organization within an as yet unarticulated Arab nation. Its emergence will eliminate both foreign and indigenous oppression; the former is defined as the state of Israel, an imposed imperialist puppet, and the latter is defined as the existing, discredited Arab political and economic institutions. In Habash's headquarters his opponents in Amman and Cairo are privately, if not publicly, defined as local, anachronistic, if persistent, power barons who prevent the inevitable moment of unity. Habash sees the entire Arab world as a single nation waiting to be born through the armed Palestinian struggle. As an "Arab Marxist-Leninist" he would anticipate continued fraternal intercontinental cooperation with his ideological allies after victory but not the disappearance of the Arab nation—much less the Palestinian nation—as a separate and special entity.

Whatever Habash may claim, it is apparent that a revolutionary movement actively engaged in undermining (either by subversion or rebellion) a dozen recognized regimes is playing a significant transnational role. It is doubtful if there is a single Arab regime, outside Southern Yemen, which has not now or in the recent past jailed members of Habash's movement to protect a "legitimate" nation-state. While Habash's movement claims to act as the germ of an all-Arab counterstate, the existing regimes view his activities much as the regimes in Latin America regard Castro's campaign of subversion—an effort by a proclaimed revolutionary to put his allies in power.

[12] The organizational structure of the Arab National Movement is as confused as most other things in the Middle East. Apparently in 1966 Habash organized the Popular Front for the Liberation of Palestine (PFLP), basically the Palestinian branch of the Arab National Movement, which has since split into various personal and ideological fragments. Outside the PFLP elsewhere in the Middle East the movement is at present of minimal importance, more a state of mind than an organization, except in Southern Yemen which is somewhat isolated from main Arab currents.

II. Transnational Revolutionary Action

Most revolutionary organizations thus aspire to act as counterstates until the moment of power when their aspirations become reality and their high command or central committee begins to operate as a recognized government. During the armed struggle, however, the organization, which may be a broad-based front, an underground army, or an exiled commando column, acts as a private government.[13] Despite the domination of Guevara's insurrection by non-Bolivians even the few men in his *foco* conceived of themselves as an alternative to the regime in La Paz. At the same time, since many of the movements have deep ideological affinities with other revolutionary organizations and governments, they also act as integrated leadership units of a transnational revolutionary society of the masses, of the peasants and workers, of the oppressed and scorned. These transnational contacts, though seldom given more structure than Tricontinental conferences or the exchange of fraternal delegations, retain a high level of national feeling.

Only a few revolutionaries like Guevara and Habash have carried domestic revolution across national boundaries as a matter of ideology and policy, although some, like the ANC inside Rhodesia, have fought joint campaigns as a matter of necessity. Most movements find "revolution in one country" a sufficient challenge. The "bishops of revolution" are national clerics, not institutionalized nuncios of a single, formal, universal church.

Those movements, however, which have explored the possibilities of transnational violence have produced spectacular results. The ability to carry the armed struggle beyond national boundaries in the name of national ends without necessarily remaining hostage to retaliation has proven an exciting option for several movements. As an invisible counterstate the movement is difficult to punish in normal ways even for international crimes. Thus, the PFLP has seized and destroyed international airliners and largely evaded retribution. This transnational strategy is much like the Irish invasion of Canada, the *Irgun* blowing up the British embassy in Rome, or the Cuban refugees trying to shell the United Nations. Perhaps revolutionaries, like scholars, have grasped

[13] The organization of contemporary revolution has tended to follow one of several relatively distinguishable courses: 1) the front policy which eschews ideological commitment and combines political and military leadership in a single command; 2) the military-core, or at least the party-militant, organized as an "army" that also makes political decisions; and 3) the political center which directs military acts. By and large, the three descend in size from the front to the political-revolutionary unit. As often as not the revolutionary organization can be a blend of the three or operate under special circumstances (EOKA under Grivas in Cyprus was almost purely military, organizationally largely separate from the political center of Archbishop Makarios III in exile). The most effective variety of revolutionary organization during the armed struggle may be found faulty or irrelevant once power is achieved (in Southern Yemen the military high command simply began running the country while in Cyprus the exiled Makarios was brought back as president of a totally new government and Grivas was sent into exile, at least temporarily). Essentially, whatever the nature of the revolutionary organization, until the moment of recognition the movement acts as a counterstate even if its only activity is guerrilla warfare.

the interrelated, transnational direction of the world that they have so long proclaimed ideologically. At present the incidence of transnational violence is insufficient to provide a base for significant analysis. In the past such revolutionary tactics have seldom played the major part in any armed struggle.

Most of the activities of revolutionary movements can be examined nearly as easily as those of legitimate states or parties, not always adverse to sponsoring occasional transnational violence themselves. Although actors without national ties are relatively rare, revolutionary movements in their peculiar position as private governments—counterstates, illegal members in good standing of a world revolutionary society—still must by definition have more transnational contacts than de jure, if revolutionary, governments. Some of these contacts differ little from conventional diplomatic ties; others are special to the revolutionary world; and several are almost without national counterparts.

The purest, least nation-bound relationship is that with the world movement. But since the "world movement" is difficult to define, these ties are more emotional than organizational. The real ties are those to the mother cell of revolution or to allies in the field. The latter can be negotiated to present a single united front in one battle area, as the Palestinian fedayeen have done, or to draw together those in different areas with the same or similar foe, as the African liberation movements have sought to do. Efforts to move to a higher plane and to tie together all revolutionaries, even those in a single continent, have been successful only if they have excluded all movements of incompatible ideological color. Thus, the only real relationships between revolutionary movements are agreements between like-minded parties for mutual aid and comfort or between an illicit alternative regime and a friendly legitimate ally.

III. Government-Movement Relations

While most transnational contacts parallel more conventional relations, the contacts between a legitimate state and a revolutionary movement are an exception.[14] This transnational relationship between the revolutionaries and

[14] With several notable exceptions most of the active revolutionary organizations accessible to study have exiled-based headquarters. The result is a great variety of host-state–revolutionary-movement relationships, sufficient, in fact, to serve as subject matter for an extensive dissertation. These relationships range from intimate friendship to total opposition: 1) The revolutionaries' ally may be an enthusiastic host dedicated to the revolutionary cause ideally and/or pragmatically—for example, Syria's support of *Al Fatah,* 1965–1967; 2) the host state may be theoretically enthusiastic toward the movement but pragmatically reluctant to assume the cost of sponsorship—Jordan's toleration of *Al Fatah,* 1967–1970; 3) the host state may be neutral, pursuing a policy of benign neglect for specific advantage—France's attitude toward the *Irgun,* 1946–1948, and toward the Palestinian fedayeen, 1968–1970; 4) the host state may evidence legalistic disapproval so that revolutionary exiles may exist but not function effectively without risk—the present situation of the anti-Castro Cubans in the United States; 5) the host state, considering the exiles enemies of the regime, prohibit operations of any kind—for example, Vichy France and the Spanish republicans.

their ally or allies is most vital since few movements act in isolation or without sanctuaries. Often the ally, as the dominant partner, can manipulate the relationship from a safe distance as the regimes in Moscow, Peking, and Havana have done. At times the revolutionaries' dedication to a mutual but embarrassing cause can hamper the legitimate ally's freedom of action as was the case with Grivas and Greece. When the revolutionaries are based on the allied regime's territory, complications and strains are inevitable. Usually the alliance is not only between unequal partners but also between partners with different priorities. At rare times, particularly when the revolutionary cause is identical or nearly so with the aspirations of the host state's population, the "normal" symbiotic host-exile relationship may be all but reversed, and the official regime becomes little more than a legitimate facade for a revolutionary base dominated by the desires of the exiles. This has increasingly been the case in Jordan and to a degree in Lebanon since 1967.

Fearful of revolt, King Hussein of Jordan has been forced to tolerate the provocative and turbulent presence of the fedayeen. The fedayeen were not interested in day-to-day government, issuing postage stamps or running the sewerage system. They only wanted Hussein to administer a revolutionary base camp even if it meant that Jordan were destroyed as a result of their own armed struggle. Thus, with vast popular support and a cause supposedly Hussein's own, their Palestinian counterstate rivaled the king's legitimate regime but without "legitimate" responsibilities. Intricately balanced loyalties in Lebanon divide those who place a first or high priority on the fedayeen campaign at the expense of Lebanese national interests and those who see a stable Lebanon as more important, even to the fedayeen, than a futile if admirable campaign against the power of Israel. Lebanon risks civil war in too closely monitoring the fedayeen. Because of the influx of Arab refugees and the universal Arab appeal of the fedayeen neither Jordan nor Lebanon have been able to gain full control of the exile base even, in the case of Jordan, after a small "civil" war.[15]

Elsewhere host governments have responded to the presence of exiled revolutionaries either by creating their own variety, as the Syrians have done, or by regulating the revolutionaries' activities and contacts, as both Zambia and

There are, of course, deviant cases. The IRA, illegal in both Northern Ireland and the Republic of Ireland, is "tolerated," when quiescent, in the latter but never in the former.

Relationships between host governments and revolutionary movements are often a factor of the strength of the movement. Similarly, the range is considerable—from a weak movement or one which has failed to gain indigenous support, given sinecure out of ideological loyalty and minor hope of future gain, to a movement that dominates or threatens to dominate the host government.

[15] Curiously, a previous "Palestinian example" exists. The grand mufti of Palestine, Haj Amin Husseini, exerted an almost controlling influence over Iraqi politics *after* his flight from the British Mandate as a wanted rebel in 1939 and his second flight from Baghdad in the face of British intervention in April–May 1941. The purpose of this manipulation, briefly successful, was to create an anti-British, anti-Zionist Iraqi base to wage a campaign for an Arab Palestine. As an exile in Germany he was given funds and passing notice but had reached the far end of the host-exile relation in a single bound.

Tanzania have done. Even when the population of the host country is not dedicated to the revolutionary cause, the presence of a large body of armed men, perhaps deeply frustrated by their own armed struggle, can clearly be a present danger. Thus, host states without ample internal security are usually the most eager for the revolutionaries to achieve an indigenous base and thereby ease the strains of revolutionary loyalty.[16]

Most revolutionary movements want their relations with sympathetic governments legitimated as rapidly as possible since the difference between supplicant and partner, even if a minor partner, is considerable. This is often why governments-in-exile are declared and yet not recognized unless a measure of de facto control really exists. The virtues of being a de facto supplicant rather than a de jure partner are obvious to the host ally as are the dangers of accepting responsibility for an illicit transnational relationship by transforming it into a legitimate international transaction. Thus, the elimination of the transnational host relationship is a consummation devoutedly to be desired by the revolutionary movement. The shift toward legitimacy is an outward symbol of revolutionary progress.

IV. Conclusion: Revolutionary Actors and Transnationalism

The major curiosity is that every revolutionary organization aspires to eliminate the necessity for most "revolutionary" transnational contacts as rapidly as possible and to begin acting as a normal, if militant, government no longer dependent on the mesh of world revolutionary society or the uncertain world of illicit agreements, minisummits, and secret conferences. The overwhelming desire of every revolutionary organization is to achieve power.

The refusal of most revolutionary movements to submerge their national differences in the sea of world revolution is indeed inexplicable if the world is rushing toward a new transnational tribe. The revolutionaries may be an aberration or an anachronism, but they most certainly are not yet truly devoted to transnationalism. Since revolutionaries, whatever their ultimate goals, must achieve political power in order to instigate the desired changes in society and since political power is largely divided into nation-state units, their immediate goal is obviously to snatch control of one of the units. With rare exceptions the prime political loyalty of most citizens is to the nation-state. Pragmatically, the revolutionaries have to be nationalists, although they are generally so by conviction rather than by convenience. Politically, the man without a nation-state is still rare. There is ample evidence to show that the attractions of nationalism have grown rather than diminished, and more submergent peoples—Bretons, Ibos, Welsh, Kurds—have seemed intent on

[16] Some revolutionary allies have, of course, no loyalty except to their own regime. Iran, for example, has aided the Kurdish revolt in Iraq while denying their own Kurds self-determination and information about the activities of Iraqi Kurds.

emerging into statehood. On the other hand, no nation organized as a state, with the possible exception of that on Zanzibar, has dissolved itself willingly or for a long period into a larger entity. Unlike a labor union, an automobile manufacturer, or a scientific society, the revolutionary movement gains by a concentration on an exclusive nationality, even if for world revolutionary purposes, as long as the nation-state holds the people's first political loyalty. To broaden the scope of the struggle is to risk dilution; to narrow the scope offers the hope of success.

Success for revolutionary movements has been illusive despite the ills of the world, the fragility of so many legitimate regimes, and their own dedication. Thus, the failure of most movements to win their battles in the world struggle assures the continued opportunity to examine revolutionaries as transnational actors. The number of organizations presently committed to the armed struggle boggles the imagination: four covert armies in Northern Ireland; two-dozen exile revolutionary headquarters in Algiers; guerrilla wars in Chad, Laos, the Philippines, the Sudan, and most Latin American countries; violent separatists in Wales, Brittany, and the Basque provinces of Spain; and bombs in airplanes, police stations, and suitcases. Revolution is clearly a growth area, but the prospects for an effective bid for world revolution by a transnational organization still look no better than they have in the past. If the future of revolution remains relatively surprise-free, the kinds of transnational contacts now existent will not be greatly transformed.

Revolutionary movements are usually transnational by necessity, not by design. The prospects of a truly transnational revolution look as bleak as ever since neither the hold of national loyalty nor the particular ambitions of various revolutionary sponsors seem to be on the decline. Surely, with so many movements competing for laurels and with so many inefficient and brutal regimes, there should be one or two successes which would remove the odd movement from the scope of transnational investigators. The long-range prognosis for the investigator remains good. Revolutionary organizations that seek to move to a higher plane, leaving behind their transnational relations, should be with us for a long time, a boon to scholars if not to international stability.

PART III

ISSUE AREAS

THE essays in part III describe systems of interaction—"the ways the game is played"—in specific issue areas. While the essays in part II focus on different types of transnational organizations, the following essays approach transnationalism from a different direction. Without prejudging their importance we want to discover the significance of transnational organizations and interactions in regard to various types of subject matter.

We asked the authors in part III to identify and assess the relative importance of different types of actors and interactions. We asked them to describe the relationships between transnational actors, governments, and intergovernmental organizations and how these relationships have changed over time. We asked them to speculate on the factors that might account for variation over time and among issue areas. Finally, we asked them to assess the effects of transnational relations on the allocation of values—"who gets what"—in their area.

Part III does not really test the hypotheses implicit in these questions. There are too few essays, and our choice of subjects was affected in large part by our knowledge of the availability of able (and willing!) authors. Nonetheless, the essays paint a broad picture of the importance of transnational actors and trends in transnational relations in a variety of issue areas.

Most of the authors agree that transnational activity has increased in their issue areas. This is particularly clear in the areas of international finance and air transport. Although this increase has not been as marked in the nuclear energy field, Lawrence Scheinman describes trends that indicate increased transnational activity in the future. On the other hand, Robert W. Cox points out that while transnational economic activity by trade unions has increased, their transnational political activity has declined.

The importance of transnational relations varies greatly between issue areas. It seems most important in economic matters. Lawrence Krause indicates that the size of liquid assets in the hands of some twenty banks can overwhelm monetary authorities in the short run. Robert L. Thornton provides examples of pilots' associations and airlines sometimes prevailing over governments. Cox indicates the way in which trade unions and multinational business enterprises working together may defeat the objectives of governments.

Diana Crane, Edward Miles, and Scheinman, on the other hand, see governments more firmly in control of their issue areas. Nonetheless, transnational relations are important. Crane portrays the evolution of transnational activity beginning with an informal network or "invisible college" of scientists who form nongovernmental organizations when the flow of information exceeds the capacities of the simple informal structure. These transnational organizations sometimes coordinate their lobbying activities to change governmental policies—for example, Miles cites the involvement of radio astronomers in frequency allocation. At the same time, however, scientists lack material resources and must obtain the favor of governments to carry out large-scale research. Governments, in turn, must increasingly rely on intergovernmental and international nongovernmental organizations to coordinate large-scale research.

We expected to find the role of transnational actors in areas of national security less important because governments would insist on tighter controls. To some extent this is borne out by the essays. Thornton indicates that airlines are weakest vis-à-vis governments when national security issues are at stake. Miles argues that the allocation of radio frequencies is state-centric because of its high security content. The political activities of trade unions that threaten the security of weak governments are precisely those which Cox says have declined. Scheinman finds less transnational activity in his issue area—one which is closely related to security.

Finally, it is worth noting that several authors point to the importance of technological change as a factor increasing transnational activity in their issue areas. Krause and Cox emphasize the way in which improved telecommunications have created effective private decision domains in banking and industrial production that extend beyond national boundaries. Miles illustrates how corporations able to profit from technological change have rendered ineffective an intergovernmental agreement on the extent of national control of the seabed and have posed important problems regarding the control of satellite communications. Scheinman indicates that changes in reactor technology will make this area more difficult for governments to control in the future.

These essays indicate that the poker game of world politics is played differently at different tables. The stakes and winnings differ from table to table. Transnational actors sit at all the tables but the hands they hold vary greatly. The essays in part III allow us to look over a few shoulders. As any kibitzer knows, that is a first step toward learning the rules of the game.

Private International Finance

Lawrence Krause

I. Introduction

The major international economic institutions established after World War II, such as the International Monetary Fund (IMF) and the General Agreement on Tariffs and Trade (GATT), had the economic disintegration of the Great Depression as their historical heritage. The lessons learned from that experience were twofold: National governments can and should take an active role in achieving national economic stabilization objectives, and one state's economic policies can and often will work at cross-purposes with those of another. The role of international institutions in such circumstances is to harmonize national policies so that international conflict is avoided.

The architects of the IMF, who met at the United Nations Monetary and Financial Conference at Bretton Woods in 1944, were charged to bring order into postwar international financial relations. In particular, they were asked to establish a monetary framework that would promote liberal rules regarding international trade and payments. During the 1930s a destructive practice had arisen whereby countries excessively depreciated their exchange rate in order to promote exports and inhibit imports, thus increasing domestic employment. The employment gain was, however, at the expense of more unemployment in other countries which then either retaliated in kind or adopted other types of restrictions. Naturally, the operational goals of the IMF became the promotion of exchange stability, the maintenance of orderly exchange arrangements between members, and the avoidance of competitive exchange depreciations.

It is important to recognize that the Bretton Woods Agreement represents a state-centered view of international finance. National governments through their power to spend money, determine taxes, and control financial institu-

Lawrence Krause, a member of the Board of Editors of *International Organization*, is a senior fellow of the Brookings Institution, Washington, D.C. The views expressed in this essay are his own and do not necessarily reflect the views of other staff members, officers, or trustees of the Brookings Institution.

tions were thought to be fully responsible for, if not completely in control of, national economies. Agreement between national governments was thought to be not only the necessary condition but also the sufficient condition for achieving international financial harmony. While doubts existed as to whether governments would be willing to show the required degree of international cooperation because of competing domestic needs, there was little doubt that governments had sufficient power to do so with well-known policy tools. However, the state-centered view of international finance no longer appears adequate to explain the current condition of international finance.

The kind of international cooperation between governments which the IMF was designed to promote is now taken for granted. Economic depression and fragmentation no longer exist, but international financial problems remain. The problems of today are no doubt less severe than those of the 1930s, but they are vexatious nonetheless. Ironically, current problems may have evolved because of the very ability of national governments individually and collectively to solve the problems of the earlier era through the IMF. Widespread depression has been replaced by widespread but uneven inflation. Exchange rate instability has been replaced by excessive stability of exchange rates. The postwar period has been one of economic success, but with progress have come new problems.

The decade of the 1950s witnessed some of the major changes that characterize today's scene. With complete economic recovery from the war the governments of Western industrial countries moved away from controls of private economic activity. Exports and imports were freed from licensing requirements. Business firms were permitted to borrow from and lend money to foreigners. Rather than being forced to channel all transactions through central banks, financial institutions were permitted to deal directly in foreign money markets. Furthermore, the major countries formally established currency convertibility in the IMF which legally bound them to convert their domestic currency into foreign currencies (and the reverse) for all current account transactions—like the exporting and importing of goods and services—at fixed exchange rates. Also, most industrial countries ended their discriminatory treatment of different national currencies in international financial transactions.

These policy changes, along with the growth of liquid assets in private hands, have led to substantial private short-term capital flows between countries. Private capital flows can have great influence on domestic economic conditions and the balance-of-payments positions of countries, possibly undermining governmental policies. Governments have found, however, that they cannot prevent "disruptive" capital flows without reinstating all the old restrictions which had previously been liberalized. Thus, governments have come to the frustrating realization that the only way that they can fully control their economies is by interfering with private economic decisions to such an extent that they will jeopardize economic prosperity—the very goal they are seeking.

II. Economics and Consequences of Private Capital Flows

Money is the most fungible of all commodities. It can be transmitted instantaneously and at low cost—indeed, with the mere stroke of a hypothetical pen. It can be inventoried without physical deterioration and without warehousing cost. It can change its identity easily and can be traced only with great effort, if at all. These characteristics work to the disadvantage of governments in their efforts to tax, regulate, and control economic activity.

Recent technological advances have improved the efficiency of international financial transfers and have thus made the situation even worse from the point of view of governments. Rapid means of personal travel have enabled financial managers of different countries to become intimately acquainted with one another. The degree of personal trust and camaraderie that has evolved exceeds that achieved at the governmental level even though international cooperation between monetary officials is the most advanced of any governmental activity. Advances in telegraphic and voice communications have facilitated the movement of massive amounts of funds and reduced the transfer to a matter of mere routine.

The most significant development in this field has, however, been the widening of the horizons of businessmen. In all advanced countries business leaders view their markets in terms of a constantly increasing number of countries. Trade liberalization and the factors mentioned earlier have brought this about. As a result the financing of trade and investment has been internationalized. Financial firms have generally followed or at times led business firms in direct international involvement. This has meant that financial impulses have spread from country to country, affecting the real economy as well as financial markets. If, for example, monetary conditions ease in the United States, American investors are likely to look abroad for assets of higher yield and thereby spread United States monetary ease to other countries, causing stimulative economic impulses in its wake.[1]

The primary consequence of large private international capital flows is the unplanned and possibly uncontrollable integration of the financial markets of industrial countries. Governments have witnessed developments in money markets which have gradually eroded their ability to control the use of monetary instruments for domestic economic needs. The experience of the Federal Republic of Germany (West Germany) in 1969 is a case in point.

[1] This essay was completed prior to the eruption of the international financial crisis during the spring of 1971. Such crises, as elaborated in other sections of this essay, are inherent in the present international monetary system. The following illustration of West German difficulties fits the current situation almost without alteration.

Early in 1969 West German authorities recognized that restraining measures would be needed for domestic purposes. Foreign and domestic demand for West German goods was rising rapidly, labor shortages were developing despite a large inflow of foreign workers, order backlogs were growing alarmingly long, and prices were beginning to rise.[2] The West German competitive position was not eroding because prices in competing countries were rising as fast as, or faster than, those in West Germany and, therefore, international competition could not be counted on to restrain the incipient inflation. The West German balance of payments was basically quite strong since large current account surpluses were being recorded, but West German authorities were managing to keep the current account surplus from increasing domestic liquidity by encouraging large outflows of long-term capital. Fiscal policy was used to restrain the domestic economy as the government was able to achieve a cash surplus in its domestic budget; but fiscal policy could not do the entire job, and monetary policy was needed to reinforce the restraint.

The Deutsche Bundesbank tried to increase monetary stringency by a series of moves like increasing the reserve ratios of the banks and raising the central bank interest rate. As monetary tightness began to be felt, however, West Germans became less willing to lend to foreigners and private foreign money was attracted into West Germany. As long as foreign funds were available, the liquidity of West German firms could not be effectively squeezed by the Bundesbank. Adding to the difficulties of the Bundesbank was the belief among speculators that the West German exchange rate was going to be appreciated, despite all official denials. This led to waves of speculative inflows of liquidity which, in the first instance, the Bundesbank was forced to monetize.[3] Thus, within a ten-day period in May 1969 the Bundesbank provided DM 17 billion ($4.25 billion at the old parity), a sum which was itself more than 20 percent of the money supply at the start of the year. Only part of this burst of liquidity was subsequently reversed. The Bundesbank found that monetary trends were being primarily determined by external factors of private origin which led to a steadily quickening increase in the money supply despite the need for restraint. The monetary situation was brought back to a semblance of order only after the currency was appreciated following a period in which it had been allowed to float in exchange markets.

The West German experience illustrates a number of consequences that result from the integration of the financial markets of industrial countries. First, the size of liquid assets in private hands that can, given enough incentive, be moved across borders is so great as to overwhelm the monetary au-

[2] *Report of the Deutsche Bundesbank for the Year 1969* (Frankfurt am Main: Deutsche Bundesbank, April 1970), p. 1.

[3] According to IMF rules countries must sell domestic currency for foreign currency to keep the spot exchange rate within one percent of parity. Most central banks intervene before this one percent is reached.

thorities. Second, the IMF rules which limit the amount of exchange rate variability promote speculative capital flows. Third, private financial managers are in a position to form strong views on currency values and will not be put off by official denials. A fourth consequence, a lesson of the French experience in 1969, is that attempts to restrict capital flows by direct intervention are likely to fail because of the many private channels through which that capital can move. However, the flow can be moderated somewhat by governmental action.

Increasingly, the private sector has encroached on governmental sovereignty in financial markets. This conclusion can be either applauded or decried depending on one's view of the wisdom of governmental policy and the desirability of integration. It should be noted that the integration referred to is functional and is independent of political integration in units like the European Economic Community (EEC). Thus, the Frankfurt money market is more closely integrated with those in Zurich, London, and New York than with those in Paris and Rome. If national governments are not prepared to yield their national monetary sovereignty, then a number of changes in the rules governing the international monetary system must be made. To examine this possibility a closer look at the nature of financial transfers is required.

III. Ingredients of International Financial Transactions

An international financial transaction can consist of any one of three distinct but related activities. The first activity involves transferring the control of funds from one political jurisdiction to another. This usually, but not necessarily, involves crossing national boundaries. If an American deposits money in a New York branch or agency of a Canadian or Japanese bank, an international transaction has occurred although no funds have (as yet) left the United States. The second activity involves entering the foreign exchange market to transfer purchasing power from the currency of one country into that of another. The transaction may require an immediate exchange of currencies (spot market) or may specify some date in the future (forward market transaction). The third activity involves an act of investment (lending or borrowing). Every financial instrument that is traded domestically is also traded internationally with the possible exception of home mortgages. Thus, foreign investors may buy short-term or long-term instruments, liquid or illiquid, of private firms or governments.

While all international financial transactions involve changing political jurisdictions, they may not require exchange market activity. An example is the Eurodollar market in which United States dollars are held outside the United States but not converted into foreign currency. Likewise, an act of investment in the ordinary meaning of the term may not take place if, for example, funds are transferred for the purpose of speculating in currency values or avoiding tax collectors.

Each step in an international financial transfer affects the economies of the countries involved. Transferring the ownership of dollars, for example, from an American to a West German firm influences monetary conditions in West Germany even though no exchange market activity is involved.[4] The West German firm can use dollars directly for financing some business activities like providing export credit for its customers or purchasing imported raw materials or machinery. Deutsche mark funds previously used for this purpose might then be freed for the purchase of domestic resources so the effect can be quite pervasive.

Should West German monetary authorities think that the monetary inflow was undesirable, they might use three general approaches to inhibit it—attempt to prohibit it directly, make it more expensive, or make it more risky. The prohibition approach can be disposed of quickly. Even if the Bundesbank found an administratively viable method to prevent the transaction within the country, the West German firm could still borrow dollars outside West Germany in every capital market in the world. Since capital transactions can easily be disguised as current account transactions, there is no feasible way to police a prohibition short of examining every transaction between residents and foreigners—obviously an unreasonable and undesirable activity. The other approaches do offer some possibilities and are discussed subsequently.

An international financial transaction that leads to an exchange rate transaction, i.e., the West German firm converts the borrowed dollars into deutsche mark, generates direct command over domestic resources through an increase in the domestic money supply. If the Bundesbank is the purchaser of the dollars, then "high powered" money is created which could permit a multiple expansion of the money supply through the banking system. The Bundesbank can offset the secondary expansion through opposite open-market operations—assuming that it has enough deutsche mark assets to sell—but the primary expansion cannot be offset without creating incentives to increase foreign borrowing even further. The Bundesbank is thus forced back on the alternatives of making the foreign borrowing more expensive or more risky.

International financial transactions that go beyond the money market into other kinds of investments have more profound influences on economic activity and are subject to many more governmental regulations. Direct investment by foreign business firms has the most significant implications and cannot be examined adequately here.[5] Foreign purchase of domestic bonds is

[4] For brevity the discussion will be confined to the effects of this activity on capital-receiving countries, although capital-sending countries experience similar consequences.

[5] For a discussion of direct investment see the essays by Raymond Vernon and Louis T. Wells, Jr., in this volume.

also of interest because the bond mechanism channels funds more directly into particular uses. Thus, purchases of new flotations of bonds by manufacturing firms are likely to support expansion of capacity in manufacturing while local government bonds support various types of municipal investments. When foreigners buy bonds, domestic liquidity is increased and a particular activity is stimulated. Governments could conceivably restrict the ownership of such financial instruments to domestic residents to prevent these effects, but legal obligations arising through the Organisation for Economic Co-operation and Development (OECD) and the EEC limit this option. Furthermore, a domestic constituency, the bond-issuing entities, would be hurt if the government did restrict inflows of this type and could be expected to oppose such action. Even foreign purchases of outstanding bonds and equities (common stocks) have effects beyond liquidity creation since they indirectly improve the market for new issues and contribute to stock market booms and the like. Domestic asset holders benefit from foreign demand for these instruments and also oppose governmental interference. Indeed, it is generally the government of the capital-exporting country that attempts to influence these capital flows for balance-of-payments purposes.[6]

Another dimension of the implications of international financial transactions can be seen by focusing on the actors, rather than the instruments, involved. Almost anyone can enter into such transactions. Business firms and banks have already been mentioned. Other financial institutions such as insurance companies and mutual funds are also frequent traders. Even individuals can be induced into the market if given enough incentive. Because of the multiplicity of actors it is almost useless for governments to exercise their considerable leverage over commercial banks to affect the flows since other actors will behave like banks if the incentive exists.

The personal ties that develop between the transnational participants in major financial markets suggest that there is substantial interaction between the actors. Each participant may, however, view his own actions as affecting an impersonal "market" and feel little responsibility for contributing to disturbances. When transactions do become personalized, some accommodation is usually made for an actor in an exposed position. Such an instance occurred when the West German government temporarily closed its exchange market following the 1969 West German election, leaving some banks unable to meet contractual obligations outside the affected country. Of course, crises can drastically alter the situation. A flamboyant mutual fund director or a commodity speculator acting as a bank director is likely to evoke little sympathy among his associates once his activities become public knowledge. In part this may

[6] The United States attempts to influence purchases of foreign stocks and bonds by the interest equalization tax (IET), foreign direct investment through the mandatory Office of Foreign Direct Investment (OFDI) program, and foreign lending by banks through a so-called voluntary program administered by the Federal Reserve System. These programs have had limited success.

reflect personalities, but it also reflects the basically conservative nature of the actors.

The participants in international finance vary rather considerably in size and importance. It is fair to say that no one actor dominates the market, although a group of perhaps twenty major banks, acting in concert, could have an overwhelming effect on money markets in the short run. As noted previously any individual, firm, or government can behave like a bank so it is hard to maintain monopoly control for very long. The importance of American actors in all financial markets is probably less profound than is that of United States–based multinational corporations in world production. It should also be noted that some of the most innovative actors in the market have not been Americans. Long-established financial centers in places like Zurich give international balance to this activity.

The personal contacts between the actors seem to have created a fair degree of horizontal coordination across national lines. Actors, however, still experience vertical conflict, mainly with governments. For example, banks in different countries cooperate with one another and see themselves in competition or in conflict with governments trying to control them. Governments see their authority eroded by actions of financial agents, and the nationality of that agent makes little difference. A French bank or business firm can borrow in the Eurodollar market and circumvent tight money in France just as easily as the Bank of America branch in France. If the French government wants to stop this weakening of restraints, it must find instruments that work equally well on domestic and foreign-owned financial institutions. The sovereignty lost by one government is not added to that of another government but to the private sector. European officials sometimes improperly blame the United States government for their monetary problems when in fact the United States is subject to the same "difficulties," if to a lesser extent.

Individual governments, while far from omnipotent, do feel responsibility for preventing disorderly financial conditions in their national markets and are often forced to bail out private institutions in trouble even though they have little real ability to prevent a bad situation from developing. The existence of separate national monetary authorities following independent policies while capital flows are reasonably uninhibited gives the private actor the ability to operate in the market of his choice. By borrowing in the cheapest market and lending in the dearest he can defeat both tight and easy monetary policies.

A government that stands firm in its monetary resolve and relentlessly pursues its policy will find itself the villain of the financial world. If attempting restraint, it will attract official reserves from all over the world and cause distress abroad; if attempting ease, it will soon lose much of its own reserves. A further condition that weights the contest between the governmental and private sectors on the side of the private sector is the fact that private financial resources are greater than the sum of governments' foreign reserves and are growing at a faster rate. Thus, governments may well lose their nerve before the private sector does.

IV. The Magnitude of International Financial Transactions

Private international financial transactions have come of age in recent years. Some feeling for judging the impact of these flows can be obtained by examining the magnitudes involved in relation to appropriate domestic monetary aggregates. Governments are most concerned about the consequences of these flows for domestic stabilization objectives and therefore are most bothered by short-term capital movements.[7] Because short-term capital movements are quite volatile, difficult to anticipate in magnitude, and next to impossible to control, governments are forced to react to them in an ex post facto manner. The size of these flows is thus an index of the degree of strain involved. Since short-term capital flows can affect both the domestic money supply and official stocks of international reserves, both of these aggregates need to be examined.

The relevant data for a number of industrial countries is shown in table 1. The situation of West Germany is illustrative of the kind of difficulties involved. During 1968 West Germany had a short-term capital inflow of $1.8 billion. If other factors had remained unchanged, the capital inflow would have increased the West German money supply by 9 percent. If West German monetary authorities had had less than a 9 percent growth rate of money supply in mind for the year, then they would have had to reduce the basis for money creation from domestic sources in order to meet their target. For a whole host of practical and institutional reasons, monetary authorities cannot repress segments of domestic liquidity in order to meet aggregate targets and therefore the targets themselves are missed. Thus, West Germany may have permitted greater stimulative monetary conditions than it desired. In a sense West Germany may have imported inflation, but this was not due to deliberate monetary policies of other countries as such.

Figures for 1969 indicate a $1.2 billion short-term capital flow into West Germany which represented a 5 percent increase in the money supply. However, 1969 was a more difficult year for West Germany in this regard than was 1968, and thus a deficiency of the measurement is illustrated. The short-term capital flows in table 1, taken from balance-of-payments accounts, are net figures over one calendar year. If there were a large inflow matched by a large outflow within the same calendar year, the net capital flow figure would

[7] Long-term capital movements are more predictable, subject to different types of controls, and can thus be integrated more easily into domestic monetary policy.

Table 1. Private short-term capital flows and monetary aggregates

Selected industrial country	Private short-term capital flows (in millions of US $)		Money supply (in billions of US $)		International reserves (in millions of US $)		Private short-term capital flows as percentage of money supply		Private short-term capital flows as percentage of international reserves	
	1968	1969	end 1967	end 1968	end 1967	end 1968	1968	1969	1968	1969
Canada	-1,089	-1,273	11.03	12.64	2,717	3,046	9.9	10.1	40.1	35.8
France	-1,551	747	40.66	43.69	6,994	4,201	3.8	1.7	22.2	17.8
Italy	-2,409	-2,399	30.15	33.83	5,463	3,342	8.0	7.1	44.1	44.9
Japan	55	-1,220	36.94	42.37	2,030	2,906	.1	2.9	2.7	42.0
United Kingdom	-2,021	- 6	35.36	37.33	2,695	2,422	5.7	.0	75.0	.3
United States	3,075	5,691	191.90	203.80	14,830	15,710	1.6	2.8	20.7	36.2
West Germany	1,810	1,210	20.38	22.10	8,153	9,948	8.9	5.5	22.2	12.2

SOURCES: Figures for private short-term capital flows are drawn from the *Annual Report of the Executive Directors for the Fiscal Year Ended April 30, 1970* (Washington: International Monetary Fund [1970]), table 25, p. 76. Figures for money supply and international reserves are drawn from *International Financial Statistics*, August 1970 (Vol. 23, No. 8), pp. 68, 132–136, 182, 188, 322, and 328.

not pick this up, although the monetary results of such a combination of short-term flows may be quite profound. Thus, the measures of table 1 should be considered as indices of monetary strain which may seriously underestimate the phenomenon.

The consequences of short-term capital inflows for West Germany's international reserves were also quite marked. In 1968 the $1.8 billion short-term capital inflow represented a 12 percent increase in reserves. It is impossible to know whether the West Germans desired such an increase, but, whether they did or not, increases in foreign reserves alone do not pose a problem other than the domestic monetary effects already discussed.

An examination of the figures for France illustrates a similar problem for governmental economic managers but with a different cause. In 1968 France experienced a $1.6 billion outflow of short-term capital. This outflow represented 4 percent of the French money supply. Following the events of May–June 1968 the French government wanted to stimulate the economy to make good the production losses and to reduce unemployment since unemployment had contributed to the social unrest. To do this monetary policy was eased, but a substantial portion of the increased liquidity leaked out through private international financial transactions. While the monetary authorities could adjust to this phenomenon by simply creating even more money, they could not stand the loss of international reserves which the flow had caused. The flow amounted to over 20 percent of French international reserves and forced the central bank to sell gold which had symbolic as well as actual consequences. Thus, the central bank was forced to restrain its monetary stimulation.

A further examination of table 1 indicates the special position of the United States. Compared with other countries, the $3.0 billion short-term capital inflow in 1968 and the $5.7 billion inflow in 1969 are quite large. Yet, these inflows did not pose a serious inflationary problem for the United States. The American economy is so large that its monetary system can absorb fluctuations in private international financial flows of such magnitudes without losing its equilibrium. The 1968 figure represented only a 1.6 percent increase in the money supply, an amount which the Federal Reserve System could easily offset if it desired. The 1969 inflow was larger, 2.8 percent of the money supply, but the Federal Reserve System could and did act to offset the domestic monetary impact.[8] If the United States experiences monetary inflation or contraction, it cannot blame foreign governments or foreign private actors for these disturbances.

The United States is not seriously affected by private capital movements in

[8] In June 1969 the Federal Reserve System imposed reserve requirements on bank liabilities to foreign branches on amounts in excess of a base figure. This device limited increases in liabilities without forcing wholesale liquidations.

its official reserve position. The United States dollar is the world's principal reserve currency. Private outflows of capital can be financed by increasing official dollar liabilities to foreigners, and private inflows can be offset by reducing United States liabilities to official foreign actors. Since the United States is the creator of dollars and dollars are international reserves, the United States cannot run out of reserves. What the United States can, of course, do by improper policy is to undermine the whole international monetary system based on the dollar.

One can carry the uniqueness of the United States too far, however, since the United States economy is not immune to foreign influence. Massive amounts of private funds flow in and out of the United States each week. A normal weekly flow between the Eurodollar market and the United States totals approximately $5 billion in each direction. The intricacies of this market are such that American financial institutions can ease out from under the restraints of the Federal Reserve System at least for a limited period of time. Thus, in the first half of 1969 the Federal Reserve's Open Market Committee was misled into believing that it was permitting a noninflationary 2 percent growth of money when in fact a 4 percent growth of money was actually occurring through a technical interaction between the New York and Eurodollar markets. The committee's strong reaction to this discovery resulted in excessively tight money during the second half of 1969. A similar mistake in the future cannot be ruled out.

V. Governmental Response to Diminishing Monetary Sovereignty

Governments have long been aware of the limitations on their monetary sovereignty, although the extent of the constraint has only recently been demonstrated. The inability to reach macroeconomic targets through monetary policy is governments' most serious concern but not their only one. Structural problems and equity concerns have also arisen. Not all segments of domestic economic activity are equally adroit at avoiding monetary tightness. Thus, construction activity in both the private and public sectors may be seriously squeezed while manufacturing firms continue to obtain all the financing they require from abroad. Also, when banks have limited capacity to extend or renew loans to their customers, they tend to favor large firms with sizable financial resources over smaller firms. Since many large firms operating in Europe are subsidiaries of American parent corporations, monetary tightness in Europe has had the unintended result of favoring American-owned enterprises over their European-owned competitors. To paraphrase a European banker, when one of the largest corporations in the world wants to become your customer, how can you turn him away?

Responding to the challenge to their monetary sovereignty, governments have been promoting intergovernmental cooperation within existing international institutions. The institutions directly involved are the Bank for International Settlements (BIS), the OECD, and especially the IMF.[9] The existence of overlapping institutions has not been a serious problem since governmental delegations to each institution often tend to be composed of the same people wearing different hats. In addition, these same people frequently engage in bilateral consultations. But there are differences that can affect the substance of proposals to solve particular problems. The BIS, for example, because of its particular historical origin has representatives only from the central banks of the largest industrial countries.[10] For example, the liquidity shortage problem of the mid-1960s was alleviated in part by the swap facilities instituted by members of the BIS. This development outside the IMF excluded less developed countries and was thus inadequate to solve the world's liquidity needs. The IMF did in time address itself to the liquidity problem and special drawing rights (SDRs) resulted. In general, international cooperation in financial matters is highly developed compared with other areas of international concern.

The difficulty with the present pattern of international cooperation is that it is inadequate to solve the challenges facing nation-states and the international monetary system as a whole. When governments cooperate, they tend to content themselves with solving minor problems or with simply talking about problems until a major crisis occurs. Because of the technical nature of the issues only the technicians are fully aware of the problems, and they tend to be conservative because of their financial backgrounds. The ability to make basic changes requires political decisionmaking power, and even central bank presidents are not able to determine policies of their governments. The limited political power of the officials most intimately acquainted with financial problems blocks imaginative solutions even if proposals were brought forward in time. When financial crises burst upon the scene, governments are goaded into action which may be wise or foolish depending on the perception of alternatives and the national interests of the countries involved. At times good solutions such as the two-tier gold system can be found, but at other times only moderating steps are taken which at best only prolong and enlarge the crisis.[11] When the crisis is over, political leaders lose interest in finance and return the operations of the system to the technicians. Thus, ad hoc decisionmaking is perpetuated. The myth that international cooperation between men

[9] The Monetary Committee of the EEC, composed of the finance ministries of member countries, is an important factor promoting monetary cooperation within the community.

[10] The BIS, with headquarters in Basel, was established in May 1930 to facilitate World War I German reparations. The bank is "owned" by the central banks of the seven founding members in Europe plus nineteen others, including the United States and Japan, which have subsequently subscribed.

[11] Lawrence B. Krause, "Recent Monetary Crises: Causes and Cures," in *Readings in Monetary, National Income and Stabilization Policy,* ed. W. L. Smith and R. L. Teigen (rev. ed.; Homewood, Ill: Richard D. Irwin, 1970), pp. 556–570.

of goodwill is sufficient to meet the challenges as they arise is maintained because the problems are thought to stem from the action of governments and thus to be easily resolved through governmental cooperation. As suggested above it is the evolution of private international financial transactions that is challenging governmental sovereignty. Governmental cooperation is inadequate to meet this challenge because governments differ in their views of the desirability of these transactions. Until these basic differences are exposed and understood, cooperation will be inadequate because the goals being sought are hidden from view.

VI. Economic Welfare and Private International Financial Transactions

Actors in private international financial transactions view themselves as promoters of economic welfare. Their belief rests on the same theoretical foundation which supports freedom for private transactions in the international trade of goods and services. International trade improves economic welfare by promoting specialization of production which increases the total amount of goods and services that can be produced with a given amount of resources. International trade tends to equalize the rates of return to factors of production, for example, the wage rates of labor and the interest rate paid to owners of capital. If full equalization is not obtained—a likely event—economic welfare can be improved further if the factors of production themselves move from countries in which returns are low to countries in which they are higher. Thus, capital flows in response to interest rate differentials should theoretically improve the welfare of both sending and receiving countries by shifting capital to countries in which it is in short supply from countries in which it is abundant.

The defenders of free capital movement resent the second-class status that capital movements occupy in relation to movement of goods in the eyes of international institutions. The Bretton Woods Agreement permits governments to restrict capital movements without review (for example, for balance-of-payments purposes) but takes a strong stand against current account restrictions. Capital movements have been progressively liberalized by most countries, but actions which tend to restrict capital movements do not elicit cries of outrage. The many steps taken by the United States to limit private capital outflows have been accepted rather passively by governments, with the important exception of Canada. The private financial community believes that the perpetuation of capital restrictions reduces the economic welfare of Americans as well as of foreigners and that it should be vigorously opposed.

Many central bankers view the economic welfare implications of private international financial movements very differently. They concede that some improvement of welfare is involved in long-term capital flows but deny that gains result from the movement of volatile short-term funds. Short-term funds are described as "hot money" and their movement as an act of speculation rather than of investment. They point out that short-term interest rates reflect the rate of domestic price inflation. Thus, the structure of the "natural" rates of interest among countries, which corresponds to the concept of capital's contribution to output, may be drowned by wildly different rates of inflation. Inflation may distort the flow of capital from more productive to less productive uses.

As is usual in such disputes, there is truth on both sides. The distinction between long-term capital and short-term capital is arbitrary—indeed, only one day at the margin—and welfare judgments cannot therefore be made. Short-term capital is used to finance international trade and long-term investment and is an integral part of the economic integration of industrial countries. However, the welfare-gain presumption from capital movements is based on the assumption of equilibrium exchange rates. Differential rates of price inflation in a fixed-exchange-rate world can result in disequilibria and thereby undermine the welfare-gain presumption.

Not all central bankers oppose short-term capital movements; some would even opt for almost unrestricted capital flows. These differences in views could be a source of conflict. The situation would be improved if the welfare-gain presumption could be clarified. A simple clarification would be to assume that private capital movements are conducive to welfare unless it can be shown that the movements arise solely in response to inflationary factors or to extraordinary speculative factors. In those instances when short-term capital flows are not desirable, governments need a usable mechanism to limit them.

VII. Restoring Monetary Sovereignty

Since national governments are held responsible for the health of their economies, a method must be found for restoring monetary policy as a usable instrument to reach aggregative economic targets. If there are instances when economic welfare is not served by private international financial transactions, then economic efficiency need not be impaired if the mechanism for restoring monetary sovereignty at times reduces international capital flows from what they would otherwise have been. Monetary sovereignty could be regained by dismembering the international economic system, but this approach holds no attraction for anyone. Nor have governments been willing to consider the extreme alternatives of a world central bank which would make national monetary sovereignty unnecessary or of freely fluctuating exchange rates which would permit so much national independence that international co-operation might falter. Some academics like pure solutions, but few political leaders are so inclined.

Those governments that thought they could rely on direct intervention in capital markets to obtain monetary objectives have been badly shaken by the French experience which demonstrated the unworkability of such controls. Other governments have been content to operate the system as it exists, their monetary sovereignty limited but not altogether eliminated. Much of the leeway that governments still have when using monetary policy for domestic goals is dependent on the existence of imperfections in capital markets which are rapidly disappearing. Imperfections are caused by ignorance, inexperience, and undercapitalization—hardly firm bases for governmental policy. A new or improved mechanism is clearly required.

In designing a mechanism that will integrate international capital flows into domestic monetary policy it would be best not to have that mechanism depend on frequent decisions by political leaders. The attention of political leaders can be attracted to the dull business of international finance only by an unusual event or a crisis. While top political leaders must remain responsible for the major outlines of economic policy, the day-to-day operations of the system and the translation of directives into action should rest with the monetary authorities. Once monetary authorities are disabused of the idea of direct controls, they will of necessity turn to the price system as a regulator of capital flows. In other words, private international financial transactions can be regulated by influencing their direct cost and by influencing the risks inherent in owning foreign assets.

Fortunately, it is not difficult to design a mechanism to utilize the price system more effectively. If central banks would permit greater fluctuations in spot exchange rates around established parities, then greater risks would be incurred by investors taking positions in foreign assets. If, for example, West German monetary authorities wished to tighten their monetary conditions and attracted foreign capital as a result, the deutsche mark would strengthen in the exchange market. If the deutsche mark were permitted to appreciate by 2 or 3 percent (instead of the less than one percent now allowed), investors would face a possible 4 to 6 percent loss of value if the exchange rate reversed itself and weakened by the maximum amount. Private investors might then attempt to hedge against the exchange risk by taking opposite positions in the forward exchange market. However, governments can influence the cost of obtaining cover in the forward market by also operating in that market (technically, by increasing the spot-forward differential). The greater the width of the band in which the spot exchange rate is permitted to move, the greater is the leeway given monetary authorities to use monetary policy for domestic needs. To effectuate a wider band, however, a change must be made in the IMF since a one percent limitation in each direction is written into the IMF Articles of Agreement.[12]

[12] Opposition to widening the band has been expressed in Europe, particularly by the Commission of the European Communities, because it does not want greater monetary independence among EEC

Wider bands by themselves will not solve the lingering problem of excessive rigidities in exchange rate parities. If countries permit a disequilibrium situation to develop and refuse to adjust their exchange rates promptly, then monetary upsets will occur involving massive amounts of short-term capital movement. The difficulty arises, however, because of the inaction of governments, not because of the capital flow. The speculator in currencies is merely taking advantage of the situation and is no more to be condemned than the exporter of goods who is able to sell his wares only because of an overvalued currency in the importing country. The entire international economic system will work better if the adjustment mechanism is improved. Exchange rates that are adjusted promptly, and therefore more frequently, will also be likely to require only small changes to restore equilibrium. Under these circumstances domestic economic policy will be easier to design and operate as the disruptions of large appreciations and depreciations will be avoided.

VIII. Conclusion

The world is experiencing a growing degree of economic integration between all countries, but particularly between industrial countries. This is true of all phases of economic life.[13] Integration of financial markets is of particular concern because private international financial activities have seriously infringed on governmental sovereignty. Governments feel themselves adrift in their economic policy. They see their policies defeated or leading to unintended and undesirable consequences. Among industrial countries only the United States appears to have a truly independent monetary policy, and even that is circumscribed. Foreign governments are resentful of the inflation or deflation they "import" from the United States, and it is even more disturbing to realize that it is unintended and unplanned. Governments have neither adapted their own policies nor altered the international monetary system as the economic world has changed, and they are paying the price.

The situation today is different from what it was during the 1950s and most of the 1960s. Changes requiring adjustment were just as great then, but adaptation could be accomplished by actions of the United States government alone. Now economic power is more diffused as Europe and Japan have prospered, and new discriminatory economic groupings have been formed that exclude the United States. Private economic interests have gained ascendency

members. Changing the IMF articles, however, would not be mandatory for the members. EEC countries could retain narrow bands among themselves but permit wider fluctuations of their currencies jointly against the United States dollar and other currencies. This would not relieve the West German monetary authorities, for example, from monetary upsets occurring in other member countries, but would permit some independence from United States monetary conditions.

[13] Richard N. Cooper, *The Economics of Interdependence: Economic Policy in the Atlantic Community* (Atlantic Policy Series) (New York: McGraw-Hill Book Co. [for the Council on Foreign Relations], 1968).

in areas previously under the complete control of governments. Adaptations of institutions and policies have become difficult since they involve international negotiations. While progress has occurred, for example, the introduction of SDRs, the time required for such an obvious improvement was substantial, and petty national politics weakened the plan in some important respects.

The 1970s promise to be just as eventful as the recent past. In fact, one may be even more pessimistic in regard to the adaptive ability of institutions in view of the further weakening of overall political cohesion between Western countries. Many governments are looking for scapegoats on which to blame failures of economic policy. The United States and the gnomes of Zurich are very convenient for this purpose. Self-serving diatribes are not the proper ingredients for analysis of difficult problems.

The ability of governments to overcome their unwillingness to face the new realities will determine whether the international monetary system will evolve with or without crisis. The private sector is moving quickly. Governments must overtake it if they are to lead and to direct the changes of the 1970s.

Governments and Airlines

Robert L. Thornton

Air transport across national boundaries has increased greatly in scope and intensity since the end of World War II. Although the vast majority of such transport involves private individuals and corporations, governments play a major role in the process. They act as producers, consumers, and regulators of air transport; they have become one of the primary actors in the process. The participation of governments has greatly modified the environment and processes through which carriage is accomplished. Governments have been involved in the establishment of such organizations as the International Civil Aviation Organization (ICAO), a supranational organization in a narrowly limited way, and the International Air Transport Association (IATA), an international association of airlines, many of which are, in fact, owned or controlled by governments.

This essay analyzes the interactions between governmental, intergovernmental, and nongovernmental actors in the field of air transport. Occasional reference to seaborne transport is made for purposes of comparison. After describing the reasons for, and evolution of, governmental intervention in air transport I discuss the interplay between governments and nongovernmental organizations and the organizational forms within which this interplay has taken place.

I. Reasons for Governmental Intervention

From their inception in the late 1920s through the immediate post–World War II period international airlines were essentially governmental enterprises. Most airlines were directly owned by governments, and those that were nominally private were heavily subsidized. During the early period commercial pilots were commonly reserve officers in national forces, and, in some cases, airlines used equipment jointly with armed forces. The first transoceanic

Robert L. Thornton is assistant professor at the School of Business, Florida State University, Tallahassee, Florida.

airline—from France to South America—used a French aircraft carrier for the essential midocean link.[1] Governments prescribed navigational procedures, authorized landing rights, supervised safety standards, and inspected and licensed aircraft. Although the degree of governmental involvement in some of these areas has been reduced, much of it has continued.

The reasons for this extensive intervention in air transport can be conveniently grouped under five headings: 1) national defense; 2) peacetime national objectives; 3) consumer protection; 4) protection of locally owned companies; and 5) foreign exchange and efficiency.

National Defense

Transport systems, both surface and air, are essential to the operation of modern military forces. National defense planning commonly includes a requirement for a specific transport capability which specifies characteristics of speed, volume, safety, and control. Most military planning assumes that transport capability will be fully responsive to governmental direction during emergencies. Theoretically, it might be possible for a state to develop all the necessary capability as an integral part of its armed forces as the Military Airlift Command does in part for the United States. For economic reasons, however, such development is never carried to completion. Instead, governments plan to preempt portions of the civilian transport capability during an emergency. This means that normal civilian transport systems must be changed in type, control methods, or capacity to make them usable for defense needs. To achieve this result governments have found it necessary to interfere extensively in transport systems. Many states (France, the Netherlands, the United Kingdom) have established governmental ownership of airlines partially to assure defense needs. Within the United States an extensive system of surface freighter design control and operating subsidies exists to retain a United States merchant marine. The Civil Reserve Air Fleet (CRAF) system and covert governmental support of supplemental airlines are also cases of governmental interference in transport.

The overriding nature of defense needs is such that transport systems are molded without regard to private needs or peacetime economics. Where necessary it has meant the establishment of national arrangements to protect a capability and has transformed what might have been essentially private transactions into those in which government was a principal actor.

Peacetime National Objectives

Air transport is of service also in meeting peacetime national objectives. States have required that commercial transport be available to serve locations

[1] Oliver James Lissitzyn, *International Air Transport and National Policy* (Studies in American Foreign Relations, No. 3) (New York: Council on Foreign Relations, 1942), p. 316.

which would not generate sufficient traffic to make service attractive to a private undertaking. Such locations have generally been an underdeveloped hinterland, the Australian outback or sections of Alaska, or they have been underdeveloped client states, frequently former colonies of major powers. Generally, this has meant either governmental ownership—the Alaskan Railroad, for example—or heavy subsidy, such as British Overseas Airways Corporation (BOAC) has received. The need to provide developmental air service in former colonies has sometimes led to innovative experiments in transnational mixed enterprises. The French government was, for example, instrumental in setting up Air Afrique which is jointly owned by twelve West African governments and French private interests.[2] Similar joint enterprises have been established in former British colonies in East Africa and Southeast Asia.

Consumer Protection

One of the reasons that governments are established is to protect the wellbeing of their citizens. In the transport industry this takes two separate forms. By its nature transport exposes the citizen or his goods to unusual risks of injury or loss. Governments everywhere have therefore established safety standards, provided external navigational aids, monitored safety devices, reviewed the training of crews, and made arrangements to provide assistance during emergencies. Since such assistance has to be standardized on an international basis, governments have drawn up treaties and conventions to establish safety rules. Among those operating in the shipping field are the International Convention for the Safety of Life at Sea (1929) and the International Load Line Convention (1930). No intergovernmental agency has been established to monitor shipping safety, but there are several private international agencies for this purpose. For airlines the greater perceived risk has led to the establishment of ICAO, a specialized agency of the United Nations. Safety regulation is one of its major functions.

The second form of citizen protection undertaken by governments has been economic. To the extent that the number of competitors in the transport industry has been limited, competition has sometimes been judged inadequate to protect the consumer from oligopolistic price gouging. Governments have paid close attention to the activities of the various price-setting, cartel-like arrangements within the transport industries but have found it impractical to set prices by governmental directive. Instead, governments have established controls over the various private international liner conferences, which set prices for surface shipping, and the IATA, which sets prices for scheduled airline service.

[2] *World Airline Record* (6th ed.; Chicago: Roadcap & Associates, Publishers, 1965), pp. 25–26.

Protection of Locally Owned Companies

If, for reasons such as defense, governments have determined a transport company under local control is essential, they will attempt to assure that these companies are economically viable. Generally, the measures taken have either been to provide that certain cargo be exclusively transported by local companies or to restrict the number of competitors or the frequency of their service to a level which will best protect the economic health of the local companies. Frequency restriction and limits on the number of competitors have been widespread within the air transport industry. Governments bargain carefully before granting the right to serve airports within their territory or the right to carry traffic from a second country to third-country destinations.

The urgency of obtaining traffic rights and the requirements that governments act as bargaining agents have put governments deeply and inextricably into the transport business. In this respect surface shipping and air transport differ. Surface shipping does not involve traffic rights which must be negotiated bilaterally between governments.

Foreign Exchange and Efficiency

Governments have realized that a local transport company may offer certain economic advantages to a state even if it may not be particularly profitable. Commonly, such advantage comes from a company's foreign exchange earnings which will assist a state's financial reserves whether profit in the accounting sense accrues or not. Thus, a government may find it worthwhile to subsidize a shipping line or an airline merely for the accompanying foreign exchange earnings.

The existence of substantial economies of scale and marketing advantages as company size increases from small to medium has meant that, other things being equal, governments will assist a corporation to grow until it reaches its minimum viable size. Where this size cannot logically be reached through traffic generated in or received by the home country, governments have sometimes bargained vigorously with other states to gain rights to third-country traffic. The need to reach the minimum viable size has sometimes resulted in an airline which is a joint effort of several countries. Scandinavian Airlines System (SAS) is a striking example of international cooperation resulting from an urgent need to reach an efficient size.[3] In this case an innovative, truly multinational corporation has been created. The company is more interesting because its ownership structure within each of the Scandinavian countries which sponsors it is a complex mixture of governmental and private interests.

[3] *Report on the Scandinavian Airlines Systems (SAS)* (ICAO Circular 30-AT/5) (Montreal: International Civil Aviation Organization, 1953).

II. The Evolution of Governmental Intervention

Insofar as surface shipping is concerned, governments' role in the industry has not changed much during this century. Governments require some shipping on terms which are noncommercial and pay for it with subsidies. However, the industry has been sufficiently flexible and able to support enough operators to permit competition to act as the regulator. While the various "conferences" (continuing organizations of shipping lines) have set prices in a cartel-like way, competition from tramp vessels and nonconference operators has been sufficient to prevent severe price gouging. As a result governmental interference in surface shipping is modest, much of it concerned with safety or with customs and contraband control.

Air transport presents a more complex picture. World War II ended without a means of ensuring safety, controlling prices and frequencies, or providing for governmental needs. As a result there have been several innovations in the air transport industry in intergovernmental and transnational organizations. At the end of the war the primary purpose of airlines was to meet the needs of governments. Only through governmental subsidy could transoceanic airlines exist. Governments were, however, willing to pay the bill, partly for defense needs but more commonly as a cost of maintaining adequate communications with their colonies. Belgium, France, the Netherlands, Portugal, and the United Kingdom all needed air transport urgently to maintain their empires. Since the industry was primarily a creature of governments, it was reasonable to assume that governments should own airlines, set prices, establish routes and frequencies, and provide safety standards. The International Civil Aviation Conference was convened in Chicago in December 1944 to establish the intergovernmental means to perform these tasks. While the conference was able to provide institutions to establish safety standards and to devise arrangements for aircraft registration and air navigation aids, it was unable to provide the institutions for regulation of air transport prices, frequencies, and routes. In spite of the powerful role of governments an ostensibly private organization of airline companies, the IATA, was established to handle the potent price-setting function.

The Chicago conference delegates had difficulty in prescribing ways in which price-setting was to be accomplished. The difficulties stemmed from important differences in economic strength between United States airlines, on one hand, and the other important international airlines, principally BOAC, on the other. The United States delegates favored considerable freedom for airlines in setting prices as well as in establishing schedule frequencies, a position which would have favored the low-cost, equipment-rich United States airlines. The other carriers favored strong governmental controls over these functions. Delegates to the Chicago conference were unable to reach an agreement on the problem, and the impasse was resolved finally through the Bermuda Air Agreement between the United States and the United Kingdom in February 1946.[4] With this agreement the IATA was given responsibility for price-setting but was not allowed to determine schedule frequencies.

Some compromise such as the Bermuda Air Agreement was of course necessary. Since BOAC, the British senior member of the IATA, was a government-owned corporation, the British government could expect IATA deliberations to be little removed from an intergovernmental meeting. The United States, on the other hand, would be represented by Pan American World Airways (Pan Am) and Trans World Airlines (TWA) as its chief delegates to the IATA. Pan Am and TWA, private concerns, had a strong interest in low fares and in price competition and have sometimes defied United States government wishes for low fares at IATA meetings.[5] Even BOAC has not always been an obedient servant.[6]

In the environment of the early post–World War II years it was unrealistic to assume that governments would allow airlines much freedom of action, particularly since the airlines were established to meet governmental needs and universally required subsidies to remain in operation. Airline representatives at IATA meetings were generally governmental employees disguised as officials of state-owned airlines. In the case of the privately owned airlines, principally of United States registration, decisions made at conferences required approval of governments to be effective. As an added control state officials informed airline delegates prior to meetings which actions they desired. The IATA was thus only one very small step removed from an intergovernmental organization.

One other unique and important development of the postwar years was the multinational airline. SAS (three countries), Air Afrique (twelve countries), East African Airways (three countries), and Air Malaysia (two countries) are the important examples of airlines which are jointly owned by several governments. Establishment of a multinational airline requires a clear submergence of national differences between the joint owners and successful compromise of sharply divergent views. The success of these multinational companies in overcoming strong divisive forces is evidence of the powerful economic and political bargaining forces which can be generated by increasing operating size. Evidence of the inherent strength of these transnational forces comes from the experience of Central African Airways. After the rather sharp breakup of the Federation of Rhodesia and Nyasaland this airline,

[4] "Results of the Anglo-American Civil Aviation Conference: Joint Statement by the U.K. and U.S. Delegations," Department of State *Bulletin*, February 24, 1946 (Vol. 14, No. 347), pp. 302–306.

[5] "IATA Fare Chaos Could Force Governments to Negotiate Rates," *Aviation Week and Space Technology*, April 22, 1963 (Vol. 78, No. 16), p. 41.

[6] As reported in "Industry Observer," *Aviation Week and Space Technology*, July 27, 1970 (Vol. 93, No. 4), p. 11.

which had been the federation's national airline, survived for an appreciable period jointly owned by the former members of the federation. Air Malaysia survives today as the jointly owned airline of the states which resulted from the breakup of the Malaysian federation.

While these multinational airlines provide evidence of the forces leading to the international integration of transport, these multinational companies remain governmental agents, and the transactions in which they take part are not purely private ones. In fact, these jointly owned airlines might be seen as an adjustment made to retain government's role in the industry rather than to permit a private, internationally owned airline to develop and carry out the transport function.

III. Who Controls Whom?

In spite of the careful efforts of governments to construct an international airline system immediately responsive to governmental direction, planning has not always achieved the expected results. Today the international airline system is an industrial giant with a purpose and power which have become increasingly international and intersocietal, responding to its own dynamics and obeying, but imperfectly, the demands of its governmental controllers.

There are several reasons for this partial escape from control. None of the reasons is sufficient to permit the airlines to operate as truly independent agents, but governments are finding it increasingly expensive to change the course their carriers desire to take.

Financial Independence

Unlike the early postwar years carriers are less dependent on their governments for financial support. Airline operations have prospered in most years and on the average have become sufficiently profitable to attract the necessary capital into the industry. Thus, since they no longer pay for a service, governments have less leverage on their flag airlines. It is no longer possible to manipulate subsidies to force compliance with governmental needs. Airline managers are now chosen for their ability to achieve profitable operations. Pliability takes second place to competence in manager selection. A government would pay a high price in political criticism if its flag airline could not make reasonable profits when other similar airlines could. A major target of this new profit orientation has been the unprofitable but politically desirable route. Increasingly, service on these routes has been neglected, shortchanged, and fought against by the airlines, frequently with success.[7]

[7] "Austrian Airlines to Scrap Domestic Routes," *Aviation Week and Space Technology*, February 2, 1970 (Vol. 92, No. 5), p. 38.

A Corporate Citizen

Airlines have become large, well-publicized organizations that employ many people. As such they have taken their place among the groups which can make claims for support from governments. They have become the governments' customers, and governments feel strong pressures to meet the needs of their clients. This is a complete reversal of the government's role as a controlling agency. Airlines have now become powerful actors that can, in a limited way, control their governments. Able airline presidents find themselves capable of coercing transport ministers even when they are technically employees of the transport ministry. Thus, Cheikh Fal, president of Air Afrique, has been able to drop Air Afrique's money-losing domestic routes even though these routes are very important to the welfare of the states they serve.[8]

IV. A Transnational Air Transport System

International air transport is a system in the broadest modern sense of the word. Interline transfers, ticketing, schedule rationalization, currency manipulation, baggage handling, and emergency support are interlocked and interdependent, even though the elements of the system are companies from different countries. No one state can exert unreasonable controls without upsetting the system; the system is important to established business and to the individual citizens of the state that uses it.

The air transport system has broadened its system characteristics to include a group of related industries which enhances the ability of the system to influence individual governments. In many countries hotels, sightseeing arrangements, restaurants, and local tourist shops are a major industry. Practical considerations of providing maximum service to the customer have forced these local businesses to become part of the international air transport system, forming a much larger and more influential tourism system. Because the airlines tend to be the largest integrated actor in the tourism industry, they dominate it, and airline decisions can strongly affect the success of the other members of the system. Again, the tourism system approaches the status of a supranational group. Its international and intersocietal nature enables it to exert a powerful restraining force on governments.

The IATA is the central focus of the system. The internal workings of the IATA have been of interest to theorists for some time. Unfortunately for the student, its deliberations are secret, and leaks have been remarkably absent. Most analysts believe that the IATA is an oligarchy in which decisions are made by representatives of a relatively narrow group of powerful airlines. As in any oligarchy there are strong differences in interests between members of

[8] Ward Wright, "Air Afrique Emphasizes Measured Growth," *Aviation Week and Space Technology,* November 29, 1965 (Vol. 83, No. 22), p. 30.

the power group. Where a government attempts to act against the interests of the airlines, they band together, using as spokesman the airline least subject to governmental retaliation in that particular case. Where, however, there are conflicts between the oligarchs, they run for help to their respective governments. Recently, for example, both Quantas Airways and Japan Air Lines have successfully protected themselves from competition by the powerful United States airlines by persuading their governments to impose limits on the flight frequency of United States carriers.[9]

The Last Refuge of Government

Many forces have weakened governmental control of airlines. However, airlines are still dependent on governments to negotiate route structures and the rights to fly these routes. The ability of any one government to negotiate a particular route structure is a function of that government's international power. This power need not be from sources within the transport industry, for, given the overriding need, a government may pay a price through concessions in other areas, e.g., in tariff changes or defense pacts, to obtain a route. Conversely, a government might trade an airline route at the expense of the profitability of its flag airlines for a more urgently needed foreign concession in another field.

At one time the route-making capability of governments was overwhelming, but it has been reduced in potency. Most of the world's important routes have already been decided, and, while it is theoretically possible to cancel an existing route and begin anew, in practice this is rarely done. Once an airline is awarded and has flown a particular route segment, it becomes almost an unfriendly act for a foreign government to revoke the concession. Similarly, where a state has but one important international airline, it is impracticable to apply pressure on its own airline through acts detrimental to that carrier's best interest since the carrier's and its government's interests too closely coincide. It is possible, however, to act in favor of a higher priority national objective which is in conflict with the flag airline's interest.

Because different governments make different demands on their airlines, the probability of conflict between a government and its flag airline is not the same for all states. When an airline is limited to being an earner of foreign exchange and is not an instrument of foreign policy, the chance for conflict is small since airline profits will usually result from the same policies as do foreign exchange earnings. SAS, KLM Royal Dutch Airlines, and Sabena Belgian World Airlines are examples of airlines whose governments act merely as their agents in obtaining necessary flight authorizations and are paid for their services in foreign exchange earnings.

9 "U.S., Australia Agree on Capacity Limits," *Aviation Week and Space Technology,* July 13, 1970 (Vol. 93, No. 2), p. 25.

For other governments airlines have multiple uses, and many of the uses are not necessarily compatible with the flag airline's own idea of its purpose. Conflict is most likely in those states which use airlines as tools of foreign policy. In such cases it is important for the government to retain power over the flag airlines. A most successful means of retaining power has been to maintain flag airlines as privately owned corporations and to have more than one flag airline. Profit will be an urgent need, and the government can regulate long-term profitability very well indeed by allocating route authorizations as it wishes. It is doubtful that the United States airline structure was established to retain governmental control. Nevertheless, it has served that objective very well. A good case could be made for ascribing Pan Am's current difficulties with excessive competition on its routes, authorized by the Civil Aeronautics Board (CAB), to its defiance of its regulator. Pan Am has historically had many friends in Congress, and it has not hesitated to use them to put pressure on the executive department. It is an interesting fact that the Western countries with the most complex international objectives, France, the United Kingdom, and the United States, all have multiple international flag carriers.

A Complex Interplay

The separate actors in the international transport drama are all playing complex and changing roles. Sometimes a government and its airline act as a team in the execution of foreign policy. Before World War II, for example, Pan Am engaged in a commercial duel with Germany's Lufthansa for control of air transport throughout South America. Actually, Pan Am was partially serving as a United States government agent in preventing the expansion of German commercial interests in a sensitive area and protecting United States bases, particularly the Panama Canal, from German attack should war occur.[10] So completely did the United States government rely on Pan Am as its agent in the area that it was sometimes said that the Pan Am representative, who even did the work of securing landing rights from governments, was more respected and more influential than was the local United States ambassador. Since the airline was urgently needed in the transport-short continent and Pan Am was well subsidized—the highest rate of air mail pay authorized by the United States government went to Pan Am—it is no wonder that its local representative was an influential man.

Sometimes an airline uses its national government to achieve its private profit objectives. Sometimes airlines are pawns in the aerospace game, acting, as British carriers have, as outlets for aircraft produced primarily to keep a military manufacturing capacity in being.

Sometimes nongovernmental interests can defy both governments and the

[10] Melvin Hall and Walter Peck, "Wings for the Trojan Horse," *Foreign Affairs*, January 1941 (Vol. 19, No. 2), pp. 347–369.

international system. An example of probable circumvention of governmental and ICAO control by nongovernmental actors occurred in the 1966 air corridors controversy. To provide needed airspace in the North Atlantic air route ICAO had agreed to reduce the lateral separation between aircraft from 120 to 90 miles.[11] This decision would have encouraged the airlines to install complicated navigational systems in their aircraft. These systems were available only from United States companies since competing companies did not have a satisfactorily accurate system available. A pilots' revolt on the grounds of inadequate safety was led by BOAC pilots. Spreading to the pilots' union, the International Federation of Air Line Pilots Association (IFALPA), the revolt prevented the decision from becoming effective. It was subsequently rescinded, although United States government authorities vigorously denied the existence of any threat to safety.[12] Representatives of United States equipment manufacturers are convinced that the original impetus for the pilots' revolt was provided by foreign manufacturing interests that sought time to ready competing gear. If this is true, it was the strongly emotional appeal of air safety which made it possible to sell the revolt to the pilots of all airlines since they did not have the statistical data or training to evaluate the issue dispassionately. In this case a joint decision of governments, taken in a supranational body, seems to have been overturned by private action of manufacturers from one country acting through a private international organization. Surely, conflict within the British government must have occurred when it agreed to the original ICAO decision. Quite possibly the defeated element within the British government went outside the government to achieve its goal.

Airlines sometime join forces against an offending government, selecting the safest weapon to bring the offender's policy into line. Foreign airlines are sometimes used by flag carriers against their own governments. Thus, in 1969 the CAB and the Department of State, acting to meet defense needs, seem to have tried to protect United States supplemental carriers from competition by preventing the scheduled airlines from carrying charter passengers and by keeping a substantial fare differential between charters and scheduled flights. This approach was defeated when Alitalia, the Italian carrier, denounced the IATA fare schedule and announced an extremely low transatlantic fare to Rome which would surely have driven the United States supplemental carriers out of the market.[13]

It cannot be proven that Alitalia was consciously acting as an agent for all the scheduled airlines, including Pan Am and TWA, but the fact remains

11 "Pilots, ATA Battle on Separation Rulings," *Aviation Week and Space Technology*, April 25, 1966 (Vol. 84, No. 17), p. 36.

12 "120-mi. Aircraft Lateral Separation Restored to Ease Traffic Problem," *Aviation Week and Space Technology*, June 20, 1966 (Vol. 84, No. 25), p. 35.

13 "Airlines Gird to Match Alitalia Cuts," *Aviation Week and Space Technology*, September 29, 1969 (Vol. 91, No. 13), p. 30.

that the act effectively served their purposes. No United States carrier could have so strongly opposed a United States policy.

Occasionally, international agencies are even used in private battles between two compatriot airlines. Presently, Continental Air Lines is, allegedly, using the United Nations Trusteeship Council as an instrument to break the Pan Am hold on the South Pacific. Air Micronesia, a Continental subsidiary, seems to be persuading Micronesian officials to urge the Trusteeship Council to request that Air Micronesia be continued as local carrier. The CAB has already recommended to President Richard M. Nixon that the job be transferred to Pan Am.[14]

Governments must exert great effort to ensure that their flag airlines—even those which are wholly state-owned—strive to meet national objectives rather than purely commercial ones. BOAC is presently locked in sharp battle with its government and sole owner to prevent the creation of a private British competitor. The government's stated objective is to increase the overall British share of the market. There is no doubt, however, that BOAC will be less able to operate independently if a competitor is set up, and this may very well be a secondary governmental objective. As a result the management of BOAC is doing everything in its power—from threatening lawsuits to supporting its own labor unions' threat to strike—to prevent the establishment of the new competitor.[15]

V. Conclusion

Obviously, the state-centered view of world affairs is inadequate to explain international transport. The industry has developed a dynamism of its own, scarcely supranational but possessing sufficient power to occasionally thwart the desires of powerful governments. It operates transnationally, and its operations often affect governments. Private parties are sometimes pawns of government; private agencies may consist partly of governments; and governments on occasion serve as stalking horses for private interests.

An alternative to the state-centered model would have to be extremely complex in order to explain transnational interactions. If a model were to be used primarily to understand the air transport system, it could best be developed by using the IATA as its focus. Such a model would consider the IATA as a separate, independent but interdependent agency, capable of formulating and carrying out policies but relying on governments and other agencies for support and concurrence. To be adequate, such a model would require an explanation and a set of power equations which would cover the inner work-

[14] Laurence Doty, "Policy, Politics Block Micronesia Award," *Aviation Week and Space Technology,* July 6, 1970 (Vol. 93, No. 1), p. 27.

[15] "News Digest," *Aviation Week and Space Technology,* July 27, 1970 (Vol. 93, No. 4), p. 22; and "BOAC Ordered to Give Certain Routes to Proposed New Carrier," *Aviation Week and Space Technology,* August 10, 1970 (Vol. 93, No. 6), p. 32.

ings of the IATA itself, something which has not yet been adequately done.

The air transport industry is a force for intersocietal contact, both for pleasure and business, which reduces the importance of state boundaries. As such, it should serve as a counterforce to nationalism. Unrest and violence are bad business for international airlines, particularly for their tourism segment. To the extent that the industry in general can influence governments, international transport is in favor of negotiated solutions to world problems—with the delegates to the negotiations traveling first class, of course.

Whether the industry's nonviolent objectives also lead to justice is another question. Essentially, transport is run by an oligopoly, a cartel which places its own profitability first. Transport is escaping governmental control and may someday be a free agent responsible only to its own managers and its customers. Cartels may or may not be just. The consumer may gain through the separation of transport and nationalism. However, he may also lose as competition disappears in favor of rationalization.

Throughout the post–World War II period a great change in air transport has been under way. The change is away from air transport as a servant of national policy and, hopefully, toward air transport as a servant of the people—an intersocietal people. The change continues, and as time passes airlines may become as neutral as ocean shipping is today—so free from government as to be able to adopt Liberian registry. That day, however, is still far away.

Labor and Transnational Relations

Robert W. Cox

Since World War II national trade union organizations have become involved in the internal political affairs of other countries, usually through the labor organizations in these countries. Soviet trade unions, a precursor and model in this respect, supported Soviet foreign policy through their international trade union contacts. United States unions played an important role in promoting the Marshall Plan, winning trade union support for it in Western Europe, and countering the opposition of communist-oriented trade unions in France and Italy. British and French unions were active in the colonial territories of their countries and often continued their influence after these territories achieved independence. United States unions have been active in Latin America and in the less developed areas of the Caribbean and Africa.[1]

Robert W. Cox, a member of the Board of Editors of *International Organization,* is director of the International Institute of Labor Studies in Geneva. The institute does not endorse any views, and the views expressed in this essay are those of the author.

[1] The foreign activities of United States trade unions in the postwar period have been analyzed by John P. Windmuller, *American Labor and the International Labor Movement, 1940 to 1953* (Cornell International Industrial and Labor Relations Reports, No. 2) (Ithaca, N.Y: Institute of International Industrial and Labor Relations, Cornell University, 1954). Windmuller has continued his analyses of subsequent events in a series of articles: "Foreign Affairs and the AFL-CIO," *Industrial and Labor Relations Review,* April 1956 (Vol. 9, No. 3), pp. 419–432; "Labor: A Partner in American Foreign Policy?" *Annals of the American Academy of Political and Social Science,* November 1963 (Vol. 350), pp. 104–114; "Leadership and Administration in the ICFTU: A New Phase of Development," *British Journal of Industrial Relations,* June 1963 (Vol. 1, No. 2), pp. 147–169; "The Foreign Policy Conflict in American Labor," *Political Science Quarterly,* June 1967 (Vol. 82, No. 2), pp. 205–234; and "Internationalism in Eclipse: The ICFTU after Two Decades," *Industrial and Labor Relations Review,* July 1970 (Vol. 23, No. 4), pp. 510–527. The role of United States labor representatives in the administration of the Marshall Plan is critically discussed in David Heaps, "Union Participation in Foreign Aid Programs," *Industrial and Labor Relations Review,* October 1955 (Vol. 9, No. 1), pp. 100–108.

The foreign policies of British and French trade unions have not received the same degree of scholarly attention. The activities of these unions in colonial territories are touched upon in Georges Fischer, "Syndicats et décolonisation," *Présence africaine,* October 1960–January 1961 (Nos. 34–35), pp. 17–60; B. C. Roberts, *Labour in the Tropical Territories of the Commonwealth* (London: G. Bell and Sons, 1964); and Jean Meynaud and Anisse Salah-Bey, *Le Syndicalisme africain: Evolution et perspectives* (Etudes et documents Payot) (Paris: Payot, 1963). The theme of trade union foreign policy is analyzed in a book by Jeffrey Harrod, *Trade Union Foreign Policy: The Case of British and American Unions in Jamaica* (London: Macmillan & Co., forthcoming). Assistance to labor movements in less developed coun-

Such overseas activities have led American trade unionists to take sides in interunion disputes, to support supposedly friendly leaders against their rivals, and, in some cases, to work against national governments. For example, United States unions supported Tom Mboya in Kenya and participated, along with the British Trades Union Congress (TUC), in activities directed against the Jagan government of British Guiana. The activities of the American Institute for Free Labor Development (AIFLD) also illustrate this point. The AIFLD is sponsored by the American Federation of Labor and the Congress of Industrial Organizations (AFL-CIO) and is financed by the United States government and several large American corporations, including W. R. Grace & Company, Anaconda Company, and Pan American World Airways. One of the institute's directors has claimed that some of its graduates were active in the clandestine planning which led to the overthrow of Brazilian President João Belchior Marques Goulart in 1964.[2] The manipulation of private organizations and interests in the service of national foreign policies is an element of the "new statecraft," or what might be called total diplomacy by analogy with total war.[3] These instances of transnational action raise questions concerning the intermingling of labor, diplomacy, intelligence and business activities in foreign policy, questions about who is manipulating whom and in what interests.

More recently trade unions have become active in a different type of transnational activity: the coordination of action against multinational corporations by unions in the various countries in which they operate. Major corporations in the automotive, electronics, chemical and pharmaceutical, rubber and petroleum, and air transport industries have been initial targets of transnationally coordinated trade union action. In 1969 the International Federation of Chemical and General Workers' Unions (ICF) coordinated the confrontation of the French multinational glass manufacturing company, Compagnie de Saint Gobain, by unions in the Federal Republic of Germany (West Ger-

tries is analyzed in Harold Karan Jacobson, "Ventures in Polity Shaping: External Assistance to Labour Movements in Developing Countries," in *The Politics of International Organizations: Studies in Multilateral Social and Economic Agencies,* ed. Robert W. Cox (Books that Matter) (New York: Praeger Publishers, 1970), pp. 195–205.

2 Statement by William Doherty, Jr., former director of the social projects department of the AIFLD, reported in United States Congress, Senate, Committee on Foreign Relations, *Survey of the Alliance for Progress: Labor Policies and Programs,* study prepared by Robert H. Dockery at the request of the Subcommittee on American Republics Affairs, Committee Print (Washington: Government Printing Office, 1968), pp. 13–16.

3 The term "new statecraft" is derived from George Liska, *The New Statecraft: Foreign Aid in American Foreign Policy* (Chicago: University of Chicago Press, 1960), and has been taken up as one aspect of transnational relations by the editors of this volume. The potential of a trade union role in United States foreign policy was underscored by George C. Lodge, "Labor's Role in Newly Developing Countries," *Foreign Affairs,* July 1959 (Vol. 37, No. 4), pp. 660–671. The potential role of United States labor in the cold war was indicated in Frank T. Carlton, "Labor Policies for the Struggle with Soviet Communism," *American Journal of Economics and Sociology,* April 1959 (Vol. 18, No. 3), pp. 277–284.

many), France, Italy, and the United States. This confrontation dramatized a development which was taking place over a much wider front.[4]

The labor response to the multinational corporation, in contrast to the "new statecraft" approach, does not directly impinge upon government or national politics. It does, however, have some indirect political implications. If the practice were to develop, it might lead to the creation of new transnational industrial structures through which labor could press for increased control not only over wages but also over all other corporate decisions affecting employment in the different countries in which the firm operates. Decisionmaking through such transnational structures would almost certainly conflict with the attempts of the nation-states in which multinational corporations operate to plan and carry out national policies for wages and employment. Other questions implicit in this process concern which trade unions in which countries will have the greatest influence and obtain the greatest satisfaction in situations in which their interests may diverge. One interesting feature of the Saint Gobain case was that, although the United States branch of the company had not made profits, the American union pressed its claims on the basis of the aggregate profits of the company in its worldwide operations. Is this another way of saying that potential benefits for workers in other countries may be transferred to American workers through transnational bargaining processes? In the Saint Gobain case the other unions directly concerned were in West European countries. What will be the interunion power relations and welfare consequences when unions in developed countries and less developed countries successfully coordinate bargaining with a single corporation? It might be predicted that the unions bargaining with multinational corporations in less developed countries will become dependent on the powerful unions of the parent company's country; that they will be cut off from other more nationally oriented labor organizations in their own country; and that the high-wage policy they will follow with the support of their overseas mentors will conflict with the employment expansion needs of a poor country.

The two tendencies singled out are only part of the complex of transnational relations involving labor, but they are at present most suggestive of the emergence of something new which might affect in some measure the location of power in world affairs between state and nonstate entities. This essay suggests an approach to the analysis of the implications of these tendencies. To do this it is necessary to situate them in the larger picture of labor as a transnational issue area.

[4] An account of the Saint Gobain case from the standpoint of the unions is given by Charles Levinson, secretary-general of the ICF, *ICF Bulletin,* June–July 1969, pp. 9–18. The larger issues of transnational bargaining are approached in Hans Günter, ed., *Transnational Industrial Relations* (London: Macmillan & Co., forthcoming), which incorporates the work of a symposium convened by the International Institute for Labor Studies to examine the emergence and future potential of the trade union response to the multinational corporation and the industrial relations consequences of regional economic integration.

An issue area can be thought of as an unorganized or partially organized system of interaction. Some of the questions of particular interest to this inquiry concern the prospect of the system becoming more fully organized through the emergence of transnational structures. Transnational relations which might become more formally structured or which might tend to change the existing nation-state and interstate structures would be of special interest. Further questions concern the consequences of such structural change for the location of power in international relations and for the welfare not only of nation-states but of social groups within states affected by these transnational relations.

Some transnational interactions in the labor issue area concern labor as a factor of production. An approach grounded in classical liberal economics would probably emphasize this aspect. For example, external factors such as international payments balances and capital flows may influence the level of employment and of wages in a given country. The level of employment and of incomes, in turn, can influence flows of migration into or out of that country. Some of these migratory movements, such as the brain drain, may have far-reaching implications for future rates of development.

Other transnational interactions in this issue area concern labor as an organized or potentially organizable social and political force. The degree of working class consciousness, the growth of trade unions, and the position of labor in the power relations between the various social forces are relevant. The conditions of labor as a factor of production influence the development and behavior of labor as a social and political force. Analytically, the former can be considered as part of the environment of the latter. Labor as an articulate social and political force in world affairs is, however, the aspect which most interests this study.

Actors in the labor issue area, in addition to trade unions and other less formal channels for articulating workers' interests, include the organizations of business or management and the agencies of the state active in the labor relations field. In addition, unorganized social groups which may impinge upon the processes of the issue area should be taken into account—the peasantry and the marginal populations of towns and also groups of intellectuals—since these may become organized and thus more politically and economically effective.

The environment of the issue area includes the technology of production, labor force characteristics, the market situation affecting products (as well as that affecting labor supply and demand), and the supply of capital, the legal system, and the political power relations in the society.

Transnational interactions can affect both the environment and the actors of the issue area. Some transnational activities, like international trade and capital flows, affect the environment indirectly. Transnational activities which affect the actors, on the other hand, can be quite direct, for example, the influence of a trade union in one country on a trade union in another. In a study concerned with political relations direct contacts between actors across national boundaries will attract the most attention, but these need to be explained against the background of environmental change.

I. The Evolution of the Issue Area

Since the nineteenth century labor history has been written in terms of attempts by trade unions to achieve control over the supply of labor and thus to enhance labor's influence over wages and working conditions. Initially, this was accompanied by an ideology which stressed the international solidarity of workingmen in opposition to employers and to states which were thought of as agents of employers. This was followed by a growing realization of the potential of the state as an instrument to achieve labor's goals. Extension of the franchise, the growth of the popular press, and the rise of socialist movements were convergent tendencies incorporating industrial labor into participation in the political systems of Western Europe. Through the state labor obtained legislation regulating working conditions and social insurance. Although the old internationalist ideology was never altogether forgotten, by the last decades of the nineteenth century it had become largely irrelevant. Popular nationalism—and imperialism—moderated latent class conflict in the more industrially developed Western countries. As industry demanded and obtained protective tariffs, labor, with some time lag, demanded and obtained controlled immigration.[5] The strength of the bonds between labor and the state, proved during World War I, were reinforced by the experience of the Great Depression. These bonds were further developed by the Keynesian doctrine of national economic management accepted during the depression and were institutionalized through the participation of labor in national planning bodies in some countries following World War II. More recently there have even been attempts in some Western countries to associate trade unions and employers with the management of national incomes policies. The notion that labor conditions are to be controlled as matters of national policy has been generally accepted since the mid-nineteenth century. This has included the use of measures to control the effect of external economic influences, especially, since the 1930s, those which might affect the level of employment.

In keeping this notion in the forefront of national concern organized labor has exercised influence on government while using its bargaining power vis-à-vis employers. As organized labor's primary preoccupations were directed

[5] Edward Hallett Carr, *Nationalism and After* (London: Macmillan & Co., 1945), called this the "nationalization of socialism"; see also Franz Borkenau, *Socialism: National or International* (London: George Routledge & Sons, 1942).

toward shaping national policy and domestic bargaining, its international concerns—expressed through the International Labor Organization (ILO)—were to generalize to other countries standards achieved at home, partly as a protective device, or, when in a weaker position, to use internationally approved norms to pressure for change in national practices. The framework of policy was, however, always the national framework.

There is evidence to suggest that during the 1960s the framework of policy may have been changing in some important ways. Two structural changes which are apparently altering the policy framework have been 1) regional economic organization, particularly in Western Europe, and 2) the multinational corporation. These basic changes can be viewed as the result of something broader which lies beyond the frame of reference of this essay—the expansion of a world market economy. In this process the initiatives have come from industry, and organized labor is seeking to adapt to them.

Before examining the implications of these recent structural developments it is necessary to recall that the evolution outlined is characteristic of Western industrial societies. Perhaps the most salient distinction between these and other societies is that in developed societies industrial labor has been incorporated into the political system as a final step in the extension of full citizenship to virtually all of society;[6] in less developed societies vast peasant and other marginal populations have remained outside the polity, unassimilated and nonparticipant. When urban industrial labor becomes participant in less developed societies, it does so not as the last low-status group to be absorbed into the polity but as a relatively privileged class.

From the standpoint of labor two modes of development can be distinguished in less developed societies. The first is the Soviet model which has as its fundamental doctrine the revolutionary myth of the dictatorship of the proletariat. The industrial labor force is accorded a deferential position in society and is made the political base upon which a revolutionary elite relies for support in its task of transforming a peasant society into an industrial society. Despite the persistence of an internationalist ideology the national framework is the basic framework of policy and is jealously protected from external influence.

The second mode of development is more characteristic of nonrevolutionary less developed societies. It can be described in terms of a series of dependency relationships between segments of the society and external forces. A segment of limited industrial development is heavily dependent on foreign capital, organizational skill, and technology. This segment draws wage-labor and certain services from the more backward segments of the society which it is depen-

[6] The salient exception has been the exclusion of women up to the twentieth century. Nonintegrated low-status social groups, usually ethnic minorities, have become more visible in Western industrial societies in the second half of the twentieth century.

dent upon and yet exploits in a relationship of "internal colonialism."[7] These societies can be called "dependent" not in the formal sense of being subject to the jurisdiction of another country but in the sense that their economies, cultures, and political processes are subject to penetration and major influence from "metropolitan" societies. Organized labor occupies an intermediate position in these dependency relationships, and some segments of organized labor have a strong external orientation because the locus of decisionmaking of the industries in which they work is abroad. The formal framework of policy is still the national framework, but external influences penetrate it with relative ease.

Thus, three patterns of society can be distinguished in terms of the salient features of industrial labor's status and power within the society: 1) a *pluralistic* pattern, characteristic of most Western industrial societies, in which industrial labor is effectively organized in independent trade unions and enjoys considerable power and prestige within the society; 2) a *revolutionary centralist* pattern, modeled on that of the Union of Soviet Socialist Republics with variants developed in other countries including Cuba and the People's Republic of China (Communist China), in which labor is accorded high formal status but is organized under the tutelage of a political party elite; and 3) a *segmental dependent* pattern, characteristic of many less developed countries, in which industrial labor has intermediate status and power in the domestic system but is highly dependent on external conditions and susceptible to external influence. Other patterns or variants might be added, for example, one which would serve to analyze more adequately the position of labor in societies led by nationalistic modernizing elites that are nonrevolutionary or conservative in their social goals. However, these three will serve for a preliminary analysis of transnational relations in the labor field.

These relations have to be distinguished according to whether they take place between states characterized by the same societal pattern, by two different patterns, or, conceivably, by all three patterns. It may be assumed that the structural consequences for the international system will vary depending on whether these relations concern homogeneous or heterogeneous groups of countries. The labor issues raised by the European Economic Community (EEC) and by the operations of United States corporations in Europe are of the first type, concerning different countries within the same general pattern of society. The labor issues that arise from the penetration of foreign capital and the influence of North American and European trade unions in less developed countries involve processes linking the industrialized pluralistic and

[7] The concept of "internal colonialism" has been developed by Rodolfo Stavenhagen. See his *Les Classes sociales dans les sociétés agraires* (Sociologie et tiers monde) (Paris: Editions Anthropos, 1969), especially pp. 343ff.; and his essay "Seven Fallacies about Latin America," in *Latin America: Reform or Revolution? A Reader,* ed. James Petras and Maurice Zeitlin (Political Perspectives Series) (Greenwich, Conn: Fawcett Publications, 1968), pp. 13–31.

the less developed dependent patterns. It is possible that the extension of the operations of multinational corporations will create frameworks and processes linking all three patterns of society.

In successive historical phases the relationships between these three patterns of society have differed and so have the characteristic transnational issues in the labor area and their relative saliency. These changes can be briefly reviewed from an international perspective since World War II in terms of three periods centering on 1950, 1960, and 1970.

During the first postwar period, in labor as in other fields, the cold war created a cleavage between Western and Soviet-bloc countries. Massive official aid went from the United States to Western Europe through the Marshall Plan to promote European economic recovery. The political division of the postwar world was paralleled by a division in the world labor movement between the communist-controlled World Federation of Trade Unions (WFTU) and the International Confederation of Free Trade Unions (ICFTU). The retention by the WFTU of communist-oriented affiliates in both France and Italy seemed to defy Western policy. Anticommunism was a prominent policy among Western trade unions. American trade unions played an important "new statecraft" role in support of United States government policy in Western Europe during this phase. Agents of the AFL won their struggle with the CIO for predominance in American labor's foreign activities; as a result these activities came to be very largely preoccupied with the anticommunist struggle.[8]

The manner in which Marshall Plan aid was allocated and administered stimulated national economic planning in Western Europe which indirectly tended to enhance the importance of the national framework for labor policy. The creation and maintenance of full employment was a national goal on which states and trade unions could agree and to which they were willing to give precedence. Governments also brought trade union representatives into consultation on a wider range of national economic policy matters.

Labor issues concerning less developed countries were less salient during this first postwar period. The TUC and the three major French central confederations of trade unions—the communist-oriented *Confédération générale du travail* (CGT), the breakaway socialist *Force ouvrière* (CGT-FO), and the Christian *Confédération française de travailleurs chrétiens* (CFTC)—maintained contacts and exercised influence over union movements in British and French colonies. During the 1950s agents of the AFL became more active in several colonies which appeared to be on the threshold of independence.

European recovery had been achieved by the late 1950s, the beginning of the second or intermediate period. Recovery was accompanied by a notable diminution in the preoccupation with anticommunism on the part of most West

[8] See Windmuller, pp. 117–133.

European trade unions. The continuing prominence accorded this issue by the leadership of American labor—the fused AFL-CIO—weakened its influence in Europe and strained relations within the ICFTU. However, events such as the Soviet occupation of the Hungarian People's Republic in 1956 precluded any prospect of significant East-West contacts between trade unions.

The creation of the European Coal and Steel Community (ECSC) and subsequently of the EEC provided a new focus for efforts of European unions to influence public policy on the harmonization of national policies directly affecting labor—migration, social security, and training policies and investment and employment policies involved in the indicative economic planning efforts undertaken through organs of the EEC. This was an extension to the European level of the role unions had sought for themselves in national planning.

Official government-to-government aid of the Marshall Plan period had been succeeded by an increasing flow of private capital from the United States to Western Europe, most of it in the acquisition or creation of subsidiaries of multinational corporations. Some of the labor policies of these American-based corporations provoked nationalistic reactions from both West European industrialists and unionists (as, for example, in 1962 when both General Motors Corporation and Sperry Rand Corporation laid off workers in their French plants), but the potential of transnational bargaining was not yet perceived. In the enthusiasm for the EEC some interest was aroused in the possibilities for collective labor agreements at the community level, but transnational labor relations did not materialize in this form.[9]

The intermediate period witnessed the growing international importance of labor issues in less developed countries. From an economic standpoint official policy promulgated by agencies such as ILO, the Organisation for Economic Co-operation and Development (OECD), and the United Nations Special Fund viewed the improvement of the quality of labor, mainly through occupational training, as a "preinvestment" condition for economic development. Bilateral and multilateral programs expanded to promote this aim. From a political standpoint the struggle for the ideological allegiance of labor in less developed countries escalated. Somewhat more subtle were efforts to export models of industrial relations systems to these countries through bi-

[9] For a discussion of collective labor agreements see Georges Spyropoulos, *Le Droit des conventions collectives de travail dans les pays de la Communauté européenne du charbon et de l'acier* (Travaux et recherches de l'Institut de droit comparé de l'Université de Paris, No. 16) (Paris: Les Editions de l'épargne [under the auspices of the Centre français de droit comparé with the aid of the Centre national de la recherche scientifique], 1959), which includes a preface on this theme by Paul Durand. The reasons for the failure of collective bargaining to appear at the community level in the EEC are analyzed by Hans Günter, "International Collective Bargaining and Regional Integration: Some Reflections on the Experience in the EEC," in Günter; and Georges Spyropoulos, "Le Rôle de la négociation collective dans l'harmonisation des systèmes sociaux européens," *Revue internationale de droit comparé,* January–March 1966 (Vol. 18, No. 1), pp. 19–55.

lateral aid programs and through the intergovernmental agencies concerned in this field of policy.[10] To some extent these policies can be seen as an attempt to apply the experience of the Marshall Plan to the labor problems of the third world. This included advocacy of regional economic integration among prescriptions for development. Soviet analysis, in line with Sekou Touré's view, now stressed the primacy of the national revolution over the social revolution in the African context. This led to a tactical inference favoring covert support of "anti-imperialist" African trade union organizations rather than an overt presence of the WFTU.

Uneasy about working with European unionists through the ICFTU, United States labor policymakers developed their own agencies such as the AIFLD for Latin America. Disengaged from trade union movements in other Western countries, the involvement of United States labor in these activities along with various agencies of government and business interests became more marked and accentuated labor's role in the "new statecraft." The events of 1964 in British Guiana and in Brazil occurred during this phase.

The third, or current, period has marked a further change in the nature of the issues in the labor area. By the late 1960s it was apparent that the EEC had facilitated the expansion of multinational corporations, most of them with home offices outside the Common Market.[11] About the same time trade unionists in some of the industries most affected by the expansion of multinational corporations, particularly metal trades and chemicals, began to advocate coordinated action by unions in different countries in which these corporations had operations.[12] In West European countries the development of more decentralized collective bargaining at the plant level within traditionally centralized systems strengthened the basis for a company-by-company approach to industrial relations which could lend itself to transnational coordination. Bargaining with multinational corporations gave new meaning to the international trade secretariats (ITSs), international organizations of trade unions in the same industry. Many of these bodies are older than the international confederations of trade unions created after World War II, but they played a less prominent role than these more politicized bodies during the period when labor movements were preoccupied with the cold war. Once international labor issues were posed in terms of functional linkages across national boundaries between workers employed in the same industry or by the same corporation, the ITSs appeared to have new potential. While these

[10] See Charles A. Myers, "The American System of Industrial Relations: Is It Exportable?" *Proceedings of the Fifteenth Annual Meeting of the Industrial Relations Research Association, Pittsburgh, Pa., December 27–28, 1962*, ed. Gerald G. Somers, pp. 2–14.

[11] Jean-Jacques Servan-Schreiber, *Le Défi américain* (Paris: Denoël, 1967). The publicity associated with the publication of this book may be used to date the widespread awareness of this particular consequence of West European economic integration.

[12] A factual note on developments in this respect is "The Trade Union Response to Multinational Enterprise," *Monthly Labor Review*, December 1967 (Vol. 90, No. 12), pp. iii–iv.

structures gained new life, the ICFTU seemed to have entered a moribund phase. Furthermore, within the American labor movement the main stimulus to transnational coordination of union action and to strengthening the ITSs for this purpose came from particular individuals like the late Walter Reuther and his brother Victor of the United Automobile Workers (UAW) who had opposed the official foreign policy line of the AFL-CIO.[13] The UAW, for example, channeled its foreign aid through the International Metalworkers' Federation (IMF). The International Federation of Chemical and General Workers' Unions, another ITS, also took initiatives to coordinate action vis-à-vis multinational corporations and had ideological affinities with the Reuther brothers.

The potential of transnationally coordinated trade union action was first apparent among Western industrialized countries but may become significant for less developed countries as well in view of the rising flow of private investment to these countries. Private investment in less developed countries during the late 1960s reached a level roughly equivalent to that of official governmental aid and was on a rising curve as official aid appeared to be tapering off.[14] Much of it has been in the form of intracorporation movement of capital; as multinational corporations have moved increasingly into manufacturing for domestic markets in less develope areas, their interests are no longer confined exclusively to extractive industries. This gives unions in the corporation's home country an interest in promoting sympathetic unions in their industry in less developed countries so that they can become partners in transnationally coordinated trade union action.

This outline history of the labor issue area suggests that in 1950 transnational relations were limited to the "new statecraft" type. United States trade unions acted in concert with United States government policy as an influence on West European trade unions. By 1960 this kind of influence extended more fully to other areas, particularly Africa and Latin America. The possibility of purely nongovernmental transnational relations was by then elicited within the EEC framework, but there was little substance to it. By 1970, however, transnational labor relations, responding to the expansion of multinational corporations in Europe first and then in less developed areas of the world, seemed to be emerging as a distinct possibility.

The issues raised by these developments have different implications for the three types of societies. These implications are clearest for transnational relations that link industrialized pluralistic societies. They are becoming clearer insofar as they link industrialized pluralistic with less developed dependent societies. This essay can do no more than begin analysis of these particular

[13] On the divisions within the American labor movement on foreign policy issues see Windmuller, *Political Science Quarterly*, Vol. 82, No. 2.

[14] *Partners in Development*, Report of the Commission on International Development, Lester B. Pearson, chairman (New York: Frederick A. Praeger, 1969), pp. 76–77, 136ff.

transnational processes. This task is taken up in the following sections which attempt, first, to analyze the actors and their strategies, second, to examine the relevant structures and ideologies in the labor issue area, and, finally, to draw out the implications of transnational relations in the labor issue area for the larger international system and for the national political systems which have been considered its principal components.

Implications for transnational relations involving revolutionary centralist societies are far less clear. While Soviet activity of the "new statecraft" type is reasonably well known, if not well documented, very little is known of those relations at the corporation level which now link some Socialist countries with Western countries. Some Western-based corporations have built manufacturing plants within Socialist countries, and a number of production agreements for the manufacture of component parts have been concluded between these corporations and state undertakings in Socialist countries. There may be some potential for East-West transnational relations in the labor field in these events, but for the present one can only speculate.[15]

A few points of the analysis which follows can, fortunately, be illustrated by reference to completed research. Relevant research, however, is still scarce. The phenomena considered have only recently attracted interest, and many of the questions concern the future rather than the past. Thus, this preliminary exploration must be limited in most of its aspects to suggesting hypotheses and drawing inferences which will have to await the test of deeper study.

II. The Actors and Their Strategies

Before considering the structure of transnational relations in the labor area and their effects on national political systems and the international system, it is useful to try to analyze the actors and their strategies in the area. What motivates some actors to enter into external activities, and how do other actors respond to them? What strategies do various actors adopt? This exercise should make it possible to discern the possible coalitions and alliances which could structure relationships in the issue area. Since activity relating to processes described in the previous section has been initiated by actors in industrialized pluralistic societies, their motivations and strategies will be examined first, followed by an examination of patterns of response from actors in less developed "dependent" societies. Multinational corporations have loomed large in the processes described; their strategies are considered in relation to those of national employers.

While the distinction between industrialized pluralistic and less developed "dependent" types of societies is analytically useful, it should not obscure the

[15] See Norman Scott, "Some Possible Implications of East-West Enterprise Agreements," and Zdaněk Mošna, "Economic Reforms and Labor Relations in the Socialist Countries of Eastern Europe," in Günter.

fact that much of the impetus for activity in the labor area is now coming from business and labor organizations in the United States and can be viewed as the penetration abroad by private American organizations. The influence of this penetration has differential consequences depending upon the type of society into which it extends.

Unions in Industrialized Pluralistic Societies

Traditionally, trade unionists have advocated and justified action abroad on two grounds: the altruistic idea of the international solidarity of workingmen and the more self-interested desire to defend the country's workers' acquired standards against cheap labor abroad by raising the wage levels of foreign workers. Both arguments legitimate action to build and strengthen unions in foreign countries, but neither can be taken very seriously as a motive or explanation of trade union action abroad. In regard to the first argument, unions in European countries and the United States have not behaved in a notably less nationalistic fashion than other elements in their societies; they have shown, if anything, rather greater than average propensity to adopt nationalistic attitudes. The second, or low wage, argument is widely regarded as an economic fallacy.[16] Both arguments belong to the folklore of the labor movement.

The issue of lower wages in foreign countries has reappeared in a new form in regard to the multinational corporation. Trade unions are now worried that corporations will shift production from home-based factories to foreign countries in which labor is cheaper. The issue is no longer one of competition in world trade but of internal corporate decisions regarding the location of certain types of production. United States trade unionists have expressed concern, for example, about the efforts of the Mexican government to interest United States corporations in setting up factories in the border areas, about the investment of American manufacturing companies in the Far East, and about the licensing of the production of certain products or components in Japan for eventual sale in the United States market.[17] The prospect is that certain types of jobs may become extinct in the United States as big corporations find it more profitable to transfer certain types of production to less developed countries. This can be seen as part of a general trend in the world market economy in which manufacturing will gradually shift to lower wage, less developed countries, while the higher productivity, more advanced countries move into a postindustrial phase concentrating on the production of knowledge and sophisticated technologies.

[16] The Randall commission report, for example, rejected this argument. See the *Report of the Commission on Foreign Economic Policy to the President and the Congress,* Clarence B. Randall, chairman (Washington: Government Printing Office, January 1954), p. 62.

[17] Elizabeth Jager, "Multinationalism and Labor: For Whose Benefit?" *Columbia Journal of World Business,* January–February 1970 (Vol. 5, No. 1), pp. 56–64. The author is an economist with the AFL-CIO, although she includes a disclaimer that her views necessarily represent those of that organization.

In a decentralized trade union movement like that in the United States, unions defending workers in jobs likely to become extinct in that society are going to protest. The labor movement's view will be the view of those groups directly affected. Where the labor movement is more centralized, and thus more able to attain a collective viewpoint on some concept of a general interest of workers, the same reaction may not occur. Swedish textile manufacturers have, for example, transferred production to Portugal, a lower wage country, without obstruction from Swedish trade unions; the move was seemingly welcomed by the unions because it removed a low-wage industry from Sweden and at the same time benefited a less developed country.[18] A centralized trade union movement is, of course, only one factor which may work toward limiting protectionist reactions by labor; employment adjustments will be easier in a period of economic expansion and in countries which give public support for job transfer and retraining.

The trade union's traditional aim to control jobs may thus lead it to attempt to control managerial decisions about the investment and the location of production. Unions are generally weak on this ground and, in order to be able to confront management, they will have to acquire strength in the countries to which production could be shifted. Thus, there is a desire to build working relationships with unions in these countries or to create unions where none yet exists. Effectively coordinated action implies that such unions in other countries share certain essential characteristics with those in the corporation's home base, particularly freedom to take industrial action on a company basis. It would be difficult for Swedish trade unions, for example, to take part in transnationally coordinated action against a particular corporation since this would probably violate the agreement concluded for the whole industry by the central trade union organization. Similarly, trade unions working under the leadership of political parties for national development goals—whether of the Soviet type or the type that has existed in some less developed countries—would not be likely to cooperate with United States unions, for example, in transnational action.

A further consideration affects certain industries which are technologically highly integrated and in which the initial stages of the technological process take place in poor countries and the final stages in rich countries. For example, in the oil and aluminum industries both the employers and the employees in the final production stages have an interest in the uninterrupted supply of materials from the early stages—crude petroleum or bauxite, in the examples cited—and thus in the maintenance of labor peace in operations in the poor country supplying them. Unions and management in the rich country's plants that carry out the final stages of the technological process will thus be drawn

18 Unpublished report on a meeting of trade union experts convened by the OECD to discuss multinational corporations, Paris, November 1969.

to cooperate in promoting peaceful relations in their plants in poor countries. The pattern for plants in these poor countries is one of high wages and the creation of unions under the tutelage of similar unions from the rich country. Thus, for example, since 1953 the United States Steelworkers of America, which represents American workers in the aluminum industry, has established such a relationship with the National Workers Union in Jamaica. This organization was set up primarily to organize the bauxite workers and exclude a union with a nationalist and socialist leadership as well as one with a rural membership base.[19]

Trade union strategies for enhancing control of jobs and labor conditions in multinational corporations include: 1) promoting contacts and working relations with existing trade unions of the same type in other countries in which the corporation has operations; 2) creating and sustaining unions in their own image in less developed countries; 3) applying pressure on corporation headquarters to recognize and bargain with unions in these other countries when corporations have been reluctant to do so; 4) banning overtime and other increases in work schedules in other countries in the event of a strike in any one country in which the corporation operates in order to prevent shifts in production; 5) organizing consumer boycotts of corporation products in cases of employer intransigeance; 6) coordinating the terminal dates of collective agreements in the various foreign operations of the corporation; and 7) coordinating bargaining ultimately on a worldwide corporation basis.

There are also certain psychological incentives impelling trade unionists to action abroad which have little to do with the economic interests of union members. Foreign policy roles give trade union leaders prestige and a sense of power. This incentive may be particularly great in a decentralized labor movement like that of the United States. Where the major economic issues are the province of strong member unions, the leadership of the national organization, excluded from a meaningful role in the bread-and-butter activities of unions, finds a compensating and prestigious role in foreign policy. The leadership, because of acquiescence in a division of functions, is free from intervention by the member unions in this field and is solicited as an ally by agencies of government which may provide resources to increase the leadership's scope in foreign affairs. The weakness of the central leadership in relation to member unions explains its preoccupation with foreign policy, and this weakness also makes it a likely ally of government in the "new statecraft." There are thus structural explanations for the foreign policy of the AFL-CIO in addition to those relating to the personal views of George Meany, its president, and of his principal advisers.

The orientation that trade union leaders give to their foreign policy activities can often be seen as the projection of local trade union conflicts into global

[19] The origins and evolution of this relationship are described and analyzed in Harrod.

confrontations. The faction fights between various socialist and communist groups in the garment industry of New York City during the 1930s gave a strong anticommunist imprint to the leadership of the International Ladies' Garment Workers Union (ILGWU). During World War II David Dubinsky, president of this union, channeled funds to support the Free Trade Union Committee, an organization run by Jay Lovestone, former secretary-general of the Communist party of the United States, who had broken with Stalin and was engaged with single-minded devotion in a global battle with Stalinism.[20] The fight against communist infiltration and subversion, a domestic union battle in the 1930s, appeared to have worldwide significance following World War II. The Free Trade Union Committee was the original base for the postwar foreign policy of the AFL and subsequently of the AFL-CIO, and Jay Lovestone became the foreign minister of George Meany.

Governments in Industrialized Pluralistic Societies

During World War II trade unions became active participants in the "new statecraft." The British government, for example, actively encouraged contacts between British and American trade union leaders prior to the United States entry into the war as one means of cultivating American support for the struggle against Germany. Total war required the mobilization of all the active forces of the country on behalf of the war effort, and the trade unions played their part in it. The occupying powers in Germany and Japan associated their trade unions in efforts to mold the future of industrial relations in these countries. They thought these industrial relations systems could be made into a bulwark against a revival of the regimes which had fought World War II. In the cold war which followed, trade unions were close to the heart of ideological issues. The support of trade unions which had proclaimed their independence of government was particularly valuable for Western governments.

During the mid-1950s attention shifted to less developed countries, and Western governments appreciated the potential of trade unions for influence in these countries. Trade union movements in countries emerging from colonial status provided many new political leaders. Thus, influence with trade unions could be regarded as a means of influencing the recruitment of political leadership in new states—of favoring or penalizing local personalities according to their presumed friendliness or enmity toward Western policies.

The transnational coordination of trade union action in order to confront multinational corporations raises different issues for governments in industrialized pluralistic societies. Almost all these governments have been concerned to involve trade unions together with employers and other powerful economic interests in national policies for economic growth and the control

[20] See Windmuller, pp. 72–76.

of inflation. Governments will be likely to suspect that transnational bargaining between corporations and segments of the trade union movement over wages and the location of production may conflict with national policies for incomes and investment.[21] Although the issue is so new that overt clashes cannot be cited, the potential for conflict seems clear. It stems from the broader issue of rivalry between the nation-state and the corporation as two conflicting sources of security for the individual. These include, specifically, job security and income security but implicitly, in the longer run, the psychological security which comes from the individual's identification with a larger community. The corporation may be a source of security and a pole of loyalty for its own employees and their families, but the state is responsible for all citizens and their dependents, including the unemployed and others outside the sphere of the corporation. The state may thus on grounds of equity oppose the development of corporation-centered systems of security for limited groups of individuals. Strong trade union movements that are centralized at the national level may be expected to ally with the state on this ground, but unions which are strong at the plant level will be more inclined to try to drive a better bargain for their members with the multinational corporation at the risk of conflict with state policy. Conflict between corporation-centered and state-centered policies in regard to wages and investment may be less evident in the United States than in countries whose economies are smaller, weaker, and more susceptible to foreign influence. In these countries conflicts with national policy deriving from the activities of multinational corporations will be seen as the spreading influence of the United States economy. Nationalism will thus be a support to the state, while corporations and the segments of trade union movements which see their advantage in bargaining transnationally with corporations will appeal to internationalist sentiments.

Employers in Industrialized Pluralistic Societies

Trade unions bargaining individually with multinational corporations in different Western countries have complained about the obscurity of the center of decisionmaking power in these corporations, whether the local managers are empowered to decide labor matters or whether these must be determined by headquarters.[22] To some extent this obscurity may be a useful bargaining tactic for local managers, but it may also reflect the reality of different management practices regarding the degree of power granted to local subsidiaries.[23] Technological factors such as information processing and integrated

[21] Raymond Vernon has referred to the potential conflict between corporation and national policies in "The Role of U.S. Enterprise Abroad," *Daedalus,* Winter 1969 (Vol. 98, No. 1), p. 126. He specifically cites governmental concern with fiscal and monetary effects of corporation policies, but income and investment consequences may be seen as other aspects of the problem.

[22] Unpublished report on an OECD meeting of trade union experts.

[23] The issue of centralization versus decentralization in regard to industrial relations management in multinational corporations is discussed in J. A. Belford, "Centralized Policy Direction of the Industrial Re-

production processes are centralizing influences. So is, perhaps, the cultural factor of home-country labor relations habits. Where labor relations issues impinge upon matters of investment location and affect the relative profitability of operations in different countries, they may be expected to rise to the central corporation-wide level of decisionmaking. To some extent, however, the obscurity of which trade unionists complain is inherent in the nature of the corporation which, in Raymond Vernon's words, is a coalition, "not . . . an organism single-mindedly devoted to maximizing the firm's profits, but . . . a group of cooperating semi-independent forces with distinguishably different goals."[24] Corporate decisions about labor relations, like those about other matters, are likely to be the result of compromises between interests within the corporation as well as between the corporation and trade unions.

National employers in industrialized pluralistic societies within which multinational corporations operate may become hostile particularly when the multinational corporation appears as an invader of protected markets. Labor relations issues may provide a focus for a nationalistic reaction conditioned by a wider range of business behavior. Worker security in a system of protected markets takes the form of a reluctance of employers to lay off workers even during periods of slack demand. Multinational corporations may in some cases outbid local employers by offering higher wages when they need to attract labor but lay off workers more readily when demand falls. Local employers will protest disruption of the wage structure of the labor market, and unions will protest insecurity of employment. In such circumstances both are potential allies of government in state-centered economic policies.

The behavior of United States or other Western-based multinational corporations in less developed countries will probably draw increased attention during the next few years. One major factor conditioning the attitude of foreign management toward labor relations in their operations in less developed countries is the importance of labor costs in these operations relative to other costs of production.

Another major factor is the extent to which the technology of the industry is a vertically integrated process in which interruption at any point would be very costly.[25] The petroleum and aluminum industries illustrate a convergence of these two factors in which labor costs, particularly in those phases of pro-

lations Function in an International Company," *Proceedings of the Seventeenth Annual Meeting of the Industrial Relations Research Association, Chicago, Ill., December 28–29, 1964*, ed. Gerald G. Somers, pp. 74–84. The essay by Louis T. Wells, Jr., in this volume discusses the broader behavioral implications of centralized and decentralized models of multinational corporation management.

[24] Vernon, *Daedalus*, Vol. 98, No. 1, p. 115.

[25] These factors are analyzed more fully by B. C. Roberts, "Factors Influencing the Organization and Style of Management and Their Effect on the Pattern of Industrial Relations in Multinational Corporations," in Günter.

duction located in less developed countries, are low relative to other costs and in which there is a high degree of vertical integration of technology. The labor relations policies of corporations in these industries are thus likely to be designed to avoid trouble. It is worth paying to limit the risk of interruptions, and the costs of high wages do not make much impact on total production costs. Some employers may try to follow a high-wage policy without unions, but others will see unions as a potential ally. The latter will welcome the organization of their employees in less developed countries by unions, provided these unions are oriented to company bargaining rather than national political action.[26] Where unions in the less developed country operations of such corporations are under the influence of the unions with which the corporations bargain in their home country, the possibility of a corporation-wide symbiotic relationship between unions and management appears. The advantages of such a symbiotic labor-management relationship may be seen to include: 1) the re-creation of known patterns of labor relationships in the foreign environment; 2) the mediation by the local union of the problems of selecting and committing a work force in the less developed country; and 3) payoffs to local political authorities in the form of jobs for their supporters since the local union can screen job applicants for political orthodoxy.[27] When labor costs are a significant factor (as in plantations and certain kinds of mining), different patterns of labor relations may be more likely to prevail. Some forms of mining are based on a technology using large numbers of unskilled workers with a substantial labor turnover. The foreign firm in this case benefits from the security provided the worker by his family or tribal links in the traditional sector; it is thus spared the costs of training, permanent housing for families, and social security. Such conditions are inimical to trade union development. In some cases foreign firms have relied on alliances with local political authorities which perform a police function and maintain a repressive labor policy. These are often cases in which developed country unions are not motivated to intervene.

Trade Unions in "Dependent" Societies

Numerous motives lead trade union leaders in less developed "dependent" countries to welcome intervention by unions from industrialized countries: the desire for material aid—from buildings to typewriters—and financial subsidies to ease high costs of organization building; the desire for allies abroad to counterbalance local forces; the psychological drive to emulate the "metropolitan society"; and the personal prestige which may come to a union leader who plays an international role—deference, opportunities for travel, etc. These

26 See, for example, the article by Jack Lee in Günter.

27 Such a symbiotic union-management relationship in bauxite mining for the aluminum industry is analyzed by Jeffrey Harrod, "Multinational Corporation, Trade Unions and Industrial Relations: A Case Study of Jamaica," in Günter.

motives, however, may be offset by the fear of loss of control in the friendly embrace of powerful foreign organizations.

The attitude of the union in the "dependent" country toward penetration by developed country unions will depend on the union's relationship to its own social and political environment. These relationships are shown in figure 1 which illustrates four ideal types of trade unions according to the matrix used by David E. Apter for the classification of political systems.[28]

	Hierarchical authority	Pyramidal authority
Consummatory values	Mobilization union	Social reform labor movement
Instrumental values	Political front union	Interest group union

Figure 1. Relationships between unions and the environment

The prototype of the interest group union is the American "business union" which represents the interests of a particular group of workers, for example, those employed in a particular industry or by a particular company. The mobilization union follows the Soviet pattern, and the union is one among several organizations which serve to mobilize the active population in the service of revolutionary national goals defined by the political leadership. Political front unions are subordinated to the national political leadership but solely as instruments of control, lacking the revolutionary goals of mobilization movements. They may result from the degradation of erstwhile revolutionary movements, or they may be a protective device engineered by conservative leadership. The models for the social reform labor movement category are drawn mainly from the earlier history of Western societies, for example, those in Scandinavia and the United Kingdom in which trade unions were one element in a more comprehensive labor movement including cooperatives and socialist political parties. Unions of this type can subordinate the interests of specific groups of workers to general objectives of social reform for the benefit of the working class and other low status social groups. Interest group unions, by contrast, are not likely to recognize any conflict between the interests of the workers they represent and any broader social objectives and will act without inhibition in their members' particular interests.

28 David E. Apter, *The Politics of Modernization* (Chicago: University of Chicago Press, 1965), pp. 24ff.

There are very few examples of labor movements of the social reform type in less developed countries today, although one might consider the Ahmadabad Textile Labor Association in its Ghandian period one such example. Their existence implies a greater degree of autonomous social mobilization than has taken place in most countries of the third world. In less developed countries formal ideological affiliation may be less important than actual behavior in determining a trade union's type. Communist-controlled trade unions in countries with noncommunist political leadership may often behave more like interest group unions than like mobilization unions. In India, for example, unions belonging to the communist-controlled All-India Trade-Union Congress have bargained forcefully for their members while those affiliated with the Indian National Trade Union Congress, linked to the government through the Congress party, have been more inhibited from pressing particular claims because of their adherence to official policy objectives.[29] Communist-controlled unions in the Chilean copper industry in the past have similarly acted for the interests of copper workers unrestrained by considerations of official anti-inflationary policy.

What is most important for the present analysis is the likely relationship of these different types to emerging transnational relations in the labor field. It can be suggested that interest group unions representing workers in the sectors developed by foreign capital are the most likely partners in transnational relations involving foreign businesses and foreign trade unions. Mobilization unions, by contrast, are most likely to adopt nationalistic attitudes hostile to foreign economic penetration. Political front unions may collaborate with foreign business if dependence on foreign capital is the policy of the local rulers; they may also be used to pressure for greater returns from foreign enterprise or to satisfy nationalist sentiments if that is the policy of these rulers. Whereas the union may be a powerful autonomous agent in the industrialized pluralistic society, its role is more likely to be subordinate to that of government in the "dependent" society. The direction of trade union development —whether toward an interest group union or a mobilization union—tends to be determined by the political leadership.

Governments in "Dependent" Societies

The attitude of governments toward foreign business and trade union influence in the labor field is conditioned by the sociopolitical structure of the country and thus by the commitments of its political leadership. Two general propositions are suggested. First, the more the leadership depends on foreign capital for the development of the country's resources, the greater will be its toleration of external influence in the labor field. Toleration of external influ-

[29] Myron Weiner, *The Politics of Scarcity: Public Pressure and Political Response in India* (Chicago: University of Chicago Press, 1962), pp. 88ff.

ence may be accompanied by hard bargaining over the quid pro quo to be paid by foreign business when local leaders feel themselves in a position of strength. Second, the more the leadership seeks to mobilize new social groups into the political system and to broaden the benefits of development, the more external influences will be likely to be resisted. These two factors may counterbalance each other in some instances and lead to ambivalent situations.

Several models of policies in this field can be sketched. The first is the "banana republic" model with very little social mobilization and considerable dependence on foreign capital. The local oligarchy allies with foreign capital and represses social protest.

A second model represents a higher level of social mobilization. Local leadership co-opts urban organized labor along with middle-class urban groups into the dominant political alliance. In some populist forms, for example, Peronism, this type of alliance has been hostile to external penetration. But in more recent bureaucratic-military-corporatist forms, for example, Argentina and Brazil in the late 1960s, Indonesia after the overthrow of Achmed Sukarno, such an alliance has been less hostile.

A third model represents a revolutionary regime that follows a mobilization policy. It would have a nationalist ideology hostile to foreign capital and foreign trade unions. Examples could be cited of the hostility of African mobilization regimes to the international trade union confederations, although experience suggests that the dependent character of these societies is not easily eliminated by revolutionary seizure of power since the cutting of overt links may be replaced by less visible contacts and influences.

Business in "Dependent" Societies

A distinction should be drawn between "dependent" countries in which a significant national entrepreneurial group has developed in the industrial field and those countries in which this has not occurred. Employers' associations now exist in most less developed countries, but it is important to know in each case whether they are representative of national employers or whether they are the creation of foreign business interests as in parts of Africa and Southeast Asia. In some countries both coexist within the same organization; in other countries local and foreign business interests are represented in separate associations.

A national entrepreneurial group may provide a base for opposition to penetration by foreign business and foreign trade union organizations, but it does not necessarily become such a base. The attitudes of national businessmen will probably be determined mainly by the extent to which foreign businesses operating in the country complement rather than compete with local business.[30] Foreign investment may enter fields not previously developed, such as

[30] The point is made by Vernon, *Daedalus*, Vol. 98, No. 1, p. 121.

the assembly of automobiles, which may also provide linkages stimulating the growth of locally owned industries. In such cases local entrepreneurs can live happily with foreign business. In other cases foreign business may import sophisticated capital-intensive methods which can compete advantageously with local, more labor-intensive businesses built under import substitution policies. Foreign employers will be able to pay higher wages and still have lower production and merchandising costs than local employers in the national market. Such a situation would lead to tensions between local and foreign employers. As multinational corporations install manufacturing facilities increasingly in less developed countries, such tensions may become more frequent and more acute. Cleavages would be likely to occur not only between foreign and national employers but also between the workers employed by each.[31] National employers together with their workers (and workers' trade unions when these exist) could become allies of local political leadership in a nationalist opposition to foreign or multinational business and foreign trade union penetration.

III. Transnational Structures and Ideologies

Transnational activity of the "new statecraft" type has been prevalent in the labor area since World War II. It has been and can continue to be an important element in the influence of some states over other states, but it is not likely to affect the structure of the international system. The international system might, however, be changed if transnational processes were to create new structures and new centers of power outside the scope of interstate relations. The continuing growth of multinational corporations now appears as the force most likely to have such an effect. Since these corporations have been increasing their investments in "dependent" countries, especially since the mid-1960s, it is of particular interest to inquire whether any new structures that link industrial and labor interests in "metropolitan" and "dependent" countries have come into being or seem likely to appear. There seems to be some prospect of the development of a symbiotic relationship between certain types of trade unions and the management of multinational corporations as United States unions gain influence over and coordinate action by unions in other countries dealing with the same corporations. Is this process leading to the creation of new institutions?

The flow of transnational influence in the labor area is outlined in figure 2. The first column refers to influence within the trade union world and between trade unions and governments. "New statecraft" activities fit here as well as trade-union–to–trade-union contacts having no reference to national foreign policies. The second column refers to the situation of trade union

[31] Fernando Henrique Cardoso and Enzo Faletto, *Dependencia y desarrollo en América Latina: Ensayo de interpretación sociológica* (Mexico City: Siglo Veintiuno Editores, 1969), especially p. 143.

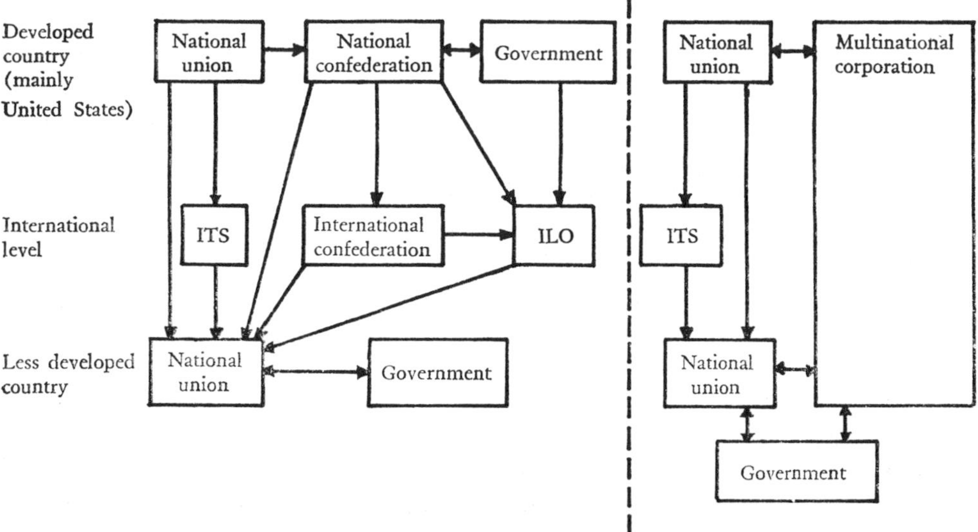

Figure 2. Transnational influence in the labor issue area

relationships with multinational corporations in both "metropolitan" and "dependent" societies. A full analysis of factors conditioning the emergence of new structures would require exploration of these relationships. Of special interest is the extent to which intermediate structures at the international level are able to function so as to aggregate and to organize the interplay of motivations analyzed in the preceding section. Three such intermediate structures seem to be worthy of attention: the ICFTU, ILO, and the ITSs.

The ICFTU has been studying the implications of the multinational corporation for labor.[32] This organization lost something of its unity with the passing of the cold war and the period of European reconstruction. The withdrawal of the AFL-CIO in 1969 weakened it further. In these circumstances the challenge of the multinational corporation might be the kind of issue which the central secretariat might use as a means to revitalize the organization and to give it a new and enlarged role. However, if it were to follow this route, the ICFTU would have to overcome the structural difficulty resulting from the fact that its members are national confederations of trade unions which do not deal directly with multinational corporations. Remote from the bargaining place, the ICFTU might perform a function for trade unions as a forum for discussion of policy and strategy and as a lobby.

The multinational corporation has also attracted interest within ILO. Like the secretariat of the ICFTU, officials of the International Labor Office are

[32] "Multinational Corporations and Labour Relations," *Economic and Social Bulletin,* March–April 1969 (Vol. 17, No. 2), pp. 1–8. A number of statements on the question have been made by the director of the Economic Social and Political Department of the ICFTU, Heribert Maier; see *The Times* (London), November 10, 1970, p. 27.

searching for ways in which to give their organization tasks which would enhance its authority and in particular make it more relevant to the present concerns of industrially advanced states as well as to less developed countries and may see such possibilities in the labor issues posed by the multinational corporation. The topic would not be entirely new to ILO for the creation of international structures to organize the major world industries was advocated in ILO during World War II as part of its postwar planning.[33] Such organizations in the form envisaged by the authors of the idea—with real decision-making power in industrial matters and labor conditions—were not established after the war. However, a series of industrial committees were created within ILO to provide representation for trade unions and management in a particular industry alongside governments. The industrial committees have adopted resolutions concerning labor conditions in their industries and have commissioned studies. The issues posed by multinational corporations have been raised at recent meetings of these committees as well as by trade union representatives in ILO's general conference.

While pressure to expand ILO's task in this area is likely to continue, certain obstacles inherent in ILO's structure will have to be overcome if it is to be successful. Like the ICFTU the trade union contituents of ILO are national confederations rather than individual unions. Thus, they are not directly involved in negotiations with multinational corporations. The same factor operates on the employer side. The national employers' confederations, which have direct representation in the ILO conference, articulate the interests of multinational corporations only to a limited degree. These corporations tend to act rather independently of the national employers' associations, and some have dissociated themselves from them. National employers' associations are in the main affiliated with the International Organization of Employers (IOE) which coordinates employer action in ILO. Multinational corporations look more to the International Chamber of Commerce (ICC), which has no representative functions in ILO, as a forum in which to consider their international policies.

ILO, on the other hand, does have the industrial committees in which representatives of some multinational corporations have taken part along with trade unionists from unions directly concerned with bargaining in the industry. If a more substantial role for these committees were to develop, the participants might seek to free themselves from subordination to central ILO machinery which is controlled by organizations somewhat remote from their interests.

[33] This proposal is discussed in Ernst B. Haas, *Beyond the Nation-State: Functionalism and International Organization* (Stanford, Calif: Stanford University Press, 1964), chapter 10; see also *The ILO and Reconstruction,* Report by the Acting Director of the International Labor Office to the conference of the International Labor Organization, New York, October 1941 (Montreal: International Labor Organization, 1941), pp. 105–108.

At the present time the international trade secretariats appear to have the greatest potential to develop as transnational structures by organizing trade union action vis-à-vis the multinational corporation. Conceivably, their role in aggregating and organizing trade union action on a transnational basis could be developed within a more comprehensive labor-management structure provided by an autonomous evolution of ILO's industrial committees. However, at this stage the future development of transnational structures in the labor area remains uncertain.

The outlines of an ideology which might eventually support new structures in this area are more clear. The emerging ideology is highly reminiscent of the doctrine of international functionalism articulated most coherently by David Mitrany toward the close of World War II.[34] Mitrany envisaged building the foundations of world peace by uniting interests across national boundaries in the performance of specific functional tasks. Individuals directly concerned with functional problems, whatever their nationality, would naturally tend to support international collaboration in order to solve these problems. Their loyalty would be to the accomplishment of the functional task; national interests would either not conflict with these functional loyalties or would be subordinated to them. The more these functional tasks could be multiplied, the smaller the area of conflict for national interests would become. Ultimately, the nation-state as an institution would wither away in a world organized functionally, rather than geographically.

This basic ideology is now being refurbished, but the hero has changed. Mitrany and the functionalists who influenced the planning of the post–World War II structure of international institutions looked to functional intergovernmental organizations like the specialized agencies of the United Nations as the type of instrument required for building peace. The hero of the new revised functionalism is the multinational corporation.

Another modification has come about with the evolution of opinion since World War II. Development takes its place beside peace as an ultimate goal of world order to be achieved by the new hero.

Elements toward the definition of the new functionalism have been contributed by corporate leaders, public officials, and academics. Roger Blough, chairman of the board of United States Steel Corporation, has said that "the multinational corporation may ultimately prove to be the most productive economic development of the twentieth century for bringing the people of nations together for peaceful purposes to their mutual advantage; and . . . it can thus provide the adhesive which can do more to bind nations together than any other development yet found by man in his pursuit of peace."[35]

[34] David Mitrany, *A Working Peace System: An Argument for the Functional Development of International Organizations* (London: Royal Institute of International Affairs, 1943).

[35] Quoted in Henry H. Fowler, "National Interests and Multinational Business," *California Management Review*, Fall 1965 (Vol. 8, No. 1), p. 5.

Henry Fowler, former United States undersecretary of the Treasury, published an article in 1965 devoted to two related questions: 1) "Will the economic recovery that has characterized the developed countries of the free world since World War II founder on the shoals of nationalism?" and 2) "Will the multinational corporations—those mighty engines of enlightened Western capitalism—be permitted to play their vital role in the less-developed countries?"[36] He argued that to clear the way for uninhibited growth of multinational corporations would serve the interests of United States foreign policy and of the "free world," would promote economic development in poor countries, and would create the conditions for world peace. George W. Ball, former United States undersecretary of state for economic affairs, has argued that the business and political structures of the world are out of phase and that the latter must be adjusted to the dynamic development of the former. He predicted that "conflict will increase between the world corporation, which is a modern concept evolved to meet the requirements of the modern age, and the nation-state, which is still rooted in archaic concepts unsympathetic to the needs of our complex world."[37] Ball has urged that the "cosmocorp," already a global institution in its behavior, become denationalized and global in law by a treaty establishing an "international companies law" to be administered by a supranational body.

Academic support has come from Frank Tannenbaum who, under the title "The Survival of the Fittest," has argued that the nation-state is a dying institution which can lead only to conflict as long as it survives. According to Tannenbaum the organization of world peace requires an extranational base which only the multinational corporation can provide. The multinational corporation could generate functional loyalties which would gradually erode and replace loyalties to nation-states. Tannenbaum has observed two systems of sovereignty in conflict: the declining system of nation-states and the rising dynamic system of supranational corporate bodies. The progress of the latter has the assurance of inevitability. As they continue to become more industrialized, the Soviet Union and Communist China would be drawn into the system of multinational corporations.[38] Of all the texts cited Tannebaum's most recalls Mitrany's functionalism.

The Economist has stressed the potential of multinational corporations to assist the development of poor countries by bringing about through their investment policies a new global division of labor, with manufacturing growing in the third world as rich countries turn increasingly to specialization in

[36] Ibid., p. 3.

[37] George W. Ball, "Cosmocorp: The Importance of Being Stateless," *Atlantic Community Quarterly*, Summer 1968 (Vol. 6, No. 2), p. 165; see also, by the same author, "Multinational Corporations and Nation States," *Atlantic Community Quarterly*, Summer 1967 (Vol. 5, No. 2), pp. 247–253.

[38] Frank Tannenbaum, "The Survival of the Fittest," *Columbia Journal of World Business*, March–April 1968 (Vol. 3, No. 2), pp. 13–20.

the production of knowledge and the processing of information. Such a trend would be facilitated in poor countries by "staid and stodgy and rather conservative regimes" whose existence now regrettably (to *The Economist*) seems less likely as a result of political developments.[39] Howard Perlmutter's research in organizational psychology also supports the proposition that multinational corporations are in the process of adapting themelves to their emerging responsibility of organizing the global economy by passing from an "ethnocentric" to a "geocentric" approach in management.[40] (The ethnocentric approach might be paraphrased as "what's good for General Motors is good for the country," and the geocentric by "what's good for General Motors is good for the world.")

The basic tenets of the new functionalism can be set forth roughly as follows: 1) Multinational corporations are the new basis for organizing the global economy; 2) to achieve this mission they will have to overcome the forces of narrow nationalism; 3) the particular manifestations of nationalism which must be overcome are restrictions on the free flow of capital and payments and the proclivity of governments to adopt national economic planning; 4) there is no basic inconsistency between the progress of multinational corporations and the national interests of the United States (this tenet is agreed to both by those Americans who advocate corporate expansion and those non-Americans who oppose it); 5) fulfillment of functional needs by corporations will develop functional loyalties which will gradually erode the emotional basis of nationalism; 6) by "transcending ideology" multinational corporations will extend into the Soviet system, reduce present tensions between East and West, and ultimately render obsolete the distinction between capitalist and Communist blocs; 7) multinational corporations, provided they are given a free hand, are the only instrument capable of achieving the economic development of poor countries; 8) the difficulties which will be encountered in perceived threats to workers' jobs and opposition to the transfer of production to new sites are essentially problems of public relations which can be dealt with by tact and good timing through corporate diplomacy; 9) managers of multinational corporations are increasingly thinking and behaving in terms of global rather than parochial or national responsibilities; 10) this development in behavior should be legally recognized through the creation of some form of international or extranational status in which corporations would become responsible to some supranational body rather than to national authorities.

There is a Saint-Simonian quality to the stress upon performance of technical functions in this ideology which goes back beyond Mitrany; it is utopian

[39] "The Giants' Causeway," *The Economist,* December 2, 1969 (Vol. 233, No. 6592), p. 11.

[40] Howard Perlmutter, "Toward Research on and Development of Nations, Unions and Firms as Worldwide Institutions," in Günter.

in its concentration on the ideal goals of its heroes rather than on the objective consequences of their actions.

Since the ideological initiative belongs to the multinational corporation, the trade union reaction to this emerging body of thought is not yet fully formed. Some unionists in both rich and poor countries simply take a negative view of the multinational corporation—those in the former see a threat to job security, while those in the latter see a threat to national independence. Another trade union reaction, however, accepts a good number of the tenets of the new functionalism, particularly the claims of economic efficiency and development potential, but remains concerned about the possible adverse implications for workers, especially in regard to job security. The problem is then seen in terms of adjusting trade union structures to exert greater control over corporate policy. This reaction leads to a policy of symbiosis of the trade union with the corporation in which both share power. Charles Levinson, secretary-general of the ICF, has articulated this view. Multinational corporations, he has stated, are "the first genuine world institutions with inherently global power and authority." Since nation-states do not control the operations of corporations, unions must urgently create a countervailing force. This can be done by transnational coordination of bargaining and also by participation of union representatives in management. Such participation, though engendering creative tensions, is feasible since management and workers have a closer identity of interest in the long-term development of the modern corporation than either group has with the shareholders.[41]

Thus, both management and trade union variants of the new functionalist ideology may prove to be compatible and together sustain new transnational structures for decisionmaking in industrial and labor affairs. It remains now to consider the possible consequences of such a development for the international system.

IV. Consequences for the International System

Two divergent, sometimes conflicting, structural tendencies in world social and economic organization are identifiable. One tendency is toward further integration within geographically defined units, whether nation-states or regional groups of states. Centrally planned economies as well as industrialized capitalist countries and less developed countries have diverse social and economic organizations involved in centralized decisionmaking for such matters of concern as investment, employment, and incomes policies.

The other tendency—exemplified by the multinational corporation—is

[41] Charles Levinson, "Towards Industrial Democracy" (Statement delivered to the First International Trade Union Conference on Industrial Democracy, Frankfurt-am-Main, West Germany, November 28–29, 1968). This text has been reprinted in the *ICF Bulletin,* January 1969 (Special Issue).

toward transnational integration within certain sectors of economic activity. Projecting this tendency has led some writers to the now often-repeated vision of a global economy in the not-too-distant future organized by perhaps 200 or 300 giant corporations.

Transnational integration may in retrospect be seen as a powerful force which made great strides in the 1960s both in Western Europe and in less developed countries. Workers and trade unions encompassed by this movement, as well as the management of the corporations which provide its thrust, become linked by interest into the transnational economy.

Strong reactions build up against this transnational integration. These reactions are fired by ideologies that stress nationalism, local control of natural resources, and social equity in development. Nationalism, as J. Bowyer Bell suggests in another essay in this volume, is the ideology of revolution on behalf of the weak and poor; transnationalism is the ideology of the dynamic rich. Forces which may strengthen national integration as opposed to transnational integration include the expansion of the public sector and the growth of a national entrepreneurial group, of national employers' organizations, and of mobilization-type labor movements. Local political leadership is the determining factor behind national integration, as private economic forces embodied in the multinational corporation are the determining factors behind transnational integration.

World economic development through a structure dominated by transnationally integrated sectors—the vision of a global economy organized by 200 big corporations—implies a separation between rich and poor which is functional rather than geographical. The rich of the world would be integrated transnationally wherever they are, while the poor remain marginal to the dominant system of production. The rich are those who seek their security in the corporation. The poor are those left outside its scope and for whom weak states are unable or unwilling to care—the marginal populations which cluster about the centers of industry, providing some supplies and services but not participating in the decisions or benefits of development.

Advocates of development through the expansion of multinational corporations hope that in the long run the poor will be absorbed and the marginal sectors disappear. This proposition, however, may engender some doubts. Multinational corporations tend to use sophisticated technology which does not employ much labor so that expansion of production in poor countries may benefit the more prosperous sectors of their economies without having much impact on poverty outside these sectors.[42] It is quite possible that statistical measures of development, such as gross national product, may show a rising curve for poor countries without development penetrating marginal popu-

[42] One result of an awareness of this probability has been stronger advocacy of population control policies, for example, by the International Bank for Reconstruction and Development (IBRD).

lations. The geographical basis for aggregating statistical data would disguise increases in the economic and social distance between the rich and the poor in less developed countries.

Historically, the geographically based power of the state has been the only power capable of counterbalancing unequal forces in the interests of welfare. There is no present or foreseeable supranational power capable of imposing a concern for the welfare of peasant populations of Asia and Latin America upon the management and organized workers of General Motors, Unilever, and Imperial Chemical Industries (ICI).

The role of the nation-state thus remains the critical factor capable of determining the future course of presently discernible transnational relations in the labor field. The basic option for the state is tolerance of transnational integration or action for national integration—in terms of the Western Hemisphere experience, between the extremes of the Canadian solution and the Cuban solution. A Canadian-type solution may be feasible where most of the population participates in the transnational society. It is, however, likely to raise considerable tensions in countries in which there is a substantial population marginal to or outside the transnational society and in which there are great disparities in incomes and life-styles which may be further exaggerated by a continuation of transnational relations. These tensions may be resolved in favor of transnational integration but with the likely accompaniment of repressive labor policies as part and parcel of the repression of social protest. On the other hand, they may be resolved in favor of nationalist revolutions and thus against transnational integration.

As the historical thrust of the multinational corporation becomes more apparent and more publicized, the reaction against it may be expected to follow with growing force. It is far too soon to prophesy the abdication of the nation-state in favor of a constellation of private supranational institutions in which labor and management share power.

Transnational Networks in Basic Science

Diana Crane

Basic science is an inherently international activity. Its principal goal is the production of new knowledge which is evaluated according to universal standards.[1] In terms of membership and goals scientific communities have been international since their emergence during the seventeenth century.[2] Basic science today consists of hundreds of research problem areas in which groups of scientists study similar problems and exchange information across national boundaries. International scientific cooperation occurs on several levels ranging from informal communication between individual researchers to multilateral agreements between governments and intergovernmental organizations (IGOs).

A useful model of these different forms of international scientific cooperation has been developed by Stefan Dedijer and A. J. Longrigg.[3] One form which they delineate consists of cooperation between individual researchers or between research laboratories and institutes. This occurs by means of communication through preprints, publications, correspondence, visits, and informal meetings. A distinct mode of organization, the so-called "invisible college," characterizes this type of communication.[4] Leading scientists in a research area maintain continual contact with each other in order to monitor recent developments in the area and adjust their activities accordingly.

In recent decades several hundred scientific international nongovernmental

Diana Crane is associate professor in the Department of Behavioral Sciences and in the Department of Social Relations at the Johns Hopkins University, Baltimore, Maryland. The author would like to thank Hilary Rose, Jean-Jacques Salomon, and Ivan Vallier for their comments on earlier drafts of this essay.

1 Basic science, as opposed to applied science, is concerned with problems whose solutions are perceived to have no immediate practical application.

2 Joseph Ben-David, "National and International Scientific Communities," in *National Scientific Communities: A Sociological Study of Developing and Developed Countries*, ed. Derek J. de Solla Price and Waldermar Voise (Paris: United Nations Educational, Scientific and Cultural Organization, 1970). (Mimeographed.)

3 Stefan Dedijer and A. J. Longrigg, "A Model of Foreign Research Policy," *Scientific World*, 1969 (Vol. 13, No. 1), pp. 17–21.

4 Derek J. de Solla Price, *Little Science, Big Science* (George B. Pegram Lecture, 1962) (New York: Columbia University Press, 1963).

organizations (NGOs) have been created. An important form of international cooperation, they engage in numerous activities from the standardization of data, units, and techniques to the organization of international conferences and symposia. Arrangements for the latter are usually handled by international professional associations. It has been estimated that each year 2,000 American scientists join 10,000 scientists from other countries at such meetings.[5]

Other forms of international scientific cooperation involve collaboration between governments. Governments reach bilateral agreements regarding the exchange of scientific information or the conduct of joint technological or scientific projects. A few IGOs maintain research facilities at which collaborative research by scientists from several countries is conducted. Other IGOs have broader functions and engage in the organization of research programs and the development of science policy rather than the conduct of research.

The key organizational problems facing scientists who conduct basic research today are: 1) how to improve the exchange and retrieval of scientific information; 2) how to organize programs to collect data at a variety of widely scattered geographical sites; 3) how to organize joint research laboratories to be used by and funded by several countries; and 4) how to allocate limited economic and manpower resources most effectively, that is, how to develop an efficient science policy on a worldwide basis.

In each of these areas one can observe increases in the activities performed either by international organizations or by national governments or both. Concomitantly with exponential increases in the numbers of scientists and the numbers of scientific papers being published, scientists have experienced increasing difficulties in locating the information which they need to conduct their research. As a result the roles of international organizations, both nongovernmental and intergovernmental, in organizing meetings and assisting the flow of information have increased. Data collection at widely separated geographical sites began in the nineteenth century. The amount and complexity of this information results in increased governmental roles expressed in formal agreements to exchange information. International research laboratories are a relatively new phenomenon and require complex agreements between governments including the commitment of large sums of money. Finally, the allocation of research funds has also undergone dramatic changes in the last three decades.

Contributions by most national governments to basic scientific research were minimal prior to World War II. In the postwar period, however, national governments have become the principal supporters of basic research. At the present time it is becoming clear that governmental resources are lim-

[5] G. C. McGhee, "International Scientific Cooperation: An American View," Department of State *Bulletin*, March 7, 1966 (Vol. 54, No. 1393), pp. 369–378.

ited and that their effective utilization will require either intergovernmental cooperation in defining priorities for basic research and controlling funds or the allocation of these tasks to supranational committees. An international science policy is becoming a necessity rather than an ideal, but its development will not be easy.

The editors of this volume have hypothesized that transnational interactions are becoming more important and that they have increasingly significant effects on international politics. In some areas they are infringing on the powers of national governments. This process can be observed most clearly in areas in which nongovernmental actors control the economic resources which support their activities.[6] Scientists do not control the financial resources which support their activities. They must continually negotiate for funds with politicians who may be favorably disposed to their cause one day and negatively the next.

In the area of basic science governments and IGOs have been steadily expanding their control over important decisions. In turn, however, scientists as transnational actors have been attempting to increase their influence on these actors by developing new types of nongovernmental organizations and associations and by strengthening their informal communities or invisible colleges through exchanges and increased mobility of personnel. In fact, what seems to be emerging is a system in which the various kinds of actors are finding it necessary to coordinate their activities with those of other actors. Unfortunately, few systematic studies of these processes have been undertaken. In the following pages I discuss what is known about the interactions between individual scientists, NGOs, IGOs, and national governments. The concluding section indicates problems which warrant further research in this area.

I. The Structure of the International Scientific Community

While acknowledging that the intellectual structure of basic science is international, some writers have argued that the social structure of science is national. The direction of scientific activity is thought to be predominantly controlled by national interests.[7] These writers are pessimistic concerning the prospects for international cooperation in science on the basis that reconciliation of national interests is so difficult as to preclude any significant increase in international scientific activity in the immediate future.

This point of view stems from the recognition that scientists as a group wield virtually no power. They control neither economic nor political resources. Instead, they exert influence based on expert knowledge. In recent

[6] See, for example, the analysis of international banking by Lawrence Krause in this volume.

[7] See, for example, Hilary Rose and Steven Rose, *Science and Society* (London: Allen Lane, 1969); and Jean-Jacques Salomon, *Science et politique* (Collections esprit) (Paris: Editions du Seuil, 1970).

years scientists in their social rather than their intellectual roles have been concerned with extending their influence and utilizing it more effectively both within and across national boundaries. This goal has led to the creation of new types of international organizations which contribute in various ways to the extension of the influence of the scientific community. In order to understand the nature of transnational processes in basic science it is necessary to describe the structure of the social community of science. The transnational social system of science includes three types of actors, scientists, administrators, and politicians, and four types of organizations, informal communication networks, NGOs, IGOs, and national governments.

Each research area in science contains its own set of informal relationships. Recent studies have shown that these relationships have a definite structure which changes over time.[8] At first a research area has few members who have little contact with one another. If they produce theoretical and experimental research of considerable interest, new members are attracted to the area. Among those who enter the field are a few scientists who develop a long-term commitment to it and become very productive. They train students in the area and collaborate with them and with other scientists. Their work provides a reference point for other researchers. Each of these highly productive scientists communicates with his coworkers and with the other leaders. Their communications produce a network that links many of the active members of the field.

Thus, the structure of international relationships in basic science consists of nuclei of collaborators connected by associations between their most active members. Since disciplines vary in their degree of consensus regarding the relative importance of research problems, there are variations between disciplines in the degree of development of such structures.[9] Disciplines characterized by a low degree of consensus about research problems tend to have distinctive national research traditions and to show few signs of international cooperation. Disciplines characterized by a high level of consensus contain research areas whose members are drawn from many different countries.

The most highly developed international communication networks exist in physics. For example, the field presently called high energy physics, which evolved from atomic and nuclear physics, has such a network as did its predecessors. The international network in that field has three major subsystems, located in the United States, the European countries which participate in the international high energy physics laboratory, the European Organization for Nuclear Research (CERN), and Japan. Approximately 88 percent of the

[8] Diana Crane, *Invisible Colleges: Diffusion of Knowledge in Scientific Communities* (Chicago: University of Chicago Press, forthcoming); Susan Crawford, "Informal Communication in Sleep and Dream Research" (Ph.D. diss., University of Chicago, 1970).

[9] Thomas S. Kuhn, *The Structure of Scientific Revolutions* (Foundations of the Unity of Science, Vol. 2, No. 2) (Chicago: University of Chicago Press, 1962).

members of the field are working in one of these three regions. Gerald Zaltman has found that Japan was relatively isolated from the flow of informal communication but that Japanese contributions to research were cited as frequently as those from the other two regions.[10] Since Zaltman's survey did not receive any replies from physicists in the Union of Soviet Socialist Republics or the People's Republic of China (Communist China), these groups were not included in his analysis. However, both Soviet and West European physicists are participating in the first experiments to be conducted at the new United States high energy physics laboratory in Batavia, Illinois.[11]

My own research has found an analogous situation in a research area of mathematics, the theory of finite groups.[12] Mathematicians in the United States, the Federal Republic of Germany (West Germany), and the United Kingdom played important roles in the informal communication network in this area; non-Western mathematicians did not appear to have much influence, and papers appearing in non-Western journals were much less likely to be cited. In a sociological research area, the diffusion of agricultural innovations, no other country or group of countries played a role comparable to that of the United States. In all three of these areas the United States had more members than any other country, but this disparity was greatest in the sociology area. Almost one-third of the non-American members of that area had fewer than two colleagues in their own countries. Only 18 percent of the members who had produced more than three papers were non-American; the comparable figure for the mathematics area was 54 percent. Finally, the relative contribution of different countries to the literature of disciplines such as physics and chemistry is related to economic factors, specifically gross national product.[13] Many countries simply cannot afford more than a minimal amount of basic science.

These studies underscore certain aspects of the informal social structure of the international scientific community. First, all countries do not participate equally in this community. Second, disciplines within each country differ in the degree of participation in this community. The prospects for successful formal scientific cooperation on an international basis vary considerably depending on the structure of these informal communication networks.

In addition to the informal networks which link scientists in individual research areas each discipline has both national and international professional associations. These organizations have two main functions. The first is to

[10] Gerald Zaltman, *Scientific Recognition and Communication Behavior in High Energy Physics* (New York: American Institute of Physics, 1968), pp. 25–46.

[11] Allen L. Hammond, "Accelerator at Batavia: The Next Step in High Energy Physics," *Science*, January 29, 1971 (Vol. 171, No. 3969), p. 364.

[12] Diana Crane, "Communication and Influence in International Scientific Communities" (Paper presented at the Seventh World Congress of Sociology, Varna, Bulgaria, September 16, 1970).

[13] Derek J. de Solla Price, "Nations Can Publish or Perish," *Science and Technology*, October 1967 (No. 70), pp. 89–90.

formalize certain aspects of the informal communication process in order to accommodate enormous increases in the numbers of scientists and in the amounts of data being collected. For example, until about twenty years ago the community of oceanographers was so small that most of its members knew one another and could exchange information on a personal basis.[14] The number of oceanographers has since increased to the point where personal evaluation of reported work is often impossible. In addition, the amount of data produced has increased astronomically from about 20 to 4,000 values per hour per observer. American professional associations in some disciplines are developing methods for improving the exchange of scientific information. Experimental schemes are being prepared which will have ramifications on the international level.[15] Numerous international professional associations organize international scientific conferences which play important roles in increasing the visibility of research across national boundaries. Studies of two international conferences in the social sciences (in psychology and sociology) indicated that substantial proportions of participants made new contacts and obtained information useful to their research.[16]

A second function of national and international professional associations is to further the interests of their disciplines. For example, these organizations concern themselves with the long-range goals of the discipline, problems of recruitment and training of new members, and the availability of research funds and jobs both academic and nonacademic. Disciplines vary in the amount of influence which they are able to exert. For example, the relevance of research to national goals as perceived by governments affects the availability of governmental grants. In the United States research in the humanities is currently being redefined in this respect, and governmental funding which was formerly unavailable is being allocated in small amounts to these fields. Disciplines also differ in the extent to which they require the cooperation of institutions to accomplish their goals. The need for elaborate and expensive research facilities is more likely to be felt in the physical and biological sciences than in the social sciences and the humanities. Thus, the former experience the necessity for international cooperation sooner than the latter.

Similarly, there are differences in the strength of national scientific communities. Probably the United States has the strongest and most active profes-

[14] Warren S. Wooster, "The Ocean and Man," *Scientific American*, September 1969 (Vol. 221, No. 3), pp. 218–234.

[15] See, for example, Philip M. Boffey, "Psychology: Apprehension over a New Communications System," *Science*, February 27, 1970 (Vol. 167, No. 3922), pp. 1228–1230; Dale B. Baker, "Communication or Chaos?" *Science*, August 21, 1970 (Vol. 169, No. 3947), pp. 739–742; Arthur Herschman, "A Program for a National Information System for Physics," in *Communication among Scientists and Engineers*, ed. Carnot E. Nelson and Donald K. Pollock (Lexington, Mass: Heath Lexington Books, 1970), pp. 307–323.

[16] Bertita E. Compton and William D. Garvey, "Information Functions of an International Meeting," *Science*, March 31, 1967 (Vol. 155, No. 3770), pp. 1648–1650.

sional associations in the world. Well-attended annual meetings strengthen the individual scientist's identification with his colleagues. The prestige of such associations motivates important scientists to serve on their committees or administrative boards, thus further strengthening them. In some European countries such associations are much less active. Each scientist advances his professional interests as an individual, experiencing little sense of identification with other scientists in his discipline. As a result the scientific community in such countries does not have significant influence on governmental policy.[17] In countries which do have strong scientific communities, such as the United Kingdom and the United States, scientists perform important roles as consultants to their governments regarding the allocation of research funds and as administrators of the programs which result. The stronger the national scientific community, the more influence it can wield on the development of national science policy and on governmental policy concerning science-related issues.

International professional associations vary greatly by discipline in terms of their accomplishments and influence. In the physical sciences some associations can point to international data collection years or decades among their accomplishments. Social science associations, on the other hand, have tended to be relatively weak and ineffectual due partly to a lack of funds.[18]

The International Council of Scientific Unions (ICSU) is an unusual combination of nongovernmental and intergovernmental organizations since it has two kinds of members, governments, whose delegates are their most widely representative scientific associations, and scientific members, which are international professional associations. The ICSU is financed by members' subscriptions and by the United Nations Educational, Scientific and Cultural Organization (UNESCO). Members of ICSU committees serve on UNESCO's committees.

As I have already suggested, the number of decisions made by national governments which can affect the scientific community has greatly expanded in the last several decades. At the present time scientific institutions are entering a new phase in which governments, because of their inability to support the steadily increasing costs of basic research, will increasingly need to coordinate their science policies with those of other countries. Concomitantly, scientific communities are developing new types of international organizations which will permit them to expand their influence in the international arena. For example, a recently formed NGO, the European Molecular Biology Organization (EMBO), is an international lobby or pressure group whose aim

[17] France is a good example of such a country. Rose and Rose, p. 143, describe how academic scientists participated in the student demonstrations of May 1968 in order to protest their lack of influence on national science policy.

[18] Eric de Grolier, *Outline of a Comparative Study on International Scientific NGOs in the Field of Social Science* (Paris: International Social Science Council, 1969). (Mimeographed.)

is to improve international research facilities in the field of molecular biology.

A different type of organization is represented by the Pugwash Conferences on Science and World Affairs which brings scientists from various countries together annually to discuss the social implications of science. Pugwash conferences have also been concerned with international cooperation in science. It has been suggested that academies of science and scholarly societies could be influential in the creation of new international centers for the study of specific scientific problems or for the encouragement of broad policy goals such as aid to scientific institutions in less developed countries.[19] Although they lack political power and funds, cooperation between such organizations could provide the drive and continuity necessary for the development of innovative international organizations. Among the latter the need for an international university has been mentioned. The first step in such a development will probably be the creation of a world federation of institutes of advanced study. Section II discusses the ways in which these various organizations interact.

II. The Exercise of Transnational Influence in Basic Science

Scientists generally lack the economic or political resources to achieve their policy objectives. Clearly, their lack of political influence means that international cooperation will be most easily achieved when the economic resources required and the political implications involved are minimal. In the following pages I examine the behavior and achievements of the scientific community in situations in which economic and political factors are minimal, for example, in the organization of worldwide data collection projects, and in situations in which these factors are extremely important, for example, in international research laboratories and the development of an international science policy. In some research areas invisible colleges have played important roles; in others, NGOs and IGOs have been of primary importance. In still other cases national governments have had the most influence. Most of the examples come from Europe since countries in this region possess highly developed scientific institutions and limited resources for basic research. As a result they face the necessity of concentrating their resources in areas in which they can compete most effectively. Regional cooperation is one way of dealing with such constraints.

The invisible college or informal community of scientists in a research area has been influential in the genesis of some forms of international scientific cooperation. For example, the inspiration behind the International Hydrological Decade (1965–1974) came from a group of scientists working in the area which

[19] W. M. Todd and J. Voss, "The Consortium of Academies: A New Way to Found International Scholarly Institutions" (Paper presented at the Twentieth Pugwash Conference on Science and World Affairs, Fontana, Italy, September 9–15, 1970).

felt that the opportunities for research in the field did not match its potential and that the importance of the field was not recognized by governmental agencies.[20]

The initiative behind the creation of CERN came from the international invisible college of physicists which had been in existence for several decades studying problems relating to high energy physics and its antecedents. Even prominent American physicists for whom no direct benefits from the laboratory were anticipated were instrumental in its creation. Participation at high levels in the defense programs of national governments during World War II had given physicists considerable influence on national science policies. Aided by the general enthusiasm for European unity which prevailed among politicians in the early 1950s, the physicists were given a remarkable degree of autonomy in the creation of an extremely complex and expensive facility.

The success of the physicists contrasts with the difficulties which European molecular biologists have experienced in their efforts to obtain a similar international facility for research in their discipline. Undoubtedly an important factor was the perceived relevance of research in the two fields to national interests. Physics was perceived as a source of weaponry while the findings of molecular biology were thought to have little utility for national defense. In addition, the weak and divided informal scientific community in molecular biology impaired the ability of the biologists to exercise influence in Europe. If a project which does not have a great deal of political potential is to be funded, it is probable that strong national and international scientific communities will be required to convince the political authorities of its usefulness. Molecular biology and the biological sciences have generally tended to be weak in European universities, and the new specialties in biology have been introduced with difficulty.[21] Strong informal ties between biologists in different European countries have also been lacking. A number of observers have commented that European biologists have closer ties with American biologists than with each other.[22]

Possibly as a result of their relative isolation from one another European biologists have been divided in regard to the need for international facilities. Some biologists have argued that their countries cannot spare scientific manpower for such centers. Others have argued that the effect of such centers would be to raise the caliber of European scientific personnel in biology and to stimulate research in the universities from which the personnel to man the

20 Michel Batisse, "Launching the Hydrological Decade," *New Scientist*, January 7, 1965 (Vol. 25, No. 425), pp. 38–40.

21 W. V. Consolazio, "Dilemma of Academic Biology in Europe," *Science*, June 16, 1961 (Vol. 133, No. 3468), pp. 1892–1896.

22 R. P. Grant, C. P. Huttrer, and C. G. Metzner, "Biomedical Science in Europe," *Science*, October 23, 1964 (Vol. 146, No. 3643), pp. 493–501; "European Technology: Hanging Together or Separately," *Nature*, September 20, 1969 (Vol. 223, No. 5212), p. 1192. One notable exception is the close association which exists between leading British and French molecular biologists.

centers would be drawn and to which it would eventually return.[23] Such facilities have the support of EMBO which, in turn, has won governmental backing for a laboratory. EMBO was influential in the creation of an organization of European governments, the European Molecular Biology Conference, whose members now appear likely to provide financial support for an international molecular biology laboratory. A committee is investigating possible sites.[24]

In some areas of international scientific cooperation—worldwide data collection programs, for example—NGOs and IGOs can accomplish a great deal with relatively little assistance from national governments. Certain types of scientific data are more useful if observations can be simultaneously made at many points on the earth's surface. This necessity led to some of the earliest examples of international scientific collaboration during the nineteenth century. The establishment of these programs requires the cooperation of numerous national scientific organizations and committees of NGOs. More than 60 countries participated in the International Geophysical Year (IGY, 1957–1958), 60 countries in the International Years of the Quiet Sun (1964–1965), and over 50 countries in the International Hydrological Decade (1965–1974).[25] Often an IGO will coordinate these programs. UNESCO, for example, is coordinating activities for the International Hydrological Decade. Assisting UNESCO are other United Nations agencies and the ICSU.

However, in some areas, such as oceanography, observers claim that there is not yet sufficient coordination of international organizations. Warren S. Wooster has complained about the "bewildering variety of international organizations concerned with ocean science or the utilization of ocean resources" and has suggested that the area would benefit from "strengthening, simplification and consolidation of the organizations which now exist."[26]

National political interests have been the biggest obstacle to international scientific cooperation. In some areas political factors have been more important than in others. For example, they have not interfered with international data collection programs, but they have not been entirely absent either. While the United States and the Soviet Union could each have created a single center capable of processing all the data collected during the IGY, it was decided for political reasons to have several centers, one each in the United States and the Soviet Union and a third composed of minicenters in different countries, each specializing in a specific research area.[27]

[23] J. C. Kendrew, "EMBO and the Idea of a European Laboratory," *Nature,* June 1, 1968 (Vol. 218, No. 5144), pp. 840–842; V. Weisskopf, "CERN and the Proposed European Biology Laboratory," *Nature,* January 27, 1968 (Vol. 217, No. 5126), pp. 317–318.

[24] Graham Chedd, "A New Lab for Europe?" *New Scientist and Science Journal,* February 18, 1971 (Vol. 49, No. 739), pp. 350–352.

[25] Batisse, *New Scientist,* Vol. 25, No. 425; McGhee, Department of State *Bulletin,* Vol. 54, No. 1393.

[26] Wooster, *Scientific American,* Vol. 221, No. 3, p. 234.

[27] Jean-Jacques Salomon, "International Scientific Policy," *Minerva,* Summer 1964 (Vol. 2, No. 4), pp. 411–434.

Increasingly, however, the complexities of international data collection require formal agreements between governments. The necessity for such agreements leads to the intrusion of political factors on international scientific cooperation. In the area of oceanography research, for example, information which was formerly exchanged on a nongovernmental basis is now being exchanged by governments through the Intergovernmental Oceanographic Commission (IOC).[28] Similarly, even ten years ago, most cooperative studies of the ocean were organized by the investigators concerned, and governments simply provided the necessary funds. Now, however, it is becoming desirable to organize more comprehensive investigations using ships from a number of different countries. The need for complex and simultaneous observations over a large geographical area makes it difficult for a single country to provide sufficient financial support. However, the organization of multiship expeditions requires a more complex form of international cooperation. Formal commitments to such expeditions by the participating governments are now being made through the IOC.

Once governments begin to take formal cognizance of the research activities of each other's investigators, political, economic, and legal factors become important. Some governments are reluctant to permit foreign scientists to conduct oceanographic research near their coastlines for fear of losing control of their maritime resources. On the other hand, unless such research is done, the true potential of these resources will remain unknown. Ironically, it is precisely those countries that lack the resources to conduct such research that have the most to gain from it and that fear foreign intrusion the most. These countries have been most active in attempts to establish an international regime for the world's oceans.

In recent years physicists have been losing control over the most important decisions affecting the future of CERN. As European politicians become less enthusiastic about the goal of European unity, they have become less willing to spend money on projects which demonstrate it. The expense of CERN's facilities is so great that it threatens to dominate the research budgets of smaller countries, some of which are seriously weighing the benefits of participation against the costs.[29]

In addition, CERN needs a more powerful accelerator which will be extremely costly. Political considerations have continually intruded on the decision to build the facility and on the choice of its location. The Dutch government was advised by its scientists to withdraw from the project but decided to participate anyway on the grounds that the project contributes to European unification, a goal of Dutch foreign policy.[30] Although British participation

[28] Wooster, *Scientific American*, Vol. 221, No. 3, pp. 225–226, 230–232.

[29] Salomon, *Minerva*, Vol. 2, No. 4.

[30] D. S. Greenberg, "European Notes: Quids Pro Quo," *Science*, July 18, 1969 (Vol. 165, No. 3890), p. 267.

was endorsed by two of the highest ranking advisory bodies in the United Kingdom, the British government at first rejected the advice of its scientific community and refused to contribute to the new laboratory.[31] When the plans were revised and the budget cut, it reversed this decision, but several other countries which had formerly supported the project expressed new doubts.[32] Finally, early in 1971, ten of the twelve member countries of CERN made the decision to go ahead with the project.[33]

While the selection of a location for the first laboratory took one year, political factors delayed a decision on the location of the second laboratory for several years. There were rumors that France was backing the selection of a site in Belgium in return for a Belgian order of French Mirage fighter planes.[34] The West Germans were pressing for a site on their territory as recognition of the fact that they have been paying a major share of the costs of CERN. They argued that they could not continue to obtain parliamentary support for such financial outlays unless the new laboratory was located on their territory. Eventually, the member countries agreed to build the new laboratory on land adjacent to the original site near Geneva.[35]

Political factors also partially explain why one proposal for international cooperation in the biological sciences failed while another succeeded. Attempts to establish a medical research laboratory under the auspices of the World Health Organization (WHO) were unsuccessful.[36] The International Agency for Research on Cancer (IARC), on the other hand, has been established even though this project received less than enthusiastic support from many scientists pessimistic about the probable results of direct cancer research. The research center, however, had the support of political decisionmakers and the additional force of public concern with cancer.[37] Unlike the proposed WHO laboratory political support for the IARC ensured the success of the proposal.

Governments rely on scientists as administrators and consultants to assist them in their decisionmaking. Since the two groups sometimes have opposing interests, the question of divided loyalties inevitably arises. For example, when the British government decided not to support the proposed 300-Gev accelerator for CERN, its principal representative to the organization, a physi-

[31] D. S. Greenberg, "300 Gev: Decision to Drop Out Angers British Science Leaders," *Science*, August 23, 1969 (Vol. 161, No. 3843), pp. 768–770.

[32] Jerome Pietrasik, "L'Accélérateur au point mort," *L'Express*, December 28, 1970–January 3, 1971 (No. 1016), p. 19.

[33] *New York Times*, February 20, 1971, p. 28.

[34] D. S. Greenberg, "CERN: Rumors but No Decision on Site," *Science*, February 27, 1970 (Vol. 167, No. 3922), p. 1231.

[35] *New York Times*, February 20, 1971.

[36] Hilary Rose, "The Rejection of the WHO Research Centre," *Minerva*, Summer 1967 (Vol. 5, No. 4), pp. 340–356.

[37] John Walsh, "International Cancer Research: New Horizons for Epidemiology," *Science*, February 2, 1968 (Vol. 159, No. 3814), pp. 513–516; Rose, *Minerva*, Vol. 5, No. 4.

cist, relayed his government's decision and then publicly stated his opposition to the policy.[38] However, there are other instances in which scientist-advisors have put national interests above scientific goals. Hilary Rose implies that the British scientists who advised their government against supporting the international medical research center proposed for the WHO were subtly influenced by institutional pressures to consider purely national interests rather than the international goals of science.[39] The strength of the informal scientific community in a discipline may make a difference. The stronger the invisible college, the more likely the scientist will support its interests in his role as advisor to government.

There is also some evidence which suggests that, while scientists have less control over the political process which precedes the creation of scientific IGOs, once such organizations have been created scientists can shape their scientific goals. Although the mandate for in-house research was not clear when the IARC was created, skillful scientific administration has made such research a reality.[40] Similarly, administration has been crucial to the successful operation of CERN.

The mode of organization selected for international research facilities may also influence their success. It has been suggested that the success of the IARC and of CERN is due to the fact that membership in these IGOs is voluntary.[41] For example, countries can belong voluntarily to the IARC upon payment of a specified annual contribution. If the WHO research center had been created, all WHO member countries would have had to contribute to its budget. Voluntary participation is desirable since it permits a project's supporters to join and does not motivate its detractors to scuttle it. Some of the latter may be persuaded to join later if the new facility demonstrates its usefulness.

International research facilities are most likely to be developed in fields that require highly sophisticated equipment and whose costs can be shared. Even with shared costs, however, the expense involved in building and maintaining such facilities is greater than that involved in the creation of NGOs and IGOs. Consequently, governments tend to be cautious in their support of such facilities. It appears that scientists have less influence in determining whether international research facilities will be created than they do in administering them once they have been established. The situation is paralleled at the national level. In most countries the ability of scientists to exert influence on the selection of priorities for research tends to be limited. Once these decisions are made, however, scientists are able to wield considerable influence in the selection of particular projects or persons to be funded.[42]

38 Greenberg, *Science,* Vol. 161, No. 3843. "Gev" is an abbreviation of "gigaelectron volt" which signifies one billion electron volts.

39 Rose, *Minerva,* Vol. 5, No. 4.

40 Walsh, *Science,* Vol. 159, No. 3814.

41 Ibid.

42 Robert P. Grant, "National Biomedical Research Agencies: A Comparative Study of Fifteen Countries," *Minerva,* Summer 1966 (Vol. 4, No. 4), pp. 466–488.

There are signs that scientists are developing means of increasing their influence on decisions which affect the future of their research. While EMBO continues to lobby for an international laboratory, it is also engaging in activities which should increase the integration of European scientific institutions. EMBO provides fellowship programs for the international exchange of scientists and organizes summer schools which bring scientists from different countries together.[43] Several national academies in Europe are collaborating on the exchange of fellows and students from one laboratory to another.[44] European federations of national professional associations are beginning to emerge.[45] Strong interdisciplinary associations would increase European scientists' awareness of each other's problems and thus contribute to European scientific cooperation.[46] Eventually, they may develop sufficient international cohesion to negotiate successfully with governments. The potential of such negotiation has been demonstrated by the creation of the International Center for Theoretical Physics in Trieste. Established over the objections of several advanced countries, it is designed to increase the participation of scientists from less developed countries in the international scientific community.

In the past national governments have controlled the resources needed for scientific research, but there are signs that in the future they will have to coordinate their allocation of resources on an international scale. Suggestions are already being made in Europe that national governments utilize scientists from other European countries to evaluate their research proposals.[47] It has been suggested that in some fields the allocation of funds would be more efficient if it were carried out entirely by supranational committees.[48] The development of a truly international science policy will be necessary if the scarce resources available for scientific research are to be used effectively.

III. Toward an International Science Policy

Increasingly, national interests in the area of basic science are likely to be furthered more by international cooperation than by competition. Unfortunately, the recent history of European scientific research organizations in applied science and technology has not been encouraging. The desire of each country to obtain a "just return" on its investment has had unfortunate effects on the planning and management of such organizations. This has tended

43 "An International Laboratory Needed," *Nature,* May 31, 1969 (Vol. 222, No. 5196), pp. 836–837.

44 "Problems of European Integration," *Nature,* February 3, 1968 (Vol. 217, No. 5127), p. 407.

45 Jack Star, "European Physicists Rush in Where Politicans Fear to Tread," *Scientific Research,* June 9, 1969 (Vol. 4, No. 12), pp. 38–41.

46 Grant, Huttrer, and Metzner, *Science,* Vol. 146, No. 3643, p. 495.

47 "Problems of European Integration," *Nature,* Vol. 217, No. 5127; *Fundamental Research and the Policies of Governments* (Paris: Organisation for Economic Co-operation and Development [for the Ministerial Meeting on Science], 1960), p. 57.

48 Adriano A. Buzzati-Traverso, "Scientific Research: The Case for International Support," *Science,* June 11, 1965 (Vol. 148, No. 3676), p. 1443.

to reflect poorly on international scientific cooperation in general. However, the problems involved in the organization of basic science are different from those of applied science and technology. The necessity for commercial profit based on technological developments leads to secrecy and competition rather than cooperation. Basic science with its emphasis on the development of a common body of knowledge lends itself more easily than applied science and technology to international cooperation, and there are indications that international cooperation in basic science will increase in the future. First, the high cost of scientific research means that more and more countries are finding that they must be selective in their support of basic research. Only the richest countries like the United States and the Soviet Union can afford to support research in any aspect of basic science. Smaller countries must pool their resources in some fields or cease to participate in those fields altogether. A recent review of the science policies of the members of the Organisation for Economic Co-operation and Development (OECD) suggests that they are beginning to use science and technology to solve social problems rather than to promote economic growth.[49] Presumably, this type of goal would be more conducive to international cooperation.

A number of problems remain to be solved before wide-scale international cooperation becomes a reality. The most suitable organizational forms for this type of cooperation are still being worked out. There is some reluctance on the part of governments to participate in the construction of large-scale new facilities along the lines of CERN.[50] However, more of these will probably be necessary in certain fields. In addition, small-scale regional institutes for groups of smaller countries may be appropriate for certain types of research problems. Much more could probably be done through the cooperative use of existing facilities. Systems for sharing expensive technical equipment will probably be developed in the future. As one writer has observed, there is a need to concentrate on the "humdrum" aspects of cooperation rather than its more dramatic possibilities.[51]

Important changes in the scientific infrastructure will also be necessary. Basic reforms in European universities must precede any substantial development of international cooperation.[52] The need for a system which will produce greater mobility of scientific personnel across national boundaries is particularly acute. This reform will require administrative arrangements for the exchange of personnel between countries on a permanent basis rather than a temporary or visiting basis. A few European countries have already announced their willingness to consider foreign nationals to fill vacancies in

[49] "Similarities and Disparities in Europe," *Nature,* August 8, 1970 (Vol. 227, No. 5258), p. 544.

[50] "Survey of Science in Europe," *Nature,* June 13, 1970 (Vol. 226, No. 5250), pp. 1009–1024.

[51] Ibid.

[52] The nature of the necessary reforms is outlined in Joseph Ben-David, *Fundamental Research and the Universities: Some Comments on International Differences* (Paris: Organisation for Economic Cooperation and Development, 1968).

their universities. Highly specialized scientific talent can be used most effectively if its mobility is not artificially restricted. Integration of research grant-allocation bodies would also be desirable. A European research council financed by nonearmarked donations from member states has been suggested as well.[53]

While governments are reassessing the need for international scientific cooperation, some scientists are continuing to lobby for it. In spite of increasing unwillingness on the part of governments to underwrite high energy physics, physicists are rumored to be seriously discussing the development of a joint Soviet-American 1000-Gev accelerator which would be twice as powerful as any facility currently operating or under construction. A recent Pugwash conference recommended the creation of a permanent body which would be entrusted with fact-finding and advisory tasks concerning international scientific cooperation and which would report to national ministries of science and appropriate international organizations.[54]

IV. Conclusion

In the area of basic science there are several different types of transnational interactions. First, there is a complex network of informal associations between scientists through which information is exchanged and collaboration occurs. These ties develop spontaneously due to the intrinsically international character of basic scientific research. However, the increasing size of the scientific community and the increasing complexity and cost of data collection have led to the development of intergovernmental and international nongovernmental organizations. When cooperation between scientists located in different countries is essential to the success of a research program, IGOs and NGOs facilitate the exchange of information, the development of contacts between individuals, and the collection of information. In turn, the invisible college uses these organizations to further its goals and to negotiate with governments.

In the past governments have independently exercised considerable control over important decisions affecting the direction of basic scientific activity, but increasing scarcity of resources for scientific research is necessitating greater coordination of activities between governments. This in turn may make decisions to support major facilities such as international laboratories less problematic. The difficult choices now being faced by smaller countries vis-à-vis participation in very costly research areas may be resolved by expanding international cooperation to include all or most of basic science. However, there are still many obstacles which will have to be overcome before such coordination is achieved.

53 "Survey of Science in Europe," *Nature*, Vol. 226, No. 5250.

54 "The Setting Up of Institutions for European Scientific and Technical Cooperation," *Pugwash Newsletter*, June 1970 (Vol. 8, No. 1), pp. 17–25.

A number of questions await further study. In their roles as advisors to governments, scientists at times support national interests and at other times international goals. There still appears to be disagreement among them regarding the extent to which international cooperation is necessary for the advancement of scientific knowledge. Systematic studies of the effects of existing international laboratories on national scientific communities would help to resolve this controversy. It would also be of interest to know whether the development of international ties between scientists either in the form of communication networks or nongovernmental organizations increases their awareness of the desirability of international cooperation. Those scientists who are in favor of such cooperation are creating new NGOs and IGOs. The NGOs tend to be international professional associations or regional federations of national professional associations. The IGOs are designed to deal with specific scientific areas and to provide a forum for scientific lobbying. Studies of the activities of organizations like EMBO and Pugwash and of their effects on governmental policies would be of great interest.

While international cooperation between scientists to further scientific goals is relatively neutral vis-à-vis the political goals of the countries concerned, this may not be the case when the object is to further political goals. Pugwash has attempted to influence policies of governments toward the arms race. One consequence of the efforts of economists working through the United Nations Economic Commission for Latin America (ECLA) to change Latin American policies was a considerable increase in the amount of tension between Latin America and the United States.[55] Case studies of organizations in which scientists' activities have political implications are needed. Pugwash, for example, seems to have evolved from a loose association only slightly more formal than an invisible college to a semiofficial organization. The consequences of this shift for its effectiveness in pursuing its objectives need to be evaluated.

The emerging structure among the plethora of scientific NGOs and IGOs should also be studied. Are IGOs emerging as dominant forces due to their greater access to financial resources? Are they assuming the role of coordinators in this area, directing the activities of the much more numerous but less powerful NGOs? This seems plausible since the latter tend to be dependent on either national scientific organizations or IGOs for financial support, a factor which limits their capacity for independent action.[56] Should IGOs eventually control the allocation of the world's resources for basic scientific research, they will become the most powerful actors in the international scientific community.

[55] Victor L. Urquidi, *The Challenge of Development in Latin America,* trans. Marjory M. Urquidi (New York: Frederick A. Praeger, 1964), p. 141.

[56] Eugene B. Skolnikoff, "The International Functional Implications of Future Technology" (Paper presented at the Sixty-sixth Annual Convention of the American Political Science Association, Los Angeles, September 1970), argues that IGOs, rather than national governments, will have to play major roles in the future if the negative effects of technology are to be averted and the advantages of technology maximized.

Transnationalism in Space:

Inner and Outer

Edward Miles

I. Interactions in the Space and Ocean Issue Areas

Interactions between different kinds of actors engaged in outer space and ocean exploration and exploitation can be grouped into five major categories of activities. These activities reflect the dominant interests of all the participants, and they are treated at a level of generality which facilitates comparison. The categories of activities are: 1) management and regulation of common resources; 2) exploitation of specific resources; 3) coordination and financing of research, including exploration and experimentation at the international level, and arrangements governing the exchange of information gained; 4) preservation of national and international security; and 5) recreation and the control of pollution.

As I describe the participants and their interaction in each of these five categories, it will become apparent that the state-centric model of international relations is adequate to explain most of the activities. The only exception is in the area of coordination and financing of research for space and the oceans in which national academies of science and international nongovernmental organizations (NGOs) play a very important role. It may also be that transnational processes are significant in the exploitation category, but much research remains to be done before any decisive inferences can be drawn.

What then are the participants? Nation-states, intergovernmental organizations (IGOs), NGOs, business enterprises, national academies of science, and universities are active in both issue areas while national professional associations of manufacturers, cooperatives of fishermen, conservation societies, and

Edward Miles, a member of the Board of Editors of *International Organization,* is associate professor of international relations at the Graduate School of International Studies, University of Denver, Denver, Colorado. The author is grateful to the editors, to Bernhard Abrahamsson, Francis Christy, Jr., and Robert Friedheim for comments on early drafts of this essay.

the like are active in the ocean area. It is important to emphasize that states are not monolithic and that it is crucial at all times to specify which parts of the nation-state are being treated as actors. For our purposes the actors may be national executives, bureaucracies, legislatures, political parties, military organizations, and particular families and individuals.

Although the state-centric model is generally an adequate framework to explain activities in outer space and the oceans, it is still true that some of the important transnational behavior which occurs in these two areas is initiated by individuals who are formally governmental actors. This behavior can, and often does, have important policy consequences. I would therefore extend the definition of "transnational behavior" employed by the editors to include those occasions in which governmental actors do not play governmentally defined roles.

For example, when drafting what eventually became United Nations General Assembly Resolution 1721 (XVI) of December 20, 1961, on the peaceful uses of outer space, individuals in the Bureau of International Organization Affairs of the Department of State had to contend with the intense competition between the United States Weather Bureau and the atmospheric scientists in the National Academy of Sciences and various universities. The issue was essentially whether the World Meteorological Organization (WMO) would control the World Weather Watch. Both the atmospheric scientists and the President's Office of Science and Technology were initially opposed to this and were inclined instead to make the WMO and the United Nations Educational, Scientific and Cultural Organization (UNESCO) jointly responsible, with cooperative links with the International Council of Scientific Unions (ICSU) for scientific planning. In a successful attempt to change the effect of the resolution being drafted by the Department of State the director of the United States Weather Bureau, Francis W. Reichelderfer, telephoned his Canadian counterpart. With his help and the support of some European friends the Canadian delegation to the United Nations was able to bring about changes in the first draft which made the resolution acceptable to both the United States and Canadian weather bureaus.[1]

II. Management and Regulation of Space Resources

The radio frequency spectrum is the most basic common resource to be regulated and managed in the issue area of outer space, and the International Telecommunication Union (ITU) is the leading IGO involved in this activity. Its

[1] This account is based on conversations with several individuals who were Department of State officials and members of the President's Science Advisor's Office at the time these events took place. In addition, the author is grateful for a long and valuable telephone interview with Reichelderfer on October 18, 1969. For a partial account of these difficulties see Eugene B. Skolnikoff, *Science, Technology, and American Foreign Policy* (Cambridge, Mass: M.I.T. Press, 1967), pp. 173–178.

primary tasks include the allocation of frequencies, the setting of technical standards for telecommunication equipment and operating procedures, and the coordination of frequency utilization including sharing between terrestrial and space services. It is clear that the state-centric model explains a great deal, if not most, of the activity which occurs in this issue area. There is a vital link between radio frequency utilization and national security in the broadest sense. The restrictions that national governments place on the ITU can be seen most sharply in the operations of one of its organs, the International Frequency Registration Board (IFRB).

Frequency allocations are bargained for in an international conference, and the IFRB is prohibited from undertaking any kind of generalized planning to determine the most efficient and equitable allocations in terms of a generally agreed-upon set of priorities. These restrictions continue beyond allocation to the problem of harmful interference and the registration of frequencies. The system of coordination which the IFRB must use, defined in the *Radio Regulations,* puts a premium on the willingness of the parties to compromise. If no agreement is forthcoming, the IFRB must be asked by the parties concerned to mediate before it can intervene. The fact that the system works in most cases is best explained by the reciprocity-retaliation sanction which is an inherent part of spectrum utilization. The formal restrictions which are placed on the IFRB are treated very seriously by the most capable members of the ITU, and this sharply curtails the informal influence which the IFRB may be able to exercise in any dispute.

In addition to restrictions on the ITU, there are other effective barriers to intersecretariat interaction concerning the allocation of frequencies. For example, in both the WMO and the International Civil Aviation Organization (ICAO) national members decide which frequencies are particularly appropriate for transmission of meteorological and navigational data. In order to obtain these frequency allocations from the ITU the secretariats of other organizations may not approach ITU officials directly. Of course, occasionally there are informal discussions between secretariat officials as they chance to meet, but these do not necessarily influence formal decisions.

The process by which IGOs decide which frequencies are needed and then lobby for them has two stages. In the first or "internal" stage an organizational position is developed by appropriate groups within the organization depending on the technical problem involved. In the WMO, for example, this stage calls for interaction between the secretariat and national representatives so that each national meteorological service is consulted about its particular needs. But even this is a delicate operation because each country jealously guards its frequency allocation rights. Once the IGO chooses its position, the second stage begins. At this point each national meteorological service takes up the question with its own postal, telephone, and telegraph administration and tries to convince it to seek these frequencies for the WMO in the ITU. Final allocations are then worked out between national representatives in ITU meetings.

As a result of these conditions coordinated interorganizational planning cannot extend beyond a very low level—sending observers to meetings—because the effective decisionmaking capacity rests with governments, not with secretariats. Admittedly, joint working groups sometimes go beyond the observer level but not sufficiently beyond it to have a major impact on governmental control.

Although I have been arguing the primacy of the state-centric model, I do not mean to imply that all activity in this area is exclusively state-centric. The three major ITU tasks have some transnational aspects, and these can be demonstrated by using two issues as examples: the allocation of frequencies for radio astronomy and the problems of frequency coordination between the ITU and the International Telecommunications Satellite Consortium (INTELSAT).

The intergovernmental Administrative Radio Conference of the ITU held in Geneva in 1959 was the first occasion that bands for space services were allocated. At that time the radio astronomers managed to receive some bands, but because they were required to share these frequencies with other users they considered their allocation to be most inadequate given the vast energy sources and transmission distances with which they had to contend.[2] In fact, it was estimated at the time that the United States took the minimal and rigid position for radio astronomy that it did because the value of the portion of the spectrum desired by the scientists on an exclusive basis would have amounted to about $100 million a year to United States communications companies.[3] In addition, the United States Department of Defense was concerned about the security aspects of allowing radio astronomy to compete for frequencies in which it was interested.

Even as the conference was in session United States radio astronomers met with representatives of the Department of State, the Department of Defense, and the Federal Communications Commission (FCC) in an unsuccessful attempt to change the United States stance. This had implications, of course, for radio astronomers everywhere because a change in the United States position would facilitate attempts by radio astronomers to obtain adequate frequency allocations.

As a result of this experience scientists from three ICSU member organizations, the International Union of Radio Science (URSI), the International Astronomical Union (IAU), and the Committee on Space Research (COSPAR),

[2] See ITU Document 8-E *(Extraordinary Administrative Radio Conference, 1963)*, Annex, pp. 29ff.; and ITU Document 46-E.

[3] United States Congress, Senate, Committee on Aeronautical and Space Sciences, *Radio Frequency Control in Space Telecommunications*, by E[dward] Wenk, Committee Print (Washington: Government Printing Office, 1960), pp. 75–78.

met in 1960 and established the Inter-Union Commission on Frequency Allocations for Radio Astronomy and Space Science (IUCAF) which was recognized by the ICSU Executive Committee in October of that year.[4] The purpose of the IUCAF was to aggregate and represent the interests of scientists involved in various aspects of radio research, radio astronomy, and space research. This body then made a series of recommendations to the IFRB for the 1963 conference.[5]

In addition to this unusual form of direct interorganizational communication between an NGO (IUCAF) and an IGO (ITU), COSPAR decided in January 1960 to establish links with the ITU. The ITU agreed to extend consultative status to COSPAR for the purpose of participating in the work of the International Radio Consultative Committee (CCIR), particularly in Study Group IV on space systems and radio astronomy and Study Group VI on ionospheric propagation.[6] Several years later, in anticipation of the second space conference planned for 1971, COSPAR urged those member academies which had not already done so to establish direct contacts with their respective national radio administrations to ensure that "they have channels whereby effective consultation will be possible if and when needed."[7] As a result of all this lobbying the IUCAF obtained frequency bands for radio astronomers allocated on an exclusive or shared basis. Twenty-two specific bands were allocated to space science research, exclusive of satellite tracking and communications.[8]

Jurisdictional problems between the ITU and INTELSAT are a very sensitive issue, and many secretariat officials and members of the ITU Administrative Council agree that the tendency of INTELSAT to develop international criteria for space systems is their major cause for concern. More specifically, they claim that INTELSAT is duplicating the ITU structure on the technical side and that its officials are attempting to set standards which are within the purview of the International Telegraph and Telephone Consultative Committee (CCITT). This is likely to lead to a major dispute on the right to award particular positions in the geostationary orbit. If open conflict occurs, it will inevitably assume North-South as well as East-West dimensions because both less developed countries and Communist countries will want control to remain with the ITU. The role perceptions and behavior of national delegates to the ITU are interesting from a transnational point of view because they again extend beyond formally defined governmental positions. Even those delegates to the ITU Administrative Council, whose countries are members of INTELSAT, appear in this case to see themselves not primarily

[4] COSPAR *Information Bulletin*, March 1961 (No. 4), pp. 8–9; and July 1961 (No. 5), pp. 10–12.
[5] ITU Document 75-E.
[6] COSPAR *Information Bulletin*, June 1960 (No. 2), pp. 4–5.
[7] COSPAR *Information Bulletin*, November 1964 (No. 20), p. 20.
[8] Ibid., pp. 10–11.

as national representatives but as members of one IGO whose jurisdiction is threatened by another.

III. Management and Regulation of Fisheries

The problems encountered in managing and regulating fisheries are similar to those which exist in radio frequency allocation in that potential and actual commercial benefits lead to severe restrictions on IGO and NGO activities. In an important way, however, it is easier to regulate frequency allocation because the reciprocity-retaliation sanction operates with such a high degree of effectiveness. In the area of fisheries not all participants have complementary interests in conservation for the same time periods. This leads to considerable depletion of stocks regardless of the activities of various IGOs and NGOs.

In the area of fisheries the state-centric model again explains most of the interaction which occurs, but the adequacy of this model is tempered by activities of IGOs in the research and, to a lesser extent, the regulatory areas. In addition, national fishery organizations are able to exert considerable influence on the international policies of their governments.

Interaction is more complex in matters concerning the oceans than in those concerning outer space. The capabilities of nation-states involved in space exploration do not vary greatly with regard to space research programs, actual exploration, involvement in satellite telecommunications, and so on. The United States and the Union of Soviet Socialist Republics are, of course, the dominant actors, but the Soviet Union has thus far not attempted to exploit its satellite telecommunications capability on a global scale. While capability rankings do not vary much in the space issue area, they do vary, sometimes widely, with different kinds of activities in the ocean issue area.[9]

The predominance of the nation-state on fisheries issues is illustrated particularly by the restrictions which are placed on the Food and Agriculture Organization (FAO) and on regional regulatory commissions. The major contributions of the FAO in the fisheries area have been in the collection, production, and dissemination of knowledge and the appraisal of alternatives

[9] On the general question of the international law, politics, and economics of fisheries see, inter alia, Shigeru Oda, *International Control of Sea Resources* (Leiden: A. W. Sijthoff, 1963); Douglas M. Johnston, *The International Law of Fisheries: A Framework for Policy-Oriented Inquiries* (New Haven, Conn: Yale University Press, 1965); Francis T. Christy, Jr., and Anthony Scott, *The Common Wealth in Ocean Fisheries: Some Problems of Growth and Economic Allocation* (Baltimore, Md: Johns Hopkins Press [for Resources for the Future], 1965); James A. Crutchfield and Giulio Pontecorvo, *The Pacific Salmon Fisheries: A Study of Irrational Conservation* (Baltimore, Md: Johns Hopkins Press [for Resources for the Future], 1969); J. L. Kask, *Tuna: A World Resource* (Occasional Paper, No. 2) (Kingston: Law of the Sea Institute, University of Rhode Island, May 1969); and Albert W. Koers, *The Enforcement of Fisheries Agreements on the High Seas: A Comparative Analysis of International State Practice* (Occasional Paper, No. 6) (Kingston: Law of the Sea Institute, University of Rhode Island, June 1970).

for particular conservation schemes. The organization also provides experts to less developed countries. But while it has, on occasion, sponsored attempts at conservation, its members have never allowed it to develop into a major regulatory agency.

Regional regulatory commissions are generally hampered by a unanimity rule in their decisionmaking, a consequent inability to respond quickly to changing conditions, and a dependence on other organizations or national members for required expertise.[10] Research undertaken in a multilateral forum is more readily accepted than research carried out on a national basis.[11] National members, especially the less capable ones, think that multilateral research is less likely to be skewed toward the interests of any single country than research which is carried out unilaterally or bilaterally. But apart from the research area the structural limitations imposed on regional regulatory commissions by national members make them incapable of reacting quickly to greatly increased levels of fishing effort on particular stocks. Again, the unanimity rule effectively prevents any adverse action involving the special interests of any member in regard to a particular stock. Finally, attempts by members to retrieve capital investment in fishing fleets in the short run can and do lead to subversion of conservation schemes with the schemes themselves tending to lag behind the rate of technological advance.

The primary patterns of interaction are therefore between national fishery organizations and appropriate agencies of the state within a single country. At the international level the focus of most of the activity is the state, although IGOs play an independent role in gathering and disseminating information. We should also note that this kind of activity in a multilateral forum can facilitate attempts to arrive at international agreement but that IGOs have not yet played a major role in solving fishery disputes. The most effective mechanism here is still "case by case negotiation among the sovereign owners."[12] Transnational processes are thus insignificant in the international management and regulation of fisheries.

IV. Exploitation of Resources

Outer Space

Unfortunately, data available for analyzing interaction in this category is insufficient, and it is not possible to draw any firm conclusions. One can, how-

[10] William Sullivan, "A Warning: The Decline of International Fisheries Management, Looking Particularly at the North Atlantic Ocean," in *The United Nations and Ocean Management, Proceedings of the Fifth Annual Conference of the Law of the Sea Institute, June 15–19, 1970*, ed. Lewis Alexander (Kingston: University of Rhode Island, 1971), pp. 43–48.

[11] C. E. Lucas, *International Fishery Bodies of the North Atlantic* (Occasional Paper, No. 5) (Kingston: Law of the Sea Institute, University of Rhode Island, April 1970).

[12] Wilbert Chapman, "Fishery Resources in Offshore Waters," in *The Law of the Sea: Offshore Boundaries and Zones*, ed. Lewis Alexander (Publication of the Law of the Sea Institute and the Mershon Center for Education in National Security) (Columbus: Ohio State University Press, 1967), p. 98.

ever, specify the kinds of questions which future research might seek to answer.

Satellite telecommunication represents the only form of profitable exploitative activity currently carried on in space. The patterns of interaction are extremely complex because telecommunication is important both for national security and business operations. Particularly in North America and Western Europe the pattern of interaction involves a mix of governmental agencies and business enterprises. In the Communist system and most less developed countries the primary actors have been governmental.

Most of the complexities which exist in this area are highlighted in the structure and functioning of INTELSAT. This peculiar organization includes both governments and business enterprises as members, and its manager, the Communications Satellite Corporation (COMSAT), is itself a mixed public and private United States firm which oversees satellite design, contracting, and operation.[13] The role of COMSAT within INTELSAT is indicative of United States dominance of INTELSAT. Due to its capability in satellite and rocket technology, the fact that it created the organization, and the size of its financial contribution the United States once controlled 53 percent of the vote and still manages the organization. Recent negotiations on the permanent arrangements governing INTELSAT operations have decreased the vote controlled by the United States to 40 percent. This control has led to a sustained challenge on the part of West European governments and business enterprises that wish to see both an internationalized manager and a larger number of development contracts given to West European companies.[14] This situation is further complicated by the opposition of less developed countries to subcontracting by United States companies to West European firms because product costs are thereby increased.

It is not clear exactly how policy is made at the national level on this issue, but it is important to realize that neither in Western Europe nor in the United States is there complete agreement between business enterprises and governments on important policy issues. For example, British aerospace firms tend to be consistently critical of what they consider the timidity of the British gov-

[13] For general information about INTELSAT see Richard Colino, "INTELSAT: Doing Business in Outer Space," *Columbia Journal of Transnational Law,* Spring 1967 (Vol. 6, No. 1), pp. 17–60; Delbert D. Smith, *International Telecommunication Control: International Law and the Ordering of Satellite and Other Forms of International Broadcasting* (Leiden: A. W. Sijthoff, 1969), pp. 142–160; Brenda Maddox, "The Connections," *The Economist,* August 9, 1969 (Vol. 232, No. 6572), pp. vii-xxxvi; Robert J. Samuelson, "Intelsat: Flying High, but Future Course Uncertain," *Science,* April 4, 1969 (Vol. 164, No. 3875), pp. 56–57; and Jonathan F. Galloway, "Worldwide Corporations and International Integration: The Case of INTELSAT," *International Organization,* Summer 1970 (Vol. 24, No. 3), pp. 503–519.

[14] See G. K. C. Pardoe, "Space Programmes in Western Europe and the U.K." (Paper delivered at the Impact of Aerospace Science and Technology on Law and Government Conference, Washington, August 28–30, 1968), now American Institute of Aeronautics and Astronautics Paper No. 68–897; and Christopher Layton, *European Advanced Technology: A Programme for Integration* (London: George Allen & Unwin [for Political and Economic Planning], 1969), pp. 162–194.

ernment in the entire space field. They fear that without a sufficient number of development contracts British industry will simply not be able to establish a base which will allow it to compete in this area. In the United States, on the other hand, COMSAT is caught in the center of a number of crucial interagency disagreements, involving the FCC, national television networks, and large electronics companies, over the organization and control of a domestic satellite telecommunication system.

Although formal negotiation and commitments in this area are carried out by governments at the international level, I am unable to make any inferences about the pattern of informal negotiation because relevant data has not yet been gathered. For example, some delegations to INTELSAT include representatives from private business, but it is not clear how many delegations have such representatives or exactly what part they play in the formulation of national policy and subsequent international negotiations. Similarly, information on the number of people in COMSAT's secretariat recruited from private business, the positions they fill, and the roles they play is not generally available.

Weather and navigation satellites are two other significant ways to exploit the space medium, but neither one is as yet a commercial venture. Navigation satellites are not widely used for aircraft, although ICAO is interested in increasing their use. Satellite systems are still too expensive for smaller ships which need them most. On the other hand, the state-centric model is significantly modified by the pattern of IGO and NGO activity in the use of weather satellites. The global nature of atmospheric circulation and the complementarity of state interests in achieving longer and more accurate forecasts has resulted in increases in IGO authority and in the influence of particular groups of scientists in formulating international policy on this issue.[15]

The Oceans

Until the early 1950s mineral exploitation in the oceans was carried out relatively near shore. As technology advanced, however, the debate concerning the jurisdiction of a coastal state over its continental shelf intensified, reaching its first threshold in 1958 at the United Nations Conference on the Law of the Sea. Extremely rapid advances in technology since that time have rendered nugatory the compromise reached in Geneva.[16] A new debate within

[15] This is described in detail in my essay, "International Administration of Space Exploration and Exploitation," in *Multinational Cooperation*, ed. Robert Jordan (New York: Oxford University Press, forthcoming), pp. 128–148.

[16] This compromise combined both geomorphological and technological criteria in defining the limits of the continental shelf. Article 1 of the Convention on the Continental Shelf defines the continental shelf as "the seabed and the subsoil of the submarine areas adjacent to the coast but outside the territorial sea, to a depth of 200 metres or, beyond that limit, to where the depth of the superjacent waters admits of the exploitation of the natural resources of the said areas. . . . " UN Document A/CONF.-13/L.55.

the UN General Assembly has taken place in the last three years focusing on the issue of jurisdiction over the continental shelf and the ocean floor beyond.[17]

The number of countries which are actually able to engage in offshore exploitation of petroleum resources is relatively small and, of those so engaged, the United States, the Soviet Union, Canada, the United Kingdom, France, and the Netherlands are the major participants. The number of countries able to engage in the exploitation of other offshore minerals, like diamonds or manganese nodules, is also very small. In general, the marine mining industry is not significant on a global scale.

In the major oil-producing countries national policymaking concerning offshore petroleum resources is characterized by a high level of interaction between governmental agencies and petroleum companies. In addition, there is direct interaction between the eight largest international companies and the governments of the ten countries which form the Organization of the Petroleum Exporting Countries (OPEC). Earlier this year the oil companies and OPEC members from the Persian Gulf area signed a five-year agreement which will increase revenues to the producing states over that period by about $10 billion, or over 40 percent.[18] The negotiation of this agreement represents a striking case of transnational interaction, with NGOs, IGOs, and states all intimately involved. The detailed history of these negotiations, however, has not yet been written. In any case, the political economy of the international oil industry is so complex that it can hardly be given adequate treatment in this essay. I simply note that transnational organizations and interactions are apparently quite significant in the exploitation of offshore petroleum resources.[19]

[17] For some of the recent literature on mineral exploitation of the oceans see, inter alia, John L. Mero, *The Mineral Resources of the Sea* (Elsevier Oceanography Series, No. 1) (New York: Elsevier Publishing Co., 1965); G. T. Coene, "Profile of Marine Resources," *Proceedings of the Conference on Law, Organization and Security in the Use of the Oceans, Ohio State University, March 17–18, 1967*, Vol. 1; Lewis M. Alexander, ed., *The Law of the Sea: The Future of the Sea's Resources, Proceedings of the Second Annual Conference of the Law of the Sea Institute, June 26–29, 1967* (Kingston: University of Rhode Island, 1968); Lewis M. Alexander, ed., *The Law of the Sea: International Rules and Organization for the Sea, Proceedings of the Third Annual Conference of the Law of the Sea Institute, June 24–27, 1968* (Kingston: University of Rhode Island, 1969); Louis Henkin, *Law for the Sea's Mineral Resources* (ISHA Monograph, No. 1) (New York: Institute for the Study of Science in Human Affairs, Columbia University, 1968); Committee on Petroleum Resources, *Petroleum Resources under the Ocean Floor: An Interim Report* (Washington: National Petroleum Council, July 9, 1968); and V. E. McKelvey and Frank Wang, *World Subsea Mineral Resources: Preliminary Maps* (Washington: United States Geological Survey, 1969).

[18] *New York Times*, February 15, 1971, pp. 1, 7.

[19] For general analyses of the oil industry see Edith T. Penrose, *The Large International Firm in Developing Countries: The International Petroleum Industry* (Cambridge, Mass: M.I.T. Press, 1969); George Stocking, *Middle East Oil* (Nashville, Tenn: Vanderbilt University Press, 1970); Michael Tanzer, *The Political Economy of International Oil and the Underdeveloped Countries* (Boston: Beacon Press, 1969); Christopher Tugendhat, *Oil: The Biggest Business* (New York: G. P. Putnam's Sons, 1968). I should note, however, that data is not generally available on the formation of coalitions between governmental and nongovernmental actors within the major oil-producing and oil-importing countries nor on the penetration of those coalitions by other external actors.

International shipping may be another area in which transnational participants, particularly national and international combinations of shipping companies, shipowners' associations, etc., play a major role in determining policy and patterns of interaction. However, this area is so complex and some of the questions that must be raised are so politically sensitive that the necessary information is again not now available.[20] Samuel Lawrence has pointed out that the considerable difficulties encountered in attempting to achieve international regulation of shipping result from a number of factors: 1) the influence of shipping interests on the governments of major maritime countries; 2) the complexity of international shipping itself in terms of routes, ports, cargoes, commodity rates, etc.; and 3) the problem of flags of convenience.[21] In international shipping the most important transnational participants may be not only companies but also families or individuals who own significant portions of a country's shipping industry.

Within the dominant shipping cartels, or liner conferences, the fixed costs of operation tend to encourage agreements to restrict competition which might otherwise force prices below operational costs.[22] These arrangements include informal "gentlemen's agreements" as well as formal cartels, and their primary aim is to set freight rates and sailing schedules.[23] Not only is there close cooperation between liner conferences with similar interests, there is also some evidence which suggests that the major lines divide the trade routes of the world among themselves.[24] In addition, there is an intricate series of links between regional liner conferences and national and international shippers' organizations and shipowners' associations.[25]

The Intergovernmental Maritime Consultative Organization (IMCO) provides a useful case history of the kinds of restrictions that members immediately place on IGOs which are supposed to regulate international activity of considerable commercial significance or at least have the potential to do so.[26] From its very inception IMCO has been burdened with some major restrictive reservations imposed by Greece and India which did not want the organi-

20 I am grateful to my colleague Bernhard Abrahamsson for bibliographic and substantive guidance on international shipping questions.

21 Samuel A. Lawrence, *United States Merchant Shipping Policies and Politics* (Washington: Brookings Institution, 1966), pp. 16–17.

22 Bernhard Abrahamsson, "Developing Nations and Ocean Transportation: An Analysis of Price and Cost of Ocean Transportation, Balance of Payments, and the Case for National Merchant Marines with Special Reference to Southeast Asia" (Ph.D. diss., University of Wisconsin, 1966), especially chapter 2; see also Daniel Marx, *International Shipping Cartels: A Study of Industrial Self-Regulation by Shipping Conferences* (Princeton, N.J: Princeton University Press, 1953); and the essay by Robert L. Thornton in this volume.

23 Abrahamsson, "Developing Nations and Ocean Transportation," p. 34.

24 Ibid., pp. 35, 39ff.

25 See, for example, Maritime Transport Committee, *Maritime Transport, 1968* (Paris: Organisation for Economic Co-operation and Development, 1968), p. 11.

26 See the excellent account by David J. Padwa, "The Curriculum of IMCO," *International Organization,* Autumn 1960 (Vol. 14, No. 4), pp. 524–547.

zation to extend its activities to "commerce and economics."[27] It was not until ten years after the signing of its convention that the required number of ratifications was obtained. In David J. Padwa's words:

> In an industry characterized by the dominance of private interests, it seemed a fair question to inquire whether the proposed organization could function adequately on an intergovernmental level. While this might be entirely feasible with respect to technical matters, the ability of the organization to discuss certain commercial questions was the source of doubts as to whether it could discharge the apparently hybrid functions assigned to it. The feeling that executive policies regarding the operation of privately owned shipping were matters best left to shipowners and nongovernmental associations was largely responsible for these doubts.[28]

IMCO's primary functions are to gather and appraise information and to make recommendations on technical problems involving navigation and the safety of life at sea. But even within this framework the secretariat is restricted by the rule that it can consider only those problems which the members unanimously agree are most urgent.[29] This provision acts as a brake on task expansion within the organization. Since 1967, however, the scope of IMCO's tasks has been enlarged to include problems of oil and radioactive pollution of the oceans. IMCO maintains communication with a number of NGOs—the International Chamber of Shipping (ICS), the International Shipping Federation (ISF), the International Union of Marine Insurance (IUMI), and the International Chamber of Commerce (ICC)—but information on the content, intensity, and effects of this communication is yet to be gathered.

V. Transnational Processes in Space and Ocean Science Research

The global space research system has a four-level structure. At the first or national level there are presently 35 countries which maintain domestic space science research programs of varying sizes.[30] At the second or bilateral level activity consists primarily of exchanges involving the United States and all other countries outside the Communist system which carry on such research. At the third level, also bilateral, there is another dimension of interaction between the United States and a large number of countries which have no research programs but on whose territory the United States maintains satellite tracking stations. Finally, the fourth or international level involves an intricate web of activity between IGOs and NGOs (mainly members of the ICSU family) and between NGOs and national academies of science.

[27] Ibid., p. 524.

[28] Ibid., p. 533.

[29] Jean Roullier, "A Youthful Agency: IMCO and Its Work since Its Establishment," IMCO *Bulletin*, November 1967 (No. 11), pp. 3–7. Roullier was secretary-general of IMCO at this time.

[30] COSPAR, *Transactions Number 5*, Reports of National Institutions on Space Research Activities Presented at the Tenth Plenary Meeting of COSPAR, London, July 1967, and Paris, April 1968.

At the bilateral level most countries must look primarily to the United States for significant cooperation in space research.[31] Even West European countries that maintain their own research programs have to seek United States cooperation in launching satellites. The Soviet Union has only recently begun to engage in bilateral cooperation with East European members of the Communist system. The United States maintains its most intense research relations with Canada, Australia, and India.[32]

The most important organizations involved in space research at the international level are the WMO and the ITU, although others, like ICAO, are becoming increasingly involved. These organizations are engaged in an expanding research program with ICSU members on particular problems in space science, especially those concerning the atmospheric sciences.[33] Among NGOs, COSPAR has played the leading role both by providing advice to the UN General Assembly and by acting as an international referee in disputes involving claims of probable harmful effects of experiments. In addition, it is the major center for the collection and dissemination of information on various aspects of space science research.[34]

The structure of ocean research is not as clearly differentiated as that of space research. Research activity at the domestic and international levels is rather clearly defined, but there is no generally available data on research activities at the level of bilateral interaction. Given this lack of information it is not possible to determine whether there is bilateral interaction between those countries that maintain the largest research programs, what forms, if any, these transactions take, and what their effects might be. On the other hand, there is some bilateral interaction, involving primarily the transfer of development aid, between developed and less developed countries. Transnational processes appear to be important here since some of this interaction is carried on by private business enterprises operating in and for aid-receiving countries, but again no data has been gathered on the number of companies and countries involved or on the effects of these transactions.

The need for international cooperation between governments and scientists engaged in oceanographic research is great. This is especially true for projects

[31] A. W. Frutkin, "International Cooperation in Space," *Science,* July 24, 1970 (Vol. 169, No. 3943), pp. 333–339; see also Homer E. Newell and Leonard Jaffe, "Impact of Space Research on Science and Technology," *Science,* July 7, 1967 (Vol. 157, No. 3784), pp. 29–39.

[32] Edward Miles, "Development of Legal Regimes to Guide Space Exploration" (Paper delivered at the Impact of Aerospace Science and Technology Conference, Washington, August 28–30, 1968), now American Institute of Aeronautics and Astronautics Paper No. 68–908; see, especially, section V, "Trends in International Agreements for Space Exploration, 1960–1967," pp. 7–9.

[33] See Hugh Odishaw, "Science and Space," in *Outer Space: Prospects for Man and Society,* ed. Lincoln P. Bloomfield (rev. ed.; New York: Frederick A. Praeger [for the American Assembly, Columbia University], 1968), pp. 75–93; H. C. van de Hulst, "COSPAR and Space Co-operation," in *The Challenges of Space,* ed. Hugh Odishaw (Chicago: University of Chicago Press, 1962), pp. 291–298; and Leonard Schwartz, "International Space Organizations," in ibid., especially pp. 242–266.

[34] Maurice Roy, "Benefits of Membership in COSPAR," COSPAR *Information Bulletin,* February 1969 (No. 48), pp. 5–10.

of rather large dimensions, like the Indian Ocean Expedition, which require participation by many ships of diverse nationalities to make standardized and sometimes simultaneous observations and measurements. Not surprisingly, therefore, there is intense and pervasive interaction between IGOs like the Intergovernmental Oceanographic Commission (IOC) of UNESCO, the FAO, and the International Council for the Exploration of the Sea (ICES), on the one hand, and NGOs like the Scientific Committee on Oceanic Research (SCOR), the International Association for the Physical Sciences of the Ocean (IAPSO), the International Association of Biological Oceanography (IABO), and the Commission on Marine Biology on the other. The NGOs are all members of the ICSU family.[35]

It is significant, however, that transnational processes in research are almost nonexistent in areas in which commercial benefits are highest. There are no NGOs which provide for "independent consideration of the technical aspects of applied marine science—fisheries, mineral resources, underwater structures, etc."[36]

Warren Wooster has described the International Geophysical Year (IGY) of 1957–1958 as the watershed for the development of the international system of marine research. Prior to this time research was limited and involved a relatively small number of scientists who knew each other personally. The exchange of information generally resulted from personal contacts and, if it involved written communication, it was communication between friends. As projects grew in size and scope during and after the IGY, however, the necessity of greater state participation and the expense of these projects called for more formal commitments from governments.[37]

The increasing involvement of governments, however, raises fears of the increasing politicization of marine science research. Since 1967 the oceans have become a more salient issue in the general North-South confrontation in IGOs. Less developed countries see the oceans as a potential source of significant wealth and appear to equate research with exploration for purposes of exploitation. The fact that the countries with the largest research capabilities are also among those engaging in the widest exploitation of the medium serves only to add fuel to this fear, and there is a tendency for coastal states to place greater restrictions on marine research activity carried on off their coasts.[38]

[35] Committee on Oceanography, *Oceanography: 1960 to 1970,* Vol. 10: *International Cooperation* (Washington: National Academy of Sciences/National Research Council, 1959); see also United States Congress, House, Committee on Science and Astronautics, *Ocean Sciences and National Security,* H. Rept. 2078, 86th Cong., 2nd sess., 1960; and Marine Science Commission, *Our Nation and the Sea* (Washington: Government Printing Office, 1970), pp. 169–208.

[36] Warren Wooster, "International Organization for Science," in Alexander, *The Law of the Sea: International Rules and Organization for the Sea,* p. 421.

[37] Warren Wooster, "The Ocean and Man," *Scientific American,* September 1969 (Vol. 221, No. 3), pp. 218–234.

[38] See William T. Burke, "Law, Science, and the Ocean," *Natural Resources Lawyer,* May 1970 (Vol. 3, No. 2), pp. 195–226; and by the same author, *Marine Research and International Law* (Occasional Paper, No. 8) (Kingston: Law of the Sea Institute, University of Rhode Island, September 1970).

Of all the IGOs concerned with the oceans, it appears that the IOC is now emerging as the central unit in the international decisionmaking system for ocean exploration.[39] In fact, consultations in 1968 between the IOC Bureau and representatives of UNESCO, the FAO, the WMO, SCOR, and the ACMRR of the FAO led to an agreement to establish the Inter-Secretariat Committee within the IOC consisting of representatives of the executive heads of the UN, the FAO, the WMO, and IMCO.[40] It is hoped that this group will coordinate basic plans, programs, and activities for the UN family in the marine sciences area.

Institutionalization of interorganizational relations between the IOC and the WMO has progressed rather rapidly in a number of areas. These involve joint working groups on problems of telecommunications requirements for the transmission of oceanographic data and on development of plans for an Integrated Global Ocean Station System (IGOSS) as a means of building an oceanographic component into the World Weather Watch.[41] Within the WMO the Executive Committee in 1969 established the Panel on Meteorological Aspects of Ocean Affairs which coordinates WMO collaboration with the IOC.[42] In addition, the Executive Committee has occasionally decided to assign a scientific officer from the secretariat to work full-time with the IOC on problems of mutual interest. Proposals by the United States for an "international decade of ocean exploration" have confronted the IOC with a major challenge because, if that unit is to coordinate such a project, its staff and financial resources must be expanded. This may mean raising its status to that of a separate UN specialized agency on ocean problems.[43]

Another issue which combines the interests of these five organizations is marine pollution. A joint group of experts was created in 1969 consisting of representatives from the IOC, the FAO, the WMO, IMCO, and observers from SCOR. As an NGO, SCOR has a formal advisory relationship with

39 See the excellent report by the joint Advisory Committee on Marine Resources and Research (ACMRR)–WMO working group on the implementation of the United Nations resolution on the resources of the sea. SCOR, *International Ocean Affairs: A Special Report* (La Jolla, Calif., September 1, 1967); see also IOC, *Intergovernmental Oceanographic Commission (Five Years of Work)* (IOC Technical Series, No. 2) (Paris: UNESCO, 1966); and Sidney Holt, "The Intergovernmental Oceanographic Commission: A Biased History" (Paper delivered at the Law of the Sea Institute, University of Rhode Island, Kingston, June 1970).

40 "Future Development of the Intergovernmental Oceanographic Commission, Meeting of Consultants Convened by the IOC Bureau, UNESCO, Paris, 11–12 October 1968," *International Marine Science,* December 1968 (Vol. 6, Nos. 3–4), pp. 55–56.

41 "Second Meeting of the IOC Working Committee for the IGOSS, WMO Headquarters, Geneva, February 24, 1969," *International Marine Science,* April 1969 (Vol. 7, No. 1), pp. 28–29; see also Intergovernmental Oceanographic Commission, *Legal Problems Associated with Ocean Data Acquisition Systems (ODAS)* (Paris: United Nations Educational, Scientific and Cultural Organization, 1969).

42 "Report of the President of CMM [Commission for Maritime Meteorology] and Report of the Fifth Session of CMM," *Abridged Report with Resolutions of the Twenty-First Session of the Executive Committee of the World Meteorological Organization, May 29–June 12, 1969* (Geneva: Secretariat of the World Meteorological Organization, 1969), pp. 32–38.

43 Marine Science Commission, pp. 174–175.

the IOC but is only indirectly linked with the WMO and the FAO on questions of air-sea interaction and scientific aspects of ocean research, respectively.[44] The FAO also has common interests with the IOC and the WMO as a result of its concern with fishery conservation and the need for data on oceanographic variables affecting the ecology of particular stocks.

IMCO has a series of other links with the WMO, the FAO, and the IOC. It shares an interest with the WMO in the relationships between meteorology, navigation, and safety of life at sea and in telecommunications techniques for the transmission of oceanographic data. The IOC also has an interest in the transmission of oceanographic data. IMCO cooperates with the FAO in setting standards to regulate what is technically called the intact stability of fishing vessels and the operation of such vessels.

It is true that there are still many areas in which requirements for successful task performance do not call for close collaboration between organizations. But since 1967, and particularly since 1969, it is clear that a crosscutting series of formal and informal links has been established between these hitherto separate units so that they do in fact constitute a single system on a series of issues. This development is a result of the convergence of three factors: 1) rapid advances in marine technology since 1958; 2) increased attempts to achieve more rational international management and regulation of ocean exploitation; and 3) United States proposals for an international decade of ocean exploration.

The state-centric model is most inadequate to explain the complexities of research in the space and ocean issue areas and must be modified. I do not mean to deny, however, that the nation-state is still the source of funds for most international activity, or that among nation-states the United States is dominant in the range of its capabilities, or even that at the international level a great deal of the activity is carried out by representatives of governmental agencies. But the physical aspects of outer space and the oceans demand a high level of international cooperation if certain problems are to be investigated. The areas are vast and therefore require standardized observations and measurements together with support systems providing for the exchange of information derived from the investigations. The organizational and management requirements of these large-scale projects reinforce this need for cooperation. The norm of internationalism, an important element in the social system of science,[45] augments nongovernmental scientific activity as does the fact that subject-matter specialization makes it easier for scientists to communicate cross-nationally.[46]

[44] SCOR *Proceedings,* April 1969 (Vol. 5, No. 1), p. 8.

[45] See, inter alia, Norman W. Storer, *The Social System of Science* (New York: Holt, Rinehart & Winston, 1966); and Robert Merton, *Social Theory and Social Structure* (rev. and enl. ed.; Glencoe, Ill: Free Press of Glencoe, 1957), pp. 550–561.

[46] I am indebted to Robert Friedheim for this point.

It is for these reasons that members of the ICSU family play an important role in stimulating and coordinating international research activities concerning outer space and the oceans. But in areas in which the commercial potential of research is high, this role is limited. For example, the inability of COSPAR to establish safety standards to prevent the contamination of Mars and other planets is due to the unwillingness of both the United States and the Soviet Union to pay the high costs that would be incurred by adopting such standards.[47]

VI. Recreation, Pollution Control, and National Security in Outer Space and the Oceans

The state-centric model of international relations is adequate for understanding most of the interaction that occurs on issues involving recreation, pollution control, and national security, although it is always necessary to specify the relevant parts of the state that are the primary actors.

On questions involving national security, that is, the development and deployment of military capabilities in space and the oceans, there are still no significant actors other than states. On these issues IGOs like the Conference of the Committee on Disarmament (CCD) and NGOs like the Pugwash Conferences on Science and World Affairs may provide forums for formal and informal discussion between state representatives, but they do not play an independent role.

Decisions about recreational uses of the oceans—sport fishing and hunting, sailing, and the maintenance of beach facilities—are generally made on the national level because most of these activities are carried on in areas in which the coastal state has exclusive jurisdiction. However, within individual states different agencies have jurisdiction over different activities. The parties involved in the decisionmaking process will also include, inter alia, representatives of the sport fishing industry, commercial fishermen, and the petroleum industry. As Richard Stroud has pointed out, "The chief sources of possible conflict [in the United States] between recreational and other uses of the water above the continental shelf appear to derive from the overseas commercial fishing operations by nationals of several foreign countries, as well as United States domestic commercial fisheries; from possible pollution of the sea by toxic chemicals such as oil, acid, pesticides, and so forth, and by disposal of atomic wastes; and from possible large-scale seismic explorations and associated activities."[48]

[47] For more details on this see Miles, in Jordan.

[48] Richard Stroud, "Sport Fishery and Recreation Demands on the Continental Shelf," in Alexander, *The Law of the Sea: International Rules and Organization for the Sea,* p. 242; cf., Marine Science Commission, *Panel Reports,* Vol. 3: *Marine Resources and Legal Political Arrangements for Their Development* (Washington: Government Printing Office, 1969), chapter 7, pp. 31 and 36.

The problem of controlling oil pollution of the oceans has recently emerged as a major concern in the ocean issue area, primarily as a result of the development of "supertankers" like the *Torrey Canyon*. This problem has both national and international dimensions, but the dominant patterns of interaction, especially in resolving conflicts over questions of liability, still take place at the national level and involve courts and the representatives of various industries.[49]

The 1954 International Convention for the Prevention of Pollution of the Sea by Oil, arranged under IMCO auspices, places the burden of regulation and enforcement of measures to combat pollution of the high seas on the flag state.[50] This provision merely incorporated customary law which had existed for a long time. While the coastal state always exercised exclusive jurisdiction over prejudicial acts occurring in its territorial sea and contiguous zone, recent events like the *Torrey Canyon* wreck encouraged claims that the coastal state and the flag state exercise concurrent jurisdiction. In any event, no IGO or NGO had any regulatory capacity whatever even though IMCO, the FAO, and SCOR are very concerned about the consequences of large oil spills in the oceans. It may be that as the magnitude of the problem increases and attempts at solution become more complex and difficult, especially when more than two states are involved, these organizations will be allowed to play a larger role than they have so far.

There is also a possibility that significant transnational interaction will emerge as a consequence of increasing radioactive pollution of the oceans. When the cost of nuclear energy decreases considerably, it will become economical to use reactors for purposes other than powering ships. One of the uses predicted is the employment of nuclear reactors as ovens in barren areas of the ocean to generate artificial upwelling and thereby to create new fisheries. As these uses multiply, the problem of radioactive pollution of the oceans and of the fish in them is likely to become more acute. If the level of radioactive pollution increases, I would expect an intensification of activity between IMCO, the IAEA, the FAO, the WHO, and SCOR. These organizations will certainly attempt to mobilize their constituents at the national level, and there will be the added possibility of short-run national and international coalitions of conservation societies and fisheries organizations.

[49] See, for example, Ved P. Nanda, "The 'Torrey Canyon' Disaster: Some Legal Aspects," *Denver Law Journal,* Summer 1967 (Vol. 44, No. 3), pp. 400–425; and Ved P. Nanda and Kenneth R. Stiles, "Offshore Oil Spills: An Evaluation of Recent United States Responses," *San Diego Law Review,* July 1970 (Vol. 7, No. 3), pp. 519–540.

[50] Nanda, *Denver Law Journal,* Vol. 44, No. 3, pp. 405–413.

VII. The Significance of Transnational Processes in Outer Space and the Oceans

For purposes of comparison I would prefer to place the categories of activity considered along a continuum rather than to treat each category as representative of a discrete condition. At the extreme left of this continuum I would place all activity for which the state-centric model is adequate. At the extreme right would be all activity for which the model is inadequate. Issues which involve national security, recreation, and pollution control would be placed near the "adequate" end while those which involve the coordination of research would be placed at the "inadequate" end. Issues involving management and regulation would have to be placed in the middle. Since we lack sufficient information on issues involving exploitation, these remain something of an unknown. It is quite possible, however, that the state-centric model will prove inadequate in this area.

The issues at the "most adequate" end of the continuum are those in which the jurisdiction of the nation-state is exclusive. For example, even though policymaking at the national level concerning pollution or recreational activities in the oceans may involve a wide range of nongovernmental participants, the locus of decisionmaking is still some agency of the state. These activities, along with many others in the space and ocean issue areas, fall into categories in which states have traditionally claimed exclusive authority. Consequently, patterns of internal organization and control over policymaking reflect these continuing concerns. They may also be buttressed by perceived national security interests, legal demands for the definition of international personality on questions involving liability for damage incurred, or the need for comprehensive definitions of responsibility to deal with the consequences of various acts which have differential impacts on nationals of the state.

In contrast, issues at the "most inadequate" end of the continuum are characterized by either a new technology which cannot be adequately exploited unless common commitments to a central organization are made by most states or by interactions occurring in an area whose physical dimensions preclude control by any single state. These characterizations define large-scale research in outer space and the oceans, and as a result there is a considerable amount of independent activity undertaken by NGOs, primarily of the ICSU family, and by particular IGOs.

The commercial potential of international shipping, and perhaps of mineral exploitation of the oceans, may lead to a rather high degree of transnational interaction involving primarily business enterprises. For example, several representatives of the petroleum industry attended the 1970 sessions of the General Assembly Committee on Peaceful Uses of the Seabed and Ocean Floor. The United States had proposed a draft treaty to which the

United States National Petroleum Council was opposed. At least one delegate, Ambassador Arvid Pardo of Malta, was quoted as having said that some United States industry representatives were lobbying against the United States proposals.[51]

Issues involving management and regulation have been placed in the middle of the continuum because, even though national concerns tend to be dominant, the pattern of interaction and decisionmaking is different from that obtaining on security issues. There is an intricate combination of governmental and business actors at both national and international levels. Wherever commercial potential is high, restrictions on IGO and NGO activity tend to be great unless the NGOs represent the interests of the business enterprises. At the same time, within our enlarged definition of transnational behavior we noted evidence of two kinds of distinctly transnational behavior: 1) when national representatives took positions and initiated action which went beyond those which were governmentally defined and 2) when well-organized radio astronomers were exceptionally effective in achieving their ends vis-à-vis agencies of governments and business enterprises.

These examples of transnational activity are important not only in themselves but also for the light they shed on the kinds of coalitions that they engender. For example, in the episode described earlier, Reichelderfer, as director of the United States Weather Bureau, acted on behalf of his bureau *and* the WMO in which he was the principal United States representative. In doing so he allied with the director of the Canadian Meteorological Service who had almost identical interests and who was able to gain the support of the relevant section of the Canadian Department of External Affairs to achieve their goals. This transnational coalition was directed primarily against a national coalition in the United States comprising the Bureau of International Organization Affairs of the Department of State, atmospheric scientists, and the President's Office of Science and Technology.

In the second example radio astronomers created a formal transnational alliance designed specifically to pressure governments. The primary target once again was a national coalition in the United States consisting of the Department of Defense and communications companies. This coalition, like that in the previous example, also significantly affected governmental behavior. Although there is no evidence that a transnational coalition of petroleum companies exists, it is at least possible that such a coalition, led by United States companies, is working to defeat or at least to modify significantly the recently proposed United States draft treaty on the seabed. There are indications that very effective coalitions of shipping companies exist which are able to restrict the activities of governments and IGOs in regulating shipping questions.

[51] Samuel C. Orr, "Resources Report: Soviet, Latin Opposition Blocks Agreement on Seabeds Treaty," *CPR National Journal,* September 12, 1970, p. 1977.

It is important to note that outer space and the oceans differ in their historical experiences. The rather slow rate of growth of ocean technology made possible the evolution of an early, well-developed, and complicated set of traditions which do not exist for outer space. Using the years 1950, 1960, and 1970 as benchmarks, research and development was the main activity in the space issue area in 1950 but only on the national level. The major qualitative jump occurred only in late 1957 and coincided with the extremely influential experience of organized NGO and IGO collaboration in the IGY. The rate of advance between 1960 and 1970 was very high. Technology increased in sophistication and diversity, and more and more emphasis was placed on practical applications.

For the oceans, on the other hand, little overt technological development occurred between 1950 and 1960. There were vast developments, however, between 1960 and 1970 which totally belied expectations of rates of advance held by participants in 1958, especially on the question of the continental shelf. These developments have important consequences for the distribution of benefits or at least for the ways in which this distribution is now perceived. Less developed countries have been awakened to the potential of the oceans as a result of the high rate of technological advance in recent years. They claim, however, that significant capabilities for exploitation rest only with those states already in the front rank. Therefore, if they are to be sure that adequate benefits accrue to them, they should seek to extend those areas of the ocean which lie within their exclusive jurisdiction. The interests which need protection are fisheries and mineral exploitation on the continental shelf and beyond. In this way the salience of this issue in IGOs has increased and so has the level of conflict. As previously noted this pattern of demands has begun to affect the international research activity of some IGOs.

Among NGOs, ICSU members are the only actors, apart from some national and international business enterprises, involved in both outer space and the oceans. In the space issue area NGOs involved in broadcasting tend to interact only with one another. Similarly, in the ocean issue area high interaction between NGOs concerned with fisheries, minerals, and shipping is precluded by differences in technology. There is, however, some crosscutting membership within each task environment. Since there is great fluidity of membership and interests among ICSU members, jurisdictional conflicts tend to arise over control of particular research programs.

Even for governments there are many advantages to activities conducted within an NGO framework. NGOs concerned with outer space and the oceans are less formal and constricting for governments than are IGOs, particularly in regard to the planning of international scientific activities, the coordination of research at the international level, and the exchange of information. NGOs are also able to muster the largest pool of international competence to work on problems like ocean exploration, data gathering, and analysis on a global basis. Moreover, NGOs tend to have greater flexibility and faster reaction times than IGOs, primarily because they are not restricted by the decisionmaking systems which exist in IGOs. For example, no IGO was concerned with the question of space exploration until after the orbiting of *Sputnik I* in October 1957, but the problem had been foreseen and discussed regularly in ICSU circles since 1954. Similarly, the Committee on Contamination by Extra-Terrestrial Exploration (CETEX) was created in 1958 within the ICSU as a result of a proposal made by the United States National Academy of Sciences. CETEX was to work toward planning landings on the moon or other planets in such a way as to avoid terrestrial contamination of these areas. This problem was entrusted to the ICSU because its members represented the most competent group of space scientists from the largest number of countries. In addition, a much freer consideration of the problem was possible within an NGO. Alternatives could be discussed without confronting governments with the necessity to take formal positions on the issues involved. Finally, it appears to be much easier to create NGOs and to modify their structures to meet changing circumstances than is the case with IGOs.

Besides lobbying for certain kinds of regulatory activity by governments and appraising the probable consequences of certain state actions NGOs can be of special importance to less developed countries as repositories of technical advice, particularly on the demands of space and ocean science research. At the same time NGOs are vulnerable to governmental influence through the funding of research grants at the national level. They can also be sensitive to major disagreements between the most capable national actors. This is clearly illustrated in the difficulties experienced by COSPAR in persuading the United States and the Soviet Union to accept its recommendations on the problem of contamination of outer space, the moon, Mars, and other planets.

VIII. Implications for International Peace and Justice

Transnational processes in outer space and the oceans do not appear to have any great potential for producing a more peaceful and just international system because they are limited in their extent and they cannot arrest the growing discrepancies in capabilities in these areas. In fact, the area in which a considerable amount of transnational activity is taking place—shipping—is oriented toward the interests of the most capable participants. Since it is the gap in capabilities which is the source of a great deal of conflict in the two issue areas, it would be useful to summarize very briefly the distributions of these capabilities.[52]

[52] Some of this data on capabilities is gross and should be used with care. For example, Peru has the largest share of the world fishing catch, but this is based on a single species. This is why it is necessary to balance the data on total catch with data on the average tonnage of a country's fishing fleet in order to obtain a reliable profile of the extent of its capability.

Concerning fisheries, for example, data for 1965 on the share of the world catch yields the following rankings: 1) Peru, 2) Japan, 3) the People's Republic of China (Communist China), 4) the Soviet Union, 5) the United States, and 6) Norway.[53] But if we compare this data with data on the total world tonnage of fishing vessels over 100 gross tons, two countries stand out. Forty-nine percent of the world's fishing vessels of 100 or more tons are owned by the Soviet Union and 13 percent by Japan.[54] Spain ranks third with 6 percent, followed by France, Norway, the Polish People's Republic, and the United Kingdom with 3 percent each, and the Federal Republic of Germany (West Germany) with 2 percent.[55] Neither Peru nor the United States appear in this list since 95 percent of all United States fishing vessels are less than 100 tons.[56] Although Peru has the largest single share of the world catch, the Soviet Union and Japan have the greatest capabilities, especially for distant-water fishing.

In the area of shipping the situation is somewhat different. The major maritime countries of the world measured in dead weight tonnage are: 1) Liberia, 2) Japan, 3) the United Kingdom, 4) Norway, 5) the United States, 6) the Soviet Union, 7) Greece, and 8) West Germany.[57] The predominance of Liberia in this category is explained almost completely by flags of convenience registration. Greece and West Germany are the only other new major actors.

The situation in marine science research is again different. There are very few significant actors—the United States, the Soviet Union, Japan, the United Kingdom, Canada, and France. I have used two variables to judge capabilities in ocean science research: the number of oceanographic research vessels and the number of scientists involved in marine research. Admittedly, these measures are gross, but comparative data over time has not yet been gathered on the amount of money allocated to ocean science research either as a percentage of gross national product or as a percentage of total research and development allocations. Rankings on the measure of research vessels are: 1) the United States, 2) the Soviet Union, 3) Japan, 4) the United Kingdom, 5) Canada, 6) France, and 7) West Germany.[58] The rankings are almost the same when the measure is the number of marine scientists: 1) the United

[53] *Marine Science Affairs: A Year of Transition,* Report of the President to the Congress on Marine Resources and Engineering Development (Washington: Government Printing Office, 1967), pp. 47–49.

[54] Francis T. Christy, Jr., "Fisheries and the New Conventions on the Law of the Sea," *San Diego Law Review,* July 1970 (Vol. 7, No. 3), table 2, p. 466.

[55] Ibid.

[56] *Marine Science Affairs,* p. 47.

[57] See UN Document TD/B/C.4/66. The dead weight tonnage measure is an indication of carrying capacity, while the gross registered tonnage measure is not. The rankings are slightly changed when utilizing the gross registered tonnage measure: 1) Liberia, 2) the United Kingdom, 3) Norway, 4) Japan, 5) the United States, 6) the Soviet Union, 7) Greece, and 8) Italy. See Maritime Transport Committee, *Maritime Transport, 1968,* table 22, p. 107.

[58] Marine Science Commission, *Panel Reports, Engineering and Resources,* Vol. I: *Science and Environment* (Washington: Government Printing Office, 1969), table 4, chapter 1, p. 14.

States, 2) the Soviet Union and Japan, 3) the United Kingdom, 4) Canada, 5) France, and 6) West Germany.[59]

Compared with the shifting distributions which exist in the ocean issue area, the distributions for space exploration and exploitation are much more stable. The United States, the Soviet Union, Communist China, Japan, and France are the most capable actors. Each of these countries has launched its own satellites. A number of other countries are also involved to varying degrees in space activities: The United Kingdom, West Germany, Australia, Canada, and India are the most important countries in this category.

It is striking that the most capable actors are virtually the same countries in both the space and ocean issue areas. The countries which are most active on the full range of issues include only the United States, the Soviet Union, Japan, France, the United Kingdom, Canada, and West Germany. For these reasons the salience of technological advance as a political issue has increased dramatically since 1965. I would hypothesize, then, that as problems of economic development become more acute and the gap in the distribution of capabilities widens, technology as a political issue will become more salient. Increasingly, the priorities of less developed countries are determined by those areas of activity in which actual or potential benefits are perceived as more immediately available and extensive. As a result it is not surprising that less developed countries consider the oceans more salient than outer space.

A study of the relationship between stratification and conflict in international systems has shown that the degree of systemic conflict is directly related to the level of status discrepancy within the system.[60] There is, however, a one- or two-year time lag between the status discrepancy measure, which reflects the discrepancy between the prestige dimension and the capability dimension, and the conflict measure. I expect, therefore, that the rate of technological advance in space and the oceans, combined with the massive investments required to support it, will lead to increased conflict in the international system because this rate of advance is fully enjoyed by only seven countries. It is instructive to note once again that it is precisely in areas in which commercial potential is highest that restrictions on IGO and NGO activity are greatest. IGOs and NGOs cannot do much to reduce the wide disparities in capability beyond expanding their tasks in education and training.

[59] Ibid., table 5, chapter 1, pp. 14–15.

[60] Maurice East, "Stratification and International Politics: An Empirical Study Employing the International Systems Approach" (Ph.D. diss., Princeton University, 1969), pp. 89–127 and 147–180.

Security and a Transnational System:

The Case of Nuclear Energy

Lawrence Scheinman

In any discussion of transnational relations the nuclear energy field can best be studied within the framework of the state-centered model of international politics. Although in most fields private activities precede governmental regulation (which follows in response to social and other considerations), the opposite is true in the nuclear energy field. Because the first development of nuclear energy so intimately involved national security, government immediately assumed a preeminent role. This role is now being modified—but still only slightly—by nascent private undertakings of an occasionally transnational nature. Nevertheless, there is already sufficient evidence of growing transnational trends to make an exploration eminently worthwhile in the context of this volume.

Two central characteristics of the nuclear energy field serve to define the parameters within which we can discuss its transnational implications: the predominant role of government and the asymmetric international distribution of nuclear resources and technology. Individually or together these characteristics have strongly influenced the pattern of nuclear transactions in the postwar international system.

I. The Predominant Role of Government

During World War II and immediately thereafter the prevalence of military considerations, awareness of the dangers of information "leaks," and only a rudimentary understanding of how atomic energy could safely and effectively be harnessed for peaceful use combined to lead the first nuclear

Lawrence Scheinman is associate professor in the Department of Political Science, University of Michigan, Ann Arbor, Michigan. The author would like to thank Edward Levine for his helpful comments on an earlier draft.

powers to assert total governmental control over nuclear energy. With time responsibility for atomic development has gradually and unevenly devolved from public to private actors. However, such decentralization has been accompanied by increased governmental regulation, both within nation-states and across national boundaries, and by the appearance of new nongovernmental and intergovernmental actors.

Regulation and Control

United States nuclear policy vividly demonstrates this evolution. The Atomic Energy Act of 1946 established a single, powerful agency—the Atomic Energy Commission (AEC)—with full responsibility for the development and conduct of nuclear activities in the United States. The act reserved all uranium in public lands to the government, made all special nuclear materials (plutonium and enriched uranium) the exclusive property of the government, and placed all facilities for the production of such materials under governmental ownership. The AEC, however, did contract operational responsibilities for research centers to private actors like Union Carbide Corporation, for management of the Oak Ridge National Laboratory, and E. I. du Pont de Nemours and Company, for management of the Savannah River materials production facilities. International cooperation for peaceful or military purposes was prohibited as was the transfer of any information, personnel, or material of a restricted nature. Most nuclear information beyond very basic science was treated as classified, making international nuclear transactions of any kind minimal. How intrusive this system of governmental control could be is demonstrated by such widely diverse acts as withdrawing uranium for the coloring of ceramics from commercial circulation, preventing American citizens from legally working on special nuclear material production outside the United States, and even questioning whether physicists who had been associated with the Manhattan District Project could teach in non-American universities without violating the prohibition on the transfer of information.[1]

Similar patterns were established in other free-world countries—France and the United Kingdom—that assumed positions of nuclear leadership. The Federal Republic of Germany (West Germany) and Japan did not undertake nuclear activities until the mid-1950s when political restrictions on their engaging in nuclear work were lifted and the economic and commercial promise of nuclear energy became more apparent. As the atomic programs of these countries never had military components, somewhat different patterns between government and private enterprise emerged. Private enterprise from the outset played more of a central role. In no country, however, is nuclear

[1] For a general review of AEC regulatory activity see William H. Berman and Lee M. Hydeman, *The Atomic Energy Commission and Regulating Nuclear Facilities* (Ann Arbor: University of Michigan Law School, 1961).

energy a purely private affair in terms of regulation, research, development, or exploitation. In addition, because of the nature of the distribution of nuclear resources and the conditions governing international nuclear exchange, the internal structure of national nuclear programs has thus far had only limited effects on the conduct of nuclear activities.

Breach of the American nuclear monopoly and the increasing probability that atomic energy could be harnessed to economically competitive peaceful purposes led to President Dwight D. Eisenhower's Atoms for Peace proposal in 1953 and to the Atomic Energy Act of 1954. The Atoms for Peace proposal, intended to encourage and facilitate the development of peaceful nuclear technology for all states, resulted in a vast program of international cooperation through bilateral, regional, and international agreements and programs. It also foreshadowed the creation of the International Atomic Energy Agency (IAEA).

The revised Atomic Energy Act opened participation in peaceful nuclear development to private industry and allowed private individuals to possess and use special nuclear materials under license from the AEC. Additional revision in 1964 "privatized" nuclear energy even further by permitting private industry to own plutonium and enriched uranium subject to AEC regulations on protection, control, and safeguards. Another step toward "privatization" occurred when the AEC began to enrich privately owned uranium on a "toll" charge basis in January 1969.[2] Thus, as of 1971 the only important vestige of the proprietary and operational features of the Atomic Energy Act of 1946 is the United States government monopoly of the technology and facilities (gaseous diffusion plants) for producing enriched uranium. Even this monopoly is currently under review, and there is an increasing probability that the gaseous diffusion plants will eventually be transferred to private enterprise.

Against this background two points in particular deserve emphasis. The first is that decentralization of operational responsibilities and readjustment of proprietary relationships do not mean decentralization of governmental regulation and control.[3] Quite the contrary, both national and international control have increased in direct proportion to the transfer of operational responsibility to private or international interests. The Atoms for Peace program meant liberalized dissemination of nuclear information and positive development cooperation, but it also meant that what could not be prevented should at least be controlled. Modeled largely on American practice, the pattern of international cooperation invariably has entailed guarantees by the

[2] United States Atomic Energy Commission, Division of Industrial Participation, *Report on the Nuclear Industry, 1970* (Washington: Government Printing Office, 1970), p. 59.

[3] Although regulatory responsibility is lodged in the AEC, agreements have been reached with a number of states in the Union regarding assumption by the states of regulatory authority over certain materials; see *Report on the Nuclear Industry, 1970*, pp. 347–348.

recipient not to divert nuclear material from peaceful to nonpeaceful purposes and provisions for safeguards and inspection techniques to ensure against this contingency. Virtually all private transactions involving the risk of diversion of special nuclear materials take place within the framework of bilateral or multilateral agreements on safeguards and nondiversion. Although surveillance of these agreements has increasingly been concentrated in the IAEA, the conditions for exchange of information or material remain firmly in the hands of national governments. This theme of controlled nuclear technological dissemination—dominant since 1954—was codified in 1968 in the Treaty on the Nonproliferation of Nuclear Weapons (NPT). The NPT in many respects represents a globalization of American and—in the past decade—of Soviet international nuclear objectives.

The second point is that the limited degree of decentralization which characterizes the American nuclear scene is much less evident in such leading nuclear countries as Canada, France, and the United Kingdom. In these countries, despite participation by private enterprise in nuclear development and growing efforts to transfer even greater responsibility to the private sector, governmental authorities keep a tight rein on both the conceptual and executory aspects of peaceful nuclear development. Even where decentralization does take place, it is not always clear that whatever consortia are created are purely private affairs rather than some form of mixed enterprise resulting from governmental participation. Therefore, what is private in one context may be quasi-governmental in a second and governmental in a third. In Canada, for example, a number of nuclear activities such as mining, processing and production of nuclear materials, and basic research and development are conducted largely through crown companies like Eldorado Mining and Refining or Atomic Energy of Canada. These companies operate as private enterprises but government holds shares and contributes some or even an overwhelming portion of their financial resources.[4] It is difficult to describe such actors as private or nongovernmental and to equate them with such transnational actors as General Electric Company, Westinghouse Electric Corporation, or Gulf General Atomics. While as a general proposition it is far from clear that legal form dictates the pattern of behavior of public corporations, available evidence suggests a close relationship between form and function in the nuclear field—at least up to the present time.

Research, Development, and Exploitation

The prevalence of government, even in the United States, is evident not only in nuclear regulation and control but also in aspects of research, devel-

[4] See J. E. Hodgetts, *Administering the Atom for Peace* (International Political Science Association Series) (New York: Atherton Press, 1964). This book contains excellent reviews of the structure of nuclear programs in Canada, France, Italy, Japan, the United Kingdom, and the United States.

opment, and exploitation. Beyond the influence of a commitment to nuclear weapons there are at least three other reasons for the pervasiveness of government in the nuclear field: the cost of nuclear research and development; the importance of nuclear energy to national industrial growth; and the international status and prestige associated with command of nuclear technology. It is clear that the nuclear "have-nots" ascribe considerable significance to peaceful nuclear capability. Countries like West Germany and Japan, which have eschewed military status in the postwar world, are particularly sensitive to the value of economic and technological leadership. While private industry has always figured prominently in the nuclear development of these countries and their patterns of development testify to greater concern for economic advancement than for political independence, concern for political independence seems to be taking a more prominent place in the more recent development of their national nuclear policies. This matter is discussed in connection with the problem of asymmetry in the nuclear field.

Less developed countries also place great value on the acquisition of nuclear technology, fundamentally for economic reasons but also for prestige. As an Indian delegate to the Eighteen Nation Committee on Disarmament (ENDC) noted, "Nuclear technology is the technology of the future and is likely to become a crucial and potent instrument of economic development and social progress."[5] In a similar vein a Brazilian representative to the same forum insisted on the right of all countries to the "whole range of nuclear technological resources required to eliminate poverty and underdevelopment."[6] It is not surprising to find the governments of such spokesmen deeply immersed in national nuclear development policy.

We can profitably turn once again to the United States to demonstrate the role of government in the areas of nuclear research, development, and exploitation. It is likely that what holds true for the United States with its powerful and wealthy private enterprises will also hold true for other countries seriously pursuing nuclear development policies but from a weaker industrial base. Decentralization has not meant a withdrawal of government from participation in nuclear development any more than it has meant a weakening of governmental control over nuclear orientation.

Christopher Layton has noted that the first research and development partnership between government and industry in the United States occurred in the nuclear field. The involvement of public authority was so great that it

[5] *India News,* March 8, 1968, p. 5, quoted in Shelton L. Williams, *The U.S., India, and the Bomb* (Studies in International Affairs, No. 12) (Baltimore, Md: Johns Hopkins Press [for the Washington Center of Foreign Policy Research, School of Advanced International Studies, Johns Hopkins University], 1969), p. 59.

[6] Quoted in C. F. Barnaby, ed., *Preventing the Spread of Nuclear Weapons* (Pugwash Monograph I) (London: Souvenir Press, 1969), p. 58.

"elevated research to the status of a national goal."[7] The average governmental investment in nuclear research and development in the three years from 1968 to 1970, for example, has been on the order of $1.5 billion exclusive of research specifically directed toward nuclear weaponry. By most estimates this represents at least two-thirds of the total peaceful nuclear research and development effort in the United States. In some cases, such as high energy physics, the entire cost has been underwritten by various agencies of the federal government; in others, like the fast breeder reactor project, government has contributed the lion's share—$100 million of a total investment of $125 million per year.[8]

Another distinctive feature of nuclear technology is the nonseparability of research from development. In order to develop a competitive reactor it is necessary to build a series of prototype or demonstration reactors. These, too, are heavily underwritten by the federal government as the high cost and high risk factors prohibit private enterprise from assuming full financial responsibility. A single prototype breeder reactor, of which the United States plans to build three, is estimated to cost about $300 million; the proven light water reactors which have cornered the world market in the past decade were developed under the naval propulsion program of the AEC and cost the federal government $2 billion. Similar patterns are found in France, the United Kingdom, and West Germany. Indeed, in the United Kingdom the largest governmental research investment in any civil technology is in the field of atomic energy.

The most significant difference between Canada, France, and the United Kingdom, on the one hand, and the United States and West Germany on the other is that in the United States and West Germany much of the conceptual and design engineering work related to research and development is contracted to private enterprise; in Canada, France, and the United Kingdom much of this work is performed by the government. The difference between the United States and West Germany lies in the magnitude of state investment and in the far more centralized and effective coordination of research and development in the United States. West German federalism lodges authority over science and technology in the individual states rather than in the federal government. The absence of a weapons program or of nationalized power production reinforces this decentralization.

Government is also substantially involved at the level of exploitation. Where power production is not nationalized, the capacity of government to exercise promotional responsibility and to influence the course of events is largely confined to setting national objectives and to creating conditions and providing incentives likely to foster these objectives; it cannot impose the use of

[7] Christopher Layton, *European Advanced Technology: A Programme for Integration* (London: George Allen & Unwin [for Political and Economic Planning], 1969), p. 28.

[8] See *Report on the Nuclear Industry, 1970*, pp. 182–188.

nuclear power to the exclusion of alternative energy sources.[9] In countries in which electricity production, the principal consumer of peaceful nuclear technology, is nationalized, government may play a role not only in the selection of power sources, reactor types, and production strategy but also in the structure of the nuclear industry itself. Thus, the governments of a number of West European countries have intervened in the electrical equipment industry to help create powerful national enterprises capable of effectively competing with external suppliers.[10] It can be hypothesized that these efforts are a defensive response to the perceived risk of extensive penetration of national energy markets by external suppliers; external suppliers are themselves amenable to home-government pressure and restraint and might therefore serve as a medium of political pressure by their government against the government of the recipient state. One must also take into account the possibility of tensions reflecting different priorities that arise between national electric power authorities and national nuclear establishments which might be exploited by external actors. In this context one might argue that private American enterprise has an impact on foreign governments which arises from its transnational penetration of nuclear technology markets. This point is developed further in section II.

American experience can also serve to demonstrate some of the practical effects of governmental involvement at the level of nuclear exploitation. The "privatization" of atomic energy was partially a response to international developments in the mid-1950s, but it was also a response to increasing private pressure in the United States to stop a potential trend toward federal power production. Having won the battle against federal power, the utilities dragged their feet about entering into nuclear power production. The cost of nuclear power compared with that of conventional sources was one reason for this hesitancy; the many risks and uncertainties associated with this new technology formed another.

In playing its dual role of regulator and promoter, the AEC set out to make nuclear power attractive to private power companies. This aim was achieved largely through two devices—the power demonstration programs and the Price-Anderson act.[11] The power demonstration programs consisted of liberal AEC aid in the form of research and development and design assistance, assistance in fuel fabrication, and waiver of fuel-use costs for designated periods of time. Governmental participation accounted for approximately 30 percent

[9] The AEC, however, through a variety of direct and indirect actions including subsidies, material procurement policies, fuel pricing arrangements, etc., can markedly influence the direction that power production takes. For an excellent review of the problems and the instruments available to the AEC see Norman Hilberry, "Nuclear Power in the U.S.," *Nuclear Industry,* August 1964 (Vol. 11, No. 8), pp. 5–12.

[10] "Westinghouse: Moving in," *Agenor,* January–February 1970 (No. 15), pp. 55–57.

[11] United States, Congress, *An Act to Amend the Atomic Energy Act of 1954, As Amended, and for Other Purposes,* P.L. 85–256, 85th Cong., 1st sess., *United States Statutes at Large,* Vol. 81, pp. 576–579.

of the total costs involved. The Price-Anderson act overcame the thorny problem of insuring against nuclear accidents. The magnitude of risk associated with a nuclear accident is such that private utilities could not secure adequate insurance from private companies. Without such insurance (at acceptable cost) they were unwilling to take a step in the direction of developing nuclear power. The Price-Anderson act called on private utilities to secure up to $60 million in private insurance and itself provided an additional $500 million in federal insurance and limited public liability to the combined amount. Guaranteed against financial loss in the event of a nuclear accident, private utilities began to move into the nuclear field with only the question of the economic competiveness of nuclear power standing between them and nuclear reactors.[12]

Reactor manufacturers capitalized on these favorable conditions by loss-leading their initial power reactor sales. This lowered the calculated cost of nuclear power and stimulated greater interest both in the United States and abroad. In the four years after Jersey Central Power and Light Company announced in 1964 that its contract with General Electric for a major nuclear power plant would provide competitive electric power when compared with modern coal-fired generators, nearly 60 other reactors were ordered by private American utilities. In the same period American industry consolidated its hold on the world market for reactors to the point that the United Kingdom considered the possibility of adopting American-type reactors in lieu of its supposedly competitive natural uranium types.[13]

Viewed from an international perspective, private industrial success would mean AEC success and would fulfill the latter's goal of promoting peaceful nuclear development. As long as the government maintained a monopoly over reactor fuel supply, American industrial penetration abroad would be tantamount to United States government penetration and would help to reinforce American efforts to guide the evolution of peaceful atomic development. There was and is a possibility that such interaction could lead the government to become hostage to its own policy, constrained by its own industrial enterprises and foreign governments and purchasers. All this suggests the conscious or unconscious use or support of transnational nongovernmental actors by government to operationalize the goals of atoms for peace, controlled nuclear transactions, and a continued central role for the United States in the evolution of world nuclear policy.

[12] A general review of the developments associated with nuclear insurance and nuclear power may be found in Sheldon Novick, *The Careless Atom* (Boston: Houghton Mifflin Co., 1969).

[13] The term "American-type reactor" refers to the enriched uranium reactors typical of the American nuclear industry.

National Options

The foregoing examples demonstrate the incentive-producing effects of governmental involvement in the nuclear energy area. Such involvement, however, can also lead to restraint in research and development and exploitation. In France and the United Kingdom governmental commitment to independent nuclear status and to development of nuclear weapons conditioned national nuclear orientation and predetermined the allocation of resources for research and development. In these countries private actors were limited to executing governmental policy and did not play a significant role in the conceptual orientation of nuclear policy. Until 1968 the French national electric authority (Electricité de France) and French industry were bound by the government to what ultimately proved to be a relatively inefficient, costly, and essentially noncompetitive line of gas-graphite reactors. Their use sustained the policy of political independence and the nuclear weapons program but placed France at a disadvantage in peaceful international nuclear competition. The United Kingdom did not fare much better.

In countries in which the government has not yet decided whether to use a nuclear weapons option, the situation is less clear. Sweden provides an interesting example of transnational impact and simultaneously reaffirms the non-monolithicity of government in the nuclear field noted earlier. In the early 1960s Sweden faced the choice of either importing American-type reactors dependent on American enriched uranium and subject to diversion safeguards or developing natural uranium reactors based on indigenous uranium resources. These reactors would have produced unsafeguarded plutonium that could have been processed for nuclear weapons should the government have eventually decided to do so. In the face of national ambivalence the quasi-governmental electric power authorities opted for the rapid acquisition of competitive nuclear power through use of American-type reactors. Their decision foreclosed the development of alternative technologies since the Swedish government hesitated to increase the national nuclear investment required to make Sweden a nuclear-weapon state at the cost of satisfying other national social and economic goals. At the same time American nuclear industry, anxious to penetrate foreign markets, and the AEC, anxious both to facilitate this penetration and to inhibit the expansion of nuclear weapons capabilities in nth countries, made effective use of the disaggregated nature of government. An appeal to the values of one segment was made in the hope of precluding the assertion of another segment. As George Quester has remarked in discussing this sequence of events, "in effect the bargains offered by the American Atomic Energy Commission had quietly undone a Swedish defense plan."[14] Parenthetically, it is worth noting that influencing initial national nuclear

[14] George H. Quester, "Sweden and the Nuclear Non-Proliferation Treaty," *Cooperation and Conflict*, 1970 (Vol. 5, No. 1), pp. 52–64, quotation on p. 54.

orientation may be one of the few types of transnational impact to be found in the first two decades of the atomic age.

It would not be unfair, particularly in relation to external activities, to characterize the relationship between private American nuclear industry and the AEC as a symbiotic one in which goals, values, and objectives are widely shared.[15] Nevertheless, even in the United States the interaction of governmental and nongovernmental actors in the nuclear field may lead to situations similar to those described for France and the United Kingdom. Two examples can be offered to support this observation. One is in the field of breeder reactor development; the other involves enrichment technology. Breeder reactor development is heavily dependent on governmental research and development contracts and the AEC development program. France, Japan, the United Kingdom, and West Germany, having lost the first round of reactor competition to the United States, are now devoting considerable attention to the breeder. American nuclear industry, concerned lest foreign competitors capture the breeder market through their more intensive programs and their early commitment to demonstration plants, has been pressing the AEC to speed up its own program, to invest more funds, and to revise its strategy so as to develop an early demonstration plant. Thus far this pressure has been to no avail. Private actors are dependent on governmental research and development policy. This does not, however, mean that private enterprise lacks influence at the policymaking level. Such influence exists and is increasing in direct proportion to the commercialization of atomic energy, but it is restrained by the heavy reliance of private enterprise on government.

Enrichment technology offers an example of the foreclosure of research and development by the government. Uranium enrichment through gaseous diffusion remains a governmental monopoly. Alternative methods of enrichment, particularly the gas centrifuge process, have been studied both in the United States and elsewhere. More than a decade ago the AEC prevailed on the Netherlands and West Germany to classify research on the gas centrifuge; domestically, it followed that action by precluding private enterprise access to existing AEC information and eventually from conducting centrifuge research and development at all, except under AEC contract with all information classified. For reasons that we presently examine, the United States lost its grip on foreign centrifuge research and development. The domestic prohibition remains intact, however, and serves to illustrate the extent of governmental intrusion into private nuclear enterprise. The potential impact of trans-

[15] It is important to emphasize that the symbiosis relates principally to international transactions and in that context is weighted heavily toward the conditions of those transactions. In the domestic arena government and private enterprise sometimes entertain significantly different goals. This is especially true for the utilities which are mostly private and whose objective is the profitable production of electric power, not the promotion of atomic energy for its own sake. It is also true of reactor and component manufacturers whose commercial interests do not always coincide with governmental classification and dissemination policies.

national activity in this area on governmental policy is great. This potential was demonstrated by the 1969 agreement between the Netherlands, the United Kingdom, and West Germany providing for joint private and governmental exploitation of gas centrifuge technology. The agreement occasioned not only a rapid response from the United States government but also caused private actors in the United States to pressure the government to change official enrichment policy. This issue is treated at greater length in section III.

II. Nuclear Asymmetry

The second central characteristic of the nuclear energy field is the asymmetric distribution of resources and technology. This leads to an asymmetric distribution of power and influence.

Technology

Nuclear technology might best be thought of as a huge spoked wheel with the United States as its center. The Union of Soviet Socialist Republics may claim parity in nuclear weaponry, but it cannot do so in nuclear power development or—as yet—in international nuclear transactions. At the present time, at least, the United States stands alone at the hub.

Basic scientific knowledge is universal in the sense that theory is available to scientists of all countries. However, nuclear information policy can be, has been, and, in sectors involving national security interests, remains subject to political restraints. Beyond these classified sectors, however, national, regional, and international information services ensure a wide and continuous dissemination of nuclear information. At the United Nations International Conferences on the Peaceful Uses of Atomic Energy, held in Geneva in 1955, 1958, and 1964, a great deal of information about fission, fusion, and reactor technology was released, but the information remained strictly within the limits of what national scientific information policy was willing to divulge. At the 1958 conference, for example, the French atomic energy authority (Commissariat à l'énergie atomique)—which has always pursued a more liberal information policy than the AEC—made an unsuccessful effort to stimulate a flow of information on isotopic separation techniques by presenting papers on its own studies containing data still classified by the AEC. While there is undoubtedly some kind of dialectical relationship between national policy and international interaction, there is little evidence that the latter is an autonomous catalyst constraining governments to respond positively to the liberalizing stimulus of international science.

Certainly, it cannot be doubted that the very occurrence of these and other conferences facilitates numerous contacts between scientists, technicians, and nuclear industrialists, stimulates nuclear aspirations and development programs in nonnuclear countries, and forges innumerable personal transnational linkages.[16] Yet, as one qualified observer of the international nuclear scene has remarked, in the last analysis "tête-à-tête meetings among governments have produced more interesting results than those of international conferences —bilateral agreements providing for the supply of substantial amounts of material and technical and financial assistance."[17] No matter how widely disseminated scientific information may be, relatively few states have the industrial infrastructure adequate to the task of translating this scientific and technological knowledge into an operational nuclear program.

Resources

The circle of nuclear sophistication grows even smaller when one considers the distribution of basic resources and certain key technologies. Uranium, which is essential to any nuclear program, is a good example. Three countries, Canada, the Republic of South Africa, and the United States, account for approximately 80 percent of proven free-world uranium ore reserves. The two most advanced nonnuclear-weapon states, West Germany and Japan, have indigenous reserves that cannot sustain a large-scale program—a precondition of competitive nuclear power production—and that certainly cannot accommodate international reactor sales competition. As a result they are dependent on the supply policies of the dominant states in this field. France, through domestic sources and privileged access to significant deposits in former French African colonies, leads Western Europe in uranium production, but even it has felt the impact of the concentration of major uranium resources.

The fact that until the mid-1960s the United States and the United Kingdom maintained virtual monopoly on free-world uranium supplies meant that they could strongly influence the conditions under which such supplies could be sold to third states by Canada and the Republic of South Africa, with which the United States had purchase agreements. One condition was that any such sale would be subject to a "peaceful-uses-only" guarantee by the recipient state and acceptance by the latter of diversion safeguards. In 1956 France tried to purchase Canadian uranium on an unrestricted basis but the United States objected. The French subsequently agreed to purchase the

[16] The IAEA annually sponsors a number of conferences, symposia, and seminars. In fiscal year 1968-1969, for example, fourteen such meetings were held with over 2,800 participants and approximately 1,000 papers were presented. See IAEA Document GC(XIII)/404 *(Annual Report of the Board of Governors to the General Conference, July 1, 1968–June 30, 1969)*, Annex D, pp. 54–55. Whatever else these meetings may accomplish, they have served to help better coordinate ongoing international research and to avoid duplication by virtue of the information transmitted and exchanged at the sessions. In the field of thermodynamics, for example, IAEA meetings revealed duplicative work in the Soviet Union and the United States and facilitated the exchange of information and the development of scientific contacts as well as the elimination of duplication and the pursuit of false paths of research. I am indebted to Edgar Westrum of the Department of Chemistry of the University of Michigan for bringing this sequence of events to my attention.

[17] Arnold Kramish, *The Peaceful Atom in Foreign Policy* (New York: Harper & Row, Publishers [for the Council on Foreign Relations], 1963), p. 7.

uranium on a restricted-use basis but at a price lower than that paid by the United States to Canada, claiming that the use limitations made the material less valuable than "free" uranium. The United States again intervened to claim that the Canadian-American agreement precluded the sale of uranium at a lower price regardless of buyer restrictions. As a result the sale was not consummated.[18] When the United States terminated its purchase-option agreements it managed to induce supplier states to agree to continue the policy of requiring all sales to be accompanied by peaceful-uses guarantees and appropriate safeguards. Thus, when in 1965 the French again approached a then surplus-laden Canadian government for the purchase of unrestricted uranium, Canada was once again prevailed upon not to sell its uranium on an unrestricted basis and the sale fell through. Frustrated, the Canadian government decided that all sales of uranium to any state, including the United States, would be subject to a peaceful-uses-only clause.[19]

The bilateral understandings between the United States and the principal free-world supplier states have gradually been internationalized in the context of the IAEA. While the United States channels its nuclear assistance primarily through bilateral agreements rather than through the IAEA, in most of its agreements it provides for the possibility of the eventual transfer of safeguards responsibilities from the AEC to the IAEA. With the advent of Soviet-American détente this policy was implemented with the result that the principle of controlled nuclear aid took on increased legitimacy. That principle was reinforced and expanded with the assignment of safeguards responsibilities to the IAEA under the NPT. Previously IAEA safeguards applied only to source or fissile materials, or to facilities supplied through the IAEA, or to states that had mutually agreed to the safeguarding of nuclear transactions by the IAEA. Under the NPT, however, signatory nonnuclear-weapon states accept safeguarding of all their nuclear facilities and materials—their entire peaceful nuclear industry.

Power Reactors

Nuclear asymmetry is even more evident in the area of power reactors and nuclear fuel. Reviewing the nuclear situation in the Western world in 1969, the Commission of the European Communities noted that "as regards nuclear power stations of 100 MWe or over, four American firms have built or contracted to build 93 with a total power of 75,000 MWe—including 74 for General Electric and Westinghouse totaling 61,000 MWe—while ten or a dozen EEC firms have only 22 stations with a total power of about 10,000

[18] Bertrand Goldschmidt, *Les Rivalités atomiques, 1939–1966* (Les Grandes Etudes contemporaines) (Paris: Librairie Arthème Fayard, 1967), pp. 139–140.

[19] Bertrand Goldschmidt, "Le Problème du contrôle international de l'utilisation de l'énergie atomique," *Revue de défense nationale*, August–September 1968 (24th Year), pp. 1167–1189.

MWe."[20] In fact, as of January 1970 countries in the European Economic Community (EEC) had slightly less than 10,000 MWe installed nuclear power. Significantly, two-thirds of that power was provided by American-type reactors built under license to European firms.[21] France had hoped to establish a competitive technology and to capture the European market but failed. In 1969 France adopted the more economical American-type reactors for electric power production.

In the international market the disparities between the United States and other countries are equally dramatic. During the past decade General Electric and Westinghouse sold 24 reactors (the number rises to 41 if one includes those sold under licensing arrangements), while Canada, France, the United Kingdom, and West Germany together were unable to market more than about a half-dozen. A number of factors account for the United States position: the powerful economic situation of the American enterprises; their ability to call on the Export-Import Bank to offer favorable-term loans to potential purchasers; and the fuel supply policy of the United States government. Licensing arrangements may also play a role. While relatively little information about these arrangements is available, it does appear that some licensing has been done on the basis of exclusive dealer contracts in which, in the name of antitrust provisions, licensees in different countries have been precluded from merging. To some extent this undoubtedly contributes to the inhibition of nuclear integration in, for example, the EEC; it also helps to weaken the competitive position of European industry vis-à-vis American licensors in third markets. As a consequence industries and their governments are encouraged to cooperate more closely in the conduct of international nuclear transactions. The West German government, for example, assisted Siemens A.G. in securing West Germany's first foreign reactor contract by offering a five-year, no-interest (and subsequently very low-interest) loan to the Argentine government in consideration of the purchase. American industry, however, dominates the reactor market and is likely to continue to do so through the lifetime of the present generation of nuclear reactors.

The experience of American industry operating in foreign environments suggests that nongovernmental actors are simultaneously in an influential and vulnerable position. On the one hand, they may serve as a channel for the promotion of particular home-government policies; on the other hand, their treatment by host governments may serve the latter as a means to influence those policies. Furthermore, as principal actors in peaceful international nuclear transactions, nongovernmental actors may themselves seek to influence the policies of both home and host governments in the interest of satisfying their own industrial interests. Evidence of this type of activity is extremely

[20] Quoted in René Foch, *Europe and Technology: A Political View* (Atlantic Papers, No. 2) (Paris: Atlantic Institute, 1970), p. 8. The units are megawatts electric (MWe).

[21] *Agence Europe,* February 10, 1970, p. 6.

limited, but it appears that the activity is aimed toward liberalizing the terms of trade. Such activity has not, however, affected the policies of controlled nuclear transactions or nonproliferation which lie at the heart of official United States nuclear policy.

More important than the reactors themselves is the enriched uranium required to fuel them. We have already commented on the near-monopolistic position of the United States in this field. While it is true that the nuclear-weapon states each have enrichment facilities, their respective capabilities are not really comparable to those of the United States. At least this is so for the Western powers. The three American gaseous diffusion plants, operating at full capacity, are capable of producing 17.1 million SWU enriched uranium annually.[22] The British facility at Capenhurst has a capacity of 400,000 SWU while the capacity of the French Pierrelatte plant is rated between 200,000 and 300,000 SWU a year.[23] In both cases this is adequate to fulfill nuclear weapon needs, or alternatively a modest power reactor program, but little more than that. Thus, the American position is truly a dominant one. In view of the predominance of American-type reactors in the world today the importance of American fuel supply policy becomes self-evident. Its importance promises to increase sharply in the near future. In 1970 only 3.6 percent of total electric capacity in Western Europe, for example, was derived from nuclear sources, but it is estimated that by 1985 nuclear sources will account for 29 percent of West European electricity production. By that time nearly 70 percent of new electricity-generating capacity in the developed part of the world is expected to be nuclear.[24] This growth pattern has tremendous implications for nuclear fuel supply policy in the future.

III. Implications of Transnational Activity

Both past practices and future problems shed some light on the developing phenomenon of transnational activity in this field.

The Commercial Atom

Up to the present time United States government policy has been to promote the international sale of enriched uranium reactors and to inhibit the

22 *Report on the Nuclear Industry, 1970*, pp. 58ff. According to the AEC "a separative work unit is not a quantity of material, but is a measure of the effort expended in the plant to separate a quantity of uranium of a given assay into two components, one having a higher percentage of uranium-235 and one having a lower percentage. Separative work is generally expressed in kilogram units to give it the same dimensions as material quantities, i.e., kilograms or metric tons of uranium. It is common practice to refer to a kilogram separative work unit simply as a separative work unit or as SWU." Ibid., p. 60.

23 Ibid., p. 68.

24 Bernard Spinrad, "The Role of Nuclear Power in Meeting World Energy Needs" (Paper presented at the Symposium on Environmental Aspects of Nuclear Power Stations sponsored by the IAEA and the AEC, New York, August 10–14, 1970).

dissemination of enrichment technology and to impede the development of alternatives to the gaseous diffusion technique perfected in the United States. Promotion of the international sale of American-type reactors serves obvious commercial interests and enables the AEC to fulfill its promotional responsibilities. The value of "toll enriching" agreements alone is estimated to be $200 to $300 million a year and may possibly reach $1 billion by 1980. The current enrichment policy has clear advantages for the United States balance of payments and equally clear disadvantages for foreign importers.

From the point of view of nonproliferation policy the promotion of American-type reactors thwarts the emergence of alternative development programs such as natural uranium reactors capable of producing large quantities of plutonium. The Swedish case demonstrated precisely this effect: Reactor systems dependent on American nuclear fuel are subject to international diversion safeguards and inspection procedures; reactors based on indigenous uranium production may escape this form of surveillance. Although direct government-to-government political pressure cannot be discounted, it would appear that the principal influence on reactor orientation is an appeal to the economic instincts of governments and their power industries. This influence is exercised largely through the highly favorable conditions for reactor purchase and through the very liberal fuel supply policies by which the United States government guarantees fuel supply up to five years in advance of actual needs at very attractive prices which most qualified observers regard as not representing real cost.[25] Unless a foreign government is determined to develop a nuclear weapons capability or is acutely sensitive to being dependent on another government for part of its energy supply (France demonstrates both aspects), the American offers generally prove seductive.

One of the most significant cases in point is that of Western Europe. In fact, West European–American relations demonstrate a number of aspects of the problems of reactor technology and fuel supply. Just as the United States was able to influence the conditions under which natural uranium would be sold by supplier states to third parties, so it has been able to affect the limits and conditions on the transfer of certain nuclear technologies. In 1955, for example, France requested the United Kingdom to build an enrichment plant in France. Relying on the Quebec agreements of 1943 in which the United Kingdom and the United States had mutually agreed not to give nuclear assistance to any third state without each other's consent, Washington prevailed on Whitehall to refuse the French request despite strong British interest.[26] Two years later the United States successfully dissuaded France's partners in the European Atomic Energy Community (Euratom) from agreeing to

[25] Critics argue that the true competitive nature of atomic energy cannot be known until enriched uranium is placed on a purely commercial basis, i.e., totally and completely separated from military participation, governmental subsidies, and industrial secrecy.

[26] See Goldschmidt, *Revue de défense nationale,* 24th Year, pp. 1177–1178.

build a European enrichment plant despite strong pressures from France on its partners to do so and despite the fact that it was increasingly probable that reactors requiring enriched fuels would soon be introduced into the community.

This event revealed interactions between governments and between governments and nongovernmental actors. On the one hand, Washington appealed politically to some of the Euratom countries to drop their interest in the idea, stressing the proliferation risks associated with enrichment facilities. Since among the six only France showed any interest in nuclear weapons, this turned out to be a powerful theme. On the other hand, the United States offered to sell a large amount of enriched uranium to these countries at extremely favorable prices. The targets here were both governments and private enterprise. Given ready access to enrichment technology an efficient diffusion plant would still cost close to $1 billion and even then would not be competitive with American fuel costs. If the purpose of nuclear development is competitive-cost energy production, the economics of the situation would be bound to impress both producers and consumers of electricity. In making such lucrative offers the United States must have counted on private industry to lobby with their governments in favor of the more economic alternative.

Simultaneously, the United States concluded an important agreement with Euratom for a joint power production program enabling West Europeans to gain rapid access to an advanced reactor technology.[27] As the first priority of most of the West European governments was not nuclear independence but acquisition of this technology, the American alternative carried the day. An important side effect of this was, of course, to facilitate American industrial penetration of the European energy market. Penetration by private American actors created the possibility that the United States government might eventually use these actors (coupled with its own continued monopoly over the fuel supply) to manipulate or at least to exert influence over the nuclear programs of a number of advanced industrial states. This policy was successful for at least the decade after 1958.

Nuclear Fuel Supply

One of the great dramas of the peaceful atom in the coming decade will undoubtedly occur in the arena of nuclear fuels. Breeder reactors will not be "on line" before the end of the decade and self-sustaining breeders (those not requiring initial enriched uranium fuel loadings) are not anticipated before the mid-1990s. Yet, as we have noted, it is estimated that by 1985 at least 29 percent of European fuel requirements will have to be fulfilled by nuclear means. The comparable figures for North America, on the one hand, and

[27] For an accessible review of this joint program see René Foch, "European Fusion and Atomic Fission," *Columbia Journal of World Business,* Spring 1966 (Vol. 1, No. 2), pp. 87–96.

Australia, Japan, New Zealand, and the Republic of South Africa on the other are 32 percent and 23 percent, respectively. The estimate for the Soviet Union is 30 percent; Eastern Europe, 10 percent; Latin America, 13 percent; Asia, 14 percent; and Africa, 2.2 percent.[28]

Even with upgraded capabilities the United States cannot continue as the sole source of uranium enrichment, even for the Western world. Western Europe and Japan in particular are increasingly sensitive to the problem of nuclear fuel dependence. Both government and private enterprise are actively involved in assessing the situation, but it is difficult to determine which is the tail and which is the dog. One source of concern is the question of American productive capacity; another is whether the United States, despite its guarantees on fuel supply, will truly treat domestic and foreign requests on a nondiscriminatory basis. One problem for foreign importers is that under the current Atomic Energy Act export of fissile materials remains dependent on legislative authorizations. West Europeans may still remember that, despite executive willingness to transmit information on nuclear submarines to France in 1958, the Congressional Joint Committee on Atomic Energy successfully opposed consummation of the agreement.[29] Importing countries might well wonder whether, for political reasons, a similar situation might not emerge in another context.

Possibly in response to conclusions that foreign-owned enterprises and governments may draw from the fuel supply problem, American private industry has been increasingly active in lobbying for the transfer of fuel supply from the AEC to private industry, and it well may be that traditional United States government enrichment policy will be overturned as a result of combined foreign and domestic pressures. Other considerations that may stimulate foreign governments to independent action include the fact that American fuel deliveries remain subject to quantitative restrictions and qualitative limits (limits on the degree of enrichment without review and evaluation of the request by the United States) as well as to reexport limitations which could impede West European competition with American industry in third markets. Indeed, it is alleged that American industry has occasionally hinted to prospective reactor purchasers that West European competitors might have difficulty supplying the necessary fuel.

Finally, there is the overriding political question of whether advanced industrial states ought to remain fully dependent on external suppliers for a significant portion of their energy production. Such dependence could have spillover effects not only on energy development but also on the rate of industrial expansion and the general competitive position of these countries. Control over fuel supply might be used by the United States as a lever to attain

[28] See Spinrad, "The Role of Nuclear Power in Meeting World Energy Needs," passim.

[29] On this event see Goldschmidt, *Revue de défense nationale,* 24th Year, pp. 1178–1179.

other nonnuclear objectives in the state in question. While these matters are still in a preliminary phase of development, it does appear that European governments and industry are forging closer and stronger links and alliances in an effort to protect national energy markets from excessive external penetration and dependence. In a sense, we are witnessing a response to what Harold Wilson once called the threat of American industrial helotry.

In contrast to the rather nationalistic response of West European states to competition with American reactor manufacturers, their response in the area of fuel supply has been an agreement between the Netherlands, the United Kingdom, and West Germany to develop and exploit centrifuge technology.[30] No longer able to control fuel technology development in other countries, the United States is faced with the growing probability that a new enrichment technique will be developed that will be economically competitive. These three states, which had responded positively to an American request to classify research on centrifuge technology to prevent proliferation, are not prepared to forego exploitation of the economic and political potential of this technology. The safeguards provisions on the nuclear industries of nonnuclear-weapon states, contained in the NPT, weakened the security rationale of the earlier American position and facilitated the tripartite arrangement.

It is unlikely that the United States can offset this development by offering economically attractive alternatives because the issue of independence now shares the decisional context with economic considerations. Rather, Washington is faced with the alternative of releasing its own gaseous diffusion technology under international safeguards and controls (in the hope of forestalling further development of centrifuge technology) or of offering to contribute a major input to a multilateral arrangement whereby the United States would be directly involved in the centrifuge program and thus able to exert influence through participation. If, however, independence of fuel supply is the primary West European concern, then it is likely that such an offer would not be accepted. Transnational linkages between these countries involve both governmental and private participants, but the relationship between these two types of actors is not yet clear. There can be no doubt, however, that these linkages have contributed to undermining the dominant position of the United States in fuel technology and production. As centrifuge research and development progresses, it is likely that the AEC will be forced to reevaluate its domestic policy of precluding centrifuge research and development to American industry except on a classified basis and under AEC contract. This is likely to lead to even further "privatization" of nuclear energy and to bring nuclear energy one step closer to normal commercial activity.

[30] The best continuing treatment of the centrifuge problem is to be found in *Report on the Nuclear Industry*, published annually by the AEC, and in *Agence Europe*.

Safeguards

Safeguards offer a final example of the relationship between asymmetry and transnationalism. While we are just beginning to confront the problems of nuclear fuel supply today, those surrounding safeguards are already familiar. Under American influence supplier states have required of recipient states not only a guarantee that nuclear aid would be used for peaceful purposes but also safeguards to verify fulfillment of that commitment. Prior to the mid-1960s—when the industrial potential of nuclear energy began to be realized—the major interest of the governments and industries of most states was to gain access to nuclear technology, facilities, and material. Beneficiaries of nuclear dissemination more or less quietly accepted this condition despite an occasionally bruised sovereign ego. Discriminatory limitation on use and surveillance was a price they were willing to pay.

The NPT was negotiated in the transitional era between the preindustrial and the industrial atomic ages heralded by the emergence of economically competitive nuclear power. A rapid growth and use of reactors would mean the creation of large quantities of plutonium which would lead to increased American demands for comprehensive safeguards provisions. Thus, the NPT called for safeguards not only on materials or facilities imported from supplier countries but also on the entire peaceful nuclear complex of the signatory nonnuclear-weapon states. Competitive nuclear energy also means increased commercial opportunities. Private enterprise in several industrially advanced nonnuclear-weapon states, particularly in Japan and West Germany, has expressed fear of potential commercial discrimination against the industry of these states in favor of those in weapon states. Charges of unfair competition, discriminatory treatment, and risk of industrial espionage were quickly assimilated by governments that were not overly content with the NPT per se but that were ill situated to raise frankly political objections to a treaty whose purpose was to minimize the risk of war through curtailing the spread of nuclear weapons.

The target of these claims—whatever their credibility—was American industry. The United States government responded in December 1967 by offering to place all United States nuclear facilities not directly related to national security under the same system of international safeguards that applied to Japanese, West German, or any other industry. During the same time period members of the Japan Atomic Industrial Forum, the principal organized spokesman for nuclear industry in Japan, were invited to observe IAEA inspectors carry out safeguards procedures at Yankee Atomic Electric and Power Company in Rowe, Massachusetts. Spokesmen for Yankee and for the American Atomic Industrial Forum subsequently remarked publicly on the nonintrusive nature of international safeguards and inspection techniques.

Thus, the United States government and private enterprise responded to claims of private foreign actors known to have considerable influence over national nuclear policy. On the other hand, the credibility of foreign private and governmental claims which were masking unarticulated political concerns were swept aside through an offer of industrial equalization. These events would seem to demonstrate the coercive hold of government over private enterprise in the United States (government subjecting private enterprise to international inspection after only minimum preconsultation) as well as a complex set of interactions between governments and private actors, governments and governments, and private actors inter se.

Arms Control and Disarmament

There is finally the question of the relationship between weapons policy and transnationalism. One form in which transnational activity may play a role in arms control was demonstrated in the Swedish case discussed earlier. Technological decisions in one country may be affected by actions of the government or private enterprise in another country. These technological decisions may in turn affect later strategic options and thus have a bearing on whether a state becomes a military nuclear power.

A second form in which transnational activity may affect arms control is through the activity of international nongovernmental organizations which address the arms control and disarmament problem, perhaps best exemplified by the Pugwash Conferences on Science and World Affairs.[31] Created in 1957 as a forum for the discussion of the dangers associated with nuclear warfare and weaponry and the means by which to cope with these problems, Pugwash has provided a channel for regularized informal exchange between scientists from East and West.[32] The conferences are credited, by some of their participants and by outside observers, with having played a positive role in developing some of the arms control measures now in force.[33] As one American participant stated: "It is a demonstrable fact that these Conferences have had a

[31] The following discussion does not give consideration to diplomatic negotiations, to situations in which it might plausibly be argued that governmental actors are not playing strictly official roles, or to the possible effects of "world public opinion" on national arms control policies. These phenomena stretch the concept on "transnational activity" to a point where it risks losing its analytic power. For a treatment of these issues see Antoinette Joseph, "Some Observations beyond Scheinman's Article on Transnational Processes and Nuclear Energy" (Paper prepared for the seminar, "Problems of Supranational Integration," Harvard University, spring 1971).

[32] The best history of the Pugwash conferences is to be found in J[oseph] Rotblat, *Pugwash—The First Ten Years: History of the Conferences on Science and World Affairs* (London: Heinemann Educational Books, 1967).

[33] See, for example, Robert Cooley Angell, *Peace on the March: Transnational Participation* (New Perspectives in Political Science, No. 19) (New York: Van Nostrand Reinhold Co., 1969); and Duane Thorin, *The Pugwash Movement and U.S. Arms Policy* (New York: Monte Cristo Press, 1965). Although the Thorin book strongly reflects the biases prevalent in the McCarthy period of the early 1950s, it does offer a useful introduction to some of the orientations, activities, and personalities involved in the Pugwash phenomenon.

discernible influence on the progress of international negotiations on the problem of disarmament. . . . our Conferences have developed . . . ideas upon which our governments have drawn and built in their efforts toward negotiation."[34] Pugwash lays claim to having introduced the concept of "black box" techniques for seismic detection of nuclear explosions which broke the deadlock over the test ban negotiations and eventually led to the Treaty Banning Nuclear Weapon Tests in the Atmosphere of 1963, as well as contributing to the idea of a partial test ban and to such other arms control measures as the "hot line" or electronic key fail-safe systems (a unilateral arms control measure). Some American former participants insist that bilateral Soviet-American talks in the Pugwash context influenced Soviet thought on the antiballistic missile (ABM) and the multiple individually targetable reentry vehicle (MIRV).

How ought Pugwash be evaluated? Despite the fact that Pugwash is one of the more tangible, systematized, and institutionalized forms of transnational activity, there has not as yet been adequate study to allow the assertion of causal propositions. We shall content ourselves with three observations about Pugwash and transnational activity. First, it is questionable whether Pugwash consistently qualifies as a nongovernmental organization. A number of participants on the Soviet side are ranking members of the Soviet Academy of Sciences, which is not merely an honorific but an official and operative organization. American scientists in consultative positions with the United States government did not at first participate in Pugwash, but in the years immediately preceding the Partial Test Ban Treaty of 1963 individuals such as Walt W. Rostow, Jerome B. Wiesner, and Franklin W. Long did participate. Although none of the Soviet or American scientists participated as official representatives of their government, one wonders to what extent persons in such positions can easily change roles from public to private actors and vice versa. Thus, while Pugwash may have exerted influence on arms control and disarmament policies, it may have done so not as a purely nongovernmental organization but as a hybrid official and unofficial actor.

A second observation is related to the preceding comments. The nature of the participants leads one to question whether Pugwash is to be regarded as an autonomous source of influence on governmental policies or whether it serves governments as a channel of communication outside the framework of intergovernmental diplomacy. If it were such a channel rather than an autonomous source of influence this would not, of course, destroy its credibility as a transnational actor; rather, it would serve to demonstrate how transnational actors may be used by official actors to achieve governmental ends.

Finally, there is the problem of causation. In the absence of further study and evidence it is not really feasible to do more than generalize about the impact of Pugwash's transnational activity on official policy. One defensible

[34] This is the opinion of Bernard T. Feld, cited in Thorin, p. 53.

point would seem to be that Pugwash has played a role in arms control and disarmament measures by influencing governments toward accommodation through the positive experience of participants who have some relevant standing in their respective national communities. Participants can come away from group interaction with positive or negative reactions; to the extent that their reactions are positive, they may contribute to the manner in which the actors conduct future analysis or the nature of recommendations they may offer in their capacity as advisers to government. While this kind of effect is extremely difficult to measure, it must be taken into account. One very positive kind of contribution that transnational interaction can make, and that Pugwash is alleged to have made, is to strip away the ideological and politics-laden dimensions of disarmament and to reduce problems to manageable levels of technical interchange. Given our current knowledge about Pugwash it would seem more appropriate, if more conservative, to evaluate it as a contribution to, but not the determinant of, national and international arms control and disarmament policy.

IV. Conclusion

Several propositions might be offered by way of summarizing transnationalism, nuclear asymmetry, and the interaction of public and private authorities in the nuclear energy issue area. First, as nuclear asymmetry diminishes, the phenomenon of transnationalism becomes more evident. The reduction of asymmetry reflects the successful dissemination of nuclear technology and the emergence of industrial and commercial interests which, within defined limits, exert their force and influence on the evolution of national and international nuclear transactions. This point is largely quantitative—industrialization and commercialization breed transnationalism. It does not pass judgment on the effects of this process.

Second, while government has been and continues to be the dominant actor in the field of nuclear energy—whether one looks at problems of arms control, research and development, regulation, or exploitation—it is becoming increasingly evident that transnational activities are beginning to have a conditioning effect on governmental policies. As transnational activities have increased, the capacity of government to exercise unilateral control or predominant influence has correspondingly decreased. For the United States this means a weakening of its unilateral capacity to orient the evolution of the international atom; for other governments it would appear to signal not only intensified pressure by indigenous industry for greater protection of national markets and the creation of conditions for more equitable opportunities to compete in international markets but also increased governmental sensitivity to the importance of technological independence. Yet, transnational activities have not been sufficiently intense to deflect government from its determination to control the nuclear world closely or to deflect governmental policy in a direction that would be detrimental to this objective. This is another way of expressing the symbiosis between public and private actors noted earlier. Private enterprise, at least in exporting and supplier states, has not tried to undermine or circumvent established policies related to national security interests. Private actors in nonnuclear-weapon states have not acted in a manner that would encourage their governments to threaten the prevailing consensus on the interdependence of international security and nonproliferation. Whether private actors might unwittingly upset the current delicate balance through new transnational linkages or national technological developments is another question.[35]

Third, as the United States has begun to lose its almost unilateral control of the nuclear energy field, it has turned to multilateral mechanisms as a compensatory approach to the problem of orchestrating world nuclear transactions. Safeguards development and responsibilities, for example, have been increasingly turned over to the IAEA. This prompts the observation that the creation of a universal international organization like the IAEA serves as a constraint on national nuclear policy. Having created the organization, states, particularly the United States, have found themselves constrained to assume responsibility for its survival and to take its existence into account when shaping national and international nuclear policy. Thus, at least in the regulatory field, intergovernmental organization has slowly evolved a role in the management of nuclear energy. It would seem likely that in the present decade the continuing industrialization and commercialization of the atom will bring significant changes in the pattern of transnational nuclear transactions.

[35] One future possibility is the linkage of industrial enterprises across national boundaries with reference to the intrusiveness or cost of safeguards systems. Should these systems and their operation prove onerous or discriminatory between enterprises in nuclear-weapon states and those in nonnuclear-weapon states, it is entirely possible that private actors might join forces to simplify or minimize safeguards operations. One thinks primarily of linkages between West German, Japanese, Swedish, and Italian industry in this regard. The suggestion of transnational linkages does not, of course, mean that vertical pressures by industries on their governments to achieve the same results would not take place.

PART IV

TOWARD PEACE AND JUSTICE?

TRANSNATIONAL relations are significant in current world politics, but it is not obvious that their effects are uniformly benign. It is therefore important to ask how transnational relations affect such deeply held values as peace, welfare, democracy, and self-identity. Who is helped and who is hurt by transnational relations?

Most writers tend to assume that transnational contacts between peoples improve the prospects for world peace. "Much of this conviction," Donald P. Warwick argues, "derives from sources other than empirical evidence." Neither the effects of greater transnational contact on individuals nor the effects of attitude changes on peace are simple relationships. In view of the world's diversity and asymmetry Warwick's emphasis on cultural similarity, in particular, has a chastening effect on optimistic assumptions.

Moreover, even when transnational participation creates accommodative attitudes in individuals, the effect of those individuals on their governments is uncertain. If some governments but not others are affected, this one-sidedness could hinder rather than promote the prospects for peace. Warwick cautiously suggests that transnational contacts are less likely to have positive effects on governmental policies directly than indirectly, by promoting wider awareness of different cultural perspectives. Although these effects may be useful, they are certainly no panacea for peace.

In contrast to the praise that is usually devoted to "people-to-people contacts," multinational business enterprises have been the objects of sharp controversy for many years. Peter B. Evans contributes to this debate by taking a critical view of the effects of the multinational corporation on the economic development and national autonomy of poor countries. Focusing on knowledge, skills, and entrepreneurship, rather than on capital, as the key contributions of the multinational corporation, Evans argues that the ideas and values transmitted by the enterprise often distort the economic as well as the political and social development of the host country. He does not, however, discuss mixed policies, falling between the extreme alternatives of laissez faire acceptance or isolationist rejection of multinational enterprise, which may be open to less developed countries. Nor does he explore how relationships between companies and countries may change over time. Evans maintains that less developed countries need autonomy, not just as a matter of taste but as a means of economic and social development. Autonomy does not conflict with development, he argues, but is rather a necessary condition for development.

While disagreeing with Evans about the net economic effects of multinational business enterprises on poor countries, Raymond Vernon agrees that they will generate problems because lopsided interdependence is psychologically and politically dangerous. Vernon's essay, which is a slightly revised version of his testimony before the Subcommittee on Foreign Economic Policy of the Joint Economic Committee of the United States Congress, addresses the practical policy problems arising from the activities of multinational business enterprises in an asymmetric world. He suggests that if the world economy is to benefit from the great economic rewards that multinational enterprises generate, governments will have to agree to limit their jurisdictions and to coordinate policies in selected fields of high interaction. Thus, for example, he proposes that governments agree to something like a Calvo Doctrine that separates diplomatic protection from overseas business behavior in return for nondiscriminatory treatment.

The equitable distribution of economic benefits is only one element of a just world. A prosperous world economy manipulated by transnational technocrats without some provision for popular participation would certainly violate democratic conceptions of legitimacy and lead to considerable discontent among people holding democratic ideals. In his essay Karl Kaiser stresses the new problems that transnational relations pose for democratic control of foreign policy. He is concerned about the dispersal of power among "technical" ministries, transgovernmental coalitions, international bureaucrats, and autonomous transnational actors. It is becoming difficult to identify and locate the object of democratic control, much less to exercise that control effectively. Kaiser suggests institutional reforms as first steps toward a solution, but he also pleads for further thought about democratic control of transnational relations.

The essays in part IV do not offer definitive answers to the questions that we or the authors pose. Vernon and Evans clearly disagree about the effects of multinational business enterprises on economic development and welfare. Warwick's judgments about transnational participation are tentative. Kaiser concludes that his suggestions could solve some problems of democratic control but that they would also create new ones. Yet, the very diversity of approaches alerts us to the complexity of the subject and to the dangers of complacency, either about transnational relations or our knowledge of them. Only to the extent that we understand transnational relations can we hope to encourage those aspects of them that are likely to promote peace, democracy, welfare, and justice.

Narrow nationalisms will be broadened and ideological cleavages lessened, then, by processes that produce more accommodative attitudes and orientations among the élite by whom policy-makers are influenced. Such changes will relax somewhat the constraints hitherto felt by the shapers of foreign policy simply because the most important segment of their constituencies has begun to move in a new direction.

—Robert Cooley Angell, *Peace on the March: Transnational Participation* (New Perspectives in Political Science, No. 19) (New York: Van Nostrand Reinhold Co., 1969), p. 21.

Transnational Participation and International Peace

DONALD P. WARWICK

THE extract above echoes one of the firmest tenets in the internationalist credo: Greater contact between the peoples of the world will foster attitudes favorable to peace. But is this conviction anything more than a comforting article of faith? What evidence is there that transnational contacts do, in fact, produce greater understanding and accommodation, and what is the impact of changes in individuals on relations between nation-states?

In *Peace on the March* Robert Cooley Angell provides the most systematic attempt to date to deal with these issues. He has argued that transnational participation—role-playing in structures involving persons from more than one country—is increasing and that its effect is to produce more accommodative attitudes. The most important group of participants is that composed of individuals such as party leaders, journalists, spokesmen for pressure groups, and intellectuals—the "influentials." Attitude changes in these individuals are particularly significant because of the influence they wield over the political leadership of their countries. Angell has envisaged a "political pyramid, with the policy-makers at the apex, the élite in close touch with them, and arrows of influence coming up from other levels in the pyramid, strongly from the

DONALD P. WARWICK is chairman of the Department of Sociology and Anthropology at York University, Toronto, Canada.

high levels, more weakly from those lower down. A person near the top probably has at least ten times the influence of a person near the bottom."[1] The line of causality is thus straightforward: Contacts between people from different countries have significant effects on the attitudes of influentials, and these effects are, on balance, in the direction of greater accommodation and international understanding. Because of their position in the elite structure of their own societies influentials have disproportionate access to foreign policy decisionmakers and, in fact, attempt to influence them in the direction of their own attitudes. Finally, the decisionmakers respond to such influence by working harder to reduce ideological cleavages and international conflict.

Both the theoretical assumptions and empirical evidence in *Peace on the March* can be challenged on many grounds. One is forced to conclude that, despite a valiant effort at data-mobilization, Angell does not prove his point. In this essay I would like to pursue the two central questions which Angell has raised: 1) What are the effects of transnational participation on the attitudes, values, and beliefs of the participants and 2) what is the relationship between these changes in individuals and international relations?

I. Socialization and the Transnational Participant

How does a social experience between persons from different countries affect an individual's attitudes toward his own and other countries? The answer to this question depends on how one conceptualizes both personality and processes of social influence. Theories of socialization offer one useful approach to the problem because they underscore the interaction between an individual and a given social setting, such as the family, a school, or an organization. In general socialization refers to the process by which individuals acquire the knowledge, motives, feelings, skills, and other traits expected in the groups of which they are or seek to become members. It is a process which begins at birth and continues in many areas throughout a person's life.[2]

When international contacts are set within the total context of an individual's socialization process, one source of variation in outcomes becomes immediately apparent—other forms of socialization which occur simultaneously. Thus, a Foreign Service officer on overseas assignment is socialized not only into the culture of the host country but also into the web of expectations of the embassy, the norms of the Foreign Service, the bureaucratic structure of the Department of State, and his role as an overseas family member. Similarly, a Latin American student in the United States is subject to influence not only from United States culture and its regional or local variants but also from the

[1] Angell, pp. 21–22.

[2] For a more detailed treatment of the socialization process see my essay, "Socialization and Personality," in *Managment of the Urban Crisis: Government and the Behavioral Sciences,* ed. S. Seashore and R. McNeill (New York: Free Press, 1971), pp. 377–414.

immediate university setting, friendships (or their absence) struck during his stay, romantic attachments and disasters, norms governing his behavior as a professional—physician, chemist, sociologist—and pressures emanating from his family, friends, and even his future employer in his own country. Any and all of these factors may affect the attitudes toward foreign policy which he develops during his stay. Of course, even the same type of transnational contact, such as student exchange programs, will have different effects on different individuals according to their initial personality dispositions. To understand the net impact of any form of transnational participation we must thus focus not only on that experience but also on its interaction with the background of the participant, the immediate cross-pressures to which he is subjected, and his long-range plans, aspirations, and possibilities.

The socialization approach suggests three major sources of variation in the personality effects of transnational participation: 1) the prearrival characteristics of the participant, 2) the character of his transnational experience, and 3) postreturn conditions related to his transnational experience. In addition, this approach is attentive to the specific personality characteristics affected by interpersonal contacts.

II. Prearrival Characteristics

The outcomes of transnational experience will depend not only on the pressures and opportunities of that experience but also on the initial predispositions, resources, attitudes, and motives of the participant. Five prearrival characteristics are especially likely to affect his susceptibility to influence: 1) his motives for engaging in transnational interaction; 2) his stage in the life cycle; 3) his attitudes toward his home country; 4) his attitudes toward the host country; and 5) his communication skills.

Initial Motives for Contact

To understand how transnational experiences affect the participant, we must first know how and why he came to have such an experience. Here we might think of two polar extremes: a nineteen-year-old American soldier who is sent to Vietnam largely against his will and a college sophomore of the same age who spends six months in Peru learning about that country and Latin American culture. Various studies, including my own research on the socialization of university students, suggest an interaction between initial motives and the outcomes of social experiences.[3] One could predict, in general, that students with motives similar to those of the student in the example cited will return to their home country with more accommodative attitudes than the modal soldier. Of course, in some cases initial motives may be overturned by subsequent ex-

[3] Theodore M. Newcomb et al., *Persistence and Change: Bennington College and Its Students after Twenty-Five Years* (New York: John Wiley and Sons, 1967), chapters 9 and 10.

perience, but in general one would expect a positive relationship between the voluntary initiation of contacts and attitude change favorable to international accommodation.

This discussion also raises the question of whether transnational participation produces accommodative attitudes or simply reinforces existing tendencies. Do people enter into transnational situations to express accommodative attitudes, or are these attitudes the result of the contact? The only way to deal concretely with this question is to carry out a series of before-and-after measurements with appropriate controls. However, research at Bennington College indicates that to the extent that individuals choose experiences that are consistent with their existing motives, interests, and aspirations, the effects of socialization are likely to take the form of accentuation or reinforcement rather than sharp change in direction. This finding suggests that some of the attitudes which Angell has attributed to transnational participation may represent self-selection rather than social influence. But even if the net impact of transnational contacts is only the reinforcement of favorable attitudes, this may be a significant kind of change. It can spell the difference between a participant who has accommodative attitudes and does nothing to express them and one who enters wholeheartedly into the foreign policy fray.

Stage in the Life Cycle

A second condition likely to account for differences in the effects of participation is the participant's readiness for change at the time of contact. Such readiness depends in large measure on the individual's stage in the life cycle. While people can change at any time if pressures become sufficiently great, there is some truth to the adage about old dogs and new tricks. Erik Erikson has given an elegant description of the psychosocial crises in the life history of an individual, each of which opens the way to further influence and change.[4] High school and college students are normally at a stage marked by the quest for identity and guiding values and may thus be more open than their elders to fundamental changes in international attitudes. Hence we might predict that, other things being equal, both the extent and depth of change in orientations toward other countries will be greatest in individuals between the ages of 14 and 25 and will decrease thereafter. One of the problems in testing this hypothesis, of course, is that the "other things" are almost never equal. It is difficult to find an eighteen-year-old who has reached midcareer in a large organization. Nevertheless, it would be a great aid to our understanding of transnational participation if relationships were sought between attitude change and common patterns of life-cycle characteristics, for example, middle-aged married men with children, middle-aged single men without children, young married couples without children, and so on.

[4] Erik H. Erikson, *Childhood and Society* (New York: W. W. Norton & Co., 1950).

Attitudes toward the Home Country

Readiness for change may also depend on the strength of the participant's attachment to national reference groups at the time he enters a transnational situation. Individuals differ greatly in the extent to which their home country serves as a source of standards for self-evaluation or norms for conduct. In some cases extreme attachment to one's native land resulting from a deeply embedded and largely irrational ethnocentrism may foreclose the possibility of extensive change in attitudes. For some participants, especially those about to enter countries viewed with suspicion in their homeland, there may be a fear that openness to interpersonal influence may be interpreted as disloyalty. Such persons may enter the new country with a narrow, instrumental, vocational orientation largely as a means of self-protection. This general hypothesis receives some support from a study of exchange students in the United States.[5] The range of student contacts with members of the host country were negatively correlated with their degree of involvement with the home country. While there may be other explanations for this finding, it does underscore the importance of continuing attachments to one's native land.

Attitudes toward the Host Country

Closely related to the participant's initial motives for engaging in transnational interaction is his attitude toward the host country or countries involved. We could predict that openness to interpersonal influence in this situation will increase with the participant's overall attraction to the country. Such attraction, in turn, will depend on the individual's perception of the rewards available in the country, including prestige, skills, or economic opportunities; the attitudes of that country's nationals toward himself and his country; and the role of identification with the other country in his own future. For example, if a participant enters a transnational situation with highly ambivalent attitudes toward the other participant's country, he may respond by adopting a strictly instrumental orientation to the relationship. That is, contacts with the other person would be seen primarily as an avenue to certain technical skills that will help him to advance when he leaves. Under such conditions there should be relatively little change in the direction of the participant's accommodative attitudes.

Communication Skills

The importance of language and other communication skills has perhaps been overworked in discussions of transnational interaction, but they remain crucial. In addition to its sheer adaptive value, language ability may have a strong conditioning effect on the opportunities for interaction, the depth of

[5] Richard T. Morris, with the assistance of Oluf M. Davidson, *The Two-Way Mirror: National Status in Foreign Students' Adjustment* (Minneapolis: University of Minnesota Press, 1960).

interpersonal contacts, and their long-term impact on personality. Language difficulties have been known to deal severe blows to the self-esteem of individuals accustomed to communicating at a high level of efficiency. The implications of these difficulties may be diverse. On the one hand, initial inability to communicate may generate strong motivation to master the language and then to use the newly acquired skill as much as possible. On the other hand, the experience may be so frustrating that the individual withdraws into the safety of a national enclave and rationalizes his own deficiencies by denigrating the host culture. This example suggests that under some conditions transnational experiences may lead to a lessening of accommodative attitudes. Those of us who have lived overseas can think of examples in which foreign nationals became extremely hostile to the host country during certain periods in their sojourn. These resentments may be heightened if, as a result of poor language skills, the individual actually loses standing in his profession or occupation.

In short, considering only the precontact situation of the participants, we could predict that attitude changes in the direction of international accommodation will be greatest when: Participants undertake transnational interactions on their own initiative; they are highly attracted to the countries of their fellow participants; they are adolescents or young adults (roughly between the ages of 14 and 25); they perceive that the transnational experience will not create political, economic, or social problems on their return; and they enter the transnational situation with adequate communication skills. However, a more complete and effective approach to understanding the effects of transnational participation is to relate prearrival characteristics to variations in the transnational experience.

III. The Transnational Experience

One of the cardinal weaknesses of existing research on transnational participation is that little effort has been made to conceptualize the processes of influence in the transnational experience itself. In *Peace on the March,* for example, the author has recognized that different causal factors may be at work in different situations, but he has given little indication of what they might be. Yet, if we wish to understand the effects of transnational contacts for either theoretical or applied purposes, it becomes highly important to identify these causal factors and to specify and explain their effects.

Theories of attitude change offer one useful way of conceptualizing the dimensions of transnational experience. We might point to three stages in the process of attitude change: unfreezing, changing, and refreezing.[6] The *un-*

[6] Kurt Lewin, "Group Decision and Social Change," in *Readings in Social Psychology,* ed. Theodore M. Newcombe et al. (Prepared for the Committee on the Teaching of Social Psychology of the Society for the Psychological Study of Social Issues) (New York: Holt, Rinehart & Winston, 1958), pp. 197–212.

freezing stage deals mainly with opening an individual to change and overcoming those personal and social factors which create resistance to change. *Changing,* in turn, refers to the processes by which a person comes to adopt new patterns of attitudes, beliefs, or behavior. Finally, *refreezing* is the process by which these new patterns are tied into various kinds of personal and social supports and thus are stabilized. For transnational interactions we would want to answer three questions corresponding to these stages: 1) What are the conditions which lead the individual to become open to influence from his fellow participants and to question his previous attitudes and beliefs? 2) What are the specific ways in which attitudes related to international accommodation are communicated to the participant? 3) What are the forces leading to retention or rejection of these attitudes on a long-term basis, especially after the participant returns to his home country?

Cultural Congruity

The concept of culture refers to the social heritage of a group, including shared norms and expectations, values, beliefs, skills, and knowledge. The general hypothesis that I would suggest—one which receives some support from Angell's study—is that the outcome of transnational interactions will depend on the congruity of the cultures involved. More specifically, a high degree of incongruity in norms, beliefs, and expectations is likely to generate strong resistance to change. Several studies of student exchange programs touch on this issue and attempt to handle it with concepts such as "culture contrast" and "dissimilarity in normative patterns." There is some evidence that Japanese and other Oriental students, at least in the 1950s, experienced greater problems of adaptation in the United States than did Europeans. Research on Japanese students has shown that one problem for this group is "status-cue confusion" which results from different cultural norms regarding social differentiation.[7] When a Japanese student who was accustomed to a high degree of status ranking entered an informal social situation in the United States, he often found himself bewildered and sometimes withdrew from future contacts of this type. Such cultural incongruity was not found, however, in all forms of Japanese-American interaction. In standardized, impersonal, or quasi-bureaucratic situations, including the classroom, the student appeared to be on more familiar ground, and his behavior was not markedly different from that of his American counterparts. This research underscores the importance of paying explicit attention to the meshing of cultures in transnational interaction rather han assuming that the impact of such interactions will be the same regardless of the cultures involved. It is worth noting that much of the research in transnational contacts has focused on the interactions

[7] J. W. Bennett, H. Passin, and R. K. McKnight, *In Search of Identity: The Japanese Overseas Scholar in America and Japan* (Minneapolis: University of Minnesota Press, 1958).

of Europeans with Americans or with other Europeans. It may be that the blend of cultures represented in these situations is much more favorable to accommodative attitudes than are more varied mixtures.

Status Discrepancy

Closely related to cultural congruity is the question of status discrepancy in transnational interactions. Here it is helpful to distinguish between national status, the way in which a participant's country is regarded in other cultures, and personal status, the way in which the participant himself is evaluated. In the case of *national status* research has found that the single most powerful influence on the attitudes of Indian scholars toward the United States were American views of India as perceived by the Indians.[8] This sensitivity to the host country's views of a student's homeland has also been noted in studies of Mexican, Japanese, and Scandinavian students. Richard T. Morris, for example, has used national status as the major independent variable in his study of 318 foreign students at the University of California at Los Angeles.[9] He has specified three types of national status: 1) subjective, the status which a student attributes to his own country in comparison with others; 2) accorded, the status given to a student's country by members of the host culture; and 3) objective, the status given to the student's country by an impartial observer using clearly defined criteria. Morris's main hypothesis was that an exchangee's attitudes are affected only by a discrepancy between subjective and accorded status, rather than by accorded status alone. The data generally supports this hypothesis which is consistent with a large body of social psychological theory and research. Interestingly, however, the discrepancy between expected and accorded status does not predict to the depth of contact with members of the host culture. Accorded status alone relates positively to depth.

The early experiences of an individual in another culture often bring about changes in *personal status* as well. Perhaps the most evident changes are in social, economic, and academic standing. An Indian student who has had previous graduate training in his own country may be reduced from a position of esteem to the rather dubious standing of a first-year graduate student at a large American university. Even more subtle are changes in the very criteria used in according personal status. An individual accustomed to ascriptive evaluations may experience confusion as well as status loss when subjected to the achievement-oriented standards of the West.

Status discrepancies become important considerations in attitude change to the extent that they create defensiveness or hostility toward coparticipants. If a participant in a transnational interaction feels that he is being assigned an

[8] R. D. Lambert and Marvin Bressler, *Indian Students on an American Campus* (Minneapolis: University of Minnesota Press, 1956).

[9] Morris.

inferior status, he may react to the entire experience by developing intense, nationalistic attitudes as a form of psychic defense. The close connection between national and personal status has recently been pointed out:

> The question of whether they are being accorded the status they are due is likely to rise in the minds of participants in any group situation. It is, however, particularly likely to come up in a multinational setting. Here, national status tends to be tied in with personal status: Participants may become sensitive about the status accorded their own national group. Such sensitivities have often been noted among representatives from African and Asian nations who feel (sometimes with justification) that Americans and Europeans are undervaluing their countries and patronizing them. The reverse reaction has also been noted. Some Europeans may feel that they are taken for granted and representatives from developing countries are given more attention. . . . A participant's satisfaction with his experience as a whole is likely to depend, to a large extent, on the degree to which it helps to enhance his status and self-esteem.[10]

Similarly, the extent to which transnational participants develop accommodative attitudes is likely to be related to their overall satisfaction with the experience.

Duration of Contacts

It might appear at first blush that the longer the transnational contact, the greater is the possibility of influencing international attitudes. This "common sense" hypothesis may, however, obscure a much more complex situation. In some cases very brief, touristic contacts may lead an individual to fall in love with a country or city while extended residence could generate more ambivalent feelings. Although Angell has disregarded these shorter contacts because of their seeming superficiality, they would seem to be worthy of further study.

Perhaps a more useful approach to the problem of duration than the unilinear emphasis is one recognizing different time-associated patterns of adaptation and influence. One of the most consistent findings in the literature on overseas experience is that, regardless of nationality, an individual's adjustment over time follows a "U" curve. This curve has at least four distinguishable stages: 1) the spectator phase, marked by interest and exhilaration with the new environment; 2) the adaptive phase, a period in which the discovery of cultural discrepancies and perhaps even subjection to misunderstanding or insults lead the person to question his earlier optimism; 3) the "coming-to-terms" phase, involving pressures to achieve a satisfactory, if not ideal, modus vivendi; and 4) the predeparture phase, in which the person's attitudes may

[10] Herbert C. Kelman and Raphael S. Ezekiel, *Cross-National Encounters* (Jossey-Bass Behavioral Science Series) (San Francisco, Calif: Jossey-Bass, Publishers, 1970), p. 310.

be changed by the anticipation of his return.[11] The particular cycle followed by the individual, especially the ways in which he works out the normal difficulties of living abroad, may have very profound effects on his attitudes toward international accommodation. A person who never passes the adaptive phase may leave the host country more of an isolationist than when he came. Similarly, short-term tourism may have the advantage of operating almost exclusively in the honeymoon phase and may thus produce slight but important positive effects. For this reason I would disagree with Angell's exclusion of tourism as a category of transnational participation.

The Organizational Context

The great majority of transnational contacts take place within the context of formal organizations or associations. Diplomats, soldiers, Peace Corps volunteers, missionaries, and international businessmen are all, in varying degrees, accountable to and dependent on organizations. The organizational setting within which they work is also a prime source of their socialization while abroad. Pressures placed on them in this setting can reinforce the development of accommodative attitudes or cancel out incipient tendencies toward accommodation growing out of other kinds of socialization. It is highly important, therefore, to understand the degree to which transnational participation is mediated by organizations and the pressures within the organizations which may bear upon accommodative attitudes. Several concepts from organization theory and the literature on socialization are especially helpful in this analysis.

A basic question in any form of transnational interaction concerns the degree to which the participants are dependent on or controlled by formal organizations. It may be helpful to consider two polar extremes. The first consists of essentially unmediated transnational contacts such as those between a tourist and a member of the host country who happen to meet in a cafe. Many contacts developed by traveling university students would also fall into this category. The other extreme involves tightly mediated contacts such as those between a Soviet and a United States diplomat in Washington or Moscow. The relationship between organizational dependence and the effects of transnational participation is likely to be complex and interactive. In many cases the potential for attitude change in the participant will be greater in the unmediated than in the mediated situation. However, much will depend on what is expected of the individual in the organization and how this relates to his interactions outside that setting.

Every organization holds certain expectations covering the behavior, atti-

[11] See Cora Du Bois, *Foreign Students and Higher Education in the United States* (Studies in Universities and World Affairs) (Washington: American Council on Education [for the Carnegie Endowment for International Peace and the Institute of International Education], 1956).

tudes, and beliefs of its employees. The degree to which interactions between an employee and a national of another country will lead to accommodative attitudes will clearly depend on how closely the individual is tied to his organization and on how the organization regards such accommodative attitudes. If the organization were fiercely nationalistic, totally opposed to international accommodation, and used conformity to this ideology as a consideration in promotion, we might well expect that shifts toward accommodative attitudes produced by after-hours contacts would be slight. If, on the other hand, a unit's overall mission is to promote international accommodation, the organizational culture may be the single most important positive force in the development of accommodative attitudes. Organizations show great differences in the extent to which they develop distinctive cultures and hold their members to these cultures in distributing such rewards as assignments and promotions. Given the importance of the career ladder in the occupational lives of many transnational participants it is essential to focus specifically on the effects of organizational expectations and rewards on transnational interactions. One would expect, for example, that organizational pressures favoring accommodative attitudes would be stronger in the Peace Corps and branches of the United Nations than in the United States Army.

IV. Postreturn Conditions

Theories of attitude change point out the importance of "refreezing"—the integration of newly formed attitudes with one's normal behavior and environment. In transnational contacts the most critical part of the refreezing process occurs when the interaction ends. It is thus misleading to judge the long-term impact of transnational interactions on the basis of attitude measures taken during the experience or very shortly thereafter. Sound analysis requires close attention to a participant's situation on his return and the implications of his transnational experience for that situation. Some participants may develop internationalist attitudes during their stay in another country only to abandon them a few months after they return. Organizational pressures, such as those directed against internationalists in the Department of State during the McCarthy period, may have strong and immediate "corrective" effects. The opposite situation may also arise when the returnee finds that internationalism holds decided career advantages for him such as the possibility of a lucrative position as director of an international division.

An essential factor in the postreturn situation is the personal, social, or political capital (positive or negative) accruing to the participant as a result of his experience. Research on Indian returnees who had studied in the United States indicates that some students who had been highly critical of the United States during their stay became strong defenders of this country on their return seemingly because of the professional "capital gains" produced by their foreign training.[12] In Mexico, on the other hand, a returning student might have to adopt (or at least feign) anti*yanqui* attitudes to reestablish his nationalist credentials. In more extreme cases he may even be removed from a former position or suffer other kinds of setbacks because of his links to "imperialist powers." These considerations highlight the need for longitudinal studies of participants in transnational interactions rather than the usual "one-shot" survey taken during or shortly after the experience, however useful the latter may be.

V. Personality Effects of Participation

Thus far the term "accommodative attitudes" has been used as a catchall concept to cover personality changes favorable to the reduction of international conflict. However, in a detailed analysis of transnational participation one should specify the dimensions of personality under discussion. *Peace on the March* and other studies of international exchange suffer from two major weaknesses in this regard. First, they treat personality changes at too general a level. While the concept of "accommodative attitudes" is useful as a shorthand expression, a thorough understanding of transnational participation requires attention to the specific knowledge, beliefs, motives, and attachments implied by the concept. Unless we are quite specific, we will never know if "accommodation" is used in a roughly comparable way by different authors. Second, there is often a tendency to bias the selection of personality dimensions in a positive direction. Because most of us who write about transnational participation favor it, it is very easy to omit or gloss over personality changes which are harmful to international accommodation. The most effective solution to both problems is to begin with a general conceptual scheme of personality.

Elsewhere I have suggested seven sets of personality tendencies which can be used in assessing the impact of various kinds of socialization and interpersonal influence.[13] These include: cognition, interpersonal orientations, motivational dispositions, concept of self, moral standards, personal capacities, and psychic strain and defense mechanisms. Several examples will illustrate their salience in the context of transnational interactions.

Cognition refers to the ways in which an individual perceives and stores information and uses it in forming concepts, reasoning, problem-solving, and decisionmaking. Research to date suggests a number of possible effects of transnational participation on an individual's cognitive structure. One is a movement toward greater subtlety, complexity, and differentiation in one's images

[12] John Useem and Ruth Hill Useem, *The Western-Educated Man in India: A Study of His Social Role and Influence* (New York: Dryden Press, 1955).

[13] Warwick, in Seashore and McNeill.

of the other country.[14] A United States citizen who lives in Latin America may discover that there are wide variations in the historical background, aspirations, present problems, and resources available in the Latin American countries. He may also come to a better understanding of their incipient nationalist strivings and the bases of anti-American sentiment. While he may not necessarily reduce his attachments to his own country nor become more favorable to his host country, he may at least be more inclined than before to look at the latter on its own terms. But here as elsewhere knowledge is not virtue. Improved understanding can be used for waging "better" wars as well as promoting international peace. The difference between accommodative understanding and hostile intelligence lies more in the intentions of the possessor than in the information possessed.

Transnational interactions may also have important effects on the participant's *interpersonal orientations,* especially his trust of persons from different countries. Herbert C. Kelman has observed that a continuing pattern of cooperation and exchange between two nations can create a

> *predisposition within each nation to trust the other nation, to perceive it as nonthreatening, and to be responsive to it. . . .* Thus, while it would be naive to assume that a pattern of cooperation and exchange is a sufficient condition for peace between two nations, such a pattern should decrease the likelihood that the nations will resort to violence in resolving their conflicts. If conflicts arise between nations whose citizens have a history of close and friendly contact, there should be less of a tendency to perceive threatening intent in the other and to formulate the issue in black-and-white terms, and a greater readiness to communicate with one another and to seek accommodation.[15]

This passage also illustrates the close connection between interpersonal orientations and cognitive structures. Individuals who trust each other are more likely than those who do not to use a differentiated and nuanced cognitive map in locating their respective actions and intentions. But how does such trust grow out of transnational interactions? One means is through the establishment of mutually satisfactory interpersonal networks based upon professional ties or other common interests. In this way "individuals and groups from different countries become committed to international cooperation not as an abstract value, but as a concrete vehicle for carrying out personally important activities and pursuing their immediate and long-range goals. They become involved in a network of interdependent individuals and groups, without reference to national differences, and are likely to develop a sense of loyalty to it."[16] Such transnational ties act as a positive force for international

[14] Herbert C. Kelman, "Social-Psychological Approaches to the Study of International Relations: The Question of Relevance," in *International Behavior: A Social-Psychological Analysis,* ed. Herbert C. Kelman (New York: Holt, Rinehart and Winston [for the Society for the Psychological Study of Social Issues], 1965), p. 573.

[15] Ibid., pp. 573–574.

[16] Ibid., p. 575; see also Kelman and Ezekiel.

accommodation and an effective deterrent against a rapid polarization of conflict along national lines.

The development of accommodative attitudes will also depend on the individual's *motivational dispositions* and on his *concept of self*. These two characteristics are tightly interwoven. Each person develops a characteristic hierarchy of dispositions—various conditions (wealth, power, dependency, achievement) which provide satisfaction across a variety of situations. The question here concerns the conditions under which the set of events loosely identified as international accommodation will rise in this overall hierarchy of motivational dispositions. How do people come to derive satisfaction from accommodative rather than hostile attitudes toward other countries? One critical condition is the degree to which transnational identifications form part of an individual's concept of self and identity. It may be, for example, that one of the greatest effects of service in the Peace Corps is the lifelong stamp it leaves on the volunteer's self-definition. To the extent that human behavior is directed toward the maintenance of a certain self-image, the impact of transnational participation on the self can be a powerful motivating force.

In considering personality effects it is also important to focus on the negative aspects of transnational interactions. Especially important is the extent to which these interactions are a source of *psychic strain* for a participant or those with whom he deals. Such strain appears most often in interactions between individuals from developed and less developed countries. University teachers from Latin America, for example, sent to the United States for advanced training in their fields, are likely to undergo considerable strain when they return to their former positions. One commonly noted effect of such experiences is an increase in the individual's level of aspirations for himself, his university, and his country—the "demonstration effect." After two or three years in a United States university these individuals may come to judge their success by United States standards. The potential for frustration upon their return is great. Teachers in the natural and physical sciences may feel thwarted by the lack of laboratory and computer facilities, the poor quality of their students, and the low degree of professionalism among their colleagues. They may also create resentment among their colleagues by using their United States training as a bludgeon for introducing reform in the university or advancing their own interests in other ways. They may be attacked by the more radical students and faculty as agents of United States imperialism or bearers of *gringo* attitudes. Thus, both the returnee and those around him may experience negative consequences as a result of his sojourn abroad, at least in the short run. Under these conditions one would have to be very careful in making specific predictions about the relationship between transnational interaction and accommodative attitudes. It may be that for the first year or two after his return the balance of effects would be negative, while later, as the participant lowers his own aspirations and becomes more accommodative at home, this balance would shift to the positive side.

VI. Participation, Socialization, and Foreign Policy

The discussion thus far has dealt with the impact of transnational participation on the attitudes, values, beliefs, and behavior of participants. Whatever these effects may be, we cannot assume that they will automatically influence foreign policy or, if such influence does take place, that it will be in a specific direction. The processes and outcomes of international relations are too complex to allow for simple, unidirectional statements about the effects of attitude change. Moreover, at present we know relatively little about the specifics of foreign policy decisionmaking, especially outside of the United States and the major powers. Theories and case studies abound, but most deal with a relatively narrow range of phenomena. Political scientists have focused rather heavily on the processes and products of decisionmaking during major crises like the Korean War or the Cuban missile crisis. While such decisions deserve close scrutiny because of their direct links to war and peace, one cannot assume that the processes at work during crises can be generalized to more routine foreign policy situations. Information is very scarce, for example, on the influences operating in noncrisis decisionmaking in such agencies as the Department of State, the Department of Commerce, the Department of the Interior, and the Department of Agriculture. Given the general paucity of explanatory models in this field it is difficult to be precise about the role of attitude change produced by transnational participation. Still, it is worth considering three questions: 1) Do transnational participants attempt to exert direct influence on foreign policy decisionmakers and, if so, how? 2) In what ways, if any, do these participants influence public opinion? 3) What is their net impact on foreign policy?

Direct Influence on Foreign Policy

James N. Rosenau has written one of the few studies dealing with the first question.[17] At a government-sponsored conference on foreign aid attended by over 1,000 United States "influentials" he succeeded in administering a questionnaire to 647 participants. His questions covered various aspects of their transnational activities as well as their previous contacts with members of the executive and legislative branches. His results showed that foreign experience made little difference in the frequency of attempts to influence legislators but that it did seem to be related to greater contact with officials in the executive branch. Angell has cited these results as fairly conclusive evidence in

[17] James N. Rosenau, *National Leadership and Foreign Policy: A Case Study in the Mobilization of Public Support* (Princeton, N.J: Princeton University Press [for the Center of International Affairs and the Woodrow Wilson School of Public and International Affairs], 1963).

support of his hypothesis about elite influence on foreign policy. But is contact with governmental officials equivalent to attempts to influence them? Perhaps so, but before deciding we would have to know what transpired during the contact, whether influence attempts were perceived as such by the officials, and how they were received. Despite this empirical study and many speculative essays on elites in the United States we still know very little about the personal impact of "influentials" on top policymakers.

Public Opinion

Transnational participation may have its greatest impact on foreign policy through its effects on the climate of public opinion. As Kelman has observed, "the moods of the general public and their broad orientations toward national and international affairs are an essential part of the climate within which foreign policy decision-making takes place."[18] The overall influence of public opinion on foreign policy, however, varies considerably from one country to another and even from issue to issue in the same country. Still, this seems to be a fruitful area for exploring the effects of transnational contacts. In dealing with this question it is helpful to distinguish between three publics: 1) the "general" public; 2) the "effective" public, composed of national leaders who occupy positions that allow for considerable influence on a variety of issues; and 3) "issue" publics, composed of leaders who are identified with a specific clientele or interest group.[19]

Research on the role of the general public in foreign policy has vacillated between denying that it has any influence and vastly overstating its influence. Several studies suggest that the collective mood of the public in the United States is a significant force in decisionmaking but not on all issues.[20] To date little systematic research has been carried out on this question in other countries, although there is ample anecdotal evidence underscoring the significance of public opinion elsewhere.

Perhaps an even more salient source of influence consists of national leaders whose views make up effective public opinion. Some would argue that the views of key influentials such as newspaper editors, congressmen, and heads of trade unions *are,* in effect, public opinion in the foreign policy field. Rosenau has claimed that "they guide and mold mass opinion and they also reflect it, and in this dual capacity the flexibility, intensity, and depth of their opinions constitute the essential subsoil in which foreign policy alternatives must be rooted."[21] In other words, certain foreign policy options may never be tried

18 Kelman, in Kelman, p. 581.

19 See ibid.; and Rosenau.

20 Milton J. Rosenberg, "Images in Relation to the Policy Process: American Public Opinion on Cold-War Issues," and Harold D. Lasswell, "The Climate of International Action," in Kelman, pp. 278–334 and 339–353, respectively.

21 Rosenau, p. 17.

or even considered because of a fear of strong negative reaction by this group. Other options may acquire such great salience that they would be difficult to ignore when espoused by the same leaders. Future research might explore the extent to which these national leaders are influenced by transnational participation and how the effects of their experiences relate to the public expression of views on foreign policy. The same strategy might be applied to research on members of the third public—leaders or lobbyists whose influence on foreign policy is limited to specific issues—tariff regulations, fishing rights, farm commodities, or monetary policy.

A useful research model on issue publics has been developed in a study on the role of businessmen in shaping United States foreign trade policy.[22] The study found that foreign travel was an important factor affecting the perspectives and attitudes of businessmen toward tariffs. Businessmen who traveled frequently were more likely to view questions of foreign trade in national terms, while their less traveled counterparts saw them more in terms of their own industry. The foreign trade policies supported by those who did little traveling were very closely related to and predictable from their companies' special interests. The attitudes of men who were well traveled, on the other hand, were not necessarily more liberal, but they did seem more subject to influence by the country's foreign policy. These results underscore the precariousness of simple generalizations about the effects of transnational participation on attitudes related to peace. In this example one might argue that the effect of travel was essentially unrelated to peace. If the United States happened to be pursuing a peaceful foreign policy, increased identification with the national viewpoint might increase business support for this stand. But if the government was bent on maintaining a cold-war posture, the exposure of businessmen to foreign travel would probably contribute to hardening the United States position. A euphoric view of the benefits of "international un derstanding" receives little support from this study.

VII. Foreign Policy and International Peace

The final and perhaps most important question to be raised concerns the effects of transnational participation on the foreign policy of individual countries and the prospects for peace between nation-states. Despite the optimism expressed in *Peace on the March* and similar works we are on very slippery terrain both theoretically and empirically. Angell, for example, has assumed that the influence process is relatively simple: One member of a social elite who has had the benefits of international experience seeks out another who is

[22] Raymond A. Bauer, Ithiel de Sola Pool, and Lewis Anthony Dexter, *American Business and Public Policy: The Politics of Foreign Trade* (Atherton Press Political Science Series) (New York: Atherton Press, 1963).

in a decisionmaking position and somehow convinces him to take a more accommodative foreign policy stand. Angell has not denied the role of public opinion in producing accommodation, but he has placed much more emphasis on direct contact between governmental and nongovernmental "influentials." Implicit in his model is the notion that there is a clearly defined group of men who can be called foreign policy decisionmakers, that they are regularly approached by other members of the elite, and that, when approached, they are open to influence on questions of international affairs.

A major limitation of an elitist approach to foreign policy lies in the identification of "foreign policy decisionmakers." While there is no doubt that the president of the United States, his national security advisor, the secretary of state, and other high officials qualify under this rubric, it is also true that responsibility for foreign policy is widely diffused through the federal executive system. In crisis situations decisions are escalated to the top of the system so that it is not difficult to locate the decisionmakers. Even here, however, executive agencies such as the Central Intelligence Agency (CIA), the Department of State, and the Department of Defense play a crucial role as sources of information and policy "inputs." Country officers in the Department of State may not be assigned a part in the final drama, but they do play some role in writing the script. Moreover, there is a vast range of foreign policy decisions and actions which simply never reach the National Security Council, the White House, or even the upper reaches of a foreign affairs agency. In fact, the diffusion and fractionation of foreign policy has been a source of consternation for the president and the Department of State during the entire postwar period. As William Crockett, former deputy undersecretary of state, has observed, "there is also an absence of an overall statement or plan of U.S. Foreign Policy against which all agencies match their programs, prepare their budgets and carry out their operations. . . . Now each agency virtually sets its own foreign policy."[23]

One example of a nonglamorous, noncrisis area of policy is United States overseas activity in water resources development. In 1969 the Department of State requested funds from Congress to establish a "Water for Peace" program essentially to coordinate the various water resources activities carried out abroad by other agencies. Congressional hearings showed that no fewer than 40 agencies were at work in this field. If one accepts the view that water resources, like oil, can be a potentially explosive area in international relations (for example, water diversion between India and Pakistan) he would be hard-pressed to find a single elite charged to set United States policy on that question. Yet, mistakes in this area could conceivably accumulate to provoke major confrontations between states.

If a simplified elite model is inadequate to handle the effects of transna-

[23] Letter to the author, December 1970.

tional participation, what are the alternatives? I would propose a stratified diffusion model which would allow for considerable dispersion of foreign policy decisionmaking but would also recognize the disproportionate influence of the upper levels. Thus, in the United States the president and the secretary of state would clearly have greater influence on foreign policy than a lower echelon employee in the Department of Commerce. Still, this approach would recognize that the employee may exercise genuine decisionmaking autonomy in an area of responsibility with some potential for affecting war and peace. I would further emphasize the importance of transnational awareness in preventing the development of crises by producing increased alertness to the sensitivity of certain nonobvious issues such as water. Perhaps a water resources specialist who had spent some years in Mexico before entering federal service could have warned the government of problems created for farmers in the Mexicali Valley by irrigation practices north of the border. As it happened, this was a sore point in United States–Mexican relations for some years.

In the final analysis it is exceedingly difficult to specify the impact of accommodative attitudes within a country on international relations. War and peace depend not only on the intentions of individual countries but also on the perceptions of these intentions by other countries. A country which develops an image of extreme accommodation may invite aggression by a more bellicose neighbor. As Kenneth N. Waltz has observed, "There is in international politics no simple rule to prescribe just how belligerent, or how peaceful, any given state should strive to appear in order to maximize its chances of living at peace with neighboring states. One cannot say in the abstract that for peace a country must arm, or disarm, or compromise, or stand firm. One can only say that the possible effects of all such policies must be considered."[24] An across-the-board reduction of ethnocentrism by all states might well produce accommodative policies on many sides and increase the prospects for a peaceful world. But a one-sided change or a lopsided change would not necessarily have such benign effects.

In sum, transnational participation seems to hold considerable potential for influencing the knowledge, motives, and attitudes of the participants. Under favorable conditions these effects may predispose an individual to an accommodative foreign policy stand. The relationship between effects on individuals and on world peace, however, is complex and not always positive. Research on these questions is both scarce and ambiguous in revealing causal connections, especially those between individual change and foreign policy. Existing studies certainly call into question the conventional state-centered view of world affairs but at the same time provide little basis for an empirically derived alternative model. This essay has suggested a number of concepts, such

[24] Kenneth N. Waltz, *Man, the State and War: A Theoretical Analysis* (Topical Studies in International Relations, No. 2) (New York: Columbia University Press, 1959), p. 222.

as socialization, which may prove useful in clarifying the effects of transnational participation and in developing new approaches to international relations. Most of us who write in this area are convinced that transnational contacts have benign effects on the prospects for world peace, but much of this conviction is derived from sources other than empirical evidence. The only way in which we can know whether our beliefs have any basis in fact is through a more extensive program of research. The efforts to date have been tantalizing, but hardly satisfying.

National Autonomy and Economic Development:

Critical Perspectives on Multinational Corporations in Poor Countries

PETER B. EVANS

WHETHER or not less developed countries can better realize their economic aspirations by strengthening their ties with developed countries will remain in dispute as long as there are rich and poor countries. Dispute will be particularly sharp while the main instruments of such interconnection are identifiable institutions like the multinational corporation. It is easier to map the growth of the multinational corporation than to assess its consequences, but the need for an assessment cannot be ignored. As this essay's subtitle suggests, my main concern is consideration of arguments which are critical of the role of the multinational corporation.

The growth of the multinational corporation is undeniable.[1] The value of the foreign subsidiaries and branches of United States–based corporations is more than $65 billion. Their sales have been rising faster than domestic sales

PETER B. EVANS, currently a research associate of the Center for International Affairs, Harvard University, Cambridge, Massachusetts, is assistant professor of sociology at Brown University, Providence, Rhode Island.

[1] The most comprehensive survey of direct overseas investment by United States firms is that of Samuel Pizer and Frederick Cutler, *U.S. Business Investments in Foreign Countries: A Supplement to the Survey of Current Business* (Washington: Office of Business Economics, Department of Commerce, 1960). The United States Department of Commerce *Survey of Current Business* runs a regular feature on foreign investment; the most recent article in this series is David T. Devlin and George R. Kruer, "The International Investment Position of the United States: Developments in 1969," *Survey of Current Business,* October 1970 (Vol. 50, No. 10), pp. 21–37. Another excellent recent source, though one unfortunately lacking in financial data, is James W. Vaupel and Joan P. Curhan, *The Making of Multinational Enterprise: A Sourcebook of Tables Based on a Study of 187 Major U.S. Manufacturing Corporations* (Boston: Division of Research, Graduate School of Business Administration, Harvard University, 1969); see also the essay by Louis T. Wells, Jr., in this volume.

of United States corporations, and their earnings are equivalent to about 20 percent of the net profits of American corporations.[2] Statistics on investment by corporations based in other developed countries are more difficult to obtain, but it appears that in recent years foreign investment by West European firms is increasing even more rapidly than that of American firms.[3] While locally owned firms will probably always retain some segment of their country's economy, it has been predicted that in another twenty years 600 or 700 corporations will control most of the business of the non-Communist world.[4] None of the 600 or 700 corporations is likely to be headquartered in poor countries, but almost all will have subsidiaries in them. About one-third of United States foreign investment is located in less developed countries, and almost all the major multinational corporations have subsidiaries in these countries.[5] Such international economic interconnection presents a poor country with a threat to its autonomy quite different from that posed by other states.

With the growing predominance of the multinational corporation increasing numbers of a poor country's economic actors become responsible to superiors and stockholders who are citizens of other countries. If a similar chain of command existed in public organizations, the poor country would be deemed a colony. Because multinational corporations are private economic organizations, chains of command leading outside the state may multiply without ostensible loss of political sovereignty. Yet, national autonomy, the ability of a nation-state as a collectivity to make decisions which shape its political and economic future, has been diminished. But is this loss a threat to general economic progress or only to the power of the elite?

Evaluation of the role of national autonomy in fostering economic progress depends on the evaluation of the effects of international corporate investment. If one sees the economic and social effects of the increased economic involvement of multinational corporations in less developed areas as beneficial, then

[2] Dividends, interest, fees, and royalties from United States direct investments were $9.54 billion in 1969; see Devlin and Kruer, *Survey of Current Business,* Vol. 50, No. 10, table 5, p. 26. Corporate profits after taxes were $50.5 billion; see *Survey of Current Business,* June 1970 (Vol. 50, No. 6), p. S-2. A recent survey of a number of large corporations found foreign earnings equal to 26 percent of total earnings; see "Worldwide Profitability 1964: 117 U.S. Firms Report," *Business International,* June 11, 1965, p. 186. For a look at trends over time in both sales and profits see Harry Magdoff, *The Age of Imperialism: The Economics of U.S. Foreign Policy* (New York: Monthly Review Press, 1969), pp. 179, 183–184.

[3] Sidney E. Rolfe and Walter Damm, eds., *The Multinational Corporation in the World Economy: Direct Investment in Perspective* (Praeger Social Studies in International Economics and Development) (New York: Praeger Publishers [for the Atlantic Institute, the Committee for Economic Cooperation, and the Atlantic Council of the United States], 1970), p. 12.

[4] George A. Steiner and Warren M. Cannon, *Multinational Corporate Planning* (Studies of the Modern Corporation) (New York: Macmillan Co., An Arkville Press Book, 1966), p. 4. Stephen Hymer has estimated that present trends could produce "a regime of 300 or 400 multinational corporations controlling 60% to 70% of the world industrial output." Quoted in the *Wall Street Journal,* December 7, 1970, p. 1.

[5] Vaupel and Curhan, p. 11.

the nation-state cannot help but appear as an anachronistic impediment to further rationalization of the international economy. By creating irrational, chauvinistic barriers in the path of multinational enterprise the nation-state hampers the progress of its citizens. If, on the other hand, one sees the multinational corporation as an instrument—conscious or unwitting—for the preservation or exacerbation of the economic disparities that currently separate rich and poor countries, then the nation-state becomes the focus of political organization, an instrument to be used to secure economic autonomy and thereby to foster economic progress.

The multinational corporation, as an efficient technocratic solution to the problems of international economic organization, has numerous supporters in both rich and poor countries. They consider international investment by private corporations an important, perhaps the most important, factor in stimulating progress in poor countries. Without these "mighty engines of enlightened Western capitalism" the prospects for the future prosperity of these countries would be dim indeed.[6] The multinational corporation not only transfers capital to poor countries, it also provides them with the organizational and technological know-how necessary for the creation of a modern industrial society. The links between parent company and subsidiary are nurturing channels through which flow the resources needed by a less developed country for its economic growth.

Since this assessment of the role of the multinational corporation eliminates economic rationales, its proponents rely on political or psychological explanations for opposition to multinational enterprise. A recent text on multinational corporations has summarized this point of view nicely: "Two major sets of consequences emerge from the extension of corporate production across borders. The first set is economic consequences and is held almost universally to be beneficial. The second set is phrased in political or emotional terms; this includes the threat—often more apparent than real but nevertheless action provoking—which foreign investment poses to local autonomy, or sovereignty, or control."[7] Raymond Vernon has taken a similar position, marveling "at the tenacity with which man seeks to retain a sense of differentiation and identity, a feeling of control, even when the apparent cost of the identity and the control seems out of all proportion to its value."[8] For these observers the quest for national autonomy is a luxury, a psychologically desirable one perhaps, but one for which an economic price is paid.

Those who oppose the encroachments of multinational corporations in the third world spend little time analyzing psychological propensities for autonomy or self-differentiation. Since they are convinced that the effects of those

[6] The quotation is from Steiner and Cannon, p. 120.

[7] Rolfe and Damm, p. 26.

[8] Raymond Vernon, "Economic Sovereignty at Bay," *Foreign Affairs,* October 1968 (Vol. 47, No. 1), p. 122.

"mighty engines of Western capitalism" are not to facilitate economic growth but to retard it, increased autonomy is an essential step toward hastening economic progress. While these opponents may agree that a sense of autonomy and control are psychologically gratifying, their main interest is explicating and documenting the retarding effects of asymmetric interconnectedness usually characterized as imperialism.

I. Providing Capital for Poor Countries

Spreading capital from rich to poor countries is one function classically attributed to international investment, but on examination the direction of the capital flow appears in doubt. Historical retrospects by critics have suggested that the Industrial Revolution in Great Britain was fueled by capital extracted from its colonies and that the development of the colonies suffered in consequence. Paul A. Baran, for example, has related India's failure to develop to the extraction of its surplus capital by British firms, an outflow which he claimed reached 10 percent of its national income in the beginning of the nineteenth century.[9] Clifford Geertz has suggested a similarly negative role for the Dutch when comparing Indonesia's development with that of Japan.[10]

Recent examinations of financial relations between the United States and Latin America also suggest that less developed countries end up exporting more funds than they receive. From 1950 to 1965 remittances of income to United States parent companies exceeded net new private investment by $7.5 billion.[11] An examination of United States Department of Commerce figures for the period 1965–1969[12] reveals an additional gap approaching $3 billion.[13]

Some critics attribute the loss of capital by poor countries to exorbitant rates of return on foreign investment in these countries. Baran has noted that the

[9] Paul A. Baran, *The Political Economy of Growth* (New York: Monthly Review Press, 1957), p. 145.

[10] Clifford Geertz, *Agricultural Involution: The Process of Ecological Change in Indonesia* (Association of Asian Studies Monographs and Papers, No. 11) (Berkeley: University of California Press [for the Association of Asian Studies], 1966), pp. 135–136.

[11] Magdoff, p. 198. For a thorough analysis of the economic relations between the United States and Latin America in the period up to 1961 see Economic Commission for Latin America, *External Financing in Latin America* (New York: United Nations, 1965).

[12] See Devlin and Kruer, *Survey of Current Business*, Vol. 50, No. 10, and the preceding four articles in the same series.

[13] For supporters of the multinational corporation these negative effects are counterbalanced by contributions of foreign firms to exports and import substitution. Such an argument fails to deal with the question of whether foreign firms could be replaced by indigenously controlled organizations which would not be obligated to remit income abroad. It is also interesting that supporters of the multinational corporation see its activities as benefiting the balance-of-payments position of the United States over the long run, a position which would seem to rule out a positive effect on the balance-of-payments position of host countries. See Jack Behrman, *Direct Manufacturing Investment, Exports, and the Balance of Payments* (New York: National Foreign Trade Council, 1968), written in reply to G. C. Hufbauer and F. M. Adler, *Overseas Manufacturing Investment and the Balance of Payments* (United States Treasury Tax Policy Study, No. 1) (Washington: Government Printing Office, 1968).

profits of British, Dutch, and Belgian companies with investments in colonies were well in excess of the rate of return normal in their countries of origin.[14] More recent data also substantiates this point.[15] An analysis of British investment has confirmed the profitability of Asian and African ventures but suggests that high rates of profit were not possible without the organized political support of the home country.[16] The lower rates of returns to British companies operating in Latin America can probably be explained by the fact that "there was greater stability within the Commonwealth and Empire and greater capacity to determine the investment climate."[17]

A look at the current profitability of American foreign investment suggests that higher rates of return are still achieved on investments in poor countries. The rate of return on investments in less developed countries in 1969 was more than double the rate of return on investments in developed countries. Separate examination of investment in extractive (mining and petroleum) industries and in manufacturing industries shows that high rates of return on extractive investment account for the difference. The following tabulation indicates earnings on United States direct investment in 1969 as a percentage of book value.[18]

	All investment	Manufacturing	Extractive
Developed countries	8.3	10.8	3.0
Less developed countries	18.8	8.9	27.6

While a combination of political dependency and concentration on extractive industry appears most conducive to exorbitant rates of return, the returns on investment in manufacturing industries may be underestimated by this analysis. In the first place, "fees and royalties" collected by United States firms from their direct investments are excluded. Were they added to earnings, rates of return would be increased by 15 to 20 percent.[19] The overpricing of intermediate goods sold by parent companies to their subsidiaries may be an even more important source of extra returns from manufacturing investment in less developed countries. A recent study of the pharmaceutical industry in Colombia suggests that return to parent companies from overpricing inter-

[14] Baran, pp. 228–233.

[15] Ernest Mandel, *Marxist Economic Theory,* Vol. 2, trans. Brian Pearce (New York: Monthly Review Press, 1968), pp. 453–459.

[16] J. Fred Rippy, *British Investments in Latin America, 1822–1849: A Case Study in the Operations of Private Enterprise in Retarded Regions* (Minneapolis: University of Minnesota Press, 1959).

[17] Ibid., p. 184.

[18] Devlin and Kruer, *Survey of Current Business,* Vol. 50, No. 10, table 6, parts A and D, p. 26.

[19] Ibid., table 5, p. 26. Unfortunately, these figures are not broken down by industry or into the categories of "developed" and "less developed" countries.

mediate products is many times the return received from dividends and interest.[20]

Even if profit rates on foreign investment were not excessive relative to domestic rates of return, foreign investment might still create a drain on the capital resources of a less developed country in the long run. The lack of a termination date is an important feature of direct investment.[21] With bonds and loans a borrower must eventually repay more than he borrows, but amortization at least diminishes his future obligation. With direct investment the recipient looks forward to interminable remittances and no guarantee that they will be matched by inflows of new capital. Initially a less developed country may receive more in new investment than it must pay out in remitted income, but over the years the balance is likely to shift to its disadvantage. A comparison of Latin America, where United States investment has a long history, with Africa, where it is relatively recent, will serve as illustration. From 1965 to 1969 Africa received about as much new capital from the United States as it remitted in income. Remitted income from Latin America, on the other hand, was over three and one-half times the amount of new capital received.[22]

Yet, multinational corporations could be making excessive profits and repatriating more capital than they invested and still contribute significantly to the economic growth of less developed countries. If the organizational and technological know-how they contribute serves as the spark to the industrialization process, departure of capital is not an unreasonable price to pay. It must only be understood that the contribution of the multinational corporation lies primarily in the transfer of intangibles rather than in the transfer of capital.[23]

II. The Impact of Extractive Investment

Unfortunately, according to critics of the multinational corporation the past utilization of the organizational and technological resources of the corporation has diverted the productive energies of poor countries in directions unconducive to self-sustained economic growth. In 1950 H. W. Singer criticized

[20] Constantine Vaitsos, "Transfer of Resources and Preservation of Monopoly Rents" (Paper presented at the Conference of the Development Advisory Service of Harvard University, Dubrovnik, June 1970), pp. 63–64.

[21] Albert O. Hirschman, *How to Divest in Latin America and Why* (Essays in International Finance, No. 76) (Princeton, N.J: International Finance Section, Department of Economics, Princeton University, 1969).

[22] Figures are taken from Devlin and Kruer, *Survey of Current Business*, Vol. 50, No. 10, table 6, parts B and E, p. 29, and previous articles in the same series; figures for Africa exclude the Republic of South Africa. Note that the difference between Latin America and Africa is not due to differences in profit rates; rates of return are higher for Africa.

[23] This is essentially the position of Harry G. Johnson in his recent essay, "The Efficiency and Welfare Implications of the International Corporation," in *The International Corporation: A Symposium*, ed. Charles P. Kindleberger (Cambridge, Mass: M.I.T. Press, 1970), pp. 35–56.

investment in extractive industries in less developed countries: "If we apply the principle of opportunity costs to the development of nations, the import of capital into underdeveloped countries for the purpose of making them into providers of food and raw materials for the industrialized countries may have been not only rather ineffective in giving them the normal benefits of investment and trade but may have been positively harmful."[24] Singer based his criticism of extractive investment on the idea that it is designed to operate as an "enclave" relatively unconcerned with the growth of the local economy because the goods it produces are sold outside it.[25] Baran has argued more strongly still that the effects of foreign investment in extractive industries are detrimental. He has concluded that "whichever aspect of economic development we may consider, it is manifestly detrimental to the prosperity of the raw materials producing corporations."[26] Development would mean increased labor costs and probably higher taxes but would do nothing to increase the demand for the goods the extractive exporter is selling. When the attenuated interest of investors in extractive industries in local development is coupled with the high rate at which they remit their profits to the United States, it hardly seems necessary to invoke a psychological need for differentiation in order to explain hostility toward these foreign investors.[27]

Defenders of extractive investment usually cite the resources made available to governments via taxation.[28] This argument also leads us to the importance of political independence in effecting the redistribution of returns from the investor to the host country. If less developed countries have been successful in retaining a larger portion of the income of extractive investment within their borders, it is because the state retained sufficient political autonomy to bargain with international firms. The existence of "aggressively nationalist groups" within a country has been a benefit to less developed states in their bargaining.[29]

24 H. W. Singer, "The Distribution of Gains between Investing and Borrowing Countries," *American Economic Review,* May 1950 (Vol. 60, No. 2), pp. 473–485.

25 For a good analysis of "enclave investment" see Charles E. Rollins, "Mineral Development and Economic Growth," *Social Research,* Autumn 1956 (Vol. 23, No. 3), pp. 253–280. For a more theoretical approach Albert O. Hirschman's idea of backward and forward linkages is useful; see his book, *The Strategy of Economic Development* (Yale Studies in Economics, No. 10) (New Haven, Conn: Yale University Press, 1958), pp. 110–112.

26 Baran, p. 197.

27 See the tabulation on p. 329. Not only are the earnings on extractive investments high, the proportion remitted to United States parent companies is also high. In 1969 income received by United States parent companies on investments in less developed countries amounted to 19 percent of book value in mining and over 29 percent in petroleum; see Devlin and Kruer, *Survey of Current Business,* Vol. 50, No. 10, table 6, parts A and E, pp. 28–29.

28 See, for example, Raymond Vernon, "Foreign Enterprises and Developing Nations in the Raw Materials Industries," *American Economic Review,* May 1970 (Vol. 60, No. 2), pp. 122–126. Vernon also discusses the role of the oil companies in maintaining artificially high prices. See also Michael Tanzer, *The Political Economy of International Oil and the Underdeveloped Countries* (Boston: Beacon Press, 1969).

29 Edith T. Penrose, *The Large International Firm in Developing Countries: The International Petroleum Industry* (London: George Allen and Unwin, 1968), p. 199.

Since mining and petroleum currently account for about 50 percent of the value of United States investment in less developed countries, just as they did in 1950, arguments about the effects of extractive investment must continue to have an important place in any critique of the multinational corporation. In this same period, however, the value of American investments in manufacturing in less developed countries has increased from $850 million to $4.7 billion.[30] Investment in manufacturing industries may be a more stimulating outlet for the knowledge and skills of the multinational corporation, but it also raises a new set of problems.

III. The Impact of Manufacturing Investment

The manufacturing firm, unlike the extractive exporter, has a direct stake in the growth of the local market. Because of this stake the manufacturing firm participates more actively in the life of the host country. The goods that it offers embody a way of life. In order to ensure their consumption the manufacturer must take on a role which bears a more than coincidental resemblance to that of the original international organization—the Roman Catholic church.[31] For the church the transmission of values from Western Europe to less developed countries has been more an end than a means; the manufacturing firm becomes involved in the transnational transmission of ideals and values, although more as a means than an end. By introducing its wares and, even more important, by trying to convince people to consume them the manufacturing firm joins the church as an outsider helping to shape the culture of less developed countries.

The transfer of ideas may have no less economic impact than the transfer of capital, though it fits poorly into quantitative economic models. Supporters of the multinational corporation are likely to speak in terms of the transfer of neutral "skills" or "know-how" which will be useful to recipients in a less developed country in achieving whatever ends they may desire. Those who argue for greater autonomy are suspicious of the usefulness of the tools, but in addition they are afraid that the tools dictate the ends more nearly than the technocrats of developed countries would like to admit. Their arguments involve a range of issues from the ways in which people spend their paychecks to the kind of political philosophy they are likely to favor. These arguments are worth considering at some length.

As a transmitter of ideas and values, as well as a producer of goods, the multinational corporation becomes a means of encouraging consumptive emulation across societal boundaries. Thorstein Veblen's analysis of the ways the "leisure class" makes its own peculiar cultural standards normative for the

[30] See Pizer and Cutler; and Devlin and Kruer, *Survey of Current Business,* Vol. 50, No. 10.
[31] See the discussion of the Roman Catholic church by Ivan Vallier in this volume.

social order as a whole now applies transnationally.[32] Products and ideas developed in rich countries shape the values and ideas of citizens of poor countries. Or, to adapt Karl Marx's statement on the class nature of ideas, the nation which has the means of material production at its disposal controls the means of mental production and, in turn, the ideas of those who lack the means of mental production.[33]

A short excursus on advertising expenditures should help make this argument more concrete. The United States Department of Commerce has estimated that sales of American manufacturing affiliates in less developed countries in 1968 were approximately $9 billion.[34] Those corporations which own the bulk of United States overseas investment spend, on average, 4 percent of their sales receipts on advertising.[35] We may estimate then that American manufacturing corporations are spending approximately $360 million each year in order to shape the consumptive habits of citizens of less developed countries. Rough as this estimate may be, it should stand as an indication of the magnitude of such expenditures. Expenditures by multinational corporations on the education of consumer preferences are less than the education budgets of national governments but not incomparably less. In Brazil, for example, use of the above percentages suggests that advertising expenditures by American manufacturing affiliates alone are over one-third of recurring public expenditures on all forms of education.[36]

The contradiction between imported consumptive tastes and the productivity of local economies is disturbing. Ivan Illich, founder of the Center for Intercultural Documentation in Cuernavaca, has expressed his distress about this situation as follows: "The plows of the rich can do as much harm as their swords. . . . Once the Third World has become a mass market for the goods, products, and processes which are designed by the rich for themselves, the dis-

[32] Thorstein Veblen, *The Theory of the Leisure Class: An Economic Study of Institutions* (New York: Mentor Books, 1953); see also Stephen Hymer's discussion of "the international trickle down" in his article, "The Efficiency (Contradictions) of Multinational Corporations," *American Economic Review,* May 1970 (Vol. 60, No. 2), pp. 441–448.

[33] Karl Marx and Friedrich Engels, *The German Ideology: Parts I and III* (New York: International Publishers, 1960), p. 39.

[34] R. David Belli, "Sales of Foreign Affiliates of U.S. Firms, 1961–65, 1967 and 1968," *Survey of Current Business,* October 1970 (Vol. 50, No. 10), pp. 18–20.

[35] The multinational corporations used in this estimate are from Vaupel and Curhan, pp. 6–8. Data on their advertising was found in "U.S. Industry's Ad Budgets," *News Front,* March 1966 (Vol. 10, No. 2), pp. 40–43. The percentage is based on firms included in both the *News Front* and the Vaupel and Curhan lists.

[36] Total recurrent public expenditure on education in Brazil was reported to be $148 million in 1966; see the UNESCO *Statistical Yearbook 1968* (Paris: United Nations Educational, Scientific and Cultural Organization, 1969). Sales of American manufacturing affiliates may be interpolated for 1966 at about $1.44 billion (Belli, *Survey of Current Business,* Vol. 50, No. 10) which, under our method, results in an estimate of resources devoted to advertising of $57.6 million or 39 percent of education expenditures of Brazil. Inclusion of European subsidiaries and investments suggests an allocation of resources to advertising by foreign-owned manufacturing firms approaching total recurrent public expenditures on education.

crepancy between demand for these Western artifacts and the supply will increase indefinitely. . . . Each car which Brazil puts on the road denies fifty people good transportation by bus. Each merchandised refrigerator reduces the chance of building a community freezer."[37] The example of the passenger car is a classic illustration of the diffusion of inappropriate patterns of consumption. A mode of transportation, developed in response to the historical, economic, and technological conditions of early twentieth-century America, was introduced by the multinational corporation and has become the mainstay of transportation systems in countries whose economic and social requirements make it altogether inappropriate. It has been estimated that automobile production facilities created by multinational corporations in Latin America are already ten times as great as they need be to meet the demands of the regional market.[38] Yet, despite the resources devoted to their production, passenger cars are a form of transportation which can benefit only a minority of the population.

While ownership of a private automobile is beyond the reach of the average citizen of less developed countries, production of passenger cars absorbs resources which might be used to produce trucks, buses, bicycles, and other forms of transportation more within the reach of all citizens. Automobile production may exert pressure on foreign exchange reserves by requiring increased importation of gasoline or of the raw materials and capital goods necessary to produce cars. Cars tend to be heavily concentrated in a few cities, and the resources necessary to build a road network to support such an individualistic mode of transportation are not available. Congestion in the cities of many less developed countries is frequently worse than in most Western cities; pollution levels are also higher. The average city dweller in a less developed country must sit in a bus each morning and evening stranded in a sea of passenger vehicles, breathing exhaust fumes and wishing he were able to add to the anarchy by purchasing his own automobile.

It is important to keep in mind that the disjunction between private consumptive longings and the welfare of the community does not have to be resolved in favor of the former. Barry Richman, an English management consultant, was struck by the extensive use of bicycles by the personnel of the factories he studied in the People's Republic of China (Communist China). Even managers and administrators, who in many poorer countries invariably move by car, rode bicycles to work.[39] Consumer sovereignty is a concept of dubious empirical validity, and in less developed countries "freedom to con-

[37] Ivan Illich, "Outwitting the 'Developed' Countries," *New York Review of Books*, November 6, 1969 (Vol. 13, No. 8), p. 20.

[38] Jack Baranson, *Industrial Technologies for Developing Economies* (Praeger Special Studies in International Economics and Development) (New York: Frederick A. Praeger, 1969), p. 73 and chapter 6, passim.

[39] Barry M. Richman, *Industrial Society in Communist China: A Firsthand Study of Chinese Economic Development and Management* (New York: Random House, 1969), pp. 805–809.

sume" is severely curtailed by poverty for all but the affluent elite. If collective decisionmaking at the national level could result in an allocation of productive resources more appropriate to the economic and social circumstances of the citizenry, it is hard to see how the freedom of the average individual can be said to have been diminished.

Without belaboring the issue further it seems plausible that multinational corporations help transmit standards of consumption which may well represent a misallocation of resources from the point of view of the welfare of the community as a whole. If this is true, then the distortion of consumer desires has a retarding effect on economic progress, and poor countries could achieve greater progress by exercising a greater degree of autonomy in shaping their consumptive norms. As Veblen has pointed out, the mark of a good borrower of technology is the ability to extricate the technology from the fetishes that grow up around its use in the culture of its origin.[40] It is possible to reject the goods which rich countries have chosen as embodiments of their technology without rejecting the technology itself.

IV. Importation of Strategy

Consumer choices are not the only decisions affected by the internationalization of less developed economies. Decisions about the allocation of productive resources are also directly affected. These decisions, however, are more likely to be made in corporate headquarters in New York or Tokyo than in capitals of less developed countries. It might be argued that the geographical location at which an economic decision is made should have no effect on its outcome. If a rational man in Dar es Salaam will make the same decision as a rational man in New York, then the locus of decisionmaking is hardly vital. If, on the other hand, the outcome of a decision depends on the environment of the decisionmaker, the change becomes important.

Increasingly, social scientists have adopted the latter view and look upon rationality as dependent on social position. No decisionmaker can consider all the information that might be relevant—to say nothing of all the possible interconnections between the relevant facts. Time constraints and limited cognitive capacity ensure that rationality is always "bounded."[41] The social posi-

[40] Thorstein Veblen, *Imperial Germany and the Industrial Revolution* (New York: Viking Press, 1942), especially p. 38.

[41] See James G. March and Herbert A. Simon, with the collaboration of Harold Guetzkow, *Organizations* (New York: John Wiley and Sons, 1958), pp. 137–165, for a discussion of the cognitive limits on rationality. See also Charles E. Lindblom, "The Science of Muddling Through," in *Public Administration: Readings in Institutions, Processes, Behavior*, ed. Robert T. Golembiewski, Frank Gibson, and Geoffrey Y. Cornog (Chicago: Rand McNally & Co., 1966), pp. 293–304, for a similar perspective. Donald P. Warwick's essay in this volume provides some good examples of bounded rationality in a public organization. For a discussion of the differences in perspective among the different functional segments of private corporations see Paul R. Lawrence and Jay W. Lorsch, with the assistance of James S. Garrison, *Organization and Environment: Managing Differentiation and Integration* (Boston: Division of Research, Harvard Graduate School of Business Administration, Harvard University, 1967).

tion of the decisionmaker will determine the relative salience of different pieces of information and the ways the various pieces will be put together. Each decisionmaker brings to a problem not only a particular subsample of the relevant information but also a particular set of theories on how his information should fit together.

It has repeatedly been the case historically that strategies of development concocted in advanced countries have been accepted by less developed countries despite their dubious appropriateness. In 1786 Queen Maria I of Portugal decided that factories should be abolished in Brazil because they diverted the attention of the populace from agriculture and mining.[42] It was, she felt, to the benefit of all concerned that the metropole should concentrate on manufacturing and the colony on primary production. Spain had already instituted the same policy for its colonies. In the nineteenth century Great Britain, which had the strongest manufacturing economy, carefully pointed out the universal economic advantages of free trade.

Looking at Latin America in the nineteenth century, Celso Furtado has noted the detrimental effects of the fervent belief in the gold standard inculcated by European economic theories. Of Brazil, Furtado has written: "All efforts were spent in a task that historic experience has shown to be in vain: that of subjecting the economic system to the monetary rules prevailing in Europe. This strenuous effort at mimicry, arising from an unshakable faith in the principles of a doctrine with no basis in reality, was to continue for the first three decades of the twentieth century."[43]

A more contemporary example of imported economic ideology is the law recently instituted in Brazil which gives substantial tax relief to companies whose stock is "highly negotiable."[44] Billed as an effort to achieve the "democratization of capital" and derived from the American example, this strategy has the effect of benefiting multinational corporations and a small community of investors at the expense of locally owned, family-run corporations. Its usefulness to the economic progress of the country as a whole remains to be seen.

Another contemporary issue is the patent system. Developed countries in general and multinational corporations in particular are firm believers in the value of patents. The rationality of the patent system for less developed countries is highly questionable both on theoretical and practical grounds.[45] Yet,

[42] Andre[w] Gunder Frank, *Capitalism and Underdevelopment in Latin America: Historical Studies of Chile and Brazil* (New York: Monthly Review Press, 1967), p. 161.

[43] Celso Furtado, *The Economic Growth of Brazil: A Survey from Colonial to Modern Times,* trans. Ricardo W. de Aguiar and Eric Charles Drysdale (Berkeley: University of California Press, 1963), p. 177. Albert O. Hirschman's discussion of the Kemmerer mission in Chile provides a parallel analysis; see his *Journeys toward Progress: Studies of Economic Policy-Making in Latin America* (New York: Twentieth Century Fund, 1963), pp. 175–183.

[44] United States Department of Commerce, *Brazilian Income Tax Legislation* (Overseas Business Reports, No. 67–26) (Washington: Government Printing Office, 1967).

[45] On the practical side see Vaitsos; for some theoretical arguments see Johnson, in Kindleberger.

until very recently most less developed countries accepted the theory of patents promulgated by developed countries and belonged to the International Union for the Protection of Industrial Property.

It is not necessary to view the promulgation of these development prescriptions as arising from any consciously exploitative motives. Such motives may exist, but they need not be invoked in explanation. Even if it is assumed that the queen of Portugal was motivated only by the desire to promote the economic betterment of the populace of her dominions, it is not surprising, given the milieu in which she reached her decision, that the destruction of Brazilian factories should seem the most rational course.

Just as imported development strategies have proven irrational to their borrowers, strategies that looked irrational to developed countries have proven efficacious to late starters. David S. Landes has illustrated this nicely in his analysis of the differing rationales of British and German entrepreneurs in the latter half of the nineteenth century—when Germany was a "less developed country": "The British manufacturer remained faithful to the classical calculus . . . making those investments which, given anticipated costs, risks, and sales, yielded the greatest margin over what existing equipment could provide. . . . The significance of this approach is best appreciated when contrasted with the technological rationality of the Germans. This was a different kind of arithmetic, which maximized, not returns, but technical efficiency."[46]

The German kind of arithmetic, irrational as it may have appeared to established British entrepreneurs, proved efficacious. In broader terms Alexander Gerschenkron has shown that each of the European countries needed a distinctive system of banking, governmental involvement, and industrial organization suited to its own material circumstances in order to industrialize.[47] Japan, with its direct governmental involvement in the creation of new industry and its cartelized, paternalistic method of industrial organization, also chose a path that looked irrational in terms of the cultural prescriptions of its predecessors but proved appropriate to its own circumstances.[48]

Too great a reliance on development rationales evolved in other times and circumstances entails the same kind of disadvantages as absorption of alien standards of consumption. Greater reliance on indigenous ideas provides no guarantee of producing better strategies, but it increases the possibility of innovations shaped by the particular situation of a less developed country. Poor

[46] David S. Landes, "Technological Change and Development in Western Europe 1750–1914," in *The Cambridge Economic History of Europe*, Vol. 6, Part 1: *The Industrial Revolutions and After: Incomes, Population and Technological Change (I)*, ed. H. J. Habakkuk and M. Postan (Cambridge: Cambridge University Press, 1965), pp. 580–581.

[47] Alexander Gerschenkron, "Economic Backwardness in Historical Perspective," in *The Progress of Underdeveloped Areas*, ed. Bert F. Hoselitz (Chicago: University of Chicago Press, 1952), pp. 3–29.

[48] For discussion of Japanese industrial organization see Seymour Broadbridge, *Industrial Dualism in Japan: A Problem of Economic Growth and Structural Change* (Chicago: Aldine Publishing Co., 1966); and M. Y. Yoshino, *Japan's Managerial System: Tradition and Innovation* (Cambridge, Mass: M.I.T. Press, 1968).

countries are desperately in need of such innovations: Only by discovering rules that work for them do they have a chance to achieve parity. Following the rules that created the present system of international stratification can hardly be expected to eliminate this system.

Even if less developed countries completely rejected the development theories proffered by developed countries, they would still be circumscribed in their choice of strategy by the predominance of foreign-owned firms in their economies. The presence of foreign-owned firms substantially limits the ability of a poor country to shape its own industrial structure. Gerschenkron's paradigm of European development and the experience of Japan suggest that the more backward a country, the more essential is initiative and direction by its government. Yet, governments of poor countries are often forced into roles more passive than those of governments in developed countries. European governments have been very active in engineering mergers to bring together locally owned firms and strengthen national industries.[49] The government of a less developed country, faced with an economy full of subsidiaries attached to foreign-based, private corporations, is much more limited in the kinds of organizational initiatives that it may take.

The automobile industry again provides a good example. As noted earlier production facilities for automobiles in Latin America exceed regional needs. At the national level the situation appears even more extreme. Argentina produces about 3 percent of the number of cars made in the United States, yet it was recently reported that Argentina had thirteen manufacturers competing in the local market. Since the assembly of automobiles is an industry with undeniable economies of scale, the cost of manufacture is grossly inflated by this fragmented industrial structure.[50]

What action is open to a less developed country faced with an industrial structure that is inefficient because it is a "miniature replica" of those of developed countries?[51] The government of a small country is unlikely to be able to persuade FIAT, Volkswagenwerk, and General Motors Corporation to merge for its convenience. As long as it allows foreign-owned firms to compete freely for its internal market, it must either import automobiles and lose

[49] Some discussion of trends in European mergers can be found in Philip Siekman, "Europe's Love Affair with Bigness," *Fortune,* March 1970 (Vol. 81, No. 3), pp. 94–99, 166, 168, 171; in "Europe's Merger Boom Thunders a Lot Louder," *Business Week,* November 23, 1968 (No. 2047), pp. 53–56; and in Bengt Rydén, "Concentration and Structural Adjustment in Swedish Industry During the Postwar Period," *Skandinaviska Banken Quarterly Review,* 1967 (Vol. 48, No. 2), pp. 51–58.

[50] See Jack Baranson, *Automotive Industries in Developing Countries* (World Bank Staff Occasional Papers, No. 8) (Baltimore, Md: Johns Hopkins Press [for the International Bank for Reconstruction and Development], 1969), pp. 44–53.

[51] The "miniature replica" idea was introduced by H. Edward English in his examination of the Canadian situation, *Industrial Structure in Canada's International Competitive Position: A Study of the Factors Affecting Economies of Scale and Specialization in Canadian Manufacturing* (Montreal: Canadian Trade Committee, Private Planning Association of Canada, 1964). For a broader analysis of the problems of industrial organization in poor countries see Meir Merhav, *Technological Dependence, Monopoly, and Growth* (New York: Pergamon Press, 1969).

foreign exchange or produce them locally at production costs that may be as much as twice those at facilities utilizing efficiencies of scale.

V. Political Ramifications

Since effective utilization of human resources is as important to a less developed country as utilization of its land and minerals, it has been argued that a close bond between elites and masses is critical to a country's development.[52] Yet, a populist orientation is rare in traditional societies, and the experience of colonialism is likely to increase the separation between elites and masses.[53] The multinational corporation may also help to maintain an external orientation among elites.

Nationals working at the local level strive to absorb the cultural perspective of the organizations that provide their livelihood and their work environment. The ability to identify with the corporation as an organization and to acquire the cognitive and stylistic norms that prevail within it is an important prerequisite of executive success. The socialization of local elite personnel is reinforced by the employment of foreign personnel in key high-level positions. If corporations are successful in inculcating a sense of organizational identity, the probability that the local economic elite will act on the basis of national identification diminishes.

The relation between foreign economic linkages and attitudes toward domestic politics has been nicely illustrated in a recent paper on Brazilian entrepreneurs. It was found that entrepreneurs in firms dependent on foreign corporate support felt that the proper functioning of society required only an alliance of upper-class groups. Entrepreneurs in firms independent of foreign economic interests were much more likely to feel that salaried employees and wage workers should share in political power.[54]

This analysis implies that policies favoring foreign investors should rarely be found in conjunction with policies that stress a higher level of participation and effort from the populace. An impressionistic glance at less developed countries appears to confirm this hypothesis. Tanzania's choice of the policy of *kujitegemea* ("self-reliance") in 1967, for example, was spelled out in a two-pronged manner.[55] One prong was the nationalization of foreign-owned

52 T. B. Bottomore, *Elites and Society* (Baltimore, Md: Penguin Books, 1966), p. 108.

53 See, for example, Hugh H. Smythe and Mabel M. Smythe, *The New Nigerian Elite* (Stanford, Calif: Stanford University Press, 1960). J. E. Goldthorpe notes that Mackerere University graduates in East Africa often appeared as "indigenous expatriates" when they ventured into rural areas in *An African Elite: Mackerere College Students, 1922–1960* (East African Studies, No. 17) (Nairobi: Oxford University Press [for the East African Institute of Social Research], 1965).

54 Vilmar Faria, "Dependéncia e ideologia empresarial" (Paper presented at the Ninth Latin American Congress of Sociology, Mexico City, November 1969).

55 For further elaboration refer to the Arusha Declaration which may be found in Julius K. Nyerere, *Freedom and Socialism: Uhuru na Ujamaa—A Selection from Writings and Speeches* (New York: Oxford University Press, 1968), pp. 231–250.

investment; the other was an attempt to increase the economic and political participation of the people of the country by diminishing the distance between the people and their leaders and convincing them that it was only through their own cooperative efforts that the country would grow. A contrasting example is that of the military government which ascended to power in Brazil in 1964. It was successful in improving the climate for foreign investors but was suspicious to the point of paranoia of widespread political participation.[56]

If regimes can hope to mobilize either foreign investors or their own constituents but not both, then the alienation of the populace from its government must be counted as one of the "opportunity costs" of policies favoring foreign investors. This cost may be especially large in very poor countries in which agriculture is primitive and dominant and the low productivity of agricultural labor is a major concern.

A related argument revolves around the role of the state as a bargaining agent. It has already been noted that governments with little political independence, for example, colonies, were most likely to provide foreign investors with exorbitant returns. It was also observed that the prevalence of nationalist sentiments within a populace might be a useful resource to governments in bargaining with foreign investors. If economic dependency reduces political autonomy, then the very countries which have the largest amounts of foreign investment will be least likely to secure their fair share of the fruits of this investment. China in the nineteenth and early twentieth centuries might be considered a case in point.[57]

A determinate relation between economic dominance by foreign-owned firms and a particular combination of political strategies cannot be proven by a few examples. Nonetheless, the examples suggest that the predominance of foreign-owned firms has political consequences which, in turn, have implications for the future economic progress of a poor country. If a state's ability to mobilize the energies of its populace and to bargain effectively are considered economic assets, then penetration by multinational corporations must be considered an economic threat to the degree that it undermines political autonomy or increases the distance between the citizenry and its leaders.

VI. Consequences of Greater Autonomy

A range of arguments leads to the conclusion that the increased economic interconnectedness between rich and poor countries fostered by large corpora-

[56] See Octavio Ianni, *Crisis in Brazil,* trans. Phyllis B. Eveleth (New York: Columbia University Press, 1970), pp. 127–196.

[57] For a discussion of the problems of the Chinese elite see Barrington Moore, Jr., *Social Origins of Dictatorship and Democracy: Lord and Peasant in the Making of the Modern World* (Boston: Beacon Press, 1967), pp. 181–201. For a comparison of the experience of Japan with that of China see G. C. Allen and A. G. Donnithorne, *Western Enterprise in Far Eastern Economic Development: China and Japan* (London: George Allen & Unwin, 1954).

tions is not without negative consequences. Some of these arguments, for example, that multinational corporations inculcate an inappropriate set of consumer desires and promulgate unsuitable development theories, are not amenable to quantitative estimation. Other arguments—that less developed countries lose capital as a result of direct investment or that profit rates are excessive—are potentially subject to rigorous analysis though a great deal of work is yet to be done. Despite the need for more information and analysis it does not seem wise to assume that increased international interconnectedness via the multinational corporation automatically increases benefits to both rich and poor countries. Less developed countries cannot count on having their welfare maximized by relying on the unseen hand of economic interchange mediated through the organizational framework of the multinational corporation.

Rejection of reliance on foreign-owned firms almost inevitably leads to diminished reliance on private enterprise in general. Leaving industrialization in less developed countries to private enterprise is tantamount to leaving it in the hands of foreign enterprise. Individual entrepreneurs in less developed countries are rarely a match for their gigantic competitors.[58] More often they find that their self-interest demands playing a cooperative, subordinate role. Managing the subsidiary of a multinational corporation is usually a more attractive possibility than competing against it.

Weakness of the local entrepreneurial class forces countries in search of greater autonomy toward more socialist forms of economic organization. Emphasis on collective rather than individual decisionmaking increases. Much more initiative will be required of the state. Throughout the discussion the importance of the state as the only organization with sufficient leverage to bargain with the multinational corporation has been stressed. Far from being an anachronistic impediment, the state appears to be the only organization that citizens of a poor country might utilize to defend their interests.

Having decided to move in the direction of a more autonomous society in which the state is a major entrepreneur, the poor country is then faced with the knotty problem of creating a state whose actions and decisions reflect the interests and desires of the populace. In most poor countries the state is primarily the instrument of the elite. If increased national autonomy results only in the creation of more cumbersome, ineffective bureaucracies or in the

[58] For one example of the demise of local entrepreneurs see Eduardo Galeano, "The Denationalization of Brazilian Industry," *Monthly Review,* December 1969 (Vol. 21, No. 7), pp. 11–30. For more general discussion of the predominance of foreign capital in the case of Brazil see Mauricio Vinhas de Queiroz, "Os Grupos Multibillionarios," *Revista do Instituto de Ciencias Sociais,* January–December 1965 (Vol. 2, No. 1), pp. 44–80. Michael Kidron's work on India is illustrative in this regard; see his book, *Foreign Investment in India* (New York: Oxford University Press, 1965). An interesting case study may be found in the analysis of one of the largest Latin American firms (Industrias Reunidas F. Matarazzo) in "The Business Globe: Matarazzo—Not One Company but 300," *Fortune,* July 1960 (Vol. 62, No. 1), pp. 71–72, 77.

more effective domination of the local populace by a local elite, it is hardly a step forward. Presently constituted public bureaucracies are poor models. The building of efficient, responsive public organizations must become a primary goal for a poor country in quest of greater autonomy.

A poor country which rejects interconnectedness based on the multinational corporation must also find new means of relating itself to other countries. Autonomy does not mean autarky any more than "self-reliance" means "self-sufficiency."[59] The possibility of autarky would make the achievement of autonomy much easier, but autarky is not possible for any but the largest of the less developed countries. For most poor countries greater autonomy must mean increased control over external economic relations, not their absence. Arguments against the further strengthening of the ties that currently bind poor countries to developed countries should not be construed to imply the wisdom of isolation. One way for less developed countries to achieve increased control would be cooperating in areas in which they face similar problems, for example, coordination between poor countries exporting the same product.[60] Replacing a private, asymmetric type of integration with a more public, symmetric interconnectedness may offer the best hope of greater autonomy.

Moving toward greater autonomy is essentially choosing to orient economic decisions around the political constituency of the nation-state rather than to allow the locus of decisionmaking to gravitate toward private, profitmaking corporations based in rich countries. There is good reason to believe this policy is an economically rational choice, but it provides no ready-made solutions to the problems of poor countries. It is rather the selection of a new paradigm, a new framework in which to seek solutions.

[59] For a good discussion of the latter distinction see "After the Arusha Declaration," in Nyerere, pp. 385–409.

[60] The Organization of Petroleum Exporting Countries (OPEC) represents such an attempt, albeit, not an entirely successful one; see Tanzer, pp. 70–74.

Multinational Business and National Economic Goals

RAYMOND VERNON

THIS essay elaborates several basic propositions. First, the extraordinary changes in international communication and international transportation during the past 40 or 50 years have profoundly altered the horizons of business decisionmakers, giving enormous stimulus to the creation of multinational business enterprises. Second, in narrow economic terms the multinationalization of business activity has added to the efficiency of the world economy. Third, the advances in transportation and communication, reinforced by the existence of multinational business enterprises, have stimulated interaction between national economies and reduced the effectiveness of national controls, particularly in advanced countries. Finally, despite the increasing porosity of national boundaries these countries have been expanding and refining their national economic and social goals in ways that require more controls at national borders or more joint controls between cooperating states.[1]

The sense of exposure at national borders is not uniform in all countries. It is felt more acutely, for example, in countries whose culture emphasizes the need for control and in countries that have a history of national self-sufficiency. In addition, the sense of exposure is greater for countries that play host to the subsidiaries of multinational business enterprises than for countries —notably the United States—that are identified with the parent companies of such systems.

The sense of exposure has contributed to a mounting feeling of tension.

RAYMOND VERNON is Herbert F. Johnson Professor of International Business Management at the Graduate School of Business Administration, Harvard University, Boston, Massachusetts.

[1] This essay is a revised version of my testimony before the Subcommittee on Foreign Economic Policy of the Joint Economic Committee, *A Foreign Economic Policy for the 1970's, Hearings,* 91st Cong., 1st sess., December 4, 1969, pp. 139–152. The issues presented here are developed at greater length in my recent book, *Sovereignty at Bay: The Multinational Spread of U.S. Enterprise* (Harvard Multinational Enterprise Series) (New York: Basic Books, Publishers, 1971).

The tension seems likely to grow as long as nation-states fail to confront its causes. How can the United States and other countries respond to the situation in constructive terms, that is, in terms that respond to national goals while giving scope to the potential contributions of the multinational enterprise?

I. The Basic Propositions Elaborated

A multinational business enterprise can be thought of as a cluster of corporations of different nationalities that are joined together by a parent company through bonds of common ownership, that respond to a common strategy, and that draw on a common pool of financial and human resources. In comparison with the average business enterprise most structures of this type are very large. Most of them are established in industries that are oligopolistic in nature, ranging from oil and mining to automobiles and chemicals. Most of them—perhaps three out of four—are headed by parent companies located in the United States.

Entities of this type have grown at a very rapid rate since the beginning of the twentieth century. This sustained growth rate made them visible by the middle of the 1950s and conspicuous by the end of the 1960s. By that time, according to one estimate, about 15 percent of the $3 trillion total value of world production was produced through subsidiaries and branches of enterprises that were "foreign" to the countries in which they were located. Perhaps equally important is the fact that the multinational enterprises whose "foreign" activities accounted for this phenomenon were the leaders in their home economies as well. The 200 leading United States–based multinational enterprises, for example, were, quite apart from their overseas role, responsible for well over 30 percent of manufactured output in the United States.

As mentioned earlier the factors that have produced the rapid proliferation of multinational business enterprises include the astonishing improvements in the efficiency of transportation and communication. Associated with that development have been new capabilities for the rapid transmission of productive ideas. The increases in efficiency resulting from these developments have been primarily associated with large organizations.[2] Some of these efficiencies derive from the ability of large enterprises to invest giant sums in industrial innovation—for example, IBM has invested $2 or $3 billion in the development of third-generation computers. Some efficiencies derive from a capacity to create international logistic systems that are capable of operating specialized facilities at different production sites and of distributing components and materials for different markets. Some efficiencies are related simply to the heightened ability of the extended firm to transmit and reuse knowledge internally.

[2] This point is elaborated in my essay, "Organization as a Scale Factor in the Growth of Firms," in *Industrial Organization and Economic Development: In Honor of E. S. Mason*, ed. Jesse W. Markham and Gustav F. Papanek (Boston: Houghton Mifflin Co., 1970), pp. 47–66.

The ways in which the fruits of these advantages are shared vary according to time and place. There is a strong presumption, of course, that managers in multinational enterprises are enriched to some extent by the widening of their opportunities; the same presumption would probably exist with respect to the stockholders of these enterprises. Various studies also suggest that the economic impact of these enterprises on host countries is favorable. A portion of the increased global output is usually captured by host countries through improvements in the efficiency with which local production factors are used and by increases in tax receipts, wages, and profits. The classic exploitation models that are so commonly applied to describe the operations of foreign investors do not stand up very well under close examination, at least not for the period since World War II. Generalizations about the harmful effects of foreign investment on the balance of payments of host countries, about the creation of "immiserizing" growth, of "backwash" areas, and so on derive little support from serious studies of contemporary investment operations.[3]

On the other hand, it would be much too simple to say that everyone always benefits. Host countries that are not in a position to press hard for their share of the rewards or that are inept in exploiting their bargaining position fare less well than others that are better situated or more skilled. In addition, the introduction of new technology and new enterprise rarely fails to cause some adverse side effects. Entrepreneurs in less developed countries—especially entrepreneurs in traditional sectors—are sometimes hurt by the introduction of powerful foreign enterprises. Some workers in the country of the parent firm, notably labor in the United States, are adversely affected in the short term and medium term. But these are exceptions to the general proposition, not the stuff of which the proposition is made.

In general the relatively simpleminded notion that open borders increase opportunities for the efficient exploitation of the world's resources seems to stand up well under examination, as does the related proposition that the gains from such increased efficiencies are widely shared. The consequent increase in the porosity of national boundaries, however, has numerous consequences, many of them difficult for sovereign states to bear.

First of all, a few words on the overt manifestations of the trend toward open boundaries are in order. International trade has tended to grow during the past decade or two at an exceedingly rapid rate, even more rapidly than domestic trade in most countries. More important, perhaps, is the fact that the quality of that trade has shown dramatic changes. The relative importance of consumer goods has declined and that of industrial goods increased. More and more, countries are exchanging sophisticated specialties, based on some unique capacity that each of the trading partners has developed. In addition, the cases in which a manufacturing plant in one country has come to rely

[3] See, especially, Vernon, chapters 3 and 5.

on a regular flow of inputs from a source located in another country have increased in frequency.

Accompanying the increase in international trade has been an increase in the flow of important ideas and controlling tastes. There has been an exponential growth in the exchange of scientific information. At the same time international tastes have converged toward common norms. Skiers in New England and those in Gstaad now draw their equipment from a common pool of products—Japanese, Austrian, French, and American—all made to standardized specifications.

The openness of boundaries has been evident not only with regard to goods and ideas but also with respect to money. The gross flows of short-term and long-term funds across national borders are not well recorded in international statistics, but there is no doubt as to their trend. These flows, stimulated by the greatly increased ease of communication, have risen to unprecedented levels. At the same time new institutions such as the Eurodollar market and the Eurobond market have attested to the international fluidity of funds.

The result of the increased connections between national economies has been fairly dramatic. Price and growth trends in advanced countries have exhibited striking parallels, at least as compared to historical norms. The economic spectacle of the 1920s, when Germany suffered hyperinflation while the United Kingdom stagnated, is out of the question today. Money travels readily between advanced countries to markets where it is needed most. Industrial goods overleap the trivial trade barriers that still exist. Only pockets of high trade restrictions remain, for example, those applied to defense-related industries and to temperate-zone agricultural products.

Of course, all of these generalizations require elaboration and qualification. Japan, for example, has adopted all the consumptive norms and technologies of the West while trying to resist the forces that propel advanced economies toward mutual interdependence. Even in the case of Japan, however, accommodations to the trend have been increasing in scope and number. Less developed countries have tended on the whole to increase restrictions at their borders. But at the same time they have become increasingly aware of the advantages of drawing on the capital, technology, and markets of other countries.

The multinational business enterprise has played a significant role in these developments. Affiliates of a multinational enterprise, operating as either buyer or seller, are involved in about 50 percent of United States exports. Approximately 25 percent of United States exports are between such affiliates, and there are indications that the analogous measures for the United Kingdom are not much lower. Overseas subsidiaries under the control of United States parent companies hold assets of over $100 billion. About $3 or $4 billion flows out of the United States annually in connection with the expansion of these overseas subsidiaries, while $6 or $7 billion is returned by such subsidiaries in the form of profits, interests, royalties, and administrative charges.

The lopsided nature of the phenomenon of the multinational business enterprise—the fact that it is principally associated with United States industry—hardly needs documentation. Most large enterprises of this type, perhaps three out of four, are under the control of United States parent companies. Furthermore, leading United States companies associated with multinational operations, generally speaking, are about twice as large as European firms of a similar character. The phenomenon, therefore, is asymmetric. This asymmetry adds to the difficulties of constructive political response.

On the other hand, the common assumption that asymmetry will increase without limit has no factual basis. It is sometimes assumed that the phenomenon of the large multinational enterprise, if unchecked, will grow until it has absorbed most of the national industries of the advanced economies. It is easy to see why such a projection is popular. The advantages of big international business are considerable in some fields: in industries based on industrial innovation, in consumer industries with strong brand orientation, and in some industries that specialize in the processing of raw materials. What is less well recognized is that the advantages for multinational enterprises are far from universal. Such enterprises have no special advantages in more mature industries, such as steel or textiles or standard chemicals, nor can they be expected to remain strong in the raw material industries as these mature. The great bulk of business enterprises in most countries is likely to remain securely in national hands in the future just as it has in the past.

Still, with 10 or 12 percent of the national production of countries outside the United States lying in the ambit of United States–based enterprises, the possibility of tension remains high. It can be especially high for those countries that think of United States enterprise as an inseparable part of a coordinated political entity made up of United States industry and the United States government. The notion that overseas subsidiaries constitute an extended arm of United States hegemony seems altogether plausible to a considerable number of observers in both the United States and foreign countries.

But the facts themselves are much more complex. The United States government sometimes collaborates closely with its multinational enterprises as, for example, in the passage of the Hickenlooper amendment and the coordinated planning of oil distribution which accompanies each Suez crisis.[4] On the other hand, the United States government has frequently been at odds with its multinational enterprises—note, for example, its antitrust suits against the oil companies, the nonferrous metal producers, the pharmaceutical companies, and other leading entities in the multinational field; its imposition of restric-

[4] First Hickenlooper amendment to the *Foreign Assistance Act of 1961, United States Code,* Vol. 22, section 2370(e).

tions on the export of capital by United States parent companies; and its regulations limiting the transfer-pricing latitude of such companies. In general, relations between United States–based multinational enterprises and the United States government are much less intimate and less closely coordinated than those of any other major advanced country. An impersonal arm's-length quality pervades this relationship in the United States to a degree that would be intolerable for most other countries.

Despite that fact, however, other countries are bound to respond with a special sense of uneasiness to the presence of United States–based enterprises. Whenever the United States government seeks to extend its influence by means of its enterprises, as it has been known to do in the case of trading-with-the-enemy controls and antitrust policies, the affected countries are reminded of the great potential power and reach that the United States government represents. Occasional reminders of that power are sufficient to keep the uneasiness very much alive.

There has been a strong temptation on the part of all countries when confronting their needs and their concerns with regard to the operations of multinational enterprises to try to solve the dilemma on their own terms. Most countries are disposed to consider unilateral restrictions on trade or on capital investment whenever such restrictions seem a possible answer to their problems. Most, however, will go no further than considering such restrictions; having walked up to the possibility, they will walk away again. Fear of losing some useful outside resource—capital, technology, or markets—will usually put a damper on the strong urge to move ahead with restrictions on a unilateral basis. Many Canadians, for example, would like to restrict investment by United States enterprises. But at the same time they are fearful, justifiably fearful, that they would lose a vital element of their national economic life if they did so. Some Canadians are also afraid—again with some solid basis for their fear—that the United States might retaliate, especially by terminating the preferential status that Canada usually demands and receives whenever the United States imposes restrictive regulations on the foreign transactions of its nationals. So Canada is likely not to act or, if it does act, to do so with special caution.

The same is true of France, Japan, or Mexico, even of Chile and Peru. Having identified national goals on which they place high value, all would like to interpose some barrier on the movement of goods, money, or people across their borders. Yet, all of these countries want capital, technology, and access to markets, and they are fearful of their loss through the imposition of such restrictions. That fear inhibits the unilateral actions toward which their desires push them.

One could say at this point that perhaps it is just as well. After all, any country within a community of nation-states ought to accept the common discipline that applies to members of the community. This might well be both an equitable and practicable response were it not for the dominance of the United States in the economic affairs of the non-Communist world. As other countries see it, the United States is relatively invulnerable to the problems of international economic interdependence. Its enterprises have unequivocably gained the most from the era of open boundaries. Yet, the United States stands to lose the least if it should decide to cut those ties. If the United States feels that its balance-of-payments position is imperiled, it can unhesitatingly restrict capital export; if it feels that copper is in short supply, it can restrict the export of that product. Unlike other countries the United States can place restrictions at its borders without real concern that retaliation would seriously hurt its economy.

It is possible that if the United States refuses to recognize this basic problem of the inequality of nation-states, the problem will eventually recede. Other countries, unwilling to bear the cost of doing anything else, will accept the full impact of United States enterprises and United States government measures in their jurisdictions. There is a considerable likelihood, however, that they will not. Goaded by a sense of being overwhelmed, of losing mastery in their own household, they will strike out from time to time to reassert their identity and independence. The challenge for the political scientist is to find the means to help accommodate these conflicting needs.

II. An Approach to Policy

Over the past 25 years the United States has led the advanced countries of the non-Communist world in an extraordinary series of steps that have enlarged the flow of international trade and capital. The work of the International Monetary Fund (IMF) and the General Agreement on Tariffs and Trade (GATT), abetted by United States initiative, has been almost phenomenally successful in opening up the national economies of the more advanced countries to one another. Restrictive measures, imposed by countries in an effort to deal with their trade and payments problems, have been exceptions to the general trend. The advanced countries cannot go much further in the elimination of barriers to international trade and payments, however, without taking several new giant steps in the coordination of national economic policies. Otherwise, they run the risk of being pulled up short by piecemeal national restrictions.

However, the coordination of national policy involves sensitive issues of sovereignty. All one can suggest at this stage is a start in the appropriate direction, choosing those courses of action that have at least an outside chance of success. Using the criteria of feasibility and relevance, there are a series of interrelated measures that could be undertaken. Some would be applicable only to advanced countries, while others might eventually be extensible to relations with less developed countries.

A course of action appropriate for advanced countries would include several distinct but related measures. First, it would require the joint development of a series of commitments which would impose limits on the jurisdictional reach of each country into the territory of others. Second, it would involve the coordination of national policy in selected fields, namely, in those fields in which the agreed curtailment of jurisdiction may seem to expose any of the countries concerned to the possibility of national injury from the others. Third, it would require a sorting out of national identities. Finally, it would demand that national power and national jurisdiction be pooled in a few carefully selected fields.

Limiting National Jurisdiction

There are a number of areas in which advanced countries might conceivably agree to limit their efforts to reach into the jurisdiction of other states as they pursue their respective national objectives. One of these areas is capital movement. Now that multinational enterprises lace the world's economies, controls over capital exports by any country have a new meaning for all the others. Such controls affect not only the flow of money across international boundaries but also the very existence of operating enterprises in the territories of other countries.

An international agreement between advanced countries not to restrict the export of capital from parent company to subsidiary seems quite feasible.[5] To be sure, it would probably have to be qualified by the exceptions familiarized by GATT and the IMF, for example, those for balance-of-payments difficulties and issues of national defense. It would also have to provide for some kind of complaint and adjudication procedure. But such initiatives lie well within the experience and capabilities of advanced countries.

There is another area, however, in which international precedents are less promising. By threatening a United States parent or affiliate company with sanctions the United States government is often in a position to compel a subsidiary in another country to respond to United States law or policy. The United States government has done this from time to time in the areas of antitrust and trading-with-the-enemy legislation, securities regulation, and the regulation of capital flows across international boundaries.

These steps are not taken by the United States government capriciously or without cause; often, significant United States interests are involved. Nor are these steps taken without a certain amount of hesitation. Indeed, sometimes

[5] For a more general proposal of this nature see Paul M. Goldberg and Charles P. Kindleberger, "Toward a GATT for Investment: A Proposal for Supervision of the International Corporation," *Law and Policy in International Business,* Summer 1970 (Vol. 2, No. 2), pp. 295–325.

they are modified or deferred altogether in recognition of the sense of national outrage and national violation that such measures generally invoke in other countries. But even when they are deferred, the latent power of the United States leaves other countries with a feeling of exposure that is still very marked.

In the areas just enumerated and perhaps in others one could envisage a series of agreements—probably in treaty form—by which the signatories would undertake not to use their sovereign power over the parent firms under their jurisdiction in order to influence the behavior of subsidiaries located in the jurisdictions of the others. This would represent a major extension of a trend already embodied in a few informal executive agreements in organizations like the Organisation for Economic Co-operation and Development (OECD) and with selected countries like Canada.

Coordinating National Policy

It would be indispensable, however, to link such a set of commitments to a second set: an undertaking on the part of advanced countries to engage in continuous coordination of national policies in the areas in which they have limited their jurisdictional reach. The United States could hardly be expected to stay its hand if it thought that the foreign subsidiaries of its national firms were overtly engaged in a series of actions that seemed to threaten the country's vital interests nor would any other country be expected to exercise similar restraint. The keynote of such coordination, of course, would have to be compromise. But past experience with international coordinating mechanisms, such as GATT and the IMF, suggests that national views need not be identical in order to maintain some tolerable degree of coordination and harmonization. It would be a great deal easier for any country to accept the differences in national policies if it thought that there was a mechanism for working out the problems associated with these differences.

Some serious thought should also be given to the reconciliation of the impact of national tax laws on the taxation of income generated by multinational enterprises. With the growing strength and reach of such enterprises and with the increasing capacity of management coordination from the center it is becoming more and more artificial and arbitrary to separate out the profit seemingly generated by the subsidiaries in each taxing jurisdiction as if the profit were organically distinguishable from that generated in other jurisdictions. In reality the profits are often the consequence of the collective efficiency and vitality of the interrelated companies that comprise the enterprise as a whole. The situation, in short, is gradually moving toward that encountered inside the United States in which each state tries to tax a large national corporation and its subsidiaries operating inside the state. This policy might well suggest a possible approach to embody in an international treaty:

a formula that arbitrarily allocates the aggregate profit of the collective entity to the jurisdictions in which it does business. This approach could be applied eclectically at first, that is, to a class of enterprises whose interests were genuinely divided between different countries and to a group of countries capable of effective collaboration in developing a modus vivendi.

The principles involved in this type of tax regime, whether applied selectively or otherwise, would be revolutionary in their implications. At present, profits generated by the subsidiaries of United States parent companies are generally not taxed until they are returned to the parent in the form of dividends. The suggested approach would look upon such profits as taxable when earned by the subsidiary. But a change of this dimension might be regarded as infeasible. If that proved to be the case, there is another possible approach involving international agreement and collaboration. This alternative would seek to develop a set of ground rules for international agreement concerning the most sensitive and contentious aspects of the taxation of the profits earned by entities making up a multinational enterprise. These ground rules would cover such subjects as the fixing of transfer prices, the use of debt in lieu of equity, the allocation of central office charges, and other such issues that promise to be at the center of future tax disputes.

Sorting Out Nationality

There is still a third measure that is inseparable from the rest of those proposed here. If it is useful for the countries concerned to commit themselves to the limitation and coordination of their jurisdiction over distant subsidiaries, it is no less important that the subsidiaries should be placed in a position that makes them bona fide nationals in the countries which gave them their juridical existence and their corporate personality. There is much to be said for the revival and rehabilitation of the much maligned and much abused Calvo Doctrine—the principle that foreign-owned subsidiaries should be foreclosed from appealing to the diplomatic support of the governments of their parent companies on pain of losing their rights as nationals. The principle, however, should be carried to its logical conclusion. At the same time that subsidiaries are obliged to give up their right to appeal for help through their parent companies, they must be granted guarantees of national treatment by the countries that have given them corporate life.

Those who are on the firing line in the business world feel uneasy about such a proposal. It cannot be said that this is wholly unjustified. "National treatment" under most systems of national law represents no guarantee against arbitrary discrimination. The concept that all business enterprises similarly situated are entitled to the same treatment under law is a concept that is confined to very few countries. In most instances the right of the sovereign to discriminate in favor of chosen instruments is well established and well accepted. It may be, therefore, that explicit guarantees of national treatment would be less useful for foreign-owned subsidiaries than guarantees of certain explicit minimum rights.

But foreign-owned subsidiaries cannot forever claim both national treatment and foreign protection. They may have to give up some of the advantages of being foreign to retain some of the advantages of being national. Certain of those latter advantages are already being lost. Foreign-owned subsidiaries are rapidly being placed in the status of second-class nationals in the countries in which they are operating. Discrimination against them is practiced all over the world with regard to credit access, governmental procurement, the granting of import licenses, and many other subjects. That tendency will grow stronger, not weaker. As regional organizations such as the European Economic Community (EEC) and the Latin American Free Trade Association (LAFTA) expand their activities into the area of business regulation, the tendency may extend to those institutions as well.

Adjudication and Enforcement

The steps just outlined could not be pushed very far, however, unless the countries concerned agreed at the same time to establish tribunals empowered to receive and adjudicate the disputes that would inevitably be generated from time to time as the result of the agreements contemplated. Like the Court of Justice of the European Communities such a tribunal would have to be empowered with jurisdiction in complaints not only of member states but also of foreign-owned subsidiaries.

One group of complaints could be expected to come from signatory states charging from time to time that other states were still seeking to influence the actions of subsidiaries by way of the parent firms in their jurisdiction. Another group of complaints could come from the subsidiaries themselves seeking to enforce their right to national treatment or its equivalent.

Alternatives for Advanced Countries

As multinational business enterprises link the economies of advanced countries more firmly, the imperfect harmonization of national policies that affect their operations will take on increasing importance. The problem is likely to arise not only for policies immediately related to the enterprises themselves, such as corporate taxation, but also for policies that affect enterprises less directly. There are limits to the utility of defining at this stage the areas in which advanced countries should start to coordinate their national policies. Too much speculation too early could put the general approach in a straitjacket. In addition to the policy areas suggested thus far, there is also the possibility of progress in a number of others.

For example, without benefit of a treaty, states have been learning to coordinate some aspects of their national monetary and fiscal policies. Changes in the value of national currencies take place with more international discussion or more careful national calculation of the external consequences than ever before.[6] Coordination in this field is almost bound to increase within the EEC. Despite a widely held assumption to the contrary developments within the EEC may make it easier to press for greater transatlantic coordination at the same time.

Agricultural policy represents still another area in which national coordination may prove possible. Such coordination was suggested to the EEC by the United States government in past years, but it received little enthusiasm or follow-up. It may be that the EEC was not ready for the proposal when it was made, but this attitude may change as the costs of the present autarchic agricultural policy begin to be driven home in Europe.

There are various other areas which invite speculation regarding the possibilities of future cooperation between advanced countries: measures to implement the various agreements of the Kennedy Round of tariff negotiations and to contain the unrelenting pressures toward national protectionism, measures to institute and extend the role of special drawing rights (SDRs) in international payments, and so on. Cooperation between advanced countries in areas such as these is of utmost importance and is likely to continue. More uncertain is the possibility of launching fresh policies that would reduce the tensions between the United States and less developed countries.

Less Developed Countries

There is not much the United States can do over the next decade to lower the level of tension that multinational business enterprises generate in less developed countries. That tension is a by-product of the rapid change that is going on inside most of these economies. If the objective performance of United States–based enterprises had anything to do with the level of tension that their presence generates, that level would be declining rather than increasing. Subsidiaries of United States–based enterprises have provided the main channel for the expansion of exports of manufactured goods from Latin America in recent years. Through these enterprises Latin American governments now acquire about 70 percent of the profits from the sale of their raw materials abroad. It is conceivable that more foreign aid, more foreign markets, or more foreign investment would reduce tension a little, but not significantly. Indeed, as the case of Libya suggests, the effect of increased economic well-being in many of these countries could well be to raise tensions in the short run, not lower them.

[6] A striking exception to this general trend was the United States government decision in August 1971 to break the tie between the United States dollar and gold. That step could conceivably set back the trend described in the text for some time.

The United States would, however, find it easier to manage those tensions if its ties to United States parent companies were less explicit and direct. This would mean, among other things, the abandonment of the approach epitomized by the Hickenlooper amendment, that is, the abandonment of the practice of tying foreign aid to the equitable treatment of foreign investors. It could mean United States acceptance of the Calvo Doctrine in countries that were willing to grant national treatment to the subsidiaries of United States companies and were willing to submit to the jurisdiction of an international tribunal. It would certainly mean a greater emphasis on multilateral aid instrumentalities and less use of bilateral aid programs, a trend already in evidence.

In addition to its efforts to achieve a lower profile, the United States has the opportunity to provide wider markets for less developed countries. The United States has been laggard in implementing the generalized tariff preferences advocated by the United Nations Conference on Trade and Development (UNCTAD). Even though other obstacles to export expansion, especially the complacent and risk-avoiding approach of locally owned enterprises, private or public, are more important, the political and psychic symbolism of the preference proposal is now so strong that it has a significance distinct from its economic and business implications.

III. Conclusion

More important than any of the individual proposals in this essay is the basic point that underlies most of them. We are at a moment in history in which increased economic interdependence among advanced countries looks close to inevitable. But it is a lopsided interdependence, one in which the United States is seen as gaining most from the continuation of the trend and losing least from its interruption. From a political and psychological point of view that is a dangerous situation. If the tension that the situation generates is to be mitigated, it will be by action that comes hard to the nation-state: curbing the full exercise of the overwhelming economic power of the United States and pooling that power with others. That type of action will take wisdom and restraint of a kind that is rare in history.

Transnational Relations as a Threat to the Democratic Process

Karl Kaiser

Transnational relations and other multinational processes seriously threaten democratic control of foreign policy, particularly in advanced industrial societies.[1] The intermeshing of decisionmaking across national frontiers and the growing multinationalization of formerly domestic issues are inherently incompatible with the traditional framework of democratic control. The threat is all the more serious because it is sustained not by enemies of democracy but unknowingly by people who consider themselves to be acting within Western democratic traditions and because it results in part from the very forces of internationalism, interdependence, and economic advancement that have come to be regarded as indispensable. The consequences of these developments and the ongoing erosion of control over military and foreign policy, dramatically demonstrated by the debate on the Vietnam War, amount to a fundamental challenge to the democratic structure of Western societies. This essay analyzes the threat of transnational relations by reexamining the arguments for limited democratic control of foreign policy in light of recent structural changes in world politics and the consequences of transnational relations for the democratic process and its institutions. It concludes by indicating some approaches that could strengthen the democratic dimension which is being eroded.

I. Limited Democratic Control of Foreign Policy

A democratic foreign policy is a foreign policy which is legitimated by reflecting the consensus and seeking the consent of the majority of a country's

Karl Kaiser is professor of political science and director of the Institute for Political Science at the University of the Saarland, Saarbrücken, West Germany.

[1] This is a revised and shortened version of my essay, "Das internationale System der Gegenwart als Faktor der Beeinträchtigung demokratischer Aussenpolitik," which appeared in *Politische Vierteljahresschrift,* 1970 (Special Issue No. 2), pp. 340–358.

citizens. Legitimacy is therefore created by a public process of interaction in which legislatures, interest groups, and the public effectively control the activities of those institutions that act in the name of the country and commit the polity as a whole.[2]

Foreign policy has traditionally been assigned a special place in democratic states. Alexis de Tocqueville's observation that a democracy lacks the very qualities necessary to be effective in foreign policy has influenced and reflected thinking on this problem. It has often been concluded that foreign policy is an area in which democratic control should be applied only to a limited extent.

Two main arguments have been advanced to justify the partial removal of foreign policy from democratic control, and both make certain assumptions about the international system. The first argument centers on the structure of decisionmaking. Only the executive, it is maintained, possesses the information necessary to make decisions in foreign policy. Furthermore, many activities in this field involve negotiation, and democratic participation in the form of public discussions and parliamentary statements or pressure could weaken the negotiating position of a foreign minister and thereby hurt the national interest. In this case negotiations should be scrutinized only after they have been concluded.

The second argument refers to the object of foreign policy. It suggests that since foreign policy deals with matters of military security, survival, national interest, and rank and prestige, it should be subjected only to limited pressures from public opinion or parliaments. Parliaments and the public are said to change their opinions erratically and irrationally and to be generally incapable of fast action. As one of the great skeptics of the possibility of democratically controlled foreign policy has written: "Every democrat feels in his bones that dangerous crises are incompatible with democracy, because he knows that the inertia of masses is such that to act quickly a very few must decide and the rest follow rather blindly."[3]

As a point of departure this essay uses the traditional distinction between foreign policy and domestic politics formulated by democratic theory. As the two policy areas merge, however, this distinction becomes increasingly inadequate, and it is necessary to point out some important consequences for the democratic control of policy. Whether or not one accepts the traditional assertion that foreign policy should be partially removed from democratic control, one still needs to be concerned with the implications of transnational relations for the democratic process.

[2] The terms "legislature" and "executive" are used in this essay in full awareness that they are problematic. They are related to the doctrine of separation of powers which, as elaborated later, is less and less valid under modern conditions, particularly in Europe. Nor are the terms "parliament" and "government" quite satisfactory in an essay that deals with democratic systems in general since the former does not apply to the United States and the latter has a different meaning in American and English usage.

[3] Walter Lippmann, *Public Opinion* (New York: Free Press, 1966), p. 172.

II. Structural Change in Decisionmaking: Multinational Politics

Transnational relations have brought about important changes in the decisionmaking structure of world politics. The theoretical framework of transnational relations elaborated by the editors of this volume corresponds approximately to that of multinational politics which I have developed in greater detail elsewhere.[4] This essay can only summarize the major characteristics of multinational politics and refer to some of its particularly relevant dimensions.

Processes which cannot be assigned unequivocally to politics *between* states and in which *states* are not the sole actors are growing in importance in world politics. These processes can be subsumed under the ideal type of "multinational politics." Within multinational politics bureaucracies allocate values either jointly in decisionmaking frameworks that are intermeshed across national frontiers or separately as a result of transnational interaction at the societal level. Three forms of multinational politics can be distinguished.

In the first form, *multibureaucratic decisionmaking,* the decisionmaking structures of different national governmental and international bureaucracies intermesh within specific issue areas for the allocation of values. The relationship between an aid-receiving country and an aid-giving country or international organization is illustrative of this form of multinational politics. A governmental bureaucracy participates in the decisionmaking process of a less developed country within specific issue areas. Participation can take various forms ranging from joint planning to the common execution of programs, occasionally drawing personnel from both countries. Such a process cannot be analyzed or explained by concepts of domestic politics because an "outsider" participates whose role and behavior are determined by a variety of domestic and foreign policy considerations. Conversely, traditional concepts of international relations are equally inadequate because the objects of decisionmaking are typically "domestic" issues like education and social or economic programs. There are numerous examples of multibureaucratic decisionmaking, in particular, joint technical projects like the Concorde between France and the United Kingdom, the gas centrifuge involving the Federal Republic of Germany (West Germany), the Netherlands, and the United Kingdom, the European "airbus," and the development of a European rocket within the European Space Vehicle Launcher Development Organization (ELDO). Similarly, one can point to the manifold forms of decisionmaking within the North Atlantic Treaty Organization (NATO). The intergovernmental character of NATO, with its unanimity rule and the resulting claim that national sovereignty is maintained, diverts attention from the fact that national bureaucracies from several countries jointly allocate major resources in a process of

[4] See Karl Kaiser, "Transnationale Politik: Zu einer Theorie der multinationalen Politik," *Politische Vierteljahresschrift,* 1969 (Special Issue No. 1), pp. 80–110. A revised English version will appear in *International Organization,* Autumn 1971 (Vol. 25, No. 4), forthcoming.

negotiation and mutual adjustment, most of which is concealed from the public.

Transnational politics, the second form of multinational politics, consists of political processes between national governments that have been set in motion by transnational relations. Transnational politics presupposes transnational relations (or transnational society) within specific issue areas in which relatively unrestricted interaction can occur between actors in the societies of various nation-states—currency exchange, movement of capital, persons, ideas, etc. The free movement of investment capital, for example, ties together different societies. Decisions made by relatively autonomous nongovernmental actors within such issue areas affect the decisionmaking context of governments, limit their maneuverability, and induce them to take measures vis-à-vis their own society or other governments.

Transnational politics presupposes a high degree of horizontal interaction between national systems and is therefore a particularly modern phenomenon. It arises from progress in areas like transportation and communication, from the development of advanced industrial society with its expansion of social interaction beyond national boundaries, and from the growing multinational welfare of an emerging system of interdependent states. But transnational politics also presupposes vertical interaction between society and government, an interaction which grows with the degree of democratization and the extent to which the regularized intervention in the social and economic life of society becomes a constituent element of the political system. Not even a high degree of horizontal interaction can lead to transnational politics unless there is vertical interaction. The laissez faire state would hardly be affected by disturbances in its own society resulting from transnational relations, although a modern welfare state or a socialist state would.

Governments reacting to disturbances in their societies created by transnational relations in the field of currency movement, for example, have jurisdiction over only a fraction of the problem which permeates several systems simultaneously. Theoretically, they have two options. They can, on the one hand, cut their links with the outside world and restrict or halt transnational relations in a given issue area. However, the social and political costs of this option are high for it implies a radical change of the system and its relationship to the environment. On the other hand, governments can coordinate policies with the other governments affected, possibly by involving international organizations. In the area of currency movement, for example, one finds elements of both options in various mixes; the result is a complex series of interactions between ministries of finance, economics, and foreign affairs, central banks, international organizations, and major transnational actors such as large banks.

In the third form of multinational politics, *multinational integration* between states, the preparation, formulation, and implementation of political decisions shift from an exclusively national to a joint, multinational framework on a regional basis in which governments, societal actors, and, if necessary, international organizations participate. This is a dynamic process in which the participants aim to further increase joint decisionmaking and interaction. Integration therefore combines the intergovernmental relationship of multibureaucratic decisionmaking and the interaction of governmental bureaucracies and transnational actors in transnational politics. For example, in the agricultural sector of the European Economic Community (EEC) decisions are made within a complex system in which national bureaucracies, the Commission of the European Communities, the Social and Economic Committee, the Council of Ministers, the Committee of Permanent Representatives, the standing committees, and the agricultural interest groups participate. Many combinations of interaction and coalition are possible, following or cutting across national borders. Less than one-third of all decisions of the West German Ministry of Agriculture can be made in a purely national context; the rest are made within the decisionmaking framework of the EEC.

No doubt, these types of transnational relations (to shift from the terminology of multinational politics to that used in this volume) are in most cases of greater relative importance to Western Europe and other non-Communist areas than to the United States. In fact, the United States is not involved at all in one of them, namely, integration. Nevertheless, the United States does participate in forms of multibureaucratic decisionmaking and is politically affected by transnational interaction, although from a position of greater power than any of the other countries.[5]

Two aspects of transnational relations are particularly relevant to the problem of democratic control. Activities of transnational actors, such as large banks or multinational corporations, which can be of crucial importance to the national systems may bypass governmental institutions. Second, systems of decisionmaking and allocation of values exist which cut across frontiers and intermesh different national and international bureaucracies. Since our existing systems of democratic control are organized along national lines, transnational relations are bound to raise some intriguing questions for the future of democratic control.

III. The Objects of Foreign Policy and Democratic Control

The contemporary international system of muted bipolarity based on nuclear deterrence has two contradictory consequences for the democratic control

[5] The relevance of transnational relations to the United Kingdom and West Germany has been examined in my essay, "Interdependence and Autonomy: Britain and the Federal Republic in their Multinational Environment," in *Britain and Germany: Changing Societies and the Future of Foreign Policy*, ed. Karl Kaiser and Roger Morgan (London: Oxford University Press, 1971), pp. 17–40.

of foreign policy. On the one hand, it restricts the possibility of democratic participation to an unprecedented degree in times of crisis: Under nuclear conditions the old rule that crisis is the hour of the executive applies more than ever. On the other hand, the contemporary international system with its nuclear stalemate has not only decreased the relevance of force as an instrument of foreign policy but has also reduced, at least for all developed states except the superpowers, the relative importance of "traditional" dimensions of foreign policy such as survival, security, and defense which in the past have been at the root of restrictions of democratic control of foreign policy.

As other essays in this volume explain in greater detail, the emergence of a multinational system of interdependent welfare states and of growing transnational relations increases the relevance of social, cultural, technological, and economic factors in the external relations of advanced industrial societies in the non-Communist world. As a result the "traditional" security dimension of foreign policy has less relative importance in day-to-day affairs, although survival remains, of course, axiomatic for all states.

These developments appear to present two options for democratic control. First, even according to the most orthodox interpretation the area of foreign policy which can be democratized expands, in particular, the economic and technical areas. Consequently, the established procedures of democratic control could be applied in these sectors. But a second possibility also exists. These areas, which traditionally belong to domestic politics, could be transferred to the realm of foreign policy in which restricted democratic control is justified by the allegedly special rules of security, national interest, and prestige. In a number of new and "nontraditional" areas one can identify such a trend, for example, in science, monetary relations, or development aid. Due to the comparatively more active role of the United States Congress in controlling the executive such examples are drawn primarily from Europe. West Germany, for example, has used most of its development aid as a means to prevent the recognition of the German Democratic Republic (East Germany), while France has used its aid to preserve its influence in its former colonies. For both countries aid policy was relegated to the foreign policy area with restricted democratic control. Science policy, particularly in the new fields of electronics, basic nuclear research, and outer space, is an area in which European governments indulge in animated competition that is barely controlled by their parliaments.

With the increasing relevance of transnational relations and of the "nontraditional" areas in foreign policy, foreign ministries, notably in medium and small powers, are losing their traditional monopoly over the regulation of the external affairs of their countries. Two forces are encroaching on that role. First, "technical" ministries concerned with science, the economy, or finance are assuming growing importance in external affairs. For example, in 1969 the West German Federal Ministry of Education and Science was involved in a number of multinational organizations—e.g., the European Atomic Energy Community (Euratom) and the European Space Research Organization (ESRO)—and in a number of multinational activities—building a gas centrifuge for fissile material (with the Netherlands and the United Kingdom), the West German satellite *Azur* (in cooperation with a number of European countries), and the development of a European rocket (within ELDO). Even a "domestic" agency like the Federal Ministry of the Interior is the partner of corresponding ministries in France or the Netherlands in, for example, regional planning.[6] In several fields, notably atomic industry and agriculture, the respective technical ministries have become the foreign ministries of their respective sectors.

Transnational organizations, particularly multinational corporations which often conduct their own foreign policy, are a second force that encroaches on the foreign ministries' role as sole regulators of external relations. While in many cases multinational corporations conform to the policies of their parent country or host countries, their margin of autonomy is considerable. Such autonomy is essential in a market economy, but the activities of such actors can be of considerable importance to a country, depending on the size of the home and host countries and on the size and activities of the multinational corporation. For example, the foreign activities of petroleum companies can take place without much supervision, although the home country has to bear the consequences of their behavior abroad and any ensuing effect on the supply and prices of petroleum.[7]

This variety of semiautonomous societal actors and "technical" ministries increasingly conducting the external relations of their polities indicates that discussions of democratic foreign policy which posit a single "executive" formulating foreign policy as a reaction to demands from "outside" (other such "executives") and from "below" (the democratic base) are obsolete. Reality is much more complex. Attempts to democratize foreign policy do not necessarily have an obvious institution, such as a foreign office or a chancellery, as their object. A critical review of the democratic dimension of foreign policy would have to include other "technical" ministries as well. The shift of foreign policy to these "technical" ministries in which national security cannot readily be used as an argument against democratization opens the door to expanded democratic control. The situation is less clear with regard to transnational organizations. With an increasing percentage of transnational activities bypass-

[6] *Jahresbericht der Bundesregierung 1968* (Bonn: Deutscher Bundesverlag [for the Presse- und Informationsamt der Bundesregierung], 1969), pp. 92–126, 525–554.

[7] On these questions see Raymond Vernon, *Multinational Enterprise and National Security* (Adelphi Papers, No. 74) (London: Institute for Strategic Studies, January 1971).

ing democratically controlled national institutions and possibly affecting the polity as a whole one must ask whether they too should not be subject to some form of control.

The shift of political weight from legislatures to executives and bureaucracies and the ensuing weakening of democratic control are typical of those advanced industrial societies that have become interventionist welfare states. The international system within the non-Communist world is therefore changing in two ways: first, as a result of domestic developments which have common roots in certain evolutionary tendencies of modern capitalism and, second, as a result of the increasing multinationalization of the functions of the modern welfare state. This multinationalization expresses itself through a growing number of interconnections between societies and various forms of cooperation between governments. The loss of power of parliaments in many Western countries is aggravated by the multinational connections with the environment, although this process has not gone as far in the United States as it has in other countries. Section IV examines the consequences of these multinational connections for the democratic process more closely.

IV. The Decisionmaking Structure and Democratic Control

The intermeshing of decisionmaking across national frontiers characteristic of the interdependent world of multinational politics is of crucial importance to the question of democratic control of foreign policy because the *object* of democratic control and the *location* of that object are becoming increasingly unclear in these decisionmaking structures. In trying to establish a chain of responsibility for an agricultural decree within the EEC, for example, one would have to point to a variety of national and multinational actors which may participate in its formulation. In joint ventures like technical projects or weapons development one can observe a number of governmental bureaucracies participating in joint decisionmaking. Similarly, one can find additional examples from other areas of transnational politics.

In trying to control the results of the intermeshing of decisionmaking parliaments can cancel each other out. Agreements are developed in a complicated multinational process of negotiation and compromise. Because of the interpretation of sovereignty and the rights of national parliaments which prevails in Western democracies a parliament can call to account only its own national government. But each government is at least partially able to escape its responsibility to its parliament by pointing to the involvement of other governments and to their shared responsibility for common measures. The "sovereign right" of parliament to change such an agreement or to stop its implementation is, in fact, mainly theoretical because of the costs that such actions might entail. A carefully balanced compromise could collapse, the political atmosphere could be jeopardized, or resources could be wasted.

The executive can also use the complexity and special rules of multinational decisionmaking to block undesired intrusions by parliament or public opinion prior to the conclusion of an agreement. Under established custom it is relatively easy for the executive to suggest that such negotiations must be treated confidentially until they are concluded and that the involvement of other governments imposes particular restraints on the disclosure of their content or state of progress.

However, democratic control might suffer from multinational decisionmaking even if the executive thoroughly intends to submit its activities to such control. Within an area as relevant to the political and economic wellbeing of Western countries as that of monetary matters important and often dramatic developments take place outside parliamentary influence or without public opinion being sufficiently informed. It could be argued that the system of interaction is so complicated that even executive leaders no longer comprehend the forces and processes at work, let alone master them.

As the number and activities of international organizations expand, an area grows in which major decisions are made without much democratic control by the peoples and institutions which are affected or which support these activities financially. In the field of development aid, for example, decisions by the International Bank for Reconstruction and Development (IBRD) or other multinational aid organizations determine the fate of millions, selecting the human beings to be saved from likely starvation or death through disease, choosing the country, industry, region, social group, and political regime to be supported. In many cases there is no feedback to the democratic base of the recipient or donor countries. The same applies to many other functional international organizations, although their activities may not be as dramatically important as the examples just mentioned.

Almost all of these international organizations are intergovernmental, and their decisions are based on unanimity. For this reason it is possible to argue that national sovereignty is not impaired and that national governments, and through them the parliaments by which they are theoretically controlled, exercise control over these institutions. But control is not applied to a large sector of their activities in which the international bureaucracy enjoys considerable leeway. While in some cases a legislature can try to exercise influence through its appropriation process, its possibilities are limited. Unlike the United States Congress, European parliaments have barely tried to exert such influence. The officials of these international organizations cannot be called on to testify before the legislature nor can their records be requested or specific programs and policies influenced. Legislatures are therefore completely dependent on publicly available information or the material which the executive provides. Even in those areas in which governments do in fact try to exercise control the multinational character of decisionmaking makes their links with the national mechanisms of democratic control ineffective. In all cases of multibureaucratic decisionmaking which involve governments and international organizations the assertion that national sovereignty is maintained through the unanimity rule has become an effective facade that conceals the ongoing erosion of democratic control over increasingly important matters.

The loss of parliamentary influence is even more obvious when supranational organizations, for example, the European Communities, are involved. Due to the limited prerogatives of the European Parliament and the inefficacy of the efforts of national parliaments to assert themselves in European affairs many activities of the Commission of the European Communities are de facto removed from democratic control.[8] It becomes difficult to locate responsibility and to apply democratic control when governments reach decisions by unanimity and more difficult still when decisions are made by majority vote.

As the welfare of advanced industrial societies is increasingly based on multinational involvement and links between societies and governmental bureaucracies, democratic control may be weakened either by the tendency to apply the special rule of foreign policy or by the inherent difficulties of controlling multinational decisionmaking as it constantly expands. Interdependence, internationalism, economic advancement, scientific and technical progress—forces we generally welcome and endorse—simultaneously undermine the democratic process. Under these circumstances how can democratic control be strengthened?

V. Strengthening Democratic Control

The ongoing erosion of the democratic process makes a discussion of the possibilities of strengthening democratic control imperative. There is a striking absence of concern about the implications of the evolving forms of multinational politics for the democratic process. The lively debate on the future of our democratic institutions that takes place on both sides of the Atlantic Ocean neglects this dimension. Only in the field of European integration has the remoteness of European bureaucracy from the weak European Parliament and national parliaments been criticized. The lack of systematic work in this field does not allow for more than a few preliminary remarks and examples, drawn primarily from Western Europe.

[8] Thus far attempts to strengthen the European Parliament, among them efforts to introduce direct election of European parliamentarians, have failed. Walter Hallstein's attempt to increase the parliament's budgetary prerogatives in 1965 resulted in the French boycott of the institution.

What is gained by a reduction of the democratic control of areas affected by transnational relations? To a considerable extent the answer is the ability to negotiate effectively, to clearly formulate and to enter into commitments, and to react quickly to a changing environment. In terms of the central role of legislatures, enhancing democratic participation without losing these advantages is difficult to imagine given the complex system of interdependence among welfare states and the inherent difficulties of democratic control. How, for example, can legislatures control developments and governmental action in the area of monetary relations? Obviously legislatures, whose role in domestic politics is already challenged by the growing power of bureaucracy, face a further weakening of their position as a result of the changes in the international system. Thus far the challenges that multinational politics poses for states have been answered primarily by strengthening executive and bureaucratic institutions. But few have questioned how these developments could be accompanied by appropriate measures of democratic participation or how the role and methods of legislative control could be revised.

To begin such a discussion one could refer briefly to the relationship between the legislature and the executive, a relationship which has been debated in Europe for some time. Although it is conducted in terms that reflect the particular problems of parliamentary regimes found in Europe, the discussion is likely to be conducted even more actively in the United States after the autonomous manner in which several adminstrations have conducted the Vietnam War is revealed.

Within this debate it is argued that the separation of powers, although one of the principal foundations of parliamentary democracy, has been eroded in most parliamentary regimes.[9] The executive and the legislature, though formally separate, cooperate closely. Indeed, they combine in governing, for example, in the formation of the government by the majority, in the manipulation of the majority by the government, or in the preparation of legislation by the governmental bureaucracy. The type of parliamentary regime prevalent in Europe today can therefore be called "parliamentary government."

[9] For this debate see Thomas Ellwein, *Einführung in die Regierungs- und Verwaltungslehre* (Untersuchungen zum Regierungsprozess in der Bundesrepublik Deutschland, Vol. 1) (Stuttgart: Kohlhammer, 1966); Wilhelm Hennis, "Aufgaben einer modernen Regierungslehre," *Politische Vierteljahresschrift,* December 1965 (Vol. 6, No. 4), pp. 422–441; Wilhelm Kewenig, *Staatsrechtliche Probleme parlamentarischer Mitregierung am Beispiel der Arbeit der Bundestagsausschüsse* (Aktuelles Recht, Vol 7) (Homburg: Verlag Gehlen, 1971); Ulrich Scheuner, "Der Bereich der Regierung," in *Rechtsprobleme in Staat und Kirche: Festschrift für Rudolf Smend* (Göttinger Rechtswissenschaftliche Studien, Vol. 3) (Göttingen: Verlag Otto Schwartz & Co., 1952); Ulrich Scheuner, "Das parlamentarische Regierungssystem in der Bundesrepublik: Probleme und Entwicklungslinien," in *Strukturwandel der modernen Regierung,* ed. Theo Stammen (Wege der Forschung, Vol. 119) (Darmstadt: Wissenschaftliche Buchgesellschaft, 1967), pp. 296–312; Dolf Sternberger, "Parlamentarische Regierung und parlamentarische Kontrolle," in Stammen, pp. 274–295; and Heinz Rausch, ed., *Zur heutigen Problematik der Gewaltentrennung* (Darmstadt: Wissenschaftliche Buchgesellschaft, 1969), particularly the contributions by Werner Kägi and Winfried Steffani.

Parliamentary control, as we have understood it in the past, presupposes a genuine separation of powers in which legislative action and its execution are separated so that parliament can effectively control executive acts. But this is no longer the case under conditions of "parliamentary government." The juxtaposition of parliament and the executive, the former allegedly controlling the latter, has become almost a fiction, for the majority acts as an auxiliary organ of the government while the parliamentary minority has only very restricted power. Parliamentary control of the legality and legitimacy of governmental acts, parliament's traditional function which has evolved from its defensive role against the formerly absolutist state, has diminished in importance while the need to control the adequacy and efficiency of governmental policy has become more and more relevant. In addition, governmental measures have become increasingly complex, oriented toward the long run, and more far-reaching in their social implications. Ex post facto parliamentary control can become almost meaningless once a program is initiated or irreversible damage done, hence the growing necessity for concomitant control. It is for these reasons that parliaments become increasingly involved in the "executive process."

Thought about the democratic dimension of multinational politics and possible reform measures has to take into account the ongoing revisions of the relationship between parliament and government. It must also consider the ensuing necessity for parliamentary participation in the "executive process" in order to control concomitantly the legitimacy, adequacy, and effectiveness of governmental policy. Parliament's will to control is tamed by its majority which forms the very executive which parliament is to control. It lies in the logic of parliamentary government to thoroughly reassess the role of the opposition and to strengthen its power.

The most likely and most threatening result of the intermeshing of decisionmaking in multinational politics and of the growing transnational links is technocratic rule. While the need for a rationalization of policy under conditions of interdependence is obvious, there is also a need to preserve the primacy of politics without which there can be no democracy. Parliaments with modern and adaptive parties that are responsive to their democratic basis remain the best suited instrument for democratic control. Thus far the case for forms of direct democracy, such as the council system suggested for the macroorganization of political systems, appears unconvincing given the conditions of large advanced industrial societies which constantly expand the perimeter of their activities through transnational relations.[10] If contemporary parliaments, notably those in Europe, are to retain their central role of democratic control, they must abandon their present restraints and passivity. A minimum

10 For an informative survey of this debate see the section "Räte als politisches Ordnungsprinzip," in *Politische Vierteljahresschrift,* 1970 (Special Issue No. 2), pp. 53–152.

program dealing with the challenge of multinational politics would require a more vigorous exercise of control by parliament.

A possible approach to dealing with the challenge of transnational relations could be to further develop parliamentary government by involving parliamentarians in governmental decisionmaking. One could examine whether the occasional participation of parliamentarians in national delegations to important international negotiations could be transformed into a regular custom. This would be desirable since the intermeshed decisionmaking of multinational politics poses even more sharply the problem that arises during the ratification of international treaties: Once a compromise is negotiated, it is almost impossible to change. Regularized participation in multinational decisionmaking would offer parliaments a chance to exercise influence and therefore to strengthen the democratic dimension.

Such a system could be further developed by creating special parliamentary representatives. Like the ombudsman they would be experts in specific fields and responsible only to parliament. They could participate in multinational decisionmaking, represent parliamentary points of view, and act as observers and informants for parliament. Their minimum task would be to make multinational processes more transparent, thereby re-creating one precondition for a modicum of parliamentary control. The committee staffs in the United States Congress, the United States General Accounting Office, or the West German Bundesrechnungshof contain the modest beginnings of such a solution.

Democratic control of multinational politics requires a high degree of expertise, and such a requirement is likely to grow with the complexity of the issues in the emerging multinational system of interdependence. From this point of view the reorganization of democratic control according to specific issue areas deserves closer examination. The older idea of representative social and economic councils of elected experts should also be considered as such councils might be in a better position to implement democratic control than parliaments composed of generalists. If traditional parliaments are unable to control multinational corporations or international monetary institutions, such councils might offer a better chance.

Interest groups have come to play an important role in domestic politics in Western countries. In fact, they perform an auxiliary and even a legitimating role in the governmental process. While transnational interest groups may not yet fulfill such functions, their actions are of vital importance to the polities involved. Like their national counterparts their activities and their links with national and international bureaucracies require scrutiny and publicly exercised democratic control. The need for control could apply even more to other important transnational actors such as multinational corporations. Their actions such as investment, transfer of profits, or price policies are relevant to a number of national systems which will often have to bear the economic and political costs of what they do.

The level at which democratic control is applied will have to be reconsidered. It will remain at the national level for many, if not for most, problems. But in multinational decisionmaking one would have to examine whether there is a chance for democratic participation at the multinational "nerve centers," perhaps through elected experts. The shape of the resulting institutions is difficult to imagine at this point, but a break with some of our cherished institutions, in particular with the national focus of political organization and democratic control, appears inevitable if we are to preserve democratic participation.

Much can be done at the national level. With the growing importance of "nontraditional" areas and of "technical" ministries in regulating external affairs the first task would be to prevent the relegation of these matters to the foreign policy area with its alleged special rules of restricted democratic control. Of course, the danger always exists that such positive steps toward democratization will be canceled out by the intermeshed character of multinational decisionmaking which makes democratic control inherently difficult.

But the response to the threat of technocracy lies not only in strengthening parliament. The challenge of bureaucratization and of technocracy in its wake, intensified by the emergence of transnational relations between interdependent industrialized states, is so fundamental that it requires a response at different levels of our political systems. At the first level a reform of bureaucracy itself is required—of internal methods of control, of the type of personality performing the function, and of the way the bureaucracy submits itself to control mechanisms of the political system. At the second level a change in the quality of society is necessary. Only an active society which is "aware, potent and committed,"[11] not blindly active but responsive to essential human values and publicly active, can function as an effective counterforce to national and international technocracies and preserve, if not rebuild, a working democratic system.

VI. Conclusion

Democratic control should be introduced in a number of fields which have traditionally been shielded from it and which have represented the well-protected realm of professionals and experts. To many, such a development would seem to make rational policy more difficult. In fact, there is little doubt that these measures of democratic control, while solving some problems, will also create new ones. But political science is only at the beginning of a systematic

[11] Amitai Etzioni, *The Active Society: A Theory of Societal and Political Processes* (New York: Free Press, 1968), p. 5.

examination of the question. Most likely other proposals will emerge once more empirical work has been done.

The evidence that transnational relations erode the democratic process appears reasonably strong. The forces of progress in our interdependent world happen to further a multinationalization of previously domestic activities and to intensify the intermeshing of decisionmaking in multinational frameworks. This inherently expansive process could, in the name of progress, efficiency, and interdependence, ultimately undermine our Western systems of democracy unless we develop new forms of democratic control.

Transnational Relations and World Politics:

A Conclusion

JOSEPH S. NYE, JR., AND ROBERT O. KEOHANE

WORLD politics is changing, but our conceptual paradigms have not kept pace. The classic state-centric paradigm assumes that states are the only significant actors in world politics and that they act as units. Diverse domestic interests have effects on international politics only through governmental foreign policy channels. Intersocietal interactions are relegated to a category of secondary importance—the "environment" of interstate politics. As Karl Kaiser has pointed out, the reality of international politics has never totally corresponded to this model. Nevertheless, the model was approximated in the eighteenth century when foreign policy decisions were taken by small groups of persons acting within an environment that was less obtrusive and complex than the present one.[1]

Simplification of reality is essential for understanding. A skeptical scholar or diplomat might admit that the state-centric model misses much of the complexity of transnational relations described in this volume, but he might argue that such a simplification is justified because 1) in direct confrontation with transnational actors governments prevail, 2) transnational relations have always existed, and 3) transnational relations do not significantly affect the "high politics" of security, status, or war. We believe that these objections are to a large degree mistaken and that a broader world politics paradigm is necessary if scholars and statesmen are to understand such current problems as the unequal distribution of power and values in the world, the new setting of

[1] Karl Kaiser, "Transnationale Politik: Zu einer Theorie der multinationalen Politik," *Politische Vierteljahresschrift,* 1969 (Special Issue No. 1), pp. 80–109. An English translation of this important essay will appear in *International Organization,* Autumn 1971 (Vol. 25, No. 4), forthcoming.

United States foreign policy, statesmen's feelings of "loss of control," and the new types and tasks of international organization.

I. Why Change Paradigms?

Before elaborating our world politics paradigm and discussing these problems we set forth our reasons for rejecting the major arguments for the adequacy of the state-centric approach.

"Governments Win Direct Confrontations"

When transnational relations are discussed, those who wish to preserve the limited state-centric view are likely to stress the point that, in direct confrontations with transnational actors, governments generally prevail. Robert Gilpin argues this point in his essay in part I. It is certainly true that national governments are often able to win such confrontations since they have much greater resources of force and popular legitimacy. The Ford Foundation can be expelled from a foreign country or disciplined by the United States Congress. A local Catholic hierarchy can be cut off from Rome. The assets of a multinational business enterprise may be nationalized, and its efforts to impose retaliatory sanctions may come to no avail. IBM and Ford Motor Company may be prevented from investing in the Union of Soviet Socialist Republics. Invading revolutionary guerrillas—or guerrillas operating from a base in an independent state—may be decimated by military force. At a nonorganizational level individuals whose attitudes become too cosmopolitan because of transnational contacts may be deprived of political effectiveness at home.

However, the question "who wins confrontations?" is insufficient. It focuses only on the extreme cases of direct confrontation between a government and a nongovernmental actor. Winning may be costly, even for governments. Transnational relations may help to increase these costs and thus increase the constraints on state autonomy. Expelling a foundation cuts off resources that may be vital to certain important groups. As Ivan Vallier points out, the Roman Catholic church today is better able than ever before to transfer resources across borders. Even where access is restricted, it remains a significant political factor. Nationalization of the local assets of a multinational business enterprise may prove costly in terms of capital, technology, or markets foregone. Restrictions on American business involvement in Eastern Europe may mean that such dealings are handled through European subsidiaries and thus are more easily isolated from the American political process. It may also mean that the market is left to European rivals.[2]

[2] There are currently several hundred joint ventures of private Western and Communist business enterprises in Eastern Europe. "Europe Economic Survey," *New York Times*, January 16, 1970, pp. 49–73; see also Marshall I. Goldman, "The East Reaches for Markets," *Foreign Affairs*, July 1969 (Vol. 47, No. 4), pp. 721–734.

Because of the rise in the costs to national governments of "winning" in direct confrontations with transnational actors there are more incentives for bargaining. More relevant than "who wins" direct confrontations are the new kinds of bargains, coalitions, and alliances being formed between transnational actors and between these actors and segments of governments and international organizations. The essays in this volume provide a wide variety of examples: coalitions between the Roman Catholic church and nation-states; new ecumenical alliances between religious groups; coalitions between locally owned companies and governments to gain protection against foreign companies; coalitions between vertically integrated corporations and trade unions to ensure continuity of supplies; coalitions between government and unions to influence or even help overthrow foreign governments; coalitions between scientists to strengthen their position in lobbying for resources at home; coalitions between trade unions to coordinate pressure on multinational business enterprises; coalitions between foreign intellectuals and United States foundations to protect social scientists against their governments; coalitions between revolutionary groups to strengthen their legitimacy in their struggles against governments.

There is considerable variety among the actors involved, the resources available to them, and the outcomes of their coalitions. For example, boycotts of companies and individuals in the entertainment world by Arab governments are coordinated through regional intergovernmental organizations. In one instance (that involving the Norwich Union Fire Insurance Society in the United Kingdom) a boycott proved effective in changing the leadership of a British corporation. In other cases the costs of boycott were too high, and governments did not enforce the agreed-upon sanctions.[3]

Robert L. Thornton's essay on air transport, to take a different type of activity, illustrates a variety of coalitions and outcomes that are suggested by figure 2 in the introduction. In the 1966 air corridors controversy a transnational actor, the International Air Line Pilots Association, lobbied successfully to prevent an intergovernmental organization, the International Civil Aviation Organization (ICAO), from endorsing the position advocated by the United States government. In general the nongovernmental International Air Transport Association (IATA), run by an oligarchy of airlines, is far stronger than the intergovernmental ICAO in which each state has one vote and minor governments can create obstructions. In some cases airlines have aligned with governments for protection against other airlines or governments. As Thornton describes it, Pan American World Airways and Trans World Airlines tacitly approved of an Alitalia position in the IATA that thwarted the United States government position on charter airline fares. United States airlines

[3] Robert W. MacDonald, *The League of Arab States: A Study in the Dynamics of Regional Organization* (Princeton, N.J: Princeton University Press, 1965), pp. 118–123.

could not have resisted the United States government as well on their own. In its rivalry with Pan American over South Pacific air routes Continental Air Lines is allegedly attempting to enlist the support of an intergovernmental organization—the United Nations Trusteeship Council—to strengthen its position. The complexity of these coalitions in the political struggle to allocate important resources in the field of air transport is not caught by the state-centric paradigm. Nor, we might add, do national governments always prevail.

A sophisticated analysis of contemporary international politics cannot ignore this variety of bargaining situations or the differences in outcomes among issue areas. The state-centric view often fails to forecast outcomes correctly, and state-centric theories are not very good at explaining such outcomes even when the forecasts are correct.

"Transnational Relations Have Always Existed"

Raymond Aron was among the first to introduce the concept of "transnational society" into international relations theory. He used the term to describe commercial interchanges, migration of persons, common beliefs, ceremonials, and organizations that cross frontiers. However, he arrived at the skeptical judgment that transnational society as he defined it was relatively unimportant for understanding basic interactions in world politics. In his words: "Before 1914 economic exchanges throughout Europe enjoyed a freedom that the gold standard and monetary convertibility safeguarded even better than legislation. Labor parties were grouped into an International. The Greek tradition of the Olympic Games had been revived . . . religious, moral and even political beliefs were fundamentally analogous on either side of the frontiers. . . . This example, like the similar one of Hellenic society in the fifth century, illustrates the relative autonomy of the interstate order—in peace and in war—in relation to the context of transnational society."[4]

Aron is certainly correct when he points to the existence of transnational relations before 1914, as the essay by James A. Field, Jr., abundantly indicates. More generally, as Oran Young has observed, "over the bulk of recorded history man has organized himself for political purpose on bases other than those now subsumed under the concepts 'state' and 'nation-state.'"[5]

Our contention, however, is neither that transnational relations are new nor that they supersede interstate politics but that they affect interstate politics by altering the choices open to statesmen and the costs that must be borne for

[4] Raymond Aron, *Peace and War: A Theory of International Relations,* trans. Richard Howard and Annette Baker Fox (Garden City, N.Y: Doubleday & Co., 1966), p. 105.

[5] Oran R. Young, "The Actors in World Politics," in *The Analysis of International Politics,* ed. James N. Rosenau, B. Vincent Davis, and Maurice A. East (Glencoe, Ill: Free Press, forthcoming); see also Adda B. Bozeman, *Politics and Culture in International History* (Princeton, N.J: Princeton University Press, 1960).

adopting various courses of action. In short, transnational relations provide different sets of incentives, or payoffs, for states. These altered payoffs were not sufficient to ensure peace in 1914 despite the hopes of men like Norman Angell, who argued in 1910 that "the wealth, prosperity, and well-being of a nation depend in no way upon its political power."[6] Nevertheless, World War I by no means refutes the contention that transnational relations influence interstate politics; it merely warns us against the incautious assumption that transnational relations render war impossible between states linked by extensive transnational ties.

In any case, the analogy between 1914 and 1971 should not be taken too seriously when discussing transnational relations any more than it should be regarded as the key to understanding great-power politics. Transnational relations today take different forms than in 1914, and in our view the contemporary forms have greater political significance than the pre-1914 versions. On the one hand, mutual sensitivity of societies has increased; on the other hand, the growth of transnational social and economic organizations has created powerful and dynamic transnational actors capable of adapting to change and of consciously attempting to shape the world to their interests.

SENSITIVITY OF SOCIETIES. The importance of transnational relations depends less on the sheer quantity of such relations than on their political salience and the resulting sensitivity of societies to one another. There are two major reasons for this increased sensitivity. First, improved technology has removed many of the imperfections of communications that once helped separate societies. Second, as we indicate in the introduction and as Edward L. Morse suggests in his essay, a given volume of transnational activity may, paradoxically, have greater effects on interdependence when governments are ambitiously attempting to control their economies than in situations of relative laissez faire.[7] Thus, Gilpin's assertion that "the role of the nation-state in economic as well as in political life is increasing" in no way contradicts our assertion that transnational relations are becoming more important. On the contrary, it reinforces our point. In the liberal nineteenth-century world transnational society remained somewhat separate from interstate politics, but today the result of ambitious governmental policies is that transnational relations affect intergovernmental relations and have themselves become politicized. New subjects enter the realm of international relations. As the May 1971 international monetary crisis made clear, governments must often be concerned

[6] Norman Angell, *The Great Illusion: A Study of the Relation of Military Power in Nations to Their Economic and Social Advantage* (3rd rev. and enl. ed.; New York: G. P. Putnam's Sons, 1911), p. 34.

[7] Richard N. Cooper, *The Economics of Interdependence: Economic Policy in the Atlantic Community* (Atlantic Policy Series) (New York: McGraw-Hill Book Co. [for the Council on Foreign Relations], 1968); see also Andrew Shonfield, *Modern Capitalism: The Changing Balance of Public and Private Power* (Oxford Paperbacks on International Affairs) (London: Oxford University Press, 1969), chapter 2.

with the internal economic policies of other governments.[8] This is sometimes referred to as the "domesticization" of international politics. It might better be called the "internationalization" of domestic politics. An important result is that subunits of governments are provided greater opportunities for transnational contacts and coalitions.

By facilitating the flow of ideas modern communications have also increased intersocietal sensitivity. Certainly there have been indirect "contagions" of ideas in earlier periods such as the European revolutions of 1848 or Latin American university reforms in 1917. Field refers to St. Petersburg, Smyrna, Nagasaki, and Canton as "windows on the West" for the transmission of culture in an earlier time. Today, however, television has created a "window on the West" in the living rooms of the elites of the third world. Widely separated elites, whether functionally similar social groups, students, military officers, or racial minorities, become more rapidly aware of each other's activities.[9] Seymour Martin Lipset has noted that "student culture is a highly communicable one, the mood and mode of it translate readily from one center to another, one country to another."[10] Indeed, although many of the leaders of the student disturbances that shook Europe in the late 1960s were aware of each other's activities, they first came into direct contact when British television producers brought them together after the events.[11]

Not all the political effects of transnational communications are so dramatic. The incremental growth, spread, and change of knowledge, doctrines, and attitudes alter the context within which governments operate and change the payoffs available to them. While these ideas and attitudes are often transmitted by transnational organizations, they are also transmitted by individuals through personal travel and communication—subject to the qualifications mentioned in Donald P. Warwick's essay.

TRANSNATIONAL ORGANIZATIONS. Not all types of transnational organizations have increased in importance. Those with explicitly political goals seem to have declined in importance. The close links between Communist parties and the international brigades of the 1930s find only the palest of reflections in the Havana-based Tricontinental or the expeditions of radical American stu-

[8] For example, "when the Nixon Administration, with at least one eye on the 1972 election, switched signals and called for easing the money supply and lowering interest rates to stimulate business and employment, the outflow of Eurodollars from the United States was set in motion, and the stage was set for monetary trouble abroad." *New York Times*, May 10, 1971, p. 52.

[9] "Hating the Pigs," *The Economist*, August 15, 1970 (Vol. 236, No. 6625), pp. 17–18, gives an example of the similarity of phrasing of demands by racial minorities in the United Kingdom and the United States. For a discussion of transnational communications affecting patterns of military coups or insurrections see Samuel P. Huntington, ed., *Changing Patterns of Military Politics* (International Yearbook of Political Behavior Research, Vol. 3) (Glencoe, Ill: Free Press, 1962), pp. 44–47.

[10] Seymour Martin Lipset, "The Possible Political Effects of Student Activism," *Social Science Information*, April 1969 (Vol. 8, No. 2), p. 12.

[11] Anthony Sampson, *The New Europeans: A Guide to the Workings, Institutions and Character of Contemporary Western Europe* (London: Hodder and Stoughton, 1968), p. 419.

dents to cut sugar cane in Cuba. As J. Bowyer Bell points out, current revolutionary guerrilla groups have a transnational myth to sustain morale and legitimacy rather than a transnational organization to coordinate operations. Robert W. Cox shows that a similar trend away from political organization has occurred in labor movements. The international confederations that aggregated labor interests at a very general level and engaged primarily in transnational political struggles have been replaced in prominence by the international trade secretariats which aggregate more specific economic interests and organize to coordinate operations against multinational business enterprises. The greater reliance of the Roman Catholic church in recent years on moral and humanitarian influence, rather than on political alliances with governments, is consistent with this trend away from explicit political activity by transnational organizations.

In contrast to political organizations, however, transnational organizations whose principal goals are social and economic have increased in importance. These organizations, of course, may have very significant political consequences. By far the most important of these organizations is the multinational business enterprise. Multinational enterprises existed at the beginning of this century but on a smaller scale and with much less important effects.[12] Modern communications technology has greatly increased the feasibility of imposing a central strategy on widely scattered subsidiaries and consequently has increased the challenge that enterprises present to state sovereignty. Unlike those of the Hudson's Bay Company, the activities of today's multinational business enterprises often do not coincide with the decision domains of particular states. Their effects on world trade and production can be judged by the fact that the production of overseas subsidiaries of the ten leading capital-exporting states was nearly twice the volume of trade between those countries.[13] Raymond Vernon indicates that overseas subsidiaries may account for approximately 15 percent of world production. Finally, multinational business enterprises have had strong effects on other transnational actors. Trade unions, banks, and public relations firms have all been lured into increased transnational activity by following the lead of the multinational business enterprise.[14]

Arnold Wolfers pointed out over a decade ago that the ability of international nongovernmental organizations "to operate as international or transnational actors may be traced to the fact that men identify themselves and their interests with corporate bodies other than the nation-state."[15] Transna-

[12] See Mira Wilkins, *The Emergence of Multinational Enterprise: American Business Abroad from the Colonial Era to 1914* (Cambridge, Mass: Harvard University Press, 1970).

[13] Robert L. Heilbroner, "The Multinational Corporation and the Nation-State," *New York Review of Books*, February 11, 1971 (Vol. 16, No. 2), pp. 20–25.

[14] See the essays by Lawrence Krause and Robert W. Cox in this volume; see also Herbert Schiller, "The Multinational Corporation as International Communicator" (Paper delivered at the Sixty-sixth Annual Convention of the American Political Science Association, Los Angeles, September 1970).

[15] Arnold Wolfers, *Discord and Collaboration: Essays on International Politics* (Baltimore, Md: Johns Hopkins Press, 1962).

tional actors therefore flourish where dual loyalties are regarded as acceptable. In totalitarian societies, and in areas in which one version or another of integral nationalism has taken hold, dual loyalties are regarded as treasonous and transnational forces as potentially corrupting and dangerous. It is hard to imagine a good Soviet citizen avowing loyalty to General Motors Corporation or a contemporary Chilean nationalist identifying himself with Anaconda Company or Kennecott Copper Corporation.

In the modernized Western world and its ancillary areas the acceptability of multiple loyalties is taken for granted. Yet, this toleration seems to be extended more readily when the transnational actor is explicitly economic in purpose than when it is explicitly political. Thus, it seems less incompatible to be loyal to both IBM and France, to FIAT and the United States, or to the Roman Catholic church and Belgium than it does for a loyal citizen of the United Kingdom to pledge allegiance to transnational communism or for Americans to identify with Israel. In the West, therefore, nationalism probably hinders overt political organization across boundaries more than it hinders transnational economic activity. Dual loyalties may be more feasible when the foci of loyalty seem to operate in different areas with different goals.[16] When the competition is directly political, the individual is often forced to choose.

These are mere speculations about the reasons for the mixed trends in transnational organizations, reflecting the rise of economic actors in modernized areas of the world and the decline of transnational political organizations. Whatever the reasons for the trends, however, the increased scale of social and economic organizations and their increased effects on the political sensitivity of societies to each other constitute an important new aspect of world politics.

"Transnational Relations Do Not Affect High Politics"

Distinctions between high and low politics are of diminishing value in current world politics. Stanley Hoffmann has described this situation with a useful metaphor: "The competition between states takes place on several chessboards in addition to the traditional military and diplomatic ones: for instance, the chessboards of world trade, of world finance, of aid and technical assistance, of space research and exploration, of military technology, and the chessboard of what has been called 'informal penetration.' These chessboards do not entail the resort to force."[17] Hoffmann observes that each "chessboard"

[16] According to Harold Guetzkow "multiple loyalties are quite admissible *provided* the different objects are furnishing compatible solutions to different needs." *Multiple Loyalties: Theoretical Approach to a Problem in International Organization* (Publication No. 4) (Princeton, N.J: Center for Research on World Political Institutions, Woodrow Wilson School of Public and International Affairs, Princeton University, 1955), p. 39.

[17] Stanley Hoffmann, "International Organization and the International System," *International Organization,* Summer 1970 (Vol. 24, No. 3), p. 401.

has rules of its own but is linked as well to others by "complicated and subtle relations." High and low politics become difficult to distinguish. Thus, during the international monetary crisis of May 1971 it became clear that an implicit bargain had been struck between American and West German statesmen and central bankers by which the willingness of West German authorities to hold United States dollars was a condition for a large United States army in Europe.

This volume has shown that on a number of Hoffmann's "chessboards," or issue areas, transnational relations are extremely important. As sensitivity to other societies increases, new subjects are brought into the realm of world politics. Issue areas that were formerly quite distinct from political calculation have become politically relevant, particularly insofar as governments have attempted to extend their control over domestic economic activity without sacrificing the benefits of transnational intercourse. Since these issue areas are often of great significance to governments, they cannot be merely dismissed as "low politics," allegedly subordinate to a "high politics" of status, security, or war. Butter comes before guns in New Zealand's diplomacy.

In these issue areas, furthermore, force may be neither appropriate nor effective. Insofar as force is devalued for a particular area of interaction, transnational interactions and the activities of transnational relations are likely to be important—even for France, the United Kingdom, and the United States.

We find ourselves in a world that reminds us more of the extensive and curious chessboard in Lewis Carroll's *Through the Looking Glass* than of more conventional versions of that ancient game. The players are not always what they seem, and the terrain of the chessboards may suddenly change from garden to shop to castle. Thus, in contemporary world politics not all players on important chessboards are states, and the varying terrains of the chessboards constrain state behavior. Some are more suited to the use of force, others almost totally unsuited to it. Different chessboards favor different states. For example, relations between Norway and the United States are quite different on shipping questions than on questions involving strategic arms. When international oil prices are negotiated, Iran is more important than it is on world trade issues in general. High and low politics have become tightly intertwined.

II. The World Politics Paradigm

Although we use the word "paradigm" somewhat loosely, we wish to make it clear that we seek to challenge basic assumptions that underlie the analysis of international relations, not merely to compile a list of transnational interactions and organizations. Nor are our concerns merely academic. "Practical men, who believe themselves to be quite exempt from any intellectual influences," are usually, as John Maynard Keynes once pointed out, unconscious captives of paradigms created by "some academic scribbler of a few years back."[18]

In the introduction we define world politics as political interactions between any "significant actors" whose characteristics include autonomy, the control of substantial resources relevant to a given issue area, and participation in political relationships across state lines. Since we define politics in terms of the conscious employment of resources, "both material and symbolic, including the threat or exercise of punishment, to induce other actors to behave differently than they would otherwise behave," it is clear that we are positing a conception of world politics in which the central phenomenon is bargaining between a variety of autonomous or semiautonomous actors.

The difference between our world politics paradigm and the state-centric paradigm can be clarified most easily by focusing on the nature of the actors. The world politics paradigm attempts to transcend the "level-of-analysis problem" both by broadening the conception of actors to include transnational actors and by conceptually breaking down the "hard shell" of the nation-state.[19]

This can be illustrated by a diagram that compares the range of actors included within our world politics paradigm with that included in the state-centric model. Figure 1 displays the characteristics of actors in world politics

	Position		
	Governmental	Intergovernmental	Nongovernmental
Maximal central control	A States as units	C International organizations as units	E Transnational organizations as units
Minimal central control	B Governmental subunits	D Subunits of international organizations	F Subunits of transnational organizations; also certain individuals

A + C = Actors in the state-centric paradigm
B + D = Actors in transgovernmental interactions
E + F = Actors in transnational interactions

FIGURE 1. ACTORS IN WORLD POLITICS

[18] John Maynard Keynes, *The General Theory of Employment Interest and Money* (London: Macmillan & Co., 1957), p. 383.

[19] See J. David Singer, "The Level-of-Analysis Problem in International Relations," *World Politics*, October 1961 (Vol. 14, No. 1), pp. 77–92.

on two dimensions: 1) the degree to which they are governmental or nongovernmental in position and 2) the extent to which they consist of coherent and centrally controlled organizations rather than subunits of governments or of transnational organizations.

The first dimension distinguishes actors according to formal position—governmental, intergovernmental, or nongovernmental. It therefore corresponds to the "inverted U" diagram in figures 1 and 2 of the introduction which illustrates our concept of transnational interactions. As a first approximation we found this easily verifiable distinction a useful way to identify certain aspects of world politics that are missed by the state-centric view.

As we also indicate in the introduction, however, there is another dimension of world politics that the classic state-centric paradigm with its assumption of states as unitary actors fails to take into account. This second dimension, centralization of control, involves the realization that subunits of governments may also have distinct foreign policies which are not all filtered through the top leadership and which do not fit into a unitary actor model. Thus, scholars have recently developed a "bureaucratic politics approach" to foreign policy analysis, explaining decisions of governments in these terms.[20]

Bureaucratic politics is not limited to governments but can be applied to nongovernmental actors as well. Multinational business enterprises are frequently unable to act as unitary actors, and we have seen that the Roman Catholic church, the Ford Foundation, guerrilla movements, and organizations of scientists are hardly monolithic.[21] Furthermore, just as American military officers may negotiate with their Spanish counterparts and Congressman Wilbur Mills with Japanese textile companies, so may local divisions of a multinational business enterprise or of the Roman Catholic church strike bargains and form coalitions with national governments or subunits thereof.[22]

The combination of these two dimensions in figure 1 portrays a complex model of world politics in which the state-centric paradigm focuses on only two of the six cells. Another way of illustrating this point is shown by figure 2. The state-centric paradigm covers only four of the 36 possible types of politically important interactions across state boundaries that are identified by the

[20] See, especially, Graham T. Allison, *Essence of Decision: Explaining the Cuban Missile Crisis* (Boston: Little, Brown and Co., 1971); or, by the same author, "Conceptual Models and the Cuban Missile Crisis," *American Political Science Review*, September 1969 (Vol. 63, No. 3), pp. 689–718; and also Richard E. Neustadt, *Alliance Politics* (New York: Columbia University Press, 1970).

[21] In his essay, "The Multinational Corporation: Measuring the Consequences," Robert B. Stobaugh argues against images of the multinational business enterprise "as one economic entity controlled by one 'economic man' in headquarters rather than of what the enterprise really is: an organization of numerous staff groups and subsidiaries, some of which are large and powerful in their own rights and among which considerable negotiation takes place." *Columbia Journal of World Business*, January–February 1971 (Vol. 6, No. 1), p. 62.

[22] For details about the Spanish case see Robert O. Keohane, "The Big Influence of Small Allies," *Foreign Policy*, Spring 1971 (Vol. 1, No. 2), pp. 161–182; on the politics of textile quota legislation see the *New York Times*, March 16, 1971, p. 51.

world politics paradigm. This gives us an idea of the richness of possible transnational coalitions that determine outcomes in world politics and that are now largely relegated to the subsidiary and largely undifferentiated category of "environment."

Actor	A States as units	B Governmental subunits	C International organizations as units	D Subunits of international organizations	E Transnational organizations as units	F Subunits of transnational organizations; also certain individuals
A States as units	IS	TG	IS	TG	TN	TN
B Governmental subunits	TG	TG	TG	TG	TN	TN
C International organizations as units	IS	TG	IS	TG	TN	TN
D Subunits of international organizations	TG	TG	TG	TG	TN	TN
E Transnational organizations as units	TN	TN	TN	TN	TN	TN
F Subunits of transnational organizations; also certain individuals	TN	TN	TN	TN	TN	TN

IS = Interstate interactions
TG = Transgovernmental interactions
TN = Transnational interactions
TG + TN = Transnational relations
TG + TN + IS = World politics interactions

FIGURE 2. BILATERAL INTERACTIONS IN WORLD POLITICS

Adding the second dimension, centralization of control, allows us to specify a paradigm of world politics that brings together traditional international politics, the bureaucratic politics approach to foreign policy analysis, and transnational actors as defined in the introduction. Yet, it also poses certain conceptual problems. As defined in the introduction, transnational interactions could be easily identified by the involvement of nongovernmental actors. Thus, definition on the basis of formal position—governmental or nongovernmental—led to a clear delineation between transnational and interstate interactions. This narrowed the issues and omitted problems of central control, but it did achieve an initially useful simplification and clarification. Unlike that of formal position, however, the concept of centralization of control is a continuum—there can be more or less central control, and lines that are drawn will necessarily be somewhat arbitrary. How, then, do we distinguish various types of behavior along this dimension?

Our first step is to introduce a new type of interaction in addition to "transnational interactions" and "interstate interactions" as defined in the introduction. Transnational interactions necessarily involve nongovernmental actors, whereas interstate interactions take place exclusively between states acting as units. Transgovernmental interactions, however, are defined as interactions between governmental subunits across state boundaries. The broad term transnational relations includes both trans*national* and trans*governmental* interactions—all of world politics that is not taken into account by the state-centric paradigm.

As we have defined world politics, any unit of action that attempts to exercise influence across state boundaries and possesses significant resources in a given issue area is an actor in world politics. Thus, this concept of transnational relations calls attention to the activities of subunits of governments or intergovernmental organizations as well as to the behavior of individuals and nongovernmental organizations. Yet, we still need to specify when an actor is behaving "as a unit" and when its subunits possess significant autonomy.

On an abstract level we distinguish transgovernmental from interstate interactions by the extent to which actors are behaving in conformity to roles specified or reasonably implied by the formal foreign policy structure of the state. The problem of discovering deviations from formally prescribed roles is difficult and sometimes impossible because of the ambiguous specification of role at high levels of authority. Nonetheless, such deviation was found among European agricultural ministers in the example cited in the introduction. At lower levels of authority the transgovernmental behavior of those in formal governmental positions is much easier to identify, for example, the coalition of United States and Canadian weather bureaus to overcome a Department of State decision on control of international meteorological research.[23] The difficulties of delineation in this murky area of control are admittedly great, but it would hardly be sensible to promulgate a supposedly "new" paradigm for world politics without including reference to transgovernmental politics.

[23] The example is from the essay by Edward Miles in this volume. Our inclusion of this second dimension is due in large part to his arguments.

To explain this more complex world the study of world politics must proceed by the analysis of particular issue areas and the relations between them. It must take into account the differences in the way the game of world politics is played on Hoffmann's different chessboards or, to escape from bipolar imagery, poker tables. Who are the players? What are their resources? What are the rules? How do the players, resources, and rules differ from game to game? Most important, how are the different games related to each other? Are winnings and resources transferable, and, if they are, at what discount?

A Plan for Research

We are suggesting an approach to the study of world politics through analysis of different types of issue areas (which we define loosely, following Cox, as unorganized or partially organized systems of interaction) and of the relationships between them. The elaboration of this paradigm suggests three foci for research: 1) analysis of issue areas, 2) research on transnational and transgovernmental actors, and 3) studies designed to illuminate relationships between issue areas.

First, we would want to know the types of interaction and interdependence that characterize each issue area. We would further want to know what role transnational actors play within the issue area and how they interact with each other and with components of governments. We would want to know to what extent governments (or some governments) act as centralized units or are characterized by transgovernmental coalitions. We would want to know how these differences have varied over time and how they vary in relation to such factors as salience to the public, technological change, and the number and symmetry of the actors. The essays in part III of this volume suggest a few preliminary answers.

The essays in part II exemplify the second research focus. By studying the internal organization of transnational actors we can shed light on the roles they play. For example, not all trade unions are lured into transnational activity nor are the effects of all multinational business enterprises similar. Both are affected by the nature of their internal structure. Cox points out that unions organized at the plant level are more likely to fight the corporation transnationally and to develop an ideology of internationalism. Unions more strongly organized at the national level are more likely to ally with the government and evidence strong feelings of nationalism. Louis T. Wells, Jr., shows that multinational manufacturing enterprises are more likely to weaken a government's control of economic matters if the firm is organized on a product basis. It would be interesting to know, for example, how the adverse effects alleged by Peter B. Evans vary according to differences in the internal organization of the transnational actor.

Similarly, further research should be focused on the process of formulation of "private foreign policies." The Roman Catholic church has very explicit procedures. The Ford Foundation, as described by Peter D. Bell, seems deliberately to shun such questions. Yet, they are unavoidable. At what point, for example, does a transnational organization withdraw from a country? Does a foundation behave more like a church or more like a bank? How are private foreign policy decisions made?[24]

The third major research focus would explore the linkages between issue areas. Here the essay by Gilpin is very suggestive. Gilpin argues for the primacy of the security issue area and suggests that in the postwar period there were explicit bargains, between the United States and the Federal Republic of Germany (West Germany) and between the United States and Japan, by which security resources were exchanged for trade and financial benefits. He argues further that changing conditions may undo these bargains and adversely affect transnational activity. One problem with Gilpin's argument, however, is that any situation of reciprocal advantage can, often incorrectly, be interpreted as a result of bargaining; one might then infer that if one set of benefits is altered, the other will likewise change. But in the absence of clear historical evidence about the perceptions and actions of decisionmakers the inference that a conscious bargain was made and maintained over a period of time is not necessarily valid. There is a danger here of interpreting the past too much in terms of the present: United States decisionmakers in the 1950s were much less concerned about America's international financial position than they are in 1971. Thus, even if bargains were struck between the United States and West Germany and the United States and Japan, it is not clear that these bargains involved an interplay of issue areas. They can also be interpreted solely in terms of mutual security: the exchange of bases or assured access to a forward position in return for protection. Since then economic elements have become more important. Finally, even if Japan in particular is now receiving economic advantages that cannot continue because political conditions have changed, it does not necessarily follow that the contradiction will be resolved in the direction of restrictions on transnational interactions. It might also be resolved within the economic issue area by increasingly opening the Japanese economy to American business—that is, by an extension of transnational relations. Yet, regardless of the validity of Gilpin's conclusions, his approach raises crucial questions that are ignored when analysts fragment

24 Transnational actors, like governments, may be unable to make decisions due to bureaucratic politics. Charles P. Kindleberger cites a major oil company that was unable to reconcile the opposing views of its subunits in regard to oil imports into the United States and thus had no position in this seemingly vital issue. See his essay, "European Integration and the International Corporation," in *World Business: Promise and Problems,* ed. Courtney C. Brown (Studies of the Modern Corporation) (New York: Macmillan Co., 1970), p. 105; see also, by Kindleberger, *Power and Money: The Economics of International Politics and the Politics of International Economics* (New York: Basic Books, Publishers, 1970), p. 13.

reality into "strategic" and "economic" sectors and deal only with one or the other.

Thus, our third research focus, and Gilpin's essay, point to crucial questions of world politics. What bargains are struck across issue areas? How fungible are resources in a given issue area—how easily transferable are they to another poker table? Does dominance in the security area provide a state with leverage in another area in which it may be weak? To what extent are all issue areas politicized, and to what extent can some of them be insulated from political competition? Answers to such questions would shed light on the elusive concept of "power" in world politics. If the poker games are not closely interconnected and resources are only fungible at a discount, how useful is a concept such as power, resting as it does on the analogy with money in an economic system?

In summary, we believe that the essays in this volume support our contention that the state-centric paradigm provides an inadequate basis for the study of changing world politics. Transnational actors sometimes prevail over governments. These "losses" by governments can often be attributed to the rising costs of unilateral governmental action in the face of transnational relations. For a state-centric theory this is represented as "environment." But it is theoretically inadequate to use the exogenous variables of the environment to account for outcomes in the interaction of various actors in world politics. State-centric theories are not very good at explaining such outcomes because they do not describe the complex patterns of coalitions between different types of actors described in the essays. We hope that our "world politics paradigm" will help to redirect attention toward the substance of international politics, in which the major theoretical as well as practical questions can be found, and away from the relatively unenlightening application of subtle reasoning or sophisticated methodology to problems that have been narrowly defined by a limited theoretical outlook or the wrong units of analysis. Perhaps for a while we have had enough computer-assisted voting analyses of the United Nations General Assembly except for the routine descriptive purpose of keeping up with recent trends. We may even have a sufficiency of macrohistorical studies of "bipolarity" and "multipolarity" that focus entirely on the strategic level of interaction. The "world politics paradigm" does not provide scholars with an instant revelation, but it does provide them with at least one path toward relevance.

III. Asymmetry and the Allocation of Values

Broadening the scope of international politics beyond the state-centric view provides a clearer understanding of and base for further thought about one of the most important structural problems of current world politics—the extremely asymmetric relations between states. We have been struck by the lack of serious theorizing about this aspect of international relations. This is attributable at least in part to the prevalence of the state-centric view. The myth of state sovereignty and the emphasis on security issues make the world seem less imbalanced than it is. The popularity currently enjoyed by a variety of theories of imperialism is one result of this vacuum. In the introduction we explain our reasons for believing that the word "imperialism" obscures more than it enlightens. Nonetheless, the problem of asymmetric relations that underlies theories of imperialism is both real and important.

Transnational activity is very unequally distributed. Sensitivity to its impact varies greatly. Multinational business enterprises, foundations, organizations of scientists, international trade union secretariats—all have their origins in advanced Western countries. Kjell Skjelsbaek's data on the distribution of international nongovernmental organizations shows that in 1966, 53.5 percent of all national representations came from Eastern Europe and .5 percent from Communist Asia. Moreover, 88.7 percent of the headquarters of all international organizations were located in the developed Northwest. Data on transnational activity by individuals has shown a similar pattern of distribution—greater participation by individuals from developed Western states.[25]

Several factors account for this uneven distribution. Among the most important seem to be: 1) modernization, 2) decreased costs of transportation and communication, and 3) pluralistic ideology. Skjelsbaek argues that the specialization that accompanies modernity creates an increasing number of discrete interests with a capacity to organize first nationally and later transnationally. The increased economic specialization of advanced countries leads them to become each other's best trading partners. The simple pattern of industrial countries trading manufactures for raw materials from poor countries has been greatly modified. Trade between developed market economy countries accounts for approximately one-half of world trade, while the share of less developed countries (and of raw materials) has been declining.[26]

Several essays in this volume discuss the effects of decreased transportation and communications costs. Advances in communications technology have played a major role in facilitating the development of a central strategy for multinational business enterprises. Lawrence Krause argues that rapid communications have greatly increased the sensitivity of money markets to each other, a point reinforced by the influx of almost $2 billion to West Germany in a few days during May 1971. While these developments in communications technology also affect less developed countries, they generally touch only a small elite and penetrate these societies less deeply.

25 Robert Cooley Angell, *Peace on the March: Transnational Participation* (New Perspectives in Political Science, No. 19) (New York: Van Nostrand Reinhold Co., 1969).

26 Michael Zammat Cutajar and Alison Franks, *The Less Developed Countries in World Trade: A Reference Handbook* (London: Overseas Development Institute, 1967); see also Shonfield.

Not only does the economic and social structure of the developed market economy countries make them the locus of transnational activity, their prevailing pluralistic ideology provides much more legitimacy for such activities than is available in Communist countries or in many less developed states. Moreover, as Cox illustrates, transnational actors tend to develop ideologies of transnationalism to add to their legitimacy, thus reinforcing their positions in areas of strength. It is now stylish for corporations to be "multinational."

If transnationalism has become the ideology of some of the rich, nationalism remains the ideology of many of the poor. In many of the new states transnational processes are (or seem to be) remnants of colonial rule. Politics often revolves around nationalists' efforts to diminish transnational ties. Transnational actors originating in rich countries are vulnerable to charges of illegitimacy. In many less developed countries insecure political elites turn to nationalist ideologies in an effort to integrate or distract populations which are undergoing social mobilization at rates too fast for their institutions to handle. In these circumstances it is not surprising to find resentment of transnational actors that seem to threaten an already shaky sense of sovereign control. The ability to tolerate a public "defeat" by a transnational actor is smaller in Bolivia than in Belgium.

We are not arguing that transnational actors always weaken governmental control in less developed countries. On the contrary, the superior performance of multinational business enterprises in paying taxes and increasing exports or the activities of Planned Parenthood or the Ford Foundation in the field of birth control may actually increase governmental capacities. Nor are we arguing that all elites in less developed countries resist transnational relations. Indeed, governmental elites are often happy to have their countries gain the resources of capital, technology, and markets that multinational business enterprises can provide. Local trade union elites are often happy to gain the organizational resources provided by international unions. Local university elites are frequently pleased to gain the material and moral support of the Ford Foundation which diminishes their vulnerability to control by their governments. The local Catholic clergy is often willing to have the support of additional resources from Rome.

The trouble lies in the gap between elites and masses in less developed countries. The increased mutual sensitivity of societies that is created by transnational relations touches only a tiny proportion of the population. As elites are absorbed into a transnational network, the gap between elites and masses is increased and intolerable political tensions may be created. Transnational trade union activity may create a grossly overrewarded "labor aristocracy" at the expense of the welfare of peasants. One effect of multinational business enterprises or American foundations may be the reinforcement of a local salary structure geared to the world economy rather than to local social conditions. This in turn would mean a grossly inequitable class structure. Experimentation with altered incentives is curtailed by the threat of brain drain since mobile individuals can escape the country. The creation of a single global economy is rational, perhaps, to achieve optimal allocation of global resources, but it is also a severe limitation on national autonomy. The transnationally mobile are rewarded at the expense of the nationally immobile.

As Cox observes in his essay, "Historically, the geographically based power of the state has been the only power capable of counterbalancing unequal forces in the interest of welfare. . . . A Canadian-type solution [of openness to transnational forces] may be feasible where most of the population participates in the transnational society. It is, however, likely to raise considerable tensions in countries in which there is a substantial population marginal to or outside the transnational society and in which there are great disparities in incomes and life-styles which may be further exaggerated by a continuation of transnational relations."[27]

IV. United States Foreign Policy

The issues raised by transnational relations are relevant to all countries, or at least to all modernized Western countries. Yet, as we indicate in the introduction, transnational phenomena raise specific and unique problems for the United States. From a transnational perspective the United States is by far the preponderant society in the world.

United States preponderance in transnational activities has its origins in American patterns of social organization and the American "style" as well as in the size and modernity of its economy. As Field points out, Americans in the nineteenth century were active transnationalists, even when the United States was by no means predominant in the world. Now, the size of the United States means that its largest social units, including some corporations, foundations, and universities, often have annual budgets greater than those of the governments of the countries in which they operate. Furthermore, as a result of this modernity American economic techniques are often more advanced than those of countries on which United States–based transnational actors descend. Thus, by virtue not only of size but also of technological leadership, the United States is somewhat less vulnerable to the effects of transnational relations than are other societies.[28]

This situation raises important issues for United States foreign policy. First, it means that the term "neo-isolationism" is highly misleading when we think

[27] Cox, in this volume, p. 584.

[28] See Kenneth N. Waltz, "The Myth of National Interdependence," *The International Corporation: A Symposium*, ed. Charles P. Kindleberger (Cambridge, Mass: M.I.T. Press, 1970), pp. 205–223; and Raymond P. Vernon, "International Investment and International Trade in the Product Cycle," *Quarterly Journal of Economics*, May 1966 (Vol. 80, No. 2), pp. 190–207.

in transnational rather than state-centric terms. Although United States government foreign policy may be turning inward, the same is not necessarily true of the private foreign policies of its transnational actors. Thus, an analogy to the 1930s is inappropriate. Second, it means that the preponderant size of the United States is one of the major problems of contemporary world politics. From a state-centric perspective the United States seems highly constrained by the structure of world politics, although analysts have often overstressed the constraints and underemphasized United States freedom of action.[29] Yet, from the perspective of transnational relations the United States often seems to have too much freedom of action—whether in exporting inflation to Europe or unwittingly undertaking the "Coca-Colonization" of the world. It would be difficult to argue that the United States is too constrained in transnational relations.

United States policy toward the third world looks particularly different when viewed in transnational perspective than it does when conceived in terms of the state-centric model. Future problems in United States relations with less developed countries will increasingly revolve around the activities of United States–based transnational actors rather than around the cold-war and anticolonial issues of the past. In many cases it may be extremely difficult to avoid the collision course that Vernon foresees. The interests of United States–based transnational actors are often incompatible with the interests of governments that desire to maintain or extend national political control. Only if the American government is able to disengage itself somewhat from the interests of United States–based business enterprises, and only if American statesmen are willing to make short-term sacrifices of interest, will it be possible for the United States to play a creative role in these conflicts.

If Evans were correct about the limitations placed on national autonomy and economic development by the activities of multinational corporations, a complete disengagement of the United States from the third world might be beneficial. In our view, however, such a complete disengagement would probably not produce autonomous national development in most poor countries but would involve high costs both for these countries and to some extent for the United States. We believe, therefore, that United States foreign policy should attempt to assist poor countries to control, choose between, and profit from transnational actors. In some situations complete disengagement may be necessary; in others, a more active policy may have greater benefits for both parties. Insofar as possible, as we indicate in section VI of this essay, cooperation in helping less developed countries control transnational incursions should be sought from other developed states through intergovernmental organizations.

[29] For a dissenting view see Kenneth N. Waltz, "International Structure, National Force, and the Balance of World Power," *Journal of International Affairs*, 1967 (Vol. 21, No. 2), pp. 215–231.

Yet, if the United States has been predominant in transnational relations, it does not dominate all the issues in which it is interested, nor can it hope to remain as immune from the effects of transnational changes in the future as it has in the years since World War II. Vernon points out that cultural patterns and antitrust legislation produce a more arm's-length relationship between government and business in the United States than is true of other developed countries, and American business leaders have recently begun to complain about this aspect of free enterprise.[30] Vernon also argues that American labor has been one of the few clear losers in welfare terms (at least in the short run) as a result of the shift of production abroad. Edward Miles shows that the United States is less predominant in the ocean issue area than in outer space. Thornton notes that the United States does not always win in the IATA. Krause points out that although the United States is less vulnerable than other countries to loss of control in the monetary field, it is still vulnerable to some extent, and it no longer has the power unilaterally to make policy in this field as it once did.

If we look toward the future, it is apparent that American dominance will be further diminished. This is not likely to be welcomed by the United States government for, as Vallier argues, a country which perceives benefits from its current position in transnational networks will be likely to attempt to preserve the system—a new and subtle form, some might argue, of imperialism. Yet, European countries and Japan are generating more transnational actors of their own, often with more direct governmental support than is provided in the United States.[31] Some people argue that the United States will have to cope with these challenges—by increasing governmental support for United States–based multinational business, as some industrialists desire, by erecting higher tariff barriers, or by other measures. Since neither statism nor protectionism is likely to be attractive to most American leaders, one can expect attempts to find other solutions, perhaps by negotiating changes in the policies of "Japan, Incorporated" or Common Market countries. In any event the outcome will be only partially determined by American policies, and the efforts of other governments will be equally important in shaping the future.

The growth of transnational relations also raises a number of important questions about the management of United States foreign policy. World politics has become more complex. One response to this has been an increase in the machinery of formal intergovernmental diplomacy. In 1914 the United

[30] For example, William H. Moore, chairman of the board of Bankers Trust Company, was recently quoted to have said that "the government and the private sector, for the good of the United States, are going to have to join hands in many projects." *New York Times,* July 13, 1971, pp. 43, 45. When business magazines discuss Japan's export activities, the same theme—the need for more active cooperation between business and government in the United States—is often stressed.

[31] Stephen Hymer and Robert Rowthorn, "Multinational Corporations and International Oligopoly: The Non-American Challenge," in Kindleberger; see also Louis Kraar, "How the Japanese Mour That Export Blitz," *Fortune,* September 1970 (Vol. 82, No. 3), pp. 126–131, 170. 172.

States was represented in only ten foreign capitals. In 1970 it was represented by 117 embassies, nine missions to international organizations, 67 consulates-general, 56 consulates, four special offices, and nine consular agencies. At the same time, however, the increased sensitivity of societies and the internationalization of domestic politics have led to a situation in which every Cabinet department and fifteen of 31 principal agencies outside the Cabinet have responsibilities requiring actions beyond national borders. In some embassies Department of State personnel account for as little as 20 percent of the total. In London in the early 1960s, 44 distinct federal bureaucracies were represented in the United States embassy, although in Moscow (where transnational relations were very limited) the embassy reflected more traditional forms of diplomacy.[32]

Increased contact between subunits of different governments both through bilateral diplomacy and representation in multilateral organizations enhances the likelihood of transgovernmental coalitions and makes central control of foreign policy more difficult. The situation is even further complicated by private foreign policies that interact with public ones. On issues involving ocean resources, for example, it is easy to imagine a coalition between international oil companies, some elements in the Pentagon, certain bureaucratic units of the Department of the Interior, and some segments of other governments facing an opposing coalition between international scientific organizations, the Department of State, other elements of the Department of the Interior and the Department of Defense, and certain foreign governmental units. Such situations raise serious questions not just about the democratic control of foreign policy but about *any* control of foreign policy.

V. Loss of Control

The increased complexity described in our world politics paradigm helps us understand the seeming paradox that statesmen in a country as preponderant in world politics as the United States often complain about a "loss of control" over their international political environment. People in government often claim that they spend most of their time just trying to find out what is happening, and some have been heard to question whether a coherent foreign policy is possible in a period of rapid, disorienting change. As we argue in the introduction, however, to speak of a "loss of control" is somewhat misleading. States have never been in full control of their external relations,

[32] Henry M. Wriston, *Diplomacy in a Democracy* (New York: Harper & Brothers, 1956), p. 26; Ellis Briggs, "American Diplomacy—The Pelican in the Wilderness," *Foreign Service Journal*, March 1971 (Vol. 48, No. 3), pp. 38–40; see also John Franklin Campbell, *The Foreign Affairs Fudge Factory* (New York: Basic Books, Publishers, 1971). For these citations and statistics we are indebted to a seminar paper prepared at Harvard University for Joseph Nye by G. Robert Dickerman of the United States Information Agency (USIA).

quite apart from the impact of transnational relations. In 1914, for example, the structure of the interstate balance of power severely constrained statesmen. Today the complexity of bureaucracy in modern welfare states and the weakness of institutions in many less developed countries also contribute to the statesman's sense of loss of control. Finally, the impact of transnational relations creates a "control gap" between the aspirations for control over an expanded range of matters and the capability to achieve it. The problem is not a loss of legal sovereignty but a loss of political and economic autonomy. Most states retain control over their policy instruments and are able to pursue their objectives. They are just less able to achieve them.[33]

It seems clear from these essays that this loss of control is not uniform for all types of state objectives. Governments sometimes act as loosely related coalitions of bureaucracies, but they also have central executive and legislative organs which try to integrate these coalitions into a coherent whole. When these central political organs are successful, the unitary model of state behavior becomes a fair approximation of reality, and we would expect to find a lesser role for transgovernmental interactions or for transnational relations in general. It seems that central governmental control tends to be stronger in matters of security than in issues of economic welfare; the "myth" of national security remains an important resource of executive control, and chief executives are likely to spend a large proportion of their time on security issues. But, as Graham T. Allison has shown, even in this area bureaucracies compete to interpret the myth.[34] It is in the nature of bureaucracies to resist policy integration that sacrifices the interest of their special domains for the sake of some allegedly more general interest. Thus, a lack of definition of what constitutes "security" may lead to bureaucratic fragmentation even in this area.

As Evans points out, some governments may be as concerned about loss of control over cultural autonomy and national identity as they are about difficulties in assuring their security against armed attack. Some countries, such as Burma, have been able to isolate themselves from transnational networks, but at considerable economic cost; other countries have attempted more selectively to limit the impact or freedom of action of transnational organizations and transnational communication. For less developed states these policies are politically attractive but difficult to carry out effectively. Controlling transnational communication may become more difficult when direct satellite-to-home broadcasting becomes feasible, and, as multinational copper and oil firms develop greater resources in politically stable areas, the rewards of nationalization may decline.[35]

[33] We are indebted for this point to Richard Cooper, "Economic Interdependence in the 1970's," *World Politics*, forthcoming.

[34] Allison, *Essence of Decision;* or Allison, *American Political Science Review*, Vol. 63, No. 3.

[35] For an interesting discussion of the perils as well as benefits of nationalization see Theodore H. Moran, "The Multinational Corporation versus the Economic Nationalist: Independence and Domination in Raw Materials," *Foreign Policy*, December 1971, forthcoming.

The sense of loss of control is probably most acute, at least among developed countries, in regard to welfare objectives. In part this reflects the expansion of the tasks of government in response to popular pressure. As governments seek to extend control over their own societies, they become increasingly dependent on transnational forces impinging on them from outside their boundaries. Aspirations for increased domestic control broaden the range of relevant issues at the transnational level, thus complicating the problem of controlling the external environment. Complexity and frustration in foreign affairs are among the consequences of the modern capitalist welfare state.

While the range of relevant issues at the transnational level has been greatly broadened by the introduction of the welfare state, technology has increased the mobility of factors and the sensitivity of markets, and societies, to one another. Advances in transportation and communications technology are destroying the fragmentation of markets that is a necessary condition for autonomous national policies. Morse, Krause, Evans, Vernon, and others provide numerous examples of loss of control in the welfare area, largely as a result of technological and organizational change.

Faced with this situation, governments that are unwilling to take a passive position have three major policy options: 1) They can attempt to restore fragmentation of markets through unilateral defensive policies, although this may invite retaliation and eventually prove harmful to the welfare of their citizens; 2) they can follow aggressive policies of extraterritorial extension of national laws to cover mobile factors, but this may also breed resentment and costly retaliation; 3) they can adopt cooperative policies involving joint coordination of policy through international institutions.[36]

For most states cooperative policies have obvious advantages: Conflict can be reduced by joint action and policies coordinated for optimal results. Yet, as Kaiser points out in his essay, this may lead to another kind of loss of control in which legislatures and other democratically responsible bodies continue to lose influence to bureaucrats and technocrats. Once again the close linkage between domestic and international politics becomes clear, and the dangers as well as the opportunities of such interconnections become more readily apparent.

Cooperative policies of response to transnational relations may strengthen ties of interdependence or help create new international organizations, but they do not necessarily do either. States may decide, for example, to amend the rules of an existing institution like the International Monetary Fund (IMF) to create greater exchange rate flexibility, hoping to weaken the mutual sensitivity through the balance-of-payments mechanism and to restore a certain degree of "fragmentation." The net effect may be a reduction of friction

[36] Cooper, *World Politics,* forthcoming. In addition, Cooper suggests an exploitative or parasitic policy option, for example, tax havens and flags of convenience, open to a few small countries.

by restricting interdependence. This would be a joint defensive policy rather than a unilateral one. More frequently, however, cooperative action is likely to create new international institutions to cope with increasing interdependence. This brings us to our final concern—the new tasks that transnational relations create for international organizations.

VI. Transnational Relations and International Organizations

Increases in the importance of transnational relations usually reflect the twin dynamic forces of advancing technology and organizational sophistication. Large organizations such as multinational business enterprises profit from new technology and help generate even greater technological advances; their successes stimulate competitors and other threatened organizations into transnational action as a means of protecting their interests. Yet, transnational relations and the advances that promote them often impose significant external costs on interest groups or governments that cannot be controlled without joint international action. By and large, however, governments and secretariats of intergovernmental organizations have been slow to respond to this challenge.

Recent developments in ocean technology and the law of the sea illustrate this point. As Miles observes, in less than a decade the supposed natural limits to national jurisdiction assumed by the 1958 United Nations Conference on the Law of the Sea were rapidly pushed outward by corporations engaged in undersea exploration. The United Nations General Assembly has been able to agree that the seabed should be the common heritage of mankind but unable to agree on where that heritage begins. The exploitation and development of modern technology by transnational organizations have therefore created difficult political problems that may exceed the capacities of intergovernmental organizations to find universally acceptable solutions.

Transnational organizations are also partially responsible for problems of pollution and wastage of natural resources which will be the subject of the United Nations Conference on the Human Environment in 1972. More dramatically, transnational guerrilla groups have accentuated problems of air safety by spectacular hijackings of airplanes. In quieter ways, networks of scientists have collaborated in pressing for intergovernmental cooperation in science policies, and United States–based foundations have taken the lead in sensitive areas such as birth control. The most significant transnational challenge to international organizations arises, of course, from multinational business enterprises. Vernon suggests a number of ways to reduce friction that will depend on coordination of national economic policies through international institutions, and Cox mentions that the International Labor Organization (ILO) is beginning to take account of the importance of multinational business. Paul Goldberg and Charles Kindleberger have elsewhere suggested the possibility of a "GATT" to monitor multinational business enterprises.[37]

A larger question, however, that transnational relations pose for international organizations is the problem of asymmetry. Science and technology, as used by transnational organizations, are having ambivalent effects on world economic interdependence in the 1970s—linking rich countries and reducing their involvements with poor countries. Thus, the North-South cleavage may be widened rather than bridged by the increasing importance of transnational relations.

Such asymmetries are bound to lead to resentments, particularly on the part of countries that strive to develop an indigenous modern identity. These problems are particularly acute for those countries in which only a small part of the population benefits from transnational relations. Resentments of the transnational interactions that impinge on local culture and of the narrow elites that benefit from these processes may lead to internal strife and increasing self-isolation by poor countries. One might conclude from the essay by Evans that such a period of isolation and separation would be beneficial. Only in this way, one might argue, will the third world achieve new societies with economic and cultural autonomy.

Isolation would, however, have costs as well as benefits. These costs would include not only the loss of the potential benefits of capital and technology but also the greater danger that developed countries would turn increasingly inward as well. Producers in rich countries would develop "safe" resources, for example, shale oil and nuclear energy, and synthetic substitutes at higher costs. Then, following the classic pattern of producers prevailing over consumers in questions of economic nationalism, tariffs and protective quotas would be erected around the West European and American markets.[38] Once in place these barriers would be hard to dismantle. Such a situation is not likely to be healthy for the objectives which the United Nations was established to achieve.

To the extent that the United Nations becomes simply an arena for harangues over intergovernmental aid and an administrator of technical assistance, financial support received from rich countries will recede to a level sustained only by a humanitarian constituency. Perhaps with generational change this constituency will grow. A more imaginative strategy would be for the UN to develop capacities that would assist less developed countries to deal with transnational relations and thus enable them to avoid being caught on the laissez faire or statist-isolationist horns of the dilemma we have sketched.

[37] Paul M. Goldberg and Charles P. Kindleberger, "Toward a GATT for Investment: A Proposal for Supervision of the International Corporation," *Law and Policy in International Business*, Summer 1970 (Vol. 2, No. 2), pp. 295–325.

[38] See Harry G. Johnson, ed., *Economic Nationalism in Old and New States* (Comparative Study of New Nations Series) (Chicago: University of Chicago Press, 1967).

Obviously, the UN cannot play this role alone, but its secretariat could provide leadership in the establishment of impartial monitoring of transnational relations, creation of tribunals to mediate disputes, and creation of a divestment fund to ease disengagement.

Kindleberger has argued that harmonization of rules for the multinational business enterprise is necessary if the institution is going to be effective in promoting world welfare. He has suggested a conference on the multinational corporation under the auspices of the UN and the creation of "an international agency which would collect information on direct investment on a systematic basis, overall and case by case, and would have power to prohibit an investment that substantially reduced competition in a given commodity, even if both governments consented. . . . "[39] In addition, "there should be an international Ombudsman, staffed by experts from the smaller countries, to which companies could appeal if they were being unduly squeezed by overlapping sovereignty of two countries. . . . it would be desirable if they bound themselves in advance to adhere to its decision."[40]

The idea that the United Nations should develop a capacity to monitor, mediate, and establish norms for transnational economic activities is an excellent one. The idea of employing the tired old institution of conference diplomacy is a mistake. Given the political schisms of today's world the classic model of the diplomatic conference with a closely associated secretariat is bound to drive the developed countries to create "shadow" institutions where "business can be done." The suggestion that the United Nations Conference on Trade and Development (UNCTAD) develop a capacity to oversee the actions of multinational corporations is unlikely to be accepted even by men of goodwill in Washington. Similarly, many aspects of inspection and monitoring of governmental behavior have become too difficult politically for the United Nations Secretariat to handle by itself. The task of monitoring the problems created by transnational economic activities in the 1970s would best be handled by institutions only indirectly related to the General Assembly. The role of the assembly (and the reason for at least some linkage) is to discuss, criticize, and publicize decisions reached in smaller and less overtly political bodies.[41]

Transnational relations present opportunities as well as problems for international organizations. The hard shell of national sovereignty appears less daunting from a transnational perspective. International organizations provide

[39] Charles P. Kindleberger, *American Business Abroad: Six Lectures on Direct Investment* (New Haven, Conn: Yale University Press, 1969), p. 207.

[40] Ibid.

[41] One of the useful tasks undertaken by UNCTAD has been to study and publicize the activities of the liner conferences—important transnational actors in ocean shipping. See J. S. Nye, "UNCTAD," in *The Anatomy of Influence: Decision-Making in International Organizations*, ed. Robert W. Cox and Harold K. Jacobson (New Haven, Conn: Yale University Press, forthcoming).

meetings and myths that help foster and legitimate transnational personal contacts and transgovernmental coalitions. Transnational and transgovernmental actors can be seen as potential allies for the secretariats of international organizations. Greater efforts might be made to involve the representatives of national and international private associations directly.[42] More institutional imagination will be needed in the future if governments and international organizations are to cope with the problems posed by transnational relations and to avoid the classic international organization syndrome of designing institutions to fight the last battle rather than to prevent the next one.

VII. A Final Word

This volume does not attempt to prove that states are obsolete. We do not contend that transnational relations will necessarily bring world peace or even reduce the likelihood of certain types of conflict. Transnational relations are dependent on the political relations between states as well as vice versa, and world peace in the future will surely depend not only on the forms taken by transnational activities but also on the creativity shown by leaders of states, international organizations, and transnational organizations themselves.

Although transnational relations are not entirely new, they are an important part of world politics, and their importance has been increasing in the years since World War II. The essays in this volume show why we believe that the simplifications of the state-centric approach divert the attention of scholars and statesmen away from many important current problems and distort the analyses of others. We have suggested a "world politics paradigm" that includes transnational, transgovernmental, and interstate interactions in the hope of stimulating new types of theory, research, and approaches to policy. We think that these essays, written within a common framework and in response to our specific questions, illustrate the potential utility of our approach. The authors pose many difficult problems, but they also attempt to provide some suggestions, if not solutions.

We plead guilty, however, to raising far more questions than we or our authors answer. These questions are amenable to research from a normative as well as an empirical point of view. We hope that they will stimulate new types of scholarly research projects and graduate theses. But the questions are not simply "academic." We also hope that they will stimulate new policy perspectives on the part of statesmen in governments and international organizations. If these new perspectives contribute to greater understanding of world politics, which may indirectly contribute to peace and justice, then this imperfect volume will have succeeded.

[42] Cox and Jacobson found surprisingly few efforts to foster such coalitions.

Selected Bibliography

This bibliography is designed as a short introduction to the literature on transnational relations as discussed in this volume. The authors have provided lists of important works from their fields of inquiry, and we have simply reorganized these lists under topic headings, eliminating redundancy when necessary.

I. General Aspects of Transnational Relations

Transnational Relations and World Politics

Allison, Graham T. "Conceptual Models and the Cuban Missile Crisis." *American Political Science Review,* September 1969 (Vol. 63, No. 3), pp. 689–718.

Aron, Raymond. *Peace and War: A Theory of International Relations.* Translated by Richard Howard and Annette Baker Fox. Garden City, N.Y: Doubleday & Co., 1966. xviii +820 pp.

Burton, John W. *Systems, States, Diplomacy and Rules.* Cambridge: Cambridge University Press, 1968. xii + 251 pp.

Cottam, Richard W. *Competitive Interference and Twentieth Century Diplomacy.* Pittsburgh, Pa: Pittsburgh University Press, 1967. 243 pp.

Cox, Robert W., and Harold K. Jacobson, eds. *The Anatomy of Influence: Decision-Making in International Organizations.* New Haven, Conn: Yale University Press, forthcoming.

Hoffmann, Stanley. "International Organization and the International System." *International Organization,* Summer 1970 (Vol. 24, No. 3), pp. 389–413.

Kaiser, Karl. "Transnationale Politik: Zu einer Theorie der multinationalen Politik. *Politische Vierteljahresschrift* (Cologne), 1969 (Special Issue No. 1), pp. 80–109.

Keohane, Robert O. "The Big Influence of Small Allies." *Foreign Policy,* Spring 1971 (Vol. 1, No. 2), pp. 161–182.

Lindberg, Leon N., and Stuart A. Scheingold. *Europe's Would-Be Polity: Patterns of Change in the European Community.* Englewood Cliffs, N.J: Prentice-Hall, 1970. vi + 314 pp.

Mendershausen, Horst. "Transnational Society vs. State Sovereignty." *Kyklos* (Bern), 1969 (Vol. 22, No. 2), pp. 251–275.

Rosenau, James N., ed. *Linkage Politics: Essays on the Convergence of National and International Systems.* New York: Free Press, 1969. xii + 352 pp.

Scott, Andrew M. *The Revolution in Statecraft: Informal Penetration.* (Random House Studies in Political Science, P551.) New York: Random House, 1965. vii + 194 pp.

Wolfers, Arnold. *Discord and Collaboration: Essays on International Politics.* Baltimore, Md: Johns Hopkins Press, 1962. xvii + 283 pp.

Transnationalism as a Historical Phenomenon

Cobden, Richard. "England, Ireland, and America." In *The Political Writings of Richard Cobden.* Vol. 1. London: T. Fisher Unwin, 1903. Pp. 5–119.

Curti, Merle. *American Philanthropy Abroad: A History.* New Brunswick, N.J: Rutgers University Press, 1963. xix + 651 pp.

Curti, M[erle], and K[endall] Birr. *Prelude to Point Four: American Technical Missions Overseas, 1838–1938.* Madison: University of Wisconsin Press, 1954. xi + 284 pp.

Drucker, Peter F. *The Age of Discontinuity: Guidelines to Our Changing Society.* New York: Harper & Row, Publishers, 1969. xiii + 402 pp.

Fairbank, John K., Edwin O. Reischauer, and Albert M. Craig. *East Asia: The Modern Transformation.* (History of East Asian Civilization, Vol. 2.) Boston: Houghton Mifflin, 1965. xvi + 955 pp.

Field, James A., Jr. *America and the Mediterranean World, 1776–1882.* Princeton, N.J: Princeton University Press, 1969. xv + 485 pp.

Heindel, Richard Heathcote. *The American Impact on Great Britain, 1898–1914: A Study of the United States in World History*. Philadelphia: University of Pennsylvania Press, 1940. ix + 439 pp.

Koht, Halvdan. *The American Spirit in Europe: A Survey of Transatlantic Influence.* (Publications of the American Institute, University of Oslo, in cooperation with the Department of American Civilization, Graduate School of Arts and Sciences, University of Pennsylvania.) Philadelphia: University of Pennsylvania Press, 1949. ix + 289 pp.

Landes, David S. *The Unbound Prometheus: Technological Change and Industrial Development in Western Europe from 1750 to the Present.* Cambridge: Cambridge University Press, 1969. ix + 566 pp.

Latourette, Kenneth S. *A History of the Expansion of Christianity.* 7 vols. New York: Harper & Brothers, 1937–1945.

Lewis, Bernard. *The Middle East and the West.* (Indiana University International Studies.) Bloomington: Indiana University Press, 1964. 160 pp.

Rippy, J. Fred. *Latin America and the Industrial Age.* New York: G. P. Putnam's Sons, 1944. x + 277 pp.

Servan-Schreiber, J.-J. *The American Challenge.* Translated by Ronald Steel. New York: Avon Books, 1969. 254 pp.

Stead, W. T. *The Americanization of the World; Or, the Trend of the Twentieth Century.* New York: H. Markley, 1902. 444 pp.

Wilkins, Mira. *The Emergence of Multinational Enterprise: American Business Abroad from the Colonial Era to 1914.* Cambridge, Mass: Harvard University Press, 1970. xiv + 310 pp.

Whitaker, Arthur P. *The Western Hemisphere Idea: Its Rise and Decline.* Ithaca, N.Y: Cornell University Press, 1954. x + 194 pp.

Woodruff, William. *Impact of Western Man: A Study of Europe's Role in the World Economy, 1750–1960.* New York: St. Martin's Press, 1967. xvii + 375 pp.

TRANSNATIONAL ECONOMIC RELATIONS

Condliffe, J. B. *The Commerce of Nations.* New York: W. W. Norton & Co., 1950. xi +884 pp.

Cooper, Richard N. *The Economics of Interdependence: Economic Policy in the Atlantic Community.* (Atlantic Policy Studies.) New York: McGraw-Hill Book Co. (for the Council on Foreign Relations), 1968. xiv + 302 pp.

Deutsch, Karl W., and Alexander Eckstein. "National Industrialization and the Declining Share of the International Economic Sector, 1890–1959." *World Politics,* January 1961 (Vol. 13, No. 2), pp. 267–299.

Deutsch, Karl W., Chester I. Bliss, and Alexander Eckstein. "Population, Sovereignty, and the Share of Foreign Trade." *Economic Development and Cultural Change,* July 1962 (Vol. 10, No. 4), pp. 353–366.

Feld, Werner. "Political Aspects of Transnational Business Collaboration in the Common Market." *International Organization,* Spring 1970 (Vol. 24, No. 2), pp. 209–238.

Gardner, Richard N. *Sterling-Dollar Diplomacy: The Origins and Prospects of Our International Economic Order.* Enl. ed. New York: McGraw-Hill Book Co., 1969. cviii + 423 pp.

Geiger, Theodore. "Trends in Atlantic Relations during the 1970's." *Atlantic Community Quarterly,* Summer 1970 (Vol. 8, No. 2), pp. 210–223.

Gilbert, Felix. *To the Farewell Address: Ideas of Early American Foreign Policy.* Princeton, N.J: Princeton University Press, 1961. 173 pp.

Hoffmann, Stanley. "Obstinate or Obsolete? The Fate of the Nation-State and the Case of Western Europe." *Daedalus,* Summer 1966 (Vol. 95, No. 3), pp. 862–915.

Imlah, Albert H. *Economic Elements in the Pax Britannica: Studies in British Foreign Trade in the Nineteenth Century.* Cambridge, Mass: Harvard University Press, 1958. xiii + 224 pp.

Kolko, Gabriel. *The Politics of War: The World and the United States Foreign Policy, 1943–1945.* New York: Random House, 1968. x + 685 pp.

Kuznets, Simon. *Modern Economic Growth: Rate, Structure, and Spread.* (Studies in Comparative Economics, No. 7.) New Haven, Conn: Yale University Press, 1966. xvii + 529 pp.

Morse, Edward L. "The Politics of Interdependence." *International Organization,* Spring 1969 (Vol. 23, No. 2), pp. 311–326.

Patterson, Gardner. *Discrimination in International Trade: The Policy Issues, 1945–1965.* Princeton, N.J: Princeton University Press, 1966. xiv + 414 pp.

Perroux, François. *L'Economie du XXe siècle.* 3rd enl. ed. Paris: Presses Universitaires de France, 1969. 765 pp.

Schmitt, Hans O. "Integration and Conflict in the World Economy." *Journal of Common Market Studies* (Oxford), September 1969 (Vol. 8, No. 1), pp. 1–18.

Staley, Eugene. *War and the Private Investor: A Study in the Relations of International Politics and International Private Investment.* Garden City, N.Y: Doubleday, Doran & Co., 1935. xxv + 562 pp.

———. *World Economy in Transition: Technology vs. Politics, Laissez Faire vs. Planning, Power vs. Welfare.* (Publications of the Council on Foreign Relations.) New York: Council on Foreign Relations (under the auspices of the American Coördinating Committee for International Studies), 1939. xi + 340 pp.

Strange, Susan. "International Economics and International Relations: A Case of Mutual Neglect." *International Affairs* (London), April 1970 (Vol. 46, No. 2), pp. 304–315.

Svennilson, Ingvar. *Growth and Stagnation in the European Economy.* Geneva: United Nations Economic Commission for Europe, 1954. xvi + 342 pp.

Viner, Jacob. *The Customs Union Issue.* (Studies in the Administration of International Law and Organization, No. 10.) New York: Carnegie Endowment for International Peace, 1950. viii + 221 pp.

Waltz, Kenneth N. "The Myth of National Interdependence." In *The International Corporation: A Symposium,* edited by Charles P. Kindleberger. Cambridge, Mass: M.I.T. Press, 1970. Pp. 205–223.

Young, Oran R. "Interdependencies in World Politics," *International Journal* (Toronto), Autumn 1969 (Vol. 24, No. 4), pp. 726–750.

The Effects of Transnational Participation

Angell, Robert Cooley. *Peace on the March: Transnational Participation* (New Perspectives in Political Science, No. 19.) New York: Van Nostrand Reinhold Co., 1969. ix + 205 pp.

Bauer, Raymond A., Ithiel de Sola Pool, and Lewis Anthony Dexter. *American Business and Public Policy: The Politics of Foreign Trade* (Atherton Press Political Science Series.) New York: Atherton Press, 1963. xxvii + 499 pp.

Coombs, Philip H. *The Fourth Dimension of Foreign Policy: Educational and Cultural Affairs.* (Policy Books.) New York: Harper and Row, Publishers (for the Council on Foreign Relations), 1964. xvi + 158 pp.

Fisher, Roger, ed. *International Conflict and Behavioral Science: The Craigville Papers.* New York: Basic Books, Publishers, 1964. xii + 290 pp. See especially chapter 5.

Kelman, Herbert C., and Raphael S. Ezekiel, with the collaboration of Rose B. Kelman. *Cross-National Encounters.* (Jossey-Bass Behavioral Science Series.) San Francisco, Calif: Jossey-Bass, Publishers, 1970. xiv + 345 pp.

Kelman, Herbert C., ed. *International Behavior: A Social-Psychological Analysis.* New York: Holt, Rinehart and Winston (for the Society for the Psychological Study of Social Issues), 1965. xiv + 626 pp. See especially chapters 1, 4, 8, 10, 15, and 16.

Lambert, R. D., and Marvin Bressler. *Indian Students on an American Campus.* Minneapolis: University of Minnesota Press, 1956. xi + 122 pp.

Morris, Richard T., with the assistance of Oluf M. Davidsen. *The Two-Way Mirror: National Status in Foreign Students' Adjustment.* Minneapolis: University of Minnesota Press, 1960. xii + 215 pp.

Rosenau, James N. *National Leadership and Foreign Policy: A Case Study in the Mobilization of Public Support.* Princeton, N.J: Princeton University Press (for the Center of International Affairs and the Woodrow Wilson School of Public and International Affairs), 1963. xvii + 409 pp.

Rosenau, James N., ed. *International Politics and Foreign Policy: A Reader in Research and Theory.* Rev. ed. New York: Free Press, 1969. See especially chapter 26. xii +511 pp.

Selltiz, Claire, J. R. Christ, J. Havel, and S. W. Cook. *Attitudes and Social Relations of Foreign Students in the United States.* Minneapolis: University of Minnesota Press, 1963. xiv + 434 pp.

Transnational Relations and Democratic Control

Kaiser, Karl. "Das internationale System der Gegenwart als Faktor der Beeinträchtigung demokratischer Aussenpolitik." *Politische Vierteljahresschrift* (Cologne), 1970 (Special Issue No. 2), pp. 340–358.

———. "Interdependence and Autonomy: Britain and the Federal Republic in their Multinational Environment." In *Britain and West Germany: Changing Societies and the Future of Foreign Policy*, edited by Karl Kaiser and Roger Morgan. London: Oxford University Press, 1971. Pp. 17–40.

———. "Transnationale Politik: Zu einer Theorie der multinationalen Politik." *Politische Vierteljahresschrift* (Cologne), 1969 (Special Issue No. 1), pp. 80–109.

II. Transnational Actors

International Nongovernmental Organizations

Angell, Robert C. "An Analysis of Trends in International Organizations." Peace Research Society (International) *Papers*, 1965 (Vol. 3), Chicago Conference, pp. 185–195.

Galtung, Johan. "Non-Territorial Actors and the Problem of Peace." Revised version of a paper presented at the World Order Models Meeting, Northfield Inn, Northfield, Massachusetts, June 18–24, 1969.

Judge, Anthony J. N. "Classification of International and National Organizations and the Relationship between Them with Special Reference to International Non-Profit Organizations." Extract from a report of a preliminary investigation of the possibility of using computer data processing methods within the Union of International Associations, Brussels, 1968. Mimeographed.

Kriesberg, Louis. "U.S. and U.S.S.R. Participation in International Non-Governmental Organizations." In *Social Processes in International Relations: A Reader,* edited by Louis Kriesberg. New York: John Wiley & Sons, Inc., 1968. Pp. 466–485.

Lador-Lederer, J. J. *International Non-Governmental Organizations and Economic Entities: A Study in Autonomous Organization and* Ius Gentium. Leiden: A. W. Sijthoff, 1962. 403 pp.

Rodgers, Raymond Spencer. *Facilitation of Problems of International Associations: The Legal, Fiscal, and Administrative Facilities of International Non-Governmental Organizations.* (Documents for the Study of International Non-Governmental Relations, No. 9.) Brussels: Union of International Associations, 1960. 167 pp.

Skjelsbaek, Kjell. "Development of the Systems of International Organizations: A Diachronic Study." *Proceedings of the International Peace Research Association Third General Conference.* (IPRA Studies in Peace Research.) Assen, the Netherlands: Royal Van Gorcum, 1970. Pp. 90–136.

———. "Peace and the Systems of International Organizations." Magister's thesis, University of Oslo, 1970.

Smoker, Paul. "Nation State Escalation and International Integration." *Journal of Peace Research* (Oslo), 1967 (Vol. 4, No. 1), pp. 61–75.

———. "A Preliminary Empirical Study of an International Integrative Subsystem." *International Associations* (Brussels), November 1965 (17th Year, No. 11), pp. 638–646.

Speeckaert, G. P. *The 1,978 International Organizations Founded since the Congress of Vienna: A Chronological List.* (Documents for the Study of International Non-Governmental Relations, No. 7.) Brussels: Union of International Associations, 1957.

White, Lyman Cromwell, assisted by Marie Ragonetti Zocca. *International Non-Governmental Organizations: Their Purposes, Methods, and Accomplishments.* New Brunswick, N.J: Rutgers University Press, 1951. xi + 325 pp.

Yearbook of International Organizations. 1st through 12th eds. Brussels: Union of International Associations, 1908–1968.

The Multinational Business Enterprise

Aharoni, Yair. *The Foreign Investment Decision Process.* Boston: Division of Research, Graduate School of Business Administration, Harvard University, 1966. xviii + 362 pp.

Baran, Paul A. *The Political Economy of Growth.* New York: Monthly Review Press, 1957. 308 pp.

Baranson, Jack. *Automotive Industries in Developing Countries* (World Bank Staff Occasional Papers, No. 8). Baltimore, Md: Johns Hopkins Press (for the International Bank for Reconstruction and Development), 1969. xiii + 106 pp.

Behrman, Jack N. *National Interests and the Multinational Enterprise: Tensions among the North Atlantic Countries.* Englewood Cliffs, N.J: Prentice-Hall, 1970. 194 pp.

Brash, Donald T. *American Investment in Australian Industry.* Cambridge, Mass: Harvard University Press, 1966. xv + 366 pp.

Carey, Omer L., ed. *The Military-Industrial Complex and United States Foreign Policy.* Pullman: Washington State University Press, 1969. 66 pp.

Dos Santos, Theotonio. *El nuevo carácter de la dependencia.* (Cuaderno No. 10.) Santiago: Centro de Estudios Socio-Económicos, Universidad de Chile, 1968. 98 pp.

Dunning, J. H. *American Investment in British Manufacturing Industry.* London: George Allen & Unwin, 1958. 365 pp.

Frank, Andre[w] Gunder. *Capitalism and Underdevelopment in Latin America: Historical Studies of Chile and Brazil.* New York: Monthly Review Press, 1967. xx + 295 pp.

Gervais, Jacques. *La France face aux investissements étrangers: Analyse par secteurs.* Paris: Editions de l'entreprise moderne, 1963. 234 pp.

Hellmann, Rainer. *The Challenge to U.S. Dominance of the International Corporation.* Translated by Peter Ruof. New York: University Press of Cambridge, Mass., Dunellen, 1970. xix + 348 pp.

Hobson, J. A. *Imperialism: A Study.* 3rd rev. ed. London: George Allen & Unwin, 1938. 386 pp.

Hollerman, Leon. *Japan's Dependence on the World Economy: The Approach toward Economic Liberalization.* Princeton, N.J: Princeton University Press, 1967. xv + 291 pp.

Hou, Chi-ming. *Foreign Investment and Economic Development in China, 1840–1937.* (Harvard East Asian Studies, No. 21.) Cambridge, Mass: Harvard University Press, 1965. xiii + 306 pp.

Johnstone, Allan W. *United States Direct Investment in France: An Investigation of the French Charges.* Cambridge, Mass: M.I.T. Press, 1965. xv + 109 pp.

Kidron, Michael. *Foreign Investments in India.* New York: Oxford University Press, 1965. xv + 368 pp.

Kindleberger, Charles P. *American Business Abroad: Six Lectures on Direct Investment.* New Haven. Conn: Yale University Press, 1969. vii + 225 pp.

Kindleberger, Charles P., ed. *The International Corporation: A Symposium.* Cambridge, Mass: M.I.T. Press, 1970. vii + 415 pp.

Lenin, V. I. *Imperialism: The Highest State of Capitalism—A Popular Outline.* (Little Lenin Library, Vol. 15.) Rev. trans. New York: International Publishers, 1939. 128 pp.

Levitt, Kari. *Silent Surrender: The Multinational Corporation in Canada.* New York: St. Martin's Press, 1970. xxi + 185 pp.

Magdoff, Harry. *The Age of Imperialism: The Economics of U.S. Foreign Policy.* New York: Monthly Review Press, 1969. 208 pp.

Mandel, Ernest. *Marxist Economic Theory.* Vol. II. Translated by Brian Pearce. Rev. ed. New York: Monthly Review Press, 1968. Pp. 389–797.

Merhav, Meir. *Technological Dependence, Monopoly, and Growth.* New York: Pergamon Press, 1969. xi + 211 pp.

Miliband, Ralph. *The State in Capitalist Society.* New York: Basic Books, Publishers, 1969. x + 292 pp.

Penrose, Edith T. *The Large International Firm in Developing Countries: The International Petroleum Industry.* London: George Allen & Unwin, 1968. 311 pp.

Rodgers, William. *Think: A Biography of the Watsons and IBM.* New York: Stein & Day, 1969. 320 pp.

Rolfe, Sidney E. "The International Corporation." Paper presented at Twenty-second Congress of the International Chamber of Commerce, Istanbul, May 31–June 7, 1969.

Safarian, A. E. *Foreign Ownership of Canadian Industry.* Toronto: McGraw-Hill Co. of Canada, 1966. xiv + 346 pp.

Standard Oil Company of New Jersey. *The Multinational Company and National Development.* New York: Standard Oil Company, 1970.

Tanzer, Michael. *The Political Economy of International Oil and the Underdeveloped Countries.* Boston: Beacon Press, 1969. x + 455 pp.

Vagts, Detlev F. "The Multinational Enterprise: A New Challenge for Transnational Law." *Harvard Law Review,* February 1970 (Vol. 83, No. 4), pp. 739–792.

Vernon, Raymond. *Sovereignty at Bay: The Multinational Spread of U.S. Enterprises.* (Harvard Multinational Enterprise Series.) New York: Basic Books, Publishers, 1971. x + 326 pp.

Wilkins, Mira, and Frank Ernest Hill. *American Business Abroad: Ford on Six Continents.* Detroit, Mich: Wayne State University Press, 1964. xiii + 541 pp.

FOUNDATIONS

Andrews, F. Emerson, ed. *Foundations: Twenty Viewpoints.* New York: Russell Sage Foundation, 1965. 108 pp.

Curti, Merle. *American Philanthropy Abroad: A History.* New Brunswick, N.J: Rutgers University Press, 1963. xix + 651 pp.

Elliott, William Y. *Education and Training in the Developing Countries: The Role of U.S. Foreign Aid.* New York: Frederick A. Praeger, 1966. xv + 399 pp.

The Ford Foundation in the 1960s. Statement of the Board of Trustees on Policies, Programs, and Operations. New York: Ford Foundation, July 1962. 16 pp.

Fosdick, Raymond B. *A Philosophy for a Foundation.* New York: Rockefeller Foundation, 1963. 27 pp.

Horowitz, Irving Louis, and Ruth Leonora Horowitz. "Tax-Exempt Foundations: Their Effects on National Policy." *Science,* April 10, 1970 (Vol. 168, No. 3928), pp. 220–228.

Kiger, Joseph C. *Operating Principles of the Larger Foundations.* New York: Russell Sage Foundation, 1954. 151 pp.

———. "Foundations and International Affairs." *Foundation News,* July 1965 (Vol. 6, No. 4), pp. 65–68.

Lewis, Marianna O., ed. *The Foundation Directory.* 3rd ed. New York: Russell Sage Foundation (for the Foundation Library Center), 1967. 1198 pp.

Philanthropic Foundations in the United States: A Brief Description. New York: Foundation Center, 1969. 35 pp.

Report of the Study for The Ford Foundation on Policy and Program. H. Rowan Gaither, Jr., chairman. Detroit, Mich: Ford Foundation, November 1949. 139 pp.

Ross, Irwin. "Let's Not Fence in the Foundations." *Fortune,* June 1969 (Vol. 79, No. 7), pp. 148–150, 164–172.

Sjoberg, Gideon, ed. *Ethics, Politics, and Social Research.* Cambridge, Mass: Schenkman Publishing Co., 1967. See especially chapter 1.

Sutton, Francis X. *American Foundations and US Public Diplomacy.* New York: Ford Foundation, 1968.

Weaver, Warren. *U.S. Philanthropic Foundations: Their History, Structure, Management, and Record.* New York: Harper & Row, Publishers, 1967. xvi + 492 pp.

THE ROMAN CATHOLIC CHURCH

Bull, George. *Vatican Politics at the Second Vatican Council, 1962–5.* (Chatham House Essay, No. 11.) London: Oxford University Press (under the auspices of the Royal Institute of International Affairs), 1966. vi + 157 pp.

Crozier, Michel. "Sociologie des organisations et institutions internationales." *Social Science Information* (Paris), August 1967 (Vol. 6, No. 4), pp. 53–62.

Galtung, Johan. "International Relations and International Conflicts: A Sociological Approach." In *Transactions of the Sixth World Congress of Sociology, Evian, September 4–11, 1966.* Vol. 1, pp. 121–161.

Graham, Robert A. *Vatican Diplomacy: A Study of Church and State on the International Plane.* Princeton, N.J: Princeton University Press, 1959. xii + 442 pp.

Jemolo, A. C. *Church and State in Italy, 1850–1950.* Translated by David Moore. Philadelphia: Dufour Editions, 1961. 344 pp.

Kunz, Josef L. "The Status of the Holy See in International Law." *American Journal of International Law,* April 1952 (Vol. 46, No. 2), pp. 308–314.

Mecham, J. Lloyd. "The Papacy and Spanish-American Independence." *Hispanic American Historical Review,* May 1929 (Vol. 9, No. 2), pp. 154–175.

Pichon, Charles. *Le Vatican.* (Les Grandes Etudes contemporaines.) Paris: Editions A. Fayard, 1960. 571 pp.

Shils, Edward. "Charisma, Order, and Status." *American Sociological Review,* April 1965 (Vol. 30, No. 2), pp. 199–213.

Unitatis Redintegratio [Decree on Ecumenism]. In *The Documents of Vatican II,* edited by Walter M. Abbott. Translation edited by Joseph Gallagher. (Angelus Book, 31185.) New York: Guild Press, 1966. Pp. 341–366.

CONTEMPORARY REVOLUTIONARY MOVEMENTS

Black, Cyril E., and Thomas P. Thornton, eds. *Communism and Revolution: The Strategic Uses of Political Violence.* Princeton, N.J: Princeton University Press, 1964. ix + 467 pp.

Chaliand, Gérard. *Armed Struggle in Africa: With the Guerrillas in "Portuguese" Guinea.* Translated by David Rattray and Robert Leonhardt. New York: Monthly Review Press, 1969. xvi + 142 pp.

Debray, Régis. *Strategy for Revolution.* Edited by Robin Blackburn. New York: Monthly Review Press, 1970. 225 pp.

Eckstein, Harry, ed. *Internal War, Problems and Approaches.* New York: Free Press, 1964. x + 339 pp.

Gann, Lewis. *Guerrillas in History.* Stanford, Calif: Hoover Institute Press, 1970.

Gott, Richard. *Guerrilla Movements in Latin America.* London: Nelson, 1970. x + 452 pp.

Guevara, Ernesto Che. *Venceremos! The Speeches and Writings of Ernesto Che Guevara.* Edited and annotated by John Gerassi. New York: Macmillan Co., 1968. xix + 442 pp.

Gurr, Ted Robert. *Why Men Rebel.* Princeton, N.J: Princeton University Press (for the Center of International Studies, Princeton University), 1970. xi + 421 pp.

Harkabi, Y. *Fedayeen Action and Arab Strategy.* (Adelphi Papers, No. 53.) London: Institute for Strategic Studies, December 1968. 43 pp.

Marcum, John. *The Angolan Revolution.* Vol. I: *The Anatomy of an Explosion, 1950–1962.* (M.I.T. Studies in Communism, Revisionism, and Revolution.) Cambridge, Mass: M.I.T. Press, 1969. xiv + 380 pp.

Mercier Vega, Luis. *Guerrillas in Latin America: The Technique of the Counter-State.* Translated by Daniel Weisshart. New York: Frederick A. Praeger, 1969. 246 pp.

Mondlane, Eduardo. *The Struggle for Mozambique.* (Penguin African Library, AP 28.) Harmondsworth, Middlesex, England: Penguin, 1969. 221 pp.

Sharabi, Hisham. *Palestine Guerrillas: Their Credibility and Effectiveness.* (Supplementary Papers.) Washington: Center for Strategic and International Studies, Georgetown University, 1970. vii + 56 pp.

Tricontinental (Havana), April 1966 (Vol. 1, No. 1), and following. Theoretical organ of the Executive Secretariat of the Organization of Solidarity of the Peoples of Africa, Asia, and Latin America, published in Havana.

III. Issue Areas with Transnational Activity

INTERNATIONAL FINANCE

Bergsten, Fred, George Halm, Fritz Machlup, and Robert Roosa. *Approaches to Greater Flexibility of Exchange Rates: The Burgenstock Papers.* Princeton, N.J: Princeton University Press, 1970. 436 pp.

Giersch, Herbert, ed. *Integration Through Monetary Union? Symposium June 1970.* Tübingen: J. C. B. Mohr (Paul Siebeck), 1971. 178 pp.

Levin, Jay H. *Forward Exchange and Internal-External Equilibrium.* (Michigan International Business Studies, No. 12.) Ann Arbor: Program in International Business, University of Michigan, 1970. x + 133 pp.

Machlup, Fritz. "Euro-Dollar Creation: A Mystery Story." *Banca Nazionale del Lavoro Quarterly Review* (Rome), September 1970 (No. 94), pp. 219–260.

McKinnon, Ronald I. *Private and Official International Money: The Case for the Dollar.* (Essays in International Finance, No. 74.) Princeton, N.J: International Finance Section, Department of Economics, Princeton University, April 1969. 40 pp.

Marris, Stephen. *The Burgenstock Communiqué: A Critical Examination of the Case for Limited Flexibility of Exchange Rates.* (Essays in International Finance, No. 80.) Princeton, N.J: International Finance Section, Department of Economics, Princeton University, May 1970. 74 pp.

Mikesell, Raymond F. *The U.S. Balance of Payments and the International Role of the Dollar.* Washington: American Enterprise Institute for Public Policy Research, July 1970. 147 pp.

Mundell, Robert A., and Alexander K. Swoboda, eds. *Monetary Problems of the International Economy.* Chicago: University of Chicago Press, 1969. x + 405 pp.

Willett, Thomas D., Samuel I. Katz, and William H. Branson. *Exchange-Rate Systems, Interest Rates, and Capital Flows.* (Essays in International Finance, No. 78.) Princeton, N.J: International Finance Section, Department of Economics, Princeton University, January 1970. 40 pp.

LABOR

Carlton, Frank T. "Labor Policies for the Struggle with Soviet Communism." *American Journal of Economics and Sociology,* April 1959 (Vol. 18, No. 3), pp. 277–284.

Fischer, Georges. "Syndicats et décolonisation." *Présence africaine* (Paris), October 1960–January 1961 (Nos. 34–35), pp. 17–60.

Günter, Hans, ed. *Transnational Industrial Relations.* London: Macmillan & Co., forthcoming.

Harrod, Jeffrey. *Trade Union Foreign Policy: The Case of British and American Unions in Jamaica.* London: Macmillan & Co., forthcoming.

Heaps, David. "Union Participation in Foreign Aid Programs." *Industrial and Labor Relations Review,* October 1955 (Vol. 9, No. 1), pp. 100–108.

Hero, Alfred O., Jr., and Emil Starr. *The Reuther-Meany Foreign Policy Dispute: Union Leaders and Members View World Affairs.* Dobbs Ferry, N.Y: Oceana Publications, 1970. 228 pp.

Jacobson, Harold Karan. "Ventures in Polity Shaping: External Assistance to Labour Movements in Developing Countries." In *The Politics of International Organizations: Studies in Multilateral Social and Economic Agencies,* edited by Robert W. Cox. New York: Praeger Publishers, 1970. Pp. 195–205.

Jager, Elizabeth. "Multinationalism and Labor: For Whose Benefit?" *Columbia Journal of World Business,* January–February 1970 (Vol. 5, No. 1), pp. 56–64.

Lodge, George C. "Labor's Role in Newly Developing Countries." *Foreign Affairs,* July 1959 (Vol. 37, No. 4), pp. 660–671.

Myers, Charles A. "The American System of Industrial Relations: Is It Exportable?" *Proceedings of the Fifteenth Annual Meeting of the Industrial Relations Research Association, Pittsburgh, Pa., December 27–28, 1962,* edited by Gerald G. Somers. Pp. 2–14.

Romualdi, Serafino. *Presidents and Peons: Recollections of a Labor Ambassador in Latin America.* New York: Funk & Wagnalls, 1967. xvi + 524 pp.

Spyropoulos, Georges. "Le Rôle de la négociation collective dans l'harmonisation des systèmes sociaux européens." *Revue internationale de droit comparé* (Paris), January–March 1966 (Vol. 18, No. 1), pp. 19–55.

"The Trade Union Response to Multinational Enterprise." *Monthly Labor Review,* December 1967 (Vol. 90, No. 12), pp. iii-iv.

Windmuller, John P. *American Labor and the International Labor Movement, 1940 to 1953.* (Cornell International Industrial and Labor Relations Reports, No. 2.) Ithaca, N.Y: Institute of International Industrial and Labor Relations, Cornell University, 1954.

———. "Foreign Affairs and the AFL-CIO." *Industrial and Labor Relations Review,* April 1956 (Vol. 9, No. 3), pp. 419–432.

———. "Labor: A Partner in American Foreign Policy?" *Annals of the American Academy of Political and Social Science,* November 1963 (Vol. 350), pp. 104–114.

———. "Leadership and Administration in the ICFTU: A New Phase of Development." *British Journal of Industrial Relations* (London), June 1963 (Vol. 1, No. 2), pp. 147–169.

———. "The Foreign Policy Conflict in American Labor." *Political Science Quarterly,* June 1967 (Vol. 82, No. 2), pp. 205–234.

———. "Internationalism in Eclipse: The ICFTU after Two Decades." *Industrial and Labor Relations Review,* July 1970 (Vol. 23, No. 4), pp. 510–527.

OUTER SPACE

Bloomfield, Lincoln, ed. *Outer Space: Prospects for Man and Society.* Rev. ed. New York: Frederick A. Praeger (for the American Assembly, Columbia University), 1968. 203 pp.

COSPAR *Information Bulletin,* March 1960 (No. 1), and following.

McDougal, Myres, Harold Lasswell, and Ivan Vlasic. *The Public Order of Space.* New Haven, Conn: Yale University Press, 1963.

Maddox, Brenda. "The Connections." *The Economist,* August 9, 1969 (Vol. 232, No. 6572), pp. vii-xxxvi.

Miles, Edward. *The International Decision-System for Space Exploration.* In preparation.

Odishaw, Hugh, ed. *The Challenges of Space.* Chicago: University of Chicago Press, 1962. xviii + 379 pp.

Schwartz, Leonard. *International Organizations and Space Cooperation.* Durham, N.C: World Rule of Law Center, 1962. 108 pp.

THE OCEANS

Alexander, Lewis, ed. *The Law of the Sea: Offshore Boundaries and Zones.* (Publication of the Law of the Sea Institute and the Mershon Center for Education in National Security.) Columbus: Ohio State University Press, 1967. xv + 321 pp.

Johnston, Douglas M. *The International Law of Fisheries: A Framework for Policy-Oriented Inquiries.* New Haven, Conn: Yale University Press, 1965. xxiv + 554 pp.

Law of the Sea Institute. *Proceedings of the Annual Conferences.* Kingston: University of Rhode Island, 1966 and following.

Lawrence, Samuel A. *United States Merchant Shipping Policies and Politics.* Washington: Brookings Institution, 1966. xiii + 405 pp.

McDougal, Myres S., and William T. Burke. *The Public Order of the Oceans: A Contemporary International Law of the Sea.* New Haven, Conn: Yale University Press, 1962. xxv + 1226 pp.

Marx, Daniel. *International Shipping Cartels: A Study of Industrial Self-Regulation by Shipping Cartels.* Princeton, N.J: Princeton University Press, 1953. xii + 323 pp.

SCOR *Proceedings,* August 1965 (Vol. 1, No. 1), and following.

BASIC SCIENCE

Baker, Dale B. "Communication or Chaos." *Science,* August 21, 1970 (Vol. 169, No. 3947), pp. 739–742.

Ben-David, Joseph. *Fundamental Research and the Universities: Some Comments on International Differences.* Paris: Organisation for Economic Co-operation and Development, 1968. 111 pp.

Dedijer, Stefan, and A. J. Longrigg. "A Model of Foreign Research Policy." *Scientific World* (London), 1969 (Vol. 13, No. 1), pp. 17–21.

Grant, Robert P. "National Biomedical Research Agencies: A Comparative Study of Fifteen Countries." *Minerva* (London), Summer 1966 (Vol. 4, No. 4), pp. 466–488.

Price, Derek J. De Solla. *Little Science, Big Science.* (George B. Pegram Lectures, 1962.) New York: Columbia University Press, 1963. 119 pp.

———. "Nations Can Publish or Perish." *Science and Technology,* October 1967 (No. 70), pp. 84–90.

Rose, Hilary. "The Rejection of the WHO Research Centre." *Minerva* (London), Summer 1967 (Vol. 5, No. 4), pp. 340–356.

Rose, Hilary, and Steven Rose. *Science and Society.* London: Allen Lane, 1969. xviii + 294 pp.

Salomon, Jean-Jacques. "International Scientific Policy." *Minerva* (London), Summer 1964 (Vol. 2, No. 4), pp. 411–434.

———. *Science et politique.* (Collections esprit.) Paris: Editions du Seuil, 1970. 406 pp.

Storer, Norman. "The Internationality of Science and the Nationality of Scientists." *International Social Science Journal* (Paris), 1970 (Vol. 22, No. 1), pp. 80–93.

Wooster, Warren S. "The Ocean and Man." *Scientific American,* September 1969 (Vol. 221, No. 3), pp. 218–234.

NUCLEAR ENERGY

Atoms in Japan, monthly publication of the Japan Atomic Industrial Forum.

Berman, William H., and Lee M. Hydeman. *The Atomic Energy Commission and Regulating Nuclear Facilities.* Ann Arbor: University of Michigan Law School, 1961. xvi + 336 pp.

Foch, René. *Europe and Technology: A Political View.* (Atlantic Papers, No. 2.) Paris: Atlantic Institute, 1970. 55 pp.

Goldschmidt, Bertrand. *Les Rivalités atomiques, 1939–1966.* (Les Grandes Etudes contemporaines.) Paris: Librairie Arthème Fayard, 1967. 340 pp.

Hewlett, Richard G., and Oscar E. Anderson. *A History of the Atomic Energy Commission.* Vol. 1: *The New World, 1939–1946.* University Park: Pennsylvania State University Press, 1962. xv + 766 pp.

Hewlett, Richard G., and Frances Duncan. *A History of the Atomic Energy Commission.* Vol. 2: *Atomic Shield, 1947–1952.* University Park: Pennsylvania State University Press, 1969. xvii + 718 pp.

Hodgetts, J. E. *Administering the Atom for Peace.* (International Political Science Association Series.) New York: Atherton Press, 1964. xi + 193 pp.

International Atomic Energy Agency. *Report of the Board of Governors to the General Conference.* Vienna: International Atomic Energy Agency, annually since 1957-1958.

Kramish, Arnold. *The Peaceful Atom in Foreign Policy.* New York: Harper & Row, Publishers (for the Council on Foreign Relations), 1963. xi + 276 pp.

Layton, Christopher. *European Advanced Technology: A Programme for Integration.* London: George Allen & Unwin (for Political and Economic Planning), 1969. 293 pp.

Novick, Sheldon. *The Careless Atom.* Boston: Houghton Mifflin Co., 1969. x + 225 pp.

Nuclear Industry, December 1953 (Vol. 1, No. 1), and following. This is the monthly magazine of the Atomic Industrial Forum.

Scheinman, Lawrence. "Nuclear Safeguards, the Peaceful Atom and the IAEA." *International Conciliation,* March 1969 (No. 572), 64 pp.

Shortall, John W., ed. *The Atomic Handbook: Europe.* Vol. 1. London: Morgan Brothers, 1965.

United States Atomic Energy Commission, Division of Industrial Participation. *Report on the Nuclear Industry.* Washington: Government Printing Office, annually since 1964.

United States Congress, Joint Committee on Atomic Energy, *AEC Authorizing Legislation for the [annual] Fiscal Year.*

Willrich, Mason. "The Treaty on Non-Proliferation of Nuclear Weapons: Nuclear Technology Confronts World Politics." *Yale Law Journal,* 1968 (Vol. 77, No. 8), pp. 1447–1519.

Air Transport

Bebchick, Leonard. "The International Air Transport Association and the Civil Aeronautics Board." *Journal of Air Law and Commerce,* Winter 1958 (Vol. 25, No. 1), pp. 8–43.

Caves, Richard E. *Air Transport and Its Regulators: An Industry Study.* (Harvard Economic Studies, No. 120.) Cambridge, Mass: Harvard University Press, 1962. x + 479 pp.

Cheng, Bin. *The Law of International Air Transport.* (Library of World Affairs, No. 47.) London: Stevens and Sons (under the auspices of the London Institute of World Affairs), 1962. xliii + 726 pp.

Corbett, David. *Politics and the Airlines.* London: George Allen & Unwin, 1965. 350 pp.

Fulda, Carl H. "International Aspects of Aviation." *Journal of Air Law and Commerce,* Winter 1967 (Vol. 33, No. 1), pp. 63–74.

Gill, Frederick W., and Gilbert L. Bates. *Airline Competition: A Study of the Effects of Competition on the Quality and Price of Airline Service and the Self-Sufficiency of the United States Domestic Airlines.* Boston: Division of Research, Graduate School of Business Administration, Harvard University, 1949. xv + 704 pp.

Keyes, Lucile Sheppard. "The Making of International Air Fares and the Prospect for Their Control." *Journal of Air Law and Commerce,* Spring 1964 (Vol. 30, No. 2), pp. 173–192.

Lissitzyn, Oliver J. *International Air Transport and National Policy.* (Studies in American Foreign Relations.) New York: Council on Foreign Relations, 1942. xviii + 478 pp.

Sackrey, Charles M., Jr. "Overcapacity in the United States International Air Transport Industry." *Journal of Air Law and Commerce,* Winter 1966 (Vol. 32, No. 1), pp. 24–93.

Sealy, Kenneth R. *The Geography of Air Transport.* London: Hutchinson University Library, 1957. 207 pp.

Thayer, Frederick C., Jr. *Air Transport Policy and National Security: A Political, Economic, and Military Analysis.* Chapel Hill: University of North Carolina Press, 1965. xxiii + 352 pp.

Van Zandt, J. Parker. *The Geography of World Air Transport.* (America Faces the Air Age, Vol. 1.) Washington: Brookings Institution, 1944. viii + 67 pp.

Wassenbergh, H. A. *Post-War International Civil Aviation Policy and the Law of the Air.* 2nd rev. ed. The Hague: Martinus Nijhoff, 1962. xii + 197 pp.

Wheatcroft, Stephen. *Air Transport Policy.* (Live Issues, No. 4.) London: Michael Joseph, 1964. 200 pp.

———. *The Economics of European Air Transport.* Cambridge, Mass: Harvard University Press, 1956. xxii + 358 pp.

World Airline Record. 6th ed. Chicago: Roadcap & Associates, Publishers, 1965. 493 pp.

INDEX

Actors
Ford Foundation's relations with, 122–27
governmental, xxv–xxvi
Holy See as, 135
in foreign policy, 362
in nuclear energy field, 284, 285, 286, 289–90, 292, 296
in oceans, 252–53, 271, 272, 274–75,
in outer space, 252–53, 259, 271, 272
international, variety of, 31–32
international organizations as, 85–86, 87
labor, strategies of actors in, 215–26
nation-states as, xiv, 3, 6, 85, 87
NGO's as, 85, 87
nongovernmental, xiv, xv
of developing countries, 326
oil companies, as, x, xxvi
transgovernmental, 383–84
transnational, x, xiii–xiv, xv, xix–xx, 56
developing countries and U.S. policy on, 390
foundations as, 116–17, 127–28, 404
governments and, confrontations with, 372–74
international finance, role in, 179–80
issue areas and, 169–71
Japanese, 391
Jews as, 7
loyalties and, 378
multinational corporations as, 14–15, 49, 54, 86, 87, 104–8, 113–14, 368–69, 402–3
nation-states as, 150–52
NGO's as, 377, 402
revolutionary movements as, 154, 164–65, 405
Roman Catholic Church as, 129–52, 404
Western European, 391
world politics and, 384–85
types of, relations between, 87
Advertising, in developing countries, xviii ,333
AFL-CIO, 214, 218, 219
Africa
Air Afrique, 193
Catholic population of, 133
education of Africans, transnational, 12–13
Ford Foundation in, 119–20, 127
NGO's, participation in, 80, 81, 82, 83
nuclear fuel supply needed for, 293
partition of, 6
railways in, 14
revolutionary organizations, 157–59
status, sensitivity on, 313
trade unions in, 213, 214
United States and
investment in, 330
trade union activity in, 204, 205, 214
African National Congress, 157
Agriculture
19th century, 7–8
development of, 6
EEC and, xiv, 44, 354, 360, 383
Ford Foundation and, 121
foundations sponsoring research in, 123
innovations in, sociological research on, 239
Ahmadabad Textile Labor Association, 224
Air Afrique, 193, 196
Airlines
as actors, 198
bibliography, 408
governments and, 191–203
control by, 197–98, 199
intervention by, 191–97
transnational actors in, 373–74
Air Malaysia, 196, 197
Algeria, revolutionaries in, 168
Alitalia, 201–2, 373–74
Aluminum, 217–18, 221–22
American Colonization Society, 7
American Federation of Labor, 211
American Institute for Free Labor Development, 204, 213
Americanization, 22
Americas, immigration into, 7
Anaconda Company, 205
Anarchism, 6
Angell, Norman, 375
Angell, Robert Cooley, 305–22 *passim*
Angola, 157
Antiballistic missiles, 297
Anticolonialism. *See* Colonialism

Antipodes, immigration into, 7
Anti-Semitism, 7
Arab League, 80, 81
Arab states
 NGO's, participation in, 80, 81
 revolutionaries in, 154, 161–63
 United States, relations with, xxii
Arbitration, 71
Argentina
 automobile industry in, 338
 Ford Foundation in, 127
 guerrilla revolution in, 156
 government and labor in, 225
 Holy See, relations with, 137
Armenia, relief for (19th century), 11
Arms control. *See* Disarmament and arms control
Aron, Raymond, 374
Asia
 Catholic population of, 133
 Communist Asia, and participation in NGO's, 80, 81, 83
 Ford Foundation in, 119, 127
 Japanese power in, collapse of, 60
 nuclear fuel supply needed for, 293
 Southeast Asia, air service in, 193
 status, sensitivity on, 313
 telegraph network of, 15
 Western Asia, and participation in NGO's, 80, 81
Atlantic cable, 15
Atlantic Community, 27, 119
 See also North Atlantic; North Atlantic Treaty Organization
Atomic cultural lag, 33
Atomic energy. *See* Nuclear energy
Atomic Energy of Canada, 279
Australia
 as nation-state, 151
 Catholic population of, 133
 NGO's, participation in, 80, 81–82
 nuclear fuel supply needed for, 293
 outer space, as actor in, 275
 Qantas Airways, 199
Automobiles
 in developing countries, 334
 in Latin America, 334, 338

Ba-ath states, 154
Bakunin, Mikhail, 156
Ball, George W., 48–49, 51–52, 230
Bank for International Settlements, 185
Baran, Paul A., 328, 329, 331
Barings, 13
Basques, 168
Bauxite, 217–18
Bea, Augustin Cardinal, 147
Belgium
 air transport, 195, 199
 Catholicism in, 142, 143
 CERN, possible location in, 246
 Sabena Belgian World Airlines, 199
Bell, David E., 126
Bell, J. Bowyer, xvi, xviii, xxvii, 93, 94, 95 153–68, 233, 377
Bell, Peter D., xvi, xviii, xxvii, 93, 94, 95, 115–28, 385
Bermuda Air Agreement, 196
Bicycles, 334
Biology
 European Molecular Biology Organization, 241–42, 243–44
 medical research, 246
 molecular biology, research, 241–42, 243–44
Bipolarity of world, 32, 33, 46
Birth control, 395
 Ford Foundation activity in, 388
 foundation support of, 116
 Humanae Vitae, 140, 144, 147
Blough, Roger, 229
Bolivia, Guevara's final mission to, 159
Brazil
 advertising expenditures in, 333
 church and state, separation of, establishment of principle of, 137, 148
 entrepreneurs in, 339
 factories in (18th century), abolition of, 336, 337
 Ford Foundation in, 121, 123, 124–25, 127
 Goulart, President, overthrow of, 205, 213
 government and labor in, 225
 guerrilla revolution in, 156
 military government's policy on foreign investment and political participation, 340
 multinational corporations in, 333, 336
 on nuclear technology, 280
 Roman Catholic Church in, 137, 138, 143
 transportation in, 334
Bretton Woods, 61
British Commonwealth, Ottawa Agrement, 57
British Guiana, 205, 213
British Overseas Airways Corporation, 193, 195, 196, 201, 202
Brittany, 21, 168
Brookings Institution, 125
Bundy, McGeorge, 126
Burma, immigration into, 7

Calvo Doctrine, 302, 352, 355
Canada
 ocean science research by, 274, 275
 oil, offshore resources of, exploitation of, 261
 outer space, as actor in, 275

position on
nuclear energy, 279, 281, 287–88, 289
U.S. investment in, 186, 348
World Weather Watch, 253, 266, 271, 383
Roman Catholic Church in, 137, 143
uranium ore reserves in, 287–88
U.S. investment in, 16, 68–69, 351
Cancer research, 246, 247
Canton, 9
Cape Verde Islands, 11
Capital
developing countries, providing for, 328–33
export of, proposed agreement not to restrict, 350
flow, 6, 25, 36–37, 186–87, 346
consequences of, 175–77
economics of, 175–77
long-term, 187
multinational corporations and, 97
short-term, 181–83, 187
Cardin, Joseph Cardinal, 142
Caribbean
Indian immigration into, 7
U.S. trade union activity in, 204
Carnegie, Andrew, 14
Castro, Fidel, 120, 155, 156, 157, 159
Central African Airways, 196–97
Central Europe, Catholic population of, 133
Ceylon, Catholic population of, 133
Chad, guerrillas in, 168
Chemicals industry, 213
Chile
Christian Democratic party, 121
church and state, separation of, 137, 138, 148
copper industry, unions in, 224
Ford Foundation in, 121
Roman Catholic Church in, 137, 138, 143
China
Chincha Islands, laborers exported to, 8
Chinese Educational Mission, 12
education of, transnational, 12, 13
emigration from, 7
flood control in, 14
foreign investment in (19th and early 20th centuries), 340
railways in, 14
China, People s Republic of
Catholic population of, 133
fishing, world catch, share of, 274
labor in, 210
NGO's, participation in, 80, 81, 83
outer space, as actor in, 275
position on
revolution, 154, 155
Roman Catholic Church, 136
transportation in, 334–35
U.S. embargoes against, xxi
Chincha Islands, 8
Cobden, Richard, on Americanization, 22
Cochrane, Lord, 5
Cold war, 58, 59–61, 211
Colombia
Catholicism in, 136, 138
family planning in, Ford Foundation support of, 116
Colonialism
anticolonialism, 153
capital and, 328
See also Imperialism
Comité Revolucionário de Moçambique, 157
Commission on Marine Biology, 265
Committee on Space Research, 255–56, 264, 268, 273
ITU, links with, 256
Communications
development of, 14–15, 16, 25
multinational corporations and, 343, 344, 387
societies' sensitivity increased by, 376
Communism
in 1930s, 376
Roman Catholic Church and, 136–37, 141–44
trade unions controlled by
anticommunist activities against, 211–12, 219
in Chilean copper industry, 224
Communist countries
Holy See, attitude toward, 136
international trade and, 39, 41, 42
multinational corporations in, 215
transnationalism and, 388
Computers, xxi, 344
Conference of National Organizations in the Portuguese Colonies, 157
Congress of Industrial Organizations, 211
Conservation, and oceans, 269
Consumers in developing countries, 332–35
Contamination by Extra-Terrestrial Exploration, Committee on, 273
Continental Air Lines, 202, 374
Continental shelf, 272
U.N. discussion of, 260–61
Cooper, R. N., xvii, xxii, 37, 42, 44–45
Copper industry in Chile, 224
Cotton, 7–8
Cox, E. E., 122
Cox, Robert W., xviii, 170, 204–34, 377, 388, 389
Crane, Diana, 170, 235–51
Crete, 18
Crockett, William, on U.S. foreign policy, 322
Cuba
and Ford Foundation, 120

Holy See, relations with, 136
labor in, 210
Latin America, aspirations in, 156
Latin American Solidarity Organization, 159
revolution, as advocate of, 155
United States and, xxi, xxii
Culture, transnationalism and, 17–19, 311
Curti, Merle, 119
Cyprus, 80, 81–82, 154
Czechoslovakia, Roman Catholic Church in, 144

Decisionmaking
by developed countries, 43
by international organizations, 42
by supranational groupings, on economic activities, 43
foreign policy and, 42, 319, 320, 322, 323, 363–65
in multinational politics, 358–60
Dedijer, Stefan, 235
Defense, cost of, 16
de Gaulle, Charles, 64–65
Democratic process
foreign policy and
decisionmaking in, 363–65
limitations on democratic control of, 356–57
objects of, 360–63
multinational politics and, 365–66, 367–69
transnational relations and, 356–70
de Tocqueville, Alexis, 4, 357
Deutsch, Karl, 43, 44
Developed countries
decisionmaking by, 43
developing countries and, 41, 43, 332–33
governmental activities as link between modernization and transnational phenomena, 47
international trade between, 42
labor in, 209, 216–22
multinational corporations based in, 23, 326, 353–54
national economic policies
adjudication and enforcement, 353
coordination of, 351–52
multinational corporations, nationality of, sorting out, 352–53
national jurisdiction, limiting, 350–51
transnational capital investment, in, 36
transnationalism centered in, 388
welfare objectives, loss of control over, 394
Developing countries
automobiles in, 334
capital for, 328–33
consumption in, and community welfare, 332–35
developed countries and, 41, 42–43
economic development in, strategies for, importation of, 335–39
economic policies, importance of, 27
elites in, 339, 376, 388
entrepreneurs in, 345
exports of primary products, 40, 41
extractive industries in, 329, 330–32
European trade unions' influence in, 211
fertility rates in, 41
international trade by, 40, 41
labor in, 209–10
actors in, 222–26
allegiance of, 212–13
mortality rates in, 41
multinational corporations in, xix, 23, 221, 230, 302, 303, 345
advertising by, xviii, 333
and political independence, 331
idea transferral by, 332–33
local industrial structure and, 338
national autonomy, loss of, 326–28
political ramifications, 339–40
tensions generated by, 354–55
welfare and, 302, 303
national autonomy of, 325–42
nationalism in, 388
North American trade unions' influence in, 210–211
patent system in, 336–37
political independence, importance of, 331
position on
INTELSAT, 259
nuclear technology, 280
ocean research, 265
private investment in, 214
resources of, 335–39
trade unions in, 214, 222–24
transnational integration in, 233
transnational pressures on, 20–21
transnational relations and, xxvi, 396–97
transportation in, 334
United States and, 326, 390
See also United States, multinational corporations based in
Disarmament and arms control, 251
Eighteen-Nation Committee on Disarmament, 268, 280
transnationalism and, 296–98
See also Pugwash Conferences on Science and World Affairs
Disease, Rockefeller Foundation work in relief of, 116, 119, 120
Domestic society, compared to international, 30–31
Dubinsky, David, 219
Dühring, Karl, 50

du Pont de Nemours and Company, E. I., 277

East Africa, Indian immigration into, 7
East African Airways, 196
Eastern Europe
 Catholic population of, 133
 Ford Foundation in, 126
 NGO's, participation in, 80, 81, 83
 nuclear fuel supply needed for, 293
 political liberalization of, attempt at, 27
 Soviet Union and, 59
 United States and, 59–60, 119
 Western Europe and, comemberships in NGO's, 90
 See also Europe
Easton, David, xxiv
Economic activities
 political activities, relationship between, 47, 49–53
Economic Commission for Latin America, 251
Economic development
 aid for, and foreign policy, 361
 Ford Foundation and, 121
 strategies for, importation of, 335–39
 See also Developing countries
Economic values, 25–26
Economist, The, on multinational corporations and developing countries, 230–31
Ecumenical movement, 145–47
Education, 12–13
Egypt
 ancient, excavation of, 18
 synarchy in, 10
 UK occupation of, 6
Eighteen Nation Committee on Disarmament, 268, 280
Eisenhower, Dwight, Atoms for Peace proposal, 278
Eldorado Mining and Refining, 279
Elites
 in developing countries, 339, 376, 388
 transnational participation by, and peace, 305–6, 321–22
Emigration, 7
Employers
 ILO, representation in, 228
 in dependent societies, 225–26
 in industrialized societies, 220–22
 International Organization of Employers, 228
Engels, Friedrich, 50, 51, 52
English, as world language, 12, 17–18
Environment, United Nations Conference on the Human, xxix, 395
Esperanto, 17
Erikson, Erik, 308
Europe
 armaments in, production of, 16
 as world center, 8–9
  of banking, 13–14
 balance of power in, 55
 economic advance of (19th century), 3
 emigration from, 7, 34
 German power in, collapse of, 60
 industrialization in, 337, 338
 multinational corporations in, as transnational actors, 14–15
 nation-states in, development of, 354
 railways in, 6
 status, sensitivity on, 313
 telegraph network of, 14
 United States and, xxvii, 16, 99
 See also Eastern Europe; Western Europe
European Atomic Energy Community, 291–92, 362
European Coal and Steel Community, 61, 212
European Communities, 288, 365
European Economic Community, 62, 179
 agricultural policy of, xxiv, 44, 354, 360, 383
 capital mobility as result of, 37
 currency area, single, possible conversion to, xxviii
 decisionmaking by, 42
 labor in, 36, 210
 monetary policy in, coordination of, 354
 multinational corporations, expansion of, facilitation of, 213
 nuclear power stations in, 288–89
 trade unions and, 212
 transactions by, 44
 U.S. investment in, 64
European Molecular Biology Conference, 244
European Molecular Biology Organization, 241–42, 244
European Organization for Nuclear Research, 238, 243, 245–46, 247
European Parliament, 365
European Space Research Organization, 362
European Space Vehicle Launcher Development Organization, 358, 362
Evans, Peter B., xviii, xxiv, 302, 303, 325–42, 390
Exploration, 5
Extractive industries, 107–8, 329, 330–32
Extranationalism, 86

Family planning. *See* Birth control
Far East culture, 18
Fedayeen, 166
Fenians, 5
Field, James A., Jr., xviii, xix, xxvii, 1–2, 3–22, 374, 376, 389

Firestone Tire and Rubber Company, 107
Fisheries, 268, 269, 272
FAO's contributions to, 257–58
management and regulation of, 257–58
state-centric model, adequacy for, 257
world catch, 274
Food and Agriculture Organization
fisheries, contributions to, 257–58
IMCO, cooperation with, 267
oceans and, 265, 266–67, 269
Ford, Benson, 124
Ford, Edsel, 117
Ford, Henry, 117, 124
Ford, Henry II, 124
Ford Foundation, xvi, xviii, 93, 94, 95, 385
actors, relations with, 122–27
AID, collaboration with, 123
assets of, 117
Board of Trustees, 117
decisionmaking in, 120–22
family planning, support of, 116, 388
foreign aid, position on, 126
Gaither report, 118, 119
in Africa, 119–20, 127
in Asia, 119, 121, 127
in Eastern Europe, 126
in Latin America, 116, 121, 123, 124, 125, 127
in Middle East, 119, 126
International Division, 118, 119, 120
philosophy of, 120–21
population activities of, 116, 124
programs and purposes, 117–20
rice strain developed under auspices of, 116
Rockefeller Foundation and, 123
structure of, 117–18
United States relations with, 125–26
wheat strain developed under auspices of, 116
Ford Motor Company
Brazilian rubber, venture in, 125
Ford Foundation, relations with, 124–25
Foreign investment
in extractive industries, 330–32
in manufacturing enterprises, 332–35
See also Capital; International finance
Foreign policy
actors in, 362
decisionmaking in, 319, 320, 322, 323
democratic control of
limitations on, 356–57
objects of foreign policy and, 360–63
strengthening of, 365–69
nuclear deterrence and, 360–61
transnational participation, socialization and, 319–21
Foundations
as transnational actors, 116–17, 127–28
birth control and, 116, 388, 395
foreign policies of, 385
United States and, 115–16
See also Ford Foundation; Rockefeller Foundation
Fowler, Henry, 230
France
19th century position of, 4, 55
Air Afrique, establishment of, 193
air transport, 192, 195, 200
businessmen and government, relationship between, 112
capital accumulation in, 13
capital flow from, 177, 183
Catholicism in, 142
church and state, separation of, 137, 138, 148
currency devaluation, 44
fishing vessels over 100 gross tons, 274
industrialization of, 56
monetary problems of, 188
nuclear capability, xxi
ocean science research by, 274, 275
oil, offshore resources of, 261
outer space, as actor in, 275
painters, 18
position on
nuclear energy, 246, 277–90 *passim*
U.S. investment in Western Europe, 64–65
Roman Catholic Church in, 143
Communism and, 144
Holy See, relations with 137, 138
worker-priest movement, intervention against, 140
trade unions in, 204, 206, 211
United Kingdom, Concorde with, 358
Free trade, 58–59
See also International trade
Functionalism, 229–32
Furtado, Celso, 336

Gaither, H. Rowan, 118, 119
Garibaldians, 5
Geertz, Clifford, 328
General Agrement on Tariffs and Trade, 173, 349, 351
tariff reductions under, 23, 27
trade expansion under, 63
See also International trade; Tariffs
General Assembly
continental shelf, discussion of, 260–61
seabed, discussion of, 260–61, 270–71, 395
transnational activities and, 397
World Weather Watch, discussion of, 253
General Electric Company, 279, 283
General Motors Corporation, 212
General Postal Union, 15

German Democratic Republic
Germany, Federal Republic of, and, 61, 90, 361
Germany
19th century
capital accumulation in, 13
customs union of, 52
entrepreneurs in, 337
industrialization of, 52, 54, 56
unification of, 4, 50, 56
composers, 18
Europe, collapse of power in, 60
inflation in (1920's), 346
Lufthansa, 200
trading bloc, organization of, 57
Germany, Federal Republic of
agriculture, decisions on, 360
capital flow into, 178, 181, 182, 387
currency revaluation by, 44
economy of, 61
exchange market, closing of, 179
fishing vessels over 100 gross tons, 274
German Democratic Republic and
NGO's comembership in, 90
nonrecognition of, 361
trading partner, separation from, 61
mathematics, theory of finite groups, communication network of, 239
monetary crisis in, 175–76
monetary policy of, 188
multinational organizations, involvement in, 362
ocean science research by, 274, 275
outer space, as actor in, 275
position on
NPT, 295
nuclear energy, 246, 277, 280, 281, 285, 289, 358, 362
United States, 65, 379
Roman Catholic Church in, 143
versus communism, 144
shipping, share of world's, 274
trade unions in, transnational activity of, 205–6
United States, relations with, 64–65, 385
Gerschenkron, Alexander, on European industrialization, 337, 338
Ghana
Ford Foundation in, 127
independence of, 119
Ghandi, Mahatma, 224
Gilpin, Robert, xviii, xix, 2, 48–69, 372, 375, 385–86
Global interactions, xii
Goldberg, Paul, 396
Gold standard, in Latin America, 336
Gordon, Charles, 10
Goulart, João Belchior Marques, 205, 213
Governments
airlines and, 191–95, 197–98, 199, 201
control, loss of, 392–95
executive branch of, and foreign policy, 361, 364, 367
ITU, restrictions on, 254
labor, relations with, 208–9
monetary sovereignty of, 177, 184–85, 187–89
nuclear energy, role in, 276–86, 298
radio frequency allocation, 254
revolutionary organizations, relations with, 165–67
trade unions and multinational corporations, attitude on, 219–20
transnational actors, confrontations with, 372–74
See also Nation-states
Grace and Company, W. R., 205
Great powers
transnational relations, xx
Greece
Cyprus and, 154
IMCO and, 262–63
relief for (19th century), 11
shipping, share of world's, 274
Green Revolution, 116
Grieg, Samuel, 10
Grivas, George, 154, 166
Group of Ten, 42, 43
Guano, 8
Guatemala, guerrilla revolution in, 156
Guerrillas, 156, 377
Guevara, Ché, 156, 157, 159, 160–61
Gulf General Atomics, 279

Habsburg Empire, 4
Hamlin, Cyrus, 17
Hart, Sir Robert, 10
Hawaii, 7, 9
Hellman, Rainer, xxvii
Hickenlooper amendment, 111, 347, 355
Hobson, J. A., 22, 406
Ho Chi Minh, 156
Hoffmann, Stanley, 378–79
Horowitz, Irving and Ruth, 121
Hookworm, 116
Hudson's Bay Company, 377
Humanae Vitae, 140, 144, 147
Human Environment, United Nations Conference on the, xxix, 395
Hussein, King, 166
Hydrology
International Hydrological Decade, 242–43, 244
Hymer, Stephen, xxvii, 51

IBM, xxi, 344
Ideas, transmission of, 332–33, 344–45
Illich, Ivan, 333–34
Immigration, 7, 208
Imperialism, xxvi, 8, 15, 22
India
 Ahmadabad Textile Labor Association, 224
 All-India Trade Union Congress, 224
 Catholic population of, 133
 Congress party, 121, 224
 culture, vogue of, 18
 economic development, and United Kingdom's extraction of capital, 328
 education of Indians, transnational, 12–13
 emigration from, 7
 English language in, 12
 Indian National Trade Union Congress, 224
 outer space, as actor in, 275
 position on
  IMCO, 262–63
  nuclear technology, 280
 telegraph network of, 15
 trade unions in, 224
 United States and, 111, 312, 315–16
Indian Ocean Islands, 7
Indochina, 13
Indonesia, 225, 328
Industrial goods, international trade in, 345–46
Industrialization, 5, 25
 See also Industrial Revolution
Industrialized countries. *See* Developed countries
Industrial Revolution, 6, 7–8, 9, 50, 328
Integrated Global Ocean Station System, 266
Inter-American Commercial Arbitration Commission, 71
Interdependence, international, 44–45
 asymmetry of, 38, 40–43
 economic, 27–34, 36–37
 great power interactions and, 38, 40–43
 international trade as measure of, 38, 39–40
 population mobility and, 35–36
Interest groups, 368–69
Intergovernmental Oceanographic Commission. *See* subheading under United Nations Educational, Scientific and Cultural Organization
Intergovernmental Maritime Consultative Organization
 FAO, cooperation with, 267
 functions of, 263
 IOC, cooperation with, 267
 NGO's, communication with, 263
 ocean, radioactive pollution of, activity concerning, 269
 restrictions on, 262–63
 WMO, cooperation with, 267
Intergovernmental organizations. *See* International organizations
International Agency for Research on Cancer, 246, 247
International Air Transport Association, 71, 86
 decisionmaking by, 198–99
 establishment of, 191, 195
 ICAO, compared with, 373
 inner workings of, 198–99, 202–3
 price-setting by, 193, 195, 196
 United States and, 391
International Association for the Physical Sciences of the Ocean, 265
International Association of Biological Oceanography, 265
International Astronomical Union, 255–56
International Atomic Energy Agency, 279
 creation of, 278
 oceans, radioactive pollution of, activity concerning, 269
 safeguards under, 288, 295, 299
International Bank for Reconstruction and Development
 development aid by, 364
 population control, advocacy of, 233
International Bureau of Weights and Measures, 15
International Center for Theoretical Physics, 248
International Chamber of Commerce, 228, 263
International Chamber of Shipping, 263
International Civil Aviation Conference, 195–96
International Civil Aviation Organization
 control by, 201
 establishment of, 191
 IATA, compared with, 373
 outer space research by, 264
 radio frequencies of, 254–55
 safety regulation under, 193
International Code of Signals, 17
International Commission of Jurists, 71
International Confederation of Free Trade Unions, 211, 213, 214
 multinational corporations, study of, 227
International Council for the Exploration of the Sea, 265
International Council of Scientific Unions, 241, 265
 as actors, 272
 IUCAF, recognition of, 256
 outer space and, 264, 272
 World Weather Watch and, 253
International economic affairs, 27, 42, 43, 56–57
 See also International finance
International Federation of Air Line Pilots Association, 201, 373

International Federation of Chemical and General Workers' Unions, 205–6
International finance
bibliography, 405
crises in, 23, 37–38, 375–76, 379, 387
currencies, devaluation of, 31
foreign policy and, 361
ingredients of, 177–81
intergovernmental cooperation in, 185
magnitude of, 181–84
nation-states and, xix, xx–xxi, xxii
private
actors in, 186
economic welfare and, 186–87
transnational financial activity and, xxviii
transnational organizations, effect on, xxi
transnational actors' role in, 179–80
See also International Monetary Fund
International Geophysical Year, 244, 265, 272
International Hydrological Decade, 242–43, 244
International Labor Organization, 209, 212, 227–29, 395–96
International Ladies' Garment Workers Union, 219
International monetary affairs. *See* International economic affairs; International finance; International Monetary Fund
International Monetary Fund, 349, 351, 394
as decisionmaking structure, 42
Bretton Woods Agreement, 173–74
exchange rate, control over, 188
intergovernmental cooperation within, 185
special drawing rights, 43, 185, 190, 354
International Olympic Committee, 71
International organizations
as actors, 85–86, 87
decisionmaking by, 42, 43
fisheries and, 257
multinational corporations' challenge, 395–96
oceans and, 252, 265, 266
outer space and, 252, 264
scientific, 238, 241–42, 247, 250, 251
transnational relations and, xxviii–xxix, 395–98
International Organization of Employers, 228
International politics, 67–68
See also Multinational politics
International Red Cross, 71
International scientific community
structure of
actors, 238, 246–48, 250
organizations, 238–42, 250–51
International shipping. *See* Shipping, international
International Shipping Federation, 263
International society, compared to domestic society, 30–31
International Telecommunications Satellite Consortium
Communications Satellite Corporation, 255, 256–77, 259, 260
U.S. dominance of, 259
International Telecommunication Union
Administrative Radio Conference of, 255
COSPAR, links with, 256
INTELSAT and, 255, 256–57
International Frequency Registration Board, government restrictions on, 254
outer space research by, 264
radio frequency spectrum, management of, 253–57
tasks of, 254
International trade, 5, 27, 45, 349
as transnational process, 38–45
before 1914, 45
economic welfare, promotion of, 186
growth of, 36, 42, 63
Communist countries' isolation from, 39, 41, 42
in industrial goods, 345–46
interdependence and, 31, 42
multilateral trade, post-World War II, impossibility of, 61
nation-states' effect on, xx
of developing countries, 40, 41
U.S. policy on, role of businessmen in, 321
World War I and World War II, between, 38, 39–40, 57–58
International trade secretariats. *See* subheading under Trade Unions
International Union for the Protection of Industrial Property, 337
International Union of Marine Insurance, 263
International Union of Radio Science, 255–56
International Years of the Quiet Sun, 244
Inter-Union Commission on Frequency Allocations for Radio Astronomy and Space Science, 256
Iran, xxii
Iraq, 154
Ireland, 7, 11
Ireland, Northern, revolutionaries in, 168
Irgun Zvai Leumi, 154
Israel
Irgun Zvai Leumi, 154
Menahem Begin, 154
NGO's, participation in, 80, 81–82
U.S. relations with, 36
Issue areas, 169–299
transnational relations and, importance of, 379
world politics and, study of, 384–86
Italy
Alitalia, 201–2, 373–74

composers, 18
painting, primitive, rediscovery of, 18
Roman Catholic Church in, 142, 144
trade unions in, 204, 206

Jamaica
bauxite workers in, 218
Japan
art of, 18
Asia, collapse of power in, 60
businessmen and government, relationship between, 112
Catholic population of, 133
economic development in, 328
economic policy of, 346
education of, transnational, 12–13
emigration from, 7
fishing, world catch, share of, 274
fishing vessels over 100 gross tons, 274
industrialization in, 54, 56, 337, 338
Japanese Iwakura Mission, 12
NGO's, participation in, 80, 81–82, 84
nuclear fuel suply needed for, 293
ocean science research by, 274, 275
outer space, as actor in, 275
physics, high energy, communications network of, 238, 239
position on
NPT, 295
nuclear energy, 280, 285, 293
role of, 22
shipping, share of world's, 274
synarchy in, 10, 11
trading bloc, organization of (pre-World War II), 57
transnational actors from, 391
transnational business by, xxvii
United States and
Japanese students in, 311, 312
Pax Americana, 63
relations with, 65–67, 385
world economy, role in postwar reconstruction of, 62
Japan Air Lines, 199
Jersey Central Power and Light Company, 283
Jews, 7
Jordan, fedayeen in, 166

Kaiser, Karl, 302, 303, 357–70, 394
Kelman, Herbert, 317, 320
Kennedy Round, 354
Kenya, 127
Keohane, Robert O., and Joseph S. Nye, Jr., ix–xxix, 371–98
Keynes, John Maynard, 208, 379–80
Kiger, Joseph C., 121, 122
Kindleberger, Charles, 396, 397
KLM Royal Dutch Airlines, 199
Knowledge, growth of, 9–13, 46
Korea, Democratic People's Republic of
NGO's, participation in, 80, 81, 83
Kosciuszko, Tadeusz, 5
Krause, Lawrence, xvii, xviii, xix, xxi, 169–90, 387
Kuznets, Simon, 38, 40

Labor
actors in, strategies of, 215–26
bibliography, 406
cold war and, 211
government, relations with, 208–9
history of, 208–15
international labor movement, 6
mobility of, 6
multinational corporations and, 209
society, patterns of, and labor's status within, 210
transnational ideologies and, 226–32
transnational relations and, 204–34
transnational structures and, 226–32
Labor unions. *See* Trade unions
Lafayette, Marquis de, 5
Landes, David S., 337
Language, world, 17–18
Laos, guerrillas in, 168
Lasswell, Harold, definition of politics by, xxvi
Lateran Treaty, 130, 135
Latin America
air transport in, 200
automobiles in, 334
Catholic population of, 133
Cuban aspirations in, 156
Ford Foundation work in, 120
gold standard in (19th century), 336
guerrillas in, 168
multinational corporations in, 354
NGO's, participation in, 80, 81
nuclear fuel supply needed for, 293
revolutionary organizations in, 159–61
Roman Catholic Church in, 136, 137–38, 142–44
social science research in, 116, 124
Soviet aspirations in, 156
telegraph network of, 15
trade unions in, 214
United States and
investment in, 16, 330
studies in United States concerning, 116
teachers studying in United States, 318–19
tension between, 251
trade union activities, 204, 213

Latin American Solidarity Organization, 159
Lawrence, Samuel, 262
Layton, Christopher, 280–81
Lebanon, fedayeen in, 166
Lenin, 22, 156
Less developed countries. *See* Developing countries
Levinson, Charles, 232
Levitt, Kari, 48–49, 51
Liberalism, 5
  classic economic, 49–50, 51, 52
  of foundations, 121
Liberia
  founding of, 7
  rubber plantations in, 107
  shipping, share of world's, 274
Libya, 354
Lipset, Seymour Martin, 376
List, G. F., 49
London, City of, 56, 57
Long, Franklin W., 297
Longrigg, A. J., 235
Lovestone, Jay, 219
Lufthansa, 200

McCarthy, Joseph, 315
Machinery, international trade in, 42
Malaria, 116
Malay (bazaar), as lingua franca, 17
Manchu Empire, 4
Manufactured goods, international trade in, 42
Manufacturing firms, 100–7, 332–35
Mao Tsetung, 156, 157
Maria I of Portugal, 336, 337
Marriage, international, 19
Mars, 268, 273
Marshall Plan, 27, 61, 204, 211, 212, 213
Marx, Karl, 156, 333
Marxism, 50, 51, 52
Mathematics, finite groups, theory of, communications network in, 239
Mboya, Tom, 205
Meany, George, 218, 219
Mediation, 71
Mehemet Ali, 10
Menahem Begin, 154
Metal trades industry, 213
Mexico
  church and state, separation of, 137, 138, 148
  Holy See, relations with, 137–38
  Mexicali Valley, 323
  United States, students in, 312, 316
Micronesia, 202
Middle East, Ford Foundation in, 119, 126
Migration, 34–35
Miles, Edward, 170, 171, 251–75, 391
Mill, John Stuart, 49
Mining industries, 329, 332
MIRV, 297
Missionaries, xviii, 9, 11–12
Mitrany, David, 229, 230, 231
Modernization, 5–9, 46–47
Moltke, 10
Monetary sovereignty, of governments, 184–85, 187–89
Mongolian People's Republic, 80, 81, 83
Mormons, 7
Morris Richard T., 312
Morse, Edward L., xix, 2, 23–47, 375
Morse Code, 17
Mozambique, 157
Multinational corporations, 13–17, 20–21, 93, 94, 95
  adjudication proposed for, 353
  as transnational actors, 14–15, 49, 54, 86, 87, 104–8, 113–14, 368–69
  capital, movement of, policy on, 97
  centralization by function, 108–9
  developed countries, economies linked by, 353–54
  developing countries and, 221, 230, 302, 303, 335, 338, 339–40, 345, 354–55
  extractive enterprises, 107–8, 329, 330–32
  functionalism and, 229–32
  governments, influence of, 110–13
  growth of, 23, 99–100, 377, 387
  ICFTU study of, 227
  ILO and, 227–29
  importance of, 67, 68, 69
  international organizations, challenge to, 395
  labor and, 209
  manufacturing enterprises, 100–7, 332–33
  national autonomy, loss of, and 326–28
  nationality of, 352–53
  nation-states and, 48–49, 67, 68, 69, 114, 362
  North Atlantic corporations, tendency to develop regime of, 51
  patent system and, 336
  taxation of, 97, 105, 110–11, 336, 351–52
  trade unions and, 97, 205–6, 218, 219–20, 226–32
  transnational actors, effects on, 377
  UNCTAD and, 397
  United States-based. *See* subheading under United States
  Western Europe-based, 347
Multinational politics, 358–60, 365–66, 367–69
Mycenae, 18
Myrdal, Gunnar, 35

Nagasaki, 9
Namibia, 111

Nationalism, 21
developing countries and, 388
growth of, 3–5
revolution and, 153, 233
National security, 276–99 *passim*
ocean issue area and state-centric model, relevance for, 268
outer space and state-centric model, relevance for, 268
Nation-states
as actors, xxiv, 3, 6, 85, 87, 150–52
as bargaining agents, 340
asymmetry in relations between, 387–89
demise of, 67
development of, 3–5, 6, 28
fisheries, predominance in, 257
international monetary system and, xix
international trade, effect on, xx
multinational corporations and, 48–49, 67, 68, 69, 114, 230, 326–28, 362
national autonomy, loss of, 325–42 *passim*
nature of, 50–51
oceans and, 252–53
outer space and, 252–53
revolutionary organizations and, 153, 154
Roman Catholic Church and, 135–40
sovereignty, transnational relations and, 397
transformation of, 20–21
transnational activities, role in, xviii, xix, xx, 150–52
welfare, role in, 234
See also Governments; State-centric model
Netherlands
air transport for, 192, 195, 199
KLM Royal Dutch Airlines, 199
oil, offshore resources of, 261
position on
Indonesian economic development, 328
nuclear energy, 245, 285, 286, 294, 358, 362
New Zealand
Catholic population of, 133
NGO's, participation in, 80, 81–82
nuclear fuel supply needed for, 293
Niishima Jo, 12
Nixon, Richard M., 202
Nixon Doctrine, 66
Nongovernmental organizations
as actors, 85, 87, 377
development of, 16, 73–83
dimensions of, 73–80, 387
oceans, involvement in, 252, 265, 272
outer space, role in, 252, 265, 272
peace, possible consequences, 88–92
scientific, 235–36, 238, 239–42, 247, 250, 251
transnational relations and, xv
world wars, effect of on founding, 75
Nonnuclear weapons states, 287, 294, 295
North America
Catholic population of, 133
economic advance of, 3
NGO's, participation in, 80, 81–82
nuclear fuel supply needed for, 292–93
telegraph network of, 15
North Atlantic
air route, ruling on, 201
productivity of, 15
See also Atlantic Community
North Atlantic Treaty Organization, 63, 358–59
Northwest, NGO's, participation in, 80, 81–82
Norway
fishing, world catch, share of, 274
fishing vessels over 100 gross tons, 274
shipping, share of world's, 274
Nuclear energy, 26
actors in, 289–90, 292, 296
asymmetry in distribution of
power reactors, 288–90
resources, 287–88
technology, 286–87
breeder reactor development, 281, 285, 292
enrichment technology, 277, 278, 284, 285–86
nuclear deterrence and foreign policy, 360–61
oceans and, 269
plutonium, 277, 284
state-centric model, relevance for, 276
transnational activities in, 290–99
United Nations International Conference on the Peaceful Uses of Atomic Energy, 286
See also European Organization for Nuclear Research
Nuclear weapons
treaties concerning, xxviii–xix, 279, 288, 294, 295
Nyasaland, 196
Nye, Joseph S., Jr., and Robert O. Keohane, ix–xxix, 371–98

Oak Ridge National Laboratory, 277
Oceania, 133
Oceans
actors in, 252–53, 275
fisheries, 257–58, 272
national security and, 268
NGO's, role in, 252
nuclear energy and, 269
oil and, 270–71
pollution of, 266–67, 269, 270
recreational use of, 268, 270
research on, 240, 244, 245, 264–268, 274–75
resources of, 260–63, 270, 272
state-centric model, adequacy for, 252–53, 269, 270–73

technology, history of, 272
transnational processes and, 270–75
United States and, 391
Oil
companies, x, xxii, xxv, 68, 261, 362
importance of, 16
oceans, pollution of, 269
offshore resources, exploitation of, 261, 270–71
production of, 217–18, 221–22, 261
supply of, 217–18, 329, 332
United States investment in, 332
Oregon, settlement of, 7
Organizational revolution, 13–17
Organization for Economic Cooperation and Development, 179, 351
as decisionmaking structure, 42
intergovernmental cooperation within, 185
labor and, 212
science policies of members of, 249
Organization for European Economic Cooperation, 61
Organization of African Unity, 157–58
Organization of the Petroleum Exporting Countries, 261
Orthodox Christianity, 146–47
Ottawa Agreement, 57
Outer space
actors in, 252–53, 271, 275
contamination in, 268, 273
history of, activities in, 272
national security and, 268
NGO's, role in, 252, 264
research on, 258, 263–64
resources of, 253–60
state-centric model, adequacy for, 252–53, 270–73
transnational processes in, 270–75
United States and, 391
Output, mobility of, 25

Pacific, United States and, 119
Pacific Islands, Indian immigration into, 7
Padwa, David J., 263
Paine, Tom, 5
Pakistan
Ford Foundation in, 121, 126–27
U.S. aid to, 111
Pan-African Congress, 157
Pan American World Airways, 196, 200, 201, 202, 205, 373
Pan-Germanism, 4
Pan-Slavism, 4
Parliaments, and foreign policy decisionmaking, 361, 363–65, 366–69
Patent system, 336–37
Paul VI, 144, 147, 149
Pax Americana, 2, 54, 55, 63
Pax Britannica, 55–57, 63
Peace
Ford Foundation work toward, 118–19
foreign policy and transnational participation, 321–24
movement, international, 5
NGO's, and possible consequences for, 88–92
oceans, transnational processes in, potential for, 273–75
outer space and, 273–75
transnational participation and, 305–24
Peace Corps, 318
Perlmutter, Howard, on multinational corporations, 231
Perroux, François, 54
Persian Gulf, oil-producing states in, agreement with oil companies, 261
Personality changes, and transnational participation, 316–19
Peru
fishing, world catch, share of, 274
guano production in, 8
guerrilla revolution in, 156, 159
Holy See, relations with, 137
U.S. aid to, 111
Philhellenes, 5
Philippines, 133, 168
Physics
high energy physics, 250
CERN, 243, 245–46
communications network in, 238–39
International Center for Theoretical Physics, 248
international communications network in, 238–39
Pidgin, 17
Pius XI, 142
Planets, contamination of, 268, 273
Planned Parenthood, 388
Plutonium, 277, 284
Poland
fishing vessels over 100 gross tons, 274
Holy See, relations with, 136–37
Roman Catholic Church in, 144
Political activities, relationship with economic activities, 47, 49–53
Politics, definition of, xxiv
Pollution
of oceans, 266–67, 268, 269, 270
of outer space, 268, 273
transnational organizations and, 395
Population
activities in, foundation support of, 116, 124
control, 233

mobility of, 25, 34–36
movement of, 6, 7
Populorum Progressio, 144
Portugal
church and state, separation of, 137, 138
colonies of
air transport for, 195
Brazil as colony, 336, 337
revolutionaries operating against, 157
Holy See, relations with, 137, 138
Swedish textile production transferred to, 217
Price-Anderson Act, 282, 283
Primary products, international trade in, 40, 41, 42
Production, factors of, mobility of, 25
Protestantism, 145–47
Prussia, customs union engineered by, 52
Public opinion, foreign policy and transnational participation, 320–21
Pugwash Conferences on Science and World Affairs, xx, 126, 250, 251, 268
evaluation of, 297–98
functions of, 242, 296–97

Qantas Airways, 199
Quester, George, 284
Quotas, xx

Radio astronomy, 255–56, 271
Radio frequency spectrum, 253–57
Railroads, rise of, 6–7
Raw materials, U.S. investment in extraction of, 107–8
Reciprocal Trade Agreements Act, 57
Recreation, and oceans, 268, 270
Red Crescent, 11
Red Cross, 11
Reichelderfer, Francis, 253, 271
Resources for the Future, 125
Reuther, Victor, 214
Reuther, Walter, 214
Revolutionary movements, 93, 94, 95, 154
as transnational actors, 164–65
governments, relations with, 165–67
guerrillas, 156, 377
transnationalism and, 167–68
Rhodesia, 157, 158
Nyasaland, break-up of federation with, 196
Rice, 116
Richman, Barry, on China, People's Republic of, transportation in, 334
Rockefeller Foundation, 116, 117, 119, 123, 124
Rockhill, W. W., 14
Rolfe, Sidney, xvi
Roman Catholic Church, 377, 385
Catholic Action, 142
Communism and, 136–37, 141–44
Council of Laymen, 149
laity in, 149
Lateran Treaty, 130, 135
manufacturing firms, compared to, 332
membership, 132–33
moral authority of, 133
nation-states and, 135–40
organization of
Holy See, 130, 134, 135–40, 147
Roman Curia, 149
specialization, areas of, 131, 132
territorial units, 130
vertical organization (parish priests), 130–31
Orthodox Christianity and, 146–47
pope, 130–31
Protestantism and, 145–47
reputation of, 133–34
systemic trends, 147–50
Theological Commission, 134–35
Vatican City, State of the, 130, 135
Roman Empire, 53
Romanov Empire, 4
Rome Treaty, 37
Rose, Hilary, on WHO, medical research center for, 247
Rosenau, James N., 319–20
Rosetta stone, 18
Rosicrucian order, 74
Rostow, Walt W., 297
Rothschilds, 13, 56
Rowthorn, Robert, xxvii
Rubber, 107, 125

Sabena Belgian World Airlines, 199
Saint Gobain, Compagnie de, 205, 206
St. Petersburg, 9
Satellites
actors involved in, 275
telecommunication, 259, 260
tracking stations, 263, 264
Scandinavia
social reform labor movement in, 223
United States, students in, 312
Scandinavian Airlines System, 194, 196, 199
Scheinman, Lawrence, 170, 171, 276–99
Science
advance of, 5
foreign policy and, 361
international science policy, 248–50
transnational activity in, xxvii, 242–48
See also International scientific community
Scientific Committee on Oceanic Research, 265, 266–67, 269

Scotland, nationalism in, 21
Sea
law of, UN conference on, 260, 395
nuclear weapons in, xxviii–xxix
UN and, xxviii
See also Oceans
Sea, United Nations Conference on the Law of the, 260, 395
Secularism, 26
Self-determination, 5
Separation of powers, 366–67
Shakespeare, William, 18
Shanghai, 9
Shipping, international, 272
commercial potential, 270–71
conferences on, price setting by, 193
transnational activity in, 273, 274–75
transnational participants in, 262–63
world distribution of dead weight tonnage, 274
Siam, 10
Singer, H. W., 330–31
Singer, J. David, xiii
Skjelsbaek, Kjell, xxv, 70–92, 387
Slave trade, abolition of, 6
Slavery, abolition of, 6
Small states, xx
Smith Adam, 49–50, 50–51
Smyrna, 9
Socialism, international, 4, 6
See also Communism
Socialist countries. *See* Communist countries
Socialization. *See* subheading under Transnational participation
Societies, sensitivity of, and transnational relations, 375–76
Sociology
agricultural innovations, diffusion of, communications network in, 239
South Africa
African National Congress, 157
immigration into, 7
NGO's, participation in, 80, 81–82
nuclear fuel supply needed for, 293
UN directives, refusal to honor, 111
Southeast Asia, U.S. power in, 66
South Pacific
airlines in, 202, 374
Catholic population of, 133
South West Africa, 157
South West Africa Peoples Organization, 157
Soviet Socialist Republics, Union of
19th century posiiton of, 55
arms control, discussion with United States on, xx
authors, translated into English, 18
Catholic population of, 133
Eastern Europe and, 59–60
fishing, world catch, share of, 274
fishing vessels over 100 gross tons, 274
IGY and, 244
interdependence with world, 37
Latin America, aspirations in, 156
labor in, 209, 210
multinational corporations, possible extension to, 231
nuclear fuel supply needed for, 293
ocean science research by, 274, 275
oil, offshore resources of, 261
outer space, role in, 257, 273, 275
Pugwash Conferences, participation in, 297
revolution, as advocate of, 154, 155
Russian navy (18th century), 10
scientific research in, 249
shipping, share of world's, 274
superpower, emergence as, 4
trade unions of, 223
United States and
interdependence, levels of, 33
NGO comemberships, 91
relations with, as center of international system, 46
situations compared, 60–61
understanding between, Ford Foundation interest in, 119
Spain
Basques in, 168
Chincha Islands, conquest of, 8
fishing vessels over 100 gross tons, 274
Holy See, relations with, 137
Speeckaert, G. P., 78
Sperry Rand Corporation, 212
Sputnik, 273
Staley, Eugene, 53, 67, 68
State-centric model
adequacy of, 23–24
rejection of arguments in favor of, 372–79, 386
air transport, adequacy for, 202–3
asymmetric relations between states and, 387
fisheries and, 257
nuclear energy field and, 276
ocean issue area and, 252–53, 267, 268, 269, 270–73
outer space issue area and, 252–53, 267, 268, 270–73
transnational relations and, xxiii–xxv, 371–72,
U.S. foreign policy and, 390
world politics paradigm, difference between, 380–83
Status, transnational experience and, 312–13
Stead, W. T., 22

Steam, at sea (19th century), 6, 15
Steel, 14, 218
Sterling area, 57
Stroud, Richard, 268
Student culture, 376
Sudan, guerrillas in, 168
Suez Canal, 6
Sukarno, Achmed, 225
Supranationalism, 86
Survival, interdependence and, 33
Sutton, Francis X., 121, 123
Swahili, 17
Sweden
 nuclear policy of, 284–85, 291
 textile production, transferred to Portugal, 217
Synarchy, transnational, 9–13
Syria
 Iraq, conflict with, 154
 relief for (19th century), 11
 revolutionaries in, 166

Tannenbaum, Frank, 230
Tanzania
 revolutionaries in, 166
 self-reliance of, 339–40
Tariffs, xx, 45, 354, 355
 industry's demand for, 208
 reduction of, 23, 27
 resurgence of, 9
 Western European, 62
 See also General Agreement on Tariffs and Trade
Taxation, multinational corporations and, 97, 105, 110–11, 336, 351–52
Technocracy, 367, 379
Technology
 development of, 5, 32–35
 politics, conflict with, 53
 skills in, mobility of, 6
Telecommunications, advances in, 16
 See also International Telecommunications Satellite Consortium; International Telecommunication Union
Telegraph, Atlantic cable and, 15
Temperance movement, 6
Texas, settlement of, 7
Thornton, Robert L., xix, 170, 191–203, 373–74, 391
Touré, Sekou, 213
Tourism, 198
Trade unions
 in developing countries, 222–24
 international trade secretariats, 213–14, 229, 377
 multinational corporations and, 97, 205, 218, 219–20, 226–32
 transnationalism and, xviii, xxvii, 216–20
Trades Union Congress, 205, 211
Transaction analysis, 34
 interdependence, as measure of, 39, 44–45
 transnational society, as measure of, 39
Transnational actors. *See* Actors, transnational
Transnational communication, xix
Transnational finance, xix, xxviii
 See also International finance
Transnational interactions, definition of, xii–xvi
Transnationalism
 air transport and, 198–202
 arms control and disarmament and, 296–98
 asymmetry in, 387–88
 Communist countries and, 388
 culture and, 17–19
 developed countries, centered in, 388
 development of, 3–22
 economic integration and, 232–33
 extranationalism, compared with, 86
 labor movement and, 226–32
 nuclear energy and, 284–85, 290–99
 oceans and, 252, 257–75
 oil production and, 261
 outer space and, 252–75 *passim*
 Pax Britannica, as Golden Age of, 56
 revolutionary actors and, 167–68
 science and, 235–51
 shipping and, 262–63
 U.S.-Japanese relationship and, 66
Transnational organizations
 as actors, xxv
 definition of, 70, 72
 founding of, reasons for, 70–71
 growth of, xxv
 importance of, 376–78
Transnational participation
 peace and, 305–24
 personality and, 316–18
 socialization and, 306–7
  foreign policy and, 319–21
  post-return conditions, 315–16
  prearrival characteristics, 307–10
  transnational experience, 310–11, 315
Transnational processes
 economic activities as, 24–27
 interdependence, international ecoonmic, and, 27–34
Transnational relations
 asymmetry caused by, 396
 definition of, xv
 democratic control and, 356–70
 developing countries and, xxvi

government's loss of control and, xxii–xxiii
history of, 374–78
imperialism and, xxvi
international organizations and, xxviii–xxix, 395–98
interstate politics, effects on, xvi–xxii
Japan and, xxvii
labor and, 204–34
societies' sensitivity and, 375–76
state-centric paradigm and, xxiii–xxv
trade unions and, 219–20
U.S. foreign policy and, xxvii–xxviii
world politics and, ix–xxix, 371–98
decisionmaking structure of, 358–60
values and, xxv–xxvi
World War I and, 375
Transportation
development of, 6–7, 16, 25, 34
equipment, international trade in, 42
in developing countries, 334–35
multinational corporations and, 343, 344, 387
transnational, xix
Trans World Airlines, 196, 201, 373–74
Travel, transnational, xix
Tricontinental, 155–56, 376
Tripartite Monetary Agreement, 57
Trotsky, 156
Trusteeship Council, 202, 374
Turkey
railways in, 14
synarchy in, 10

Union of International Associations, 72
Union of Soviet Socialist Republics. *See* Soviet Socialist Republics, Union of
United Automobile Workers, 214
United Kingdom
19th century condition of, 4, 337
air transport, 192, 193, 195, 196, 200, 202
Bermuda Air Agreement, 196
BOAC, 193, 195, 196, 202
colonies
air transport for, 195
capital provided by, 328
trade unions' influence in, 204, 211
entrepreneurs in (19th century), 337
fishing vesesls over 100 gross tons, 274
France, Concorde with, 358
Holy See, relations with, 137–38
Industrial Revolution in capital for, 328
Iran, relations with, xxii
labor movement in, social reform, 223
maritime position of, 6
mathematics, theory of finite groups, communications network of, 239
monetary situation in (1920's), 346
ocean science research by, 274, 275
oil, offshore resources of, exploitation of, 261
Ottawa Agreement, 57
outer space, as actor in, 259–60, 275
Pax Britannica, 55–57
position on
free trade, 39
nuclear energy, 245–47, 286, 287, 290, 291, 358, 362
trade union leaders' contact with U.S. leaders, 219
WHO, proposed medical research center for, 247
railway, invention of, 6
scientific community in, 241
shipping, share of world's, 274
trade unions in, 204, 205, 211
Trades Union Congress, 205, 211
United Nations
Conference on the Human Environment, xxix, 395
Conference on the Law of the Sea, 260, 393
Conference on Trade and Development, 355, 397
Educational, Scientific and Cultural Organization
Intergovernmental Oceanographic Commission, 245, 265, 266–67
International Council of Scientific Unions, financing of, 241
International Hydrological Decade, coordination of activities for, 244
World Weather Watch, control of, 253
International Conference on the Peaceful Uses of Atomic Energy, 286
Secretariat, geographical distribution in, xvi
Special Fund, 212
transnational relations, possible role in, 307
Trusteeship Council. *See* Trusteeship Council
United States
Agency for International Development, 111, 116, 123, 126
air transport in, 192–202 *passim*, 373–74
Arab states, relations with, xxii
arms control, discussion with Soviet Union on, xx
as nation-state, 150–51
as superpower, emergence of, 4
Atomic Energy Commission, 277, 282–83, 284, 285, 294
Bermuda Air Agreement, 196
Canada, investment in, 16, 68–69, 348, 351
capital flow from and to, 183–84, 186
Central Intelligence Agency, 322

China, People's Republic of, embargoes against, xxi
church and state, separation of, 137, 138
Civil War, transnationalism during, 11
Cuba and, xxi, xxii
Department of Defense, 322
Department of State, 322
developed countries, investment in, rate of return, 329
developing countries and investment in, 326, 329, 332
Eastern Europe and, 59–60, 119
EEC and, 64, 65, 69
English writers in, influence of, 18
Euratom, agreement with, 292
exports, 346
fishing, world catch, share of, 274
Ford Foundation and, 118, 125–26
foreign aid by, 111
foreign investment by, 99, 107–8, 111, 330
foreign policy of, 366
  Congress and the executive, 361, 364
  decisionmaking process, 322, 323
  diplomatic representation, 392
  state-centric model and, 390
  transnational relations and, xi, xxi, xxvii–xxviii, 389–92
foundations in, international activities of, 115–16
Germany, Federal Republic of, relations with, 63–65, 379, 385
humanities, research in, 240
IATA and, 391
IGY and, 244
immigration into, 7, 11
India and, 111, 312, 315–16
industrialization of, 54, 56
INTELSAT, dominance of, 259
interdependence with world, 37
Israel, relations with, xxii
Japan, relations with, 65–67, 69, 311, 312, 385
labor in, 218, 391
Latin America and
  studies about, 116
  study in United States, by university teachers, 318–19
  subsidiaries in, 16
  tension between, 251
mathematics, theory of finite groups, communications network of, 239
merchant marine of, 6
Mexico and
  Mexicali Valley, problems over, 323
  students in United States, 312, 316
monetary policy, 189
multinational corporations based in, xxvii, 98, 99
  assets, 346
  as transnational actors, 14–15
  exports by, 346
  extractive enterprises, 107–8
  foreign policy, as instrument of, xxi, 111–12
  growth of, 231, 325–26, 344
  manufacturing enterprises, 100–7
  profits, 346
  taxation of, 351–52
  tensions arising from, 347–49, 354–55
  US government and, xxi, 111–12, 347–48
    restrictions by, 350–51
National Academy of Sciences, 273
Pakistan, aid to, 111
Pax Americana, 2, 54, 55
Peru, aid to, 111
physics, high energy, communications network of, 238, 239
position on
  Commonwealth discrimination, 59
  France, nuclear capability of, xxi
  decisionmaking by supranational groupings on economic activities, 43
  developing countries and transnational actors, 390
  EEC agricultural policy, 354
  GATT, 349
  Germany, Federal Republic of, acceptance of U.S. dollars, 379
  IAEA, 288, 299
  IMF, 349
  international trade, 57, 58–59, 61–62, 321
  multinational corporations as transnational actors, 54
  nuclear energy, 277–93 *passim*, 298, 299
  oceans, 391
    exploration, international decade for, 267
    research, 274–75
  oil, offshore resources of, 261, 270–71
  outer space, 275, 391
    contamination of, 273
    research, 257, 263–64
    satellite tracking stations, 263
  radio astronomy, frequencies for, 255–56
  seabed, draft treaty for, 270–71
  special drawing rights, 43
  tariffs, 57, 355
  Vietnam war, 366
  water resources development overseas, 322, 323
  Western Europe, reconstruction of, 61–62
  World Weather Watch, 253, 271, 383
Pugwash Conferences, participation in, 297
railroads in, 6
Roman Catholic Church in, 138, 143

Scandinavian students in, 312
science, transnational activity in, as focus of, xxvii
scientific community in, 240–241, 249
shipping, share of world's, 274
sociology, research in, 239
Southeast Asia, power in, 66
Soviet Union and
comparison of situations of, 60–61
interdependence, levels of, 33
NGO comemberships, 91
relations with, 46, 59–60
understanding between, Ford Foundation interest in, 119
synarchy by, 10–11
trade unions in, 220, 223
communism, activities against, 219
foreign activities of, 204–20 *passim*
transnationalism and, xxvii, 216, 217
transnationalism and, 16, 150–51, 389, 391
Weather Bureau, 253, 271, 383
Western Europe and, xxvii, 16, 66, 67, 99, 210
Western Pacific, power in, 66
world affairs, participation in, Ford Foundation interest in, 118
world leadership of economy, failure to assume (after World War I), 57
United States National Petroleum Council, 271
United States Steel Corporation, 14
United States Steelworkers, 218
Uranium, 277, 278, 284, 287–88, 290, 292, 293
Urbanization
Uruguay, guerrilla revolution in, 156
Utah, settlement of, 7

Vallier, Ivan, xviii, 93–94, 95, 129–52
Values, transnational relations and, xxv–xxvi
Vatican City, State of the, 130, 135
Veblen, Thorstein, 332–33, 335
Venezuela
guerrilla revolution in, 156
Holy See, relations with, 137
Vernon, Raymond, xviii, xix, 302, 303, 327, 343–56, 377, 390, 391, 395
Victor Emmanuel II, 135
Vietnam
Catholic population of, 133
war in, 366
Vietnam, Democratic Republic of (North Vietnam)
NGO's participation in, 80, 81, 83
Viner, Jacob, 52–53, 67
Vo Nguyen Giap, 156, 157

Wales, separatist movement in, 21, 168
Waltz, Kenneth, 30, 31–34, 37, 323
Warwick, Donald P., xvii, 301, 303, 305–24, 376
Weather
satellites, 260
World Weather Watch, 253, 266, 271, 383
See also World Meteorological Organization
Welfare
control over, loss of, 394
of developing countries, 389
state, growth of, 26
Wells, Louis T., Jr., 93, 94, 95, 97–114
Western countries
elites of third world and, 276
trade unions in, 214
See also Developed countries
Western Europe
agricultural policy in, xxiv, 44, 354, 360, 383
airbus for, 358
biological research (molecular) in, 241–42, 243–44
Catholic population of, 133
Eastern Europe and, 90
economy of (post World War II), reconstruction of, 61
electrical equipment industry in, 282
European Organization for Nuclear Research, 238, 243, 245–46
integration of, 44
labor in, 208, 209
multinational corporations and, 210, 212, 326, 347
NGO's, participation in, 80, 81–82
nuclear fuel supply needed for, 292
nuclear policy of, 291–92, 293, 294
outer space research by, 264
parliaments in, 364, 365, 366, 367–68
scientific community in, 241, 248, 249–50
student disturbances in, 376
technological revolution in, 25
trade unions in, 206, 211–12, 213, 214
transnationalism and, 25, 233, 391
United States and, 63, 64–65, 66, 67, 379
See also Europe
Western Hemisphere Idea, 4
Westernization, 5, 12
Western Pacific, U.S. power in, 66
West Indies, sugar planters in, 9
Westinghouse Electric Corporation, 279
Wheat, 8, 116
Whitney, Eli, 7–8
Wiesner, Jerome B., 297
Wolfers, Arnold, x, 377
Women, rights of, 6
Wooster, Warren, S., 244, 265

World Council of Churches, 71, 147
World Federation of Trade Unions, 71, 211, 213
World Health Organization
medical research laboratory, attempt to establish, 246, 247
oceans, radioactive pollution of, activity concerning, 269
World Meteorological Organization, 253, 254–55, 264, 266–67, 271, 383
World politics
definition of, xxiv–xxv, 380, 383
nation-states, asymmetric relations between, 387–89
paradigm, 379–86
research plan, 384–86
state-centric paradigm, difference between, 380–83
World War I
international trade, decline in, after, 38, 39–40
NGO's founded during, decrease in, 74, 75
transnational relations, 375
World War II
consequences, 60
NGO's founded during, decrease in, 75
trade unions during, 219
World Weather Watch, 253, 266, 271, 383

Yellow fever, 116
Yemen, 154
Young, Oran, 44, 374
Yugoslavia, Roman Catholic Church in, 144
Yung Wing, 12

Zaltman, Gerald, 239
Zambia, revolutionaries in, 166
Zimbabwe African National Union, 157
Zimbabwe African People's Union, 157
Zionism, xxii

Publications Written under the Auspices of the Center for International Affairs, Harvard University

Created in 1958, the Center for International Affairs fosters advanced study of basic world problems by scholars from various disciplines and senior officials from many countries. The research at the Center focuses on economic, social, and political development, the management of force in the modern world, the evolving roles of Western Europe and the Communist bloc, and the conditions of international order. Books published by Harvard University Press are listed here in the order in which they have been issued. A complete list of publications may be obtained from the Center.

Books

The Soviet Bloc: Unity and Conflict, by Zbigniew K. Brzezinski (jointly with the Russian Research Center), 1960. Revised and enlarged edition, 1967.

Rift and Revolt in Hungary: Nationalism versus Communism, by Ferenc A. Váli, 1961.

The Economy of Cyprus, by A. J. Meyer, with Simos Vassiliou (jointly with the Center for Middle Eastern Studies), 1962.

Entrepreneurs of Lebanon: The Role of the Business Leader in a Developing Economy, by Yusif A. Sayigh (jointly with the Center for Middle Eastern Studies), 1962.

Communist China 1955–1959: Policy Documents with Analysis, with a foreword by Robert R. Bowie and John K. Fairbank (jointly with the East Asian Research Center), 1962.

In Search of France, by Stanley Hoffmann, Charles P. Kindleberger, Laurence W. Wylie, Jesse R. Pitts, Jean-Baptiste Duroselle, and Francois Goguel, 1963.

Somali Nationalism: International Politics and the Drive for Unity in the Horn of Africa, by Saadia Touval, 1963.

The Dilemma of Mexico's Development: The Roles of the Private and Public Sectors, by Raymond Vernon, 1963.

The Arms Debate, by Robert A. Levine, 1963.

Africans on the Land: Economic Problems of African Agricultural Development in Southern, Central, and East Africa, with Special Reference to Southern Rhodesia, by Montague Yudelman, 1964.

Public Policy and Private Enterprise in Mexico: Studies, by M. S. Wionczek, D. H. Shelton, C. P. Blair, and R. Izquierdo, edited by Raymond Vernon, 1964.

Democracy in Germany, by Fritz Erler (Jodidi Lectures), 1965.

The Rise of Nationalism in Central Africa: The Making of Malawi and Zambia, 1873–1964, by Robert I. Rotberg, 1965.

Pan-Africanism and East African Integration, by Joseph S. Nye, Jr., 1965.

Germany and the Atlantic Alliance: The Interaction of Strategy and Politics, by James L. Richardson, 1966.

Political Change in a West African State: A Study of the Modernization Process in Sierra Leone, by Martin Kilson, 1966.

Planning without Facts: Lessons in Resource Allocation from Nigeria's Development, by Wolfgang F. Stolper, 1966.

Export Instability and Economic Development, by Alasdair I. MacBean, 1966.

Europe's Postwar Growth: The Role of Labor Supply, by Charles P. Kindleberger, 1967.

Pakistan's Development: Social Goals and Private Incentives, by Gustav F. Papanek, 1967.

Strike a Blow and Die: A Narrative of Race Relations in Colonial Africa, by George Simeon Mwase, edited by Robert I. Rotberg, 1967. Second printing, with a revised introduction, 1970.

Development Policy: Theory and Practice, edited by Gustav F. Papanek, 1968.

Korea: The Politics of the Vortex, by Gregory Henderson, 1968.

The Brazilian Capital Goods Industry, 1929–1964 (jointly with the Center for Studies in Education and Development), by Nathaniel H. Leff, 1968.

The Process of Modernization: An Annotated Bibliography on the Sociocultural Aspects of Development, by John Brode, 1969.

Taxation and Development: Lessons from Colombian Experience, by Richard M. Bird, 1970.

Lord and Peasant in Peru: A Paradigm of Political and Social Change, by F. LaMond Tullis, 1970.

The Kennedy Round in American Trade Policy: The Twilight of the GATT?, by John W. Evans, 1971.

Korean Development: The Interplay of Politics and Economics, by David C. Cole and Princeton N. Lyman, 1971.

Development Policy II — The Pakistan Experience, edited by Walter P. Falcon and Gustav F. Papanek, 1971.

Transnational Relations and World Politics, edited by Robert O. Keohane and Joseph S. Nye, Jr., 1972.

Latin American University Students: A Six Nation Study, by Arthur Liebman, Kenneth N. Walker, and Myron Glazer, 1972.